DICTIONARIES IN EARLY MODERN EUROPE

Dictionaries tell stories of many kinds. The history of dictionaries, of how they were produced, published and used, has much to tell us about the language and the culture of the past. This monumental work of scholarship draws on published and archival material to survey a wide range of dictionaries of western European languages (including English, German, Latin and Greek) published between the early sixteenth and mid seventeenth centuries. John Considine establishes a new and powerful model for the social and intellectual history of lexicography by examining dictionaries both as imaginative texts and as scholarly instruments. He tells the stories of national and individual heritage and identity that were created through the making of dictionaries in the early modern period. Far from dry, factual collections of words, dictionaries are creative works, shaping as well as recording early modern culture and intellectual history.

JOHN CONSIDINE is Associate Professor of English at the University of Alberta.

DICTIONARIES IN EARLY MODERN EUROPE

Lexicography and the Making of Heritage

JOHN CONSIDINE

CAMBRIDGE
UNIVERSITY PRESS

CAMBRIDGE UNIVERSITY PRESS
Cambridge, New York, Melbourne, Madrid, Cape Town, Singapore, São Paulo, Delhi

Cambridge University Press
The Edinburgh Building, Cambridge CB2 8RU, UK

Published in the United States of America by Cambridge University Press, New York

www.cambridge.org
Information on this title: www.cambridge.org/9780521886741

© John Considine 2008

First published 2008
Reprinted 2009

Printed in the United Kingdom at the University Press, Cambridge

A catalogue record for this publication is available from the British Library

Library of Congress Cataloguing in Publication Data

Considine, John (John P.)
Dictionaries in early modern Europe : lexicography and the making of heritage /
John Considine.
p.   cm.
Includes bibliographical references and index.
ISBN 978-0-521-88674-1 (hardback : alk. paper)
1.   Lexicography–Europe–History. 1.   Title.
P327.45.E85C66 2008
413′ .028094–dc22
2007051326

ISBN 978-0-521-88674-1 hardback

For Sylvia

Contents

Acknowledgements

The writing of this book was supported by a Standard Research Grant from the Social Sciences and Humanities Research Council of Canada (SSHRC), and by generous funding from the University of Alberta. I am very grateful for both. This funding supported the research assistantships of Ernst Gerhardt and Peter Midgely, to whom I am indebted, as I am to Kris Calhoun, Leona Erl and Anna Minarchi for their administrative support.

I am very greatly indebted to the libraries that have given me access to their collections: the Kongelige Bibliotek, Copenhagen; the University of Alberta Libraries, Edmonton; the British Library, London; the Bodleian Library, Oxford (I owe a particular debt to Alan Carter, Russell Edwards, William Hodges and Jean-Pierre Mialon of Duke Humfrey's library); the Bibliothèque Nationale and the Bibliothèque de l'Arsenal, Paris; the Kungliga Bibliotek, Stockholm; the library of the University of Toronto and all the other libraries, too numerous to list, that have sent me material by inter-library loan. I greatly appreciate the courtesy and patience of their staff. I would also like to express my warm appreciation of the genius of the architects of the new British Library and of the Black Diamond building of the Kongelige Bibliotek, Sir Colin St John Wilson and Schmidt, Hammer & Lassen K/S respectively.

This book is not a reworked thesis, but it had one of its origins in work on Henri Estienne that I began as a graduate student, and that owed much to the advice of my supervisor, Robin Robbins, and of Peter Burke, Anthony Grafton, David Norbrook, Fred Schreiber, Michael Screech and Nigel Smith. Another point of departure was my experience of work on the staff of the *Oxford English Dictionary*, where Philip Durkin, Simon Hunt, John Simpson and Edmund Weiner helped me to understand how dictionaries are made. Robert Ireland introduced me to du Cange. I am very grateful to all of these friends and teachers.

Earlier versions of some of the material presented here were offered as conference papers at meetings of the International Association for Neo-Latin Studies, the International Society for Historical Lexicography and Lexicology, and the Rocky Mountain Medieval and Renaissance Association, and as seminar papers at Oxford and Princeton, and I am grateful to everyone who heard my papers and discussed them with me. At Cambridge University Press, Linda Bree has given this project years of patient encouragement, two anonymous readers have offered welcome criticisms, and Maartje Scheltens has guided me in the last stages of my work; out of house, J. Bottrill has been a patient and supportive project manager, and Joanne Hill an ideal copy-editor.

Most important of all has been the love and support of my parents, of my son Nicholas, and of Sylvia, to whom this book is dedicated.

Conventions and abbreviations

I have, except for some single words and very short passages, given translations or paraphrases of my sources in my main text and originals in my footnotes. Quotations from vernacular languages are given in old spelling, preserving i/j and u/v variation but normalizing, e.g., vv in English to w, ʒ in Old English to g. Use of accents, cedillas and other diacritics in vernacular texts has only been normalized in the case of superscript e in German, which has been replaced by the umlaut. Quotations from Latin are normalized by the removal of diacritics and the expansion of digraphs; & is retained for *et*, and the expansion of other abbreviations is indicated. Quotations from Greek are normalized by the expansion of all ligatured and abbreviated forms. Black-letter and Anglo-Saxon typefaces are given in italics. Underlinings in manuscript are represented by underlinings.

The forms of names are always a problem in the intellectual history of this period. If in doubt as to whether to cite a given name in vernacular or classicizing form, I have generally preferred the one that seemed more familiar to me. (For what it's worth, my earlier intention was to give vernacular forms wherever this would not be positively absurd, i.e., Melanchthon rather than Schwarzerd but van Gorp rather than Goropius and Zsámboky rather than Sambucus – but as the years went by, this arrangement seemed increasingly unsatisfactory, and Goropius and Sambucus, among others, had their learned names restored to them.) I have given alternative forms of some names in parentheses where they first appear. Classical Greek names and a few later ones have generally been Latinized, and a few Greek and Latin names have been Anglicized, familiarity being the criterion again: Marcus Musurus, not Markos Mousouros; Aristotle, not Aristoteles. The form of Byzantine Greek names generally follows the usage of the *Oxford dictionary of Byzantium*.

References in footnotes are to author and short title, plus date or other publication details when these are particularly significant or are necessary to distinguish editions; fuller bibliographical information has been provided in the bibliography. This is divided into three sections: manuscripts and annotated copies of printed books; printed books written before 1800; printed books written after 1800. The identifications of publishers in the imprints of early printed books have been reported in their original form, since they may convey significant information: 'ex officina Roberti Stephani' in 1536 and 'ex officina Roberti Stephani typographi Regii' in 1543 certainly say different things, as does 'Oliua Roberti Stephani' in 1558, and the form of words 'excudebat Robertus Stephanus in sua officina' in 1538 may also have been selected deliberately. Although this policy leads to bibliographical records in which the vernacular and classicizing forms of a name both appear, e.g., 'St Justin Martyr, *Epist[ola] ad Diognetu[m], & Oratio ad Graecos*. Ed. Henri Estienne. [Geneva:] excudebat Henricus Stephanus, 1592', I think this inconsistency is an acceptable price to pay for the presence of the imprint. The names of publishing towns have been given in the vernacular, and Anglicized where appropriate.

Quotations from and references to classical sources generally follow what I understand to be the modern *textus receptus* and division into books, chapters, etc., and particular editions have therefore not been specified. Translations from classical sources are my own unless otherwise stated, but owe a general debt to Loeb translations where those have been available. Translations from post-classical sources and texts in modern languages are my own unless otherwise stated. Quotations from patristic sources are accompanied by references to the *Patrologia graeca* and *Patrologia latina*. Quotations from and references to the Bible follow the New RSV unless otherwise specified.

In citations, facsimile, microfilm and digitized reproductions of early printed books are not generally distinguished from originals: often the same edition has been consulted in several different forms at different times, and identifying them all would not have been particularly useful. However, where I have discussed an individual copy of a book for the sake of its annotations and I know it to be available in facsimile or on microfilm, I have said so; I have also identified locations or facsimiles of one or two particularly elusive items. I have made particular use of the reproductions of English books in the microfilm series *Early English books 1475–1640*, *The Thomason Tracts*, *Early English books 1641–1700*, and *The eighteenth century* (and of the digitized images of these microfilms available in the databases *Early English books online* and *Eighteenth-century collections online*), and of continental printed books in the IDC microfiche series *Philological tools* and *Harmonia linguarum* and in the *Gallica* collection which the Bibliothèque Nationale generously makes freely available online.

I have tried to disencumber footnotes of the following: (i) gratuitous identifications of mistakes or omissions in the work of others; (ii) general bibliographical information, e.g., 'for a good overview of the subject, see X, Y and Z' as opposed to the identification of the sources for the statements I have made; (iii) references to the standard sources of biographical, bibliographical and lexicographical information, unless these are actually being quoted directly. Standard sources which I have consulted routinely include the following.

Biographical: for antiquity, the *Oxford classical dictionary*, 3rd edn, and the *Neue Pauly*; for the Byzantine world, the *Oxford dictionary of Byzantium*; for early modern writers, Bietenholz and Deutscher's *Contemporaries of Erasmus*, Maillard, Kecskeméti and Portalier's *L'Europe des humanistes (xiv*^e*–xvii*^e* siècles)*, and the *Oxford encyclopedia of the Reformation*; the *Dictionary of scientific biography*; the *Biographie nationale* and the *Nieuw Nederlandsch biografisch woordenboek* for the Low Countries; the *Oxford dictionary of national biography* for the British Isles; the extant volumes of the *Dizionario biographico degli italiani* for Italy; those of the *Neue deutsche Biographie* for Germany; the *Nouvelle biographie française* for France; and the predecessors of all these.

Bibliographical: the *English short-title catalogue* and the printed volumes of *STC* and *Wing*; the catalogues of libraries in the United Kingdom available online through COPAC; the printed catalogues of the British Library and the Bibliothèque Nationale; the Swedish library catalogues available online through LIBRIS; the *Gesamtkatalog der Wiegendrucke*; the published volumes of the *Index aureliensis*; the *National union catalog*; the catalogues available online through OCLC WorldCat.

Lexicographical: the *Deutsches Wörterbuch*; Liddell and Scott's *Greek lexicon*; the *Oxford English Dictionary*, 2nd and revised online editions (*OED*); the *Oxford Latin Dictionary*, the *Thesaurus linguae latinae*, and the standard dictionaries of patristic and medieval Latin; the *Trésor de la langue française*; the *Woordenboek der Nederlandse taal*.

I have used the following abbreviations:

ASD	*Opera omnia Desiderii Erasmi Roterodami* (see bibliography s.n. Erasmus)
BL	British Library, London
BN	Bibliothèque Nationale, Paris
Bodl.	Bodleian Library, Oxford
CWE	*Collected Works of Erasmus* (see bibliography s.n. Erasmus)
HCS	*History of classical scholarship* (see bibliography s.n. Pfeiffer)

LB	*Desiderii Erasmi Roterodami opera omnia* (see bibliography s.n. Erasmus)
LLT	*Linguae latinae thesaurus* (see bibliography s.n. R. Estienne)
MED	*Middle English Dictionary*
OED	*Oxford English Dictionary* online
PG	*Patrologia graeca*
PL	*Patrologia latina*
STC	*Short-title catalogue*, 2nd edn
TGL	*Thesaurus graecae linguae* (see bibliography s.n. H. Estienne)
WNT	*Woordenboek der Nederlandse taal*

CHAPTER I

Introduction

THIS HEROIC AND INDEED HERCULEAN WORK: DICTIONARIES AND THE HEROIC

In the 1550s, the son of the best lexicographer in Europe was writing the introduction to his own first dictionary – a collection, with commentary, of all the Greek words used in the works of Cicero, which would be published under the title of *Ciceronianum lexicon graecolatinum*. His name was Henri Estienne, and the *Latinae linguae thesaurus* edited by his father Robert was the definitive dictionary of the Latin language. Robert had for some years been working on an enormous dictionary of classical Greek, and Henri explained that his dictionary of Cicero's Greek was intended to make a small contribution to this great undertaking, 'this heroic and indeed Herculean work'.[1]

Nearly two centuries later, another dictionary preface was being written. This time, the dictionary was of a whole language rather than one writer's usage, and of a living language, Irish, rather than a classical one. It was called *The English Irish dictionary* in English, the language of its definitions, and *An focloir bearla Gaoidheilge* in Irish. The dictionary would be published in Paris, and would be used by the clergy and clerical students of the Irish College there, and no doubt by those of some or all of the thirty or so other Irish colleges of continental Europe, whose students would return to Ireland to serve a people some of whom spoke no English.[2] Work had been done on it by Hugh MacCurtin (Aodh Buí Mac Cruitin), hereditary ollave, or praise-poet, to the chiefs of the clan O'Brien, and author of a celebratory account of Irish antiquity and an Irish grammar.[3] The preface appears to

---

[1] H. Estienne, *Ciceronianum lexicon graecolatinum* sig. **3r, 'in heroico illo ac plane Herculeo opere'.

[2] See Simms, 'The Irish on the Continent, 1691–1800' 644–6.

[3] For MacCurtin, see Ó Cuív, 'Irish language and literature, 1691–1845' 394 and 396–7; the books are MacCurtin, *Brief discourse in vindication of the antiquity of Ireland* and MacCurtin, *Elements of the Irish language, grammatically explained in English*.

have been by MacCurtin's senior collaborator, Father Conor O'Begley, although its argument is reminiscent of MacCurtin's preface to his grammar. Its author writes as follows:

That a people so naturally ambitious of Honour and so universally covetous of Glory, as several generous BRITISH Historians have described the IRISH to be, can so strangely neglect cultivating and improving a Language of some Thousands of Years standing may seem very surprising to all learned Foreigners, and I believe will do so to the IRISH, themselves, when they recover out of their Error, and take a little time to consider how much they deviate, in this particular, from the Practice and Policy of their Ancestors, and how inexcusable they are for neglecting so sacred a Depositary of the Heroick Atchievments of their Country.[4]

Estienne and O'Begley, far removed as they were in time, had a number of points in common. They were, for instance, both exiles from their own countries, the Irishman O'Begley writing in France and the Parisian Estienne writing in Geneva. They both reinvented their names to reflect the cultural concerns that also informed their lexicography, Henri Estienne classicizing to Henricus Stephanus and Conor O'Begley Hibernicizing to Conchobhar Ó Beaglaoich. They both worked on languages which they could speak, but which they perceived to be undervalued or endangered. And – the point that matters most here – they both made an association between dictionaries and the heroic. Estienne saw his father's work on his dictionary in progress as 'heroic and indeed Herculean'. O'Begley saw the dictionary that he and MacCurtin had made as giving access to language that was a treasury of 'Heroick Atchievments'.

The association between dictionaries and the heroic which Estienne and O'Begley both made is to be found again and again in post-medieval writings on lexicography. David Garrick boasted in 1755, on the completion of Samuel Johnson's dictionary of English, which Garrick supposed to be superior to the dictionary of the Académie française, that 'Johnson, well arm'd like a hero of yore Has beat forty French and will beat forty more', and these words were much reprinted.[5] In the next century, a correspondent of Joseph Wright's admired the 'heroic exertion' of his work on the *English Dialect Dictionary*, adding: 'When I told my

---

[4] MacCurtin and O'Begley, *English Irish dictionary* sigs. ã2r–v; cf. MacCurtin, *Elements of the Irish language* sig. A4r, 'how strange it seems to the world, that any people should scorn the Language, wherein the whole treasure of their own Antiquity and profound sciences lie in obscurity'.

[5] Garrick, 'Talk of war with a Briton'; for printings, see Knapp, *Checklist of verse by David Garrick*, item 220.

wife she said "I don't know how he has done it – what a brave man!" '[6]
The association is a double one: dictionaries have repeatedly been presented as heroic works and their makers have been characterized as heroes.

This is at first sight somewhat counter-intuitive. Dictionary-making is not
a conspicuously heroic business, as I know from personal experience. I took
great pleasure in my work as a full-time lexicographer in the 1990s, but I
certainly, and rightly, had no sense of myself as a heroic figure as I worked. A
visitor to my place of work, one of the greatest lexicographical centres of the
late twentieth century, the main office of the Dictionary Department of
Oxford University Press, might at first glance have mistaken it for one of the
offices of an insurance company. It was, as I remember it, a room in which a
hundred or so men and women sat at desks partitioned off from each other
by low dividers covered in a greyish fabric, busy with data entry or other
paperwork, or making photocopies, or conferring with each other, or eating
sandwiches. The air quality was not very good; there always seemed to be a
telephone ringing somewhere; periodically a hundred or so workstations
bleeped one after the other as a group e-mail circulated. Nor was this, except
with regard to its size, an unusual workspace for dictionary-making. The
dictionary room at the top of Samuel Johnson's house in eighteenth-century
London, or the sixteenth-century publishers' *officinae* in which dictionaries
like Robert Estienne's *Latinae linguae thesaurus* were made, appear also to
have been cluttered, busy, unheroic.

Johnson himself summed up the paradoxical relationship between the
lived experience of dictionary-making and the association of dictionaries
with the heroic when, in his own dictionary, he called the lexicographer a
'harmless drudge'. On the one hand, that sounds like an entirely fair
description. It has been taken at face value. On the other hand, *drudgery*
was a word that Johnson used to express scornful irony, comparing 'the
charming Amusement of forming Hypotheses' with 'the toilsome
Drudgery of making Observations' in his life of Boerhaave, writing in the
Plan of a dictionary that 'the work in which I engaged is generally considered as drudgery for the blind', commenting sarcastically in the
Adventurer on 'the low drudgery of collating copies, comparing authorities, digesting dictionaries', and remarking in the preface to the dictionary itself that Learning and Genius do not bestow so much as a smile
upon 'the humble drudge that facilitates their progress'.[7] Johnson's

[6] R. Oliver Heslop, letter to Joseph Wright of 14 June 1895, quoted in E. M. W[right], *Life of Joseph Wright* 376.

[7] Samuel Johnson: 'Life of Dr. Boerhaave' 115; *Plan of a dictionary of the English language* 1; *The adventurer* 232 (no. 39, for 20 March 1753); *Dictionary of the English language* sig. A2r.

definition both acknowledges the possibility of seeing lexicographers as drudges and expects the intelligent reader to see them as something much more like heroes.

This book originates in an attempt to understand the association between dictionaries and heroic narratives. Doing that may incur the reasonable suspicion of practising lexicographers: the response of some of my former colleagues at the *Oxford English Dictionary* to the original sketch from which this book arose was, more or less, that they were painstakingly engaged in exact and fully documented scholarly research into language, and that heroic narratives really had nothing to do with their work. I do not want to denigrate the integrity, accuracy and completeness that characterize the best post-medieval dictionaries. Nor do I want to underestimate the traditional histories of lexicography that trace the influence of one dictionary upon another, or describe the minutiae of dictionary-making. I want instead to propose some new contexts in intellectual and cultural history for the history of lexicography.

The idea that dictionaries have the sort of imaginative qualities that characterize poetry or fictional narrative has certainly been proposed before, albeit rather casually. The novelist and journalist Arnold Bennett described the *Oxford English Dictionary*, of which he had been buying each new part as it was published for forty-odd years, as 'the longest sensational serial ever written'. Elizabeth Lea, as she then was, writing to Joseph Wright before their marriage, told him that the *English Dialect Dictionary* was 'really more poetical than any other work of the age'. Eric Partridge, writing in his memoir *The gentle art of lexicography*, recounts the doubtless apocryphal story of the old lady who, having borrowed a dictionary from the library under the misapprehension that it was a novel, remarked on returning it that it was 'A *very* unusual book indeed – but the stories are extremely short, aren't they?'[8]

I want to respond to perceptions like these of dictionaries as narrative or poetic or indeed sensational, and to argue that, notwithstanding the misgivings of my former colleagues, many dictionaries can be read as, to some extent, works of the imagination, and as presences in the imaginative lives of their readers. Rather than documenting early modern lexicographers' debt to the dictionaries of the Middle Ages, for instance, I want to look at the place of early modern dictionaries in the imaginations

[8] Arnold Bennett, 'Books and persons' column in the *Evening Standard*, 5 January 1928, reprinted in Mylett, *Arnold Bennett: The Evening Standard years* 115; Elizabeth Lea, letter of 17 June 1896, in Wright, *Life of Joseph Wright* 230; Partridge, *Gentle art of lexicography* 14.

of their makers and readers. I want to ask why lexicography was a heroic matter to a number of its practitioners. I want, in other words, to think about the kinds of anxiety and pride and imagination and love that inform dictionaries.

One way to begin to address the questions about the social and cultural history of dictionaries outlined above is to examine the possibility that Estienne and O'Begley were both saying something interesting and profound about lexicography when they associated it with the words *heroicus* and *heroic*. The argument of this section is that they were. On the one hand, dictionaries have much in common with those kinds of writing which are more usually called heroic, or which take the heroic as their subject. This is O'Begley's point: the dictionary orders a treasury of heroic achievements. On the other hand, the makers of dictionaries are often seen as heroic figures. This is Estienne's point: the dictionary-maker is a hero, another Hercules.

Neither Estienne nor Begley meant to call lexicography heroic in the sense 'courageous'. This has been done. Just as the correspondent of Joseph Wright's who referred to his 'heroic exertions' went on to say that he had been described as 'brave', other admirers of Wright's referred to his 'courage' and 'pluck'.[9] Other examples could no doubt be adduced. The idea that lexicography calls for a kind of moral courage is, however, vague. Its weakness becomes apparent when a statement like the following is considered: 'Indeed linguists afford some notable examples of heroism if heroism may be said to include pioneering sometimes in perilous isolation and under risk of derision. Henry Sweet and the Grimm brothers were perhaps heroes in this sense, and the Russian linguists who fell foul of Stalin.'[10] This is true, but it is too general to be of interest. Although linguists, and among them lexicographers, have certainly been known to show great moral courage, so have the members of many other professions: that point does not make a specific association between dictionaries and the heroic. What Estienne and Begley meant starts to become clearer when some instances of the Latin word *heroicus* which Estienne applied to his father's work are examined.

[9] Wright, *Life of Joseph Wright* 377 (quoting a letter of the early 1890s from an unnamed American), 394 (quoting a letter of 11 January 1896 from F. J. Furnivall).
[10] Williams, 'George Borrow: The word-master as hero' 117.

The earliest extant occurrences of *heroicus* are in Cicero, who referred in *De natura deorum* to the wicked Medea and Atreus as *heroicae personae*, 'characters of heroic legend'. A little earlier in the same book, Cicero had written that one of the several solar deities known to the learned was said to have been born at Rhodes *heroicis temporibus* 'in the heroic period'.[11] He was here evidently not using *heroicus* in the sense that *heroic* has in modern English: he had no intention of associating either a dubious solar deity or two of the villains of Greek myth with courage. His point was that they could be located in a distant time, in which a number of exemplary and foundational stories, often peopled by larger-than-life characters, were set. Ulysses and Nestor had, Cicero said elsewhere, lived in that time: they were wise men *heroicis aetatibus* 'in the heroic age'.[12] One of the greatest early modern philologists, Joseph Scaliger, likewise suggested that the period at the beginning of Greek history, the records of which mixed historical and legendary material together, should be called *heroicum* rather than *mythicon*.[13] That same distant time is called heroic in early uses of the word in other languages. For instance, the first occurrence of Italian *eròico* documented in the *Grande dizionario italiano* is a reference to the 'eroici tempi' in which meritorious persons such as Codrus, Cyrus or Charlemagne came to be venerated as heroes.[14] Similarly, the first occurrence of *heroic* in any variety of English is, according to the *Oxford English Dictionary*, in the dedication of a political text called *The complaynt of Scotland*, written in Middle Scots in 1549. Addressing Mary of Lorraine, widow of James V, the author said that

your heroic virtue is more to be admired than was that of Valeria, the daughter of the prudent consul Publicola, or of Cloelia, Lucrece, Penelope, Cornelia, Semiramis, Tomyris, Penthesilea, or of any other virtuous lady whom Plutarch or Boccaccio has described.[15]

Here, *heroic* describes a kind of virtue manifested in ancient narratives, which, in an early modern high culture that traced many of its institutions to the ancient world, were to some extent foundational narratives

[11] Cicero, *De natura deorum* 3.71 and 3.54.   [12] Cicero, *Disputationes tusculanae* 5.7.
[13] Scaliger, *Thesaurus temporum* (1606), quoted and discussed Grafton, 'Tradition and technique' 26.
[14] Davanzati, 'Orazione in morte del granduca Cosimo primo' (1574) in *Opere* II:463, 'Così naturalmente ancora si facevano i re di quegli eroici tempi, quando i popoli eleggevano spontaneamente colui che gli avanzasse di meriti o di virtù sue o de'suoi maggiori, come fu Codro in Grecia, Ciro in Persia e poi Carlo in Francia.'
[15] Wedderburn [?], *Complaynt of Scotland* 1, 'ʒour heroyque vertu, is of mair admiratione, nor vas of valeria the dochtir of the prudent consul publicola or of cloelia, lucresia, penelope, cornelia, semiramis, thomaris, penthasillie, or of ony vthir verteouse lady that plutarque or bocchas hes discriuit.'

for that culture. But heroic virtue is not, for the author of the *Complaynt*, confined to the remote world of antiquity; it can be re-enacted now, and in this case its present enactment even surpasses the past. Similarly, in Shakespeare's *The first part of Henry the Sixt*, there is a reference to the 'Heroick Lyne' of the sons of Edward III of England and their progeny.[16] Here, as in the Scots example, the heroic belongs in the past – the word describes the ancestors of men living in the time of the play – but also in the present as descended from that past, for the heroic line still flourishes, embodied in its living representatives. The heroic world is that past world on which the present is founded, and which informs or is re-embodied or emulated by the present.

This helps to explain what Conor O'Begley meant by 'Heroick Atchievements', and to suggest why there really is an important association between lexicography and the heroic. Begley's argument was that language makes a link between the present and the foundational past of any culture, the past to which its larger-than-life predecessors belong, the heroic past. Its distance from the observer may vary greatly, from the gulf of time between Cicero's contemporaries and the solar deity born in the heroic age to the century or so between the lifetimes of Edward III and Henry VI. What defines it is not this distance but its difference from the present, and its place in the cultural ancestry of the present. The people of the heroic age are the forerunners of the living, its institutions are the forerunners of living institutions and its language is connected with living language.

The connection between the living and the heroic age is one of inheritance or heritage. Inheritance may be a matter of literal genealogical descent from a heroic person or family, for instance the descent from Edward III which is so important in Shakespeare's history tetralogies, or the descent from Trojan colonists which was so widely claimed in Europe in the medieval and early modern periods. A theme that will recur in this book is the relationship between lexicography and family background, as in the cases of Robert Estienne, his son Henri and Henri's grandson Meric Casaubon – or as in that of the new edition of Francis Holyoake's Latin–English dictionary by his son Thomas, 'heir not only to the legal rights and material inheritance of his father, but to his industry and erudition', and indeed heir to the dictionary too, 'which his dying father gave to him as one of his charges'.[17] Another, related to it, is the sense that

---

[16] Shakespeare, *First part of Henry the Sixt* in *Works* sc. 13 (II. v in other editions), TLN 1031.

[17] Thomas Barlow, epistle 'lectori benevolo' in Holyoake, *Large dictionary* sig. A2r, 'non tantum juris ac patrimonii, sed industriae ac eruditionis paternae haeres' and sig. A2v, 'Lexicon a Parente editum (quod etiam in mandatis sui dedit moriens pater)'.

the lexicographical work of one generation is inherited from the one before it. A number of early modern dictionaries can be surveyed together as links in a chain of inheritance, as in the case of the first wordlists of Old English: from Laurence Nowell to John Joscelyn, from Joscelyn to Sir Simonds D'Ewes, from D'Ewes to William Somner and into the web of filiations from one seventeenth-century antiquary to the next.[18] A third theme, related to the previous two, is the relationship between lexicography and material inheritance, particularly the inheritance of land, as in the cases of Sir Simonds D'Ewes and of Sir Henry Spelman and his heirs. Finally, although dictionaries are not autobiographies (the claim has, incidentally, been made by Anthony Burgess with reference to Johnson's *Dictionary*), one of the stories to which the lexicographer can hardly help alluding, more or less fully and explicitly, is that of his or her own life.[19] The lexicographer becomes part of the story that she or he tells, and thus becomes not only the transmitter of a heroic heritage but heroic in his or her own right. The same may of course be said of other scholars who recover ancient texts: for instance, a student of the literary historian W. P. Ker wrote: 'We came to look upon Ker as an epic hero ... whose unfaltering guidance led us and allowed us to share in the voyage to the enchanted places of the mind.'[20]

The word *heritage* calls for further consideration. It unites the themes of this book very helpfully, but, by using it, I do not want to claim that this book makes a specialized contribution to the academic discipline called 'heritage studies'. I want to use the word flexibly and non-technically, in the range of senses suggested by, for instance, its excellent definition in the *Canadian Oxford Dictionary*: 'things such as works of art, cultural achievements and folklore that have been passed on from earlier generations; a nation's buildings, monuments, countryside, etc., esp. when regarded as worthy of preservation; ... that which is or may be inherited; inherited circumstances, benefits, etc.' The distinction between *heritage* and *history* in David Lowenthal's *The heritage crusade and the spoils of history* is stimulating. Lowenthal's argument there is that *heritage* is not simply a name for the cultural monuments of a nation or a people; it is, rather, the product of a particular kind of creative relationship with the past:

heritage is not an inquiry into the past but a celebration of it, not an effort to know what actually happened but a profession of faith in a past tailored to present-day

---

[18] For antiquaries' filiations, see Parry, *Trophies of time* 6.
[19] Burgess, 'The *OED* Man' 1094, answered by Walker, 'Johnson's Dictionary'.
[20] Quoted in [MacCunn and MacCunn], *Recollections of W. P. Ker* 30.

purposes ... The historian, however blinkered and presentist and self-deceived, seeks to convey a past consensually known, open to inspection and proof, continually revised and eroded as time and hindsight outdate its truths. The heritage fashioner, however historically scrupulous, seeks to design a past that will fix the identity and enhance the well-being of some chosen individual or folk.[21]

In so far as a heroic age is an age in which the foundational myths of a culture are located, it is also an age in which the heritage claimed by a culture is seen as having its wellspring. The heroic achievements of the Irish people which O'Begley saw as stored up in their language are the heritage of speakers of Irish. Once a heritage has been identified, it may help to unite the people who lay claim to it, and there is therefore a sense in which questions of heritage and questions of community bear reciprocally on each other. The 'spurious past' concocted by ancient Greeks as they reflected on 'fossils and landscape ... ruins and relics' is discussed by Sir John Boardman in his *Archaeology of nostalgia*, with the conclusion that it 'played an important part in the Greeks' own creation of national identity and pride'.[22]

Dictionaries have sometimes been records of the emerging sense of identity of particular speech-communities or reading communities, groups defined by use of a common spoken language or by commitment to the study of a common body of texts. These communities are often ill-defined, and an individual may belong to more than one.[23] By no means are they always nations, and this is not a book about nationalism: the members of a speech-community may constitute a nation, but they may also spread over several nations, or be a minority in one nation, or both. The members of a reading community – the Latin-reading commonwealth of the learned, for instance – may have quite a strong sense of collective identity while remaining physically scattered. One particular kind of reading community which will appear from time to time in this book is the group of people who work together, in one place or as a network of correspondents, to make a dictionary. So, for example, James Murray remarked in his presidential address to the Philological Society in 1880 that readers from the United States had contributed very helpfully to the project that would become the *Oxford English Dictionary*, and went on to say 'that I find in Americans an ideal love for the English language as a glorious heritage, and a pride in being intimate with its grand memories, such as one does sometimes find in a classical scholar in regard

---

[21] Lowenthal, *Heritage crusade* x–xi.   [22] Boardman, *Archaeology of nostalgia* 190–1.
[23] See Burke, *Languages and communities* 5–6.

to Greek, but which is rare indeed in Englishmen towards their own tongue'.[24] In such a case, the dictionary may help to define two communities, that of its contributors and the larger one whose language it documents.

The consideration of heritage and community in linguistic terms is important. Certain objects, including buildings, and certain places are indeed tangible embodiments of heritage, an important theme of Lowenthal's book.[25] But objects and even places are vulnerable to time and fortune, in a way in which less tangible items of cultural heritage are not. Names may outlast the things named, and songs may outlast their subjects; moreover, words and tunes are portable. So, a concern with heritage that leads to the valorization of certain places and antiquities and to the collection of culturally significant objects may also lead to the valorization and collection of words, music, traditional knowledge and other intangibles. 'Folklore,' as Lowenthal reflects, 'the authentic voice of unlettered ancestors, became a prime facet of 19th-century patrimony, folksong an agent of chauvinism.'[26] There, the word *authentic* is charged with irony: the oral and customary traditions covered by the term *folklore* are not always as immemorial as those who value them like to believe. Traditions may be invented, as in the cases discussed in Eric Hobsbawm and Terence Ranger's famous collection *The invention of tradition*; the dividing line between 'oral' and 'literate' culture, between folklore and learning, is permeable.[27]

The collection of information about heritage might, in early modern Europe, belong to aristocratic culture, as in the case of the collection of genealogical information, an enterprise in which tradition was often manufactured by venal heralds and eager clients.[28] An interest in heraldry might be accompanied by an interest in lexicography, as in the cases of Sir Henry Spelman and Charles du Cange. Legal history might likewise be directed primarily to questions of landholding, a matter of most interest to the landholding classes. But it might also lead to a discovery of popular heritage, for customary law such as the common law of England or that of the *pays de coutumes* of early modern France was regarded as by definition the creation of the people rather than of nameable legislators; J. G. A. Pocock remarks of it in his classic *The ancient constitution and the*

---

[24] Murray, 'Ninth annual address' 123.   [25] Cf. also Boardman, *Archaeology of nostalgia* 45–126.
[26] Lowenthal, *Heritage crusade* 63.
[27] On oral and literate cultures, see esp. Fox, *Oral and literate culture in England, 1500–1700*.
[28] See, e.g., the examples in Edelman, *Attitudes of seventeenth-century France toward the Middle Ages* 51–3, and cf. Lowenthal, *Heritage crusade* ad indicem s.v. *genealogy*.

feudal law that it 'may have furnished one of the roots of European romanticism: for it constantly opposed the folk to the legislator, the primitive, the inarticulate and the mutable to the rigidities of ordered reason'.[29] Legal historians were, like heralds, an important class among early lexicographers. They needed to understand the wording of the laws and their cultural background, and language gave access to both.

Landowning and legal history were not the only things that brought an interest in land, language and cultural heritage together in early modern Europe: so also did the experience of travel through the country to which the traveller felt that he belonged, and a recurring theme in this book will be the relationship between lexicography and different kinds of topographical writing and collection. An important way in which writing, collection and travel might be associated with lexicography in the early modern making of heritage was the collection of inscribed objects. These might occasionally be stone tablets and the like, collected either as physical objects or by transcribing them.[30] But more often the inscribed objects were books, and particularly manuscripts. The status of certain manuscripts, for instance the Gothic Bible called the Codex Argenteus, as heritage objects handled by makers of dictionaries and wordlists will become apparent from time to time in this book; the feelings of awe and reverence that they sometimes excited show their status as heritage objects rather than simply as the raw material of scholarship. Librarianship and lexicography may go together: Georg Henisch was librarian at Augsburg and an innovative lexicographer of German; Charles du Cange contributed to the catalogue of the Greek manuscripts of the Bibliothèque du roi as well as using them in his dictionary of post-classical Greek; in the nineteenth century, the prodigious Johann Andreas Schmeller catalogued 18,000 manuscripts in the Bayerische Staatsbibliothek and compiled the first Old Saxon vocabulary and a major dictionary of Bavarian dialect words (not to mention publishing the *editio princeps* of the *Carmina Burana*); later in that century, Falconer Madan, librarian of the Bodleian Library, contributed both to the Greek lexicon of Liddell and Scott and to the *Oxford English Dictionary*.[31] Apart from such cases, and apart from the fact that making dictionaries is often best done in a library,

---

[29] Pocock, *Ancient constitution and the feudal law* 15.

[30] For collections of inscribed stones, see, e.g., Hepple, 'William Camden and early collections of Roman antiquities'; for epigraphic collections on paper see IJsewijn, *Companion to Neo-Latin studies* 2:365–79.

[31] For Henisch, see pp. 135–8 below; for du Cange and the royal manuscripts, see Barret-Kriegel, *Jean Mabillon* 53 and Leibniz, letter of 1692 to Daniel Larroque in Leibniz, *Sämtliche Schriften und Briefe* 1.8:547–9 at 548; for Schmeller's catalogue, see Hobson, *Great libraries* 140; for Madan and Greek, see

dictionaries and libraries are both collections of textual items, and they are both means of preserving and transmitting textual heritage. So, for instance, the anxiety about cultural loss that underlies the making of dictionaries such as O'Begley's can be seen underlying the foundation of the Bibliotheca Ambrosiana in Milan at a time when Italian cultural achievements appeared to be in a state of disturbing decline.[32]

The importance of books and manuscripts in heritage-building led to eagerness to fit them into stories about the past: when Matthew Parker, the most important sixteenth-century English patron of the editorial and lexicographical study of Old English, claimed that his manuscripts of Homer and of Cicero's *Rhetoric* had belonged to Theodore of Tarsus, his seventh-century predecessor in the see of Canterbury, he was surely actuated by no particular feature of the manuscripts themselves, which both belong to the fifteenth century (the Homer, indeed, is written on paper, which should have given Parker a hint as to its date), but by a desire to see them as part of the heritage of English learning.[33] Once collections of manuscripts had been formed in a particular culture, they and the knowledge to be gleaned from them might become objects of pride and even jealousy. This is the note to be detected in Humfrey Wanley's remarks to a friend on the *Palaeographia graeca* of the French Benedictine Bernard de Montfaucon: 'excepting some few things I could have made as good a book from our English libraries and collections alone: in lieu whereof, I can assure you that they can both correct and supply him'.[34] A regular concomitant of this pride was a sense that the owner of a manuscript or collection of manuscripts had a duty to make them available. So, for instance, the editor of *The principall nauigations, voiages and discoueries of the English nation*, Richard Hakluyt, complained in 1589 that 'these voyages lay so dispersed, scattered, and hidden in seuerall hucksters hands, that I now woonder at my selfe, to see how I was able to endure the delayes, curiosity, and backwardnesse of many from whom I was to receiue my originals'.[35] The assumption about the proper subordination of individual ownership to the national good that underlies these words is characteristic of the sense of heritage – 'private property

Roberts, 'Madan', and for his contributions to the *Oxford English Dictionary*, see Gilliver, '*OED* personalia' 242, and cf. Madan's collection of papers relating to *OED*: Bodl. 30254 c. 2.

[32] Hobson, *Great libraries* 186.

[33] Sisam, *Studies in the history of Old English literature* 271.

[34] Wanley, letter to Arthur Charlett of 19 November 1715, in Sisam, *Studies in the history of Old English literature* 273n2.

[35] Hakluyt, *Principall nauigations* (1589) sig. *2v.

blurs into public patrimony; privilege entails stewardship', as Lowenthal puts it – and it will be a recurring motif in this book.[36]

Another way to collect lexical objects was to make a virtual collection of texts, in other words to establish a literary canon, and to set this up as a part of the heritage of a given culture. These might be texts that had been produced in an earlier stage of that culture, as in the cases of some of the great nineteenth-century series such as the *Monumenta germaniae historica* in Germany and the Rolls series and the publications of the Early English Text Society in Great Britain. In such cases, the question of the cultural inheritance to which a given text belonged might turn out to be a vexed one. So, for instance, the *editio princeps* of *Beowulf* was made in 1815 by an Icelandic scholar whose interest in what he was handling was sharpened by his belief that it was an English translation of a Scandinavian original.[37] The *Monumenta germaniae historica*, to take another example, extend far beyond what is German in the strictest sense of the word, including texts of Frankish, Flemish and Lombard provenance, and this policy has been seen in terms of cultural appropriation.[38] The texts that were made by publication into part of the heritage of one culture might have been unquestionably produced by other cultures, such as the ancient Greek texts from the French royal library which were printed in the 1540s by Robert Estienne in the Greek types called the *Grecs du roi*, and the great series of Paris editions of Byzantine authors published from the Imprimerie Royale from 1645 onwards. Both of these series of French publications tended, if not to make Greek authors a French possession, at least to stake a French claim to them, or to integrate them with the story of the glory of France. Likewise, an eighteenth-century French author referred to du Cange as 'ce héros paisible' who brought glory to his country by scholarship, as opposed to the 'héros bruïans' who govern countries or defend them in war.[39] Because a dictionary is often something very like a lexical index to a literary canon, proprietorship of intangible heritage becomes a question in lexicography as it does in canon-formation. A recent example of sensitivity to this point is the title of the *Alberta Elders' Cree Dictionary*, which assigns proprietorship away from the chief editor of the dictionary (who is not of Cree ancestry) and the university press that published it, and to the elders of the people who speak the language.

A dictionary may be one of the most substantial records of a heritage. To return to the appeal of the *Complaynt of Scotland* to the values of

---

[36] Lowenthal, *Heritage crusade* 65.   [37] See Stanley, *In the foreground: Beowulf* 13.
[38] Geary, *Myth of nations* 28.   [39] Baron, *Éloge de Charles Dufresne, Seigneur Du Cange* 4.

antiquity, there were monuments of the Roman past in sixteenth-century Scotland, but they were very few, and for the most part physically insignificant. If a sixteenth-century Scot was to be uplifted by a heritage of Roman virtue, it had to be through language. And this was possible: the availability of grammars and dictionaries, and of a canon of ancient texts (which informed a vigorous canon of Scottish neo-Latin) ensured that Latin could be learned and read, that Latin words could live, warm and active, in the mouths of Queen Mary's contemporaries. Likewise, Henri Estienne's passionate love for the culture of ancient Greece had to feed on words, on texts, rather than things; the Ottoman occupation of the eastern Mediterranean precluded his enjoying the physical intimacy with Greek antiquities that was an important and exciting part of the Hellenophile experience from the nineteenth century onward. O'Begley and his colleagues in Paris may have had some physical mementoes of Ireland with them, but they were in more or less voluntary exile from the country itself and, even if they had been at home, their Catholic, Irish-speaking culture was marginalized and dwindling there; the part of Ireland they could carry about and regenerate at will was the Irish language.

A language is more than a collection of words, and the complete study of a linguistic heritage goes beyond lexicography. However, it is easier to observe and collect old words than to observe and collect grammatical features. So it was that a reflection on linguistic change attributed to one of the most learned Englishmen of the mid seventeenth century, John Selden, was expressed in purely lexical terms:

If you looke upon the language spoken in the Saxon time & the language spoken now, you will find the difference to be just, as if a man had a Cloake that hee wore plaine in Queene Eliz: dayes, & since has putt in here a peece of redd & there a peece of blew, heere a peece of Greene & there a peece of Orange Tawney. Wee borrow words from the French, Italian, Latine, as every pedantick man pleases.[40]

This is taken from Selden's table talk, and even if he spoke those very words, his considered judgement might have been more sophisticated. It is striking, though, that he or the recorder of his conversation was able to imagine for a moment that the significant changes to English that had taken

---

[40] Selden, *Table Talk* 67–8; a contemporary use of the same image is G[eorge] T[ooke], prefatory epistle to 'The Belides, or eulogie of that noble martialist Major William Fairefax' in Tooke, *The Belides or eulogie and elegie of that truly honourable John Lord Harrington Baron of Exton* 22, 'another Netherlander, has objected our English to me, for made up of severall shreds like a Beggars Cloake'.

place between 'the Saxon time' and his own were a matter of the borrowing of words, not of grammatical development. That understanding of language privileged dictionaries over grammars.

Words are a living and portable inheritance from the past, and they embody a culture with particular fullness. Every cultural institution and concept has its distinctness summed up in its individual name, and its history is accessible through the history of that name. This is the *raison d'être* of Raymond Williams' famous lexicological study *Keywords*, and indeed of an earlier essay on the same lines, Léon Brunschvicg's *Héritage des mots, héritage d'idées*. The relationship between words and cultural phenomena is not confined to the intellectual culture surveyed in those books. Dictionaries, by collecting the names of all the distinctive institutions of a culture, are depositories of the whole culture in microcosm. So, for instance, a nineteenth-century dictionary of the Karen language, spoken by one of the peoples of Myanmar, has the suggestive title *Thesaurus of Karen knowledge, comprising traditions, legends or fables, poetry, customs, superstitions, demonology, therapeutics, etc., alphabetically arranged, and forming a complete native Karen dictionary with definitions and examples illustrating the usages of every word*.[41] Likewise, Jack Thiessen, the author of three dictionaries of the variety of Low German spoken by Mennonites of Prussian and Ukrainian heritage in Canada and elsewhere, wrote in the foreword to the first: 'This modest effort has one goal: the goal of promoting a unique sense of Gemeinschaft which was guided by a peculiar dialect star and which star accompanied a world which I experienced and of which one could say: it still had a semblance of happy order.'[42] Again, a review of a dictionary of the Iban language, spoken in Borneo, notes that it 'is far more than a mere recording of words and their meanings; it is a major reference work on Iban oral tradition and custom.'[43]

Since the heroic world is by definition past or coming to an end, its language is often perceived by the living members of a culture to be distinct from theirs. A dictionary may make a bridge between heroic language and living language in one of three ways. First, when the language of the heroic age is quite distinct from that of the living, a dictionary may offer the possibility of translation. It will in that case gloss the words of the heroic language with those of a living language, giving speakers of the latter access to texts written in the former. Second, when the language of the heroic age is an ancestor of that of the living, a

---

[41] Kau-Too, *Thesaurus of Karen knowledge*, title-page.
[42] Thiessen, *Mennonite Low-German dictionary* viii.   [43] King, 'Clever Talk'.

dictionary may offer the possibility of etymological connection. It will in that case include in its discussion of the words of the living language an explanation of the derivation of each from the dead heroic language. Third, when the language of the heroic age is an earlier form of that of the living, a dictionary may offer the possibility of revival or enrichment. It will in that case offer lexical items from the dead language side by side with items from the living language. In all three cases, the work done by dictionaries contributes to the retrieval and revival of cultural heritage. From the Renaissance desire to reanimate texts, wisdom and virtue from Greek and Roman antiquity to the desire of many twentieth-century Blacks in the United States to understand and recultivate their African roots – from the *Anacreontea* to Kwanzaa – the listing and shaping of words has been part of the business of heritage; dictionaries have been made and used to give access to the heroic past.

Sometimes, they have also shown that the past is inaccessible: the sense of loss may be a part of the sense of heritage. The Mennonite heritage documented in Jack Thiessen's dictionary 'still had a semblance of happy order', a form of words which suggests that, when Thiessen was writing, he saw that sense of happy order as a thing of the past. Dictionaries recover words and store words: they are sometimes called *thesaurus* or *trésor*, 'treasury'. But sometimes the words gathered in a dictionary are both a surviving linguistic heritage and a sign that a material heritage has been lost, and sometimes they are the record of a dying linguistic heritage. Grief for an unrecoverable, unattainable past is itself a kind of possession, and one that has been a foundation for lexicography.

Finally, every lexicographer whose work is rich enough to express a heritage will be affected by a double inheritance, cultural and personal. My use of a given language ties me to the other members of my speech-community, and to our shared past, or at least it ties me to a heritage, an imaginative regeneration of that past. The scope and kind of this heritage will be determined by the place and time in which I live, since the past has been imagined differently in different places and different times. My interest in it may connect me to an intellectual heritage of teachers and their teachers.[44] But a second narrative which interweaves with this narrative of culture is that of perceptions of individual inheritance. My use of the language of my childhood brings me back to that childhood, and to the parents who taught me to speak, and to the family among whom I spoke. My use of a language learned after childhood brings me back

---

[44] Cf. Lowenthal, *Heritage crusade* 33 and n7.

to the circumstances that led me or forced me to learn it. My statements about language are, unless they are of an inhuman dryness, most unlikely to escape some colouring from my heritages. If I make a dictionary, it will tell a story about heritage.

This book obeys two sets of limits and transgresses one. The first set that it obeys is geographical and linguistic: the dictionaries discussed in this book were made in western Europe (including the British Isles) and nearly all of them describe Latin, Greek, or Germanic or Romance languages. This criterion has the advantage of making the book more cohesive, but it is really imposed by the limits of my linguistic competence. If I were to discuss dictionaries of the Slavonic languages or of Hebrew, both of which were studied in early modern Europe, I would be working entirely from secondary sources, as I would if I moved into non-European traditions of lexicography such as those of Arabic or of the languages of India and the Far East. I am unwilling to do so. Within the area that I do discuss, I make no attempt at comprehensiveness, and many important dictionaries are mentioned in passing or not at all: this is not a general history of western European lexicography but a discussion of one group of themes in lexicographical thought, based on a selection of case-studies.

The second set of limits that the book obeys is imposed by choice: I am interested in understanding what people thought in the sixteenth and seventeenth centuries, not in deciding how good they were at anticipating what we know in the twenty-first, and so although I have not deliberately made incorrect statements on the authority of early writers, I have tried as far as possible to avoid judging their statements with hindsight as right or wrong. For instance, I report Goropius Becanus' identification of the name *Adam* with the Dutch elements *hat* 'hate' plus *dam* 'dam', but it seems unnecessary to labour the point that this etymology was wrong, and I am certainly not interested in making patronizing remarks about Goropius' ignorance of the name's actual origins in Hebrew.

The phrase 'lexicographical thought' introduces the set of limits that my argument transgresses: I have not confined myself to the discussion of dictionaries in any narrow sense of the word, but have also considered a number of short wordlists and other studies of words. As J. G. A. Pocock has put it, one 'may seek to distinguish between "historical thought" and "historiography"; perhaps better . . . one may say that the writing of "history" was not always carried on by the writing of "histories"'.[45] Similarly, lexicographical thought, which is the subject of this book, has not always been expressed in the writing of dictionaries; Guillaume Budé, who never published a dictionary but had a major influence on lexicography, is a good example. Some histories of lexicography have been notably impoverished by a failure to look beyond dictionaries at the related works contemporary with them.

This book falls into eight chapters of three or four sections each. This first chapter has introduced the association between dictionaries and ideas of heritage, and the next six will look at three different textual and linguistic heritages with which early modern dictionaries engaged. The heritages of the classical world are discussed in chapters 2 and 3, chapter 2 taking the story from the first dictionaries of the age of print to the work of Robert Estienne in the 1530s and 1540s, and chapter 3 being devoted to the work of Henri Estienne from the late 1540s to the early 1590s. The heritages of the early medieval Germanic world are then discussed in chapters 4, 5 and 6: chapter 4 introduces the topic of the rediscovery of vernacular heritages and deals with Germany and the Netherlands in the sixteenth century and the first ten or twenty years of the seventeenth; chapter 5 turns to England from the early sixteenth century to around 1650; and chapter 6 discusses England and Scandinavia, and the international figure of Franciscus Junius, in the third quarter of the seventeenth century. Seventeenth-century treatments of the heritages of the worlds of post-classical Latinity and Byzantine Greek are then discussed in chapter 7. Chapter 8 comments on three ways in which seventeenth-century lexicographical thought built on and went beyond these heritages, and chapter 9 brings some conclusions together.

---

[45] Pocock, 'Ancient constitution revisited' 255.

CHAPTER 2

The classical heritage I: Philology and lexicography

THE LABOURS OF HERCULES: LEXICOGRAPHY AND THE CLASSICAL HERITAGE AT THE TIME OF ERASMUS

A literary canon is defined in order to embody a cultural heritage. When the philologists of Hellenistic Alexandria made lists of the authors whose writings merited particular attention, they were selecting a heritage, saying that these authors were connected with their own period, and encouraging the reinforcement of that connection by imitation.[1] The theme of the imitation of selected ancients – the *classici* as they were called as early as the second century AD – has a long history, from Statius' closing of his epic *Thebais* with the injunction to the poem to follow the footsteps of Virgil's *Aeneid* and worship them at a respectful distance, through Chaucer's injunction to his poem *Troilus and Criseyde* to 'kis the steppes, wheras thou seest pace Virgile, Ovyde, Omer, Lucan and Stace'.[2] There has been a classical heritage for as long as there has been a canon of classical authors in whose footsteps a reader might try to follow.

In the fourteenth and fifteenth centuries, the canon that had been known and available in ancient Rome was known no longer to be fully available, and earnest efforts to recover it were being made: this is the familiar story of the textual rediscoveries of the Renaissance. An intersection of this story of the recovery of a textual heritage with the story of lexicography took place in 1508, as Erasmus worked on a dictionary of ancient sayings and allusions, the *Adagia*, in the combined household and printing works, the *officina*, of Aldus Manutius in Venice. 'I perceived quite clearly', he wrote,

that this was no job for one man or one library ... and I have finished it ... with the assistance of only one library. It was of course the library at the house of

---

[1] Pfeiffer, *HCS* I 203–7.
[2] See, e.g., Curtius, *European literature and the Latin Middle Ages* 247–64.

Aldus, and so it was as rich and well supplied with good books as any anywhere, particularly Greek, being as it were the source from which all good libraries world-wide spring and increase.[3]

Erasmus remarked elsewhere on the way that manuscripts poured into the *officina*:

How often were ancient copies sent him unsought from Hungary or Poland, and complimentary presents with them, so that with all needful diligence he might publish them ... When I, a Dutchman, was in Italy, preparing to publish my book of *Adagia*, all the learned men there had offered me, unsought, authors not yet published in print who they thought might be of use to me and Aldus had nothing in his treasure-house that he did not share with me ... Just consider what advantages I should have lost, had not scholars supplied me with texts in manuscript.[4]

He went on to ennumerate some of the manuscripts that were sent to the Aldine *officina* for his use: the works of Plato and of Plutarch, the *Deipnosophistae* of Athenaeus, Eustathios of Thessalonica's commentaries on Homer, Pausanias' description of Greece.[5] Although some were unsought, others clearly were solicited: Aldus reminded an eastern European friend in 1502 that in the past 'you promised, whatever the cost, to send and search for books in the land of the Dacians, where men say there is a tower full of ancient books'.[6]

As Aldus and Erasmus knew, not all owners of manuscripts were generous with them; the ideal that 'privilege entails stewardship' was not universal. In the early 1490s, Aldus had been unable to borrow manuscripts he needed; by 1497, he could say proudly that Greek manuscripts were regularly sent to him for his use, but still added the hope that 'if there should be people so evilly disposed that they grieve at a good

---

[3] Erasmus, *Adagia* III i 1 ('Herculei labores'), *ASD* II–5:36, 'Plane perspiciebam hunc laborem nec vnius esse hominis nec vnius bibliothecae ... quem nos soli ... absoluimus vna duntaxat adiuti bibliotheca, nimirum Aldina copiosissima quidem illa quaque non alia bonis libris praecipue Graecis instructior, vt ex qua ceu fonte omnes bonae bibliothecae per omnem vsque orbem nascuntur ac propagantur' trans. adapted from *CWE* XXXIV:179.

[4] Erasmus, *Adagia* II i 1 ('Festina lente'), addition of 1526, *LB* II:405, 'Quoties ad illum ab Hungaris ac Polonis missa sunt ultro vetusta exemplaria, non sine honorario munere, ut ea justa cura publicarent orbi? ... Cum apud Italos ederem Proverbiorum opus homo Batavus, quotquot illic aderant eruditi ultro suppeditabant auctores nondum per typographos evulgatos, quos mihi suspicabantur usui futuros, Aldus nihil habebat in thesauro suo, quod non communicaret ... Hic mihi cogita quanta pars utilitas abfutura fuerit, nisi docti libros manu descriptos suppeditassent', trans. altered from *CWE* XXXIII:14.

[5] Ibid.; see Geanakoplos, *Greek scholars in Venice* 263–5 for discussion.

[6] Manutius, dedication of Valerius Maximus (1502) in *Aldo Manuzio editore* 1:67, 'pollicitus es tua quamvis magna impensa ad Dacas usque mittere inveniendi librorum gratia, quod ibi antiquorum librorum plena turris esse dicatur', trans. Lowry, *World of Aldus Manutius* 197.

common to all, they may either burst of envy, or, succumbing to their grief, be overcome by wretchedness and at last hang themselves, since they will shortly see all of the extant books of Aristotle printed on our press'.[7] That hope suggests that there were indeed people so evilly disposed as not to see their manuscripts as part of a common scholarly heritage, and Erasmus describes one of them just after his happy reminiscence of the generosity of the Italian owners who had sent their codices to him at Aldus' *officina*: a northern European owner of a copy of the Byzantine encyclopedic dictionary called the *Suda*, in which proverbial material had been marked in the margins, steadfastly refused to lend it because 'everything is now becoming public property' that had previously been reserved by scholars for their own use, safe from the common gaze. He goes on to remark: 'There lie hid in the colleges and monasteries of Germany, France, and England very ancient manuscripts' which their owners are most unwilling to make available.[8]

In his attitude to the selfish withholding of manuscripts from publication, Erasmus showed his sense that those manuscripts, and the lexical items that he wanted to publish from them in his dictionary of ancient culture, were parts of a heritage. In his attitude to his own work on them, he showed his sense that he, as the maker of a dictionary, was a heroic figure; this sense developed at just the time when he was reading Greek manuscripts in the *officina* of Aldus Manutius. He identified himself, appropriately enough, with a Greek hero, Hercules. He had included the tag 'Herculei labores' in his first, very brief, collection of adages, the *Adagiorum collectanea* of 1500: 'The proverbial "Herculean labours" describes those which are indeed useful to others, but bring nothing but envy to the person who performs them.'[9] In 1507, writing to ask if Aldus would be interested in printing his translations of two plays by Euripides, he applied the tag to Aldus himself: 'you devote yourself to reviving and disseminating good writers, taking infinite pains indeed but failing to receive an adequate reward; and you strive at enormous tasks in the

---

[7] Manutius, preface to *Thesaurus cornucopiae* (1496) in *Aldo Manuzio editore* I:II, 'Spero fore et illud, ut, siqui sunt tam pravo ingenio, ut communi omnium bono moereant, aut rumpantur inuidia aut succumbentes moerori misere conficiantur et denique suspendant se, quandoquidem quaecunque extant Aristotelis volumina videbunt brevi nostris excusa formis.'

[8] Erasmus, *Adagia* II i I ('Festina lente'), addition of 1526, *LB* II:405, 'fassus est, haec jam evulgari, per quae docti hactenus fuissent vulgo mirandi. Hinc illae lachrimae. Latitant in collegiis ac monasteriis Germanorum, Gallorum & Anglorum pervetusti codices, quos exceptis paucis adeo non communicant ultro, ut rogati vel celent, vel pernegent, vel iniquio precio vendant usum, decuplo aestimatorum codicum', trans. *CWE* XXXIII:15.

[9] Erasmus, *Adagia* III i I ('Herculei labores'), *ASD* II–5:23, 'Herculei labores prouerbio dicuntur, qui aliis quidem vtiles auctori praeter inuidiam nihil afferunt.'

manner of Hercules ... which for the time being profit others rather than yourself'.[10]

Once he had taken up residence in the Aldine household, he found the tag particularly applicable to the work in which he participated there. His vastly enlarged new edition of the *Adagia* included, as one of its longest entries, an essay-like treatment of 'Herculei labores', in which he writes that 'if any human toils deserve to be awarded the epithet of "Herculean", it seems to belong in the highest degree to those at least who devote their efforts to restoring the monuments of ancient and true literature'.[11] He was now claiming the epithet for himself as well as for Aldus, and went on to expatiate on this, explaining the 'immense labours and the infinite difficulties' which the *Adagia* had cost him.[12] His reading programme had been comprehensive: 'it is all the writers that ever were, ancient and modern, good and bad alike, in both Latin and Greek and every known subject – in short, it is the whole range of the written word that a man must, I will not say, run through, but analyse and examine'.[13] But even after this, there were the secondary sources to read, some of which made his work harder rather than easier, and there was the problem of collating texts, and the fact that so much classical literature had been lost, and the physical difficulty of obtaining and reading manuscripts, and even of handling one's own notes: 'Suppose you have read everything, made notes of everything, have everything ready at hand: is it all, in this vast medley of materials, instantly available?'[14] He concluded in an addition to the entry made in 1515 for a yet further expanded edition that his labours had been Herculean and more than Herculean, for he had worked at once on revising the *Adagia* and on editing the letters of Saint Jerome, 'two frightful monsters at the same time, each of which demanded so much

---

[10] Erasmus, letter to Aldus Manutius, 28 October 1507, in *Opus epistolarum* 1:437, 'restituendis propagandisque bonis authoribus das operam, summa quidem cura, at non pari lucro, planeque Herculis exemplo laboribus excerceris, pulcherrimis quidem illis et immortalem gloriam allaturis aliquando, verum aliis interim frugiferis magis quam tibi', trans. *CWE* 11:131; cf. Jardine, *Erasmus, man of letters* 41f.

[11] Erasmus, *Adagia* III i 1 ('Herculei labores'), *ASD* II–5:27, 'Quodsi vllis hominum laboribus hoc cognominis debetur, vt Herculani dicantur, eorum certe vel maxime deberi videtur, qui in restituendis antiquae veraeque literaturae monimentis elaborant', trans. *CWE* XXXIV:170.

[12] Ibid., *ASD* II–5:28, 'quam immensis sudoribus, quam infinitis difficultatibus', trans. *CWE* XXXIV:171.

[13] Ibid., *ASD* II–5:28, 'hic quicquid est scriptorum, veterum recentium, bonorum simul et malorum, in vtraque lingua, in omniiugi disciplina, breuiter in omni scripti genere, necessum fuit non dicam euoluere, sed curiosius ac penitus excutere rimarique', trans. *CWE* XXXIV:172.

[14] Ibid., *ASD* II–5:33, 'Vt nihil non legeris, nihil non annotaris, nihil non apparaueris, itane statim in tam immensa rerum turba succurrit?' trans. *CWE* XXXIV:175; cf. Blair, 'Reading strategies'.

effort that it demanded many a Hercules'.[15] Thereafter, he used the reference in more letters, and had ΗΡΑΚΛΕΙ ΠΟΝΟΙ, 'the labours of Hercules', included as the tail-edge title of the book he is holding in Holbein's portrait of 1523. Correspondents of his picked it up as well.[16] So did Aldus, whose complaints about the volume of correspondence he received and the interruptions he had to put up with were followed by the proclamation that he had put up a notice above the door of his room, with the following inscription:

Whoever you are, Aldus asks you again and again: if there is anything you want from him, please state your business quickly and get on your way, unless you are going to take his work on your shoulders, as Hercules did for weary Atlas.[17]

The image of Hercules was to be taken up by other scholars and learned publishers. The labour of cleaning the Augean stables was often alluded to, since it was one of washing away the accretions of ages, like a Renaissance scholar purging a text of layers of error: as Alciato put it, Hercules 'cleans out filth, and brings new refinement to men's minds'.[18] So, for instance, Thomas James, first librarian of the Bodleian, remarked that the Papist editors of a recent edition of the works of Gregory the Great had unsurprisingly produced a seriously defective text: a team collating the Rome edition with four manuscripts in Oxford 'have found so many passages added, removed, changed and interchanged that a single Hercules will not be enough to make this Augean stable clean again'.[19] The seventeenth-century Dutch philologist Cornelius Schrevelius was said to have cleared errors out of the text of a Greek dictionary which he was revising for the house of Elzevier 'with such labour, that he can be said, as it were, to have purged the Augean stable of its filth'.[20] A few years later, the printer Roger Daniel was praised in a preface to his new edition of a geographical dictionary for his improvements to the text, the

---

[15] Ibid., *ASD* 11–5:33, 'Nobis ... cum duobus monstris immanibus fuit congrediendum, quorum vtrumuis tantum habebat negocii, vt multos Hercules requireret', trans. *CWE* xxxiv:181.

[16] Erasmus, *Opus epistolarum, ad indicem* s.n. *Hercules*.

[17] Manutius in *Rhetorica ad Herennium* (1521) in *Aldo Manuzio editore* 1:129, 'Quisquis es, rogat te Aldus etiam atque etiam ut, siquid est quod a se velis, perpaucis agas, deinde actutum abeas; nisi tanquam Hercules, defesso Atlante, veneris suppositurus humeros', trans. Lowry, *World of Aldus Manutius* 166.

[18] Alciati, *Emblematum libellus* fo. 15r, 'expurgat sordes, & cultum mentibus addit'.

[19] James, *Bellum Gregorianum* sig. A2r, 'comperimus tot addita, detracta, mutata, commutata, vt ne vnus quidem *Hercules* sufficeret ad hoc *Augiae* stabulum repurgandum'.

[20] Louis Elzevier, epistle to the reader in Scapula, *Lexicon graeco–latinum* (1652) sig. *2r, 'tanto labore, ut vel *Augiae* stabulum a sordibus suis repurgasse, dici possit'.

rhetorical question 'but who shall cleanse the Augean stable?' having as its answer that Daniel himself had undertaken the job.[21]

The revised *Adagia* that Erasmus produced in the Aldine *officina* was a magnificent achievement; no other work of early modern scholarship is as widely enjoyed today. The book is by no means simply a collection of proverbs: its lemmata are a mixture of proverbs, quotations and single words. It is in fact a dictionary, one of the first big dictionaries of post-medieval Europe. None of its entries is a simple one-word gloss, and some are long essays, which were to be expanded further in later editions. Its concern with the cultural significance of lexical items makes it a forerunner of many of the dictionaries that will be discussed in this book, and distances it radically from earlier dictionaries. Erasmus himself played up this distance. Writing of the *Catholicon* of Giovanni Balbi, a major thirteenth-century dictionary available in several incunabular editions, he exclaimed 'Immortal God! What absurdities the author of the *Catholicon* brings in in his entry for the word *Tristegon*! What an unhappy age was that, when books like this were the sanctuaries, as it were, from which literary oracles were sought!' and referred to 'the most unlearned of all works, which is called *Catholicon*'.[22] His decision not to present the *Adagia* in alphabetical order can be explained in several ways, but perhaps one reason for it was that he wanted to make it clear that he was not doing the same sort of lexicography as his medieval predecessors.[23]

Nor was he: Erasmus had read very extensively in ancient literature, setting up an influential ideal of comprehensive, encyclopedic knowledge of 'the whole range of the written word', and had synthesized his reading brilliantly. He had also shown succeeding generations of the learned how a scholar might make even a work of splendid learning sparklingly autobiographical. But even as he laboured, a new way of approaching the ancient world was being prepared. For as Erasmus worked on the *Adagia* he used, as was noted above, manuscripts that preserved texts such as the *Deipnosophistae* of Athenaeus and Pausanias' description of Greece. He used, that is to say, texts whose attraction is not so much their style or

---

[21] William Dillingham, preface in Ferrarius, *Lexicon geographicum* sig. *3v, 'At quis Augiae stabulum expurgabit?'

[22] Erasmus, *In novum testamentum annotationes* (1535) on Acts 20:9 (*LB* VI:511F), 'Deum immortalem! quas naenias adducit auctor Catholicon de hac voce *Tristegum*. O miserum illud seculum! quum ex hujusmodi libris velut ex adytis petebantur oracula litterarum' and on Hebrews 11:37 (*LB* VI:1017E), 'auctor operis omnium indoctissimi, quod vocant *Catholicon*'. For more on Erasmus and medieval grammars and dictionaries, see Tunberg, 'Latinity of Erasmus' 151–2, and for the *Catholicon* in an early sixteenth-century context, see Moss, *Renaissance truth* 15–19.

[23] Cf. Moss, *Renaissance truth* 21, 28.

their philosophy as their richness as sources for the material culture of the ancient world: the kinds of fish that people ate, the vessels from which they drank their wine, the location of public buildings. As these texts were printed (the Aldine *editio princeps* of Athenaeus, for instance, appeared in 1514 and that of Pausanias in 1516), scholars without Erasmus' privileged access to manuscripts could start to ask themselves questions about topics such as these.

Answering these questions entailed doing philology, in one particular sense of the word, which is suggested by the classic discussions of Hellenistic and early modern scholarship by Rudolf Pfeiffer.[24] The business of philology is, in this sense, the systematic and comprehensive knowledge of the past, founded on the study of texts: 'some knowledge', as Juan Luis Vives put it, 'of matters such as chronology, geography, histories, fictions, proverbs, sayings, apophthegms, domestic and rural affairs' and more.[25] A book like the *Adagia*, which uses ancient texts to build up a picture of the common wisdom of people in the ancient world, is in this sense a fundamentally philological book. The history of this sense of *philology* is a long one. The first person to call himself φιλόλογος 'philologist' was the Alexandrian Eratosthenes, whose interests included the Greek language (including technical vocabulary), literary history, chronology and geography.[26] The Latin equivalent *philologus* was taken as a name by the polymath Lucius Ateius, author of a *liber glossematorum* on rare or obsolete words. Scholars who are in this sense philologists often, like Eratosthenes and Ateius, collect rare words, but they use them to study culture: the sense of *philology* applicable to their work should be distinguished from *philology* meaning 'the study, always empirical and often historical, of language', as in the name of the discipline of comparative philology. In fact, the *philologi* discussed by Pfeiffer have less in common with comparative philologists than with the *antiquarii* of a famous article by Arnaldo Momigliano, which reflects on the distinction between *antiquitates*, as studied (and perhaps given that name) by Varro, and political history: for Varro, *antiquitates* 'meant a systematic survey of Roman life according to the evidence provided by language, literature, and custom'.[27] Momigliano

---

[24] Pfeiffer, *HCS* I 156ff. and Pfeiffer, *HCS* II 101–2, 170ff. (and cf. 118); on Pfeiffer's conception of philology, cf. Lloyd-Jones, 'Rudolf Pfeiffer' 267f.

[25] Vives, *De tradendis disciplinis* lib. 3, 271, 'philologia, id est cognitio aliqua reru[m] nempe temporum, locorum, historiae, fabulae, prouerbioru[m] sententiarum, apophthegmatum, rei domesticae, rei rustic[a]e'.

[26] Pfeiffer, *HCS* I 156–70.

[27] Momigliano, 'Ancient history and the antiquarian'; see also his *Classical foundations of modern historiography*, esp. 54ff., and cf. Cornell, 'Ancient history and the antiquarian revisited'.

remarked in his article that the two great dictionaries of Charles du Cange were 'to be reckoned among the products of antiquarian research' in this sense, and the connection between antiquarianism and language was generally important in the early modern period.[28] One reason for this was that, for Varro's early modern readers, the survival of a substantial part of his *De lingua latina* and the loss of most of his *Antiquitates rerum humanarum et divinarum* meant that his reputation as, in Cicero's words, 'diligentissimus investigator antiquitatis' and 'praestans omnique doctrina' – 'most diligent investigator of antiquity' and 'outstanding in every branch of learning' – was bound up with his treatment of language, and especially etymology.[29] So, they were particularly disposed to see language as a tool for the study of the *res antiquaria*.

The philological study of ancient texts, and the philological lexicography that went with it, really began in the first half of the sixteenth century. To be sure, much humanistic work before the sixteenth century had had a very similar aim. Imitation of the style, and therefore the language, of ancient texts was a way to appreciate the culture that underlay them. This is why the Renaissance began: educated Italians not only had a sense of themselves as the spatial heirs of ancient Rome, but also appreciated the way in which privileging and imitating the style and language of texts from ancient Rome might help them to find models for their own culture – urban, republican, characterized by the presence of a lay intelligentsia and by the sense that public service through civic office was a high ideal – when such models were lacking in the chivalric literatures of transalpine Europe.[30] Moreover, the humanistic imitation of ancient models and the philological interest in everyday life in the ancient world came together in the re-creation of Latin as a language to be spoken in the classroom and even in everyday conversation, a project for which manuals were published in the late fifteenth and early sixteenth centuries, and which was realized in a few cases such as those of Montaigne, Camille Morel and Henri Estienne.[31] But the point remains that the recovery of a

---

[28] Momigliano, 'Ancient history and the antiquarian' 291n1.

[29] On the survival of Varro's works and his early modern reputation, see Brown, 'Varro' (quotations from Cicero at 453).

[30] See Witt, '*In the footsteps of the ancients*' esp. 22ff.

[31] For the general background, see Tavoni, 'Western Europe' 8–9, Burke, "Heu domine, adsunt Turcae" 45ff and Burke, *Languages and communities* 45–7, supplemented by Salmon, 'Missionary linguistics' 332; for spoken Latin as an educational ideal, Trinquet, *Jeunesse de Montaigne* 193–304 *passim* and, e.g., Vives, *De tradendis disciplinis* lib. 3, 278; for case-studies, Trinquet, *Jeunesse de Montaigne* 354–8 (discussing Montaigne, *Essais* 1.26); Will, 'Camille de Morel' 90; and Armstrong, *Robert Estienne* 92–3.

moral and intellectual culture through the profound understanding of canonical style and language that comes with good and creative imitation is not the same as the recovery of a whole culture, including its physical details, that comes with attention to a wider textual corpus, and a more comprehensively investigated language. In the words of Wilamowitz,

> what matters to us is the negative point that no concern with history or philology played any part either in the search for the old literature or in its dissemination. The humanists would long remain men of letters, publicists, teachers, but in no way did they become scholars ... we must not expect philology of the humanists.[32]

There is a significant difference between the kind of humanistic lexicography that serves the student of Latin or Greek prose composition, and the kind of philological or antiquarian lexicography that serves the cultural historian.[33] The first of these kinds of lexicography is exemplified by the Greek dictionary of Giovanni Crastone (1476) and the Latin dictionary of Ambrogio Calepino (1502). Both of these were influential expressions of and contributions to the humanistic recovery of the classical lexical heritage, and both call for discussion before the lexicographical work that followed theirs can be considered.

Giovanni Crastone (Crestone, Crestoni, Joannes Crastonus) was a Carmelite, who played a significant part in the first generation of print-assisted Greek scholarship. He translated the Greek grammar of Konstantinos Laskaris into Latin in 1480, and thus made the learning of Greek considerably easier, and he produced the *editio princeps* of the Greek translation of the Psalms. He also made a Greek–Latin dictionary. This, the *Lexicon graeco–latinum* (it is sometimes known by its Greek title, Λεξικὸν κατὰ στοιχείων), appeared as a large, handsome folio of 520 pages and about 18,000 entries in 1476, the second or third book ever to be printed in Greek.[34] For nearly fifty years it was 'the vital book for every humanist who wanted to learn Greek seriously'.[35] Crastone's role was that of editor rather than sole creator: the printer, Buono Accorso of Milan,

---

[32] Wilamowitz-Moellendorff, *Geschichte der Philologie* 10, 'Wichtig ist ... das Negative, daß historisch-philologisches Interesse weder an dem Suchen noch an der Verbreitung der alten Literatur beteiligt ist. Noch auf lange Zeit sind die Humanisten durchaus nur Literaten, Publizisten, Lehrer, dagegen Philologen keineswegs ... Wir dürfen eben von den Humanisten keine Philologie verlangen,' trans. in Wilamowitz, *History of classical scholarship* 21, 23 (adapted).

[33] For the idea of 'humanistic lexicography', see Bierbach, *Grundzüge humanistischer Lexicographie in Frankreich*.

[34] Entry-count from Delaruelle, 'Dictionnaire greco–latin de Crastone' 233.

[35] Ibid. 221, 'le livre indispensable à tous les humanistes qui voulaient apprendre sérieusement le grec'.

explained in his foreword that Crastone had undertaken the emendation of earlier work by Laskaris and others, which had been done 'I shall not say thoughtlessly, but not very elegantly and accurately'.[36] The *Lexicon graeco–latinum* was on the whole a collection of glosses, sometimes single words, sometimes lists of two or three possible equivalents. Illustrative quotations were not provided. A Latin–Greek version, *Lexicon latino–graecum*, was to appear, suggesting the didactic role of the dictionary: Crastone's target audience was interested in understanding what classical Greek words meant, but also in writing original compositions in Greek. These would be belletristic, as can be seen from the claim in Accorso's preface that the dictionary presents 'nearly all the words both of orators and of poets which are in general use'.[37]

Crastone was making his dictionary at the very beginning of the printing of Greek texts, and it soon called for revision. A number of new editions were produced from the fifteenth century into the 1520s.[38] Five of these are particularly interesting. One, published by Aldus Manutius in 1497, presented Crastone's work with some ancient lexical opuscula and a copious index; its selection by Aldus as part of his programme of Greek publication demonstrates its status as the pre-eminent Greek lexicon of the late fifteenth century. Another, published in 1519, is an example of a self-consciously Herculean dictionary, presented with a specially designed title-page border in which the Gallic Hercules is to be seen leading a crowd by the chains of eloquence coming from his mouth.[39] A third, published by Froben in 1524, has an epistle to the reader by Erasmus.[40] Two others never reached print. One of these survives in the form of a copy annotated before 1513 by Johannes Cuno, which subsequently passed into the hands of Beatus Rhenanus, and is mentioned in a letter of Erasmus.[41] The other was undertaken by Johannes Reuchlin for the Basel printer Johannes

---

[36] Buono Accorso, dedicatory epistle in Crastone, *Lexicon graeco–latinum* sig. A2r, 'uidissetq[ue] quae et a Consta[n]tino Lascari & ab aliis quibusdam inmedium elata forent: no[n] dicam inconsyderate sed minus eleganter & p[ro]prie: uoluit p[ro] sua bonitate tanto errori occurrere'. For the ultimate source, see Delaruelle, 'Dictionnaire greco–latin de Crastone' 228f.

[37] *Gesamtkatalog der Wiegendrucke* item 7816, giving the text of the relevant part of the dedication: 'omnia fere uerba quae in usum co[m]unem cadunt uel oratoru[m] uel poetaru[m]'.

[38] A late example, perhaps the last, is the edition published without author's name as *Dictionarium graecum* by Melchior Sessa and Petrus de Ravanis in Venice in 1525; Delaruelle, 'Dictionnaire greco–latin de Crastone' 246n1, notes a *Lexicon graecolatinum* printed by Gerard Morrhe in Paris in 1530 apparently based on Crastone's dictionary but so much augmented as to constitute a different work.

[39] For the title-page border, see Meier et al., *Andreas Cratander* 68–9.

[40] The letter is Erasmus, *Opus epistolarum* v:483–5 (no. 1460), with a very useful prefatory note.

[41] Now in the Bibliothèque Humaniste, Sélestat: see Hieronymus, *Griechischer Geist aus Basler Pressen* 4–5 (item 3), and also Erasmus, letter to Froben of 22 October 1518, in *Opus epistolarum* III:421–2 (no. 885).

Amerbach, and survives in the form of Reuchlin's copy of the 1476 edition, very heavily annotated up to the world ἐπιτρέπομαι.[42] Reuchlin can be said on the evidence of these annotations to have done lexicographical work on all three of the learned languages of his time: Greek, Latin (his *Vocabularius breviloquus*, which is heavily indebted to medieval sources, was printed by Amerbach in 1478) and Hebrew, in the reworking of David Kimchi's twelfth-century dictionary that forms the first two books of his *Rudimenta hebraica* of 1506.[43]

The career of Reuchlin's Latin dictionary came to an abrupt end: it was printed twenty times in the fifteenth century, but only twice thereafter (1501 and 1504). This was because it was superseded by that of Ambrogio Calepino (Calepinus, de Calepio), to which we now turn. Calepino, the son of a nobleman, who lived as an Augustinian religious from the age of eighteen onwards, was the maker of the best-selling Latin dictionary of the sixteenth century. It was printed in 211 editions between 1502 and 1779, many of these being expansions of the original work, which added equivalents in more and more languages to Calepino's Latin wordlist; these even included Japanese, in an edition of 1595.[44] Its reputation became proverbial in several European languages, and its name came to be used as a generic term for 'dictionary', and to be appropriated by other lexicographers as that of Webster has been in twentieth-century America.[45] The dictionary was a response to the new printed dissemination of classical Latin texts, and aimed to document their vocabulary while excluding that of the post-classical world. It is particularly notable for its use of illustrative quotations from ancient authors, a feature that had already been identified as desirable by the eleventh-century lexicographer Papias, who had not, however, managed to incorporate it in his work.[46] 'Here', as one historian of the lexicography of Latin has said of Calepino's work, 'we have in front of us, although in a quite rudimentary form, the prototype of the modern Latin dictionary.'[47] The

---

[42] Now Universitätsbibliothek, Basel, DB III 1: see Hieronymus, *Griechischer Geist aus Basler Pressen* 1–2 (item 1).

[43] For these, see Geiger, *Johann Reuchlin*, esp. 68ff. (for the *Vocabularius*) and 110ff. (for the Hebrew dictionary); Geiger's account of editions of the *Vocabularius* is corrected in Benzing, *Bibliographie der Schriften Johannes Reuchlins* 1–5.

[44] Labarre, *Bibliographie du Dictionarium d'Ambrogio Calepino*.

[45] For the generic use, see, e.g., *OED* s.v. *calepin*, and for the appropriation, by Cesare Calderini in the *Calepinus Parvus* (editions from 1613 to 1770), see Labarre, *Bibliographie* III–12.

[46] Papias describes his *Elementarium* (1053) as enlarged 'sententiis ... et multis id genus superadditis' in its preface, ed. in Daly and Daly, 'Some techniques in mediaeval Latin lexicography' 230 (trans. 231–3), but, as is pointed out ibid. 235, the promised *sententiae*, i.e., illustrative quotations, are not present in his text.

[47] Krömer, 'Lateinische Lexikographie' 1715: 'Damit haben wir, wenn auch ganz rudimentär, den Typ des neuzeitlichen lateinischen Wörterbuchs vor uns'.

dictionary's focus on classical texts makes it an example of the humanistic tradition of lexicography, quite different from the work of the medieval lex-icographers: it is a handbook for just the sort of good and creative imitation that characterizes the Latin writings of the Renaissance. The title-pages of a number of early editions describe the work as synthesizing previous good authorities, both ancient and modern, such as the *Cornu copiae* of Niccolò Perotti (an encyclopedic commentary on the works of Martial and their contexts, rich in lexicographical material) and the works of Varro, Donatus and others. This is a statement about the virtues and the deliberate limitations of the dictionary: the claim is for conformity with the best tradition of judgements about the Latin language, rather than for originality or compre-hensiveness.[48]

Although Calepino's was a humanistic dictionary, its procedure was nevertheless less critical than that of the best humanistic scholarship. Vives was to call Calepino 'a man well suited to gathering material from others, but not well suited to supplying their deficiencies', and to remark more harshly that 'although he undertakes to teach others, he needs a teacher himself'.[49] His dictionary was deficient in at least four quite important ways. It was, first, alphabetized only to the first three letters, permitting sequences such as *calo- callu- calli-*. Second, the quotations from ancient authors are sometimes missing, and they are very summarily referenced, to author and work or even to author alone (here, Calepino suffered to some extent from the limitations of the texts available to him, since early printed editions of classical authors lacked the page numbering that makes it easy to give precise references to every quotation).[50] Third, the treatment of the different senses of words is often insufficiently subtle: quotations do not always illustrate the same senses as definitions, and significant senses go untreated. Fourth, the page layout of early editions is not very clear; for instance, the quotations are not set off typographically from the surrounding text. Here again, Calepino was slightly too early to use the opportunities of printed publication to the fullest. This can also be seen in his self-effacing editorial material. Editions from 1509 onwards have an epistle to the reader, printed after the text, but it is short (half a quarto page), and says very little about the writer and his relationship

---

[48] See Labarre, *Bibliographie* nos. 9, 11, 12, etc. (editions from 1511 onwards); and for Perotti's lexicographical material, see Pade, 'Niccolò Perotti's *Cornu copiae*' 53–6.

[49] Vives, *De tradendis disciplinis* lib. 3, 297, 'homo congerendis quidem illis idoneus, explendis uero quae deerant, non idoneus'; Vives, *De ratione studii puerilis* ep. 2 in *Opera* 1:11, 'Calepinus uero ... accessit ad alios docendos, quum ipse potius egeret doctore.'

[50] For the slow development of page numbering, see Kenney, *Classical text* 152f.

with his book, except that he hopes to show 'evidence, not of my learning, which is extremely limited, but of my labour and industry'.[51] His labour and industry led to the best Latin dictionary of the first half-century of print, but to one that would be superseded for scholarly purposes in the next half-century.

YOU HAVE REMADE THINGS WHICH HAD ALMOST BEEN OBLITERATED: GUILLAUME BUDÉ AND THE ORIGINS OF PHILOLOGICAL LEXICOGRAPHY

The kind of lexicography that superseded that of fifteenth- and early sixteenth-century humanists such as Crastone and Calepino was made possible by a friend of Erasmus and Reuchlin, Guillaume Budé. Born in 1468, Budé came late to scholarship, moved to it by the example of his father, who owned a considerable library.[52] He fell in love with the Greek language, and, 'burning with mad desire' to read Homer and other authors, he engaged Georgios Hermonymos as his tutor in Greek. Hermonymos was quite an important scribe – indeed, a scribe of, *inter alia*, dictionaries, who offered in a letter of 1478 to transcribe a Greek dictionary for Reuchlin – but he was apparently a remarkably poor teacher.[53] Budé persevered, enlisted the help and borrowed the manuscripts of Aldus' friend Ianos Laskaris, and attained so great a mastery of the language that, despite the slow start which led him to call himself *opsimathes*, a late learner, he was recognized after his death by as good an authority as Joseph Scaliger as having been 'le plus grand Grec de l'Europe'.[54] His Greek was good enough for him to write many letters in it (fifty-four survive), but it was applied in his major works to the purposes of a scholar rather than an orator. Budé was, as Pfeiffer put it, 'a φιλόλογος in the sense of Eratosthenes', whose conviction was that 'encyclopedic knowledge, not eloquence, leads to true human culture'.[55] This conviction can be seen at work in three of his most important publications.

---

[51] Calepino, *Vocabularius* (1522) 381, 'si non eruditionis, quae perexigua est, laboris saltem et industri[a]e testimonium non ingratus lector exhiberet'.

[52] Grafton, *Commerce with the classics* 148.

[53] For Budé's lessons with Hermonymus, see Grafton, *Commerce with the classics* 146, quoting Budé, 'flagrare me studio insano [Hermonymus] intelligeret' 147n23, and cf. McNeil, *Guillaume Budé* 9–10, esp. 9n31 and 10n33; for the letter to Reuchlin, see Grafton, *Commerce with the classics* 150.

[54] For the lessons with Laskaris see Grafton, *Commerce with the classics* 160–1; for *opsimathes*, see McNeil, *Guillaume Budé* 10n34; Scaliger's judgement is quoted Pfeiffer, *HCS* II 101.

[55] Pfeiffer, *HCS* II 101–2.

The first was the *Annotationes*, published in 1508, on the first twenty-four of the fifty books of the late antique legal compendium called the *Digesta* or *Pandectae*, a key text in Roman law, on which there was a well-established tradition of medieval commentary associated in particular with the name of the thirteenth-century jurist Accursius.[56] Here, Budé established a characteristic scope and method: he criticized the medieval commentators on the basis of his superior knowledge of the meaning of Latin and Greek words and of the *realia* of everyday life in the ancient world, discussing some five thousand individual points in a series of seven hundred questions, arranged in no particular order. Because the materials from which the *Digesta* were compiled were of varying dates, the *Annotationes* had to be informed by an understanding of linguistic and cultural change: 'Budé's philological method', in Donald Kelley's words, 'required not only encyclopedic learning but a sense of anachronism.'[57] They also had to be informed by a general understanding of the culture for which the law was made: the comprehensiveness of Roman law meant that it bore on many different aspects of Roman culture, and so the law could not be explained unless the culture was understood.[58] The philological method of study that Budé pioneered in the *Annotationes* inspired a newly philological approach to the study of law in French universities such as Bourges, and came therefore to be known as the *mos gallicus jure docendi* (as opposed to the scholastic *mos italicus*).[59] Budé's discussions in the *Annotationes* often led him to patriotic commentary on contemporary French institutions: he was characteristically interested both in the alterity and in the modernity of the ancient world.[60] Some of his criticisms of the medieval commentators on the *Digesta* and their followers were forcefully worded, just as were Erasmus' of the *Catholicon*, and for the same reason: this was the book in which Budé needed to establish himself as having a new relation to the past, a sense of the classical heritage as accessible through philological enquiry. He would return to the language of the law towards the end of his life, in his posthumously published *Forensia*, a glossary of ancient legal terms.[61]

---

[56] For the *Annotationes*, see Kelley, *Foundations of modern historical scholarship* 53–80 and McNeil, *Guillaume Budé* 15–24.

[57] Kelley, *Foundations of modern historical scholarship* 73.

[58] See the discussion in Pocock, *Ancient constitution* 8–10.

[59] See Kelley, *Foundations of modern historical scholarship* 92ff. and Kelley, 'Civil science in the Renaissance'.

[60] Kelley, *Foundations of modern historical scholarship* 76f.

[61] For the *Forensia*, see Schreiber, *Estiennes* 90–2 (item 98) and Armstrong, *Robert Estienne* 112–13.

The *Annotationes* were followed by a study of Roman coinage and systems of measurement called *De asse et partibus eius* (1514). Now Budé was working in the genre of monograph rather than commentary, although his exposition still lacked a powerful overarching structure, and his style was confessedly repulsive, that of a philologist rather than a humanist.[62] His explanation of the value of ancient coins and measures illuminated the understanding of the ancient world in a way that is hard to reimagine: every passage in every ancient author in which money was mentioned now made more sense. So, for instance, a sixteenth-century reader remarked that it had been one thing to know that the courtesan Laïs had offered Demosthenes sex at a price of forty sestertii, but another to learn that this meant the remarkable sum of 1750 livres in contemporary money.[63] Thomas More was not alone in his admiration when he wrote to Budé, 'I have read through your *De Asse* more attentively than some ancient works ... you have remade things which had almost been obliterated': the book ran to ten editions and fifteen abridgements in fifty years.[64]

Third among Budé's major philological works was a mighty volume of some seven thousand notes on the Greek language, the *Commentarii linguae graecae* (1529, with an enlarged posthumous edition in 1548). These too have a foundation in Budé's juristic interests: the opening sentence of the main text begins 'In public judicial charges, which are called δημόσια ἀδικήματα, the accusations are called κρίσεις, and γράφαι, and sometimes δίχαι.'[65] What follows immediately is a discussion of the rather complex vocabulary of Greek legal procedure, and, as this suggests, Budé was making no more concessions to his readers in what became the more than 1100 folio pages of this work than he had in the *De asse*. Equally uncompromising is what precedes this material, a dedicatory epistle to François I, written entirely in Greek, and therefore Greek to the king, for whom a French translation had to be made.[66] The epistle in question made an important plea to François to endow a royal college in which

[62] For the *De asse*, see McNeil, *Guillaume Budé* 25–36, with discussion of style at 36, and Cooper, 'Numismatics in early Renaissance France' 12–14.

[63] A. Le Pois, *Discours sur les medailles et graveures antiques* (1579), cited Cooper, 'Numismatics' 13.

[64] More, letter of August 1518 to Guillaume Budé in More, *Correspondence* 124–5 (no. 65) at 124, 'Assem vero tuum sic attente perdisco, quomodo non quemliber veterum' and 125, 'propemodum deleta refecisti'; Cooper, 'Numismatics' 20–1.

[65] Budé, *Commentarii linguae graecae* (1548) 7, 'In criminibus publicis, quae δημόσια ἀδικήματα vocantur, accusationes ... κρίσεις, & γράφαι, & interdum δίχαι dicuntur.'

[66] The translation is preserved in BN ms fr 25445: see [Gasnault and Veyrin-Forrer], *Guillaume Budé* 27 (item 98).

philological work could be conducted, and the text of the *Commentarii* suggested one respect in which this work might have a connection with contemporary France: Greek and French, Budé pointed out, showed some remarkable correspondences in grammar and vocabulary.[67] In 1555, the theologian and humanist Joachim Périon was to assert that Budé had actually claimed that French was – as Perion himself believed – largely descended from Greek, but this was not true.[68]

Budé's publications show a complex response to the classical heritage. He was vividly conscious of its delights. He had started learning Greek 'burning with mad desire'. He chose to be a scholar, and enjoyed doing scholarship above all else: hence the stock of stories in which he limits himself, on his wedding-day, to three hours of study, or dismisses the servants who have interrupted his study with the news that the house is on fire, telling them that he is busy, and that it is his wife who is responsible for household matters.[69] Both the brilliance and the grittiness of his writing show this enjoyment, an enjoyment so great as to need no justification to others: it has been said of the *Forensia* that 'it is difficult to imagine anyone but Budé who could have written it, or who would have wanted to write it'.[70] He was not anxious to make the delights of philology available to every reader in smooth and alluring prose of his own. 'Budé was exceptionally learned, like a second Varro,' wrote his younger contemporary Celio Secondo Curione, 'but in his writing, he was tough and obscure.'[71] His rejection of alphabetical for thematic order in the *Commentarii* is of a piece with this, and of Budé's approach to the ancient Greek cultural heritage in general: in the *Commentarii*, as Ann Moss has said of Perotti's *Cornu copiae*,

A total culture is brought to life, explained, and grasped in all its complex detail, and its language, its concepts, and its material objects are authenticated from textual evidence. [The author's] method of exploring verbal proximities conveys the sense of being inside a language, of following its natural associations ... Alphabetization may be convenient, but it is a search tool to be used from outside a system.[72]

---

[67] See Trapp, 'Conformity of Greek and the vernacular' 241.

[68] Périon, *Dialogorum de linguae gallicae origine, eiusque cum graeca cognatione, libri quatuor* sig. a2r.

[69] Both stories are in de Budé, *Vie de Guillaume Budé* 21–2; the former goes back at least as far as Bayle, *Dictionaire historique et critique* 1:690.

[70] Armstrong, *Robert Estienne* 113n1.

[71] Curione, dedication in Budé, *Opera omnia* sig. AA3r, 'Budaeum tanqua[m] Varronem alterum, doctissimum fuisse: in scribendo tamen durus, obscurusq[ue] fuit.'

[72] Moss, *Renaissance truth* 20–1.

Budé had come with difficulty to his own place inside the Greek cultural heritage, his own erudition, and it seems to have suited him that others should share with difficulty in its fruits. Moreover, as he grew older, he became increasingly conscious that there were higher kinds of wisdom to be had than expertise in the ancient world, a point on which he reflected in his *De transitu hellenismi ad christianismum* of 1535: there were two kinds of *philologia*, love of the words of secular authors and love of the Word of God, and love of the Word of God was the better.[73]

The subject of pleasure is important. Budé was alone neither in publishing on *realia* nor in having these publications enthusiastically received: the scholar and diplomat Lazare de Baïf, for instance, wrote monographs on ancient ships, costume and vases, and these were published in very successful abridged versions 'for the pleasure and the use of the young', whom Vives likewise imagined mastering the vocabulary of one subject area – 'the house and all its furnishings, clothes, kinds of food, the weather' – after another.[74] The story of French Hellenism in the second quarter of the sixteenth century is full of pleasure, such as that of the young Ronsard listening to Dorat read the *Prometheus* of Aeschylus to him in French, and asking 'Et quoy, mon maistre, m'avez vous caché si long temps ces richesses?'[75] The anecdote leads us into the network of teacher–student relationships by which the newly exciting riches of the Greek language could be handed from one person to another: Budé's plea in the dedication of the *Commentarii* helped to persuade François I to found a college in which Greek would be taught, the *Collège des lecteurs royaux*, and the *lecteurs royaux* for Greek were Pierre Danès and Jacques Toussain, both of whom had been pupils of Ianos Laskaris.[76] Attendance at their lectures was not confined to the young, and their audiences included Calvin, Rabelais, Ignatius of Loyola, François de Sales, Ronsard and Henri Estienne.[77]

To turn back from this dazzling scene to Budé's philological learning – by the time he was working on the *Commentarii*, what he was doing was lexicography in all but name, and it is not surprising that he should have been encouraged to make a dictionary. In 1521, Erasmus wrote to him (in the famous letter in which the household of Thomas More is described,

---

[73] Budé, *De transitu hellenismi* sig. a2v; cf. McNeil, *Guillaume Budé* 78f.
[74] Horodisch, 'Geburt eines Kinderbuches' and Schreiber, *Estiennes* 58–60 (item 50); Vives, *De tradendis disciplinis* lib. 3, 292, 'de domo, & tota supellectili[,] de vestimentis, de cibis, de tempore'.
[75] Binet, 'Vie de Pierre de Ronsard' 119.
[76] For the foundation of the college, see McNeil, *Guillaume Budé* 86f.
[77] Pfeiffer, *HCS* II 102f.

and More himself is called 'a man for all seasons') that 'I perceive one thing in which you might render a very great service to Greek studies, if you were to make a really full lexicon, not only listing the words but explaining the idioms and turns of speech.'[78] In December, 1522, Budé responded to what appears to have been Erasmus' report of the rumour that he was indeed at work on a Greek dictionary by agreeing that he had considered, and had not wholly rejected, such a project:

> As for what Konrad [perhaps Konrad Resch, who had published one of the revised editions of Crastone's Greek dictionary in 1521] told you about the Greek lexicon, my answer is neither yes nor no. It had at one time come into my mind, but the labour of the writing put me off. In the way I had begun, it was an enormous task; not that the working up of the material is more than I can now manage, but there is such a range of subject-matter, at any rate after the labour of taking notes which I completed long ago. For I have started on a great many things, up to the point where I might perhaps not have to work very hard to finish them; but they are scattered about all over the place, and after my death will be very little comfort to my successors.[79]

At the end of the letter, he returned to the point: 'you cannot hope to get anything out of me for the common cause of good literature, still less for the compilation of a lexicon, though there is nothing anyhow that I would more cheerfully, willingly and readily take on if I had the time'.[80]

No dictionary by Budé had appeared by the time of his death. He had, however, continued to study the vocabulary of Greek, making the sort of notes that he had mentioned in his letter to Erasmus. They were not as useless to his successors as he had feared. Some of them were published as the *Forensia*. Others, from a marked-up copy of the 1529 edition of the *Commentarii*, were added to the 1548 edition.[81] Others again, of a very

---

[78] Erasmus, letter to Budé of September (?) 1521 in *Opus epistolarum* IV:575–80 (no. 1233) at 579–80, 'Video qua in re plurimum adiumenti possis adferre Graecanicis studiis, nimirum si copiosissimo Lexico nobis non tantum recenseas vocabula, verumetiam idiomata et Graeci sermonis tropos', trans. *CWE* VIII:294–9 at 299.

[79] Guillaume Budé, letter to Erasmus of 14 December 1522, in Erasmus, *Opus epistolarum* V:152–5 (no. 1328) at 153, 'quod Corradus tibi de Lexico Graeco, nec agnosco ipse nec inficior. Aliquando id in mentem mihi venerat; sed scribendi labor me deterruit. Nam vt instituoeram, res erat immensi laboris, nec tamen commentationis tam mihi intractabilis quam valde argumentosae, duntaxat post adnotandi laborem iamdiu exanclatum. Plurima enim ita orsa habeo, vt detexendis iis non magnopere fortasse assudandum mihi esset: sed sparsa, incondita, et dissipata, et quae me defuncto parum adiumenti successoribus meis allatura sint,' trans. *CWE* IX:214–18 at 216. For Resch's edition of Crastone, see Erasmus, *Opus epistolarum* V:483 (headnote to item 1460).

[80] Ibid. V:155, 'de me in commune literarum negocium nihil est quod tu speres, nedum in lexici coagmentum. Etsi nihil est certe quod libentius, iucundius promptiusque susciperem, si mihi ocium suppeteret', trans. *CWE* IX:218.

[81] Budé's marked-up copy of the 1529 *Commentarii* is in the BN, Impr. Rés. X. 67: see [Gasnault and Veyrin-Forrer], *Guillaume Budé* 27 (item 99).

miscellaneous nature, survive in seven notebooks in the private collection of a descendant of Budé's, of which the seventh is 'above all a repertory of Latin terms or phrases suitable for translating technical or figurative expressions, idioms, proverbs, and popular turns of phrase of the sort used in natural conversation', a reminder of the sixteenth-century cult of conversational Latin.[82] But does this *Nachlass* include all the scattered notes for a dictionary to which Budé referred in his letter to Erasmus?

The story is more complicated. In 1554, a Greek dictionary appeared in Geneva, edited by Claude Baduel, sometime rector of the Collège des Arts at Nîmes, bearing on its title-page the claim to be 'corrected in many places, and enlarged with a great number of additional words and phrases from a manuscript dictionary of G. BUDÉ himself'.[83] Baduel claimed in his preface that Budé had kept a 'commentarium ad priuatum studii sui vsum institutum', a private notebook in which 'he diligently gathered in a collection everything which he read and noted in the best authors in the course of his observation of and dealings with words and names'. Budé's children had, he added, reported that their father had intended to make a dictionary of these materials.[84] A little further on in the same preface, this *commentarium* had become *tres Budaei Commentarii*, three notebooks, kindly communicated to Baduel by Budé's son Jean.[85] Baduel had visited Budé at least twice in the 1530s, so it is not unreasonable to suppose that Budé 's children may have turned to him as a surviving friend, or at least acquaintance, of their father's to whom the great man's dictionary materials could be entrusted.[86] The trouble with this theory is that Baduel's dictionary is based on another *Lexicon graecolatinum*, published two years earlier at Paris under the name of Jacques Toussain, but seen through the press after Toussain's death by his pupil Fédéric Morel the elder. Comparison of the two shows a few additions in Baduel's dictionary, but few enough for the meticulous P. S. Allen to call it 'little

[82] The notebooks are described in Delaruelle, *Guillaume Budé* 246–77, and their present location is identified in Grafton, *Commerce with the classics* 152n36; the quotation is from Delaruelle, *Guillaume Budé* 268, 'surtout un répertoire des termes ou des phrases latines propres à traduire les expressions techniques ou figurées, les idiotismes, les proverbes, les manières de parler populaires qui s'emploient couramment dans la conversation'.

[83] [Baduel, ed.], *Lexicon graeco–latinum*, title-page, 'ex ipsius demum G. BVDAEI manu scripto Lexico, magna cum dictionum tum elocutionum accessione auctus, & plurimis in locis restitutus'.

[84] Baduel, epistle to the reader in ibid. sigs. *2r–*3r at *2v, 'ipse in obseruatione tractationeque verborum ac nominum, quaecunque in probatis auctoribus legerat et annotarat, collecta diligenter referebat ... Intellexi enim ex liberis illius, eum si vita longior contigisset, ex illis ipsis commentariis huiusmodi, Graecae linguae Dictionarium editurum fuisse.'

[85] Ibid. sig. *3r, 'tres Budaei Commentarij, ab filio Ioanne Budaeo ... nobis benigne communicati'.

[86] Budé's records of the visits are transcribed by Delaruelle, *Guillaume Budé* 275, 276.

more than a reprint of the Paris volume'.[87] What this suggests is that if Baduel did have access to manuscripts of Budé's, they were similar to the seven surviving notebooks (though not identical with them, according to Anthony Grafton, who has compared the notebooks and the dictionary): sources of some lexical material, prestigious enough to be announced on a title-page, but by no means the raw material for a substantial dictionary.[88] What about Toussain: did he have Budé's lexicographical collections? Again, the answer appears to be that he did not. His dictionary is indeed enriched with material from Budé, but all from the published works, both the *Commentarii* and the published letters, on which Toussain had written a philological commentary during Budé's lifetime. At no point does he claim to be using material from manuscripts of Budé's; nor does the printer, Charlotte Guillard, make such a claim in her interesting and detailed prefatory letter.

If Budé actually gathered the materials for a dictionary, rather than simply having a great number of lexical animadversions in his notebooks and written in the margins of his printed books, they are lost or unrecognized. However, the correspondence on dictionaries with Erasmus, and the fact that Baduel could sell a dictionary by claiming the extensive use of Budé's lexicographical materials in manuscript, and the fact that Toussain should have used materials from Budé's printed works extensively in his own dictionary, suggests that a significant relationship between lexicography and Budé's philology was perceived by his contemporaries. Material by Budé would also appear in the dictionaries of the publisher of the *De transitu* and the 1548 *Commentarii*, Robert Estienne, and in that of Robert's son Henri. But the most pervasive influence of Budé was more a matter of methodology than of individual borrowings. What he modelled for his successors was the precise treatment, founded on vast learning, of words as evidence for the past: words in the service not of humanistic rhetoric but of philology.

SETTING FORTH A HIDDEN TREASURE: ROBERT ESTIENNE AND THE CLASSICAL HERITAGE

The lexicographer whose works were most richly indebted to Budé's philological understanding of the classical heritage was Robert Estienne.[89]

---

[87] In Erasmus, *Opus epistolarum* IV:579–80, footnote to epist. 579 line 166.

[88] Grafton, *Commerce with the classics* 169n96.

[89] For him, see Armstrong, *Robert Estienne*; Brandon, *Robert Estienne*; and Schreiber, *Estiennes* 45–104; the unsuperseded bibliography is Renouard, *Annales de l'imprimerie des Estienne*.

Robert was born into the world of scholarly publishing: his mother, Guyonne Viart, was the widow of an important printer, Jean Higman, and his father, Henri Estienne the elder, succeeded Higman in his business, printing and selling books for the University of Paris, among the buildings of which his *officina* was situated. Robert spent his entire life in the world of the *officina*: that of his father, which passed after his death to Guyonne's third husband, the printer and publisher Simon de Colines, and then, from his qualification as a master-printer in 1526 onwards, his own, in Paris until 1551 and in religious exile in Geneva thereafter. His first modest publications were mostly aimed at the educational market. The printer's device on their title-pages, though, bore witness to piety as well as an interest in secular learning: it showed an olive tree with one branch detached and the motto *noli altum sapere* beside it. The reference is to St Paul's letter to the Christians of Rome, telling them that some of the Jews have turned away from salvation, which has been offered to Gentiles in their place. The passage is now translated as follows:

some of the branches were broken off, and you, a wild olive shoot, were grafted in their place ... They were broken off because of their unbelief, but you stand fast only through faith. So do not become proud, but stand in awe. For if God did not spare the natural branches, neither will he spare you.[90]

These words are of great importance to understanding the lives of the Estiennes. They hinge on the sense of the prohibition, translated here as 'do not become proud' and in the Vulgate as *noli altum sapere*. The Greek text has the verb ὑψηλοφρονέω, which Henri Estienne would explain as 'I have a lofty mind – but generally in a bad sense, i.e., I am too lofty and elevated in mind ... I think arrogantly of myself.'[91] However, the form of words *altum sapere*, while it can be taken as a calque on the Greek in which the sense is unchanged, has also suggested the pursuit of lofty knowledge rather than an overbearing mental loftiness to readers from late antiquity onwards: as Carlo Ginzburg has put it, 'St. Paul's condemnation of moral pride became a warning against intellectual curiosity.'[92] What, then, was the sense of the motto *noli altum sapere* on Robert Estienne's title-pages? Why did he print what he surely knew to be a potentially misleading translation of the words of St Paul? The answer

---

[90] Romans 11:17, 11:20b–21; for discussion, see Schreiber, *Estiennes* 247–9.
[91] H. Estienne, *TGL* s.v. (vol. III, col. 1770), 'Alta sum mente. sed plerunque in malam parte[m], pro Nimis alta & elata mente sum ... vel Arroganter de me sentio.'
[92] Ginzburg, 'The high and the low' 28–9; in the lightly revised version published in his *Clues, myths, and the historical method*, Ginzburg rewords to 'a rebuke of intellectual curiosity' (60).

was surely that he wanted to use the equivocality of the words of the Vulgate: he wanted to confess with every book he printed that arrogance was to be avoided, that intellectual curiosity could look very like arrogance, and that only through faith could God's judgement and condemnation be averted.[93] He was engaging with the same perceived conflict between classical philology and Christian intellectual life as Budé in the *De transitu*. The emblem appeared on a number of Robert's early publications, and was then greatly elaborated to include the figure of St Paul and a detailed naturalistic rendering of the grafted branches of the tree. The elaborated form appeared for the first time on, and was doubtless engraved for, Robert's magnificent folio Bible of 1527, the first critical edition of the Vulgate text, which 'immediately established him as the most outstanding figure in the Paris booktrade of his time'.[94] Introduced though it was by a handsomely presented statement of humility, this Bible showed that he was capable of producing a large, complex, high-profile work of learning.

There was a demand for just such a work in another field by the 1520s. As the criticisms made by Vives suggest, Calepino's dictionary was perceived to have become inadequate for high-level scholarly use. In the late 1520s, Robert Estienne investigated the possibility of producing a revised edition, and rejected it on the grounds that the lacunae and inaccuracies of the dictionary were such as to make revision an insufficient solution.[95] Nevertheless (as he tells the story) his customers insisted, 'urging with a determined outcry that I should either arrange for the compilation of, or compile by my own labour, a more perfect dictionary, from the best authors in the Latin language, together with the respective commentaries and interpretative tools'.[96] He agreed at last, and having decided that a new dictionary needed to be undertaken, and having found nobody prepared to do the work for him, he decided to make the dictionary himself, basing it on a new reading, if not of all Latin literature, at least of the major canonical authors. This was a much more laborious process than producing a mere revision of Calepino, and it was also riskier, since Calepino had such wide brand recognition. Estienne was committing

---

[93] The same question is asked in Floridi, 'Grafted branches of the Sceptical tree'; the answer given there cites 'Henri's acceptance of the motto as a consequence of his humanistic anti-dogmatism' (157).

[94] Schreiber, *Estiennes* 49 (reproduction of title-page), 51 (quotation, and discussion of emblem).

[95] R. Estienne, *LLT* (1531) sig. *2r.

[96] Ibid. sig. *2v, 'assiduo clamore postulantes, vt exquisitius aliquod dictionarium ex optimis quibusque linguae Latinae authoribus, & eoru[m] commentariis atque interpretibus, aut colligendu[m] curare[m]: aut ego ipse meo labore colligerem.'

himself boldly to the sort of re-examination of the classical heritage that
Erasmus had undertaken in the *Adagia* and Budé in the *Annotationes*. He
was moving away from a received tradition of commentary to the ancient
sources themselves, *ad fontes*; but, unlike Erasmus and Budé, he was using
alphabetical order, conscious of the needs of the reader who needed a
ready guide into the sense of a given word rather than of its whole cultural
context. 'I began', he explained,

> by carefully considering and reading through two Latin authors, of the utmost
> distinction for the variety, elegance and propriety of their vocabulary, Plautus
> and Terence, in whose works I made scrupulous note even of the tiniest points,
> so that I passed over hardly a single word which I thought might be of use either
> for speaking or for writing Latin. I then had those annotations copied out as a
> continuous text and put into alphabetical order with all diligence, treating them
> as a kind of raw material, and as a resource for a future dictionary.[97]

The emphasis on literary excellence, and on the texts as sources for
conversation and composition in Latin, is still outwardly humanistic,
though the judgement of Plautus differs strikingly from that of Vives,
who called him an *antiquarius*, and points out that he is therefore much
less pure in style than Terence.[98] The preference for the antiquarian or
philological that is apparent in Estienne's choice of Plautus is also shown
in his methodology, both in its concern with direct access to minutiae
and in its combination of lexicographical and editorial work – he not only
studied Plautus and Terence as he worked on his dictionary but actually
published new editions of them, thus setting an example to his son Henri
and to many future lexicographers (compare, for instance, the founding
of the Early English Text Society as a means of supplying edited texts to
what would become the *Oxford English Dictionary*).[99]

In 1531, five years after he had set up in business on his own account,
Robert Estienne published the fruits of this lexicographical work, his first
Latin dictionary, *Dictionarium, seu latinae linguae thesaurus* (it is always
known by its subtitle). It was a folio of 940 leaves, attractively printed,

---

[97] Ibid. 'In primis . . . duos latinae linguae authores & copia, & elegantia, & verboru[m] proprietate
praestantissimos, Plautum ac Terentium diligenter euolui, atque perlegi: in quibus etiam
minutissima quaeque adeo scrupulose annotaui, ut nullu[m] fere verbum praetermiserim: quod ad
Latine tu[m] loque[n]dum, tum scribendu[m], commodu[m] esse existimare[m]. Eas deinde
annotationes, vt essent veluti sylua quaeda[m], & quasi materies futuri dictionarii, protinus
excribendus curaui, & cu[m] omni diligentia in ordinem alphabeticu[m] redigendas.'

[98] Vives, *De tradendis disciplinis* lib. 3, 293, 'Minus multo est puritatis in Plauto, antiquarius est
enim.'

[99] For the editions of Plautus and Terence, see Schreiber, *Estiennes* 54 (item 43); for the Early English
Text Society and the *OED*, see Murray, *Caught in the web of words* 138–9.

with text set right across the page rather than in columns. Its title-page made three boasts: that it was rich in information about phraseology, that it was founded on the usage of the best Latin authors and that French equivalents were given for its Latin vocabulary.[100] Its abundance of phraseological material, presented with admirable typographical clarity, was supported by Robert's recent publication of a volume of *sententiae* from Plautus and Terence.[101] Such material would be a characteristic feature of his future dictionaries and of the very numerous dictionaries that were based on them. It had its origins partly in his desire to guide speakers and writers of Latin – hence the title-page's boast of *loquendi et scribendi formulae* – but it also helped to shed light, as Erasmus' *Adagia* had done, on a huge range of habits of speech and thought in the ancient world. The second point made on the title-page, that the best authors had been used, is unpacked in the summary of Estienne's achievement by Elizabeth Armstrong:

the non-classical elements which had hitherto been admitted to dictionaries on equal terms with correct classical Latin were weeded out; the interpretations taken from grammarians and commentators were checked both for correctness of text and for applicability to the word in a particular context; and the citations from authors were ... abundant.[102]

The third point advertised on the title-page, the presence of French, is a reminder of the position of Estienne's work at the beginnings of the Renaissance of classical learning in France. In 1531, it could not yet be assumed that there was a Latin-reading public large enough for a scholarly dictionary to have Latin as its sole defining language. The dictionary was by no means comprehensive, and it was still noticeably influenced by the work of Calepino, as Estienne himself acknowledged, but it marked a striking advance on the work of any predecessor.[103]

The relative closeness of the text of the 1531 *Thesaurus* to that of the dictionary of Calepino was partly a matter of preparation time – Estienne had only started examining the possibility of revising Calepino

[100] R. Estienne, *LLT* (1531), title-page: 'non singulas modo dictiones continens, sed integras quoque Latine & loquendi, & scribendi formulas ex optimis quibusque authoribus accuratissime collectas, cum gallica fere interpretatione.'

[101] R. Estienne, *Sententiae et proverbia ex omnibus Plauti & Terentii comoediis*: a very rare book, but registered, e.g., by Renouard, *Annales* 34, and, with a good discussion, by Schreiber, *Autumn 2005 list* 20 (item 25).

[102] Armstrong, *Robert Estienne* 87; cf. Brandon, *Robert Estienne* 35ff.

[103] For the influence of Calepino, see R. Estienne, *LLT* (1531) sig. *5r (another prefatory epistle, this one introducing errata which had occurred 'partim operariorum nostrorum incuria: partim Calepini vitio') and Armstrong, *Robert Estienne* 86.

in the second half of the 1520s – and partly one of marketing. Estienne wanted to make a better dictionary than Calepino's, but he did not want entirely to turn his back on the market that Calepino dominated. So, the dictionary that Estienne published in 1531 was meant to be marketable both to students and to learned persons.[104] In his subsequent lexicography, Estienne made a division between two classes of dictionary, one aiming at scholarly definitiveness and one meant for the educational market. This distinction was in fact called for by Vives in 1531: 'a dictionary of the Latin language should be put together from all of these [i.e.,the classic ancient authors], because none is sufficiently full and accurate. It should be in two parts, the one a simple wordlist with brief equivalents added, and the other with illustrative quotations added quite plentifully.'[105]

Estienne started to make the division in his lexicographical practice in 1536, when he brought out a second edition of the *Thesaurus*. This was enlarged with new Latin material, and had fuller French translations. It also included proper names, on the ground that although they might not be part of the linguistic core of the language, they were of cultural importance (they were also marketable, as Estienne knew from the success with which he had published onomastica).[106] It was typographically more sophisticated than its predecessor, being printed in two columns, so that although there were actually fewer leaves than in 1531 (898, down from 940), more material was still included. This edition of the *Thesaurus* cost a hundred and ten shillings, more than twice as much as any other item sold by the business.[107] A third edition appeared in 1543, with the legend 'editio secunda' on its title-page, as if the 1531 and 1536 dictionaries had been two versions of what was basically a single edition.[108] It was a much bigger book than either of them, comprising 1584 leaves printed in double columns (it therefore tends to be bound in three volumes, whereas they are bound in two), and was priced accordingly, at ten francs (still reasonable if, as Henri Estienne was to claim, the

---

[104] Brandon, *Robert Estienne* 40.
[105] Vives, *De tradendis disciplinis* lib. 3, 291, 'Ex quibus vniuersis confletur dictionarium Latinae linguae, quod nullum est plenum satis & iustum. Istudque sit duplex, alterum enumeratione tantum vocabulorum, breui interpretatione adiecta, alterum copiosius dictis authorum intermistis.'
[106] For the onomastica, see Starnes, *Robert Estienne's influence on lexicography* 86ff.
[107] R. Estienne, *Libri in officina Rob[erti] Stephani partim nati, partim restituti & excusi* sig. A3v; the next most expensive item was a legal handbook, *Promptuarium iuris*, at 50s (sig. A8r).
[108] Another explanation is that Estienne ignored the 1531 edition in his numbering because it 'n' étoit à ses yeux qu'une ébauche, et devoit désormais être considérée comme non avenue' (Renouard, *Annales* 57).

Thesaurus project cost thirty thousand francs in all).[109] In it, the French translations were abandoned, and the Latin coverage was much more extensive, the title-page proclaiming 'a new addition of material, so that there shall be virtually nothing worthy of note in the works of orators, historians, poets, and, in short, writers of every kind, which the reader shall not have readily available for him here'.[110] So, Estienne had moved from a dictionary based on Plautus and Terence in 1531 to one documenting all the significant Latinity of every kind of author in 1543.

As the *Thesaurus* itself became bigger, more learned, and more expensive, so the range of publications descended from it increased.[111] A first abridged version, 'omitting a few obsolete or uncommon words' and without the references to classical authors, but with the rest of the vocabulary explained 'in the language of the fatherland' (*sermone patrio*, a phrase that recurs in sixteenth-century comments on linguistic heritage), appeared in a single folio volume as the *Dictionarium latinogallicum* in 1538; four more editions followed.[112] Next came a French–Latin dictionary, *Dictionaire francoislatin*, in 1539–40, with a number of further editions, notably one by Jean Thierry, a former assistant on the *Latinae linguae thesaurus*, a descendant being Jean Nicot's *Thresor de la langue françoyse* of 1606, a landmark of French vernacular lexicography.[113] These were by no means pocket dictionaries – the last two editions of the *Dictionarium latinogallicum* are both folios of 1430 pages – but they were less than half the size of the big *Thesaurus*. They were meant to contribute to the establishment of the prestige of the French language. As early as the first edition of the *Dictionarium latinogallicum*, Estienne was pointing out the usefulness of 'setting forth a hidden treasure in our language', in other words of making texts written in Latin available to Francophones.[114] By the second edition of the *Dictionnaire francoislatin* in 1549, he had gone considerably further, adding French words from his own reading (including words taken

[109] For the figure of ten francs, see Renouard, *Annales* 55; for that of thirty thousand, see H. Estienne, *Les premices* sig. *6r, 'son Thresor de la langue Latine (dont tant le receuil que l'impression luy uenoyent à plus de trente mille francs)'.

[110] R. Estienne, *LLT* (1543), title-page, 'nunc accessione, ut nihil propemodum observatu dignum sit apud oratores, historicos, poetas, omnis denique generis scriptores, quod hic non promptum paratumque habeat'.

[111] An enumerative overview of all Estienne's dictionaries is given in Brandon, *Robert Estienne* 116–23, and a discursive one in Armstrong, *Robert Estienne* 88–9.

[112] R. Estienne, *Dictionarium latinogallicum*, title-page, 'thesauro nostro ita ex adverso respondens, ut extra pauca quaedam aut obsoleta: aut minus in usu necessaria vocabula, & quas consulto praetermisimus, authorum appellationes, in hoc eadem sint omnia, eodem ordine, sermone patrio explicata'.

[113] See Wooldridge, *Les débuts de la lexicographie française* 17–36, esp. 18.

[114] Quoted Renouard, *Annales* 47, 'Latentem adhuc linguae nostrae gazam exponere.'

from Rabelais), and inviting his readers to contribute words 'ès Rommans et bons autheurs François', an acknowledgement that he was interested not only in translating the treasures of Latin but also in collecting the treasures of French.[115] The *Dictionarium latinogallicum* and *Dictionnaire francois-latin* had their successors in turn, in the forms first of the little Latin–French *Dictionariolum puerorum* of 1542 (five more editions followed) and its French–Latin equivalent *Les mots francois selon lordre des lettres* of 1544 (four more editions followed); second of adaptations for the use of speakers of other languages such as German; and third of Estienne's *Grammaire francoise* of 1557, presented as 'of great use in particular to those who make use of our Latin–French and French–Latin dictionaries'.[116]

We now return to the formal features by which the *Latinae linguae thesaurus* described the Latin heritage. Unless otherwise indicated, this discussion applies in its general outlines to all three editions of the dictionary. The material to be treated falls under seven main headings: the concept of the *thesaurus* or treasury suggested in the title of the dictionary; word-ordering and its relationship to the treatment of etymology; sense-division and labelling; the treatment of Christian Latin; the treatment of recent and contemporary sources; the use of Estienne's personal knowledge and experience; and the autobiographical material in the prefaces to the successive editions of the dictionary.

The point of the title of the *Latinae linguae thesaurus* was that it was much more than a wordlist, or even a list of good words, such as would have been implied by a title such as *Glossarium* or *Vocabularius* or *Dictionarium*. Estienne was compiling something much richer: a treasury of information, a book more in the spirit of Erasmus or Budé than in that of Calepino, even though its retention of alphabetically based ordering of lemmata might make it look like a dictionary in the tradition of Calepino and the medieval glossarists.[117] He knew that the title he had chosen

---

[115] Quoted Armstrong, *Robert Estienne* 89.

[116] R. Estienne, *Traicte de la gram[m]aire francoise* 4, 'Laquelle chose pourra beaucoup seruir principalement a ceulx qui saident de nos Dictionnaires Latinfra[n]cois, & Francoislatin'; cf. also ibid. 110, 'Ce qui pourroit rester, a scauoir comment chasque mot se doibt escrire, & les plus communes manieres de parler Fra[n]cois, se trouueront au petit Dictionaire Francois Latin, que nous auons imprimé ceste presente annee M. D. LVII.'

[117] The word *thesaurus* had been used as the title of a dictionary in a 1522 edition of Calepino and in [Crastone], *Dictionum graecarum thesaurus copiosus . . . Dictionum latinarum thesaurus cum graeca interpretatione* (1510); cf. the use of *thesaurus* in the title of Guarino di Favera, ed., *Thesaurus cornucopiae* (1496), a collection of ancient grammatical treatises, which was in turn preceded by use in that of a short elementary collection of rules for grammatical constructions, Antonio Mancinelli, 'De varia constructione Thesaurus', of which the dedication is dated 1490, in his *Epitoma seu regulae constructionis* (1492).

needed to be explained in his preliminary editorial materials. Two pages of these are taken up with notes on the special features of the dictionary, explaining in 1531 that, on account of the richness with which the dictionary documents Latin phraseology, and of its copiousness, 'it has not seemed inappropriate to certain men of the highest erudition to call this work of mine a Treasury of the Latin language, as if it were a storehouse of Latin discourse'; in the second edition, the claim was made more forcefully, and in celebratory small capitals, as 'it has seemed to certain men of the highest erudition that this work of mine can justly be called a TREASURY OF THE LATIN LANGUAGE'.[118] His successors took up the title with enthusiasm: Nicot's *Thresor de la langue françoyse* (1606) has just been mentioned, and in subsequent sections we will encounter not only Henri Estienne's *Thesaurus graecae linguae* (1572) but André Madoets's *Thesaurus theutonicae linguae* (1573), Georg Henisch's *Thesaurus linguae et sapientiae Germanicae* (1616) and Jan Comenius' *Thesaurus linguae bohemicae* (before 1656).

The title *Treasury* invites a display of richness or grandeur, and, pleasing as are the first two editions, by that of 1543 the *mise-en-page* of the dictionary had been developed with considerable artistry. When a volume of this edition is opened, the elegance and generosity of layout are an immediate pleasure to the eye. The text is set out in double columns, with a well-proportioned space between them, an inner margin amply sufficient to keep the text of a bound volume from disappearing into the gutter, and a wide outer margin. Its principal headwords are in large type. They are in exact alphabetical order. Between them, at the appropriate points in the alphabetical sequence and set in small capitals, are headwords for proper-name entries. Under each large-type headword, its derivatives have their own subentries. These break the alphabetical order, but cross-references are inserted in the alphabetical sequence to steer the reader to the location of every subentry. Estienne's ordering of his lemmata was therefore alphabetically based rather than alphabetical: rather than being roughly alphabetized, as in earlier dictionaries, or smoothly alphabetized, as in later ones, lemmata were in a double order, in which alphabetically ordered root words were each followed immediately by their derivatives.

---

[118] R. Estienne, *LLT* (1531) sig. *3v, 'ob tantam formularu[m] Latine loquendi copiam & varietatem, non ab re doctissimis quibusdam placuit, hoc nostrum opus appellari linguae Latinae Thesauru[m]: quasi Latini sermonis quoddam promptuarium'; R. Estienne, *LLT* (1536) sig. *3r, 'ob tantam formularum Latine loquendi vim, & incredibilem copiam, doctissimis quibusdam visus est, hoc nostrum opus, LINGVAE LATINAE THESAVRVM iure dici posse'.

This semi-etymological ordering has four implications. First, at the level of lexicographical practice rather than linguistic theory, it suggests a powerful information management system; not only did Estienne have to keep his alphabetically ordered headings straight, he also had to order the material under those headings as rationally as possible. He referred in the prefatory epistle of 1531 to 'our diligence in ordering individual words very exactly', and said more explicitly in 1536 that this had been his great achievement in making the dictionary: 'what really earns the praise which is ours by right is, I say, our diligence in arranging our material, each word in its right order'.[119] (This sort of information management was something that printers were increasingly expected to provide as they supplied large texts with indexes; Estienne, maker of dictionaries and concordances, was especially good at it, and so full was the verbal index to Servius' commentary on Virgil that accompanied Estienne's folio edition of Virgil's complete works that it was advertised as capable of being used in place of a dictionary.[120]) Second, it implies a sense – like that displayed by Budé in the *Annotationes* – of the Latin vocabulary as something with an internal history in which one word could be seen developing from another. Third, it adds a qualitative argument about Latin to this general historical point: it forces the reader to consider the productivity of the language, its ability to generate a great number and variety of derived forms from relatively few roots. This kind of productivity is what Renaissance rhetoricians valued as *copia*, the sort of rhetorical wealth that enabled a person to expand a simple argument into a sophisticated and powerfully convincing oration. Fourth, it makes an argument about the high degree of rationality of the language. Strict alphabetical ordering implies that the language being documented is fundamentally arbitrary, that there is no connection between the form of names and the things named; so does purely thematic ordering, like that of the *Commentarii linguae graecae* of Budé or the *Commentarii linguae latinae* (1536–8) of Etienne Dolet.[121] Semi-etymological ordering, because it brings semantically related words together, suggests that formally identifiable classes of signifiers may correspond to natural classes of signifieds.

---

[119] R. Estienne, *LLT* (1531) sig. *3r, 'nostra diligentia in singulis vocibus curiosissime ordinandis' and *LLT* (1536) sig. *2v, 'Quod vero ad eam laudem, quae nostra est & propria, attinet, diligentiam dico, in singulis vocibus apte suo quoque ordine disponendis.'

[120] Virgil, *Opera* (1532), title-page, 'Index eorum quae a Seruio explicantur, ita copiosus vt vel dictionarii instar esse possit'; the Biblical concordances are mentioned in Starnes, *Robert Estienne's influence on lexicography* 56n7.

[121] For the latter, see Moss, *Renaissance truth* 27–32.

Emphasizing this connection between form and signification places Estienne's work in the great intellectual tradition of search for the perfect language.[122] This – whether it was to be devised philosophically or discovered in the form of, for instance, Hebrew – would be a language in which all things could be named in such a way that the form of the names conveyed information about the nature of the things. Hebrew looked as if it might be the perfect language not only because it was the language in which God had apparently communicated with His chosen people but also because Hebrew word-formation generates semantically and formally related groups of words in the form of sets of derivatives from three-consonant roots – hence the dictionary by David Kimchi that Reuchlin reworked was called *Sefer HaShorashim*, in Latin *Liber radicum*, 'the book of roots'. As the study of Hebrew and then Arabic became increasingly a part of the intellectual mainstream of European life, the productivity of their morphological systems became increasingly widely recognized; hence for instance the seventeenth-century observation that Hebrew, 'by reason of its *Trigrammacall Foundation*, and other regular Considerations, for the multiplications of all sorts of words ... is most capable to be *enlarged*, and fitted to express all *things* and *actions*, all *motions* and *notions*'.[123] So, by the time that the search for the perfect language had led to the invention of philosophical languages that attempted to name everything in the world by means of complex systems of derivation from roots, it was the Semitic languages that appear to have inspired their makers.[124] Well might an inventory of words that mapped the riches of the human and natural worlds be called a *thesaurus*, a treasury, as indeed such an inventory was when it was devised by Peter Paul Roget in the nineteenth century. Roget was conscious of his debt to the schemes for philosophical languages, but his *Thesaurus* attempts to categorize all human knowledge and experience from the resources of English rather than from a made-up system of roots and derivatives. Roget's *Thesaurus* and Estienne's *Thesaurus* share with the philosophical-language schemes a sense that the knowable world could be mapped by language, and that a strict and arbitrary alphabetical ordering of words was not the ideal way to do the job of mapping.

Different senses are distinguished in each entry and subentry of the *Thesaurus*. For example, *callus* had been glossed by Calepino as 'that

[122] See Eco, *Search for the perfect language*.
[123] Eliot, *Communion of churches* 17; I am grateful to Sylvia Brown for helping me with this reference.
[124] See Salmon, 'Arabists and linguists' 65–6.

hardness which develops on the hands or the feet as the result of labour'.[125] The word was, however, already shown by Estienne in 1531 to have a wider range of senses, referring to skin anywhere on the body of humans or animals which had been hardened by labour or friction, or to metaphorical toughness.[126] By 1543 he had also observed the use of the word to refer to tough matter in plants.[127] This analysis of senses was one of the great strengths of the dictionary, though Estienne played it down on the grounds that he was not so much a writer of definitions as a compiler:

> if therefore any interpretation should chance to offend the reader, he should not be annoyed with me, but rather with the authors from whom I have transcribed everything *verbatim*. For I have not (to use the words of Pliny) put my own authority at stake in these matters, but have turned to those authors who have written, or have interpreted the writings of others.[128]

This is surely related to his claim that what was most praiseworthy in the *Thesaurus* was 'our diligence in arranging our material': although he was providing definitions as a guide to the reader, he disowned them, regarding the researching and grouping of quotations as more important. In this respect, the *Thesaurus* can be seen as something as much like a verbal concordance as a dictionary.[129]

The quotations themselves are, as their importance necessitated, well referenced – a great advance on Calepino (elsewhere, Estienne made one of the most influential of all contributions to the referencing of quotations, namely the numbering of the verses of the Bible) – and generously provided. Words for which Estienne gives no quotation evidence, like *adamiani* or *alcibiadion*, stand out as anomalous. After the 1531 edition, status labels are occasionally provided, as are discussions of rarity and indeed of authenticity. So, for instance, *adindo* is labelled 'verbum antiquum', as is *abiugo*; *adinstar* is not regarded as good Latin, although

---

[125] Calepino, *Vocabularius* (1522) s.v. *callus*, 'Callus ... dicitur pro duricie illa, quae in manibus, vel pedibus ex labore nascitur.'

[126] R. Estienne, *LLT* (1531) s.v. *callum*, 'Est caro durata, & d[e]nsior facta vel labore vel alia caussa in pedibus, manibus, aliave corporis parte, vt in suis rostro, in bouis ceruice, in animalium plantis pedem ... Callum obducere, Endurcir a quelque chose.'

[127] R. Estienne, *LLT* (1543) s.v. *callus*, 'Callus ... est cutis labore viae pedibus, aut alio opere in manibus, parteve alia corporis densior facta, cuiusmodi est in suis rostro, ceruice bouis, animalium plantis pedem ... Callum fungorum ... Callum, per metaphoram ponitur.'

[128] R. Estienne, *LLT* (1531) sig. *3r, 'Siqua igitur interpretatio lectorem forte offendet, is non mihi, sed iis potius authoribus, ex quibus ad verbum omnia transcripsi, succensere debebit. Non enim (vt cum Plinio loquar) in hisce rebus fidem nostram obstringimus: sed ad ipsos authores, qui aut scripsere, aut alioru[m] scripta interpretati sunt, relegamus.'

[129] Cf. Cram, 'Concordances of words and concordances of things', esp. 86.

Apuleius uses it (his style is too inventive to conform to the best canons of correctness); and *adimpleo* is a 'verbum rarissimum'.[130] The latter label is also assigned to *advivo*, with the further observation that in the only passage in which Estienne has found this word it is a variant reading, and that if the manuscripts which have it are at fault, then the word has no authority at all.[131] Words that are given in Calepino on the sole authority of bad readings, such as *adineo* and *defoetus*, are identified as spurious. All these notes were the products of expert editorial decision-making. Only on the basis of a complete knowledge of all of ancient Latin literature could Estienne have pronounced confidently that a given word was distinctively ancient, or very rare.

Even when he was simply providing quotations without comment, Estienne's range of sources was itself a statement about his sense of what the Latin heritage meant: although he distinguishes the usage of approved authors from the medieval material that appeared in Calepino, his approved authors may belong to the Christian era. Returning to the two examples of undocumented words given above, the *adamiani* were the Christian sect or series of sects called Adamites in English, who supposedly worshipped naked and rejected the sacrament of marriage, and *alcibiadion* is a herb mentioned in a botanical treatise of the sixth century.[132] Elsewhere in the letter A – to go no further – Estienne cites Eusebius to give a context for *Apelles* as the name of a Marcionite heretic and St Jerome as authority for the word *abin*.[133] The distinction between classical and Christian Latin is an awkward one to draw, because it can neither be assigned to a single date nor associated with striking linguistic change. However, in a dictionary whose formal list of primary sources extends only to thirty-three major canonical pagan authors, from Cato to Claudian, it is striking to see these irregular extensions into Christian vocabulary. For irregular they are. If *abin* is accepted, then why not

---

[130] *Adindo* is only found in Cato, and *abiugo* in the fragments of the early dramatist Pacuvius, and the *Oxford Latin Dictionary* gives five examples from Apuleius as its only authorities for *ad instar* s.v. *instar* sense 4. It gives three other examples of *adimpleo*, two from the *Digests* of Justinian, so although it is not a common word, it is not extremely rare.

[131] The passage in question is Pliny, *Historia naturalis* 15.18, where Ermolao Barbaro has the reading *advivit* in his *Castigationes Plinianae* sigs. z5v (ad loc.) and d2r (note in index), but the manuscripts generally agree on *vivit*. The word is in fact also in Statius (*Thebaid* 12:424), and is now further recorded from epigraphic evidence.

[132] *Adamiani* is in fact from St Augustine, *De haeresibus* 31, directly or via St Isidore, *Origines* 8.5.14; *alcibiadion* is from the sixth-century Dioscorides Latinus 4.24 etc. Both are added after the 1531 edition.

[133] In the case of *abin*, he was in fact dealing with very tricky material; it is identified as a non-Latin word in Erasmus' text of the prologue to St Jerome, *Adversus pelagianos*, but there are textual problems: see *PL* 23:496.

abanet, which is in St Jerome and St Isidore as the name of a kind of garment? Why not the adverb *abaliud*, which is in Tertullian? If *adamiani* is accepted, then why not, in a dictionary rich in proper nouns, *Adam*? The reasonable answer is that the *Thesaurus* is already a monumental book, and a witness to extraordinary labour. Estienne could hardly have done more. Why, then, did he not do less, confining himself altogether to the ancient canonical authors on whose writings the great majority of the dictionary is based? He must have felt that irregular coverage of patristic vocabulary was better than none at all. The study of Christian texts was important to him: his first major work was an edition of the Bible, and his last was the definitive edition of Calvin's *Institutio christianae religionis*. Here, in a dictionary largely of the Latin of pagan authors, he is proclaiming that Christian Latin cannot be forgotten, that there is a continuity between the two.

A further sort of continuity is evident in Estienne's citation of recent authors. This is dense enough to locate the *Latinae linguae thesaurus* centrally in the philology of its own day and the recent past. Calepino is cited and animadverted upon in discussions of spurious words. So is Perotti, who appears as the authority for the word *caulina*, the name of a kind of wine produced near Capua, and for the story, under the name *Corax*, of the man of that name who killed the poet Archilochus in battle and had to plead with the oracle of Apollo that he had done so by the chance of war rather than as an act of deliberate wickedness. Among other fifteenth-century scholars, the encyclopedic anthologist Lodovico Ricchieri (Ludovicus Caelius Rhodiginus) is the source of the entry for the spendthrift *Acilius*, and provides a discussion of the sense of *aconitum*, and Ermolao Barbaro, as well as being cited in the discussion of *advivo*, is referred to at the ends of the discussions of two other Plinian words, *acoetus* and *aconiti*. Erasmus is also cited in the latter entry, and is the only source given for the words *acoluthus* and *acolytus*, both of which he treats in his edition of Jerome. Among more recent scholars, the botanist Jean Ruel is the only source for the plant-names *alcanna* and *alcaquengi*, and the principal one for the plant-names *blattaria* and *corion*. The references to Ruel, whose translation of Dioscorides had been published by Henri Estienne the elder in 1516, and who had died as recently as 1537, bring the scope of the dictionary into the circle of Robert's own learned acquaintances. Recent and living authors are acknowledged in prefaces as well as in individual entries: Erasmus, Linacre, Perotti and Valla are listed in the 1531 edition; Lazare de Baïf and Jacques Toussain are singled out in 1536; others are thanked in 1543. By the latter year, indeed, Estienne could report in the preface to the *Dictionarium latinogallicum* that he was drawing on 'philosophers, jurists, physicians, poets, grammarians and in short the whole nation of the lettered'.[134] The most vaunted of these consultants, Budé, is cited fairly frequently, for instance in a discussion of the sense of *acolastus*, where his judgement is given from the *Commentarii*, and in discussions of *abiudico*, a word which may refer to legal renunciation; of certain senses of *censere* and *censeri*; of *centuriatae leges*, a particular kind of legal instrument; and of the word *cenotaphium*. The list of primary and secondary sources in the prelims is set out in two columns until the very last item, the acknowledgement of Budé's assistance, which is brought to the reader's eye by being printed right across the page in a single block of type.[135] This, like his other references to the scholarship of the last half-century, and especially to that of his own circle, allows Estienne to make the point that the Latin language is alive in a flourishing tradition of scholarly discussion and judgement, to which he belongs.

Of all authorities, the most readily available is the lexicographer's own knowledge of things and words. It can be difficult to see when this is a source, but it must underlie some of Estienne's remarks about the real world, such as the observation at the end of the entry for *bubalus* 'buffalo' that 'a great many buffalo are to be seen at Rome. The common people of Italy still call the animal *bufalum*, with a change of only one letter from the Latin; we call it *ung buffle*.'[136] His statements of the modern equivalents of Roman place-names may, when unreferenced, be based on his own general knowledge, and he presumably inserted the unreferenced entry '*Burgundia*, a province of France' on that basis rather than leave that familiar place-name out of the dictionary altogether. The French derivative of a Latin word is, unusually, noted at *corbito*: 'our word *corbiner* seems to me to derive from this word'. Classical Latin words may also be glossed with modern Latin equivalents: these may either be at second hand, such as Ruel's explanation of *corion* as called *herbam perforatam* or *mille perforatam* by country people, and *herba Sancti Iohannis* by the common people, or apparently at first hand, as when the disease *condyloma* is identified with the note that 'the common people call it *Morbum Sancti Fiacri*'. Here, the French of 'the common people' is

---

[134] Armstrong sums up these acknowledgements (*Robert Estienne* 93–4) and quotes the preface to the *Dictionarium latinogallicum* (ibid. 93n2), 'philosophos … iurisconsultos, medicos, poetas, grammaticos, totam breviter literatorum nationum'.

[135] R. Estienne, *LLT* (1531) sig. *4v.

[136] R. Estienne, *LLT* (1536) s.v. *bubalus* (not in 1531; reprinted in 1543, where *bubalus* is a subentry s.v. *bos*), 'Visuntur Romae permulti bubali. vulgus Italorum adhuc vocat bufalum, immutata tantum vna litera: nos *Vng buffle*.'

confusingly translated back into Latin before it goes into the dictionary, but the real point stands: Estienne's dictionary presents Latin as a living heritage, as a story that carries over from pagan Rome into the Christian world, and from the ancient world into modern scholarship but also into modern language and modern lived experience.

In his dictionary, he was presenting not only a heritage but its beneficiary; not only a language but himself. Erasmus had set up the image of the philologist as hero as part of his exploration of the printed book as a double medium for the communication of knowledge and for self-promotion, and Estienne followed his lead in the 1536 edition. 'Now at last, readers', he remarked in its preface, 'I see the truth of what Terence's character Demea lamented to himself', and quoted:

There is never anyone who is so well guided by reason in his life but that affairs, time, experience always bring something new, something will warn that you do not know what you believed you knew, and what you thought at first, you will reject with experience.[137]

For Calepino, the dictionary-making process was a careful, laborious one, to which he hoped to have made a modest contribution. For Estienne, the story of his work is dramatic: and it is a drama in which he is a figure and his readers are an audience, to whom he can present his dictionary as the result of work that has engaged not only his intellect but also his emotions.

He plays several parts in the dramatic narratives of his prefaces. In the one quoted above, he speaks in the words of Demea, a character in the *Adelphi* of Terence, whom Estienne himself describes in the *Thesaurus* as 'tough and boorish', adding that 'men who are tough, boorish, and harsh are therefore called Demeae'.[138] He could surely have found other words than Demea's in which to express himself, or at the least he could have identified their author without specifying the character who speaks them, but he chose not to: his joky self-identification with a notorious boor is as much a sign of confidence as Johnson's description of his vocation as that of a harmless drudge. Estienne then goes on to describe himself listening to criticisms of the *Thesaurus* made by visitors to his shop in Paris, who did not know that the editor of the great work was listening to them, and

---

[137] R. Estienne, *LLT* (1536) sig. *2r, 'Nunc demum Lectores, verum esse video, quod Demea ille Terentianus secum queritur, | Nunquam ita quenquam bene subducta ratione, ad vitam esse, | Quin res, aetas, vsus semper aliquid apportet noui, | Aliquid moneat: vt illa, quae te scire credas, nescias: | Et quae tibi putaris prima, in experiundo repudies.'

[138] Ibid. s.v. *Demea*, 'Persona est apud Terentium in Adelphis, dura ac rustica. Vndi Demeae homines duri, rustici & asperi dicti sunt.'

says that he was, as he listened, in the same position as Apelles, lurking behind one of his pictures to hear what people had to say about it as they viewed it.[139] The part of Apelles (the painter, not the heretic) was a very different one to play from that of Demea. His entry in the *Latinae linguae thesaurus* describes him as an excellent painter, absolutely outstanding in his invention and execution, superior to all others who had come before him and who came after him, who contributed to painting than all his contemporaries put together, left volumes of writings on art for a disciple to edit and died leaving a painting of Venus unfinished, which nobody dared to complete.[140] Estienne was describing himself as being in the comic position of the nervous artist wondering what people really think about his work, but he was at the same time also describing himself as an artist, and an artist of unrivalled greatness and productivity. The third role he plays in his prefaces is a variant on that which Erasmus had played before him, that of Hercules. He wrote, in the preface to the 1531 edition of the *Thesaurus*, of 'this work of ours, to which so many labours, vigils, and what might be called Herculean hardships were to be devoted'.[141] He returned to the image of Hercules twelve years later, echoing the words of Aldus in his acknowledgement that the labour of revising the dictionary would have been impossible without the help of his colleague Johann Dietrich: 'if he had not helped me, and taken up part of the labour as Hercules did for the weary Atlas, I would never have been able to endure the weight, great as it was, of the work I had undertaken'.[142] Dietrich, indeed, seems to have done much of the final editorial work on a project that had been developed *a nobis et a nostris*, by Estienne and his employees or assistants; in other words, by 1543, Estienne seems to have acted as editor in chief of the *Latinae linguae thesaurus*, and Dietrich to have been the managing editor, perfecting the work done by Estienne and his assistant editors or sub-editors.[143] And, finally, there is a fourth role,

---

[139] Ibid. sig. *2r, 'multos memini quum saepe de industria in taberna nostra libraria eo animo sederem, quo scilicet Apelles post tabulam latere solebat, vt quid de eo labore nostro docti pariter & indocti sentirent, audirem'.

[140] R. Estienne, *LLT* (1543) s.v. *Apelles*, 'Pictor eximius … ingenio & gratia … praestantissimus. Nam … omnes prius genitos futurosque postea superauit, & picturae plura solus prope, quam caeteri omnes contulit, voluminibus etiam ad Perseum discipulum suum editis, quae doctrinam eam continerent. Is moriens Venerem reliquit, quam nemo ausus est perficere.'

[141] R. Estienne, *LLT* (1531) sig. *3r, 'hoc nostrum … opus: in quo tot labores, tot vigiliae, tot aerumnae, pene dixerim Herculeae, fueru[n]t exantlandae'.

[142] R. Estienne, *LLT* (1543) sig. *2v, 'nisi nobis auxilio fuisset, & quasi Hercules quidam fesso Atlanti in partem laboris successisset, nunquam profecto tantam operis molem sustinere potuissemus'.

[143] Ibid. 'omnia quae & a nobis & a nostris congesta erant, ipse relegeret, eaque tanquam supremus artifex inchoata & adhuc rudia perpoliret'.

that of himself, as a learned man among the learned, able like Aldus Manutius to attract scholars to his household as collaborators or as guests, and asking for comments on the dictionary from many of them.

Estienne's self-portrayal as a hero was ultimately shaped by a technology. Because statements about the past could be marshalled and communicated in print, they could be built up into the great learned compilations that are the fundamental philological texts of the sixteenth century. Technical possibilities and scholarly aims were in a symbiosis here: the work of the best philologists meant that the printers had learned texts to print, and the existence of printed texts gave the philologists more to think about. This was a symbiosis at whose most lively point stood those who both engaged in original philological research and had control over the technology that could express it. Erasmus in the Aldine *officina* is nearly there, but the really exemplary figures are Robert Estienne in the second quarter of the sixteenth century, and his son Henri in the third. It was these men who could, in an act of creative self-positioning characteristic of the post-medieval lexicographer, re-create a culture in its utmost retrievable fullness and variety, place themselves in it as gatekeepers and guides, and also stand outside it, looking back at it as a heritage.

CHAPTER 3

The classical heritage II: Henri
Estienne and his world

WE BEGAN TO BABBLE IN LATIN: HENRI ESTIENNE AND
THE INHERITANCE OF LANGUAGES

Robert Estienne's son Henri has been called 'one of the dominant literary and scholarly figures of the second half of the sixteenth century in Europe ... among the greatest French prose writers of the Renaissance ... this giant of sixteenth-century scholarship ... one of the most fascinating personalities of the Renaissance'.[1] However, the scope and complexity of his achievement have, paradoxically, led to his being generally underappreciated. The most extensive work on him has been done with reference to one part, and not the largest, of his intellectual life, namely his works in French and his discussions of the French language.[2] Beyond that, the best treatments have – unsurprisingly, given his colossal printed output – taken the form of bio-bibliographies, most recently the book quoted above, Fred Schreiber's *The Estiennes*, which is the splendid catalogue of a collection of Estienne editions now at the University of North Carolina at Chapel Hill.[3] So, no continuous biography of Estienne has replaced Léon Feugère's of 1853, and the fullest account of his work in English apart from Schreiber's is an essay by Mark Pattison which reviews Feugère's work.[4]

Henri Estienne was born in 1531.[5] By the time of his childhood, the family connection with the business of scholarly printing and publishing

---

[1] Schreiber, *Estiennes* 127–8.
[2] See esp. Clément, *Henri Estienne et son œuvre française*; and *Henri Estienne* (1988), an anonymously edited conference proceedings, with a useful bibliography.
[3] Esp. Maittaire, *Stephanorum Historia* 195–503 (bio-bibliography) and 37–47 in the second sequence of pagination (*index librorum*); Renouard, *Annales* 115–58 (bibliography) and 364–477 (biographical sketch); and Schreiber, *Estiennes* 127–245.
[4] Feugère, 'Essai sur Henri Estienne' (apparently one of several versions of his *Essai sur la vie et les ouvrages de H. Estienne* which appeared between 1850 and 1853); Pattison, 'Classical learning in France'.
[5] The date has been debated in the past, and though it was established by Clément, *Henri Estienne* 463–4, erroneous dates continue to be reproduced: see Schreiber, *Hanes collection of Estienne publications* 11 and 23n12.

was even stronger than it had been at the time of his father's. Both of Henri's paternal uncles, François and Charles, achieved independent distinction in the learned book trade, and his mother, Perrette, was the daughter of a printer and scholar, Josse Bade (Jodocus Badius Ascensius), who had published a number of the works of Budé. The making of learned books was therefore a dynastic business for Henri, a trade, and indeed a responsibility, which he inherited (so did his brothers Robert and François, who also became scholarly printers and publishers). In the household in which he grew up, the business of scholarship coloured the fabric of everyday life.

So did the language of scholarship: Latin was a living language in the Estienne household. It had to be, because Robert's 'decemvirs', the scholarly employees of the *officina* such as Johann Dietrich, had different native languages, and therefore used Latin as a *lingua franca*. Madame Estienne understood it well, as her son was to remember, and even the female servants had a working command of it, though they apparently spoke it rather ungrammatically.[6] A poem of 1538 by Dorat in which there is a vignette of life chez Estienne says just the same: what is to be heard throughout the household, summing up its character? What but

> the purity of Latin speech
> In rev'rend elegance pronounced by each?
> His wife, his handmaids, and his clients too,
> His children (lively band) hold speech with you
> Habitually in no other way
> Than Terence or than Plautus in a play.[7]

So, remembered Henri, 'I and my brother ... heard no other language than Latin in the society of my father or any of the decemvirs, and, building on the first foundations which were thus laid down, we began to babble in Latin.'[8] The word here translated 'babble' is *balbutire*, more often used in classical Latin of the defective speech of an adult than of the prattling of a very small person, and perhaps that suggests that to be a

---

[6] H. Estienne, letter to his son Paul, in Gellius, *Noctes atticae* (1585) 12, 'ipsas etiam famulas magnam Latinarum vocum partem intelligentes, multa etiam (sed quasdam deprauate) loquentes. Auiae autem tuae, eorum quae Latine dicebantur (nisi rarius aliquod vocabulum intermisceretur) haud multo difficilior erat intellectus quam si dicta sermone Gallico fuissent.'

[7] Jean Dorat, 'Ad Robertum Stephanum typographum nobilissimum' 242, 'Latini puritas | Sermonis, & castus decor | Nempe vxor, ancillae, clientes, liberi | (Non segnis examen domus) | Quo Plautus ore, quo Terentius, solent | Quotidiane colloquii'; trans. Armstrong, *Robert Estienne* 60.

[8] H. Estienne, in Gellius, *Noctes atticae* (1585) 13, 'ego, fraterque meus ... non alia quam Latina apud patrem vel quempiam ex illis dece[m]uiris vti lingua auderemus, ex quo iactis primis fundame[n]tis balbutire in ea coeperamus'.

child in the Estienne household was to be something equivalent to a defective adult – but Leibniz uses the same word of his own happy first attempts at Greek, and Henri certainly appears to have remembered his introduction to Latin with satisfaction.[9]

His intimacy with Latin was matched by an intimacy with Greek. There are, he remarked in the introduction to one of his books on French, some people

who say that talking Greek is a trade which I have mastered better than talking French. I freely admit the truth of one part of their reproach: I have in the past shown my mastery of spoken Greek – at Venice, to be precise, with a Greek gentleman called Michael Sophianos. My fluency as I did so was a result of my having learned Greek before I learned Latin. But I will deny the other part: this foreign language has not kept me from knowing how to speak my native language well.[10]

Rudolf Pfeiffer wrote that Henri's adult knowledge of ancient Greek was such that he 'really thought in Greek and could speak it; to him it was simply not a foreign language at all. In this respect he was, as far as I can see, unique.'[11] Pfeiffer's own mastery of Greek gives this assessment great force. Henri came to Greek before Latin because of a single formative experience, that of hearing passages from the *Medea* of Euripedes read aloud and discussed when he was a very small boy. Many years later, he still remembered his delight on that occasion, a delight that recalls some of the reactions to Greek in the circle of the *Collège des lecteurs royaux*: 'how great was the sweetness and loveliness with which that music of the Greek language excited my hearing!'[12] His words recall those of Petrarch, remembering an occasion when, too young fully to understand the Latin he was reading, he had been captivated 'by the sweetness and sonority of the words'.[13] The word shared by these reminiscences, *dulcedo* 'sweetness', had been used of the charm of *oratio* by Cicero, but of the pleasures of

[9] Leibniz, 'Vita Leibnitii a se ipso breviter delineata' 381, 'nondum duodecennis latinos commode intelligebam et graeca balbutire coeperam'.

[10] H. Estienne, *Proiect du livre intitulé De la precellence du langage françois* sig. ēıv, 'ceux qui disent que parler Grec est mieux mon mestier que parler François. Ie leur confesse librement vne partie de leur reproche: sçauoir est, que i'ay faict autresfois mestier de parler Grec, & nommément à Venise, auec vn gentilhomme Grec, nommé Michel Sophian: (& que ceste promptitude m'estoit venue de ce que i'auois appris la langue Greque auant la Latine:) mais ie leur nieray l'autre partie, que ce langage estranger m'ait gardé de sçauoir bien parler celuy qui m'est naturel.'

[11] Pfeiffer, *HCS* II 109.

[12] H. Estienne, preface to H. Estienne, ed., *Poetae graeci principes heroici carminis* 3, 'tanta dulcedine voluptateque meas auras illa Graecarum vocum modulatio titillabat'.

[13] Petrarch, *Epistolae de rebus senilibus* xv, 1046, 'Nihil intelligere poteram, sola me uerborum dulcedo quaedam, & sonoritas detinebat.'

wrath and plunder by Livy: the young Petrarch and the young Estienne both felt, not an insipidly aesthetic response, but a fierce excitement as each heard an ancient language.

The combined effect of Henri Estienne's childhood environment and of his intelligence and moral seriousness was to make him precociously dedicated to philology. When he was eight, his uncle Charles dedicated the second edition of a short book in Latin about gardens to 'his little Henri', beginning his dedicatory epistle:

Now I see in you, little nephew, what I wanted with a most earnest desire from the beginning, and I cannot say how much it delights me. For it is a great thing for a growing boy to work so hard, not only to follow his father in manners but also in intellect, that even at the beginning of his life he leaves everyone with a happy expectation of his intellectual achievements.[14]

This was very public praise for the small prodigy: Charles's epistle was written to be printed and circulated across Europe. It continued with a reference to Henri's then teacher, the *lecteur royal* and future lexicographer Jacques Toussain, boasting that his reports of his pupil could not have been more glowing if the boy had been the infant Cicero.

Henri went on to learn much of his Greek from another *lecteur royal*, the humanist Pierre Danès, who had been a friend of his grandfather Josse Bade, and remembered more than forty years later that 'nobody ever owed as much to his teacher as I confess myself to owe to him' and that 'when I was still a boy, my love for him was so great and, if you will pardon me for saying so, so jealous, that at that time I would not endure to be taught by anybody other than him'.[15] The reason why he apologized for describing himself as jealous was that the Latin word he used, *zelotypus*, is usually used of sexual jealousy. Reluctant as he was to offend his dedicatee, a relative of Danès, by wrongly suggesting an erotic element in his relationship with his old teacher, Estienne felt that no other form of words would adequately describe the intensity of his feelings. The same intensity of feeling, and the same resort to quasi-erotic language to

---

[14] C. Estienne, dedicatory epistle in idem, *De re hortensi* (1539) 3, 'CAROLVS STEPHANVS HENRICVLO SVO S. Video tandem in te nepotule, quod iampridem summo desyderio cupieba[m]: atque id qua [n]tum gaudeam, satis exprimere non possum. Magnu[m] enim est, adolescente[m] paternis non solum moribus, sed etia[m] ingenio adsequendo ita studere, vt iam ab ineu[n]te aetate foelice[m] omnib[us] ingenii sui expectatione[m] relinquat.'

[15] H. Estienne, dedicatory epistle in Macrobius, *In somnium Scipionis* (1585) sig. ā2v–3r, 'Nullus enim vnqua[m] tantum praeceptori suo debuit quantum illi debere me fateor: quum eius tantus & tam zelotypus (si cum tua venia ita loqui possum) in me adhuc puerum amor eius foret, vt nec ab alio quam a se doceri me tu[m] temporis pateretur.'

describe it, were to be features of his preface to the *Thesaurus graecae linguae*. Henri had a third teacher besides his father, Toussain's pupil Jean Dorat, a noted poet and an exceptionally charismatic teacher of Greek poetry. We have already noticed his introduction of Aeschylus to Ronsard, who remembered that 'Dorat ... M'apprist la Poësie'.[16] Henri would quote unpublished readings of Dorat's in his own work for many years to come (Dorat was to claim in 1570 that he had sometimes printed his readings without giving him credit for them, but one may surely, when dealing with a problem, recall a solution that one heard many years ago and think that one is making it up rather than remembering it).[17] In the extraordinary education that his father, Toussain, Danès and Dorat gave him, he internalized a great deal. Most importantly, he learned to engage imaginatively and passionately with Greek, seeing it as a possession that had come down to him, an inheritance bestowed upon him. Poetry clearly had much to do with that passion. Henri was not a significant poet himself, or so at least it seemed to the author of the standard account of his writings in French, who wrote that 'il a peu mérité le nom de poète'.[18] But he was perhaps at least a poet manqué, a poet doomed at last to wake a lexicographer.

Latin was the *lingua franca* of Robert Estienne's household, and Greek was the language of which Henri wrote most passionately. But the Estienne *officina* did not exist in isolation from the city of Paris, the city of Henri's birth, his fondness for which is referred to in a poem by Jean de Baïf and suggested by his sojourns in the city even after he had emigrated for reasons of conscience to Geneva.[19] Henri was a speaker of Parisian French, which he regarded as the preferable variety of the language.[20] He inherited his father's interest in the French language: a year after Robert had published his French grammar, the *Traicté de la grammaire françoise* of 1557, Henri translated it into Latin as *Gallicae*

[16] Pierre Ronsard, 'L'hynne V: de l'autonne' in *Oeuvres* (1587) VII:171–86 at 174.
[17] See Demerson, *Dorat et son temps* 172, 174 and Silver, *Intellectual evolution of Ronsard I: The formative influences* 38–9; for the use of Dorat's conjectures by his former students, see also Pfeiffer, *HCS* II 106–7 and Mund-Dopchie, 'Le premier travail français sur Eschyle' 264f.
[18] Clément, *Henri Estienne* 143.
[19] For the poem by Baïf, see Nolhac, *Ronsard et l'humanisme* 66 and n1; Estienne's sojourns in Paris include one of eighteen months after the publication of his *Deux dialogues du nouveau langage françois italianizé* in 1578 (see, e.g., Schreiber, *Estiennes* 171), but also, e.g., in 1584–5, when Paulus Melissus dined with him in Paris (Nolhac, *Ronsard et l'humanisme* 222n6) and he published the 'Noctes aliquot Parisinae' (see Schreiber, *Estiennes* 174–5).
[20] Estienne makes the point, e.g., in his *Hypomneses de gall[ica] lingua* sig. *2v; for discussion, see Padley, *Grammatical theory in western Europe: Trends in vernacular grammar* II:341 and Demaizière, 'Deux aspects de l'idéal linguistique d'Henri Estienne: Hellénisme et Parisianisme'.

grammatices libellus. Between 1565 and 1582, he produced a series of books on language, in several of which he can be seen working out the relationship between the vernacular and classical heritages.

The first of the treatises in question, the *Traicté de la conformité du langage françois auec le grec* of 1565, takes up the theme of the relationship between Greek and French which had been suggested in the *Commentarii* of Budé.[21] So closely was its thought entwined with that which would shape his great dictionary of Greek that Henri felt it necessary to explain in his preface that, having for so long encouraged so many learned persons to hope for the completion of 'vn grand Thesaur de la langue Grecque', he was not now palming this off as the long-awaited work on the strength of its discussion of some Greek phrases and idioms.[22] The *Traicté* is in fact a commentary on a number of grammatical and lexical similarities between Greek and French. In the first of its three sections, Henri pointed out that there were several grammatical agreements between the two languages against Latin – most conspicuously the possession of the definite article, but also matters such as the use of the partitive genitive and the nominalized infinitive, as well as many points of idiom, enumerated in the second section.[23] He left a blank page at the end of each chapter of his book for further examples to be added by the reader, whom he clearly expected to share his excitement at the accumulation of points of resemblance. Turning from grammar to vocabulary in the third section, he promised on the title-page to list 'a number of French words, some taken entirely from Greek and others partially – that is to say, retaining some letters from it by which one can identify their etymology', and devoted eighteen pages of his book to this wordlist, remarking that he could have made a much more detailed treatment, but that 'I decided that that was material for a dictionary rather than for a treatise like this one'.[24] Several of his identifications of French words with Greek originals are made on the authority of Budé, for instance the derivation of *pantoufle* 'a loose shoe, especially a cork-soled chopin' from Greek πᾶν 'all' and φελλὸς 'cork', on the questionable grounds that such shoes are made entirely out of cork.[25]

[21] See Clément, *Henri Estienne* 198ff. and, much briefer, Schreiber, *Estiennes* 141–2 (item 156).

[22] H. Estienne, *Traicté de la conformité* sig. ¶3r.

[23] Ibid. 67–76 (article), 3–4 (partitive genitive), 49f. (nominalized infinitive).

[24] Ibid., title-page: 'plusieurs mots François, les vns pris du Grec entierement, les autres en partie: c'est à dire, en ayans retenu quelques lettres par lesquelles on peut remarquer leur etymologie'; ibid. 139, 'i'ay pensé estre plustost matiere de Dictionaire que d'vn Traicté tel que cestuy-ci'.

[25] Ibid. 152, and cf. ibid. 137 for a reference to Budé as a source for the lexical information that follows.

Henri's Hellenizing claims are easily misunderstood: his argument, like those of most contemporary French writers on the same subject, was for the *conformity* of French with Greek, not for a very close genealogical relationship between the two like that which evidently existed between Italian and Latin.[26] Greek, it could be argued, was the noblest language of antiquity. If French was to be shown to be the noblest language of the contemporary world, then it must be shown to resemble Greek. Moreover, if French could be connected more closely with Greek than with Latin, it could 'be freed ... from the dominance of Latin and that degenerate (linguistically and morally) modern descendant, Italian'.[27] The latter was particularly important for Henri, who regarded Catherine de Médicis with real hatred as an enemy of the Protestant cause in France, and therefore regarded the Italian influence on the French language, which could be associated with her, as malign.[28] His reasons for providing French with affinities that separated it from Italian were, therefore, personal rather than philological, and the quality of his arguments is correspondingly emotional and impressionistic: it has been pointed out that Estienne 'insists on the conformity of *esprit* between the two languages' and that his argument comes down in the end to questions of 'richness and harmony', and Daniel Droixhe has commented on 'the ambiguity of the concept of "correspondence" or *cognatio*, which can, as in Estienne's work, rest essentially upon typological or aesthetic parallels'.[29]

So, Henri was not interested in taking his own arguments as far as Périon had taken Budé's. He influenced, but cannot have approved of, Léon Trippault's *Celt'hellenisme* of 1582, an etymological dictionary of 295 pages asserting the Greek roots of the French language, whose wordlist is followed by supplementary proofs, including the charming picture of French babies who, 'demanding food, cry out imploringly *gaga*, in place of γάλα', which is the Greek for 'milk'.[30] Trippault proclaimed in the first paragraph of his dedication that 'the language which we use has its source in that of the Greeks'.[31] He argued that Gaul had been founded by

[26] See Tavoni, 'Western Europe' 51–2 and Demaizière, 'Réflexions étymologiques d'Henri Estienne' 206–7.

[27] Trapp, 'Conformity of Greek and the vernacular' 243.

[28] Demaizière, 'Réflexions étymologiques d'Henri Estienne' 201–204.

[29] Trapp, 'Conformity of Greek and the vernacular' 243; Padley, *Grammatical theory in western Europe: Trends in vernacular grammar* II:343; Droixhe, *Linguistique et l'appel de l'histoire* 99, 'l'ambiguïté du concept de "convenance" ou *cognatio*, qui peut, comme chez Estienne, porter essentiellement sur des parallélismes typologiques ou esthétiques'.

[30] Trippault, *Celt'hellenisme* 299, 'nos enfans ... demandans nourriture, d'vne voix suppliante crieront γαγα, au lieu de γάλα'; cf. the similar discussion in H. Estienne, *Traicté de la conformité* 136.

[31] Trippault, *Celt'hellenisme* sig. *2r, 'le langage duquel vsons, a esté puisé de celui des Graecs'.

Greek-speakers such as the colonists of Massilia (Marseilles); that the Druids had, on Caesar's testimony, spoken Greek; that the Galatians, cousins of the Gauls, had read the letter of St Paul addressed to them in Greek, and that although Latin and Hebrew had certainly left their traces in the French language, its foundation was Greek.[32] The uncompromising arguments here are quite different from the procedure of Henri's *Traicté*. Henri was certainly prepared to identify the Celts as 'our ancestors' in 1574, and to call the proponent of good, un-Italianized French in his *Deux dialogues du nouveau langage françois italianizé* 'Celtophile'.[33] But he was not to put his lexicographical energies into the pursuit of a Celtic or Celto-Hellenic heritage for the French language; indeed, by the time Trippault's book was published, he was thinking differently about the affinities of French.

The progress of his thought can be seen in what at first looks like an unlikely place: *De latinitate falso suspecta*, a treatise on the Latin language, written four years after the *Thesaurus graecae linguae*. This was an attack on Ciceronianism, the cult of the usage of Cicero as the only correct Latin, and as such it contributed to an argument that had been going on since the second half of the fifteenth century.[34] Ciceronianism had its own dictionary, that of Mario Nizzoli (Nizolius), which had first appeared as *Observationes in Ciceronem* in 1535, documenting approximately 20,000 words; fifty or more further editions appeared under various titles in the next hundred years.[35] Nizzoli had dared to publish an augmented version of Robert Estienne's *Linguae latinae thesaurus* in Venice in 1550–1, and inspection of this edition in press had enraged Robert, who recognized some of the added words as ones which he had carefully identified as to be omitted from his dictionary as spurious or post-classical.[36] Attacking Nizolianism may therefore have been a personal pleasure for Henri as well as a scholarly duty.

The Ciceronians, Henri argued, condemn certain Latin usages which they suppose to be modern Gallicisms. So, for instance, they censure the use of *pausa*, supposing it to be a modern formation from French *pause* – but it is to be found in the ancient fragmentary poets Ennius and Lucilius; a number of examples of its use by Plautus are given in the

---

[32] Ibid. 299–311.
[33] H. Estienne, *Francofordiense emporium* II, 'de Celtis, majoribus nostris'; H. Estienne, *Deux dialogues du nouveau langage françois italianizé*, *passim*.
[34] See IJsewijn, *Companion to Neo-Latin studies* 2:412f. and bibliography at 418–19.
[35] Breen, '*Observationes in M. T. Ciceronem* of Marius Nizolius': entry-count at 52, edition-count at 56.
[36] Nizzoli, *Dictionarium seu thesaurus latinae linguae*; for Robert's response, see Armstrong, *Robert Estienne* 45.

Latinae linguae thesaurus; Robert Estienne's edition of Plautus contains others; and so on.[37] The cumulative effect was not only to show the weaknesses of a Ciceronianism untempered with the knowledge of other Latin texts, and particularly those written before the age of Cicero, but also to show the numerous parallels between Latin and French usage. 'This work', as Feugère pointed out, 'might, on account of the striking analogies between the two languages which it presents, also be called a *Traité de la conformité du français avec le latin*'.[38] So it might; and that suggests a reorientation of Henri's thought. No longer was he observing only the analogies between Greek and French. Now he was seeing those between Latin and French and, more specifically, between non-Ciceronian Latin and French. And these analogies, he realized, did indicate genealogical filiation. This struck him particularly as he wrote the treatise on Plautus' Latin usage which is appended to the *De latinitate falso suspecta*: after commenting on his own affection for Plautus, he added: 'For sure, it is fitting that the French love the Latinity of Plautus more than any other people do, for in many respects, his speech has a greater affinity with theirs than with anyone else's.'[39] Henri was developing the theory that French may be descended from archaic Latin, and may preserve archaic features that had been rejected from formal written Latin by the time of Cicero; a similar argument was being developed at the same time by the Italian grammarian Lodovico Castelvetro.[40] Henri's argument was, like Castelvetro's, a development of that of the grammarian Jacques Dubois (Jacobus Sylvius) that French had, along with some Greek and Hebrew loan elements, a Latin basis that differed to some degree from classical written Latin – though Dubois did not go so far as to identify this explicitly as vulgar Latin.[41] Students of French antiquity such as François Hotman proposed in the 1570s and 1580s that French was 'a mixed language, resulting from the "corruption" of Latin mixed with the language of the Gauls and then of the Franks'.[42] Henri's argument was more dramatic than theirs: he was not thinking in terms of corruption so much as of the continuation of a variety of Latin that had

---

[37] H. Estienne, *De latinitate falso suspecta* 3ff.

[38] Feugère, 'Essai sur Henri Estienne' cxcii note 1, 'Cet ouvrage, par les analogies frappantes qu'il présente entre les deux langues, porrait aussi être appelé un traité de la Conformité du français avec le latin.'

[39] H. Estienne, 'De Plauti latinitate dissertatio' 367.

[40] Tavoni, 'Western Europe' 49.

[41] For Dubois's approach to a theory of vulgar Latin, see Colette Demaizière in Dubois, *Introduction à la langue française* 12.

[42] Tavoni, 'Western Europe' 54.

been spoken and written in the age of Plautus, and had lived on as a spoken variety through the Golden Age and the fall of the Roman Empire.[43] Had he ever written the *De latinitate prisca* in which he announced his intention of treating Plautine Latin more fully, he might have been able to pursue this point to good effect.[44]

Instead, he continued his attacks on Ciceronianism in two more dialogues, *Pseudo-Cicero* and *Nizoliodidascalus*, and an edition of some specimens of Ciceronianizing Latin. His next two books on the vernacular were likewise not as rich in discussion of linguistic heritage as the *Traicté de la conformité*: the *Deux dialogues du nouveau langage françois italianizé* were concerned to attack the fashion for Italian loanwords rather than to enquire into the heritage that they were sullying, and the *Proiect du livre intitulé De la precellence du langage françois* – a production, despite its modest title, of more than three hundred pages – was written to urge the superiority of French over Italian (and, in passing, Spanish) on impressionistic and synchronic grounds. In his last, the *Hypomneses de gallica lingua* of 1582, a grammar of French written to supply the needs of foreigners and also to be of use to native speakers of French, he returned to some of the themes of the *De latinitate falso suspecta*, but without developing them very much further.[45] The *Hypomneses* was issued with two other texts: Robert Estienne's French grammar in the Latin translation made by Henri (the sheets were in fact those printed in 1558 and still unsold after twenty-four years) and, more remarkably, a short epistle on the Hebrew loanwords in French.[46] Here, Henri was printing material that helped to complicate the story of the French linguistic heritage, demanding a word-by-word etymological scrutiny which might lead beyond the classical and the indigenous heritages towards questions of cultural contact and mixing.

EMULOUS OF MY FATHER'S DILIGENCE: HENRI AND ROBERT ESTIENNE AND THE HERITAGE OF SCHOLARLY ACHIEVEMENT

Henri's early dedication to scholarship was first expressed in a printed text under his own name in 1550, when a seventy-two-line liminary poem of his in Greek was printed with Robert's third edition of the Greek New

[43] Ibid. 55.
[44] H. Estienne, 'De Plauti Latinitate dissertatio' 367, 'in libro DE LATINITATE PRISCA, fusius eadem (Deo favente) ... tractaturus'.
[45] See Demaizière, 'Réflexions étymologiques d'Henri Estienne' 208–9.
[46] Claude Mitaliers, 'Epistola ... de vocabulis quae Galli a commorantibus in Gallia Iudaeis didicerunt, in vsumque receperunt' in H. Estienne, *Hypomneses de gall[ica] lingua* sigs. o5–p4 (separately paginated).

Testament, the so-called *Editio regia*.[47] It led him, when he was old enough, to travel in search of manuscripts in order to establish himself as a scholar of independent stature rather than merely the assistant to a famous father. These travels and the extent to which they were successful will be discussed in the next section; for now, it is enough to say that he made important discoveries, but was dissatisfied when he compared them to the achievements of his father. He remembered how Alexander the Great as a young man had complained that the victories of his own father, Philip of Macedon, would leave him no-one to conquer, and drew the parallel with his own situation:

when I consider how many volumes he edited in the past, and how many more he has edited recently, and indeed very recently, and how many he now has in press, and how distinguished they are in every kind, I feel that every single opportunity for eminence in my publications has been denied me.[48]

Admiration is here joined with a gloomy discomfort: his paternal heritage, the business of being the son of Robert Estienne, was to be an onerous one for Henri.

He was always to have a strong sense of hereditary obligation as a factor in human affairs: he saw the heirs of his patron Thomas Redinger as kind to him 'as if by a hereditary law' and used exactly the same words to describe the motive that made a kinsman of his old teacher Danès study Greek.[49] So, he was to be acutely conscious of following in his father's footsteps as a scholar. In 1557 he was to request, in the first words of the introduction to his first independent work, the *Ciceronianum lexicon graecolatinum* with which this book began, that his reader consider with him the effect of a father's influence upon his children, and particularly that of the influence of his own stunningly industrious father.[50] Seven years later, the title-page of his edition of the fragments of the earliest Latin poets described them as having been 'formerly collected with the

---

[47] H. Estienne, 'φιλοθεω παντι' in R. Estienne, ed., *Novum Iesu Christi D. N. Testamentum* (1550) sig. **7r–v; for these verses, see Renouard, *Annales* II:375 and Schreiber, *Estiennes* 97 (item 105), 140 (item 155), and 179 (item 220).

[48] H. Estienne, *Ciceronianum lexicon graecolatinum* sig. **2r, 'sic ego, quum tot tantaque in omni genere, non solum quae iam olim, quae non ita pridem, quae nuper, quae nuperrime edidit, sed etiam quae in manibus nunc habet uolumina ob oculos pono ... mihi praeclusum esse ad typographicam gloriam omnem plane aditum existimo'.

[49] H. Estienne in Gellius, *Noctes atticae* (1585) 22 and Macrobius, *In somnium Scipionis* (1585) sig. ã3v, 'velut haereditario quodam iure'.

[50] H. Estienne, *Ciceronianum lexicon graecolatinum* sig. **2r, 'Quantum in utranque partem momenti in exemplo domestico ac paterno positum sit, si nunquam antea considerasti, lector, nunc saltem mecum, obsecro, considera. Dum mihi quotidie patris mei Roberti Stephani labores & uigiliae ob oculos uersantur, fit nescio quomodo ut ego ... ad laborem accendar.'

utmost diligence by Robert Estienne, and now prepared for publication by Henri Estienne his son': Robert takes first place, and it is his diligence, not Henri's, that is foregrounded.[51]

Paternal inheritance was to give Henri not only this edition, but his great lexicographical project. Robert had completed the first edition of the *Latinae linguae thesaurus* at the age of twenty-eight, and its third edition at the age of forty. Thereafter, his enormous scholarly output, combined with the business responsibilities of a busy publisher and the creative enterprise of producing some of the most magnificent typography of his own or any century, by no means exhausted his personal resources. He undertook another dictionary, which was to document Greek as his earlier work had documented Latin. He referred in rather general terms to a plan to make a dictionary of Greek 'with the proper significance of the Greek words as observed in the best authors' in a letter of 1556.[52] The normative language here suggests that Robert might have been planning something like a school dictionary. However, Henri's reference to 'that heroic and downright Herculean work' a year later suggests something more elaborate. Had Robert lived into his seventies, he might have completed his undertaking. Instead, on his death at the age of fifty-six, he bequeathed it to Henri, who wrote in a dictionary progress report of 1569, the *Epistola de suae typographiae statu nominatimque de suo thesauro linguae graecae*, that 'when he had prepared a good part of the material which was needed for a rebuilding [of the lexical record of ancient Greek], death took him from us – but in the hour of his death, he commended this work to me'.[53] In the catalogue of books that he issued as an appendix to the *Epistola de suae typographiae statu*, he added that the Greek dictionary would be 'put together on the model of the *Thesaurus* of the Latin language by his father Robert Estienne'.[54]

It was in keeping with this sense of inheritance that Henri should acknowledge on the title-page of the *Thesaurus* that he was, in making it, 'emulous of my father's diligence in his work on his Latin dictionary'.[55]

---

[51] H. Estienne, ed., *Fragmenta poetarum veterum latinorum*, title-page, 'vndique a Rob. Stephano summa diligentia olim congesta: nunc autem ab Henrico Stephano eius filio digesta'.

[52] R. Estienne, letter of 25 October 1556 to Mathurin Cordier, reprinted from his *Dictionariolum puerorum* (1557) in Armstrong, *Robert Estienne* 267–8 at 268, 'verborum Graecorum propria significatione, ex optimis authoribus'; trans. ibid. 235.

[53] H. Estienne, *Epistola … de suae typographiae statu* 31, 'Parata autem jam bona materiae quae novum aedificium requirebatur parte, mors illud nobis invidit, in qua tamen hoc ipsum opus mihi commendavit.'

[54] H. Estienne, 'Index librorum' sig. b2v, 'constructus ad exemplar Thesauri linguae Latinae a Rob. Stephano patre suo editi'.

[55] H. Estienne, *TGL*, 1: title-page, 'paternae in Thesauro Latino diligentiae aemulus'.

This was well-informed emulousness: he knew the great Latin dictionary intimately, not as an ordinary user but as a highly interactive one, who annotated a copy so heavily in or after the 1570s as to suggest that he may have hoped to prepare a revision for publication; indeed, those annotations that could be retrieved from it despite the illegibility of his informal hand and the damage that had been sustained by the book over the best part of two centuries were made one of the chief selling points of a new edition published in 1740.[56] After the publication of the *Thesaurus graecae linguae*, the same emulousness would continue, sometimes seasoned by unease. 'Look!' he imagined the worst readers of his *De latinitate falso suspecta* saying, 'he, to whose father Latinity owes such a debt, has opened the door to barbarism!' Later in the same book, he added more cheerfully that 'I will not deny that I apply myself to Plautus with an inherited love', and a few years later he would argue that those who had read the writings of his father and his uncle would realize that 'this ardent desire [of mine] to honour my fatherland is so strongly hereditary, that I could not uproot it from myself without degenerating altogether from the virtues of my ancestors'.[57]

The same comparison with his father still mattered deeply to Henri when he was in his fifties and sixties, more than a quarter of a century after Robert was dead. In the prefatory matter to the *Hypomneses de gallica lingua* of 1582, he explained that he had written the book to fulfil a wish that Robert had once entertained.[58] Three years later, he would remark proudly that, despite limited physical strength, he had endured long journeys, sleepless nights, and the business worries of managing a press, 'emulous of my father's glory, which rewarded my father's diligence'.[59] Right at the end of his scholarly career, in the dedication of the *editio princeps* of St Justin Martyr's *Epistola ad Diognetum* and *Oratio ad Graecos* in 1592, he reflected that 'there are still some people alive who can testify with what delight and with what applause' Robert's *princeps* of the major works of Justin had been received.[60] There, the implicit reflection that

[56] R. Estienne, *Thesaurus linguae latinae* (1740–3) sig. ****1v ff., reproducing selected annotations from the copy at the Bibliothèque Publique, Geneva; this copy is discussed by Clément, *Henri Estienne* 480–1, with a folding reproduction of the title-page between 478 and 479.

[57] H. Estienne, 'De Plauti latinitate dissertatio' 366, 'dissimulare nolo, haereditariu[m] mihi eum quo Plautu[m] prosequor, amore[m] esse'; H. Estienne, *Proiect du livre intitulé De la precellence* sig. ã2v, 'ceste ardante affection d'honorer ma patrie, m'est tellement hereditaire, que ie ne pourrois me la desraciner, sans forligner totalement'.

[58] H. Estienne, *Hypomneses* sig. *2r, 'pio me officio ac vere meo functurum esse putaui, si eius viuentis desiderio, etiam eo defuncto, satisfacerem'.

[59] H. Estienne in Gellius, *Noctes atticae* (1585) 6–7, 'dum gloriam paternam in paterna diligentia aemulor'.

[60] H. Estienne in St Justin Martyr, *Epist[ola] ad Diognetu[m], & Oratio ad Graecos* sig. *2r, 'quanta laetitia quantoque applausu excepta fuerint, supersunt quamplurimi qui testari possint'.

many of those who had applauded Robert Estienne were dead, that the intellectual excitements of the 1540s were now a long way away, is inescapable, and a couple of years later he entertained the theoretical possibility that, one day, nobody would acknowledge his father's work any longer: 'Many have borne witness, and more do every day, that my father, Robert Estienne, was born for the good of learning: and if all were silent, his achievement would bear witness.'[61]

He was aware of two other formidable predecessors, Erasmus and Budé. He edited and annotated the *Adagia* in 1558, prefacing them with a short epistle to the reader.[62] This begins by praising Erasmus for the learning and efficiency with which he brought out the collection:

Consider how many writers, in Greek and likewise in Latin, there were for him to read and re-read; how many passages there were to be compared with each other; how many stories, both real and fictional, there were for him to search out from the furthest recesses of antiquity; and then how many times he had to agitate his fertile mind, in order to bring forth from one or another of these sources the sense of an adage which had never been explained before.[63]

This sounds just like the experience of lexicographical work, and it is no doubt meant to: the epistle ends by looking forward to the time (still, in fact, fourteen years distant) 'when I shall have put the colophon [there is a play on the technical sense of *colophon*, 'information about the scribe or printer which is placed right at the end of a book', and its more general sense, 'finishing touch'] to the *Linguae graecae thesaurus*, to which work, under the auspices of my father, and following his lead, I devote my days and nights'.[64] Likewise, Estienne thought of Budé as he thought of the completion of the *Thesaurus*, writing in 1565 that he hoped to produce a sequel to the *Commentarii* under the title *Appendix ad commentarios linguae graecae*, which would be 'as it were, like a harbinger' to the *Thesaurus*. This, he said, picking up his father's image, would be possible

---

[61] H. Estienne in R. Estienne, *Concordantiae Testamenti Novi graecolatinae* sig. (..) 2v, 'Robertum Steph[anum] parentem meum, literarum bonarum bono natum esse, testati sunt multi, ac testantur quotidie quamplurimi: & omnibus tacentibus, res ipsa id clamet.'

[62] His annotations are still valuable: see those translated in *CWE* 35, at III iv 4 note 3, III iv 29 note 1, etc.

[63] H. Estienne in Erasmus, *Adagiorum chiliades* (1558) sig. ãiv, 'cogita enim tecum quot legendi relegendi Graeci pariter ac Latini scriptores, quot loci eorum inter se conferendi, quam multae partim historiae, partim fabulae ex antiquitatis penetralibus eruendae illi fuerint: quoties denique foecundum pectus concutere oportuerit, vt modo huius, modo illius adagii a nemine explicati sententiam depromeret'.

[64] Ibid. 'quum linguae Graecae thesauro (in quod opus paterno auspicio atque ductu dies incumbo noctesque) colophonem imposuero'.

'however much it may seem that the work of the late Monsieur Budé would give no less fear to those who desire to complete it than the picture which Apelles left incomplete on his death gave to every painter'.[65] Four years later, in the *Epistola de suae typographiae statu*, he associated the *Thesaurus* again with engagement with the works of these great predecessors, announcing an intention to reprint both the *Commentarii* and the *Adagia*.[66]

After the making of the *Thesaurus*, Erasmus and Budé were to continue to be important presences in Henri's scholarly life. His *Pseudo-Cicero* of 1577 was intended to recall Erasmus' dialogue *Ciceronianus*, written five decades earlier on the same subject.[67] He stayed in touch with at least one member of the Budé family into the 1580s, printing the *editio princeps* of the fragments of Dicaearchus from a manuscript obtained by Guillaume's son Mathieu Budé.[68] Finally, one of his last works was to be a book of adaptations of proverbs, in the preface of which he would remember the *Adagia*, but in a spirit of senile querulousness far removed from the sympathy and generosity of his preface of 1558, complaining that Erasmus and other students of proverbs had expounded them 'badly, and some of them very badly, in my opinion'.[69] Even there, he was at least remembering that the *Adagia* were important.

A third predecessor, or tradition of predecessors, seemed far from formidable to him. This was the series of lexicographers who had produced dictionaries of Greek before his own, beginning with Crastone.[70] Henri spoke scornfully of the original and the enlargements alike: what had been a slight and elementary performance, he remarked, had now been padded out by editors, so that 'the expositions which had previously been jejune [punning on the sense 'lean'] and, if I may put it this way, skeletal, came out of their hands so fat and bloated that sometimes we see nothing other in them than a Boeotian sow'.[71] Just as Erasmus had separated himself from the intellectual world of thirteenth-century

---

[65] H. Estienne, *Traicté de la conformité* sig. ¶3v, 'vn autre ouurage, quasi comme auantcoureur, intitulé Appendix ad Commentarios linguae Graecae. Car combien qu'il semble qu l'œuure du feu Monsieur Budé ne doive donner moins de crainte à ceux qui le vouldront acheuer, que donnoit à tous les peintres le tableau qu'Apelles mourant quoit laissé imperfaict.'

[66] H. Estienne, *Epistola . . . de suae typographiae statu* 5.

[67] Schreiber, *Estiennes* 167.   [68] Ibid. 179.

[69] H. Estienne, *Premices* sig. *5r, 'plusieurs prouerbes Grecs, qu'Erasme & autres auoyent ia exposez: mais mal, & aucuns tresmal, selon mon aduis.'

[70] An old overview which is still useful is Cohn, 'Griechische Lexikographie'.

[71] H. Estienne, *Epistola . . . de suae typographiae statu* 10–11, 'quae ieiunae, & (si ita loqui licet) macile[n]tae antea era[n]t expositiones, adeo pingues & crassae redditae sunt, vt in illis passim nihil aliud quam Boeoticam suem agnoscamus'; the Boeotian sow was proverbial.

lexicography by his scornful remarks about the *Catholicon*, and Budé had separated himself from that of thirteenth-century juristic studies by his similarly scornful references to the Accursian tradition, so now Henri was separating himself from the scholarship of the past. This was very important for him. In 1557, he was already assuring readers that the *Thesaurus graecae linguae*, his father's Greek dictionary as he still considered it, would not be 'any old Greek–Latin dictionary, collected from, as it were, a nasty mess of thoroughly inept notes, like some garment patched together from worthless rags, but a vast and enormous treasury of the Greek language, which he has been collecting and compiling for you for many years, and at almost infinite expense'.[72] A dozen years later, he returned more passionately to the image of the uncritical dictionary as patched up from scraps, referring in a discussion of the forthcoming *Thesaurus* to 'the people who make dictionaries by patching up or by interpolation', and to 'the patchers-up of common dictionaries, grossly ignorant and incompetent men, who should be put to manual labour, or better still, flogged'; a lexicographer who has made a particularly stupid mistake is referred to as 'the patcher-up to whom is ascribed the patching-up or enlargement of the latest edition' of Crastone's dictionary.[73]

Patching something together from scraps is a good metaphor for the lexicography that brings together material from many sources, as do the *Latinae linguae thesaurus* and the *Thesaurus graecae linguae*. For Henri, these many sources included the work of his father; the influence of Budé and other scholars; and of course a lifetime's collection of Greek words and phrases from his extraordinary reading. The passion with which he condemned the patchwork dictionaries of his less talented contemporaries was perhaps given an uneasy intensity by a sense of himself as ultimately an artist in patchwork too. And his sense that manual labour or flogging would be a good occupation for stupid lexicographers may also have been uneasy, for the image of Hercules which he appropriated is the image of a man required to labour, and lexicography could be seen by contemporaries as a

---

[72] H. Estienne, *Ciceronianum lexicon graecolatinum* sig. **2v, 'ille tibi non Lexicon Graecolatinum nescio quod, ex ineptissimarum adnotationum quadam uelut colluuie conflatum, tanquam uestimentum aliquod ex uilibus scrutis consarcinatum, sed ingentem & immensum linguae Graecae thesaurum, iam a multis annis, sumptibus prope infinitis, ex praestantissimis linguae Graecae authoribus tibi congerit atque coaceruat'.

[73] H. Estienne, *Epistola ... de suae typographiae statu* 11, 'egregii illi Lexicorum seu co[n]sarcinatores seu interpolatores'; 24, 'vulgarium lexicorum consarcinatores, imperitissimi & ineptissimi, & stiua vel flagris potius dignissimi homines'; 29, 'consarcinator ... cui adscribitur nouissimae editionis co[n]sarcinatio atq[ue] locupletatio'.

laborious, even a punishingly laborious, pursuit. Joseph Scaliger, not himself a maker of dictionaries, wrote that

> If a harsh sentence from the judges awaits someone, once
>   He has been condemned to afflictions and penalties,
> Let workhouses not fatigue him with raw material to be wrought
>   Nor let mines of metal pain his stiffened hands:
> Let him make DICTIONARIES. Need I say more? This
>   One labour has aspects of every punishment.[74]

THE RICHES OF GREEK: HENRI ESTIENNE AND THE HERITAGE OF TEXTS

The *Thesaurus graecae linguae* was a way for Henri Estienne to engage with his sense of linguistic heritage, of having received the Greek language and the French language as possessions handed down to him. It was also a personal inheritance, a project bequeathed to him by his father, and it was a project that he understood as deriving from a mixed heritage of earlier classical scholarship, of which he found some admirable and some contemptible. In its making, he was also dealing with a heritage of texts, those that had survived the processes by which they had been handed down from antiquity. The humanist rediscovery of this heritage makes a familiar and attractive story, one of decades of excitement punctuated by moments of positive rapture: 'Oh wondrous treasure! Oh unexpected joy! Shall I see you, Marcus Fabius, whole and undamaged', wrote Leonardo Bruni on hearing of Poggio Bracciolini's recovery of the lost books of Quintilian, 'and how much will you mean to me now?'[75] As we have seen, Wilamowitz saw 'the search for the old literature or . . . its dissemination' as activities that characterized humanism. This search, however, was coming to an end during the lifetimes of Robert and Henri Estienne.

The great majority of pagan Latin had, indeed, been printed as early as 1500. Incunabular editors had not quite made a clean sweep: the *princeps* of Tacitus, *Annales* 1–5 appeared in 1515, and other *principes* also appeared in the next hundred and fifty years. These included the letters of

---

[74] Quoted, e.g., by Franciscus Junius in Franciscus Junius and Thomas Marshall, eds., *Quatuor . . . euangeliorum versiones perantiquae duae* sig. ***1r, 'Si quem dura manet sententia Judicis, olim | Damnatum aerumnis suppliciisque caput: | Hunc neque fabrili lassent ergastula massa, | Nec rigidas vexent fossa metalla manus. | LEXICA contexat. Nam caetera quid moror? omnes | Poenarum facies hic labor unus habet.'

[75] Leonardo Bruni, letter of 15 September 1416 to Poggio Bracciolini, in Bruni, *Epistolarum libri viii* 1:111–13 at 112, 'O lucrum ingens! O insperatum gaudium! Ego te, o Marce Fabi, totum integrumque aspiciam? & quanti tu michi nunc eris?', trans. Gordon, *Two Renaissance book hunters* 191–2.

Symmachus, the histories of Velleius Paterculus and of Ammianus Marcellinus, the attractive poem *Pervigilium Veneris*, and the fables of Phaedrus (which had previously been known through a paraphrase). The *princeps* of the longest fragment of Petronius, the *Cena Trimalchionis*, was as late as 1664. However, these late *principes* were relatively few and far between, and their infrequency told a story. A great deal of pre-Christian Latin had evidently been lost for good. Most of Ennius, the father of Roman poetry, was gone, leaving for instance fewer than six hundred lines of the eighteen books of his national epic the *Annales*. Three quarters of Livy was gone, as were nearly half of Cicero's orations. The circulation of printed texts of ancient authors, and then of bibliographies such as Conrad Gessner's *Pandectae* – the fifth book of which was dedicated to Robert Estienne – made it possible for any educated person to understand how much, or rather how little, was extant.[76] There might, to be sure, be a few more discoveries.[77] There could be no hope, though, for a substantial overall advance in knowledge of the Latin classics, and no scholar could expect to make a reputation, or to experience any emotion other than corrosive disappointment, through a lifelong search for *inedita*.

Greek was a little slower to come into print, but the supply of *inedita* was running out by mid-century. By the year of Henri's death, 1598, the late neo-Platonist Iamblichus was just about to be published, the *princeps* of the *Bibliotheca* of Photius was three years ahead, and the only other important inedited authors who would appear in the next two hundred years were Sextus Empiricus and the mathematician Diaphantus. The losses from the original corpus of ancient Greek were even worse than those from that of Latin. A catalogue of seventy-two plays by Aeschylus was known from a manuscript; seven were extant. About two hundred titles of works by Theophrastus were listed by Diogenes Laertius; fourteen were extant. Apart from the *Iliad* and the *Odyssey*, the long poems of the Epic Cycle had all been substantially lost. When the German humanist and encyclopedist Conrad Lycosthenes was writing the preface to an abridgement of Gessner's *Pandectae* in 1551, he broke into the *ubi sunt* lament 'in what corner of the earth do they lie hidden today, the forty volumes of Clitomachus of Carthage, the forty-three of Empedocles, the sixty of the consul Alteus Capito, the three hundred of Theophrastus ... ?'[78]

---

[76] For the dedication, see Gessner, *Pandectarum siue partitionum uniuersalium libri xxi* fo. 73r.

[77] See Reynolds and Wilson, *Scribes and scholars* 192ff. for textual discoveries made since 1600.

[78] Conrad Lycosthenes, introduction to Gessner, *Elenchus scriptorum omnium* sig. a4r, 'quo terrarum angulo hodie latitant Clitomachi Carthaginensis uolumina quadraginta, Empedoclis tria & quadraginta, Altei Capitonis Romani consulis sexaginta, Theophrasti trecenta ... '

The question is one that expects the answer 'nowhere'. We are used to the canon of ancient literature that we have inherited – with a leaven of additions, especially from papyri – from the sixteenth century, and it is difficult for us to feel the grief and loss that inform Lycosthenes' words.

Henri Estienne did feel them, from the early years of his scholarly career until its end. At the very beginning of his adult life, he had before his eyes the example of the remarkable output of *editiones principes* that marked Robert's last years in Paris: the ecclesiastical history of Eusebius in June 1544, followed by two more works of his shortly afterwards; the *De ratione examinandae orationis* of the Byzantine grammarian Moschopoulos in December 1545; the *Antiquitates romanae* and many of the opuscula of Dionysius of Halicarnassus in early 1547; the works of the Greek medical writer Alexander of Tralles in January 1548; the surviving books of the Roman history of Dio Cassius four weeks later; most of the works of Justin Martyr in 1551; Xiphilinus' abridgement of the lost books of Dio Cassius in the same year.[79] But this rate of publication was possible because Robert, in his capacity as *typographus regius*, had access to a rich – but finite – deposit of manuscripts in the royal library. Such a deposit of classical *inedita* was hardly to be found elsewhere.

Henri learned this in the course of his first three research journeys, made between 1547, when he was sixteen, and around 1555.[80] These certainly led to some significant finds. Most spectacularly, when he was passing through Louvain in 1551, he read a manuscript of Greek verse that was in the possession of a Catholic exile from England called John Clement. Henri identified the verse as the work of the renowned ancient poet Anacreon, showed extracts to Pierre Ronsard and to the Italian philologist Pietro Vettori, and published the whole as by Anacreon in 1554.[81] Or was it the whole? The *Anacreontea* that Estienne published were the Anacreontic poems of the *Greek Anthology*, and these start with a poem that 'describes explicitly how the first-person-narrator dreamed of Anacreon and began to write Anacreontic imitations'.[82] Estienne left it out, which suggests that he was deliberately passing pseudo-Anacreontic

[79] Armstrong, *Robert Estienne* 124–36.   [80] For details, see Clément, *Henri Estienne* 468–9.
[81] For Ronsard's pre-publication access, see his *Oeuvres* (1587) 1:6 [second sequence of pagination] (sonnet 'Les liens d'or' and commentary by Muret), Silver, *Ronsard and the Hellenic Renaissance in France I: Ronsard and the Greek epic* 45 and 93–110, and O'Brien, *Anacreon redivivus* 158f.; for Vettori's, see his *Variarum lectionum libri xxv* 313.
[82] Schmitz, review of O'Brien, para. 12.

verse off as Anacreon's. Nobody knew that, and the edition caused great excitement, summed up in Ronsard's lines:

> Ie vais boire à Henry Estienne,
> Qui des enfers nous a rendu
> Du vieil Anacreon perdu
> La douce Lyre Teïenne.[83]

Henri had filled a hole in the lacunose classical heritage by offering the *Anacreontea* in the place of the lost authentic poems of Anacreon, but other holes could not be filled: celebrating the supposed rediscovery of Anacreon led him directly into bewailing the loss of another ancient poet, Alcaeus, fragments of whom can be reconstructed from passages where they are echoed in Horace: 'for if we can discover all these fragments hiding among Horace's odes, what would happen if the whole corpus of this Greek poet were extant?'[84] He also said that his publication of the *Anacreontea* would have been more expeditious 'had not a vain hope clung to me, that a third exemplum might be added to the two which I chanced to find, in different places and with great effort'.[85] One of these manuscripts of the *Anacreontea*, he said, was written on vellum; it can be identified with the whole or a part of the manuscript now called the *Palatine Anthology*.[86] The other was written *in cortice arboris* 'on tree-bark' and was very difficult to read.[87] The phrase *cortex arboris* need not puzzle us: Estienne must have meant papyrus.[88] But there is no corroborating evidence for a second manuscript of the *Anacreontea*, whether written on papyrus or any other medium.[89] And furthermore, when Estienne had reported his discovery of the poems to Pietro Vettori before publishing his edition, he had told Vettori that 'he had chanced to find them within the covers of an ancient book': one book, not two.[90] In fact,

---

[83] Ronsard, '[Livre V] ode xv: nous ne tenons' in his *Oeuvres* II:344–5 at 345; see Nolhac, *Ronsard et l'humanisme* 107ff.

[84] H. Estienne, notes to *Anacreontis Teii odae* (1554) 77, 'nam si haec omnia ἀποσπασμάτια inter Horatii odas latere deprehe[n]dimus, quid si corpus integrum huius Graeci poetae extaret?'; trans. and discussed O'Brien, *Anacreon redivivus* 25.

[85] H. Estienne, preface to Dionysius, *Responsio ad Gn. Pompeii epistolam* sig. *6r, 'Proferam ... & iam protulissem, nisi me uana spes tenuisset, fore ut ad duo eius exemplaria, quae diuersis in locis no[n] sine immenso labore inuenire mihi contingit, tertium accederet.'

[86] Ibid., 'ex duobus alterum in membranis...scriptum erat'. For the arguments as to the identity of this manuscript, see O'Brien, *Anacreon redivivus* 14–15.

[87] H. Estienne, preface to Dionysius, *Responsio ad Gn. Pompeii epistolam* sig. *6r, 'alterum in cortice arboris scriptum erat ... adeo antiquum, ut in singulis uerbis litera aliqua oculos fugeret'.

[88] See Mabillon, *De re diplomatica* 33.   [89] See O'Brien, *Anacreon redivivus* 15–19.

[90] Vettori, *Variarum lectionum libri* 313, 'lepidumque Anacreontis carmen, quod ... Henricus Stephanus Roberti filius ... ipse mihi dedit: inuentum a se forte (vt aiebat) in antiqui libri tegmine'.

when Estienne had suppressed the introductory poem in which the *Anacreontea* were clearly identified as inauthentic, he had put a poem from later in the sequence in its place. He must then have decided to invent a manuscript authority for this ordering.[91] The Italian philologist Francesco Robortello soon guessed as much:

Now there have been people who summon up from the underworld Anacreons and Dionysiuses of Halicarnassus. . . . There have been people, I say, who cite manuscript books, but do not mention what they are, where they are, or to whom they are known. Who knows whether these are dreams, or rubbish and pure nonsense?[92]

The ancient and scarcely legible copy of Anacreon written *in cortice arboris* was Henri's dream manuscript, the one that he secretly knew he would never find.

But despite his failures and frustrations, Henri did in the end emulate and even surpass his father in the publication of *inedita*. He may have guessed that this might be the case even as he compared himself with Alexander – who, after all, became much more famous than his own father. He produced at least twenty-two *principes*, even counting a volume in which the *principes* of several texts appear as one publication: (1) the *Anacreontea* in 1554; (2) some short rhetorical works by Dionysius of Halicarnassus, including a fragment of his *De imitatione*, in the same year; (3) the *Apologia pro christianis* and *De resurrectione mortuorum* of Athenagoras in 1557; (4) the *Disputationes* of Maximus of Tyre in the same year; (5) six fragments of the scientific writings of Theophrastus in the same year; (6) the complete *Agamemnon* of Aeschylus in the same year; (7) the fragments of the historians Ctesias, Agatharchides and Memnon in the same *annus mirabilis*; (8) ten books of Diodorus Siculus in 1559; (9) six new orations of Themistius in 1562; (10) the lexicon of Erotian to the works of Hippocrates in 1564; (11) the fragments of the poets Solon, Tyrtaeus and Mimnermus in 1566; (12) the orations of Polemon and Himerius in 1567; (13) the hymns of Synesius and the poems of St Gregory of Nazianzen in 1568; (14) pseudo-Athanasius on the Holy Trinity and some other patristic texts in 1570; (15) the glossaries of pseudo-Philoxenus and pseudo-Cyrillus in 1573; (16) a collection of Byzantine legal texts in the same year; (17) the fragments of the pre-Socratic

---

[91] Schmitz, review of O'Brien, endnote 4.

[92] Robortello, *De arte sive ratione corrigendi antiquorum libros disputatio*, quoted and translated O'Brien, *Anacreon redivivus* 19, 'Nunc exstiterunt (si diis placet,) qui excitant ab inferis Anacreontas, Halicarnasseos . . . Exstiterunt, inquam, qui manuscriptos libros citant, nec tamen proferunt, qui sint, ubi sint, cujus notae sint. Ecquis scit, an somnia illa sint, an quisquiliae, meraeque nugae?' See also Kenney, *Classical text* 31f.

philosophers in the same year; (18) the *Certamen Homeri et Hesiodi* (a poem of the second century AD) in the same year; (19) the history of Zosimus in 1581; (20) the geographical and political treatises of Dicaearchus in 1589; (21) St Justin Martyr's *Epistola ad Diognetum* and *Oratio ad graecos* in 1592; (22) the *Iberica* and *Hannibalica* of Appian in the same year. These editions were not all his unaided work as editor and publisher – for instance, the very important text of the *Agamemnon* was largely edited by Vettori – and the quality of his own editorial output was, moreover, variable, and was sharply criticized by Joseph Scaliger.[93] But their sheer number is quite extraordinary.

One point which this list illustrates is that even when the extant remains of the culture of antiquity were fragmentary, they might yet be gathered and used to regenerate that culture. *Ex ungue leonem* was a popular tag in the sixteenth century: we only need to see the claw to imagine the lion.[94] Much of Henri's most important work would be a matter of gathering fragments. This, for instance, is what he did in the *Fragmenta poetarum veterum latinorum* of 1564, in which the extant verses of Ennius and other early Roman poets were gathered, ordered and given a lexical commentary. This publication can be seen as related to the *Latinae linguae thesaurus* project; but the dictionary not only gathered fragments but made sense of them, attributing and annotating them so that they became part of a unified picture of Latin literature. The fragments of Alcaeus would be gathered (and apparently read by Ronsard) in Henri's edition of Pindar and the Greek lyric poets.[95] And likewise, the *Thesaurus graecae linguae* self-consciously re-created a lost culture, or at least the language that informed that culture, bringing together every lexical item that occurred in any text or fragment of Greek. In its preface, Henri would identify his work as a lexicographer with that of Aeneas as he sailed to re-create the sacked city of Troy.

Henri's editorial output and his lexicographical work were closely linked, as Robert's had been. He was both the editor and the printer of many of the texts on which the *Thesaurus* would draw, as he showed in its pre-liminaries, which included an *index fontium*, beginning with the Greek

---

[93] For the edition of Aeschylus, see de Gruys, *Early printed editions ... of Aeschylus* 77–96, with notes on the shares of Vettori and Estienne in the work at 89f. and 95; for Scaliger on Estienne as editor, see Kenney, *Classical text* 67.

[94] See Erasmus, *Adagia* i ix 34 ('Leonem ex unguibus aestimare'), *ASD* ii–2:356–9, trans. *CWE* xxxii:200, and Tilley, *Dictionary of the proverbs in England in the sixteenth and seventeenth centuries*, entry L313, 'A lion is known by his paw (claw)'.

[95] For Ronsard and the fragments of Alcaeus, see Silver, *Ronsard and the Hellenic Renaissance in France II: Ronsard and the Grecian lyre* iii:315f.

poets.[96] The first seventeen entries, from Homer to the Greek Anthology, are all indicated as 'ex editione Henr[ici] Steph[ani]', i.e., as texts for which he had used his own editions. The names of four poets for whom he had used Aldine editions followed, then the next two (Aeschylus and Sophocles) were identified as from his own editions; two more Aldine authors followed, and the list closed with Pindar and the fragmentary lyric poets from his own edition. The dictionary was, therefore, at the centre of an extraordinary network of printed books in which Estienne laboured – almost single-handedly, it might appear – to rearticulate the scattered remains of ancient Greek culture. A reader could find a word in the index, find its place in the etymological structure of Greek in the main text of the dictionary, go from the illustrative quotations in the dictionary entry to occurrences of the word in ancient texts, and, depending on the text, perhaps go on to its commentary to get a fuller sense of the word's cultural significance. That process of cultural reconstruction could be repeated again and again, always with the dictionary as the starting-point.

A poem that Henri composed and printed in his translation of the Greek bucolic poets shows the same sense of cultural recovery working in his mind: looking at what he supposed to be the virtuous simplicity of the peasantry whom he saw as he travelled, he started to think of them as the poor remains of an ancient culture of rustic goodness – the sort of culture that is given a voice in one of his favourite poets, Hesiod, and in the bucolic poets themselves – and to imagine a golden age being reborn from them, just as if they were the textual fragments that would be the keys to the cultures of antiquity.[97] The learned young man reflecting on the peasantry with his head full of Greek verse sounds like a figure from the nineteenth century as much as one from the sixteenth – but that is a point that should not be pushed too far. The Greek heritage changes from generation to generation.[98] The Greek textual heritage as Henri experienced it was not quite the same as ours.

We can see this when we look at the texts from which he quoted in the *Thesaurus*, examining a sample of approximately 2500 citations.[99] In this

---

[96] H. Estienne, *TGL* 1:7; an earlier version of the list is in H. Estienne, *Epistola ... de suae typographiae statu* 62–4.

[97] H. Estienne, 'Idyllion, in via scriptum, itidem in laudem vitae rusticae' in his trans. of Moschus, Bion and Theocritus, *Idyllia* sigs. E3v–E4v at E4v, 'O gens antiqui tam paruae tempore nostro | Reliquiae generis, tandem aurea posse renasci | Ex te secla puto, dum vrbis contagia vites.'

[98] Cf. Jenkyns, *Victorians and ancient Greece*.

[99] The sample was obtained by working through the entries for N in H. Estienne, *Thesaurus graecae linguae* (1831–65), excluding square-bracketed (i.e., post-Estienne) material from consideration. The figures should be regarded as approximate.

sample, 420, or about one in six, are from Homer, the *Iliad* being cited rather more frequently than the *Odyssey*. Clearly Homer was the author whom Henri most nearly knew by heart, and to whom he turned whenever he wanted a quotation for a given lexical item. There are three references to 'my manuscript of Homer', which Henri had mentioned previously in his preface to the *Poetae graeci principes* of 1566; this was a late Byzantine manuscript of the *Iliad* with some scholia that were not available in the standard printed edition of the scholia on Homer.[100] No other author rivals him in importance; the second most frequently quoted is Plutarch (whom Henri was editing as he worked on the *Thesaurus*) from whom there are about 200 citations, i.e., 8 per cent of the total. Then there is a marked gap again between Plutarch and the author in third place, Aristotle, who is cited about 110 times, over 4 per cent of the total. The next four authors are all major canonical figures, and are all cited with similar frequency: Xenophon 94 times, Aristophanes 87 times, Thucydides 85 times, Plato 84 times. The next three, however, are now rather less frequently read: in eighth place is the lexicographer Pollux, cited 80 times in the sample; in ninth place, cited 76 times, is Athenaeus, whom Erasmus had used in manuscript for his work on the *Adagia*; in tenth place, cited 72 times, is Eustathios, the major Byzantine commentator on Homer, whom Erasmus had also read in manuscript during his Aldine days.

A striking presence among the most-cited authors in the sample is Budé, whose name appears 53 times, sometimes only as the intermediate source for a quotation, but often as a source of philological commentary. A few other sixteenth-century authors appear: Erasmus eight times, Lazare de Baïf twice (as a source for ancient marine vocabulary), and Adrien Turnèbe three times (for words in Philo's *De vita Mosis* and Plutarch's *De primo frigido*, which he had edited). There are a number of self-citations, directing readers to Henri's *Lexicon ciceronianum* for Cicero's understanding of νέος in the senses 'young man, child', and to his commentary on Sophocles for that author's fondness for the verb νέμω. But there is less of a sense of 'the whole nation of the lettered' as consultants and contributors than there had been in the *Latinae linguae thesaurus*. Henri's own world is brought more noticeably into the dictionary in his comparisons of Greek usages with French ones – so that

[100] The manuscript is now Geneva, MS graecus 44, identified Nicole, *Scolies genevoises de l'Iliade* I:ix–xiii and discussed *Scholia graeca in Homeri Iliadem* (1969–88) I:xxi–xxii and lvi–lix; Henri remarks in *Poetae graeci principes* sig. **3v that readings in Eustathius agree 'cu[m] meo veteri codice' against those of all printed editions of Homer.

for instance the idiom ἀπὸ τοῦ νῦν 'from now on' is identified with a French idiom given as *D'ores en avant* / *Doresenavant* / *Doresnavant*, and the Greek word νόθος 'bastard' is shown to form an abstract noun νοθεία just as French *bastard* forms *bastardise*.[101]

After the ten major authors in order of frequency of citation are some predictable canonical names: there are 63 citations from Lucian, 53 from Hesiod, 50 from Euripides, 47 from epigrams, 44 from Sophocles, 40 from Demosthenes, and so on. There are one or two striking absences: hardly any Aeschylus (four citations, two of them from secondary sources), for instance, very little Polybius (seven citations), and less than might be expected from authors on whom Estienne had worked such as Dionysius of Halicarnassus (two citations). Some authors are notably generously represented: Wilamowitz remarked that 'the historian Herodian, an insignificant imitator who had no place there, is quoted frequently' and that 'the late author Synesius is another favourite'.[102] Herodian does indeed appear 38 times in the sample, more often than Herodotus, and Synesius is cited 19 times, as often as Galen.

Christian authors are quite well represented, suggesting Henri's sense of a strong continuity between pagan Greek and Christian Greek, comparable to the continuity between pagan and Christian Latin suggested in the *Latinae linguae thesaurus*. About 25 citations in the sample – 1 per cent of the total – are from the New Testament, with another eight from the Septuagint, and some of the lemmata are explicitly identified as belonging to the usage of the New Testament or of theologians.[103] The works of St John Chrysostom are cited ten times; those of St Gregory of Nazianzen ten times; those of St Basil and of the theologian Theodoretus four times each; those of the ecclesiastical historian Socrates and of the Biblical exegete Theophylact three times each – taken together, and excluding Synesius, who was a bishop but is best known for secular writings, these patristic writers account for between 1 and 2 per cent of citations. Their presence helped Henri to bridge the gap between his own Christian faith and his commitment to the study of pagan authors.

---

[101] H. Estienne, *TGL* II cols. 1678, 1676.
[102] Wilamowitz-Moellendorff, *Geschichte der Philologie* 25, 'z. B. erscheint sehr oft der Historiker Herodian, ein nichtiger Nachahmer, der gar keinen Platz verdiente. Auch der Spätling Synesios ist bevorzugt,' trans. Wilamowitz, *History of classical scholarship* 54.
[103] E.g., νεκρόω, glossed 'Morte macto, Eneco, Mortifico, vt theologi loquuntur', with citations from Colossians, Romans, and Hebrews, and also from Philo *De mundo* (*TGL* II col. 1014); νομοδιδάσκαλος, glossed 'Legis doctor' with the note 'Vocabulum est in Testamenti noui scriptis vsitatum', and citations from Romans and Luke (*TGL* II col. 1023).

The liminary verses in the *Editio regia* of the New Testament which had been his very first publication had ended with the infallible Word of God ordaining an end to the quasi-divine inhabitants of Olympus.[104] But then Henri had turned to the study of pagan texts, and he sometimes feared that this had been a mistake. So, for instance, he expressed the hope that his translation of the Psalms into Anacreontics and Sapphics would make up for the moral damage which his *princeps* of the *Anacreontea* might have done, so that

> Those whom the lyre once harmed with strings profane
> It shall, with Christian strings, make whole again.[105]

In the same spirit, he saw the Calvinist neo-Latin poet George Buchanan as 'easily the leading poet of our age' rather than, for instance, Ronsard or Tasso.[106] A particularly poignant expression of his sense that his learned work was at odds with his faith occurs in a record of his reading for the *Thesaurus graecae linguae*, his marked-up copy of the *Expositiones ab Oecumenio & Aretha collectae*, which is an anonymous Byzantine commentary on the Acts of the Apostles, the Epistles and Revelation.[107] Many of his underlinings in this book are philologically motivated, but one is a personal reflection. It occurs in a passage in which Acts 10:4 is being discussed: in this verse, the righteous centurion Cornelius is visited by an angel, who tells him that 'Your prayers and your alms have ascended as a memorial before God.' The commentator wrote here that 'though deeds look good, they are dead if they lack faith', and Estienne underlined the second clause, adding the words *o si placuissem Deo*, 'if only I had found favour with God!' – the construction implies that his actions may well not have found favour.[108] All of his wonderful labours in the cause of secular

---

[104] H. Estienne, 'φιλοθεω παντι' sig. **7v, 'Νῦν ἄρξασθε Θεοῦ μαθέειν νεμερτέα μῦθον | ... | καὶ τέλος ἰσοθέους θείη ναετῆρας ὀλύμπου.'

[105] H. Estienne, 'Odarion de Psalmis' in his, 'Index librorum qui ex officina Henrici Stephani hactenus prodierunt' sig. a3r, 'Quos sauciauit olim | Neruis chelys profanis | Sanabit illa neruis | Aptata Christianis.'

[106] H. Estienne, 'Index librorum qui ex officina Henrici Stephani hactenus prodierunt' sig. a4r, 'Psalmorum Dauidis paraphrasis poetica ... Autore Georgio Buchanano, Scoto, poetarum nostri saeculi facile principe.'

[107] For Henri's copy, see Schreiber, *Catalogue twenty-nine* 10–12 (item 12); for the authorship, see Beck, *Kirche und theologische Literatur im byzantinischen Reich* 418.

[108] *Expositiones antiquae* (1532) 56 (corresponding to *PG* 118:177D), quoted and discussed Schreiber, *Catalogue twenty-nine* 11; the suggestion ibid. that an underlining in *Expositiones antiquae* 342 (corresponding to *PG* 118:549D) likewise shows personal interest is less convincing, since the passage underlined is one in which there is an obvious bad reading in a Scriptural quotation (ἀπιστίᾳ 'through lack of faith' for πίστει 'through faith'; cf. the correct reading in the quotation of the same passage a few lines earlier, at a position corresponding to *PG* 118:549B) – because Henri knew that this was a bad reading, he did not comment on it in *TGL* s.v. ἀπιστία (III cols. 139–40).

learning, coupled as they were with numerous editions of the Scriptures and of Christian authors, and carried out in an exile that was the consequence of his Christian beliefs, seemed to Estienne, when he wrote those words, to be part of a lifetime of failure to serve God.

The dictionary to which all this textual activity contributed, the *Thesaurus graecae linguae* of 1572, was the most comprehensive and sophisticated lexical record of any European language that had ever been published. It ran to 4208 pages in folio (it is usually bound in four or five volumes), with the main text printed in double columns. About 64,000 words are documented in the dictionary, many at considerable length.[109] No more elaborate dictionary of ancient Greek exists even today, and scholarly libraries therefore have a nineteenth-century revision of the *Thesaurus* on their shelves beside modern works such as the lexicon of Liddell, Scott and Jones and the incomplete *Diccionario Griego–Español* and *Lexikon des frühgriechischen Epos*. The dictionary is made up of four parts: forty pages of introductory material, including dedication, *index fontium*, epistle to the reader, and reprinted orations in praise of Greek by Aldus Manutius' associate Scipio Carteromachus and others; the main text, in which lemmata are grouped under alphabetically ordered roots, i.e., in the mixed etymological and alphabetical order of the *Latinae linguae thesaurus*; an appendix of reprinted treatises on the Greek language (at least one of which, Philoponus *On the accent of homonyms*, Estienne appears to have taken from an earlier printing in an edition of Crastone); and an alphabetical index of 864 pages.[110]

The *Thesaurus* was followed a year later by a companion volume, the *editiones principes* of two early glossaries, one Latin–Greek and one Greek–Latin (formerly attributed respectively to compilers called Philoxenus and Cyrillus), presented as 'Two glossaries, brought to light from the disuse of antiquity, and extremely useful for the knowledge and enrichment of Greek and Latin'.[111] These were accompanied by a long essay by Henri on the Attic dialect. The dedicatory epistle expresses regret that the volume had not appeared sooner, remarking that a number of

---

[109] The count is my own, based on an average of 37 lemmata per column in the 1727 columns of the index, giving a total of 63,899 lemmata. In the *Prospectus novae editionis Thesauri graecae linguae* (1830), *TGL* is said to register more than 160,000 words ('ultra 160,000 vocabulorum numero constat'); can this be a typographical error?

[110] For the *TGL*'s text of Philoponus, see Daly in Philoponus, *On the accent of homonyms* (1983) xxvii–xxviii.

[111] Pseudo-Cyrillus and pseudo-Philoxenus, *Glossaria duo*, ed. H. Estienne, title-page, 'Glossaria duo, e situ vetustatis eruta: ad utriusque linguae cognitionem et locupletationem perutilia.'

readers had wanted to have it as one of the volumes of the *Thesaurus*.[112] Readers responded actively to it, and surviving copies include those that bear the annotations of Joseph Scaliger and of two seventeenth-century makers of wordlists, Franciscus Junius and Melchior Goldast.[113]

The *Thesaurus graecae linguae* was, like the *Latinae linguae thesaurus*, meant to be a record of all the ancient vocabulary of the language, together with some of its Christian vocabulary. This was a different sort of undertaking for Greek than for Latin. The monuments of ancient Greek are, despite the loss of so many texts, more extensive than those of Latin, and their total vocabulary is enormous, partly because writers in Greek were very ready to generate new words by affixation or compounding. The Estiennes could only have guessed very roughly at the proportion of extant Latin to extant Greek, which varies depending on the terminal date selected: in fact, the Greek corpus from the beginnings to 200 AD runs to twelve million words, and the Latin corpus to the same terminal date runs to about seven and a half million, but the Greek corpus to 700 AD runs to about sixty-five million words, and the Latin corpus to that date is probably less than half as extensive.[114] As early as 1557, Henri was aware that the Greek dictionary, which he still thought of as his father's, would be 'richer and more precious than the *Latinae linguae thesaurus* which he himself compiled, in the same proportion as the riches of Greek are, as all admit, greater than those of Latin'.[115]

The *Thesaurus graecae linguae* was, like the *Latinae linguae thesaurus*, designed well and printed handsomely. When volumes of both dictionaries are opened side by side, they make a similar impression, though the use of large type for a higher proportion of the lemmata in the *Latinae linguae thesaurus*, the slightly longer columns of its text and its uncluttered margins all contribute to its greater elegance. By no means, though, is the *Thesaurus graecae linguae* one of Henri's plainer books, some of

---

[112] H. Estienne in ibid. sig. *2v, 'non sum nescius hunc librum tardius et tua et aliorum multorum spe in lucem prodire: (praesertimque eorum qui lubenter uni cuipiam ex tomis mei Thesauri Graecae linguae assuendum [sc. assūendum, i.e., assumendum] curassent)'. Some copies are bound as volumes of the *TGL*, e.g., Bodl. fol. Godw. 249, where the glossaries are vol. v of the set (and the bracketed clause just quoted has been emphasized by underlining) and Buchanan b. 8, where they are vol. vi; in Bodl. B 2. 4 (2) Art. Seld. the glossaries are bound with vol. iv of a set. Even when the present bindings on the books are post-sixteenth-century, they suggest earlier practice.

[113] Goetz and Gundermann, eds., *Corpus glossariorum latinorum II*, xix–xx.

[114] Berkowitz, 'Ancilla to the Thesaurus linguae graecae: The TLG canon' 36 (but see also 54n14), 49; Rydberg-Cox, 'Automatic disambiguation' 373.

[115] H. Estienne, *Ciceronianum lexicon graecolatinum* sig. XX2v, 'certe illo Latinae linguae thesauro (quem etiam ipse cumulauerat) tanto erit opulentior, tantoque pretiosior, quanto maiores sunt illius quam huius, ut omnes fatentur, diuitiae'.

which were really concerned with getting a text into print rather than
with achieving a splendid or even a particularly graceful effect. It was
meant as a showpiece. It was dedicated with appropriate typographical
grandeur to the Holy Roman Emperor, the King of France, the Queen of
England, the Elector Palatine, the Duke of Saxony, the Margrave of
Brandenburg and, for good measure, the nine principal universities in the
realms of these potentates. The emperor appears to have been impressed
by it: when Henri travelled to Vienna years after its publication, 'he made
so much of me, and equally of my *Graecae linguae thesaurus*', that the
gratified lexicographer found it difficult to leave, and as late as 1595, Henri
recalled with pride that for two months the emperor had shown his presentation copy off to visitors as 'the finest present he had ever received'.[116]

Two formal features of the dictionary stand out. The first is its strong
concern, emulating that of the *Latinae linguae thesaurus*, with the differentiation of senses. Take, for example, the treatment of the word
ἔθνος. It is first defined as 'people, nation', with references from
Thucydides, the *Cyropaedia* of Xenophon (with a note that this text
supplies more examples than the one quoted), and Aeschines. Then, after
the sign ‖, a new sense is discussed: the word is used 'metaphorically (as
genus and *natio* are in Latin) to mean "order of men" or "community or
kind of men"'.[117] This sense is shown to have been identified by Budé,
who illustrates it from Plato; Estienne offers another quotation from
Plato, and then adds 'The use of ἔθνος in the sense "a crowd of men of a
specified kind" is undoubtedly taken from Homer by his successors: he
uses the expression ἔθνος ἑταίρων, to mean "and some others of the
same kind".'[118] Two quotations from the *Iliad* and one from the *Odyssey*
follow, with a note that *agmen* 'troop' has a similar extended use in Latin
poetry. Another break in sense is marked, and Estienne goes on to explain
that ἔθνεα can be applied to animals, citing in passing a passage in which
Virgil uses *gens* similarly. Homer, he observes, refers to ἔθνεα of geese,
cranes, swans, and even bees – Columella, he adds, uses *gens* of bees – and
other poets follow Homer, a point illustrated by quotations from Oppian
and Lucillius. Here too, Henri notes, Latin *agmen* is used like the Greek

---

[116] H. Estienne, 'Noctes aliquot Parisinae' 5, 'Maximilianus Caesar ... tanti me qua[n]ti meum
Graecae linguae Thesaurum, multo ante ad se missum, faciebat'; H. Estienne, *Premices* sig. *3v, 'il
tint ledict liure enuiron deux mois aupres de soy ... en faisa[n]t ses mo[n]stres à tous
venans ... co[m]me du plus beau present qu'il eust onque receu'.

[117] H. Estienne, *TGL* ad loc., 'metaphorice (vt Latine Genus & Natio) pro ordine & societate ac
genere hominum'.

[118] Ibid., 'Non dubito autem quin ἔθνος pro certorum hominum multitudine, ex Homero petierint
eius posteri, dicente aliquoties ἔθνος ἑταίρων, aliaque huiusmodi nonnulla.'

word. A fourth sense is marked: ἔθνος is used in place of γένος 'sex' in Xenophon, the point being illustrated with a quotation from the *Oeconomica*. The entry concludes with the note that a Byzantine etymologicon derives ἔθνος from ἔθος 'custom', as does Eustathios. This entry, massively learned as it is, represents a drop in the ocean of Henri's erudition: it takes up a third of a column in a dictionary of some six thousand columns. Multiply the illustrative quotations in the entry by eighteen thousand, and the *Thesaurus graecae linguae* can be seen to be an enormous treasury of extracts from Greek literature. The quotations are not usually as well referenced as those in the *Thesaurus linguae latinae*, but they are remarkably copious; the *Thesaurus* is one of those dictionaries that can be used as a partial concordance to the language it documents, and indeed it was recommended for use as a concordance of New Testament Greek in the next century.[119]

The second striking formal feature of the *Thesaurus graecae linguae*, which also derives from Robert's work, is its etymological macrostructure. There was a reason for the entry to conclude by remarking that two Byzantine authorities see ἔθνος 'people' as a derivative of ἔθος 'custom'. So, in Henri's opinion, were words as disparate as ἔθω 'I do habitually', ἠθικός 'moral' and καλλιεθείρα 'having beautiful hair'. These bring together a whole set of ancient Greek ideas about custom and habit, the connection with hair being that dressing one's hair is a customary action. They also show these ideas as genealogically affiliated, and therefore as growing from a single radical idea: Henri was not simply mapping a state of affairs but, implicitly, mapping a development, telling a story. He knew that the etymological structure of the *Thesaurus* would be controversial. It had been the subject of rumours before publication (another rumour, by the way, had been that the defining language of the *Thesaurus* would be Greek): 'there are', he remarked in the *De suae typographiae statu*, 'those who have heard that the words in my *Thesaurus* are brought together in an order far removed from the alphabetical, and they are very curious as to what this can be, and fear that my labour will be of no use even to those who are, as it were, veterans in the knowledge of Greek, let alone novices'.[120] But he followed through on his plan, providing the *Thesaurus* with its massive alphabetical index to disarm criticism.

---

[119] Wilkins, *Ecclesiastes* 25.
[120] H. Estienne, *Epistola … de suae typographiae statu* 7, 'Sunt … qui, quod vocabula in meo Thesauro, longe alio quam alphabetico ordine digesta esse audierint, quisnam is esse possit, valde mirentur, ac ne iis duntaxat qui in linguae Graecae cognitione veterani sunt (vt ita loquar) no[n] item tyronibus labor meus vtilis futurus sit, vereantur.'

Estienne did not take the final step which his etymological macro-structure might have suggested to him: he did not arrange his quotations in chronological order. This would in fact have been far from easy. Wilamowitz may have put his case too strongly when he remarked, à propos of the *Thesaurus*, that 'Clearly discrimination between the various periods and styles could not be expected yet'; even if he risks erring in the other direction, Anthony Grafton surely does the best scholarship of the period something closer to justice when he writes that scholars like Isaac Casaubon 'checked their texts against the new lexica they could read and the even more impressive mental lexica they had compiled by their own hard work, which divided the history of the Greek language into periods as hard and well-defined as geological strata'.[121] But the richness of Henri's quotation evidence, the implicit chronological structure of his dictionary, and his use of explicit historical statements make the *Thesaurus graecae linguae*, like the *Latinae linguae thesaurus*, an immensely important precursor to the nineteenth-century principle that every dictionary entry should be historically arranged, and should tell the story of the word it documents from the earliest witnesses to the latest.

THE EXPENSE, AND THE LOSS OF MY YOUTH: HENRI ESTIENNE'S DICTIONARY AND THE FAILURE OF PHILOLOGY

Just as his father had done, Henri Estienne used the preface to his dictionary to present himself to his readers – and, specifically, to present himself as a heroic figure. Writing about his love of the Greek language, he identified himself as Hercules: 'inflamed by my love, I was able successfully to perform that Herculean labour which it called for'.[122] Enlarging on the painful difficulty of his work, he asked his reader, 'How often would you say that, deterred by so many difficulties, I wanted to retrace my steps? Truly, as Virgil sang of Aeneas, *Love of the fatherland overcame him*, so I can state of myself, love of the language overcame me.'[123] This

---

[121] Wilamowitz-Moellendorff, *Geschichte der Philologie* 25, 'Daß die Scheidung der Zeiten und Stile noch nicht erwartet werden kann, sagt sich jeder', trans. Wilamowitz, *History of classical scholarship* 54; Grafton, *Defenders of the text* 176.

[122] H. Estienne, *TGL* I:10, 'eo [amore] accensus, Herculeum quendam laborem, qui exantlandus in ea erat, eluctari potui'; the word *exantlandus* or *exanclandus* in either of its spellings is uncommon, and its use here perhaps echoes its use by Robert Estienne in *LLT* (1531) sig. *3r, 'hoc nostrum ... opus: in quo tot labores, tot vigiliae, tot aerumnae, pene dixerim Herculeae, fueru[n]t exantlandae'.

[123] H. Estienne, *TGL* I:10, 'Quoties tantis difficultatibus deterritum pedem referre voluisse arbitraris? Verum ut de Aenea cecinit Maro, *Vicit amor patriae*: ita de me affirmare possum, Vicit amor linguae', misquoting Virgil, *Aeneid* 6:823a, 'vincet amor patriae'; cf. ibid. 823b, 'laudumque immensa cupido.'

quotation must be from memory, for it is wrongly explained. It was not Aeneas who was overcome by patriotism in the passage that Henri quotes, but Lucius Brutus, who sentenced his own sons to death when they committed treason. He was actuated by patriotism and, Virgil adds, the great desire for glory. Virgil's words are disturbing because they suggest that Brutus may have sacrificed his sons to his own glory as well as to the good of the fatherland; in 1599, Jacobus Pontanus was to sum up a number of earlier responses to the passage by noting that 'Neither will all who hear of this approve it, nor can the poet himself praise it altogether.'[124]

Henri was half-remembering, and failing or refusing to acknowledge, a story that provides a frightening analogy for intense research into a dead language, one in which superhuman (but yet morally ambiguous) restraint, loss, the need for consolation, and the desire for fame come together. But while that story was at the back of his mind, he was also thinking of another story of destructive commitment to duty: for the moment at which Aeneas could be said to have been overcome by love of a fatherland was surely that at which he chose to abandon Dido in order to go and found the New Troy. Neither of the stories jostling for place in his mind was exactly triumphant. But at least Brutus had a fatherland to defend, and Aeneas had one to re-create. Henri did not. He had gone into exile from France, settling in (and often wandering from) the troubled and impoverished republic of Geneva.[125] Greek was his chosen home and comfort, his *Heimat*, but it was very much the language of a lost world: some western European scholars in the mid-sixteenth century 'believed', in the words of the German humanist Martin Crusius, writing with hindsight in 1584 after the picture had become clearer, 'that Athens, where all intellectual activity began and was cultivated, had ceased to exist (as had a number of other cities), and had been destroyed apart from a few fishermen's huts'.[126] He was cut off both from the country of his birth and family heritage and from the world of his intellectual and emotional heritage, and his anger at the incompetence of other lexicographers of

---

[124] Pontanus, *Symbolarum libri xvii Virgilii* col. 1527, remarking that 'nec omnes, qui audierint, probabunt, nec ipse poeta omnino laudare potest', and citing Budé's demonstration that a father was not obliged to sentence his sons to death for capital offences, Plutarch's uncertainty in the life of Publicola as to whether Brutus' act was god-like or bestial, and Augustine, *De civitate Dei* 3:16, 'qui filios occidit infelix est. Et tamquam ad consolandum infelicem, subiunxit, *uincit amor patriae laudumque immensa cupido*.'

[125] For a vivid picture of the poverty and precarious situation of sixteenth-century Geneva, see Pattison, *Isaac Casaubon* 17–23.

[126] Crusius, *Turcograeciae libri octo* sig. *3v, 'illae omnium doctrinarum inuentrices & propagatrices Athenae, non amplius extare (sicut nec aliae nonnullae urbes), sed deletae, aliquot tantum piscatorijs casis relictae, crederentur'.

Greek may have arisen partly from a sense that their laziness and stupidity was a betrayal of a heritage that he loved all the more passionately because he could not fully enjoy it.

Henri saw his relationship with the Greek language as one of love, and not only as one of doomed heroic love. 'In this love of mine', he wrote elsewhere in the preface to the *Thesaurus graecae linguae*, 'I certainly did not find what the most poetic of the Latin poets has affirmed, *I want no part of what I do not know*.' His point there was that he was delighted by a hearing of Greek while the language was still a mystery to him. But who was 'the most poetic of the Latin poets'? Virgil again? The answer, unexpectedly perhaps, is Ovid, and the quotation is from the *Ars amatoria*.[127] He went on in the next paragraph to quote from the *Ars amatoria* again, and then from the *Amores* and from Tibullus. By doing so, he was rounding the reader's sense of what had gone into the dictionary: not simply the world in which the epic qualities matter and flourish, but an unexpected tenderness as well, affection as well as dedication, a whole life.

He never presents this affection as merely tranquil. Again, he gives a remarkably intimate picture of his life and emotions as a lexicographer. He says that 'in the passion of love, "things of no beauty yet seem beautiful"', a quotation that he gives first in Latin and then in Greek, identifying it as from Theocritus.[128] Henri knew Theocritus well, having edited him in the *Poetae graeci principes* six years previously, and therefore surely knew to whom this good advice is being given: the most unattractive of lovers, Polyphemus. To see the relationship of Galatea and the monster as a model for his own relationship with Greek suggested that he had a sense, not simply of the futility of his ambitions, but of their comic futility. The stately multiple dedication of the *Thesaurus* to the principal monarchs and universities of north-western Europe quotes Theocritus again. To be a good patron will win you undying fame, and what can be better than fame?

> The Atreides keep that undamaged; but in darkness
> Whence no return is granted now lies hidden
> All that they took overrunning the city of Priam.[129]

---

[127] H. Estienne, *TGL* 1:9, 'In hoc meo amore, verum non comperitur quod poetarum Latinorum ποιητικώτατος testatur, – *ignoti nulla cupido*' (quoting Ovid, *Ars amatoria* 3:97).

[128] Ibid., 'Quadam amoris vehementia, *Res minime pulchrae, pulchrae tamen esse videntur*, vel (ipsissimis Syracusani poetae verbis) τὰ μὴ καλὰ καλὰ πέφανται' (quoting Theocritus, *Idyllia* 6:19).

[129] Ibid. 1:4 (translating Theocritus *Idyllia* 17:116–20), 'Hoc manet Atridis salvum: caligine contra | Nunc adoperta latent (nullus datur unde regressus) | Quaecunque obtigerant Priami populantibus urbem.'

Here, Theocritus is also being used to speak of Henri's own work, and of futility. The fame of the Atreides had not been an enviable one. They had gone down, bloodily and painfully, into the darkness. Henri added to the effect by remarking that Theocritus might have said the same of Achilles, at whose tomb Alexander had remarked on the fortune of the youth (*adolescens*) who had Homer to praise him.[130] The word *adolescens* emphasizes the prematurity of the death of Achilles, and looks ironically towards the premature death of Alexander.

There is something uncompromising about the presentation of the royal and learned dedicatees of the dictionary with this *memento mori*. Henri made a similarly uncompromising decision when he chose that the first text his reader would encounter on turning the title-page of the *Thesaurus* would be a poem by himself, in Greek, starting with a reference to Hesiod.[131] The first words of the introduction to the reader were a couplet, also in Greek, this time straight from Hesiod: 'The tongue's best treasure among men is when it is sparing, and its greatest charm is when it goes in measure.'[132] The dictionary is being presented by means of an appeal to the sort of traditional wisdom characteristic of this author, and there is a suggestion that the dictionary itself participates in that wisdom. Like Hesiod, Henri is in the business of bringing new life to old truths – just as he is in the business of praising the dead, and of love, and of finding a fatherland.

It is possible to think more about his interest in finding a fatherland by returning to the dedicatees of his dictionary. They were not purely nominal; they received their expensive books. Not only did Henri twice go on record as saying that the emperor had received his copy, but the first volume of the set he presented to the University of Heidelberg survived the plunder of the university library in 1623 and is still extant.[133] The dedications might still, in theory, have been mercenary. Multiple dedications made in the obvious hope of multiple rewards were quite common in the sixteenth century, and they often have a comic air. There are a good few examples of books dedicated to several different patrons on the same page, or even on specially printed supplementary

---

[130] Ibid., 'idem de reliquis omnibus heroibus ... ac nominatim de Achille, canere poterat: cuius ad tumulum quum Alexander astitisset, O fortunate, inquit, adolescens, qui tuae virtutis Homerum praeconem inveneris.'

[131] Ibid., 1:2.   [132] Ibid. 1:9, quoting Hesiod, *Works and days* 719–20.

[133] The volume, inscribed 'Celeberr. Academiae Heydelberg. Henr. Steph. D. D.', and rebound in England at some time in the eighteenth century, was offered for sale by Bernard Quaritch in October 2000.

or cancel dedication pages.[134] In 1608, Thomas Dekker gave a lively account of the

> fellowes ... that buying vp any old Booke (especially a Sermon, or any other matter of Diuinity,) that lies for wast-paper, and is cleane forgotten, ad a new-printed Epistle to it, and with an Alphabet of letters which they cary about them, beeing able to Print any mans name (for a Dedication) on the suddaine, trauaile vp and downe most Shires in England, and liue by this Hawking.[135]

But although Henri could, as he knew, sometimes be seen as a comic figure, he was quite serious here: he meant to make a multiple dedication, and he meant the dedicatees to be conscious of it. He was not pretending for a moment that a given dedicatee was in a unique relationship with him: he was urging them to reflect that they were in a shared relationship.

He was, in other words, urging the claim of the *Thesaurus graecae linguae* to be a profoundly international document. By the time of its making, his interest in the conformity of Greek and French was being replaced by a sense of Greek as a language of interest to western Europeans in general. His multiple dedication belongs to the history of irenicism. It can be compared to the Protestant internationalism of his collection of Latin versions of the Psalms, in which he boasted that the translators were 'four famous poets, to whom four different regions, France, Italy, Germany and Scotland, gave birth'.[136] As early as the 1550s, he had listened (though with disapproval) to Guillaume Postel's arguments for a reconciliation of Christianity, Judaism and Islam.[137] A number of the people with whom he was in contact in the 1570s were earnestly interested in the slightly more realistic ideal of peace and some sort of confessional toleration throughout Christian Europe. One of these was the Silesian humanist and physician Johannes Crato von Crafftheim, who exchanged letters with Henri and received a presentation copy of one of his books.[138] Another was the Hungarian humanist and emblematist Joannes Sambucus (János Zsámboky), in whose letters Henri is a recurring presence.[139] A third was the English poet and hero Philip Sidney, dedicatee of two of Henri's books,

[134] For some examples from the British Isles see Williams, *Index of dedications* 243–56.
[135] Dekker, *Lanthorne and candle-light* sig. F2r (and cf. ibid. sig. F1v).
[136] H. Estienne, 'Index librorum qui ex officina Henrici Stephani hactenus prodierunt' sig. a4r, 'Dauidis psalmi aliquot Latino carmine expressi | A quatuor illustribus poetis, quos quatuor regiones, Gallia, Italia, Germania, Scotia, genuerunt.'
[137] H. Estienne, *Introduction au traité de la conformité des merveilles* 93.
[138] For Crato, see Evans, *Rudolf II and his world* 89–90, 98–100; his presentation copy of Estienne's *Hypomneses de gallica lingua* is described by Schreiber, *Estiennes* 173–174.
[139] For Sambucus, see Evans, *Rudolf II and his world* 123–7 and Karrow, *Mapmakers of the sixteenth century* 457–63, and for Estienne's place in his letters, see Sambucus, *Briefe* (1968) *ad indicem*.

to whom a number of learned men looked as a possible future leader of European Protestant internationalism.[140]

Other lexicographers shared Henri's ideals; indeed, bilingual and polyglot lexicography are natural partners of irenicism, since in each case the aim is that members of different communities should understand each other. So, for instance, Rudolfine Prague, a multilingual city and a centre of irenicism, was a centre of polyglot lexicography as well: Rudolf's artistic adviser Jacopo Strada worked for forty years on an eleven-language dictionary; the Spanish ambassador Juan Borja y Castro commissioned a Spanish–Latin–Czech dictionary; another resident of Prague, the Hungarian bishop Faust Vrančić (Faustus Verantius), produced a five-language dictionary; one of the major interests of the leading Prague publisher, Daniel Adam of Veleslavín, was bilingual and polyglot dictionaries.[141]

These lexicographical interests were of a piece with the apparently less practical Rudolfine fascination with cryptography and with the occult, whose ambitions were really theirs on a more grandiose scale: the discovery of connections, of fundamental principles of decipherment and therefore of communication and of wisdom. These are the traditions that produced the great Czech irenicist, encyclopedist and philosopher Comenius, a maker of dictionaries (the one that might have been his masterpiece, the *Thesaurus linguae bohemicae*, was accidentally destroyed in manuscript) and theorist of lexicography, who witnessed the ruin of the irenical hopes of all persons of good will in the Thirty Years' War.[142] Due to that disaster, the *Thesaurus graecae linguae* was one of the last great scholarly projects that could seriously claim to be of equal concern to the three principal monarchs of north-western Europe. The next dictionary of a pan-European language to be conceived with similar grandeur, the *Thesaurus linguae latinae* whose publication began at the very end of the nineteenth century, was emphatically, despite its use of Latin as a defining language, the product of the academies of German-speaking Europe.

---

[140] For Sidney in the context of Prague and irenicism, see Evans, *Rudolf II and his world* 121–2, and for his relations with Estienne, see Considine, 'How much Greek did Philip Sidney know? ' 68–73.

[141] For Strada's dictionary, see Evans, *Rudolf II and his world* 129 and Louthan, *Quest for compromise* 79n48; for Borja y Castro's, see Chudoba, *Spain and the Empire* 160; for Vrančić's, see Evans, *Rudolf II* 187n1, Stankiewicz, *Grammars and dictionaries of the Slavic languages* 18 and 84–5 and Claes, *Bibliographisches Verzeichnis* 211–12 (item 807) and for its expanded version, the *Dictionarium septem diversarum linguarum* of Peter Loderecker (Prague, 1605), see Jones, *German lexicography* 480–1 (item 800); for Veleslavín, see Hüllen, *English dictionaries* 368–71.

[142] For Comenius and lexicography, see Přívratská, 'Dictionary as a textbook' 155–7 and Hüllen, *English dictionaries* 372.

The internationalism of Henri's outlook goes with one of the dominant features of his career, the forced internationalism of a man driven to travel repeatedly across Europe, in search of *inedita* or on publishing business. Regular visits to the mart at Frankfurt, in which the most important bookfair in Europe took place as part of a great general market of food, weaponry, luxury goods, horses, and so on, were a necessary part of the business. The *Francofordiense emporium*, an encomium of the mart which he wrote and published in 1574, ends with a meditation on the juxtaposition there of the book trade and the arms trade, and with the prayer that the former may flourish as the latter declines, that the international book trade may become part of an international triumph of peace.[143] Throughout this text, there is a sense of pleasure in the mart: strangers are treated kindly, lodgings are good, the merchants are honest, the objects displayed for sale are fascinating and delightful. But his travels on publishing business were not always satisfactory. In one dedication, he recalls the return from a visit to Vienna, 'with my business not only unfinished but in such a state as to be despaired of', with a line of Homer running through his head, 'it is shameful to come back home empty-handed after a long delay'.[144] What cheered him up, he goes on to say, was the thought that in Vienna he had met the dedicatee whom he was now addressing – but this must really have been cold comfort.

The partial success of his journeys between 1547 and 1555 has been mentioned. It may have been at this time that he copied out a number of inscriptions at Rome and Naples, which he contemplated printing in his edition of the earliest Latin poets but decided to reserve until he had more time to deal with their textual corruption.[145] As the years went by, he knew that there were still *inedita* to be found. Contemporaries of his produced *editiones principes* now and again: the *Dionysiaca* of Nonnus in 1569, Hierocles in 1583, Andronicus of Rhodes in 1594, and so on. He knew from his notes of 1551 that the manuscript of Greek verse that John Clement had shown him in Louvain had had more in it than the *Anacreontea*, but was clearly unable to return to it when he was editing the *Planudean anthology* in 1566.[146] In 1592, he apologized for the delay in

[143] H. Estienne, *Francofordiense emporium* 27–31.
[144] H. Estienne, 'Noctes aliquot Parisinae' 5 (quoting Homer, *Iliad* 2:298 in Latin), 'quum negotio meo non solum infecto sed propemodum deplorato redirem ... illud Homericum in mentem venisset, *Turpe, moram vacuum post longam ad tecta reuerti.*'
[145] H. Estienne, ed., *Fragmenta poetarum veterum latinorum* 426.
[146] Cameron, *Greek anthology* 179–81.

printing two *inedita* of St Justin Martyr, explaining that he had, among other problems, been waiting for a manuscript of a similar text, which he had hoped to publish at the same time as Justin.[147] But knowing that there were *inedita* to be found was not the same as finding them. Even when he did come across an important unpublished text, there might be obstacles: meeting in the library of Pierre Pithou with a manuscript of excerpts from Macrobius' *De verborum graeci et latini differentiis vel societatibus*, he could find no amanuensis to make a copy for him, and was too busy to copy the whole text himself, so that in his edition of Macrobius of 1585, where he could suitably have published the *princeps* of a new text, he only published a very short extract from its preface. The *princeps* appeared three years later, edited by Johannes Opsopoeus.[148]

The business of which Henri was despairing on his gloomy journey from Vienna was very probably concerned with the financing and distribution of books rather than the hunt for manuscripts. Publication of ancient Greek on the scale that he had achieved before the appearance of the *Thesaurus graecae linguae* was at best a financially risky enterprise.[149] Henri eventually found himself unable to recoup his expenses by sales. The cultivation of patronage was an uncertain business, too: he had from 1558 to 1568 been so generously supported from the princely riches of Ulrich Fugger as to use the imprint 'excudebat Henricus Stephanus, illustris viri Huldrici Fuggeri typographus', but that had come to an end, and although he subsequently benefited from the patronage of several other German-speakers, none of them could subvent a whole publishing programme.[150] The *Thesaurus* itself was financially disastrous. It had called for a huge investment, presumably in the order of the more than thirty thousand francs which the *Latinae linguae thesaurus* had cost. Even as Henri completed it, he admitted in a liminary poem that he would not recover his investment:

Other treasuries have the power to enrich and to delight,
And make the man as rich as Croesus who was previously as poor as Irus.
But this Treasury [*Thesaurus*] has brought me from wealth into poverty,

---

147 H. Estienne in St Justin Martyr, *Epist[ola] ad Diognetu[m]* 97, 'alium quendam libellum exspectabam, luce nec ipsum antea donatum, quem, quod eiusdem argume[n]ti sit, pergratum lectori futurum sperabam'.

148 For the manuscript, now BN ms lat. 7186, and the *editio princeps*, see Macrobius, *De verborum graeci et latini differentiis vel societatibus excerpta* (1990) xli ff. and lxiv–lxv.

149 See Kenney, *Classical text* 80–1.

150 For later patronage, see H. Estienne in Gellius, *Noctes atticae* (1585) 21–2, 'De Germanis enim si bene mereri non cupiam, ingratus profecto sim, quum multorum non solum humanitatem sed liberalitatem quoque sim expertus.'

And has made an old man's wrinkles furrow my once youthful face.
But the expense is a light matter to me, and so is the loss of my youth,
If in your judgement this work was not in vain.[151]

The expense could not, though, be shrugged off. The dictionary must have
cost at least as much in the bookshop as the *Latinae linguae thesaurus*:
seventeenth-century English records suggest a price of between four and
five pounds, which would make it one of the most expensive multi-volume
sets on the market.[152] Likewise, at the auction of Jan de Laet's books in
1650, the *Thesaurus* went for 53 guilders, more than an eight-volume Bel-
larmine (*f*44) and less only than the very priciest sets such as a nine-volume
Bibliotheca patrum or a twelve-volume *Annales* of Baronius (*f*60, *f*100).[153]
The fact that these are seventeenth-century records is significant in itself.
Copies of the *Thesaurus* are now widespread – no other continental printed
book of the period before 1641 is held in as many Oxford libraries, and a
number of copies were presented to school and civic libraries in England in
the seventeenth century – but that does not mean that they sold briskly in
the 1570s.[154] One early purchaser bought his copy on an instalment plan,
and it would be interesting to know how many others did likewise.[155]

---

[151] H. Estienne, *TGL* I:2, 'Thesauri momento alii ditantque beantque, | Et faciunt Croesum qui prius
Irus erat. | At Thesaurus me hic ex divite reddit egenum, | Et facit ut iuvenem ruga senilis aret. |
Sed mihi opum levis est, levis est iactura iuventae, | Iudicio haud levis est si labor iste tuo.'

[152] Samuel Pepys tried to obtain a set for £4 in 1661, and gave £4 10s for a set on 24 December 1662,
paying an extra 10s for 'strings and golden letters' for the bindings (Pepys, *Diary* II:239, III:290,
and IV:133); Norwich City Library paid £5 for a set with the *Glossaria duo* in the following year
(Stoker, 'Doctor Collinges and the revival of Norwich City Library' 83). Cf. the prices of history
books gathered in Woolf, *Reading history in early modern England* 212–31: from the seventeenth
century, sets of the *Annales* of Baronius and of Dugdale's *Monasticon* might cost between £5 and
£6 (219, 226), and the nine volumes of the *Critici sacri* ed. John Pearson et al. were said to sell for
as much as £15 (225n71; for the publisher's own figure, £13 10s, see *Case of Cornelius Bee and his
partners*), but no other work cost as much as £5.

[153] Hoftijzer, 'Library of Johannes de Laet' 208–9; exceptional in this auction was the price of *f*400
for a large-paper *Biblia regia* in eight volumes.

[154] For Oxford holdings, see University of Oxford Early Printed Books Project, 'Background'
(subheading 'database'), which remarks that 'a few very common items have more than 15 locations
and just 1 is held in 23 locations in Oxford. (Henri Estienne's Thesaurus Graecae Linguae, 1572)';
holdings in school libraries include the set bought by Pepys, which was given by him to St Paul's
School, London, and the set donated by John, Lord Harrington, to the Free School at Coventry
between 1603 and 1614, for which see Sharp, ed., *Illustrative papers on the history and antiquities of the
city of Coventry* 175; one early donation of the *Thesaurus* was that of Sir Nicholas Bacon to Cambridge
University Library as early as 1574, for which see Leedham-Green and McKitterick, 'Catalogue of
Cambridge University Library, 1583' 199–200 (catalogue entry) and 154 (date of donation).

[155] Johannes Castelius, letter of 31 July 1574 to Abraham Ortelius in Ortelius, *Epistolae* 120–1 (letter 51)
at 120–1, 'Accepi doctiss[ime] abs te missum mihi Theatrum orbis, quod tamen pro mea tenuitate
tribus tantum terminis, ut convenimus, persolvere potero ... quo modo aiebam me prius emisse
Thesaurum Henr[ici] Stephani.'

Unlike his father, Henri did not get a cheaper version of his big dictionary onto the market. Instead, a minister and teacher from Lausanne called Joannes Scapula (Jean Espaulaz) produced a *Lexicon graecolatinum*, published as a folio volume in 1580, in which he used material from the *Thesaurus*.[156] He acknowledged this with every appearance of candour in his foreword: 'lest I deprive the author of this thesaurus, composed indeed with Herculean labour, of his rightful praise (and he has deserved well of the learned), and lest I appear to show myself off in borrowed plumes, I shall not be loth to confess what I have taken from him'.[157] In fact, Scapula's work was an abridgement of Estienne's, not an original dictionary which borrowed from the *Thesaurus*, and it is hard to avoid the conclusion that his foreword was meant to deceive his readers. The *Lexicon graecolatinum* was naturally much cheaper than the *Thesaurus graecae linguae*: to return for the purposes of comparison to seventeenth-century England, a copy was valued at nine shillings in 1635 and another was bought for nineteen shillings in 1641, suggesting a range of prices between one tenth and one quarter of that of the *Thesaurus*.[158] It doubtless undercut the big dictionary's sales. Estienne was able to report by 1594 that the plagiarism was notorious, so that at least Scapula was winning no honour from it, and by the next decade, the English satirist Joseph Hall could refer to this notoriety in a book of imaginary travels, placing 'mount *Scapula*, a very high hill', in a land of thieves near the city of Leigerdumaine, and adding the marginal note '*Scapula* stole his *Greek Lexicon* from *Steuens*, and yet durst avow this. *Hoc ego contendo Lexicon esse novum*.'[159]

Estienne's works on the French language and his satirical *Apologie pour Herodote* (1566), which ran into twelve editions in his lifetime, did not restore his fortunes; nor did his editions of the Bible. The combination of a shortage of working capital with an intense anxiety to emulate his father and satisfy his readers by publishing copiously led to a whole string of publishing projects that he announced and never completed.[160] In the *De suae typographiae statu*, he announced a forthcoming Plutarch, which did indeed appear, in the same year as the *Thesaurus*, an amazing double achievement, since the Plutarch ran to thirteen volumes – well over eight

[156] For Scapula, see Hieronymus, *Griechischer Geist* 103–6.

[157] Scapula, *Lexicon graecolatinum* (1580) sig. a4v, 'At uero ne thesauri illius Herculeo sane labore compositi autorem bene de literis meritum debita laude fraudare, aut me alienis plumis uenditare uidear: quid illi acceptum feram, fateri non grauabor.'

[158] Marsden, 'Virginian minister's library' 330; Watson, *Library of Sir Simonds D'Ewes* 253 (19s for 'A scapulas Lexicon in quires' plus 4s 6d for clasps and binding).

[159] H. Estienne, *Premices* sig. *6v; Hall, *Discovery of a new world* 135.

[160] Maittaire, *Stephanorum historia* 469–78.

thousand pages – in octavo. But he also announced plans to print Strabo, Athenaeus, Stobaeus, Aristophanes, Diogenes Laertius, Lucian, and then perhaps, as a lower priority, Cicero, Livy and Pliny, not to mention new editions of Budé's *Commentarii* and Erasmus' *Adagia*, and a new edition of the *Latinae linguae thesaurus*, a Latin–Greek–French dictionary, and some Bible editions.[161] These were to be distinguished from the nineteen works that he regarded as in press, or practically so.[162] He was thirty-eight, and looking forward to a long and productive life, but even so, these long-range plans were wildly ambitious, and it is not surprising that they were largely made in vain (though the Diogenes Laertius did appear, as, in 1591, did the letters of the younger Pliny). Ambitious as they were, even more projects would be added to them, notably a complete Aristotle, to be edited by Sambucus, and to be printed by Henri in financial partnership with Episcopius of Basel. This was supposed to be printed in 1577, but it never appeared; nor did an edition of the works of Dioscorides which he and Sambucus were discussing at about the same time.[163] By the 1580s, Henri was anxious to send something new to the Frankfurt bookfair to prove that he was still alive and working, 'for by a number of learned men of German-speaking Europe, I was mourned as if my light was broken, since for a long time they had seen nothing which had come out of my *officina*'.[164] In 1585, books that he had edited were being produced by other printers with no publisher's imprint or colophon, more or less as private publications of his own. He described himself as the *procurator* of one of these editions, the person who had commissioned it, and added gloomily that it was 'not such an edition as would have come from my *officina*'.[165] In that year, one of the liminary epistles to his edition of Gellius announced forthcoming enlarged editions of Dionysius of Halicarnassus and of Polybius, and a major edition of Aristotle (can he have hoped to use the materials of the recently deceased Sambucus?) – and, as an afterthought, one of Pausanias. New editions of Pausanias and Aristotle had, he admitted, just come out, but, he proclaimed bravely, 'I deny that I have been anticipated by

[161] H. Estienne, *Epistola de suae typographiae statu* 4–6.

[162] H. Estienne, 'Appendix' in 'Index librorum qui ex officina Henrici Stephani hactenus prodierunt' sigs. A1r–A3r.

[163] Sambucus, *Briefe* 287–8 (Aristotle) and 299–302 (Dioscorides); for the latter, see also Riddle, 'Dioscorides' 109–10 and 41.

[164] H. Estienne in Gellius, *Noctes atticae* (1585) 21, 'quod a plerisque literatis Germani[a]e viris ... tanquam lumine cassus lugear: quod a longo iam tempore nihil quod ex officina mea prodiret viderint'.

[165] H. Estienne, dedicatory epistle in Macrobius, *In somnium Scipionis* (1585) sig. ā2v, 'hanc editionem, cuius ... procurator fui, non tale[m] qualis ex officina mea prodiisset ... dico'.

those whose edition mine will, as often as you like, leave many paces behind it."[166] In fact, his Aristotle, Pausanias and Polybius never appeared, and he was anticipated in the publication of Dionysius as well, by an excellent edition of 1586 (which included the *editio princeps* of the *De Thucydide* for which Henri had once searched in vain).[167] The editor of this edition, Friedrich Sylburg, referred courteously to Henri as 'my master' in a liminary epistle – he had learned his first Greek from him, and had subsequently contributed to the *Thesaurus graecae linguae* – but by the time he wrote these words he, not the older scholar, was the leading active editor of ancient Greek, and his publishers, the house of Wechel in Frankfurt, were the leading publishers of editions of Greek texts, their output including the editions by Sylburg of Pausanias and Aristotle which had pre-empted Henri's projects.[168]

This disparity between scholarly ambition and production is clearly related to the fact that Henri suffered painful fits of melancholy for much of his adult life. He suggests the relationship himself in his report of one period when the thought of literary work disgusted him so much that he had to cover his face in his library because he could not bear even to see his books on their shelves.[169] These fits were joined with a sense of the world as a dangerous and sinister place, full of adversaries: he reported with great feeling the advice of the philosopher Panaetius that the prudent man should be like a boxer in the ring, fists up in self-defence, ready to avoid or inflict injury.[170] Towards the end of his career, his judgement seems sometimes to have been impaired, and after 1593 his productivity declined, perhaps because his physical strength was failing (he was sixty-two in that year) but perhaps because he was increasingly affected by some form of mental instability. He took to travelling obsessively. By 1594, his son-in-law Isaac Casaubon was to refer to his wanderings with sorrow: 'ἀλᾶται, πλανᾶται καὶ ἀλύει', he wrote, using three words which may each apply

---

[166] H. Estienne in Gellius, *Noctes atticae* (1585) 23, 'me ab illis pr[a]euenirinego, quorum editionem mea, quoties libuerit, multis a tergo passibus relinquet'.

[167] Dionysius, *Scripta quae exstant omnia* (1586), printing *De Thucydide* from a transcript made by Andreas Dudithius, who was in Italy in the same year as Estienne, 1554, but had better luck hunting for this particular text: see Sylburg's dedicatory and prefatory epistles sigs. (:)2r–3v, and see also Dionysius, *Opuscula* (1899) 1:xxix f. for Dudith's transcript, and 1:xv f. for the manuscript authorities.

[168] For Sylburg and Henri, see Bursian, *Geschichte der classischen Philologie in Deutschland* 229; for the acknowledgement as master, see Sylburg, epistle to the reader in Dionysius, *Scripta quae exstant omnia* (1586) sig. *5r, 'magister meus Henricus Stephanus'.

[169] H. Estienne, dedicatory epistle in Sextus Empiricus, *Pyrrhoniarum hypotypωseωn libri* III (1562) 2–3; see also Maittaire, *Stephanorum historia* 247–8, 485–8, and Pattison, 'Classical learning in France' 345–6, 354–5.

[170] H. Estienne in Gellius, *Noctes atticae* (1585) 3.

to physical or mental displacement, adding, 'I hear without a doubt that ἀλύειν is the right word for what he does, since he is neither able to return home nor to find a place which is right for him elsewhere.'[171]

Henri also became anxious that a war should be prosecuted against the Ottoman Empire, and wrote extensively on the subject, as if trying, after years of studying a common European heritage and promoting it in documents like the joint dedication of the *Thesaurus graecae linguae*, to turn the hearts of his readers towards action in a Christian cause. In 1594, he published two hundred pages on the subject encouraging the emperor Rudolf II to attack the Turkish empire, and in the *De Lipsii latinitate palaestra I* of the following year, the crusade becomes a King Charles's head, prompting Scaliger's sardonic reference to the work as *De latinitate Lipsiana adversus Turcam*.[172] Unbalanced as was the urgency with which Henri called for war on the Turks, the call itself was not idiosyncratic: the Ottoman Empire posed a real threat to central Europe. It could also be seen as the most important factor in the loss of the Greek literary heritage. A liminary poem in Sylburg's edition of Dionysius, for instance, remarks that 'the Turk has brought irreparable ruin upon the Greeks, and the Goth has given Italy many wounds', before saying unconvincingly that the works about Greece and Rome by Pausanias and Dionysius respectively more than make up for this by the glory they give their subjects.[173] Here, the Turkish presence in Greece is seen as antithetical to the textual heritage to which Estienne had devoted his life.

He was, in old age, oppressed not only with business problems and thoughts of the Turks, but by unhappiness, largely of his own making, in his relations with his family. His son Paul was to be a respectable scholar, but Henri apparently found him a reluctant one. In 1585, when Henri was fifty-four and Paul was nineteen, the father exhorted the son in the very public medium of a liminary epistle:

What means of giving you a superb education could possibly have been demanded, which were not expected of me? And therefore what do you think is not now expected of you yourself? For nearly the whole of Europe knows that not only your father has shown you the way forward, but also your grandfather,

---

[171] I. Casaubon, letter to Richard Thomson of 25 April 1594, in his *Epistolae* 8–9 at 8, 'ἀλᾶται, πλανᾶται καὶ ἀλύει. Ita enim plane audio ἀλύειν eum, ut neque domum redire, neque alibi aptas sedes reperire queat.'

[172] Quoted Schreiber, *Estiennes* 181 (item 225).

[173] Nicodemus Frischlin, 'In Pausaniam et Dionysium Halicarnasseum Friderici Sylburgii' in Dionysius, *Scripta quae exstant omnia* sig. *8v, 'Turca quidem damnum dedit irreparabile Graiis, | Atque Italo Gothus vulnera multa dedit. | Sed neque tam magnum Turcae tibi Graecia probrum, | Quantum Pausanias attulit iste decus.'

Robert Estienne, and that both have as it were trodden out the way ahead of you. If you follow in their footsteps, you will gain so much good-will for yourself, so much praise and glory; and if you leave their footsteps, you will earn yourself just as much ill-will, or indeed hatred, just as much ignominy.[174]

It is hard to imagine how this could have been other than counter-productive. The same breakdown in Henri's ability to treat others decently is to be seen elsewhere. His daughter Florence married the scholar Isaac Casaubon, a man of deep piety and evident goodness, whose compassionate description of Henri's travels has just been quoted. No more suitable son-in-law can be imagined: Scaliger, who had praised Budé as the greatest Hellenist of the earlier sixteenth century, called Casaubon the greatest Hellenist and most learned man of the con-temporary world.[175] But for all his learning and piety, Henri mistrusted him, just as he did everybody else. The wheel had come full circle from Erasmus' excitement at the access to new manuscripts in the house of Aldus at the beginning of the century: Henri, the heir to Erasmus' wonderful breadth of reading and Herculean self-conception, had become an entomber of manuscripts himself. A certain jealousy had been evident in his dealings with manuscripts from the beginning. When he stayed with Vettori around 1552, he let his host see and publish eleven lines of the *Anacreontea*, but certainly showed him no more, and very possibly gave him the impression that no more was extant, leaving Vettori to wonder in print what the rest had been like.[176] He had obtained a manuscript of the *Bibliotheca* of Photius by 1555, and thus had a pearl of great price in his hands – the *Bibliotheca* is a detailed record of the reading of a major Byzantine scholar, who had access to many texts that are no longer extant – but he never printed it in its entirety, producing individual *editiones principes* of some of the fragments it collects and then keeping it for himself.[177] Writing in 1594 to the jurist and philologist

---

[174] H. Estienne in Gellius, *Noctes atticae* (1585) 6, 'quid enim ad praeclaram tui institutionem requiri potest, quod a me non expectetur? Atque adeo quid non a te etiam ipso iam expectari putas? Scit enim tota propemodum Europa quam tibi viam non solum pater, sed ipse quoque auus, Robertus Stephanus, monstrarit, quam vterque viam tibi velut praecalcarit. Quantum vndique beneuolentiae, quantum laudis & gloriae tibi co[m]parabis, si vestigijs illorum insistas, tantum maleuolentiae, vel potius odij, tantum ignominiae tibi conflabis, si eorum vestigia relinquas.'

[175] *Scaligeriana* (1669) 64, 'C'est le plus grand homme que nous ayons en Grec, je luy cede, *est doctissimus omnium qui hodie vivunt.*'

[176] Vettori, *Variarum lectionum libri* 313, 'Si reliquae autem partes illius similes huic erant, vere potuit Cicero dicere, totam Anacreontis poesin esse amatoriam.' I am grateful to my father for discussing this passage with me.

[177] The manuscript, inscribed 'Venetiis An. 1555 August XVIII', is now BL MSS Harley 5591–5593: see Wright, *Fontes Harleiani* 315.

Conrad Rittershausen (Rittershusius), who had lent Henri a manuscript and needed it back, Casaubon admitted:

You could not possibly be more wrong, if you suppose me to have any influence with that excellent old man, or any access to his library ... when he was absent, we dared to undo the bolts and hunt through everything, so that we send your book, which we found there, to you. Believe me, it was another sack of Troy. Don't you know with what difficulty and what passage of years Leunclavius [Hans Löwenklau, who had edited Xenophon in 1569] regained his Xenophon from him?[178]

In the following year, Casaubon had to tell another correspondent that 'the ancient books he has, he begrudges others as the Indian griffins their gold, keeping them for himself, to perish'.[179]

   In his morose old age, Henri Estienne looks superficially like a failure, his intellectual work over, his business on the rocks, disappointed by or suspicious of his successors. But when his career is taken as a whole, it is hard to imagine any scholar who has ever been less of a failure. His work as lexicographer, editor, writer on language and publisher really defines the limits of what a single person is capable of achieving. No lexicographer in the Western tradition had ever achieved as much before. The achievement closest to his own was that of his father, but although Robert printed finer books than Henri, and added to his talents as a classicist the Biblical scholarship in which Henri was a comparatively minor figure, the *Latinae linguae thesaurus* documented a smaller literature, and owed more to previous lexicographers, than the *Thesaurus graecae linguae*. There would be perhaps three Western lexicographers in subsequent centuries who would achieve as much as Henri Estienne – Charles du Cange in the seventeenth, Sir James Murray in the nineteenth and Sir William Craigie in the twentieth – but none who would achieve more.

---

[178] I. Casaubon, letter to Rittershausen of 24 August 1594, in his *Epistolae* 10–11 at 10–11, 'Falleris vero toto coelo totaque terra, si me putas apud senem illum optimum quicquam posse, aut ad ipsius bibliothecam ullam habere aditum. Eo absente ausi sumus claustra revellere & omnia διφᾶν, ut tuum librum tibi mitteremus repertum, mihi crede, Ilium expugnavimus. An tu nescis qua difficultate, quo annorum spatio Xenophontem suum Leunclavius ab illo receperit?'

[179] I. Casaubon, letter to Pierre Pithou of 8 October 1595, in his *Epistolae* 25–6 at 26, 'libros quos habet veteres, ut Indici gryphi aurum, aliis invidet, sibi perire sinit'.

CHAPTER 4

Vernacular heritages I: Germany and the Netherlands 1500–1618

THE SUREST PROOFE OF PEOPLES ORIGINALL: THE TURN TO THE POST-CLASSICAL AND THE DISCOVERY OF THE GERMANIC HERITAGE

For Henri Estienne, the latter part of his lifetime was an unhappy time to be a philologist. But there were a number of courses that could be taken by a person of the generation after his who wished to do learned work. One was to study the classical world and its texts, going over ground that had been broken by the humanists, aware that it was bounded by horizons narrower than they had hoped – but aware also that the land was fertile, and that it was capable of much improvement by new techniques. There might be few major classical *inedita* awaiting discovery by seventeenth-century editors, but a text that had been edited once could be edited better, or with a better commentary. Moreover, new tools were put into the hands of readers and potential improvers of the literary monuments by the development of disciplines such as epigraphy, archaeology, codicology and numismatics.[1] These might be seen explicitly as compensating for the loss of ancient texts, so that a French antiquary could observe in the 1640s of the study of ancient coins that 'what would have been almost redundant had the writings of the ancients suffered less massive loss turned out to be the principal evidence in the face of such loss'.[2] In the history of scholarship, the earlier seventeenth century looks like the age of the antiquarians, of men like the encyclopedist and Latinist G. J. Vossius (Gerard Johan Vos), or the so-called Eratosthenes of his time, Claudius Salmasius (Claude de Saumaise).[3]

---

[1] See Momigliano, 'Ancient history and the antiquarian' 289–307.

[2] Jean Tristan de Saint Amant, paraphrased by Crawford, Ligota and Trapp in the introduction to their *Medals and coins from Budé to Mommsen* 1–4 at 3; cf. Daniel Rogers, letter of 20 October 1572 to Abraham Ortelius in Ortelius, *Epistolae* 100–3 at 102, 'Saepe enim in numismatibus et marmoreis citantur ij, quorum, alias, authores non meminerunt, uel si meminerint, lucem recipiunt ab ijs, non uulgarem.'

[3] For Salmasius as Eratosthenes, see Pfeiffer, *HCS* II 122.

Intellectual work along all these lines had its effects on lexicography. Each new edition of or commentary on a classical text (and, indeed, each new publication of an inscription) put new materials into the hands of the makers of dictionaries. In particular, the classical Latin and Greek technical vocabularies – those of, for instance, the exact sciences, architecture and music – were, as work progressed on the texts, capable of being treated with increasing refinement by lexicographers. Ancient mathematical and scientific texts could, once they had been edited and understood, be made one of the foundations of original mathematical and scientific work, and this rapidly progressed well beyond what had been achieved in antiquity and led to the creation of very extensive new terminologies, both in the Latin of the sixteenth and subsequent centuries and in the vernacular languages in which scientific inquiry was conducted; these would set up a variety of lexicographical challenges and opportunities.[4]

The scope of classical philology could also be widened by attention to the cultures at the geographical and temporal edges of the classical Mediterranean world. That might mean attention to the ancient Near East and its languages, as in the introduction to Syriac and other languages published by Teseo Ambrogio in 1539.[5] This pioneering work led to more ambitious work in the seventeenth century. Coptic, for instance, the language of Christian Egypt, was a key to the way in which Christian churches had differed from each other long before the sixteenth-century reformations or even the eleventh-century schism between the Roman Catholic and Orthodox churches. New possibilities for its study were opened up by Athanasius Kircher's publication in 1644 of a thematically ordered Coptic–Arabic glossary of about 8000 words, from a manuscript collected by the traveller Pietro della Valle some years earlier, with his own Latin translation.[6] Armenian was not only the language of another ancient church but also a relative of the major European languages (it is, in modern terms, Indo-European whereas Syriac and Coptic are not), so that its study, facilitated by a *Dictionarium armeno–latinum* of 1621, impinged on that of European heritages of both faith and language.[7] Looking beyond the Mediterranean might also mean engaging with the

---

[4] See, e.g., Swerdlow, 'Recovery of the exact sciences of antiquity' and Siraisi, 'Life sciences and medicine in the Renaissance world'.

[5] Ambrogio, *Introductio in chaldaicam linguam, syriacam, atque armenicam, et decem alias linguas*, for which see Hamilton, 'Eastern churches and Western scholarship' 237.

[6] Kircher, 'Nomenclator aegyptiaco–arabicus, cum interpretatio latina'; for this and his other Coptic studies, see Iversen, *Myth of Egypt and its hieroglyphs* 90ff.

[7] Rivola, *Dictionarium armeno–latinum* (1621); most scholars must actually have used the much more common Paris edition of 1633.

cultures and languages of the New World, Africa and Asia. The new
ethnographies and linguistic discussions that ensued from this engagement naturally generated new lexicographical work.[8]

Rather than surveying newly encountered modern languages, those
sixteenth- and seventeenth-century lexicographers who were interested in
mapping a heritage naturally chose most often to investigate the earlier
stages of their own vernaculars. This had hardly been attempted before
1500.[9] The ancient languages studied by Europeans in the Middle Ages
were, in descending order of importance, Latin, Greek and Hebrew. Latin
was the language in which intellectual work was conducted and in which
the most generally admired ancient texts had been written. The most
important medieval European dictionaries were therefore of Latin. In
some of these, such as Balbi's *Catholicon*, the defining language was Latin;
in others, meant for use at a more elementary level, the defining language
was a vernacular, and the first dictionaries to register vernacular words
were generally bilingual Latin–vernacular works. From the late fourteenth
century onwards, interest in Greek increased. It was at first taught largely
in an oral tradition, without textbooks and dictionaries, but in the second
half of the fifteenth century Greek–Latin dictionaries such as Crastone's
emerged. Hebrew was almost exclusively the preserve of Jews – a low
estimate is that 'probably no more than a few dozen Christians from 500
to 1500 could read Hebrew at all' – and there does not appear to have
been a tradition of Hebrew–Latin lexicography before 1500.[10]

The vernaculars started to be studied as they rose in prestige. For this
to happen to a language, one variety had to be recognized as a supra-
regional standard, used in government, canonical literature, worship or all
three, and therefore taking over some or all of the prestige functions of
Latin.[11] If a language was spoken in many different regional varieties,
none of which had supra-regional prestige, then each variety was bound
to be of purely local interest, and would often be part of a continuum
with other language varieties, which might extend across political
boundaries. To take a well-documented example, the village of Montaillou
was, in the 1320s, part of the Comté de Foix, a satellite of France, but much
the same language – part of an Occitan–Catalan dialect continuum – was

---

[8] Cf. Burke, *Languages and communities* 25–6.
[9] Cf. Bischoff, 'Study of foreign languages in the Middle Ages'.
[10] Friedman, *Most ancient testimony* 13–14.
[11] See Fisher, *Emergence of standard English* 65–83 and Burke, *Languages and communities* 61–110 for
   outlines, supplemented for individual languages by the entries in Price, ed., *Encyclopedia of the
   languages of Europe*.

spoken there as on the other side of the Pyrenees, in the kingdom of Aragon.[12] However, once one variety became recognized as a standard, it could become a symbol of membership of a wider community and of difference from other communities. By 1600, Montaillou was part of the kingdom of France, which had Parisian French as the official language of government, and the former Aragon was part of the kingdom of Spain, which had Castilian Spanish as the official language of government; Occitan and Catalan were non-official language varieties, and were declining in status. A standard variety such as Parisian French came to be accepted as part of the shared cultural heritage of a community, even by persons who did not use it as a household language, and thus helped to define the community that recognized it.

Linguistic communities united by a standard language variety were not always political entities, let alone nations in the modern sense.[13] Of the eight western European vernaculars to develop important standardized varieties by 1600, five – Castilian, French, English, Danish and Swedish – were the official languages of centralized monarchies. The processes by which they standardized took place at different times from the thirteenth century onward. The Old English of Winchester had had some status as a written standard from the reign of Alfred in the tenth century to the Norman Conquest in the eleventh, but lost its status thereafter.[14] Then, more enduringly, a variety of Castilian based on that of Toledo began to be recognized as a written standard during the reign of Alfonso X in the third quarter of the thirteenth century, partly through Alfonso's sponsorship of literary and learned writing in that variety of Castilian, and partly through the use of Castilian as the language of administration by the royal chancery of Castile at Toledo.[15] The same was true of the French of the Chancellerie Royale of Paris, which began to replace other varieties of the vernacular as a written language of administration as early as the thirteenth century, and the English of the London chancery, which became a written standard in the fifteenth.[16] A variety of Danish based on the writing tradition of Copenhagen and a variety of Swedish based on that of the Mälar-Uppland area of Sweden (in which Stockholm and the ancient university of Uppsala are located) developed as national standards during the sixteenth century, after the declaration of an independent

[12] Le Roy Ladurie, *Montaillou* 286.
[13] For the applicability of the word *nation*, see Hastings, *Construction of nationhood*, esp. 1–34.
[14] See Fisher, *Emergence of standard English* 68.   [15] Penny, *History of the Spanish language* 20–2.
[16] For France, see Lodge, *French: From dialect to standard* 85–152, esp. 122–3; for England, Fisher, *Emergence of standard English* 36–64.

Swedish monarchy in 1521 made it politically impossible to regard the Scandinavian languages as a single complex whole of which Swedish and Danish were simply varieties.[17] The prestige of one language variety often rose both at the expense of other varieties of the same language and at that of other languages. So, for instance, from the thirteenth century onward, Castilian not only developed an internal standard but became more prestigious than other varieties of Spanish such as Aragonese and other languages of the Iberian peninsula such as Mozarabic, Basque and Catalan, so that the union of the crowns of Castile and Aragon in 1479 completed rather than inaugurated its rise to a position of dominance.[18]

In three other cases, those of Italian, German and Dutch, standardization took place without political unification. An Italian identity transcending the local identities of the various states of the Italian peninsula emerged during the fifteenth century: hence Flavio Biondo's chorographical *Italia illustrata*, begun around 1450, which would influence the patriotic description of other national heritages such as those of Germany and England.[19] This identity can only have been strengthened by the French invasion of the Italian peninsula in 1494.[20] It led to the development of two overlapping standards for Italian: a variety that borrowed eclectically from local dialects and was sometimes called *cortegiano*, and the Tuscan dialect, whose status depended partly on that of the poetry in Tuscan of Dante, Petrarch and Boccaccio. In German-speaking Europe, High German had been gaining ground over Low German from the thirteenth century onwards. Within High German, the usage of the chanceries of the Emperor at Vienna and of the Electors of Saxony at Meissen developed supra-regional status; Martin Luther described them as having 'drawn all speeches into one', and he himself attempted to use a variety which all Germans could understand as he translated the Bible. The language of Luther's Bible translation was influential in the establishment of a written standard for German during the sixteenth and seventeenth centuries.[21] During the fifteenth and sixteenth centuries, Dutch came to be seen as a language distinct from Low German (with which it actually forms a dialect continuum); this development was in part a result of the political unification of the Low

---

[17] Haugen, 'Scandinavian languages as cultural artefacts' 272–3; Haugen, *Scandinavian languages: An introduction to their history* 38–41, 323–9.

[18] Penny, *History of the Spanish language* 18–20.

[19] See Cochrane, *Historians and historiography in the Italian Renaissance* 34–40 (esp. 40).

[20] See Burke, 'Language and identity in early modern Italy' 71ff.

[21] For the early modern movement towards the standardization of German, see Wells, *German: A linguistic history* 133–42 and 179–201.

Countries under the Dukes of Burgundy, who used French as a language of administration but were tolerant of the Dutch vernacular, and it naturally accelerated with the revolts against the rule of the heir of the Burgundian territories, Philip II of Spain, which took place in the third and fourth quarters of the sixteenth century.[22] The usage of the rich southern province of Brabant was prestigious in the earlier sixteenth century, but after the separation of the seven northern provinces (the Dutch Republic) and the ten southern ones (the Spanish Netherlands), the dialect of Holland, influenced by that of refugees from Brabant, became the standard in the north.[23]

The prestige of these eight standard varieties led to, and was reinforced by, their use in printed books.[24] Of these, the most important were translations of the Bible and liturgical books.[25] The first ten vernacular languages in which Bible translations were printed included all of the eight standardizing languages identified above: in chronological order of first printed vernacular Bible, they were German, Italian, Catalan, Czech, English and Dutch, French, Swedish, Danish and Spanish. The other two languages in this list, Catalan and Czech, actually declined in the sixteenth century. Catalan had been the administrative language of the kingdom of Aragon until its union with Castile in 1479, when Castilian took over its prestige functions; it was subsequently, but briefly, a significant unofficial language at the Papal court in the reign of Alexander VI.[26] Czech had been the literary (though not the administrative) language of an independent kingdom, Bohemia, in the fifteenth century, and a Czech grammar was printed as early as 1533, forty years before the first grammar of German and half a century before the first grammars of English and Dutch.[27] However, it lost prestige after the death in battle of the last king of Bohemia in 1526 and the inheritance of his titles by Ferdinand von Habsburg, the future Emperor Ferdinand I, and suffered further damage at the defeat of the Bohemian Estates by Ferdinand's grandson at the Battle of the White Mountain in 1620.[28]

The emerging standard vernaculars gave many sixteenth-century philologists a sense that there was such a thing as a national language, which could be treated as a shared heritage by the people of a political or cultural

---

[22] See Donaldson, *Dutch: A linguistic history of Holland and Belgium* 21–4. [23] Ibid. 99–104.

[24] The point should not be overstated: cf. Burke, *Languages and communities* 91–4 but also 106–8.

[25] Ibid. 102–6.

[26] See ibid. 84–5 and, for Catalan at the Papal court, Burke, 'Language and identity in early modern Italy' 77.

[27] For the dates of these grammars, see Law, *History of linguistics in Europe from Plato to 1600*, 234–5.

[28] See Burke, *Languages and communities* 83–4.

community. National languages therefore became possible objects of historical study for philologists interested in the post-classical and non-classical histories of Europe. At the same time, the sense of the past and the techniques for retrieving it that had been, and were being, developed by students of classical antiquity were being transferred from their original field. So, for instance, Vives remarked in 1531 on the fact that vernacular languages undergo rapid historical change, illustrating his point with the observation that the archaic Latin of the law-codes which had been preserved in the Twelve Tables was not fully intelligible to Cicero and his contemporaries.[29] This sense of change, which is now seen as characteristic of the Renaissance, sometimes coexisted with medieval myths of heritage, such as the belief of many educated Europeans that their nations had been founded by refugees from the fall of Troy.[30] Although this story might be seen as incompatible with the stories of national origins that were suggested by the historical study of language, it might also be blended with those stories: the Welsh lexicographer John Davies of Mallwyd suggested in 1632 that Brutus and his followers had arrived in the British Isles, found the aboriginal population speaking Welsh, and merged their own language with, or even adopted, that of the natives, and the Flemish antiquary Goropius Becanus had proposed sixty years earlier that the Trojans had simply spoken an ancient language very like Dutch.[31]

More stimulating were versions of the stories of the Noachides (the sons and descendants of Noah) and the Tower of Babel.[32] The latter suggested that all living languages were descended from the mutually unintelligible languages with which God confused the building of the Tower of Babel. However, the preceding chapter of Genesis suggests that the diversity of languages in the world had begun before Babel, as the descendents of Shem, Ham and Japhet developed their own languages. Both stories were elaborated by the Jewish historian Josephus in his *Jewish antiquities*, from which early modern readers learned, for instance, that the Galatians of Josephus' day were originally called Gomerites, being the descendants of Japhet's son Gomer, and that the Scythians were originally called Magogians, being the descendants of another son of Japhet's, Magog (the latter made particularly good sense since the Scythians lived

---

[29] Vives, *De tradendis disciplinis* lib. 3, 274.
[30] See, e.g., Asher, *National myths in Renaissance France* 9–43.
[31] For the sceptical position, see the arguments of George Buchanan summarized in Kendrick, *British antiquity* 84–5; the believers quoted are Davies, *Antiquae linguae britannicae ... et linguae latinae dictionarium duplex* sig. **2v and Goropius Becanus, *Origines antwerpianae* 959.
[32] For the myth of Babel, see Borst, *Turmbau von Babel*, but also Eco, *Search for the perfect language*, esp. 7ff.

to the north of the Mediterranean world and, in Ezekiel, Magog is the name of a northern enemy of Israel).[33] Josephus quotes an earlier historian called Berosus the Chaldaean, whose work survives only in fragments; to make up for this, the fifteenth-century Italian antiquary Annius of Viterbo fabricated a text of Berosus, with his own commentary, which was packed with alluring aetiological myths, and was avidly read by many of his immediate successors.[34] On its authority, early modern authors added figures to the Biblical genealogy, so that, for example, the Biblical Ashkenaz, son of Gomer, was given a son called Tuisco (a name borrowed from the *Germania* of Tacitus) from whom the Teutonic peoples were supposed to be descended.

There were two kinds of response to these aetiological stories, both of which entailed the consideration of linguistic change. The first was to ask whether one extant language, transmitted by one group among the Noachides and unaltered at the confusion of tongues, represented the perfect language spoken by Adam and Eve and God in the Garden of Eden. If so, there was a *prima facie* case for its being Hebrew, the language in which the Bible reports the words spoken in Eden; the insights into the history of Hebrew offered by comparative Semitic studies eventually made this idea unsustainable.[35] It might possibly, however, be one of the vernaculars, and in that case, reconstructing the earliest possible form of the language might give access to the wisdom of Eden. The second response was to ask whether the languages descended from those of the Noachides or of the builders of Babel fell into unrelated families, and if not, by what changes they had diverged from a common ancestor.[36] One story of affinity proposed that many or all of the languages of Europe and western Asia were descended from a protolanguage spoken in Scythia. This was defined as an area to the north and east of the Black Sea, taken to include the mountain on which Noah's Ark had come to rest, and hence conceived of as a cradle of humanity.[37] Because the Scythians were, in antiquity, one of the principal peoples of the northern

---

[33] Josephus, *Jewish antiquities* 1:123, discussed Borst, *Turmbau von Babel* 170–4; cf. Genesis 10:2 and Ezekiel 38:1–2 and 39:1–6.

[34] For pseudo-Berosus, see Asher, *National myths in Renaissance France* 44–87 (discussion) and 191–233 (texts and translations), Borst, *Turmbau von Babel* 975ff., and Grafton, *Defenders of the text* 76–103; for his local reception, see, e.g., Kendrick, *British antiquity* 69ff. (esp. family tree at 70), Tate, 'Mythology in Spanish historiography' 11ff. and Allen, *Legend of Noah* 115n12.

[35] For the position of Hebrew, see Droixhe, *Linguistique et l'appel de l'histoire* 34–50, and Droixhe, 'Crise de l'hébreu langue-mère au XVIIe siècle'.

[36] Droixhe, *Linguistique et l'appel de l'histoire* 60–5.

[37] Ibid. 76f. (German and Persian); 86ff. (Scythian hypothesis); for Scythia as cradle of humanity, see, e.g., J. Magnus, *Historia de omnibus gothorum sueonumque regibus* 18–19.

world, they were readily accepted as ancestors by a number of northern Europeans between the sixteenth and late eighteenth centuries; the Celts comprised the other major northern people known to antiquity, and the Celtic and Scythian peoples were sometimes conflated in antiquity and in the early modern period into one great Celto-Scythian group.[38]

Myths of ancient heritage apart, as early as the fifteenth century, antiquarians such as Biondo in Italy and John Rous and William Worcestre in England were seeking to understand how the processes of historical change had acted in their own countries.[39] During the sixteenth, this kind of work became much more common, especially in Protestant countries in which a Roman cultural heritage had become suspect. Stories emphasizing the long cultural autonomy of given peoples were newly valued; hence the delighted response in Germany and elsewhere to the rediscovery of the *Germania* of Tacitus, and the widespread fascination with the Druids, who represented an ancient and non-Roman tradition of learning.[40] The study of the development of vernacular languages was seen as a particularly important key to the past. 'Every people and nation has its particular chronicle in its language and traditional wisdom,' wrote the German historian Aventinus.[41] Jean Bodin agreed that one of the three best means of determining the origins of peoples was 'in the traces of language'.[42] William Camden put the case more strongly, seeing language as 'the surest proofe of peoples originall', and was still being quoted with approval a century later.[43]

Once this was accepted, then the earliest texts in that language, and therefore the earliest forms of that language, could be seen as the *fontes* of cultural history themselves. Lexicography then became a means by which to understand heritage, and a more powerful one than, for instance, even the study of genealogy, despite the obvious narrative power and cultural importance of the latter. Sixteenth-century English gentlemen could

---

[38] For an ancient conflation, see Plutarch, 'Life of Gaius Marius' 11; for early modern ones, see Kidd, *British identities before nationalism* 188ff. and Dekker, *Origins of Old Germanic studies in the low countries* 212, 223.

[39] For Rous and Worcestre, see Gransden, *Historical writing in England II*, 308–41, and for other fifteenth-century English antiquarians, see the list ibid. 503.

[40] See Owen, *Famous druids*, e.g., 31–2, 43–5.

[41] Aventinus, quoted in Ridé, *Image du Germain* II:263, 'denn ein jedes volck und nation hat ir besondere cronick nach sprach und weis'.

[42] Bodin, *Methodus* 406, 'in lingu[a]e vestigiis'.

[43] Camden, *Britannia* 13, 'certissimum originis gentium argumentum', trans. in Camden, *Britain* 16; Latin text quoted by Hepp, *Parallelismus & convenientia xii lingvarum, ex matrice scytho-celtica* (1697) sig. A2r; cf. Vredius, *Historia comitum Flandriae* (1650) 237, 'Gentium originis nullum certius argumentum est lingua.'

seldom trace their family trees back to the Anglo-Saxon period.[44] They could, however, say that the Anglo-Saxons had lived in the same landscape as them, owned the land that they owned, and even shaped some of the laws that governed them, and also that Old English was the ancestor of their own language. We see just this sense of continuity in the argument of the landowner and Anglo-Saxonist William Lisle that English readers needed Old English to understand 'these so venerable handwritings and monuments of our owne antiquity: without which we can neither know well our lawes, nor our Histories, nor our owne names, nor the names of places and bound-markes of our Country ... I haue found some good vse hereof in my owne grounds.'[45]

The philological opportunities presented by Germanic languages such as Old English were different from those presented by the Romance languages. There could be little serious doubt that the traditions of Romance languages such as Spanish, French and Italian went back to Latin, even if their speakers believed themselves to be descended from peoples such as the Goths, Gauls or Franks, whose vernacular was not Latin. In that case, in a culture that not only privileged Latin but privileged the Latin of the age of Cicero and Virgil above that of later authors, seeing the vernacular as descended from Latin meant either seeing its story as that of a decline from the excellence of Golden Latin or as that of a new *generatio* following the *corruptio* of the ancestral language.[46] Moreover, and more importantly, there was a shortage of texts from the early stages of the Romance languages, since their first speakers used Latin as a written language, regarding the spoken language as in effect a colloquial variety of the Latin that they wrote. For literate speakers of Germanic languages in the same period, however, the vernacular was quite clearly an alternative to Latin, not a colloquial form of the written language. So, they wrote texts in their vernaculars, many of which, including written texts in Old English, Old High German and Old Norse, epigraphic texts in Old Norse, and a single very important manuscript in Gothic, were available for study in the sixteenth and seventeenth centuries.

Excellent historical work was certainly done by early modern students of the Romance languages.[47] As early as the 1550s, Estienne Pasquier was engaged in a programme of research into French cultural history which would include important work on the history of the French

---

[44] See, e.g., Wagner, *English ancestry* 24–6.
[45] In Ælfric, *Saxon treatise concerning the Old and New Testament* (1623) sigs. e4v, f2r; cf. John Foxe in *Gospels of the fower Euangelistes* (1571) sig. ¶2r.
[46] See Tavoni, 'Western Europe' 47–8.   [47] Burke, *Languages and communities* 20–1.

language.[48] In the early seventeenth century, Spanish study of the history of the vernacular led to a classic treatise on the origin of the Spanish language, Bernardo Aldrete's *Del origen y principio de la lengua castellana o romance* (1606), and a classic etymological dictionary, Sebastian de Covarrubias Orozco's *Tesoro de la lengua castellana o española* (1611). Orozco was in fact documenting something more complex than a story of decline or change from Latin: he was interested in the Arabic lexical heritage, and in distinguishing Italianisms in Spanish.[49] It may also be to the point that Aldrete lived in Italy, so that he had daily reason to see the changes from Latin to Spanish as being part of a national story, with which could be contrasted the story of change from Latin to Italian.[50] Italian itself would be treated by Italian scholars such as Vincenzio Borghini and Celso Cittadini, and by the Frenchman Gilles Ménage, whose *Origini della lingua italiana* of 1669 was preceded by his *Origines de la langue françoise* of 1650.

On one occasion when a document offered equally important records of early Germanic and Romance varieties, Germanic and Romance philologists alike made excellent use of it. This was the Latin chronicle that preserves the Strasburg Oaths, records of the precise words spoken by two of the grandsons of Charlemagne to make an alliance in 842. One of them spoke French, and the record of his words is one of the very earliest monuments of Old French; the other spoke a variety of Old High German called Rhenish Franconian. The chronicle was published by the French philologist Pierre Pithou in 1588, and the language of the oaths was examined both by his French peers, such as Pasquier and Claude Fauchet, and by speakers of the Germanic languages such as Bonaventure de Smet, Justus Lipsius, Marquard Freher and Christoph Besold.[51] But generally, the early vernacular monuments available to the countrymen of Lipsius and Freher gave their lexicographical thought a more spacious field to range in than those available to the circle of Pithou.

So, rather than trying to look at the earliest beginnings of Italian, an Italian-speaker with a patriotic interest in the language might do best to consider its canonical glories (in other words the writings of Dante,

---

[48] Kelley, *Foundations of modern historical scholarship* 271–300, esp. 273, 278f.

[49] He was not alone in seeing Spanish as a language rich in borrowings: see Burke, *Languages and communities* 121.

[50] See Malkiel, *Etymology* 5–6 and Droixhe, *Linguistique et l'appel de l'histoire* 100.

[51] P. Pithou, ed., *Annalium et historiae francorum* 353–4. For Pasquier, Fauchet, and de Smet as students of the Strasburg Oaths, see Droixhe, *Linguistique et l'appel de l'histoire* 100–1; for Besold see ibid. 70; for Lipsius, see his *Epistolarum selectarum centuria tertia ad Belgas* 42; for Freher, see his *Foederis Ludovici Germaniae, & Caroli Galliae regum . . . apud argentoratum, anno 842 percussi, formulae* (1611).

Petrarch and Boccaccio), its present virtues and its future perfectibility. Many did just that, and their inquiries led to the making of grammars, and of a great dictionary of Tuscan, the *Vocabolario degli accademici della Crusca*, which was published in 1612. It was followed by a similar dictionary of French, the *Dictionnaire de l'académie française*, on which work began in the second quarter of the century, the first edition being published in 1694. Between 1726 and 1739, a Spanish counterpart, the *Diccionario de la lengua castellana*, appeared. The story of these academy dictionaries, which leads into that of the dictionaries of the eighteenth and nineteenth centuries, is beyond the scope of this study.

The principle that non-Latin origins might be expected to stimulate interest in language history may also hold for Polish, which was the subject of at least one substantial sixteenth-century dictionary and had developed some degree of literary standardization by the end of the sixteenth century, and perhaps for Czech and Russian, but these are likewise beyond the scope of this study.[52] The principle would hold in theory for the Celtic languages, but none of them was in the early modern period the language of a political unit as powerful and stable as those that used English, Dutch, Swedish and Danish, and so (with the partial exception of Welsh) they did not generally come to be studied with the same nationalistic determination until the middle of the eighteenth century, although ideas about ancient Celtic were widely used by philologists interested in the supposed Scythian or Celto-Scythian origins of their own vernaculars. Other languages such as Finnish, Lithuanian, Serbian or Faeroese were likewise not intensively studied in the early modern period.

To conclude, then, there are good reasons why particularly strong traditions of historical lexicography should have arisen in the Germanic-speaking areas of Europe in the sixteenth and seventeenth centuries. The eight emerging standardized vernaculars were naturally the first languages to be documented in printed dictionaries elaborate enough to make interesting statements about heritage. But of those eight, Italian, French and Castilian lent themselves more readily to treatment in synchronic dictionaries which would emphasize good current usage than to treatment in diachronic dictionaries which would emphasize linguistic heritage. The remaining five – German, English, Dutch, Swedish and Danish – will be the subject of the remainder of this chapter, and of the next two chapters as well.

---

[52] For the study of Polish and Czech, see Gandolfo, 'Roman Slavdom'; for that of Russian, see Toscano, 'Orthodox Slavdom'.

OUR TEUTONIC LANGUAGE: THE EARLIEST STUDY OF THE
VERNACULAR HERITAGE IN GERMAN-SPEAKING EUROPE

The early modern lexicography of German was founded on a glossarial tradition that went back as far as the first half of the eighth century; over a thousand manuscripts include Old High German and Old Saxon glosses, and their number is a vivid illustration of the German linguistic self-consciousness of the Middle Ages.[53] Turning to the early modern period itself, the standard bibliographies identify a huge lexicographical output: 858 printed wordlists and dictionaries of German (usually bilingual or multilingual) from the period 1467 to 1600, and 1150 more from the seventeenth century.[54] The great majority of these, however, are not concerned to identify and discuss a German linguistic and cultural heritage, but simply to present equivalences between words in the contemporary German language and words in other languages: 'all these books', as a classic nineteenth-century history of *Germanistik* puts it, 'have at bottom nothing to do with German philology'.[55] So, for instance, the Latin–German *Vocabularius ex quo*, first printed as early as 1467 and reprinted at least fifty-seven times in the next half-century, is of great interest as the first bilingual dictionary to be printed in Europe and as a record of the appetite for Latin in later fifteenth-century Germany, but it was not meant as a contribution to the understanding of German.[56] Conversely, the historical narratives that constructed German heritages in the Middle Ages did not depend on the study of language.[57] However, by the end of the fifteenth century, the two factors that would lead to the development of a German lexicography oriented towards a German heritage had both come into play. These were the rediscovery of the references to ancient Germanic language and culture in classical Latin, and the rediscovery of the vernacular Christian writings of medieval Germany.[58]

Several classical Latin sources refer to a people called Germani, against sections of which the armies of Rome fought intermittently from the first century BC onwards. Some of the tribes of the Germani were conquered (German cities such as Cologne and Bonn were founded by the Romans),

---

[53] Wells, *German: A linguistic history* 33 (see esp. n5), 50f.
[54] Claes, *Bibliographisches Verzeichnis*; Jones, *German lexicography*.
[55] Raumer, *Geschichte der Germanischen Philologie* 84, 'alle diese Bücher haben im Grunde mit der deutschen Philologie nichts zu thun'.
[56] For the editions, see Claes, *Bibliographisches Verzeichnis* 1.
[57] For an overview (with a cut-off point *c.* 1530), see Borchardt, *German antiquity in Renaissance myth*.
[58] Overviews in Sonderegger, 'Ansätze zu einer deutschen Sprachgeschichtsschreibung', esp. 419–27, and Raumer, *Geschichte der Germanischen Philologie*, esp. 4–60 and 83–8.

but many remained independent. The most important accounts of them are those of Caesar and Tacitus. Caesar had campaigned successfully against a Germanic people called the Suebi from 58 BC onwards, and gives some account of them in the *Bellum gallicum*, commenting on their bellicosity and on their personal vigour and hardiness.[59] The *princeps* of this text appeared in Rome in 1469, and it was translated into German as early as 1507.[60] Gratifying as its account of ancient Germanic warriors doubtless was to the sensibilities of early modern Germanic readers, it was not nearly as exciting as the *Germania* of Tacitus. This book depicts its subjects as very attractive noble savages: hardy, racially pure and autochthonous – a point which encouraged German humanists to dismiss the Trojan myth.[61] Their resistance to Rome had obvious attractions for German reformers in the sixteenth century. A manuscript of the *Germania* had been located at the monastery of Hersfeld in Germany in the first quarter of the fifteenth century, and the *princeps* of 1472 was followed by eighteen more editions in the next fifty years. The work was received with great interest, and became the basis for much patriotic writing, in the vernacular (a German translation was made in 1526) and in Latin.[62] One kind of response to it is typified by the strikingly illustrated *Germania antiqua* published in 1616 by Philippus Cluverius of Danzig (Philipp Cluwer, Clüver), whose use of Tacitus as a starting-point for his meticulous reconstruction of the Germanic cultural heritage was summed up in a footnote of Gibbon's referring to his treatment of the religion of the Germani: 'Tacitus has employed a few lines, and Cluverius one hundred and twenty-four pages, on this obscure subject. The former discovers in Germany the gods of Greece and Rome. The latter is positive, that, under the emblems of the sun, the moon, and the fire, his pious ancestors worshipped the Trinity in unity.'[63] Another was that of writers on the history of law, for whom the Germani offered a model of ancient liberties which could be compared to modern usurpations of one sort or another.[64]

---

[59] Caesar, *Bellum gallicum*, esp. 4:1–3.

[60] For early editions, translations, and commentaries, see Brown, 'Caesar' 93f. and 102–26.

[61] For an early account of the Germans as autochthonous written by a reader of Tacitus, Heinrich Bebel, see Borchardt, *German antiquity in Renaissance myth* 110f.; but cf. ibid. 60 for a claim for German autochthony as early as *c.* 1456.

[62] For the reception, see Kelley, '*Tacitus noster*'; Ulery, 'Tacitus', esp. 94 and 96; and the discussion of early editions in Hirstein, *Tacitus' Germania and Beatus Rhenanus*, esp. 23–7.

[63] Gibbon, *History of the decline and fall of the Roman empire* xxxiv–xxxv (separately paginated notes after main text: this is note 62 to book 1 ch. 9); several of the illustrations to Cluverius are reproduced in Schama, *Landscape and memory* 75ff.

[64] Pocock, *Ancient constitution* 20, 56.

The *Germania* does not provide much information about the language of the peoples it describes. Tacitus mentions a couple of stray vocabulary items: *framea* 'spear' and *glaesum* 'amber' (cf. Old High German *glas*, which has the same meaning), but not much is to be learned from them. However, he does also set out the ethnic divisions of the Germani, naming a number of the major groupings. Since there was no reason to doubt that the Germani were the ancestors of the Germanic-speaking peoples of contemporary Europe, these ethnic divisions could be taken to correspond with the differences between the Germanic languages. In fact, the names of the three main ethnic groups identified by Tacitus, Ingvaeones, Istvaeones and Herminones, had by the twentieth century come to be applied, though not uncontroversially, to linguistic groupings.[65] Each of the peoples described by Tacitus is assigned to a particular area, and this encouraged reconstruction of the ethnogeography of ancient Germania and comparison of what had been reconstructed with the map of contemporary German-speaking Europe. So, there was a close natural relationship between the study of the German cultural and linguistic heritages and the topography of ancient and modern Germany.[66] This recalls William Lisle's association of the study of Old English with the understanding of 'names of places and bound-markes of our Country'. It is no coincidence that Conrad Celtis, who gave the first university lectures on Tacitus in German-speaking Europe in Vienna at the end of the fifteenth century, also planned a great chorographical study of Germany and its antiquities, inspired by Biondo's *Italia illustrata* (the project was taken up by his pupil Aventinus) – nor that he was a great traveller, who knew Germany, and much more of Europe, by personal observation.[67]

In 1519, an edition of the *Germania* was published in Basel by Johann Froben; its editor was Beatus Rhenanus, the friend and biographer of Erasmus. Beatus' intellectual heritage goes back to the *officinae* of Aldus and the Estiennes: he had been employed as editor and proof-reader by Henri Estienne the elder, and had learned Greek from the Dominican Johannes Cuno, a former student of the Aldine editor Marcus Musurus (the copy of Crastone's Greek dictionary that Cuno gave to Beatus was mentioned at page 28 above).[68] He adorned his edition with a series of

---

[65] For discussion, see e.g., Wells, *German: A linguistic history* 38 and 438n18.

[66] Cf. Strauss, 'Topographical-historical method in sixteenth-century German scholarship'.

[67] For Celtis, Tacitus and chorography, see Spitz, *Conrad Celtis* 40–1, 66–7; for a fuller account of the *Germania illustrata* project, see Ridé, *Image du Germain* 1:198–229, and for Aventinus and the project, see Strauss, *Historian in an age of crisis* 223ff. and Karrow, *Mapmakers of the sixteenth century* 71–7.

[68] D'Amico, *Theory and practice in Renaissance textual criticism* 45 (work for Henri Estienne the elder), 47 (study with Cuno).

notes on the ancient and modern names of Germanic peoples, beginning
with the question of what exactly Tacitus had meant by the word *Germania*
itself.[69] Was there not, Beatus asked, a problem in Tacitus' statement at
the beginning of his book that Germania was separated from the territory
of the Gauls by the river Rhine, when he also stated that there were
peoples of German origin on both sides of the Rhine? Since Beatus came
from Sélestat (or Schlettstadt) in Alsace, just to the west of the Rhine, the
question was one of personal interest, closely connected with the German
patriotism that he shared with other Alsatian humanists such as the
historian Jacob Wimpfeling: was his homeland part of the ancient
Germania or not?[70]

Beatus' study of classical antiquity and his German patriotism ani-
mated each other in his discussion of this question. They also did so in his
editio princeps of the Roman historian Velleius Paterculus, which not only
added to the corpus of Latin prose but also supplemented the account in
other sources of the massacre of three Roman legions by German forces
in AD 9. Likewise, in his edition of Procopius, who records the wars
of Justinian against the Goths and Vandals, Beatus proclaimed to his
German-speaking dedicatee that 'the triumphs of the Goths and Vandals
and Franks are ours'.[71]

Several of the early students of Germanic antiquities combined their
classical learning with their new sense of a Germanic heritage by comparing the Greek and German languages. One of the first must have been
Franciscus Irenicus, in his description of Germany published in 1518.[72]
The learned bishop Johann von Dalberg, a patron of Celtis, Reuchlin and
others, was said to have compiled a wordlist of several thousand examples,
and he was followed by the historian Johann Aventinus (Turmair), whose
list of about two hundred words is, unlike Dalberg's, extant, and by the
Czech humanist Sigismundus Gelenius (Zikmund Hrubý z Jelení), whose
Lexicon symphonum of 1537 shows the *concordantia* and *consonantia* between
Latin, German, Greek and Czech in a series of multilingual wordlists.[73]

[69] Ulery, 'Tacitus' 140–1.
[70] For the German patriotism of Beatus and other Alsatians in general, see, e.g., Spitz, *Religious
renaissance of the German humanists* 55, and for Wimpfeling on Alsace in particular, see Borchardt,
German antiquity in Renaissance myth 99.
[71] Beatus Rhenanus, prefatory epistle in Procopius, *De rebus gothorum, persarum ac vandalorum*
(1531), rpt Rhenanus, *Briefwechsel* 402, 'Nostri enim sunt Gotthorum, Vandalorum Francorumque
triumphi'; cf. Borchardt, *German antiquity in Renaissance myth* 124.
[72] Borchardt, *German antiquity in Renaissance myth* 146.
[73] Gessner, *Mithridates* fos. 34v–35r (esp. fo. 34v, 'Io. Camerarius a Dalbergio … aliquot millia
dictionum collegit, quae utraq[ue] lingua, Graeca & Teutonica, idem significant'); cf. Droixhe,
Linguistique et l'appel de l'histoire 61, 93–4, and see Přívratská, 'Dictionary as a textbook' 152–3.

Another way to explore this heritage was to seek out and publish texts from the German past, often, like the Hersfeldensis of Tacitus' *Germania*, from monastic libraries. That manuscript had gone to Italy, and Conrad Celtis, seeing the flow of manuscripts from Germany over the Alps, decided that, since he was a German by birth and the first German to be crowned with the poet's laurels by the emperor, 'it was my business, by law of succession and heritage, that I should seek out these codices now lying in obscurity like a skilled hunter, and should present them to my fellow Germans'.[74] Aventinus dramatized the search process further, saying that he had 'suffered heat and cold, sweat and dust, rain and snow, winter and summer; ridden through all of Bavaria; gone through every monastery and religious house; searched diligently through bookrooms and chests; read through and transcribed all kinds of manuscript: old privileges, conveyances, letters, chronicles, summonses, verses' and so on.[75] The emperor Maximilian I was a keen patron of this work, and his encouragement was continued by his grandson Ferdinand, who author-ized the humanist and jurist Johann Sichard to visit ecclesiastical libraries in search of *inedita* in the mid-1520s.[76] The manuscripts hunted so diligently were not always in the vernacular: Sichard's *principes* were of patristic Latin, and the words of Celtis quoted above are from his ded-ication to the *princeps* of the tenth-century Latin poet and dramatist Hrotswitha of Gandersheim, edited from a manuscript that he found at a monastery in Regensburg.[77] Likewise, Conrad Peutinger published Roman inscriptions from his home town of Augsburg and an edition of Jordanes' sixth-century Latin history of the Goths, and supplied the manuscript of the thirteenth-century Latin *Chronicon Urspergense* for its first edition; he also owned a medieval copy of a very important ancient Roman map, the so-called *Tabula Peutingeriana*, which Celtis had obtained (under suspicious circumstances) and bequeathed to him.[78]

[74] Conrad Celtis, dedication of the *princeps* of Hrotswitha (1501) to Frederick the Wise of Saxony in Celtis, *Briefwechsel* 461–7 (item 267) at 463, 'cogitabam ego ad me … successionis et hereditatis iure spectare debere, ut latentes in obscuro codices velut venator egregius elicerem Germanisque meis … offerrem'.

[75] Aventinus, *Bayerische Chronik* 6–7, 'hitz und kelten, schwaiß und staub, regen und schnê winter und sumer erlitten, das ganz Baierland durchritten, alle stift und clöster durchfaren, pueckamer, kästen fleissig durchsuecht, allerlai handschriften, alte freihait, übergab, briefe, chronica, rüef, reimen … durchlesen und abgeschriben'.

[76] For Maximilian and the Germanic heritage, see, e.g., Raumer, *Geschichte der Germanischen Philologie* 10 and Borchardt, 'Medievalism in Renaissance Germany' 82–3; for his encouragement of the search for manuscripts, see D'Amico, *Theory and practice* 298n122 and Ridé, *Image du Germain* 195; for Ferdinand and Sichard, see Carley and Petitmengin, 'Pre-Conquest manuscripts from Malmesbury Abbey' 200n18.

[77] Spitz, *Conrad Celtis* 42.   [78] For Celtis and the *Tabula Peutingeriana*, see ibid. 99.

Peutinger's library did, however, include manuscripts in the vernacular as well as in Latin.[79] The story of the disinterment of such manuscripts by scholars of his generation and their successors – in other words, the rediscovery of medieval and late antique Germanic texts – intertwines with that of the development of lexicography as a means of exploring the Germanic heritage.

The process of rediscovery can be said to have started at the end of the fifteenth century, in the works of the learned Johannes Trithemius (Johannes Zeller of Trittenheim), abbot of Sponheim. Trithemius read his first Greek with Celtis, and studied more Greek, and Hebrew, with Reuchlin.[80] His interests were very wide-ranging, including Biblical scholarship, writing systems, and the occult. He wrote in a patriotic spirit on German history, which led to patronage from Maximilian I, and to embarrassment when the Emperor's interest in primary sources led him to ask for the manuscript of the chronicle of Hunibald, a source that Trithemius cited frequently, and had in fact invented.[81] Celtis saw him as a figure in the revival of ancient heritage, extolling his 'embodiment of that Druidic past of the German nation which even predates the Greeks' in a poem addressed 'ad Johannem Trithemium druidam'.[82] He was also a remarkable book-collector, who built up a library of two thousand volumes at Sponheim.[83] And, as he needed to be in order to choose so many books, he was a pioneer of bibliography, an area of expertise that led to his awareness of linguistic change.

His first major contribution in this area was a catalogue of Christian Latin writers, *De scriptoribus ecclesiasticis*, published in 1494. One of its entries is for a monk of Weissenburg called Otfrid, writings by whom Trithemius lists with the caution that 'the works which he wrote in the language of his fatherland (*patrio sermone*) are not easily to be read and understood in our age, however learned in the Teutonic language the reader may be'.[84] The works listed include one of the major monuments of Old High German, a poetic life of Christ now referred to as the *Evangelienbuch*. The successor to the *De scriptoribus ecclesiasticis*, a catalogue specifically of German writers brought out with encouragement from Wimpfeling in the following year, naturally had an entry for Otfrid

[79] For some of its contents see 'Index codicum manuscriptorum bibliothecae Peutingerianae'.
[80] Brann, *Abbot Trithemius* 16.
[81] Ibid. 96–7.   [82] Ibid. 241–2.   [83] Ibid. 9–13.
[84] Trithemius, *De scriptoribus ecclesiasticis* (1494) in his *Opera historica* 1:257, 'ea quae patrio sermone conscripsit non facile nostra aetate legi, & intelligi possunt, etiam ab homine quantu[m]cunq[ue] Theutonicae linguae perito'.

as well, remarking that his writings 'in the mother tongue (*lingua materna*)' are 'numerous and wonderful' but that his language is scarcely intelligible, 'for it differs more from our own than Tuscan does from Latin'.[85] One of Trithemius' historical writings, a chronicle of the monastery of Hirsau, also refers to Otfrid as writing in 'our Teutonic language', and also makes the point that his variety of the language is very difficult to understand.[86] Once Trithemius had said this much, the path towards the historical lexicography of German had really been pointed out. There were admirable ancient writings in German, but they were difficult to read because of their obsolete language: a dictionary was called for.

More Old High German texts were recovered and excerpted before the first substantial text was printed in full, accompanied with the first printed wordlist of the language. A major figure in this story of the recovery of heritage was Joachim von Watt (Vadianus), who was born in a town with an outstanding monastic library, St Gallen, and became its Bürgermeister. Like Celtis and others, he was interested in Latin texts from medieval Germany, and in 1510 he published a Latin poem of the ninth century, Walafrid Strabo's *De cultura hortorum*, from a St Gallen manuscript. By the late 1530s, he was making extracts from Old High German documents at St Gallen, although the work for which they were made was not printed until the next century.[87] Like Beatus Rhenanus in the edition of the *Germania*, von Watt made a study of early Germanic personal names.[88] This was a topic to which a number of German philologists attended: Beatus returned to it in his *Rerum germanicarum libri tres* of 1531, and a tract that offered 'Certain proper names of the Germans restored to their original etymologies by a student of antiquity' was published in Wittenberg in 1537; it was reprinted later in the century as by Luther.[89]

Von Watt had a number of companions in his study of the linguistic monuments, not least Sebastian Münster. He is better known for his work on the Semitic languages than for his study of Germanic materials: his contributions to lexicography included a *Dictionarium hebraicum* in

---

[85] Trithemius, *Catalogus illustrium virorum Germaniam* (1495) in *Opera historica* 1:127, 'multa & mira[n]da lingua materna ... co[m]posuit ... quae nemo facile nostra aetate legere & intelligere potest, quantumcunq[ue] sermonis nostri peritus: quippe cum sermo ille ... a nostro plus differat, quam Ebruscus [sc. Etruscus] a latino'.

[86] Trithemius, *Chronica insignis monasterii Hirsaugiensis* (before 1503) in *Opera historica* 11:15–16, 'scripsit Otfridus ... quatuor libros Euangeliorum metrice in lingua nostra Theutonica quibusdam regulis formata: vt paucissimi hodie reperiantur, qui eius scripta intelligant'.

[87] Hertenstein, *Joachim von Watt* 19–87, 202–11.

[88] Sonderegger, 'Ansätze' 423.

[89] *Aliquot nomina propria Germanorum ad priscam etymologiam restituta per quendam antiquitatis studiosum*, discussed Sonderegger, 'Ansätze' 422, 425.

1523 with an appendix of Aramaic words; a *Dictionarium chaldaicum* of 1527, treating Aramaic more fully; and a Latin–Greek–Hebrew *Dictionarium trilingue* published at the modest price of six shillings for the use of students in 1530.[90] In the latter part of his life he undertook a massive account of the known world, and particularly of Germany, called *Cosmographia* in its earlier editions (1544–8) and *Cosmographei* in its later ones (1550 onwards).[91] This was, like Celtis' unfinished chorographical project, inspired ultimately by the work of Biondo, although Münster was moved to it by the encouragement of Beatus Rhenanus; and it was, like the near-contemporary work on topography and national heritage undertaken by the Englishman John Leland, founded on extensive travels.[92] It had a strong historical orientation, as can be seen at the beginning of the treatment of Germany, which, after a very brief introductory passage, begins with a section 'On the Goths, Vandals, and Huns' (recalling Beatus' identification of modern Germans with ancient Goths and Vandals), and moves on to a comparative list of ancient and modern names for Germanic peoples.[93] It naturally collected a significant amount of textual and linguistic data: Latin inscriptions, a bilingual Czech–German list of place-names, a short Finnish wordlist, and the Lord's Prayer in several languages, including Latvian, of which Münster's is the earliest surviving printed specimen.[94] The *Cosmographei* also included an incomplete Old High German confession from a manuscript of *circa* AD 1000 which Münster had found in the course of the travels he made for the book, introduced with the words, 'and although little enough was written in the days of our forefathers, here and there in libraries I do still find sundry texts serving the purpose of instruction in the Christian faith, written more than six hundred years ago in the Old Frankish language; and so I wanted to set down this form of general

---

[90] For the making of these dictionaries, see Burmeister, *Sebastian Münster: Versuch eines biographischen Gesamtbildes* 39–43; for editions see Burmeister, *Sebastian Münster: Eine Bibliographie* 31–9 (items 17–26).

[91] For the *Cosmographei* in biographical context, see Burmeister, *Sebastian Münster: Versuch eines biographischen Gesamtbildes* 111 ff., and for its numerous editions, see *Sebastian Münster: Eine Bibliographie* 62–88 (items 66–101); see also Karrow, *Mapmakers of the sixteenth century* 410–34.

[92] For Biondo as inspiration, see Burmeister, *Sebastian Münster: Versuch eines biographischen Gesamtbildes* 157; for the encouragement of Beatus Rhenanus, ibid. 111–12; for Münster's travels, ibid. 124 ff.

[93] Münster, *Cosmographei* Book 3, 'Von dem Teütschen land', which has after the brief introductory 'Beschreibung Teütscher nation' a section 'Von den Gothen Wandeln vnd Hunen' (296) and 'Vergleichung der alten vnd neüwen namen Teütscher nation' (307–8).

[94] Münster, *Cosmographei* 779, 792 (Latin inscriptions); 937 (Czech / German place-names); 984 (Finnish wordlist); 932 (Lord's Prayer in Latvian, identified as the first printed specimen of the language in Rūķ̧-Draviņa, *Standardization process in Latvian* 29).

confession here'.[95] So Münster, an important lexicographer in another field, was also conscious that the Germanic languages called for presentation both in their synchronic aspect – as neighbours of other vernaculars and as diffused over, and forming a heritage with, the landscapes of Germany – and also in their diachronic aspect, which was linked to the present day by the continuing possibility of discovering ancient Germanic manuscripts in German monastic libraries.

Wolfgang Lazius of Vienna, another scholar with Germanistic and cartographical interests (some of Ortelius' maps of central Europe are based on his work) explored that possibility with Münster and by himself, handling a number of Old High German translations and glosses, and producing a study of 'The migrations, settled dwellings, and languages – with reference to the remains of original usage, as well as changes and dialects – of certain peoples' in 1557.[96] In this work, he showed a strong interest in the relationship between modern linguistic diversity and ancient ethnic movement and diversity, commenting, for instance, on differences between Swabian and Austrian German and relating these to the descent of Swabians and Austrians from different ancient peoples. He also presented *editiones principes* of linguistic monuments: the Old High German translation of the 138th psalm, and, more recent but more illustrious, extracts from the *Nibelungenlied*.[97] He generally treated the latter as historical evidence rather than as poetry, referring to the poem as 'History of the Goths, written more than eight hundred years ago in the old Gothic language' and calling its author *poeta ille Gothicus* 'that Gothic poet' at one point, and *poetaster ille Gothicus* 'that Gothic versifier', at another.[98]

---

[95] It first appears in the 1561 edition of the *Cosmographei*: see Steinmeyer, *Kleineren althochdeutschen Sprachdenkmäler* 314–15 (item 43); Münster's introductory note is ibid. 315: 'Und wie wol man gar wenig bey unsern voralten geschriben, so find ich doch hin und wider in Libereyen allerley das zu underricht Christlichs glaubens gedient, in Altfränkischer sprache vor 600 jaren geschriben: desz hab ich wöllen dise offne Beicht hiehär setzen.'

[96] Lazius, *De gentium aliquot migrationibus, sedibus fixis, reliquiis linguarumque initiis et immutationibus ac dialectis libri* XII, discussed Raumer, *Geschichte der Germanischen Philologie* 25–8; for more on Lazius and his patriotic and scholarly undertakings, see Louthan, *Quest for compromise* 27–42 and 67–9, and Karrow, *Mapmakers of the sixteenth century* 334–43; for his visits to libraries with Münster, see Burmeister, *Sebastian Münster: Versuch eines biographischen Gesamtbildes* 128.

[97] For the psalm, see Steinmeyer, *Kleineren althochdeutschen Sprachdenkmäler* 105–9 (item 22), commenting on Lazius' text 108; the extracts from the *Nibelungenlied* are analysed in Menhardt, 'Nibelungenhandschrift c'.

[98] Lazius, 'Catalogus et tituli codicum et autorum antiquorum, qui lucem nondum viderunt' (1551) item 37, 'Historia gothorum, gothica lingua vetusta scripta ante annos 800. et plures' and *Degentium aliquot migrationibus* 682 (references to *poeta* and *poetaster*), all three quoted Menhardt, 'Nibelungenhandschrift c' 158.

So far, the story has been one of extracts. The first substantial ancient German text to be printed in full was Otfrid's *Evangelienbuch*. In 1560, a manuscript was communicated by Henri Estienne's patron Ulrich Fugger to the Augsburg physician and historian Achilles Pirmin Gasser, who was eager to publish it, and transcribed Fugger's manuscript in preparation for an edition.[99] He then had some trouble finding a publisher, and it was not until 1571 that the reformer and historian Matthias Flacius Illyricus (Matija Vlačić), instigator of the Magdeburg *Centuries*, completed and published the edition, dedicated to and supported financially by the Protestant nobleman Adolf Hermann Riedesel. Despite the edition's associations with the Reformed Church, its title-page calls it 'an outstanding monument of the language, poetry and theology of the ancient Germans', putting the linguistic interest of the book before its poetic or theological significance.[100] Likewise, Flacius described the book in his dedication to Riedesel as 'this outstanding treasure of the antiquity of the Teutons, as Beatus Rhenanus [who had discussed and excerpted it] calls this most distinguished monument'.[101]

He went on to give a list of reasons for making the edition. One of these was that, by examining the German language in an earlier state than had previously been possible, the cultural history it encapsulates could be reclaimed. For instance, he observed, we know from Caesar that the priests of the ancient Gauls were called *druidae*, and Aventinus has argued that the Gauls spoke a Germanic language: now, by observing that the Old High German word for 'God' is *trutin* [sc. *truhtîn*], we can confirm Aventinus' point and understand that *druidae* means 'divine men' or 'ministers of God'.[102] He gave another example, the derivation of *marschalc* 'marshal' from *mar-* 'horse' and *schalk* 'servant', an etymology which had in fact already been discussed by French legal historians interested in the non-Roman bases of their national institutions.[103] Then

---

[99] Burmeister, *Achilles Pirmin Gasser* I:174. Fugger's manuscript was the present Heidelberg cod. Pal. germ. 1; for Gasser's transcript, now Vienna, Schottenkloster MS 733, see Burmeister, ibid. II:26–7.

[100] Otfrid, *Euangeliorum liber*, title-page, 'ueterum Germanorum grammaticae, poeseos, theologiae, praeclarum monimentum'.

[101] Flacius Illyricus, first dedicatory epistle in Otfrid, *Euangeliorum liber* sigs. α2r–ß3r at sig. α2r, 'Thesaurum hunc egregium antiquitatis (ut hoc praeclarissimum monumentum beatus Rhenanus uocat) Theutonum'.

[102] Ibid. sigs. α4v–α5r, 'Narrat Iulius Caesar, sacerdotes Gallorum (qui ut Auentinus probat, olim etiam Germanice sunt locuti) uocatos esse Druidas, cuius uocis Etymologiam liquido hic Liber indicat, cum toties Trutin uocat Deum: ut Druidae ide[m] sint, quod diuini uiri, aut Dei ministri.'

[103] Ibid. sig. α5r, 'Nomen Marsalck facile ex hoc libro intelliges significare ministrum equorum aut rei equestris, cum hinc animaduerteres, Salch significare ministru[m] aut famulum, nempe

he went on to present Germanic etymology as a matter of productive development from inflectional bases 'or, as the Hebrew grammarians say, roots', making the argument for the copiousness of German which the etymological structure of the Estiennes' major dictionaries had already made for Latin and Greek.[104] Another reason for making the edition, he continued, is that the study of early German forms helps us to see that the language is, like Latin, Greek and other European languages, derived from Hebrew: so, for instance,

the word *kerle* once meant 'man', as it still does in Sweden and in Saxony [in the High German of Flacius' day, the word had already been restricted to a more colloquial register, with a sense 'fellow, guy'], and if you refer that word to the Hebrew language, it actually has a most excellent etymology, for it means 'one who calls upon and worships God'.[105]

After this rich and interesting epistle, Flacius reprinted Trithemius' note on Otfrid from the *De scriptoribus ecclesiasticis*.[106] Then he presented a contribution of Gasser's to the volume, which he had already acknowledged in the epistle:

Indeed, the most eminent Doctor Achilles Gasser has greatly assisted this edition by his erudition and piety, both in copying out the original manuscript, and also in putting together a lexicon of the old words of this language [or 'discourse': *huius sermonis*], by which he has satisfied a public need and his own ardent concern for his fatherland and the true Church. He has earned and will receive the gratitude of all honest Germans and followers of the Christian faith.[107]

These words herald the first printed wordlist of Old High German; the first, indeed, of any ancient Germanic language variety. Crimean Gothic would follow in 1589, Old Dutch in 1602, Old English in 1605, Old Frisian in 1617, Old Norse in 1636, and Biblical Gothic in 1665, leaving Old Saxon (which as learned a reader as Franciscus Junius regarded as a

ministrum Principis, qui rem equestrem, equitesq[ue] & aulam curet aut regat'; cf. Kelley, *Foundations of modern historical scholarship* 203, 213.

[104] Flacius Illyricus, first dedicatory epistle in Otfrid, *Euangeliorum liber* sig. α5r, 'ex illis primis thematibus, aut (ut Hebraei Grammatici loquuntur) radicib[us]'.

[105] Ibid. sigs. α5v–6r, quotation at α6r, 'Vox Kerle olim significauit homine[m], sicut & adhuc in Suecia & in Saxonia: quam uocem si ad Hebraeam linguam referas, praeclarissimam profecto Etymologiam habet: notat enim inuocatorem & cultorem Dei.'

[106] Otfrid, *Euangeliorum liber* sigs. γ8r–v.

[107] Flacius Illyricus, first dedicatory epistle in ibid. sig. ß1r, 'Plurimu[m] sane hanc editione[m] adiuuit eruditione & pietate clarissimus uir D. D. Achilles Gassarus, tum describendo, tum & Lexicon ueterum huius sermonis uocum conficiendo, quo publicae utilitati & suo ardenti erga patriam & ueram Ecclesiam studio satisfaceret: cui ab omnibus ingenuis Germanis Christiq[ue] fidis cultoribus gratiae debentur & habebuntur.'

mixture of Danish and Old English) for J. A. Schmeller in the nineteenth century.[108]

The wordlist itself, headed 'Erklerung der alten Teutschen worten' but with the running head *Dictionarius*, occupies thirteen pages of an octavo volume, covering about three hundred Old High German words with very brief glosses in modern German.[109] It is, then, a modest production, but it is significant as a milestone. The recovery of the textual and cultural heritage of ancient Germanic peoples had at last reached a stage in its maturity that made it possible to begin taking stock of the lexical heritage. At the end of the wordlist, the reader was told that an Old High German confession (not, incidentally, the one printed by Münster) with inter-linear glosses into modern German followed, and was encouraged to use the wordlist to understand it, and then to move on to studying the text of Otfrid with the help of the wordlist.[110] The copy of the edition now in the Kongelige Bibliotek at Copenhagen shows just this process being undertaken: an early owner (apparently a speaker of Dutch) has added a dozen glosses to the wordlist, has supplied a missing interlinear gloss in the confession, and has made glosses in the text of Otfrid.[111]

Lazius' description of the maker and language of the *Nibelungenlied* as *Gothicus* is a reminder that that word was used by the mid-sixteenth century to mean 'ancient Germanic' as well as 'of the Goths'. That poem is in the language variety now called Middle High German, and its principal characters are Burgundians. But the people whom we know as Goths were objects of interest in their own right in early modern Europe. From the fifteenth century onwards, Gothic ancestry had been a source of pride to certain European peoples. For instance, both Swedish and Spanish dele-gates to the Council of Basel in 1434 claimed precedence as representatives of monarchs of Gothic, and therefore ancient, descent: early medieval

---

[108] For Junius on Old Saxon, see his remarks on his transcript of the *Heliand*, now Bodleian MS Junius 103, quoted Dekker, 'Franciscus Junius' 289.

[109] Otfrid, *Euangeliorum liber* sigs. δ1r–7r.

[110] Otfrid, *Euangeliorum liber* sig. δ7r, 'Hie haben wir dir / gütiger Leser / hernacher gesetzt: Erstlich ein form der Alten Teutschen Beicht / darnach zwo Vorred dess Meisters dises Buchs: vnd die selbige[n] / souil müglich gewesen / auff jetzige breüchlichste Teutsche spraach vertollmetschet / vnd gegen einander gesetzt / damit das du das vorgesetzt *Dictionarium*, vnd auch das gantz Buch / souil füglicher gebrauchen / vn[d] geringer verson möchtest. *Vale, & fruere.*' The confession is Steinmeyer, *Kleineren althochdeutschen Sprachdenkmäler* 327–9 (item 48).

[111] The copy is now Copenhagen: Kongelige Biblioteket 175:2, 88; for the annotator as Dutch-speaker, see the gloss of 'zuune ni gisüonta' at sig. δ8r as 'bewieent niet myn sondes'. It was in Denmark by 1751, since a flyleaf is endorsed 'Exemplar hoc in auctione *Fossii* pretio 4–4–8 venditum e[st] (Bibl. Foss. [i.e., *Bibliotheca Fossiana*, the auction catalogue of the library of Niels Foss, sold in 1751, from which the Kongelige Bibliotek bought many volumes] pag. 485. no. 1365.)', but its earlier history is not evident.

Spain had had Visigothic monarchs, and Scandinavia had some claim to be the Gothic homeland.[112] Sixteenth-century German scholars were interested in the Goths as heroic ancestors of their own.[113] They knew of them from authors who wrote in Latin and Greek, such as Procopius, Jordanes and St Isidore of Seville. They knew in particular that the Goths had had their own language, and inspection of personal names such as Ermanaric (cf. Hermann) and Theodoric (cf. Dietrich) must have suggested that this language was related to German, though other theories were floated.[114] They knew from Isidore that the language of the Goths had been written down, though they may reasonably have doubted that any manuscripts were extant. By the second quarter of the sixteenth century, the story that Goths who spoke a language like German were still living on the coast of the Black Sea had been recorded by Willibald Pirkheimer and others, but these Goths did not appear to write their language.[115]

The surprising thing is that there actually *was* – and still is – an extant manuscript of a long text in Gothic: a Gospel-book written in the sixth century, which preserves part of the translation of the Bible into Gothic made by Ulfilas in the fourth century. It is written in the distinctive Gothic alphabet, on purple vellum, in silver letters, which give it its familiar name, the Codex Argenteus. It was already incomplete by the sixteenth century, and had at one time come apart and been rebound with some of the pages out of order, but it was still an impressive object – impressive enough, indeed, for someone to have taken the trouble to rebind it even though he could not read it, and therefore could not put the leaves in the right sequence.[116] It came to the attention of two natives of Bruges, Georg Cassander and Cornelius Wouters, both of whom resided in Cologne and made a number of visits to libraries in the region, when they were in the library of the Benedictine abbey of Werden, on the river Ruhr about forty miles from Cologne. A letter of 1554 refers to a Gothic alphabet and the Lord's Prayer in Gothic which were by then in their possession; these were unquestionably transcribed by them from the Codex Argenteus.[117] Gothic

---

[112] Klindt-Jensen, *History of Scandinavian archaeology* 11.

[113] Brough, *Goths and the concept of Gothic* 22ff.

[114] See Borchardt, *German antiquity in Renaissance myth* 30 (Gothic as Slavonic), 158 (Gothic as Old Prussian).

[115] Brough, *Goths and the concept of Gothic* 67f.; Stearns, *Crimean Gothic* 6–9.

[116] The out-of-sequence leaves are reported in Jan Gruter, *Inscriptiones antiquae* (1602) 146, reproduced Van de Velde, *Studie van het Gotisch in de Nederlanden*, plate facing p. 40: 'diruptum, & nullo ordine ignorantia compactoris colligatum'.

[117] The classic summary and discussion of the sparse documentation of the rediscovery of the Codex Argenteus is Schulte, 'Gothica minora: Erster Artikel', editing the letter that provides the first evidence, from Caspar von Niedbruck to Cassander and Wouters, 6 June 1554, at 57–8.

was, after this discovery, the only Germanic language that could be studied in a substantial text more than a thousand years old. It was clearly a significant part of the Germanic linguistic heritage, and the manuscript that preserved it was a significant heritage object. The Gothic language and the Codex Argenteus will reappear at a number of points in the following narrative.

Between the first renewal of study of the Germanic heritage in the late fifteenth century and the rediscovery of the Codex Argenteus in the 1550s, no major historical dictionary of German appeared. That does not mean that the period was lexicographically barren: far from it. One scholar after another was contributing to a picture of the German language. It had, their work was showing, a history. There were ancient texts in Germanic language varieties that needed scholarly work to decode them. These texts were part of a German heritage that went back to the Germanic-speaking peoples of antiquity. The sense that old texts and old language varieties really did constitute a heritage, which developed in the first half of the sixteenth century, was a necessary precondition for the major lexicographical work in the second half of the century and beyond. This work, to which we now proceed, was undertaken by German-speaking scholars and also by their peers in the Low Countries, England and Scandinavia.

PIETY AND THE GLORIFICATION OF THE LANGUAGE OF
THE FATHERLAND: THE STUDY OF THE GERMANIC
VERNACULARS BY CONRAD GESSNER AND GEORG HENISCH

Conrad Gessner (Gesnerus, and hence often Gesner) was an extraordinary figure even in the age of polymaths like Münster. He was born in Zürich in 1516, and studied there under Erasmus' friend Johann Jacob Ammann, one of his own closest friends there being the future lexicographer Johannes Frisius (Hans Fries).[118] After continuing his studies in Strasburg, Bourges and Paris, reading widely and impressing his teachers considerably, he moved to Basel, where his first book, a revised edition of the Greek–Latin dictionary of Guarino da Favera (itself an early competitor of Crastone's, much of which it incorporates), appeared in 1537.[119] He was to complain that the printer had not even used most of the revisions on which he had worked – scholarly lexicographers generally have to resign

---

[118] Wellisch, *Conrad Gessner* 2–3.

[119] Ibid. 5–6 and 31–4, items A1.1–14. Guarino of Favera (Varinus, Phavorinus, Camers, Varino Favarino Camerte) had edited the *Thesaurus cornucopiae* for Aldus in 1497; and his dictionary was first printed in 1523.

themselves to the fact that only a small proportion of their researches actually gets published in dictionary form – and that his name did not appear on the published dictionary. It was, though, a great achievement to have been the editor, albeit anonymous and underappreciated, of a 1900-column folio dictionary at the age of twenty-one.

By his thirtieth birthday, Gessner had produced two alphabetical dictionaries of the names of plants, the latter being quadrilingual (Latin–Greek–German–French); an important and widely circulated edition and translation into Latin of the early Byzantine anthology of Joannes Stobaeus, which preserves extracts from a number of lost texts; a new edition of Calepino's dictionary with a substantial onomasticon of his own making; and the first volume of an enormous universal annotated bibliography, covering the works of about three thousand Latin, Greek and Hebrew authors.[120] In the next two decades, his most famous work was a five-volume zoological encyclopedia, best known to English readers through its shortened adaptation by Edward Topsell.[121] The lesser-known works of Gessner's which it overshadows include three more volumes of the bibliography; an edition of the works of Aelian in 756 folio pages; the *princeps* of Marcus Aurelius; an edition of Galen in 3703 folio pages; and an unfinished botanical encyclopedia.[122] His translation into Latin of the early Christian author Athenagoras was published by Henri Estienne, who also enlisted his help with his editions of Xenophon and Erotian in the early 1560s, and referred to Gessner as 'that Atlas of literary labour'.[123] Among his unfinished projects when he died was a historically oriented dictionary of Germanic proper names.[124] This extraordinary body of achievement is unified by lexicography and lexicology. On the one hand, the alphabetical listing of words was a way in that Gessner regularly imposed order on great bodies of knowledge. On the other, in his dealings with the natural world, his tendency was regularly towards the

---

[120] Wellisch, *Conrad Gessner* 6–9 and 34–50, esp. items A3 (*Historia plantarum*, 1541), A8 (*Catalogus plantarum*, 1542), A11 (*Ioannis Stobaei sententiae*, 1543), A14 (*Onomasticon*, 1544, the edition of Calepino being mentioned only in passing), A16 (*Bibliotheca universalis*, 1545).

[121] Ibid. 59–69, items A23–A28; for Topsell's version see 61, item A23/24.7.

[122] Ibid. 50ff., items A16.1.b–d (remaining volumes of the *Bibliotheca*, 1548–55), A42 (Aelian, *Opera*, 1556), A46 (Marcus Aurelius, *De seipso*, 1559), A53 (Galen, *Opera*, 1561–2), B11–12 (botanical works).

[123] For the translation of Athenagoras, see ibid. 84–5, item A44 (Athenagoras, *Apologia*, 1557); for the work on Xenophon, see Gessner, letter of 2 January 1563 to Achilles Pirmin Gasser in Burmeister, *Achilles Pirmin Gasser* III:212; for the work on Erotian, see Gessner, letter of April 1563 to Achilles Pirmin Gasser, ibid. III:228, and Wellisch, *Conrad Gessner* 95, item A60 (Estienne, *Dictionarium medicum*, 1564); for Estienne's praise, see ibid. 88; for some letters between Estienne and Gessner, see ibid. 116, item C7.

[124] See Peters, 'Einleitung' 17 and 73n55.

lexicographical, because he was very interested in the place of natural entities and phenomena in human systems of signification. In the zoological work, for instance, each animal is named in different languages, and the entries for the animals are rich in etymological discussions of their names and accounts of their places in literature and in cultural history: the work clearly has points in common with the *Adagia* of Erasmus, on which it draws.[125]

Gessner's comparison of languages and cultures is the focus of his *Mithridates*, described on its title-page as 'observations on the differences between the languages used throughout the world, both by the ancients and by different nations today', which he published in 1555 with a dedication to John Bale, at the time a Protestant exile from the British Isles. Its association with Reformed Christianity goes further than that, for the text at the heart of the book is, recalling some of Sebastian Münster's examples, the Lord's Prayer in the vernacular. Gessner printed it in twenty-two language varieties: Ethiopic, English, Armenian, Welsh, Syriac, French, German, Dutch (in the dialects of Brabant and Gelderland), Icelandic, Old High German, Greek, Hebrew, Spanish, Hungarian, Czech, Croatian, Polish, Italian, Romansh and two dialects of Sardic. This range, and the insistence on the Lord's Prayer as both a common inheritance and a text to be read in individual vernaculars, recalls the multilingual Protestant irenicism of some of the circles in which Henri Estienne moved. Gessner's spirit, like theirs, was not one of unqualified benevolent interest in all nations. He took the Lord's Prayer in Croatian from one of the works of Bartholomaeus Georgievitz (Bartholomaeus Georgii, Bartol Ourevic, Georgijevic, etc.) on the Turkish oppression of Christians in south-east Europe, a reminder that the language varieties he studied included that of a hostile nation.[126] Likewise, he observed in the dedication that 'a number of peoples have now, within my own memory, begun to express holy prayers, psalms and other things relating to the profession and cultivation of true piety in their own diverse vernacular tongues, both in private and in public worship, against the will of Antichrist'.[127] Bale would have endorsed Gessner's identification of Antichrist.

---

[125] See Ashworth, 'Natural history and the emblematic world view', esp. 310 for Gessner's debt to Erasmus.

[126] Gessner, *Mithridates* fo. 63r, citing 'Bartolomaeus Georgeuitus in libello suo de afflictione Christianorum sub Turcas, Latine ante paucos annos in Germania impresso Vuormaciae', i.e., Georgievitz, *De afflictione tam captivorum quam etiam sub Turcae tributo viventium christianorum.*

[127] Ibid. sig. A2v, 'orationes … sacras & psalmos, & quaecunq[ue] ad uerae pietatis professionem cultumq[ue] pertinent, diuersae nationes hodie (nostra memoria) priuatim publicequ[ue] in templis, inuito Antichristo, sua quaeq[ue] uernacula lingua proferre incoeperint'.

Gessner's project in the *Mithridates* was not, then, simply to amass data. He was making cultural and confessional value-judgements. Indeed, the thoughts on the relationships between languages which give the *Mithridates* its pioneering quality and make it a foundation for later lexicography are themselves shaped by such judgements. Hebrew, Greek and Latin are the three pre-eminent languages for Gessner, with Hebrew in first place: 'it is the first and most ancient of all languages, and alone appears to be pure and unmixed.'[128] The bulk of *Mithridates* deals with vernacular languages, arranged alphabetically by speakers from the Abasini, i.e., Abyssinians, speakers of Ethiopic, to the Zagovani (sc. Zagorani?), speakers of 'Illyrian', i.e., a South Slavic language variety. These are followed by notes on some exotic languages and a more detailed treatment of some languages that Gessner regards as invented, especially Utopian, with specimens given from More's *Utopia*, and 'the made-up language of gypsies and beggars', namely Rotwelsch, a secret thieves' language with Yiddish and Romani elements. The main text of the book concludes with a ten-page vocabulary of Rotwelsch from the *Liber vagatorum*, a late fifteenth-century book about vagabonds.[129] This vocabulary is the longest of the wordlists in *Mithridates*, although there are a number of others (e.g., of the *lingua indica* and the *lingua chaldaica*, and of Armenian and Hebrew), and Gessner made other, unpublished lexical collections such as one of Dutch words.[130]

All languages, in Gessner's scheme, have some signs of their Hebrew ancestry, and German also has an important affinity with Greek: 'there are innumerable words which have the same sense for us and for the Greeks' and 'there are, indeed, some who have seen a number of traces of a Hebrew origin in our language',[131] such as Aventinus, Dalberg, Gelenius, and the Lutheran humanist Andreas Althamer, whose commentary on the *Germania* succeeded that of Beatus Rhenanus. The humanist historiography of the Germanic heritage and the comparative lexicography of German and other languages, whose affinity is suggested

[128] Ibid. fo. 2v, 'Ex linguis Hebraica, ut prima & antiquissima omnium est, ita sola uidetur pura et syncera'.

[129] Invented languages ibid. fos. 71v onwards, with Utopian at 72v–73r and Rotwelsch vocabulary 73r–77v, the latter identified as from the *Liber vagatorum* by Peters, 'Einleitung' 33. For comparable vocabularies see Burke, *Languages and communities* 30–1.

[130] Gessner, *Mithridates* fos. 7v, 101r–v; Gessner refers to a 'libellus, in quo scripsi Belgica uocabula' in a note cited by Peters, 'Einleitung' 71n29.

[131] Gessner, *Mithridates* fos. 34v and 35r, 'Infinita sunt uocabula quae nobis & Graecis idem ualent ... Sunt qui Hebraicae etiam originis plurima in lingua nostra obseruarunt'; see the discussion in Peters, 'Einleitung' 37.

by the harmonization of German and Greek, come together in Gessner's comparative discussion of the Germanic languages. This was fuller and more important than any that had preceded it: the chapter 'De lingua Germanica' takes up a fifth of *Mithridates*.[132] It includes a discussion of dialect variation within German and the competing claims of the local varieties of different cities – Leipzig, Augsburg and Basel – to be regarded as the best German, and extends backwards in time to Old High German.[133] As might be expected from this attention to historical material, Gessner also took an interest in Gothic, reporting the existence of the Germanic-speaking Gothic communities on the Black Sea.[134] In 1563 he received specimens of Gothic material, deriving from the Codex Argenteus, from two correspondents, and expressed the hope that he might add them to a new edition.[135]

The making of the first adequate modern dictionary of German was a project in which Gessner had a part as well, and he brought both his comparative interests and his interests in early texts to it. This dictionary was *Die Teütsch Spraach* of Josua Maaler (Pictorius), published in 1561. As we have seen, there were German dictionaries of a kind before *Die Teütsch Spraach*. Although the medieval tradition represented by the *Vocabularius ex quo* had ended by the 1560s, it had its successors. The successful Latin–German dictionary of the Strasburg schoolmaster Petrus Dasypodius (Peter Hasenfuss), who had been one of Gessner's teachers, made humanistic lexicography that drew on the work of Calepino, Robert Estienne and others widely available in German-speaking schoolrooms from 1535 onwards; it was supplemented in 1536 with a German–Latin section.[136] It was followed by the collaborative work of the Zürich scholars Petrus Cholinus (Colinus, Choeli) and Johannes Frisius, whose German version of Robert Estienne's *Dictionarium latinogallicum*, the *Dictionarium latino–germanicum*, was published in 1541, followed after seven years by a *Dictionariolum puerorum tribus linguis* adapted by Frisius from Estienne's *Dictionariolum puerorum latinogallicum* and after another eight by Frisius' *Novum dictionariolum puerorum latinogermanicum et*

[132] See Metcalf, 'Konrad Gesner's views on the Germanic languages' and Peters, 'Einleitung' 33–43.
[133] Peters, 'Einleitung' 50; Hertenstein, *Joachim von Watt* 51.
[134] Gessner, *Mithridates* fos. 27v, 43r–v, discussed Brough, *Goths and the concept of Gothic* 68ff.
[135] See Gessner's letters of 22 April and 11 August 1563 to Gassar in Burmeister, *Achilles Pirmin Gassar* III:230–2 at 231 and III:240–2 at 240.
[136] For the sources of Dasypodius' dictionary, see de Smet, 'Einführung' [viii]–[ix]. Claes, *Bibliographisches Verzeichnis* 90 (item 341) notes 29 sixteenth-century editions. Gessner acknowledges him as a former teacher in his 'Praefatio' in Maaler, *Teütsch Spraach* sigs. *3r–*7v at *7r, 'Petrus Dasypodius ... praeceptor olim meus'.

germanicolatinum, which ran to thirty-seven further editions from 1568 to 1750.[137] Frisius' work was itself used by lexicographers in England (notably Thomas Cooper) and the Low Countries.[138] Cholinus and Frisius were concerned to present a widely acceptable variety of High German in their dictionary, just as Luther had been in his Bible translation, and wrote that their aim was to use 'the language which is most widely received in upper Germany [as opposed to the Netherlands and the northern regions of Germany], and is used most generally at once by the Swiss and the Germans, so that when this book comes into general use, we shall not appear to have been biassed towards the dialect of any particular community'.[139] And they were concerned also to promote the merits of German, 'the riches in which it is more blessed than all other languages', telling their reader that it excelled both Greek and, *a fortiori*, Latin.[140]

Gessner contributed to the *Dictionarium latinogermanicum*, and it was published by his preferred publisher, Christoph Froschauer of Zürich. Maaler's *Die Teütsch Spraach* came from the same publisher – 'as a conclusion and a crown to the Zürich family of dictionaries from Froschauer's *officina*', as Gilbert de Smet has put it – with a dedication to Gessner and Frisius which identifies them repeatedly as Maaler's 'praeceptores' and a foreword by Gessner himself.[141] *Die Teütsch Spraach* differs from its predecessors because it is a German–Latin dictionary, made 'in patriae linguae laudem', designed to show off the riches of the German language. It runs to 536 pages in double columns, with about 11,000 entries, 13,000 subentries, and 30,000 proverbs and other examples.[142] The last of these features was a result of Robert Estienne's interest in phraseology, for Maaler's dictionary was substantially indebted – as was frankly acknowledged in Gessner's foreword – to the work of Frisius and thence of Estienne. As a Latin dictionary, then, it was unoriginal, but

---

[137] There were two editions of the *Dictionarium latinogermanicum* in 1541, one in octavo and one in folio, followed by enlarged editions in 1556, 1568 and 1574 (Claes, *Bibliographisches Verzeichnis* 102, items 386–7); for Frisius' *Dictionariolum puerorum* (1548), see ibid. 110, item 416, and for his *Novum dictionariolum* (1556), see ibid. 120–1, item 460, and Jones, *German lexicography* 362–73, items 628–48 and note to item 648.

[138] For Cooper and Frisius, see Starnes, *Robert Estienne's influence on lexicography* 104–5.

[139] Cholinus and Frisius, *Dictionarium latinogermanicum*, quoted de Smet, 'Einführung' in Maaler, *Teütsch Spraach* (1971) v*–xxv* at ix*, 'lingua in Germania superiori usu maxime recepta, et Helvetijs simul ac Germanis communissima: ita ut neutrius gentis idiomati, quando communis liber futurus esset, nimium addicti videremur'.

[140] Ibid. ix*, 'diuitias ... quibus est omnibus alijs linguis felicior'.

[141] Maaler, *Teütsch Spraach* sig. *2r; de Smet, 'Einführung' in Maaler, *Teütsch Spraach* (1971) x*, 'als Abschluß und Krönung der Züricher Wörterbuchfamilie aus Froschauers Officina'.

[142] Schneider, *Einfluß von Justus Georg Schottelius* 89.

it took the treatment of German further than even Frisius and Cholinus had done. Jacob Grimm recognized it, in the preface to the *Deutsches Wörterbuch*, as 'the first real German dictionary', a text that left behind the jejuneness, the 'dryness', of the medieval dictionaries and of Dasypodius.[143]

Gessner's foreword to *Die Teütsch Spraach* is presented as a 'preface on the subject of this German–Latin dictionary, and on (i) the German language in general, with its dialects and geographical distribution; (ii) what it has in common with the Gothic and Gaulish languages; (iii) the ancient and modern authors who have written in the language; (iv) the means of enriching it'.[144] Here, all the work on the German language and its monuments conducted over the last fifty years comes together in Gessner's unified vision of the German dictionary as concerned both with the German language as a living and various entity and with the origins, affinities and continued use of that language. The foreword opens with a report of a conversation:

> When I and my excellent friend Joannes Frisius, a man famous for his intellect and his learning, were engaged in a friendly conversation – in the company, as it chanced, of Josua Maaler, our fellow-citizen, an outstanding man and a learned one, the pious and faithful minister of the Word of God at Elgg, a town in the territory of Zürich – one of the subjects on which we touched was the current vernacular languages of Europe. We observed that several of the peoples who are our neighbours, including the French, Italians and English, were beautifying and amplifying their languages more and more day by day, and that they had copious dictionaries in book form, in which individual words with their usages and meanings, and locutions as well, were explained in due order, and we regretted that our Germany lacked anyone who would furnish the same thing to our language.[145]

What followed can for the most part be guessed from that opening. After Gessner and Frisius had reflected a little further on the irony that German, which lacked such a dictionary, should nevertheless be a language

---

[143] Grimm, 'Vorwort' xxi, 'das erste wahrhafte deutsche wörterbuch ... die trockenheit des teutonista und DASYPODIUS verlassend'.

[144] Gessner, 'Praefatio' in Maaler, *Teütsch Spraach* sig. *3r, 'praefatio super hoc dictionario Germanicolatino: & lingua Germanica in uniuersum, eiusque dialectis, & quam late pateat: quid ei cum Gothica & Gallica commune: deque antiquis ac recentibus in ea scriptis, & illustrandae eius ratione'.

[145] Ibid. sig. *3r, 'Clarus ingenio & eruditione uir Ioan. Frisius, summus amicus meus, & ego, cum in familiari colloquio, (cui tum forte etiam Iosua Pictorius ciuis noster inter erat, egregius ac bene doctus uir, & diuini Verbi minister Elgouij, quod agri Tiguri oppidum est, pius ac fidelis,) inter alia de linguis hodie per Europam uulgaribus mentio incidisset: & animaduerteremus plerasq[ue] uicinas nobis gentes, ut Gallos, Italos, Anglos, aliosq[ue] suas linguas ornare ac locupletare indies magis magisq[ue] & copiosos habere dictionarios codices, in quibus ordine dictiones singulae, earumq[ue] uires & significationes, nec non locutiones explicantur: doluimus deesse Germaniae nostrae, qui idem in nostra praestarent lingua.'

of such excellence, second to none but Hebrew in its antiquity and copiousness, and also purer than languages such as English and the Romance vernaculars, Maaler offered to undertake the labour himself, for the sake 'not only of his *patria* [i.e., Zürich] but of the whole of Germany, and of all students either of Latin or of German'.[146] This, Gessner and Frisius reflected, was an undertaking by no means alien from Maaler's ministerial duties, in which he was called upon to use language with particular excellence: the dictionary would be 'an instrument both of piety and of the glorification of the language of the fatherland (*lingua patria*)'.[147]

After introducing the dictionary itself, Gessner's preface turned in more detail to the German language, referring back to its treatment in *Mithridates*, but emphasizing the point that German is the first and most ancient language. This, Gessner added, could be seen from the examination of several kinds of evidence, notably proper names and place-names – an argument placing Gessner in a tradition that goes back to Beatus Rhenanus.[148] Gessner adduced toponymic evidence for his claim that a Germanic language had formerly been spoken in Muscovy: hence the word *Muscovia* itself was, when one considered the country's water-logged terrain, explicable as German *Mossgöw* 'swampy region' (Middle High German *mos* could mean 'swamp' though modern German *Moos* can only mean 'moss'; *göw* is equivalent to modern German *Gau* 'region'). He added to this the point that Gothic was still spoken in the Crimea, although this area was now close to the borders of Muscovy, and went on to discuss the Goths and Gothic at some length, concluding firmly that 'the Goths are Germans, and they have a language in common with the other Germans'.[149] Turning from breadth of distribution to antiquity, he mentioned that the most ancient writings in German that were known to Trithemius were those of Otfrid, and quoted four lines from Otfrid's *Evangelienbuch*, explaining that they had been communicated to him by Achilles Pirmin Gasser, from whom an edition could be expected (Gasser had asked him for help finding a publisher).[150] On that note, Gessner returned to the topic of dictionaries, remarking that, among the other means by which a man may adorn his fatherland,

---

[146] Ibid. sig. *3r, 'non patriae modo, sed uniuersae Germaniae, & studiosis utriusque linguae (Latinae inquam & Germanicae)'.

[147] Ibid. sig. *3r, 'simulq[ue] pietati ... instrumento ac patriae linguae illustrandae'.

[148] Ibid. sig. *3v.

[149] Ibid. sigs. *4r–5v; quotation at sig. *5v, 'Gothos Germanos esse, & communi caeteris Germanis lingua uti'.

[150] Ibid. sig. *6v; for Gasser's enlistment of Gessner's help in finding a publisher, see Burmeister, *Achilles Pirmin Gasser* 1:174f. and the correspondence between Gessner and Gasser ibid. 111:214ff.

the cultivation of the mother tongue has its place – and to that end, dictionaries, as comprehensive as possible, and giving the distinctive meanings of all the words in the language, are not only useful but necessary.[151] A discussion of the editing of ancient texts, then, led Gessner straight to the topic of dictionary-making as a patriotic project, the link between the two being the concept of linguistic heritage.

By this stage in his career, Gessner was seeing the German heritage and its lexicographical record in strikingly inclusive terms. Although one of the spurs to his concluding outline of a *Wunschlexikon* of German was the recent appearance of 'an extremely copious Latin–English dictionary', by which he must have meant the 1559 edition of Thomas Cooper's revision of the *Bibliotheca Eliotae*, a dictionary whose ancestry went back to Calepino and to Robert Estienne's *Dictionarium latino–gallicum*, Gessner's ambitions ended up going beyond the derivative tradition to which the *Bibliotheca Eliotae* belonged. 'For my part', he wrote,

I should like to put the whole German language (or as much of it as possible) into a dictionary: the words and phrases for all arts, all things, all academic disciplines, all actions ... And if any words were not common but ... peculiar to a certain dialect, that also would be set down ... And once the dictionary was finished, I think another book should also be brought into being, in which more or less the same set of words and phrases would be rearranged in a different order, following the common places of the arts and sciences and of other things and actions.[152]

This extraordinary plan for a comprehensive union dictionary of every variety of German followed by a subject-ordered thesaurus of similar scope – a dictionary which would present the entirety of the German linguistic and cultural heritage, and would arrange it with a view both to its linguistic and to its cultural significance – was never realized. It looks forward, in its emphasis on language as a record and embodiment of culture, to much of the best German-language lexicography of the nineteenth and twentieth centuries. The turn away from dryness that

---

[151] Gessner, 'Praefatio' in Maaler, *Teütsch Spraach* sig. *6v, 'inter alia quibus quisq[ue] patriam suam ornat, linguae etiam maternam excolendae ... rationem habeat. Ad quod cum alij libri, tum quos Lexiconum seu Dictionariorum nomine appellamus, utpote uniuersales, & qui omnes uocabulorum differentias contineant, utilissimi, immo necessarij sunt.'

[152] Ibid. sig. *7r, 'Optarim equidem uniuersam linguam Germanicam, quoad eius fieri posset, & omnium artium, rerum, studiorum actionumque uocabula & phrases, Dictionario inseri ... Quod si quae dictiones non essent communes, sed glossae, hoc est, dialecto alicui peculiares, id quoque exprimendum fuerit ... Sic absoluto Dictionario, alium quoque librum instituendum censeo, in quo eadem fere omnia uocabula ac phrases alio ordine recenseantur, secundum locos communes artium, scientiarum, aliarumque rerum et actionum.'

Grimm saw in Maaler's dictionary was this belief that language is inseparable from its cultural context, and the same belief, expressed in the same metaphor, has been seen in the work of the founder of the twentieth-century *Preussisches Wörterbuch*:

that the dictionary should not be a lifeless glossary, a dessicated series of words ... [but should] represent the speech of the people in all its richness. Every word should be set forth in all its manifold phraseological potential and shades of meaning, in sayings and proverbs, in connection with popular beliefs and customs. In every word, the thought and experience of the people should be reflected, their humour, their outlook on life.[153]

Gessner's thoughts on lexicography as expressed in his remarkable preface were ahead of their time. Only one early modern German dictionary came some distance to realizing them before the course of German lexicography was changed by the work of Schottelius and his successors, which falls outside the scope of this study. This was the unfinished *Teütsche Sprach vnd Weißheit / Thesaurus linguae et sapientiae germanicae*, the 'Treasury of German language and wisdom' published in 1616 by Georg Henisch.[154] It has been said that 'Georg Henisch sought to complete the work begun half a century earlier by Maaler, but on a much greater scale.'[155]

Henisch was born in a town founded by German settlers in Hungary (now Bardejov, Slovakia). So, like the Swiss and Alsatian philologists who contributed to the study of German in the sixteenth century, or like Cluverius, his younger contemporary from Prussia, he came to the German linguistic heritage from a place on the edge of German-speaking Europe. From 1576 onwards, he was a teacher, doctor and latterly civic librarian at Augsburg. He was one of the circle centred on the attractive

[153] Riemann, *Preussisches Wörterbuch* fasc. 1, 'Einführung' 10: Walther Ziesemer had the conception 'daß sein Wörterbuch kein totes Glossar, keine trockene Aneinanderreihung von Wörtern sein sollte. Er wollte die Volkssprache in all ihrem Reichtum zur Darstellung bringen. Jedes Wort sollte in seinen vielfältigen Ausdrucksmöglichkeiten und Bedeutungsschattierungen gezeigt werden, in Redensarten und Sprichwörtern, im Zusammenhang mit Volksglauben und Brauchtum. In jedem Wort sollte sich das Denken und Fühlen des Volkes widerspiegeln, sein Humor, seine Einstellung zum Leben.' Cf. Considine, 'Mennonite Low German dictionary' 255–7.
[154] For it, see Jones, *German lexicography* 409–10 (item 707) and Kämper, 'Einführung und Bibliographie zu Georg Henisch'.
[155] Raumer, *Geschichte der Germanische Philologie* 86, 'Was Josua Maaler begonnen hatte, das suchte ein halbes Jahrhundert später Georg Henisch in viel größerem Umfang auszuführen'; Schneider, *Einfluß von Justus Georg Schottelius* 95 identifies some specific debts and Kämper, 'Einführung und Bibliographie zu Georg Henisch' 61–2 points out that Henisch's abbreviated references 'Pict[orius]', 'Helv[eticus]' and 'V[ocabulum] H[elveticum]' are all to Maaler and identifies some debts.

figure of the patrician Marcus Welser, who is linked back to the German humanists and philologists of the earlier sixteenth century by his relationship by marriage with Conrad Peutinger: it was under Welser's patronage that the *Tabula Peutingeriana* was at last published by Ortelius.[156] Henisch published widely, editing an ancient medical author (Aretaeus of Cappadocia, the earliest author by whom a migraine is described), producing astronomical and astrological works, translating a herbal into German, making the first printed catalogue of the civic library of Augsburg, and so on. When the first folio volume of his dictionary appeared, covering the letters A–G in 1802 columns, he was already sixty-seven, and would die two years later. The year of his death was that of the outbreak of the Thirty Years' War, an inauspicious one for scholarship, and no more of the dictionary was published.[157]

The title-page of the *Teütsche Sprach vnd Weißheit* is, indeed, a sad document when it is seen as that of a book published two years before the war broke out. It is partially framed with portraits of the Electors of the Holy Roman Empire; the Emperor Matthias is at the top centre, and Friedrich, the Elector Palatine who would become Matthias' enemy, next to him. At the foot is a panorama of Augsburg, which would be occupied by the Swedish army sixteen years later. Like the multiple dedications of the *Thesaurus graecae linguae*, this title-page suggests the irenic potential of lexicography, offering a dictionary for all German-speakers just before the war that would set one German-speaking community so bitterly against another. Likewise, the dedication of the *Teütsche Sprach* refers in its first sentence to 'Germany, our common fatherland'.[158] The dictionary also speaks to other Europeans, perhaps particularly the nations whose members had mercantile business at Augsburg, offering equivalents for its German vocabulary in English, Czech, French, Greek, Hebrew, Spanish, Hungarian, Italian and Polish.

The dedication begins with patriotic claims of a familiar kind for the primacy of German over all languages but Hebrew, Greek and Latin. These are specifically linked to German history: because Germany has never been conquered, its language has been preserved with particular purity, while others have been changed, or indeed corrupted, over the centuries.[159] Then the claims made by Gessner in his preface to Maaler for

---

[156] Evans, 'Rantzau and Welser', esp. 260–1.
[157] The point is made by Raumer, *Geschichte der Germanischen Philologie* 87 and by Kämper, 'Einführung und Bibliographie' 42.
[158] Henisch, *Teütsche Sprach vnd Weißheit*, sig.):(2r, 'Germaniae, communi nostrae patriae'.
[159] Ibid. sig.):(2v.

the wide distribution of German appear again, supported with the same etymology of *Moscovia*.[160] Henisch concludes:

Our German language so excels in antiquity, that it traces its origins back to the building of the Tower of Babel itself; it so excels in purity that it can, alone among languages, be called a virgin unimpaired; it so excels in wide distribution that it appears to be bounded by no limits but rather to travel all over the world; and finally, it so excels, as in brevity, so in copiousness [that it cannot be sufficiently praised] ... and it is to the adorning and enlargement of this language that I have gathered this THESAURUS of German speech and wisdom.[161]

The subtitle suggests some of the means by which this adorning will be brought about: this is to be a dictionary 'in which all the words in German, both rare and common, are contained together with synonyms, derivatives, phrases, compounds, epithets, proverbs and antonyms'.[162] Henisch expanded this claim in his dedication, explaining that he could without boasting call his work fuller and more perfect than any previous dictionary, since it included the rarest words. Moreover, it permitted 'the accommodation of words to things' as did no other dictionary, by its provision of synonyms and the like.[163] What Henisch had in mind here in particular was, I think, the subtlety with which he differentiated senses, so that the reader would be quite sure of applying the right sense of the right word to the significandum: to take his last full entry, for instance, the German word *gyren, kirren* 'cry with a harsh sound' is translated *frendere* 'gnash' (perhaps after a passage in Livy where Hannibal is described as *frendens gemensque* 'gnashing [sc. his teeth] and groaning'), but then different Latin translations are given for the same word as applied to the noises of wheels, an ungreased cart, a tree in the wind and a door opening.[164] To this very lavish provision of equivalents for different shades of meaning he added a rich selection of 'proverbs, and elegant sayings of the wise men of Germany, both of the past and of the present day, all of which are especially useful in the practice of piety, the governing of the state, the formation of character, or the administration of a household', so that for instance the treatment of

---

[160] Ibid. sig.):(3r.

[161] Ibid. sig.):(4r, 'Ad hanc igitur Germanicam nostram lingvam, quae tanta excellit antiqvitate, ut originem ab ipsa Babiloniae turris aedificatione ducat: tanta puritate, ut sola virgo illibata dicenda sit: tanta amplitudine, ut nullis terminis circumscribi, sed ubivis potius peregrinari videatur: tanta denique tum brevitate, tum copia ... ornandam atque locupletandam THESAVRUM hunc linguae et sapientiae Germanicae collegi.'

[162] Ibid. title-page: 'in quo vocabula omnia Germanica, tam rara, quam communia, cum suis Synonymis, derivatis, phrasibus, compositis, epithetis, proverbijs, antithetis, continentur'.

[163] Ibid. sig.):(4r, quoting Quintilian, *Institutiones* I [5] iii on the ideal of 'verba rebus bene accommodata'.

[164] Ibid. col. 1802; cf. Livy, *Ab urbe condita* 30. 4. 20.

gut 'good' begins with the simplest adjectival uses, but this material is followed almost at once with a dizzying array of sayings, special senses, uses of the word as singular and plural noun, and so on, which continues the entry for sixteen columns.[165] Alphabetically ordered root words were followed by derivatives as in the Estienne dictionaries, so that a given entry would provide information on a diachronic axis as well as a synchronic one; this demonstration of the ability of German to match the productive copiousness of the ancient languages had been anticipated in the writings of Franciscus Irenicus as early as 1518, and is parallelled by the praise of Old English by John Hare in the 1640s as 'most fruitfull and copious in significant and well-sounding rootes and Primitives, and withall capable and apt for diffusion from those her roots into ... a Greeke-like ramosity of derivations and compositions'.[166] Like the *Thesaurus graecae linguae*, Henisch's dictionary had an alphabetical index so that the reader could find derivatives without knowing their etymology.[167] Etymological information was provided explicitly as well as being implicit within the structure of the dictionary; Henisch observes, for instance, that Otfrid uses the form *brutigomo*, which must be the ancestor of modern German *Bräutigam* 'bridegroom', and derives a number of German words more ambitiously from Hebrew.[168]

It has been said of the *Teütsche Sprach vnd Weißheit* that it 'gives a mixed bag of proverbs and etymological ballast, with a bias in favour of rare words' and is 'a learned tome, not a practical aid'.[169] This is rather grudging. Whatever the shortcomings of Henisch's dictionary, it was a remarkable attempt to put Gessner's vision into action. He and Gessner were seeing a dictionary both as a comprehensive repository of culture, and as a comprehensive account of things. In the integration of popular wisdom into a dictionary to make it a truly representative cultural record, Henisch would have no rivals until the great national dictionaries of the nineteenth and twentieth centuries.

RESTORING ITS HERITAGE TO THE FATHERLAND: THE
GERMANIC HERITAGE IN THE LOW COUNTRIES

A starting-point for the consideration of the study of the Germanic heritage by early modern students from the Low Countries is, surprisingly,

---

[165] Ibid. cols. 1785–800.
[166] Ibid. sig.):(3v; for Irenicus' claim, see Borchardt, *German antiquity in Renaissance myth* 146; Hare, *St. Edwards ghost* 12.
[167] Kämper, 'Einführung und Bibliographie' 52f.   [168] Ibid. 55–6.
[169] Wells, *German: A linguistic history* 215.

Constantinople. From the point of view of students of ancient Greek like Henri Estienne, the fall of Constantinople in 1453 must have looked like a disaster, mitigated only by the fact that it gave further impetus to the drain of Greek intellectuals and Greek manuscripts from the eastern Mediterranean to Venice – hence Aldus' Greek helpers and Greek books – and other parts of Italy and western Europe. But late Byzantine Constantinople had been in a state of quite serious decline anyway, and under the Ottomans the city became a much more interesting and cosmopolitan place. It was the capital of their huge empire, and therefore received visitors from an enormous and linguistically diverse hinterland, and from territories further afield. One of these visitors was Ogier de Busbecq (Augerius de Busbecke, Busbequius), who was sent to Constantinople as ambassador on two missions between 1554 and 1562 by Ferdinand, king of Bohemia (who had, as Imperial Lieutenant in Austria, authorized Johann Sichard's search for manuscripts thirty years earlier).[170] He brought back a number of treasures from his travels, notably 'whole cartloads, whole shiploads, of Greek manuscripts'.[171] The most famous of these is the richly illustrated sixth-century copy of the *Materia medica* of Dioscorides which is now in Vienna; Dioscorides was known in Europe already, but this manuscript is unusually old and beautiful (its recovery may have encouraged Sambucus to work towards the edition of Dioscorides which Henri Estienne was to have published).[172] Busbecq has also been credited with introducing both the tulip and the lilac to Western Europe.[173] By combining his interest in old texts with the direct observation of the world around him, he produced one of the most remarkable, and most carefully studied, short wordlists ever made.

Constantinople was a great place for encountering remarkable linguistic data. The story of a small puzzle gives some of the flavour of this: one of Busbecq's party for part of his Turkish mission was a Bohemian-born German called Hans Dernschwam, an amateur of archaeology and epigraphy.[174] One day, Dernschwam observed a mysterious inscription in

---

[170] For his embassies see Forster and Daniell, *Life and letters of Ogier Ghiselin de Busbecq* and von Martels, 'On His Majesty's service'.

[171] Busbecq, *Legationis turcicae epistolae quatuor* fo. 162v, 'librorum Graecorum manuscriptoru[m] tota plaustra, totas naues'.

[172] Now Vienna: Österreichische Nationalbibliothek, Codex Vindobonensis med. gr. 1; see the facsimile, Gerstinger, ed., *Codex Vindobonensis med. gr. 1*.

[173] Both points have been debated: see, e.g., Haudricourt, 'Ogier de Busbecq, botaniste' and le Bourdelles, 'En marge de la communication de A. Haudricourt'.

[174] For a major epigraphic contribution of his, see Couvreur, 'Le déchiffrement du monument d'Ancyre'.

a place where foreign ambassadors were kept waiting before audiences with the Sultan and copied it carefully into his journal.[175] At the beginning of the twentieth century, the scholar preparing a modern edition of the journal was puzzled by the inscription. The best guess that he could make was that it looked vaguely runic, and so he sent a photograph of it to Copenhagen, for the attention of the philologist Vilhelm Thomsen, who identified it at once as an example of a particularly uncommon alphabet, that formerly used by the Székely, a Hungarian people resident in Transylvania. The alphabet was used in this case to baffle inquisitive Turkish courtiers, since the sense of the inscription is not complimentary to the Sultan.[176] Constantinople was, then, a centre for members of some very unusual linguistic groups – the editor of Dernschwam was baffled partly because he knew that the inscription could have been in any one of a hundred different languages. Great cities are usually strongly multi-lingual, but sixteenth-century Constantinople was more so than most. Hence Busbecq's own discovery.

He had heard that a Germanic language, perhaps that of the Goths, was spoken in the Crimea, and had encouraged his servants to locate any of its speakers if they could. Eventually his enquiries bore fruit: a member of the Gothic-speaking ethnic group was introduced to him. Although this man did not actually speak Gothic himself, he was accompanied by another who, although of a different ethnicity, had learned some of the language, and could be interviewed. It was immediately evident to Busbecq that the language to which his informant was introducing him had points in common with his own, Dutch. He could not be sure of its identity, remarking that 'whether they are Goths or Saxons I cannot decide' – as late as the end of the eighteenth century, the zoologist and collector of languages Peter Simon Pallas refused to believe that the language could be Gothic – but his record was carefully enough made for modern scholars to be sure that the language variety he heard was Gothic, although in a dialect that differed from that of the Codex Argenteus.[177]

Busbecq recorded about eighty words from this interview, together with an enigmatic fragment of song. These were listed in glossary form in the printed text of his account of this meeting. The words were divided

[175] Dernschwam, *Tagebuch* 40.
[176] For the decipherment by Thomsen, see Babinger, 'Ein schriftgeschichtliches Rätsel' and Pedersen, *Discovery of language* 201–3; see also Diringer with Regensburger, *The alphabet* 1:246–7.
[177] Busbecq, *Legationis turcicae epistolae quatuor* fos. 135r–137r (I quote fo. 136v, 'Hi Gothi an Saxones sint, non possum diiudicare'), discussed by Stearns, *Crimean Gothic*, esp. 37–48, with transcription and translation 9–15 and facsimile reproduction plates II–VI; for Pallas' comment, see ibid. 19–20 at 20; for the relationship of Crimean and Biblical Gothic, see ibid. 118–20.

into three categories. First came a list of words which Busbecq thought had evident Dutch cognates: *tag* 'day', *plut* 'blood', *stul* 'stool', and so on (cf. Dutch *dag, bloed* and *stoel*). Then came a list of words which Busbecq believed to lack such cognates, beginning with *iel* 'life or health'. Then, finally, came a short account of the cardinal numbers, whose relationship with Dutch was obviously close, and in one detail gratifyingly close to Busbecq's own dialect, that of Flanders: 'Being told to count he did so thus: *Ita, tua, tria, fyder, fynf, seis, sevene,* as we Flemings do. For you men of Brabant, who claim to speak in the Germanic way, are in the habit of ... ridiculing us as if our pronunciation of that word which you pronounce *seven* offended against good taste.'[178] The inference is clear – whether its speakers were actually Goths or Saxons, this language clearly represented a very old tradition, and it agreed with Flemish, not Brabantine, usage, prestigious as the latter might be.[179] Busbecq's fourth Turkish letter, in which the Gothic wordlists appear, was not written up for some years, although its Gothic wordlist must draw on notes taken on the spot, and it was not published until 1589.[180] In the following years, its importance was to be widely recognized; the wordlists were, for instance, reprinted from it by Bonaventure de Smet in 1597 and by Abraham van der Myl (van der Mijl, Mylius) in a very interesting comparative study of the Dutch language in 1612, and from de Smet by Caspar Waserus in his edition of Gessner's *Mithridates* in 1610.[181] Such reprints continued into the eighteenth century.[182]

Before the Turkish letters were published, however, the first specimen of the Gothic language, the text of the Lord's Prayer that is given in the Codex Argenteus, had already been printed, by another Dutch-speaker, Joannes Goropius Becanus (Jan van Gorp). Goropius had been court physician to the queen of France before retiring to Antwerp, where he practised medicine, attending Christophe Plantin after the printer had been stabbed in the street near the beginning of his career. He eventually

---

[178] Busbecq, *Legationis turcicae epistolae quatuor* fo. 136v, 'Iussus ita numerabat. Ita, tua, tria[,] fyder, fyuf [for the convincing emendation to *fynf,* see Stearns, *Crimean Gothic* 43–4], seis, seuene, prorsus, vt nos Flandri. Nam vos Brabanti, qui vos Germanice loqui facitis ... nos soletis habere derisui, ac si istam vocem pronunciemus rancidius, quam vos Seuen effertis.'

[179] For the prestige of the Brabantine dialect, cf. Gessner, *Mithridates* fo. 39r, 'Brabantica lingua inter c[a]eteras Belgicas ... elegantior hodie habetur.'

[180] For the date of composition, see von Martels, 'On His Majesty's service' 180n65.

[181] De Smet, ed., *De literis et lingua getarum* 49–53; van der Myl, *Lingua belgica* 47f. (for which see Metcalf, 'Abraham Mylius on historical linguistics)'; Waserus, 'Ad Mithridatem commentarius' fos. 102v–111v.

[182] E.g., in Malmenius, *Reliqui[ae] linguae Geticae* 18ff.

became a financial partner in Plantin's business.[183] During his residence in Antwerp, he also devoted many hours to history, producing a folio of more than 1100 pages called the *Origines antwerpianae* in 1569, and leaving materials for a posthumous volume on the same scale. It was in the *Origines* that the Gothic Lord's Prayer appeared, from a manuscript communicated to Goropius by Cardinal Granvelle's secretary Maximilien Morillon from the papers of Maximilien's deceased brother, the antiquary and student of language Antoine Morillon. Antoine appears to have had his text from Cassander and Wouters.[184]

The *Origines* made a major contribution to lexicographical thought: it was the first book to make the claim that a given vernacular was substantially identical with the perfect language spoken by Adam. Similar claims had been made before: that Irish was closer to perfection than any other language, or that the Tuscan dialect of Italian could become so.[185] But Goropius' argument went much further: for him, the living Dutch language, and particularly the dialect of Antwerp, preserved the divinely inspired language of Adam, the one language in which things were named aright, in which there was a non-arbitrary correspondence between signifier and signified. All other languages had been corrupted beyond recognition at the fall of Babel, but not Dutch, because the ancestors of the speakers of Dutch had not been present at the ill-advised building of the Tower.[186] What had happened was that, after the Flood, the Noachides had found themselves in Scythia. Most of the human race had sooner or later travelled southwards, towards what would become the site of the Tower of Babel, and there had undergone the confusion of tongues. But the family of Gomer, otherwise known as the Cimbrians or Cimmerians, had gone from Scythia to northern Europe. It was their language, not Hebrew, that had remained unconfused, and this language was preserved with particular purity in contemporary Dutch. The linguistic heritage of Eden was therefore in the mouths of Dutch-speakers.

One of the proofs of Goropius' argument was the fact that Dutch is comparatively rich – according to him, richer than any other language – in

---

[183] For Goropius and his studies, see Borst, *Turmbau von Babel* 1215f.; for his first meeting with Plantin, see Voet, *Golden compasses* I:19, and for the subsequent business relationship, ibid. II:44–9 and II:456n1.

[184] Goropius Becanus, *Origines antwerpianae* 739–40, discussed Schulte, 'Gothica minora: Zweiter Artikel' 318ff. and Van De Velde, *De studie van het Gotisch in de Nederlanden* 24–35; for Antoine Morillon, see Crawford, 'Antoine Morillon'.

[185] Eco, *Search for the perfect language* 16f. for the perfectness of Irish; 45–6 for the perfectibility of Tuscan.

[186] Goropius Becanus, *Origines antwerpianae* 533–4.

monosyllables, from which it forms more complex words by compounding. The perfect language, after all, must have been concise, because concision is a virtue, and to be perfect is to have all the virtues. It must therefore have expressed each basic concept with a single syllable, while retaining the ability to produce derived forms to express concepts derived from the basic ones. This understanding of the lexical productiveness of a Germanic language anticipated that of Henisch. Goropius' two big books are rich in highly imaginative Dutch etymologies that show how compounds were built up from primitive monosyllables: *Adam*, for instance, is explained as from *hat* 'hate' and *dam* 'dam', since Adam needed to withstand the hatred of Satan just as a dam withstands the pounding of the sea, and *Methuselah* from *maek thu salich*, 'make yourself blessed', since that is the way to live long.[187]

These etymologies were not destined to win general acceptance, although the great lexicographer of Dutch Cornelis Kiel borrowed a few – for instance the derivations of *nacht* 'night' from *nie acht*, 'never esteemed', since the night is thought of as worthless, and of *stort* 'throat' from *storten* 'pour', since fluids are poured into the body through the throat – and Goropius could still be described as 'beautifully learned in languages' by the Swedish lexicographer Ericus Schroderus in the next century.[188] Likewise, the historical narrative with which they were associated depended on equivalences that were vulnerable to criticism: for instance, although there was an ancient Germanic people called Cimbri, it was quite easy to argue that they had nothing at all to do with the Scythian people called Cimmerians. But there was some very impressive material in the *Origines*. For instance, the account of the Noachides in pseudo-Berosus conflicted with Goropius' story, and he demolished pseudo-Berosus' credibility with learning and acumen.[189] One striking feature of the pseudo-Berosan story was the identification of Noah and his family as giants, the basis for this being an understanding of Genesis 6:4 as referring to giants (as in the English translation of 1611, which has 'There were Giants in the earth in those daies') rather than simply to mighty men.[190] When Goropius was confronted with material evidence, of a kind that many earlier and contemporary writers had found convincing,

---

[187] Ibid. 539, 548.

[188] Kiel, *Etymologicum*, s.vv.; Schroderus, *Lexicon latino–scondicum* sig. a6v, 'pulchre de linguis disserente'.

[189] Goropius Becanus, *Origines antwerpianae* 337ff., for which see esp. Grafton, *Defenders of the text* 99–101.

[190] Annius of Viterbo, *Commentaria* (1498) in Asher, *National myths in Renaissance France* 194, 'Vnus inter gygantes erat ... Huic nomen erat Noa cum tribus filiis: Samo: Iapeto[:] Chem.'

that there had indeed been giants in the past just as pseudo-Berosus said –
namely an enormous tooth found in an excavation in Antwerp – he
proposed the reasonable theory that the tooth had belonged to an elephant, adding that the elephant in question had no doubt been brought
to the future site of Antwerp by the Romans. Similar finds would be
explained as the teeth of Roman elephants for decades to come.[191]

In the end, the weaknesses of Goropius' arguments were thought to
outweigh their strengths. His own publisher, Christophe Plantin, had to
admit that the arguments of the *Origines* were 'fort estrange'.[192] In the
1590 *Britannia*, Camden wrote that his derivation of *Angli* from *angle*
'fishing rod' was 'worthy to be laughed at rather than to be believed'.[193] A
couple of decades later, Abraham van der Myl exclaimed of him 'what a man
for rich erudition, terse judgement, and sharpness of understanding!' –
but that was after describing him as 'an accomplished and very learned
performer of conjuring tricks'.[194] A hundred years after that, Leibniz, who
was greatly interested in language, coined the derisive verb *goropiser* 'to
make ridiculous etymologies', and by the later eighteenth century the
Swedish etymologist Johann Ihre could describe Goropius' work as
proverbial for its absurdity.[195]

The defence against these judgements is that the *Origines* was a matter
of linguistic heritage-making rather than history. In the 1560s, what really
mattered about Dutch, from a nationalistic point of view, was its total
independence from Spanish, the language of Habsburg oppression, and
French, the other principal language of the southern Netherlands. In
order to assert this independence, Goropius had to argue that Dutch

---

[191] Goropius Becanus, *Origines antwerpianae* 175–81; cf. the discussion by Dionysius de Villiers, letter
of 1 July 1592 to Abraham Ortelius in Ortelius, *Epistolae* 414–17 (letter 215). For earlier responses to
such remains, see Boardman, *Archaeology of nostalgia* 33–43, Piggott, 'Antiquarian thought' 97 and
Piggott, *Ancient Britons and the antiquarian imagination* 48f.; for the supposed remains of giants
in the early modern period, Allen, 'Donne among the giants' and Parry, *Trophies of time* 327; for
the teeth of Roman elephants, see Parry, *Trophies of time* 33 (theory accepted by Camden and
others) and 257f., 303f. (theory doubted by Thomas Browne and rejected by Robert Plot).

[192] Plantin, letter of 13 December 1568 to Gabriel de Çayas in Plantin, *Correspondance* vol. II no. 160.

[193] Camden, *Britannia* (1590) 69, 'Nec Goropii coniectura fidem, sed potius risum meretur, qui
Anglos ab *Angle*, i[d est] hamo piscatorio deducit.'

[194] Van der Myl, *Lingua belgica* 117, 'proh, quam opulentiae eruditionis & tersi iudicij, acutique
ingenij viri!'; ibid. 87, 'artificiosus & doctissimus praestigiator'.

[195] For Leibniz' interest in language, see Schulenburg, *Leibniz als Sprachforscher* and Waterman,
Leibniz and Ludolf on things linguistic, and for *goropiser* see Leibniz, *Nouveaux essais sur
l'entendement humain* III. ii in his *Sämtliche Schriften und Briefe* VI.6; Ihre's judgement is in his
Glossarium Suiogothicum ii, 'Praeterea GOROPIUM BECANUM, cujus audacia Etymologica in
proverbium abiit'; for others, see Metcalf, 'The Indo-European hypothesis in the 16th and 17th
centuries' 241 and, e.g., Jan Van Vliet, letters to Nicolaas Heinsius and Christiaan Huyghens of 27
and 25 January 1662, in Dekker, *Origins of Old Germanic Studies* 191n5.

could not possibly be seen as, like Spanish and French, a derivative of
Latin. To go further and assert the *superiority* of Dutch, he had to show
that it was older than Latin. Then, to forestall claims that Spanish and
French were in fact descended not from Latin but from Greek or
Hebrew, he had to show that it was older than those languages. From a
philological perspective, the radical claims of the *Origines* seemed
eccentric to many contemporaries, but they are not entirely a matter of
philology: their rhetorical function was to trump other etymologies. The
Origines might be compared to Pieter Breughel's *Massacre of the Innocents*
of 1566–7, which is not an accurate representation of first-century
Palestine, and is not meant to be – it is telling a story about the sixteenth-
century Low Countries. Moreover, as we shall see when we return briefly
to Goropius in the last section of this book, his interest in the remotest
origins of Dutch led him to formulate some very interesting ideas about
the ways in which languages are related to each other.

Despite the real merits of Goropius' work, it does not bear comparison
with that of his contemporary Cornelis Kiel (Cornelis Abts alias van
Kiele, Cornelis van Kiel, Cornelius Kilianus, Cornelis Kiliaan), one of the
major figures in the history of lexicography. Kiel was, for much of his life,
a member of a household like those in which Robert and Henri Estienne
grew up: the Plantin *officina* in Antwerp. He had begun working and
living there by his late twenties. In 1558, he was employed as a compositor
with the extra responsibility of looking after the types in the printing
shop, and in 1563 he took on the more highly skilled job of proof-
reading.[196] He continued in this position for more than forty years,
becoming *de facto* the senior employee of the *officina*: he received a salary
three times the usual for a resident proofreader, lent Plantin money, and
contributed to the volume of funerary verses published on his death (he
also wrote interesting verses on the subject of proofreading).[197] When he
died in 1607, a great deal of unwritten knowledge about the operations of
the *officina* must have died with him; it has been suggested that a set of
written rules for proofreaders (including the instruction that they must
not laugh out loud when they find egregious mistakes set in large type)
can be dated to the period 1607–8 and was drawn up to compensate for
his absence from the correctors' room.[198]

---

[196] Voet, *Golden compasses* II:176, II:316; van den Branden *et al.*, *Bio-bibliografie van Cornelis Kiliaan* 35f.
[197] Ibid. 2:189 (salary), 2:456n4 (loan to Plantin); the funerary collection was Bochius, *Epigrammata funebria*; one of Kiel's poems on proofreading is reproduced and translated in Simpson, *Proof-reading* 220–221.
[198] Ibid. 2:183–185.

Kiel undertook three major translations: Philippe de Commines's *Cronique du roy Loys XIe*; a collection of sermons attributed to St Makarios of Egypt; and Guicciardini's description of the Low Countries.[199] These, however, were *parerga*: his great achievement was his Dutch–Latin dictionary. He had begun work as a lexicographer in his first few years as an employee of Plantin's, producing a Latin–Greek–French–Dutch dictionary of about 20,000 entries, the *Dictionarium tetraglotton*, for him; this was published in 1562.[200] It was substantially a new edition with added Dutch of a trilingual Latin–Greek–French dictionary, Guillaume Morel's *Verborum latinorum cum graecis gallicisque coniunctorum commentarii* of 1558, which was itself based on Robert Estienne's *Dictionarium latinogallicum* of 1538.[201] The *Dictionarium tetraglotton* was successful, and further editions appeared until at least 1634. Eleven years later, Plantin published a larger Dutch–Latin–French *Thesaurus theutonicae linguae* of about 40,000 entries, which was compiled for him by Kiel's colleague André Madoets, and was also quite largely derivative from dictionaries in a tradition going back to Robert Estienne, depending most heavily on Maaler's *Die Teütsch Sprach*.[202]

These two Plantin publications competed with a number of other dictionaries with Dutch content, several of them based ultimately on the work of Robert Estienne.[203] One reason for this competition was the emergence of Dutch as a language distinct from German: all these dictionaries were contributing to the formation of a national linguistic identity. The word *teutonicus* does not make this independence fully clear for a modern Anglophone reader, since we regard *Teutonic* as meaning 'Germanic'; but it could be used to mean 'Dutch' in the sixteenth-century Low Countries, as opposed to *germanicus* 'German'.[204] When Plantin announced in the *Dictionarium tetraglotton* that he was presenting material in the *lingua gallica* and the *lingua teutonica*, 'so that the whole youth of the Netherlands shall share a dictionary in their mother-tongue', he was offering a book which could unite the Dutch-speaking and French-speaking moieties of the population.[205] Early modern general

---

[199] Van den Branden *et al.*, *Bio-bibliografie van Cornelis Kiliaan*, items 22–9 (translations), 43ff. (verses).
[200] Bibliographical details ibid., item 6; word-count in Claes, *Bronnen van drie woordenboeken* 269.
[201] Claes, *Bronnen van drie woordenboeken* 51–141 (English summary 352–3).
[202] For its sources, see ibid. 143–266 (English summary 353); for entry-count, see ibid. 269.
[203] See Claes, *Lijst van Nederlandse woordenlijsten en woordenboeken* 5–9.
[204] See Dekker, *Origins of Old Germanic studies* 246–8, 255f., 259.
[205] Plantin, dedicatory epistle to Kiel, *Dictionarium tetraglotton* sig. π2v, '[voces] duabus Linguis, Gallica videlicet, & Teutonica ... interpretandas exhibuimus: vt totius Galliae Belgicae pubes commune habeat vernaculo idiomate Dictionarium'.

dictionaries which included Dutch (as opposed to specialized monolingual vocabularies, such as Jan van de Werwe's puristic list of legal terms, *Het tresoor der Duytsscher talen* of 1552) were in fact all bilingual or multilingual. This reflected the bilingualism of the Netherlands – Antwerp in particular was as richly polyglot a city as Rudolfine Prague – and it also demonstrated that the resources of the Dutch language were equal to those of others, vernacular and classical. As Plantin put it in the preface to the *Thesaurus theutonicae linguae,*

trying to amass and order a definitive dictionary for the first time, in a vernacular language which has not previously been regulated and made grammatical, is as feasible as, at the first attempt, to cut, accumulate, and arrange all the stones from a quarry which abounds in all kinds of stone suitable for working, and to decorate all sorts and orders of buildings, to be as sumptuous and extensive as one can imagine.[206]

The obvious tone of apology for the insufficiencies of the dictionary does not conceal a strong note of pride in heritage. The Dutch language was, even for the Francophone Plantin, a part of heritage comparable to the living rock of the fatherland, and it was capable, with the help of lexicographers, of being turned into something comparable to a great building, as 'sumptuous and extensive' as those of any other civilization.

Kiel's independent contribution to the project of registering the Dutch language appeared twelve years after his reworking of Morel's dictionary. It was an unpretentious octavo of 240 pages and about 12,000 entries, with the title *Dictionarium teutonico–latinum.*[207] This, too, drew on a dictionary descended from one of Estienne's, Frisius' *Dictionariolum puerorum germanicolatinum.*[208] However, it was much more eclectic than its two predecessors from the Plantin *officina*: whereas the *Thesaurus theutonicae linguae* drew 91 per cent of its entries from two major sources, the *Dictionarium teutonico–latinum* drew 49 per cent of its entries from its two most important sources, Frisius and Maaler, and the remaining 51 per cent from at least nine others.[209] It differed significantly from the same predecessors in another important respect: it adduced comparative

[206] Plantin, introduction in Madoets, *Thesaurus theutonicae linguae* sig. §3r, 'entreprendre d'amasser & ordonner premierement vn Dictionnaire absolut en quelque langue vulgaire, non encores reglee & mise en art; est autant faisable, comme du premier coup tirer, ramasser, & mettre en ordre toutes les pierres d'vne certaine quarriere abondante en toutes sortes de pierres propres à dresser & adorner toutes manieres & ordres d'edifices, pour sunptueux & amples qu'on les peust imaginer'.

[207] See van den Branden *et al.*, *Bio-bibliografie van Cornelis Kiliaan* item 12 and, for entry-count, Claes, *Bronnen van drie woordenboeken* 269.

[208] Claes, *Bronnen van drie woordenboeken* 267–344 (English summary 353–4).   [209] Ibid. 342–3.

material from French and German in more than a quarter of its entries, showing the place of Dutch in a network of relationships between the vernaculars, and thus asserting its equality with the languages with which it was being compared.[210] This was not only a patriotic claim but also a statement of the importance of etymology: Kiel was interested in understanding where given words had come from, aware that there were, for instance, French words which 'by long use have become naturalized (*vernaculae*) to us'.[211] He was aware of the contrast between this temperate inquiry and the ideas of Goropius, the typesetting of whose *Origines* he had presumably overseen. Although he did not name his imaginative countryman in his foreword, he remarks in its last paragraph that

Anyone should be at liberty to search for the closer derivation of our words from Greek, Arabic, Hebrew, and other ancient ones, and to discuss the whole Babylonian confusion, if this comparison with German and French cognates, which we exhibit as a specimen of our training, is not enough for them.[212]

The same patriotism, though, shaped the *Origines antwerpianae* and the *Dictionarium teutonico–latinum*. In the first paragraph of his introduction, Kiel remembered his threefold original desire: to do a good piece of work for Plantin, to further the studies of all those interested in Dutch and to deserve well *de sermone patrio*, of the language that was his patrimony, his heritage.[213] And at the very end of the dictionary, he wrote, 'I have written these things in celebration of the qualities of the *patria lingua*, so that its words may have lasting praise and honour.'[214] It is not a coincidence that the adjective *patrius* appears at the beginning and end of Kiel's work. In the *Dictionarium teutonico–latinum*, that word glosses the Dutch word *vaderlick* 'fatherly'; by the second revision of his dictionary in 1599, Kiel still used it in the entry for *vaderlick*, but also in a new and resonant one: 'vader-landsch. *Patrius, vernaculus*'. The headword here means 'of the fatherland'; the two words which translate it are both words that Kiel applied to the Dutch language. Dutch lexicography was a study of what was pre-eminently *vaderlandsch*.

---

[210] Ibid. 332.
[211] Kiel, *Dictionarium teutonico–latinum* (1574) sig. A2v, 'longo vsu nobis sunt vernaculae'.
[212] Ibid. sig. A3v, 'Cuivis tamen liberum esto nostratium Dictionum propinquiorem originem a Graecis, Arabibus, Hebraeis, & alijs antiquis petere, atque Babylonicum omne chaos discutere, si haec cum Germanicis & Gallicis affinibus facta collatio, quam tanquam specimen nostri exercitij exhibemus, non satis placeat.'
[213] Ibid. sig. A2r, 'viro optime de me merito gratificari, de sermone patrio bene mereri, & multorum studijs ... consulere'.
[214] Ibid. sig. P7v, 'Scripsimus haec patriae celebrantes commoda linguae, | Vt maneat Verbis lausque decusque suis.'

A greatly enlarged second edition of the *Dictionarium teutonico–latinum* was published in 1588.[215] The dictionary reached its final form under the original editor in 1599, when a third edition was published as *Etymologicum teutonicae linguae*.[216] By this time, Kiel had really made a new dictionary: placing the first and third editions side by side, the difference in scale is striking. The main text of the *Etymologicum* ran to 690 pages (about 34,500 entries). This was followed by thirty-five of *peregrinarum, absurdarum, adulterinarumque dictionum*, 'words which have come from abroad, or are absurd or spurious' – the first are *abandon* and its verbal derivative *abandonneren, abbreuiatie* and *abricock* – whose presence recalls the pur- istic tendencies of other Dutch lexicographers, not to mention the six- teenth-century English controversy over 'inkhorn terms'.[217] Then came thirty-eight pages of proper names in two sequences, one of them listing the current names of places, and the other listing personal names, 'parti- cularly of Goths, Vandals, Germans, Teutons, Saxons and Anglo-Saxons', with brief etymological notes.[218] This latter recalls the sixteenth-century German lists of early Germanic proper names and their etymologies.

The full form of the new title that Kiel gave to his dictionary in 1599 can be translated as 'Etymological dictionary of the Dutch language, or Dutch–Latin dictionary, comprising the principal words and phrases of the Dutch language translated into Latin, and compared in passing with a number of other languages ... a work of great value to High Germans, Low Germans, French, English or Anglo-Saxons, Italians, Spaniards and others'.[219] Kiel was asserting the international standing of Dutch even more firmly than in 1573, and he was making the claim that a dictionary whose headwords were in Dutch might still be well worth the reading for members of many other European nations, just as the Latin-language publications of the Plantin *officina* were. The foreign-language material advertised on the title-page went markedly beyond the provision of French and German comparative material in the *Dictionarium teutonico– latinum* of 1574, though generally it consisted of strings of cognates

---

[215] Van den Branden *et al.*, *Bio-bibliografie van Cornelis Kiliaan* item 13.
[216] Ibid. item 14 is the 1599 *Etymologicum*, with items 15–21 being editions from 1605 (during Kiel's lifetime, but without his input) to 1777.
[217] The English cognates of these particular words were not in fact stigmatized in early English dictionaries: cf. Osselton, *Branded words* 178.
[218] Kiel, *Etymologicum* 745.
[219] Ibid. title-page: 'Etymologicum teutonicae linguae, sive dictionarium teutonico–latinum, praecipuas teutonicae linguae dictiones et phrases latine interpretatas, & cum aliis nonnullis linguis obiter collatas complectens ... opus germanis tam superioribus quam inferioribus, gallis, anglis siue anglosaxonibus, italis, hispanis, & aliis lectu perutile.'

provided without comment, as in the case of *nieuw* 'new', where Greek, German, French, Italian, Spanish and English forms were cited, but the question of their relationship was left undiscussed. (Occasionally Kiel went further, for instance in his explanation that the archaic *lieven* 'to love', was Greek φιλεῖν, 'with the first three letters transposed'.[220]) This tentative approach to etymology is evident elsewhere: Kiel was in fact unsure as to whether he should present his book as a synchronic *dictionarium* or as a diachronic *etymologicum*. So, as he annotated an exemplar of the 1588 *Dictionarium teutonico–latinum* to make printers' copy for the new edition, he added *Etymologicum teutonicae linguae* as the first element of the title as a late decision, after the title-page had been given its first mark-up.[221]

Not all of Kiel's cited forms were from foreign languages. Although his dictionary was based on the dialect of Brabant, it included material from different Dutch and Low German dialects. 'I have diligently collected and digested', he explains in his introduction,

firstly, words used by the people of Brabant; and also many of those most used by those of Flanders, Zeeland, Holland, Friesland, and the Sicambrian lands (namely Gelderland, Cleves, and Jülich), and also by the Saxons and Alemanni or High Germans ... for this work of ours can be used in other regions of Germany, particularly northern Germany and the Netherlands, not in Brabant alone.[222]

The results of his dialect research were impressively full. Hundreds of entries are labelled: *kleynsen* 'to clean' is recorded as in use in Holland, Friesland, Sicambria, Zeeland and Flanders, with the English cognate *cleanse* duly noted; *neyen* 'to sew' is identified as Saxon and Sicambrian, with a cross-reference to the Brabantine form *naeyen*; *seghel* 'sail' is identified as archaic, with a cross-reference to the more current *seyl* and cognates from German, Saxon and English. No such elaborate treatment of dialect was being attempted in any contemporary study of English.[223] Kiel also cited forms from Old English and Old High German, using printed sources such as Flacius' Otfrid, and thus took his study of variation back through time as well as across the face of northern Europe.[224]

---

[220] Ibid. s.v. *lieven*, 'litteris tribus prioribus transpositis'; for the use of *litterae* here, see Law, *History of linguistics in Europe from Plato to 1600*, 61.

[221] Voet, *Golden compasses* 2, plates 63–6.

[222] Kiel, *Etymologicum* sig. *2v, 'Voces ... Brabantis in primis vsitatas; plurimas insuper Flandris, Selandis, Hollandis, Frisijs, & Sicambris (Gheldris ne[m]pe, Cliuiis & Iuliacis,) Saxonibus quoque & Alamanis siue Germanis superioribus vsitatissimas ... (vt non Brabantiae solum, sed & aliis Germaniae, praecipue inferioris, regionibus, noster hic labor vsui esse posset) studiose collegi ac digessi.'

[223] Cf. Stein, 'Emergence of lexicology' 31–2 and Burke, *Languages and communities* 35–8.

[224] See Dekker, '*Vide Kilian*' 518–19.

Kiel was, then, on the one hand, one of a number of philologists around 1600 whose lexicographical sympathies were widening into a generous comparativism, and on the other, a student with a specific interest in the heritage of the Low Countries and neighbouring parts of Germany. The local specificity of his work can be seen in his use of historical material as well as in his provision of dialect forms. Some articles in the *Etymologicum* are rich in encyclopedic material on cultural history, such as that for the word *veeme* and some of its derivatives, which provides information on the secret medieval German tribunals called *vehme* or *vehmgericht* from a number of sources: the Frisian jurist and antiquarian Joachim Hopper; Erasmus, who mentions the *vehme* in passing in the *Adagia*; Sebastian Münster; Trithemius; and Aventinus. A number take material, including some information about Gothic, from Hadrianus Junius' *Batavia*.[225] This book is an account, sometimes speculative, of the people called the Batavi, who are described in the *Germania* of Tacitus as the most conspicuously brave of all the German tribes in Gaul.[226] As such, it was a contribution to a central theme in the story of Dutch heritage. Although the Batavi were difficult to pin down historically, and the island between the mouths of the Rhine and the Waal on which they had lived was variously identified by various antiquaries in the sixteenth century and afterwards, they were imaginatively hugely important to sixteenth- and seventeenth-century Dutch patriots: they could be seen as heroic ancestors, independent from Rome although allied with it, well-governed, 'addicted to cleanliness and liberty'.[227] A history was manufactured for them, supported by a forged inscription, which read 'Batavi amici et fratres Rom. Imp.', on a stone supposedly unearthed near Leiden – an appropriate location, since in 1575 Leiden was given the Latin name *Lugdunum Batavorum* (many neo-Latin place-names were, like this one, creations of the Renaissance rather than revivals of ancient nomenclature).[228] This name appeared as the imprint of a great number of scholarly books, and told every consumer of Dutch scholarship about a Dutch heritage of independence. Kiel's use of a major account of the Batavi as a source in his *Etymologicum* locates his work in the story of Dutch patriotic publishing as well as in that of the European

[225] See de Smet, 'Invloed van Junius' Batavia op Kiliaans Woordenboek', and, with reference to Gothic, Van de Velde, *De studie van het Gotisch in de Nederlanden* 109–10.

[226] Tacitus, *Germania* 29, 'omnium harum gentium virtute praecipui Batavi'.

[227] Schama, *Embarrassment of riches* 54–81; quotation at 78.

[228] For the date of *Lugdunum Batavorum*, see Schöffer, 'Batavian myth' 89; for neo-Latin place-names in general, see IJsewijn, *Companion to Neo-Latin studies* 2:400–3.

study of language. The liminary verses to the dictionary likewise emphasize its importance in a story of national pride: 'Here is a champion who gives the Belgae reborn words, restoring its heritage to the fatherland (*patriae restituens patriam*)', wrote Franciscus Raphelengius, and Justus Lipsius commended Kiel to readers in the Low Countries as the man 'who, by his outstanding labour, gives you a draught of the language which is your heritage (*sermonem patrium*) ... the language which belonged to your grandfather and great-grandfather, and to mine'.[229]

Lipsius is now remembered for his place in the history of Neo-Stoicism and for his editions of Tacitus and Seneca. The interest in Germanic studies suggested by his liminary verses in Kiel's *Etymologicum*, however, led him to make a very important wordlist. Within a couple of years of his verses in praise of Kiel, he wrote a long letter to the jurist and syndic of Antwerp Henricus Schottius, which he published in 1602. It began and ended with reflections on Goropius Becanus, whom Schottius had presumably been reading with interest: 'I loved the man, and wondered at his sharp, ready, and even fortunate intellect – at least, "fortunate" would have been the word if it had turned to different subjects and material ... But who can read the theories of coming into being, or origin, which Becanus brings forth without often being moved to irritation or laughter?'[230] Lipsius concluded by pointing out that Goropius' argument 'The simplest things are the oldest: our language is such: therefore it is the first' was neither convincing in itself nor immune from comparative criticism, since Chinese was rich enough in monosyllables to be a contender, by Goropius' criteria, for the title of oldest language, a suggestion which Lipsius made facetiously but which would be advanced in earnest seventy years later by an English antiquary.[231]

Goropius' theories depended on the assumption that Dutch had remained conspicuously pure and unchanged over the centuries, and

[229] Raphelengius, 'Cornelio Kiliano linguae Teutonicae assertori, epigramma', in Kiel, *Etymologicum* sig. *2v, 'adest vindex, rediuiua vocabula Belgis | Qui reddat, patriae restituens patriam'; Lipsius, 'In Cornelii Kiliani eruditi viri Etymologicon', ibid. sig. *5r (and already in a letter to Kiel of 1 March 1597, in Lipsius, *Epistolarum selectarum centuria tertia ad Belgas* 27–8), 'qui egregio suo labore | Sermonum tibi patrium propinat | ... qui fuisset | Aut aui aut proaui tui, meiq[ue]'.
[230] Lipsius, letter of 19 December 1598 to Henricus Schottius in Lipsius, *Epistolarum selectarum centuria tertia ad Belgas* 41–62 at 41, 'virum amaui, & ingenium acre, facile, felix etiam miratus sum: felix, si in aliam rem & materiem vertisset' and 62, 'Etsi pariationes, aut originationes, quas Becanus adfert, quis saepe sine indignatiuncula aut risu legat?' The date, XIV Kal. Ianuar. MDXCIX, is rendered differently in different secondary sources, but 19 December 1598 is right: see Deneire and Van Hal, eds., *Lipsius tegen Becanus* 119.
[231] Lipsius, letter of 19 December 1598 to Schottius 62, 'Antiquissima, quae simplicissima: talis est lingua nostra: ergo & prius'; Lipsius' suggestions about Chinese loc. cit. anticipate Webb, *Historical essay endeavoring a probability that the language of the empire of China is the primitive language* (1669).

Lipsius wanted to show that this is not how languages behave. So, he quoted the Strasburg Oaths as evidence for linguistic change; and then he turned to an account of a remarkable manuscript which he had known since 1591, and which he supposed to be contemporary with the Strasburg Oaths. It was a Latin psalter owned by one Arnold van Wachtendonck, with interlinear glosses in a language variety that Lipsius called *saxonica* in one letter and *germanica* in another; it is now seen as a dialect of Old Dutch.[232] Lipsius then copied out a roughly alphabetized list of 670 of the words in the manuscript that appeared to differ most markedly from the Dutch language of his own day (apparently based on a wordlist of 822 items made under his direction, which was published in the nineteenth century), ending 'There you have what will suffice as a specimen.'[233] Since the Wachtendonck Codex, as it is now called, was one of the few monuments of Old Dutch, and was lost after Lipsius had made partial transcripts from it, his wordlists are very important records of the language.

Another contribution to the study of the earliest Germanic monuments was made in 1597 by Paulus Merula, Lipsius' successor at the University of Leiden, with assistance from Pancratius Castricomius, a member of the States-General, praised by Merula for his expertise as jurist, politician and linguist alike. An eleventh-century manuscript of Willeram of Ebersberg's double commentary on the Song of Songs, in Latin verse and Old High German prose, had come to their attention, and they prepared it for the press and published it with a Dutch paraphrase, a useful commentary and a glossary in 1598.[234] This provided philologists with an important supply of new data, and was cited by a number of lexicographers, among the first being Kiel.[235]

A collection of short texts and wordlists made at the end of the sixteenth century complements these publications of ancient material on the one hand, and the depth and comprehensiveness of Kiel's work on Dutch on the other, by offering a broader sketch of the Germanic heritage as it had been rediscovered over the last fifty or so years. This was an inquiry into Gothic by Bonaventure de Smet (Bonaventura Vulcanius, Fortunatus Faber), a native of Bruges, who was at one time Georg Cassander's

---

[232] Robinson, *Old English and its closest relatives* introduces the witnesses to the Wachtendonck Codex (203–4) and discusses its language (215–21); see also Kyes, ed., *The Old Low Franconian psalms and glosses*, esp. 1–5. For Lipsius' engagement with this manuscript, see Heesakkers, 'Lipsius, Dousa and Jan van Hout' 109f. and Van Hal 'Een "geurtje" rond de Wachtendonkse Psalmen?'

[233] Lipsius, letter of 19 December 1598 to Schottius 43–54, ending 'Habes, quod sufficiat in specimen'.

[234] See Sanders, *Der Leidener Willeram* 10–19 and 65–8, and Gumbert, 'The Willeram goes to print'.

[235] For Kiel and Willeram, see Dekker, '*Vide Kilian*' 519.

secretary, subsequently worked as a proof-corrector for Henri Estienne, and became Merula's colleague as professor of Greek at Leiden.[236] He is remembered not so much for his work on Greek as for his interest in Germanic antiquities. This can, for instance, be seen in his edition of the *Batavia* of an early Dutch humanist and correspondent of Erasmus, Cornelius Gerard (de Gouda, Aurelius, etc.), which not only added to the literature on the ancient origins of the Dutch nation but also celebrated a tradition of Dutch historical scholarship.[237] It can also be seen in his ownership of a manuscript of Willeram, collated by Castricomius for the *princeps* of 1598, and one of the Old High German translation of the Gospel harmony of Tatian, now known only from a copy which he sent to Marquard Freher and which was subsequently acquired by Franciscus Junius.[238] De Smet brought the classical and Germanic heritages together again in an edition of Jordanes and some of the other ancient authorities for the history of the Goths in 1597. His *De literis et lingua getarum siue gothorum*, also of 1597, was a natural development from this work on the recorded history of the Goths.[239] It begins with two short anonymous treatises on the Gothic alphabet, possibly by Cornelius Wouters, and some extracts from the Gospels of Matthew, Mark and Luke.[240] It then attempts to place the Gothic language in what scholars like Kiel – who would use de Smet's publication in his *Etymologicum* – were showing to be a network of European languages, some more closely connected to each other than others.[241] To this end, it contains specimens, sometimes followed by wordlists, of Gothic, Old English, Old High German (including the texts of the Strasburg Oaths), Persian, Basque, Frisian, Welsh, Icelandic and Romani. The Persian lexical items are compared with German cognates, and this had never been done before; the Romani wordlist is the second specimen of that language ever to have been printed; Gothic had never before been printed in the Greek-based Gothic alphabet.[242] De Smet's Gothic was taken both from Busbecq's wordlist and from manuscripts deriving from the Codex Argenteus, to which he

---

[236] Van de Velde, *Studie van het Gotisch in de Nederlanden* 66f.

[237] Discussed Tilmans, *Historiography and humanism* 199ff.

[238] For his Willeram, see Gumbert, 'The Willeram goes to print' 210; for his Tatian, now Bodleian MS Junius 13, see Ganz, 'MS. Junius 13 und die althochdeutsche Tatianübersetzung' 36f.

[239] The contents are analysed by Schulte, 'Gothica minora: Dritter Artikel'.

[240] The ascription to Wouters is proposed ibid. 354.

[241] For Kiel and de Smet, see Dekker, '*Vide Kilian*' 519.

[242] For the pioneering comparison with Persian, see Droixhe, *Linguistique et l'appel de l'histoire* 55–6; for the Romani wordlist, see Matras, *Romani: A linguistic introduction* 2; for the Gothic, see Fairbanks and Magoun, 'On writing and printing Gothic' 322–3.

was the first to give this name. One of these manuscripts survives among de Smet's papers at Leiden; it was apparently made by Wouters.[243]

De Smet was one of the first philologists to attend to Frisian, a minority language of the northern Netherlands and elsewhere on the North Sea coast which had been in decline since the thirteenth century, and had recently ceased to be used for official purposes.[244] He was followed by van der Myl in 1612.[245] The first wordlist to contain Old Frisian appears to have been the sixty-eight-item 'Index vocabulorum germanicorum et frisicorum' published in the first separate edition of the earliest Frisian law-code in 1617, a rare book even in its own day.[246] Although a number of early modern philologists saw a close relationship between Frisian and English, and Frisian forms were cited by English lexicographers such as Sir Henry Spelman, even the great comparativist Franciscus Junius, although he had studied Frisian and was interested in data from a wide range of Germanic languages, made comparatively little use of it.[247] Frisian was of much more marginal interest than Dutch to most philologists in the early modern period, a reminder that the first languages to be studied from a historical perspective were those that had standard forms and high cultural status: languages of public affairs and not of the home.

Having said that, the study of the Germanic linguistic heritage of the Low Countries in the early modern period was on the whole diverse and vigorous. Enquiring Netherlandish writers had discovered written Gothic in Germany and spoken Gothic in the Ottoman Empire, and their successors had studied both, with a recurring interest in the comparison between Gothic and other language varieties, and had also discovered a major record of Old Dutch. Meanwhile, the Plantin *officina* had been nurturing synchronic vernacular lexicography, most notably that of Cornelis Kiel. In his *Etymologicum*, the synchronic and the diachronic study of Dutch came together in one of the most impressive accounts of a vernacular linguistic heritage to be published in the sixteenth century.

---

[243] It is reproduced Van de Velde, *Studie van het Gotisch in de Nederlanden* after p. 76 and ascribed to Wouters ibid. 84.

[244] For the decline of Frisian, see Price, *Encyclopedia of the languages of Europe* 179.

[245] For van der Myl and Frisian, see Droixhe, *Linguistique et l'appel de l'histoire* 59.

[246] *Lex frisionum* (1617), sig. V3r–v; for its rarity in the early seventeenth century, see Bremmer, 'Late medieval and early modern opinions on the affinity between English and Frisian' 178.

[247] For the relationship in general, see Bremmer, 'Late medieval and early modern opinions on the affinity between English and Frisian'; for Junius and Frisian, see Breuker, 'On the course of Franciscus Junius's Germanic studies', esp. 132f. (overview of Junius' references to Frisian) and 141 (Spelman).

CHAPTER 5

Vernacular heritages II: England to circa 1650

In England, as in Germany and the Netherlands, there was a substantial production of Latin–vernacular and vernacular–Latin dictionaries in the fifteenth and early sixteenth centuries. The first of any importance – the *Medulla grammatice*, the *Hortus vocabulorum* and the *Promptorium parvulorum* – appeared in the first half of the fifteenth century, and can perhaps be associated with the rising prestige of the English language under the Lancastrian kings.[1] They were succeeded from the second quarter of the sixteenth century onwards by a tradition of dictionaries showing humanistic influence: this begins with the first edition of the *Dictionary* of Sir Thomas Elyot in 1538, a work indebted to Calepino, and continues with a revision by Elyot of the same work, published as the *Bibliotheca Eliotae* in 1545. The tradition was then continued by an Oxford schoolmaster, Thomas Cooper, and by lexicographers indebted to him.[2] It would be possible to trace the development of the aims of these bilingual dictionaries from the elucidation of Latin texts to the increasingly confident display of the riches of English vocabulary and phraseology. The story of this development from the fifteenth-century *Medulla* to Cooper's *Thesaurus* of 1565 could be compared to that of the movement in German lexicography from the fifteenth-century *Vocabularius ex quo* to Maaler's *Die Teütsch Spraach*, although the likeness weakens at the end, since Cooper did not commit himself as firmly as Maaler to making a dictionary of the vernacular. If this story were being told here, it could be enriched by that of the development of the major bilingual dictionaries

---

[1] For these glossaries, see Starnes, *Renaissance dictionaries* 3–37 and Stein, *English dictionary before Cawdrey* 74–120; for the English language and the Lancastrians, see Fisher, *Emergence of standard English* 16–35.
[2] Starnes, *Renaissance dictionaries* 45ff.

of English and the Romance vernaculars in which the riches of English are most copiously displayed: John Palsgrave's *Lesclarcissement de la langue francoyse* (1530), Randle Cotgrave's *Dictionarie of the French and English tongues* (1611), and John Florio's *Worlde of wordes* (1598) and *Queen Anna's new world of words* (1611). Interesting as these dictionaries are, their primary focus is always on the elucidation of foreign words rather than on the riches of the English language. Rather than discussing them, I shall turn here to the historical approach to the English linguistic heritage which was the subject of an important series of inquiries in the sixteenth and seventeenth centuries, as the earliest monuments of English, the texts written before the end of the twelfth century in Old English, were rediscovered and examined.

It is possible to discern some interest in Old English, or at least in texts written in it, in England as early as the fifteenth century.[3] However, the extent of this interest cannot have been very wide: the two clearest cases are both, as might be expected, those of persons who had access to manuscripts that had been written in Old English and preserved in monastic or cathedral libraries. Nobody tried to make such manuscripts more accessible by announcing their presence in existing libraries. No Oxford college appears to have owned a manuscript with a substantial Old English content (as opposed to scattered glosses in Old English or books with fragments of Old English manuscripts used as scrap parchment in their bindings) in the Middle Ages; the few now in college libraries were acquired in or after the seventeenth century.[4] The great donations of books made to the University of Oxford in the 1440s by Humphrey, Duke of Gloucester, included works from antiquity, the early Middle Ages and the early Renaissance, but all in Latin: early humanist Oxford, like medieval Oxford, had no use for Old English.[5] It was only after the dissolution of the monasteries that manuscripts written in Old English began to be collected, studied and printed.[6] This development was roughly contemporary with the hunt for manuscripts in German and Swiss libraries by scholars such as Celtis, Münster and Lazius.

---

[3] See Ker, *Catalogue* xlvii–xl, 'Use before 1540', and cf. the absence of references to language in the pre-fifteenth-century material covered in Rouse, *Idea of Anglo-Saxon England*.

[4] Ker, *Catalogue* 333–4 (item 265) and 429–37 (items 352–62).

[5] The original lists are in *Epistolae academicae Oxon. part 1 (1421–1457)* 179–84, 204–5, and 232–7 respectively, and are consolidated in C[raster], 'Index to Duke Humphrey's gifts'; for the humanistic quality of the donations see Ullmann, 'Manuscripts of Duke Humphrey of Gloucester' and Weiss, *Humanism in England during the fifteenth century* 62f.

[6] See esp. Wright, 'Dispersal of monastic libraries'.

There were, however, two distinctive elements in the turn to the study of Old English which did not apply across German-speaking Europe. One was that manuscripts in Old English became mobile after the massive dispersal of the English monastic libraries in the 1530s and 1540s, passing into the hands of private owners who made them available to friends, and then, in the seventeenth century, little by little into fairly readily accessible institutional collections. Another was that an important thread in the rhetoric of the English Reformation was that it represented a return to an ancient Anglo-Saxon tradition of Christianity, predating the evidently Popish practices of the later Middle Ages; Anglo-Saxon theological writers such as Ælfric were therefore grist to the reformers' mill, even if their texts had to be handled selectively in order to make the points that the reformers wanted.[7] So, early figures in the revival of interest in Old English include John Bale, the Protestant controversialist and dedicatee of Gessner's *Mithridates*; the martyrologist John Foxe; and Matthew Parker, archbishop of Canterbury, together with his son John Parker and his secretary John Joscelyn. The revival of the study of Old English was not simply an effect of the English Reformation any more than the revival of the study of German antiquities was simply one of the German Reformation. It was, for instance, well known to fifteenth- and sixteenth-century speakers of English that the contemporary language contained many recent loanwords, so that older varieties of English could be regarded as purer, and might be valued for that reason.[8] Jurists and historians of institutions needed to examine the earliest English law-codes and legal documents, and the engagement of heralds with various kinds of heritage required them to read old documents, and therefore to attend to early varieties of the English language.[9] But one reason to read Old English was certainly interest in England's Christian heritage, just as a reason to read Old High German was interest in that of Germany.

The textual and lexical heritage of the Anglo-Saxon past as recovered in the early modern period scarcely included Old English poetry. Here, too, there is an analogy with the German scholars among whom Wolfgang Lazius could use the word *poetaster* of the maker of the *Nibelungenlied*. Even Laurence Nowell, a particularly thoughtful and wide-ranging early

[7] See Leinbaugh, 'Ælfric's *Sermo de sacrificio in die Pascae*: Anglican polemic in the sixteenth and seventeenth centuries'.
[8] See, e.g., Jones, *Triumph of the English language* 115f.
[9] For lawyers and Old English, see Schoeck, 'Early Anglo-Saxon studies and legal scholarship'; for the scholarship of early modern English heralds, see Maclagan, 'Genealogy and heraldry in the sixteenth and seventeenth centuries'.

Anglo-Saxonist, hardly touched verse texts: he made a few glosses in the Old English poetical manuscript called the Exeter Book, and one in the manuscript of *Beowulf*, but his attention to these poems was clearly desultory.[10] The first lexicographer to handle material from the other major Old English poetical manuscript known in the period, the so-called Cædmon Manuscript, was not quite certain whether it was poetry or prose (Anglo-Saxon scribes wrote poetry out without line-breaks), writing that 'it appears from time to time to be made up of lines of verse'.[11] Three adventurous persons wrote and published verses in Old English in university miscellanies of the 1640s and 1650s, but these are not written in the flexible, unrhymed, divided alliterative line of the Anglo-Saxon poets, but in rhyming couplets, with little alliteration in one case and none in the others.[12] Not only was the metre of Old English verse not understood; its language was seen, as the lexicographer William Somner put it, as 'ancient, obsolete, poetic, inflated, mannered, obscure and riddling'.[13] Somner and Franciscus Junius both tried to understand it in the 1650s, but earlier lexicographers of Old English tended to leave it alone.

One of the very first people to take an interest in the earliest records of English and in the glossing of Old English was John Leland.[14] He began his learned career as a minor humanist, a poet who eulogized – and may have met – both Erasmus and Budé, and corresponded with Beatus Rhenanus.[15] But he was also a student of the English cultural heritage, from his own day backwards, with a marked interest in language as a vehicle of that heritage (hence his commemoration of Thomas Wyatt as a rival for Dante and Petrarch in the work he had written *patrio sermone*).[16] As such, he had significant medieval precursors, but the greatness of his own achievement is generally agreed: his twentieth-century admirers have called Leland, among other things, 'the father of local history and bibliography ... the father of

---

[10] Flower, 'Laurence Nowell' 24 and 27n19.

[11] Jan de Laet, letter to Ole Worm of 4 March 1643, in Timmer, 'De Laet's Anglo-Saxon dictionary' 200, 'videturque metra [*sc.* metris?] quondam constare'. Cf. Plumer, 'Construction of structure' 245ff.

[12] Utley, 'Two seventeenth-century Anglo-Saxon poems'; Turner, 'Another seventeenth-century Anglo-Saxon poem'.

[13] Somner, *Dictionarium* sig. b1r, 'veteri, obsoleto, poetico, tumido, affectato, mystico & enigmatico scriptus stylo'.

[14] For his work, see Simpson, *1350–1547: Reform and cultural revolution* 8–33.

[15] For Leland's knowledge of Erasmus, see Carley, 'Four poems in praise of Erasmus by John Leland'; for his interest in and knowledge of Budé, see Carley, 'John Leland in Paris' 12–14; for the correspondence with Beatus, see Carley and Petitmengin, 'Pre-conquest manuscripts from Malmesbury Abbey' 210f. and 222–3.

[16] Leland, *Naeniae in mortem Thomas Wyattis* sig. A3v, 'Bella suum merito iactet florentia Dantem. | Regia Petrarchae carmina Roma probet. | His non inferior patrio sermone Viatus | Eloquij secum qui decus omne tulit', discussed Foley, *Sir Thomas Wyatt* 29ff.

English topographers ... the first English antiquary of any consequence'.[17] The years of great achievement to which these statements refer began in 1533, when he received a royal commission that called upon him, as he was to put it in his 'New years gift', an epistle to Henry VIII,

> to peruse and dylygentlye to search all the lybraryes of Monasteryes and collegies of thys your noble realme, to the entent that the monumentes of auncyent wryters ... myghte be brought out of deadly darkenesse to lyuelye lyght, and to receyue lyke tha[n]kes of their posteryte, as they hoped for ... and furthermore, that the holy scrypture of God myght both be syncerely taught and learned, all maner of superstycyon, and crafty coloured doctryne of a rowte of Romayne Byshoppes, totally expelled oute of thys your most catholyque realme.[18]

He hoped, in other words, to map the monuments of ancient writers (especially English ones, whose posterity were Leland's intended readership), and thereby not only to illuminate English antiquities but also to attack the legacy of late medieval Catholicism. The first half of this double project was done in conscious emulation of Conrad Celtis and other continental European humanists; indeed, Henry's commission may have been inspired by those of Maximilian I and his grandson Ferdinand, as may similar commissions such as that issued at some time before 1537 by François I of France to Jean de Gagny, rector of the University of Paris.[19] Leland knew very well that his research called for extensive travel over England; he was, like Celtis, a highly mobile scholar. Engagement with a textual heritage and with a landscape were both important intellectual projects for Leland, and they suggest two ways in which he gave an impetus to the reclaiming of the medieval heritage of England by lexicographers in the generation after his own.

The first of these was the hunting of manuscripts. He saw the manuscripts in English libraries as numinous objects, describing the 'awe or stupor' that stopped him in his tracks at his first sight of the books at Glastonbury Abbey.[20] He also saw them as of national significance,

---

[17] For Leland's precursors, see Gransden, *Historical writing in England II* 475 and n135; for modern assessments, see Chandler, 'Introduction' xxi, quoting A. L. Clarke (1911), H. B. Walters (1934) and J. M. Levine (1987).

[18] Leland and Bale, *Laboryouse iourney* sigs. B8r–C1r.

[19] For Leland's emulation of Celtis, see ibid. sig. B7v; for François's instructions, see Carley and Petitmengin, 'Pre-conquest manuscripts from Malmesbury Abbey' 199–201, and for other cases see Ridé, *Image du Germain* 1:195.

[20] Leland, *Commentarii de scriptoribus Britannicis*, 'Vix certe limen intraueram, cum antiquissimorum librorum uel solus conspectus religionem, nescio an stuporem animo incuteret meo; eaque de caussa pedem paululum sistebam,' quoted and translated Carley and Petitmengin, 'Pre-Conquest manuscripts from Malmesbury Abbey' 201n22.

writing to Thomas Cromwell in 1536 that, if he might collect them for deposit in the royal library, 'It would be a great profit to students and honour to this realm; whereas, now the Germans perceiving our desidiousness and negligence do send daily young scholars hither, that spoileth them, and cutteth them out of libraries, returning home and putting them abroad as monuments of their own country.'[21] This echoes the fears of Celtis that German manuscripts were being exported to Italy. John Bale was also to write of 'the wonderynge of the foren nacyons' at the export of monastic manuscripts after the dissolution, and subsequently returned, in a letter to Matthew Parker, to the spoliation of the monastic libraries and his own efforts to preserve manuscripts from being 'carryed over the sea into Flaunders to be solde', saying that 'onle conscyence, with a fervent love to my Contrey moved me to save that myghte be saved'.[22] Parker himself would write to William Cecil that he rejoiced at the presence of such treasures as a Biblical manuscript with an interlinear gloss in Old English in Cecil's library 'as moche as thei wer in my[n] owne. So that thei maye be preserved within the realme, & not sent over by couetouse statyoners.'[23]

Leland studied the Old English manuscripts that he located. Two of those that he handled were borrowed from a pioneer in the study both of Old English and of the Roman topography of Britain, Robert Talbot, prebendary of Norwich, who made good use of his access to the manuscripts of Norwich Cathedral Priory as well as forming a collection of his own.[24] Others came directly from monastic collections. One of these occasioned the first direct foray into the lexicography of Old English made by any scholar of the sixteenth century. This was Leland's transcript of 181 entries from a lost manuscript, possibly from Glastonbury, of Ælfric's *Glossary*, a subject-ordered Latin–Old English glossary of 1257 entries, which accompanies Ælfric's *Grammar* in seven medieval manuscripts.[25] These works were pedagogical, and therefore fairly easy to read, and they were widely used: Talbot studied them as well, using a different manuscript from Leland's (extant with his marginalia, which show a

---

[21] Leland, letter to Cromwell of 1536 in Wright, 'Dispersal of the monastic libraries' 210.

[22] Leland and Bale, *Laboryouse iourney* sig. B1r; Bale, letter to Parker of 30 July 1560 in Wright, 'Dispersal of the monastic libraries' 211.

[23] Parker, letter to Cecil of 24 January 1566 in Wright, 'Dispersal of monastic libraries' 212.

[24] For Talbot as antiquary, see Kendrick, *British antiquity* 135–6; for his Old English manuscripts, see Graham, 'Robert Talbot's "old saxonice Bede"' (Leland's borrowings noted 313n41 and 316n70); for Talbot at Norwich, see Ker, 'Medieval manuscripts from Norwich Cathedral Priory' 3.

[25] Buckalew, 'Leland's transcript of Aelfric's *Glossary*'; the transcript is printed in Leland, *De rebus Britannicis collectanea* IV:134–6.

strong interest in place-names), and at least ten other early modern transcripts and collections of extracts as well as Leland's are extant.[26] Leland's excerpts from Ælfric, together with a list of place-names from Talbot's manuscript of the *Anglo-Saxon chronicle* and a series of excerpts with a strong topographical flavour from Elyot's Latin–English dictionary, appear in his topographical notes shortly before a draft of the 'New years gift', and probably belong like it to 1544.[27] In the 'New years gift' itself, Leland announced that he intended a grand program of topographical, historical and genealogical publication based on the work of early English authors, which would not only denounce the Pope but also 'describe your moste noble realme, and . . . publysche the Maieste and the excellent actes of youre progenytours, hytherto sore obscured . . . for lack of empryntynge of such workes as lay secretely in corners'.[28] Part of the project, a *De nobilitate britannica*, would ensure that the illustrious families of the realm should be described, 'that all noble men shal clerely perceyue theyr syneal [*sc.* lyneal] parentele'.[29] Clearly he was preparing himself by his lexicographical note-taking to interpret the *inedita* to which he had access so as to publish them.

A second heritage-related activity of Leland's, the travelling that he undertook in search of manuscripts, became significant in itself: he became, rather than simply a traveller, a topographer, fascinated by the histories of places, buildings and antiquities, and fascinated in particular by their names and the origins of those names. In 1543, he enriched a poem that he had written six years previously on the occasion of the birth of the future Edward VI, *Genethliacon Edwardi*, with a long alphabetically ordered appendix on place-names which discusses the topography and toponymy of the three regions from which the royal baby's titles were taken, Cornwall, Wales and Chester. In the next year, he wrote a defence of the authenticity of King Arthur, a heroic figure with many associations with the English landscape, with a four-page appendix of ancient place-names and their modern equivalents. Then, in 1545, the year in which he transcribed Ælfric's glossary, he wrote a poem of 699 lines, *Cygnea cantio*, which expounds the topography of the Thames Valley between Oxford and London, and has an alphabetically ordered toponymic appendix

---

[26] Buckalew, 'Nowell, Lambarde and Leland' 20 (identifying Talbot's manuscript) and 26–7.

[27] The extracts from the *Chronicle* are Bodl. MS Top. gen. c. 3, pp. 194–200 (Leland, *De rebus Britannicis collectanea* IV:122–5); those from Elyot are ibid. pp. 237–50 (Leland, *De rebus Britannicis collectanea* IV:136–48), separated from the excerpts from Ælfric only by blank pages; 'The new years gift' follows ibid. p. 280 (noticed but not printed in Leland, *De rebus Britannicis collectanea* IV:168).

[28] Leland and Bale, *Laboryouse iourney* sigs. C2r, C3r [wrongly signed C.v.].   [29] Ibid. sig. E3r.

which, in the first edition, runs to sixty leaves, three times as many as the poem and the prelims put together.[30]

When Leland died in 1552, he had been in a state of incapacitating mental illness for five years. Many of his topographical writings remained unpublished until the eighteenth century. But those that had been published had an important effect. In 1561, the antiquary Laurence Nowell, a member of a Lancashire gentry family with a tradition of churchmanship (one cousin, his namesake, became Dean of Lichfield, and another became Dean of St Paul's) acquired a copy of *Cygnea cantio*.[31] He and a friend, a lawyer called William Lambarde, both made extensive marginal notes in this volume calling attention to information on place-names. This was the beginning of Nowell's career as a reader and copyist of early British manuscripts. His work on them was marked by an interest in historical toponymy, which reached its most maturely synthesized form in a set of sketch-maps of early medieval England, with Old English place-names.[32]

These make a link from toponymy to lexicography, for they are clearly related to a 'Topographical dictionarie' of which Lambarde wrote as follows in the dedication of his pioneering county history *The perambulation of Kent* (insertions in half brackets):

I had somwhile synce gathered out of diuers auncient ⌈& late⌉ hystories of this our ⌈Iland⌉ countrye, sundrye notes of suche qualitie, as might serue for the descriptio[n] & stoarie of the most famous places thorowe out this whole realme: whiche ⌈collection⌉ (by cause it was digested into Titles by ordre of Alphabet, & concerned the descriptio[n] of places) I called A Topographical Dictionarie, And out of whiche, I ment in tyme ... to drawe (as from a ⌈certein⌉ stoare house) fitte matter for eche particuler shyre ⌈& countrye⌉.[33]

These 'sundrye notes', a gazetteer of medieval England with historical notes, were eventually published as *Dictionarium Angliae topographicum et historicum* in the eighteenth century. Other work of Lambarde's done with Nowell includes his edition of Old English laws (including some *spuria*), the Αρχαιονομια [*Archaionomia*]. His sense of the Anglo-Saxon

---

[30] Leland, *Genethliacon*, with 'syllabus et interpretation antiquarum dictionum' sigs. c2r–g5r; Leland, *Assertio*, with 'elenchus antiquorum nominum' fos. 38r–39v; *Cygnea cantio*, with poem sigs. B1r–E3r (29 pages) and 'commentarii' sigs. A1r–P2v (108 pages).

[31] For Nowell's copy of *Cygnea cantio*, now BL C. 95. c. 18 (and microfilmed in the UMI series *English Printed Books 1475–1640*, reel 103), see Flower, 'Laurence Nowell' 7–8.

[32] Flower, 'Laurence Nowell' 10–11, 14ff.; for Nowell's maps, see Barber, 'A Tudor mystery', reproducing one of the maps of Anglo-Saxon England (upside down) at 20, and for more on his toponymic studies, Rosier, 'A new Old English glossary' 190–1.

[33] Lambarde, unpublished dedication of 1570 to Thomas Wotton of the *Perambulation of Kent*, reproduced Warnicke, *William Lambarde* plate 3; see also ibid. 26f.

heritage as alive in English culture has led to his being called 'an enthusiastic, almost a utopian, "Germanist"' who 'assumed that English society was essentially Anglo-Saxon in character.'[34]

In his study of Leland's alphabetically ordered discussions of place-names, and in his making of the place-name dictionary with Lambarde, Nowell was doing a kind of specialist lexicography. This was putting the cart before the horse, though, since there was no general dictionary of Old English. Ælfric's *Glossary* was nothing like a complete survey of the Old English lexicon, but readers in the decades after Leland's death had, for the most part, to use it as a dictionary or to proceed by other ingenious means. For instance, when the Cambridge don William Lisle first wanted to read religious books in Old English around 1600, he had no dictionary, and did his best for a time by learning some Dutch and German and using those languages to help him with Old English words that appeared to have no modern English descendants; then he obtained and read Gavin Douglas' translation of the *Aeneid* into Middle Scots, consulting the original Latin when he needed to elucidate a difficult passage, and found that by this means, he got 'more knowledge of that I sought than by any of the other'.[35] Turning to Scots seemed particularly reasonable to Lisle since he had a sense of Scotland as preserving an Anglo-Saxon heritage in language and in royal genealogy: at the Norman Conquest, 'many of the Saxons fled into Scotland, preseruing in that Realme vnconquered, as the line Royall [a reference to the Saxon descent of the kings of Scotland from the marriage of St Margaret, great-niece of Edward the Confessor, to Malcolm Canmore], so also the language'.[36] The route to Old English via Scots was not in fact the directest Lisle could have taken; by his time, a number of Old English texts were available in print. Of these, the *Archaionomia* had Old English and Latin on facing pages, and the Old English Gospels could be read side by side with the Vulgate. The circulation of these first printed books in Old English must have facilitated the learning of the language. But, unlike Robert and Henri Estienne's editions, they did not lead directly to the production of a printed dictionary.

They nearly did, though. In the 1560s, Nowell was at work on the first dictionary of Old English, which he called *Vocabularium saxonicum*. He

[34] For the *Archaionomia* see Sisam, *Studies in the history of Old English literature* 232–58 and Warnicke, *William Lambarde* 23f.; the criticism is by Kelley, 'History, English law and the Renaissance' 35.
[35] Lisle, 'To the readers' sig. dır, discussed Pulsiano, 'William L'isle and the editing of Old English' 177f.
[36] Lisle, 'To the readers' sig. dır.

left it incomplete when he departed for the Continent in 1567, and he never returned from his journey. The *Vocabularium* then passed into the hands of Lambarde, who made some additions to it and hoped to print it, but it was never readied for the press. In it, Nowell treated about 6500 Old English words (with a handful from early Middle English texts: the modern distinction between the two was not yet firm).[37] His definitions were quite often single words or short phrases, either in modern English, for instance 'Cyslyb. Cheesecruddes' or 'Dædbote. Penitence, ame[n]des for evle deedes', or in Latin, often that of a Latin–Old English gloss, for instance 'Dropsag [*sc.* dropfag] Stroni[us]'.[38] Some of them, though, were encyclopedic, for instance the long note on *bleostæning*, 'Mosaicke woorkes', and the shorter ones on *breostbeorh* 'The bataylementes of a walle', *corsned* 'Cursebread [consecrated bread used in a kind of trial by ordeal]', and *pund* 'A pownd in weight & in money'.[39] This is particularly true of the entries for place-names, which draw for their information on Bede and the *Anglo-Saxon chronicle*, for instance:

Dorcceaster. Dorchester besides Oxenford where the bisshoppe see wche nowe is at Lincolne was first placed by Byrine, the bisshoppe, about ao 635, who there baptised Cynegilf, first Christian king of Westsex. The see was sith translated to Lincolne in the time of William the Redde.[40]

Here, Nowell's interest in the origins of the human geography of his own England and its neighbours is apparent. The longest entry in the dictionary is that for *Ireland*, which led Nowell to remark that 'Scotland is su[m]time signified therby as likewise Irela[n]d is called Scotland & Scotia major in old writers', and to discuss the historical relationship between the Irish and the Scots.[41] From time to time he drew analogies between Anglo-Saxon culture and that of sixteenth-century Celtic Britain, in which contemporaries of his such as Edmund Spenser and Walter Raleigh also supposed ancient practices to be preserved: *heofsang* is 'Lame[n]tation ... A song of lamentation suche as Irisshe folkes use at the buriall & death of their frendes', and *ruhsco* is 'A shoo made of a rough hide suche as the Irishe, Redsha[n]kes, and Ketrickes use'.[42] Nowell's interest in histories and origins is further apparent in his handling of

---

[37] Word-count from Marckwardt, 'Sources' 23; for Middle English sources, see ibid. 27, 34–5 and also Hetherington, *Beginnings of Old English lexicography* 11–12.
[38] Nowell, *Vocabularium* 53, 57.   [39] Ibid. 40, 49, 136.
[40] Ibid. 56. For the sources of this encyclopedic information, see Marckwardt, 'Sources' 28.
[41] Nowell, *Vocabularium* 109.
[42] Ibid. 95, 140; for Spenser on Celtic culture and the archaic, see McCabe, 'Translated states' 69f., and for Raleigh, see Piggott, *Ancient Britons* 64.

etymology. He knew, for instance, that *becc* 'brook, beck' was 'Danisshe', in other words from Old Norse, and he noted a Dutch cognate in the case of *buce*: 'The belie. Flandrice, *Buke*'.[43] After translating *beor* as 'Beere. Hydromelu[m] [ve]l mulsu[m]', he brought his interest in etymology and in material culture together by observing that 'It was a kind of drinke made w[ith] hony, wherby it hath the name of the bee, for our kinde of beere was not knowen in those dayes'; in fact, *beor* means 'ale', not 'mead', but it is Nowell's desire to reconstruct the past through language that matters.[44]

As we shall see, a number of early modern scholars used the *Vocabularium* in manuscript. Even if this had not been the case, it would still be of great interest for three reasons. The first is its pioneering nature. Hardly anyone before Nowell had had access to enough manuscripts written in Old English to be able to consider forming a dictionary of the language; he was in a new position, and he took advantage of it, becoming, as Camden was to call him, 'the man who first revived the Saxon language of our ancestors in our age'.[45] Robert Talbot had, indeed, made a list of thirty-two Old English words and phrases with their Latin equivalents in a notebook as he read two chapters of Genesis and then one chapter of Orosius in Old English versions while comparing these with the Latin; but this was hardly the beginning of serious lexicography.[46]

The second interesting feature of Nowell's dictionary is that it was strongly inductive, basing its definitions on what words appeared to mean in their context. Lexicographers of Latin had of course used quotation evidence both illustratively and as a basis for inductive work, but they had a living tradition of use of the language, and a strong medieval tradition of Latin dictionaries, to draw on for many of their definitions and sense analyses, while Nowell usually had only the sources to help him. There were in fact two exceptions to his inductive procedure. First, he did occasionally write his own illustrative quotations in Old English, just as he had translated a few Latin legal texts and passages of the Latin text of Bede into Old English.[47] Second, he used Latin–Old English glosses when he could obtain them. One particular glossary gave him about two hundred and fifty of his lemmata, including one that derives from a misreading: the manuscript gives two Old English equivalents for the Latin word *crocus*, *gæle* and *geolo*, and Nowell, supposing these to be a

---

[43] Nowell, *Vocabularium* 32 (*becc*), 41 (*buce*).   [44] Ibid. 34 (Nowell's entry), 32 (Lambarde's note).
[45] Camden, *Britannia* (1590) 118, 'Laurentius Noelus, vir rara doctrina insignis, & qui Saxonicam maiorum nostrorum linguam desuetudine intermortuam, & obliuione sepultam primus nostra aetate resuscitauit'.
[46] Graham, 'Earliest Old-English word-list'.   [47] See Nowell, *Vocabularium* 9–10.

single word, made an entry for *gælegeolo* in the *Vocabularium*.[48] He used other glossarial sources, notably the *Glossary* of Ælfric.[49]

Nowell's sources included many manuscripts other than wordlists. He had access to the Lindisfarne Gospels, an outstandingly beautiful Latin Gospel-book with an interlinear Old English gloss, whose dialect he perceived to be non-West-Saxon and therefore particularly interesting (it is Northumbrian): 170 entries in the *Vocabularium* are marked as drawn from this source, and other forms that are not thus marked are to be found in no other manuscript.[50] The Alfredian translation of Orosius is cited about a hundred times, especially for exotic place-names. Here, as in the case of the Lindisfarne Gospels and some of the glossarial works, we can point with some confidence to the manuscript that Nowell must have used: in this case, a copy of the *Anglo-Saxon chronicle* which was at the time in the possession of William Bowyer, the keeper of the archives in the Tower of London, as the Lindisfarne Gospels may have been.[51] Other manuscripts used by Nowell can also be identified, as, sometimes, can the persons who preserved them and made them available to him.[52] This identification of manuscripts helps to build up a picture of Nowell's negotiations with and indebtedness to other early modern Anglo-Saxonists. He was one of a community of scholars with a shared sense of heritage and a shared sense of duty towards that heritage and its other beneficiaries.

In the third striking feature of Nowell's dictionary, his sense of heritage is again apparent. He was a Lancashire man, probably born at Whalley, in the north of the county, and probably brought up for at least part of his childhood near Eccles, in the south. He remembered some of the local vocabulary when he was working on the *Vocabularium*, and observed that some Old English words were now extinct in south-eastern England, but had living descendants in Lancashire. He supplied and marked Lancashire words in 173 entries, usually in a form like that of the entry for *hwostan*: 'To cough. Lanc., to host'.[53] Occasionally these notes extended to include

---

[48] Marckwardt, 'Sources' 33–4; see Nowell, *Vocabularium* 80.

[49] For his use of Ælfric, see Buckalew, 'Nowell, Lambarde and Leland' 22 and 36, and for other glossaries, see Marckwardt, 'Sources' 34–5.

[50] Marckwardt, 'Sources' 24, 30–1.

[51] For Nowell's use of this manuscript (now BL Cotton Tiberius B. i), see Marckwardt, 'Sources' 28–9 and for Bowyer's ownership see Tite, *Early records of Sir Robert Cotton's library* 106; for Bowyer's ownership of the Lindisfarne Gospels, see ibid. 137; for his work as archivist, see the vignette in Wernham, 'Public records in the sixteenth and seventeenth centuries' 17.

[52] E.g., Bodl. MS Hatton 38, the Hatton Gospels, owned by John Parker, from which Nowell took seventeen words (see Marckwardt, 'Sources' 24–5), or the legal manuscript which is now Cambridge, Corpus Christi College MS 383 (see ibid. 32–3).

[53] Marckwardt, 'Unnoted source of English dialect vocabulary'; Nowell, *Vocabularium* 106.

remarks on popular culture: in the entry for *sælig*, Nowell noted that 'Of *sælig* they of Lancashyre calle their cake made for [th]e choyce of king & queene the selye cake', and in that for *heordena* (sc. *heordan*), after the Latin glosses 'Naptae, stuppae', he added 'Lanc., hardes. It is the refuse of flaxe or hemp that is beate[n] out fro[m] it in the dressi[n]g'.[54] This collection of Lancashire words is one of the most substantial accumulations of English dialect material as an object of inquiry before the work of John Ray in the 1670s.

From Lambarde, the manuscript of the *Vocabularium* passed into the hands of John Joscelyn. He had clearly begun his own dictionary of Old English, the *Dictionarium saxonico–latinum*, before he had access to the *Vocabularium*, since his first explicit citations of Nowell are appended to, or, more often, written in the blank spaces of a first sequence of entries.[55] The *Dictionarium* was much larger than Nowell's work, running to about 22,000 entries and subentries, in which Old English words are generally glossed by a Latin equivalent followed by an English one.[56] Its linguistic focus was sharper, with more regular attention to the referencing of sources and to the context in which Old English words occur, and to variant forms, and less encyclopedic material. It was also founded on a wider range of sources than was available to Nowell: Joscelyn was an owner of manuscripts, travelled to see others, and had access to Parker's great collection.[57] Many of the wordlists that he compiled from his reading of individual manuscripts were transcribed into the dictionary in their correct alphabetical sequence by John Parker, whose attractive hand makes the latter part of the manuscript of the *Dictionarium saxonico–latinum* a pleasure to work with.[58] Joscelyn left his *Dictionarium* unfinished and unpublished on his death in 1605; it was, according to a later historian, encouraged by Matthew Parker, 'that ingenious Men might be the more willing to engage in the Study of this Language', and perhaps the archbishop's death in 1575 put an end to its real chances of reaching print.[59] So, despite the foresight

---

[54] Nowell, *Vocabularium* 142, 95. The note s.v. *sælig* is, according to Marckwardt ad loc., in Lambarde's hand, but must surely be from materials of Nowell's, since Lambarde had no knowledge of Lancashire.

[55] The *Dictionarium* is BL MS Cotton Titus A. xv and xvi. For its early independence from Nowell, see fo. 1v, where 'abolgen. offendit. homilia' has the last word crossed out, and followed in smaller writing by 'offendes Laur.'; at fo. 2r, the space between the entries *acænnedum* and *accunnedon* has had inserted into it the entries *accoren / accorn* and *accorn / accren*, both with the ascription 'laur'.

[56] The entry-count is mine, supported by Graham, 'John Joscelyn' 93, counting 'well over twenty thousand' and Rosier, 'Sources of John Joscelyn's Old English–Latin dictionary' 29, counting approximately 22,500.

[57] See Ker, *Catalogue* lii.   [58] For these wordlists, see Graham, 'John Joscelyn' 98–127.

[59] Strype, *Life and acts of Matthew Parker* 536.

of a few isolated figures in the reigns of Henry VIII and his elder children, and despite strong official encouragement in the reign of Elizabeth I, which had resulted in the publication of several texts in Old English and the undertaking of two dictionaries of the language, no guide to the vocabulary of Old English was generally available in the sixteenth century.

That one was wanted can be seen by looking at the work of a last Elizabethan antiquary, William Camden. As a boy in the 1560s, and as a master at Westminster School from 1575 onwards, his appetite for monuments of the past was insatiable. 'I always had my mind bent like a tensed bow on the study of antiquities', he would remember, 'and when I had a vacation, I could not help returning to those studies, and repeatedly going off to explore this or that part of England.'[60] In the year after his appointment at Westminster, Antwerp was occupied by soldiers of the king of Spain, who sacked the city in November. A number of citizens fled, one being Abraham Ortelius (Ortels, Örtel, etc.), a collector of books and antiquities and compiler of one of the most famous books of the sixteenth century, the atlas published in 1570 as *Theatrum orbis terrarum*. Ortelius had a wide range of learned acquaintances: his *album amicorum* has contributions from Christophe Plantin and a number of members of his household, including Cornelis Kiel; from other scholars and antiquaries from the Low Countries such as Goropius Becanus, Bonaventure de Smet, and Justus Lipsius; from Henri Estienne's friend Johannes Crato (with whom he corresponded, as he did with Sambucus and Sylburg) and from the polyglot lexicographer Hieronymus Megiser (another lexicographer with whom he corresponded was Nathan Chytraeus, maker of a pioneering dictionary of Low German).[61] These are all the names of continental Europeans, but Ortelius had British contacts too, such as his friend and kinsman Daniel Rogers, a widely travelled poet and diplomat.[62]

It was therefore quite natural that Ortelius' travels between 1576 and late 1577 or early 1578 should bring him to England. Rogers had in the early 1570s been interested in making an account of Roman Britain, and this interest in antiquities coincided with that of Ortelius, who had

---

[60] Camden, 'Ad lectorem' I, 'animum semper in haec [studia antiquitatis] tanquam arcum inte[n]tum habui, cum feriarer, non potui non haec studia recolere, & subinde in has vel illas Angliae partes expatiari'. Cf. Smith, 'Vita Camdeni' xii and Gibson, 'Life of Mr. Camden' sig. BIV.

[61] Alphabetical index of entries in Ortelius, *Album amicorum* 97–9. For the correspondence with Crato, see Ortelius, *Epistulae* 70 (letter 30), 131–3 (letter 58), etc.; for that with Sambucus, see ibid. 28–32 (letters 13–14) and 104–5 (letter 44); for that with Sylburg, see ibid. 425–6 (letter 175) and 436–8 (letter 181); for that with de Smet, see ibid. 305–7 (letter 131) and 528–30 (letter 220), etc.; for that with Chytraeus, see ibid. 565 (letter 238).

[62] Ortelius, *Album amicorum* fos. IV–3r.

published a plan of the ruins of a Roman fort on the coast of Holland in 1568 and a map of the Roman Empire in 1571, and would subsequently undertake an alphabetical list of the place-names in Ptolemy, a dictionary of ancient and modern place-names, a map of the British Isles in antiquity and an illustrated description of the customs of the ancient Germanic peoples.[63] If Rogers had written on Roman Britain, Ortelius would have been able to use his work as he used that of the Welsh antiquary Humphrey Llwyd.[64] However, by the time the two met in 1576, it must have been clear that Rogers was not going to produce anything usable in the foreseeable future – whereas, at Westminster, there was a learned schoolmaster with a wide knowledge of English antiquities and chorography who might be called upon instead. The meetings of Ortelius and Camden in 1577 are commemorated by an inscription in the cartographer's *album amicorum*, and by a famous passage in an autobiographical note of Camden's: 'he urged me ... to restore antiquity to Britain, and to restore Britain to its antiquity, to the best of my ability'.[65] This meant publishing a major book, and the prospect of doing so was daunting, but,

since I wanted no glory to be lacking to my dearly beloved country, I undertook it, and by no means did I neglect the most powerful tools for digging up the truth of antiquity. I provided myself with what knowledge I could of the Welsh and Anglo-Saxon languages, I travelled over by far the greater part of this realm, I carefully read and re-read the writers of the country and other historians, and I took care to have many things which seemed relevant copied from archival records.[66]

The agenda looks very much like Leland's or Aventinus' overall, but its putting the study of language in first place is a new development, as is the insight that a Celtic language and Old English together might be needed for a comprehensive survey of British antiquities. Camden was able to learn

---

[63] Karrow, *Mapmakers of the sixteenth century* 1–31 *passim* and esp. items 1/5 (*Arx Britannica*), 1/77 (map of Roman Empire), 1/J (gazetteer to Ptolemy), 1/F and 1/Q (dictionary of place-names), 1/174 (map of British Isles), 1/R (book on Germanic antiquity).

[64] For Ortelius and Llwyd, see ibid. 344–8, and for Llwyd as antiquarian see also Kendrick, *British antiquity* 136f.

[65] Ortelius, *Album amicorum* fo. 113v; Camden, 'Ad lectorem' 1, 'mecum pluribus egit ... vt Britanniae antiquitatem & suae antiquitati Britanniam quoad possem restituerem'; cf. Smith, 'Vita Camdeni' xii and Gibson, 'Life of Mr. Camden' sig. b1v.

[66] Camden, 'Ad lectorem' 1, 'Dum tamen charissimae patriae gloriae deesse nolui, rem suscepi, & illa quae ad antiquitatis veritatem eruenda[m] plurimum habent momenti neutiquam neglexi. Britannicae & Anglo-Saxonicae linguae qualemcunque scientiam mihi comparaui, partem huius regni longe maximam perlustraui, scriptores patrios, aliosque historicos studiose volui & reuolui, atque ex Archiuis plurima quae in rem videbantur mihi describenda curaui.' Cf. Smith, 'Vita Camdeni' xi and Gibson, 'Life of Mr. Camden' sigs. b1v–2r.

Welsh as a living language, but Old English was much less simple: he was, as one of his biographers put it, dealing with 'A Language that had lain dead for above four hundred years', which had 'to be reviv'd; the Books wherein it was bury'd, to be rak'd out of ashes', while '(which was yet worse) those Fragments, such as they were' were 'so very hard to be met with'.[67] He borrowed the manuscripts of Joscelyn's dictionary and grammar from the antiquary Sir Robert Cotton – and expressed the fear that all knowledge of Old English might disappear unless 'the labours of the learned Gentlemen Maister Laurence Nowell of Lincolnes Inne, who first in our time recalled the studie heereof' and of Lambarde and Joscelyn were published – but all the same, his position was difficult.[68]

The work that Camden eventually published, the *Britannia* (1586), was a substantial volume in its own right, closer in scale to Biondo's *Italia illustrata* than to the modest account of Roman Britain that Ortelius had hoped to be able to use. It grew from edition to edition until the final Latin edition of 1607 and the first English one of 1610. Although it made a major contribution to the historical study of place-names, and there is interesting etymological material in it, its importance in the history of lexicographical thought is more for the impetus that it gave to antiquarian studies in England than for its own content. This impetus was double. On the one hand, the *Britannia* gave every educated reader in the British Isles a model for thinking about the cultural heritage of the nation. On the other, it placed Britain in a larger model of European antiquities – as Stuart Piggott has said, 'it was to have a European appeal, and ... was to establish Britain as a member of that fellowship of nations who drew their strength from roots struck deep in the Roman Empire' – and so it suggested the possibility of a closer relationship between British and continental antiquarian scholarship.[69]

This possibility is partially realized in the antiquarian work in which Camden recorded his knowledge of the sixteenth-century lexicographers of Old English, the *Remaines of a greater worke concerning Britaine*, a set of discourses in English which had been composed in parallel with the *Britannia*.[70] These include an etymological dictionary of Christian names, with 407 entries; a sparser alphabetical list of place-name elements which illustrates a long essay on surnames; and, added in the second

---

[67] Gibson, 'Life of Mr. Camden' sig. b2r.
[68] For Camden's borrowings of the works by Joscelyn, see Tite, *Early records of Sir Robert Cotton's library* 57, items 75.9–10; the quotation is from Camden, *Remaines* (1605) 19–20.
[69] Piggott, 'William Camden and the *Britannia*' 43.
[70] For the relationship between the two works, see Dunn, 'General introduction' xvi–xix.

edition, an essay on 'The excellencie of the English tongue' by the Cornish antiquary Richard Carew, which begins by setting out the intention to go mad in good company: *'delirare ... cum sapientibus,* in seeking out with what comendations I may attire our English language, as *Stephanus* [i.e., Henri Estienne] hath done for the French, and diuers others for theirs'.[71] In an essay on the languages of Britain, Camden makes clear his vision of the English language as a heritage from continental ancestors in a passage whose final version is:

This English tongue is extracted, as the nation, from the Germans the most glorious of all now extant in Europe for their morall, and martiall vertues, and preseruing the libertie entire, as also for propagating their language by happie victories in *France* by the *Francs,* and *Burgundians,* in this Isle by the *English-Saxons,* in *Italie* by *Heruli,* West-*Gothes, Vandales,* and *Lombards,* in *Spaine* by the *Sueuians* and *Vandales.*[72]

Having said this, he goes on to note an exotic theory and an exotic fact. The latter is the presence of words evidently cognate with English in Busbecq's Gothic wordlist, which he explains as evidence that 'the *Saxons* our progenitours' founded colonies in the east as well as in western Europe.[73] The former puzzles him more:

I dare not yet heere affirme for the antiquitie of our language, that our great-great-great-grandsires tongue came out of *Persia,* albeit the wonderfull Linguist *Ioseph Scaliger* hath observed, *Fader, Moder, Bruder, Band,* &c. in the *Persian* tongue in the very sence as we now vse them.[74]

What we see here is the direct consequence of the application of Camden's fine intelligence to the comparative data becoming available in the work of continental scholars (as well as Busbecq and Scaliger, he cites, among others, Goropius, Kiel, Lipsius and the sixteenth-century editions of Otfrid and Willeram) together with his understanding of the non-insular linguistic heritage of English.[75] His work therefore marks a turning-point in English lexicographical thought. Before Camden met Ortelius, the study of the English linguistic heritage had been fundamentally insular. After the *Britannia* and the *Remaines,* it would scarcely be possible to maintain that insularity.

---

[71] Camden, *Remaines* (1605) 40–87 (list of Christian names), 89–139 (essay on surnames; list of place-name elements 98–103); Carew, 'Excellencie' 36.

[72] Camden, *Remaines* (1614) 20–1; cf. *Remaines* (1605) 13–14.

[73] Camden, *Remaines* (1605) 14–15; quotation at 15.   [74] Ibid. 14.

[75] Ibid. 58 (Goropius), 39, 44, 48, etc. (Kiel), 44, 71 (Lipsius), 58 (Otfrid), 39, 51, etc. (Willeram); Camden's annotated copy of the 1598 Willeram survives in the British Library, 844. k. 4. (2).

THAT LARGE GROUND OF A KINDE OF DICTIONARY: THE
HISTORY OF ENGLISH INSTITUTIONS IN
THE DICTIONARIES OF COWELL AND SPELMAN

Before Camden's *Britannia*, there had been no adequate printed treatment of the languages of Anglo-Saxon England, and after it there were a number, of two kinds. One tradition culminates in a dictionary of the Latin vocabulary of medieval English law and institutions, and will be treated in this section; the other culminates in two major dictionaries of Old English, and will be treated in the next. To examine the former, that of the lexicographical treatment of Anglo-Latin, we need to turn back to William Lambarde.

What must have been one of the most difficult conversations of Lambarde's life took place on the fourth of August, 1601, after he had given Queen Elizabeth I a written report of his work as Keeper of the Records in the Tower of London: 'his pandecta of all her rolls, bundells, membranes, and parcells that bee reposed in her Majesties Tower att London'. She looked at this, and then began to ask questions:

in the 1st page shee demanded the meaninge of *oblata, cartae, litterae clausae,* and *literae patentes. W. L.* Hee severally expounded the meaninge, and layed out the true differences of every of them, her Majestie seeminge well satisfied ... Then shee proceeded to further pages, and asked where she found cause of stay, as what *ordinationes, parliamentaria, rotulus cambii, redisseines. W. L.* Hee likewise expounded all these to theire originall diversities, which shee tooke in gratious and full satisfaction; soe her Majestie fell upon the raigne of kinge Rich. IId; sayinge, 'I am Rich. IId; knowe yee not that?'[76]

Elizabeth knew that the deposition and killing of her cousin and predecessor Richard II might furnish a precedent to her enemies, and that stories and plays about him were dangerous.[77] This understanding of the past as immediately important in contemporary statecraft arose directly out of the reading of old records, and that reading had to be informed by knowing what certain words in the records actually meant, particularly words like *parliamentaria*, on whose interpretation very sensitive questions might turn. Elizabeth had inherited a country from her sister, but to understand that inheritance fully she needed a dictionary – *faute de mieux*, a walking dictionary like Lambarde.

What she really needed, in fact, was not so much a general dictionary of medieval English as a dictionary of keywords in legal and institutional

---

[76] Warnicke, *William Lambarde* 136–7 and 163n8.
[77] See, e.g., Barroll, 'New history for Shakespeare and his time' 442–54.

history. A dictionary of English law had been published as early as the 1520s, namely John Rastell's *Expositiones terminorum legum anglorum*, which presented about a hundred and seventy technical terms, mostly of Latin or Law French origin, with explanations in Law French and English.[78] This elementary handbook, 'for yong men very necessarye', ran to many editions under various titles, and was consulted, directly or indirectly, by all subsequent lexicographers of English law. It was not, however, meant as a major scholarly dictionary; there could be no comparison between it and the great continental law dictionaries such as the 2000-page lexicon of Johannes Calvinus. Early in the reign of Elizabeth's successor, however, an English author published a law dictionary sufficiently large and learned, if not to rival Calvinus, then at least to mention his name, with due modesty, in its preface:

> The Ciuilians of other nations, haue by their mutuall industries raised this kinde of worke in their profession, to an inexpected excellencie. I haue seene many of them that haue bestowed very profitable and commendable paines therin: and lastly one *Caluinus* a Doctor of *Heidelberge*, like a laborious Bee, hath gathered from all the former, the best iuyce of their flowers, and made up a hiue full of delectable honie. And by this example would I gladly incite the learned in our common lawes and antiquities of England.[79]

This dictionary was the *Interpreter* of John Cowell, Regius Professor of Civil Law at Cambridge, published towards the end of 1607.

The *Interpreter* caused a great deal of offence in seventeenth-century England; it was the first really controversial English dictionary. Elizabeth's conversation with Lambarde suggests why this was so. Richard II had been deposed after supposing himself to be above the law, and to say 'I am Richard II' was therefore to confront the question of the relationship between Parliament, monarch and law. This question mattered deeply to Elizabeth, and mattered even more to her successor, James VI of Scotland and I of England. To simplify a complex story, although some medieval authorities suggested that, in theory, the monarch could make laws without Parliament, and was not bound by the laws of the land, it was nevertheless generally agreed that in practice laws could only be made and subsidies raised with the assent of Parliament, the latter position being identified particularly with the common-law tradition rather than with the written doctrines of civil law in which Cowell specialized.[80] One way

---

[78] For date and editions, see Devereux, *Bibliography of John Rastell* 111–12.
[79] Cowell, *Interpreter* sig. *3r.
[80] See Chrimes, 'Constitutional ideas' 479–80 and Burgess, *Politics of the ancient constitution* 139–78, esp. (on Cowell) 149–52.

to deal with this apparent contradiction would be to describe the authority of the king as duplex: distinguishing his 'ordinary prerogative', which was 'coterminous with the common law', and his 'absolute prerogative', which 'was exercised in spheres where the common law did not hold sway (the church, international affairs) or where the common law left room for the king to act of his own will (the power of coining money, for example)'.[81] Cowell, however, saw the question not as one of duplex authority but as one of ambiguity, and he was inclined to resolve this ambiguity in the direction of the theoretical absolute power of the monarch. So, in his entry for *king*, he wrote that 'he is aboue the Law by his absolute power'.[82] Turning to *parliament*, he observed that 'of these two one must needes be true, that either the king is aboue the Parlament, that is, the positiue lawes of his kingdome, or els that he is not an absolute king ... simply to binde the prince to or by these lawes, weare repugnant to the nature and constitution of an absolute monarchy'.[83] A few other passages in the dictionary had similar implications.[84]

There was no reaction to the *Interpreter's* treatment of monarchical power for two years after its publication. It is not surprising that the objectionable passages should have escaped notice at first; they add up to a few sentences in a dictionary of 584 double-column quarto pages.[85] However, at the end of February 1610, the wit and lawyer John Hoskyns brought them to the attention of Parliament, which had been engaged in a struggle with the government over royal revenues. His aim was no doubt partly to embarrass the king by the public censure of an indiscreet overstatement of the nature of royal prerogative.[86] By the first of March, Cowell had been summoned from Cambridge to London to defend himself: a letter of that date records:

Those of the Lower House have been very much nettled and offended at one Doctor Cowell's Booke, for a certain exorbitant Position therein held by him in the interpretation and in favour of the Kings Prerogative ... Which hath been so odious to the House, that if the King will give them leave ... to proceed by their authority against the said Cowell, it is thought they will go very near to hang him.[87]

In the end, Cowell escaped hanging, but he endured a short term of imprisonment. He also found his dictionary censured, not only by Parliament

---

[81] Burgess, *Politics of the ancient constitution* 161.   [82] Cowell, *Interpreter* s.v. *king*, sig. Qq1r.
[83] Ibid. s.v. *parliament*, sig. Aaa3v.   [84] They are excerpted in Chrimes, 'Constitutional ideas' 483–7.
[85] But cf. ibid. 465–6.   [86] Ibid. 466ff.
[87] J. Beaulieu, letter to William Trumbull, 1 March 1610, quoted ibid. 469n3.

but by a royal proclamation, which ingeniously accused it of being derogatory both to Parliament and to the Crown, on the grounds that it both undervalued the powers of Parliament and meddled impertinently with the mysteries of royal authority:

vpon that large ground of a kinde of Dictionary (as it were) following the Alphabet, hauing all kind of purposes belonging to Gouernment and Monarchy in his way, by medling in matters aboue his reach, hee hath fallen in many things to mistake and deceiue himselfe: In some things disputing so nicely vpon the mysteries of this our Monarchie, that it may receiue doubtfull interpretations ... In other cases mistaking the true state of the Parliament of this Kingdome, and the fundamentall Constitutions and priuiledges therof.[88]

The proclamation went on to prohibit the sale of the *Interpreter*, and demanded that all copies should be surrendered by their owners to the appropriate authorities. The political writer and economist Roger Coke, looking back to this episode at the end of the century, remarked bitterly that 'the King ... promised to call in these Books by Proclamation, as he did, but they were out, and the Proclamation could not call them in, but only served to make them more taken notice of'.[89] In 1613, the book was rare enough for a complete transcript to be made by someone with access to a copy; he had it interleaved with blank sheets, and must therefore have been planning to expand the work or comment substantially on it.[90]

In 1637, two paginal reprints of the *Interpreter* were published by one William Sheares, with the controversial material intact.[91] This was to be seen as an act of absolutist propaganda, and was to have grave repercussions. For when William Laud, the archbishop of Canterbury, who was closely associated with the absolutist tendencies of the personal rule of Charles I, was put on trial for high treason in 1644, his alleged sponsorship of a republished *Interpreter* was made one of the charges against him. It was claimed that the book had been printed by a client of Laud's, one Richard Hodgkinsonne, who had gone to work 'in a close house without Licence', and that Laud had failed to respond adequately to complaints about the reprinting as it was in progress. Sheares had already been in trouble for surreptitious printing, and the fact that he

---

[88] 'Proclamation touching D. *Cowels* booke called the Interpreter' 226.
[89] Coke, *Detection of the court and state of England* 50–1.
[90] Now Cambridge, St John's College, MS I. 32: see Moore, *Primary materials* 3, and the fuller description in St John's College, 'Catalogue of post-medieval manuscripts'.
[91] The Hodgkinsonne edition is *STC* 5902; the Mathewes edition is *STC* 5901. Sheets from the two are sometimes mixed.

actually employed two printers, Hodgkinsonne and Augustine Mathewes, to produce editions of the *Interpreter* for him simultaneously in 1637 suggests that he was working in haste and secrecy.[92] Bad as this looked, the archbishop answered every point as best he could, adding that there could not be any danger 'in the Printing of that Book to mislead any Man: Because it was generally made known by Proclamation, that it was a Book Condemned, and in such Particulars: But for other things the Book very useful'.[93] The fact that having sponsored a reprint of a dictionary nearly thirty years old should have been made a charge in a capital trial (and Laud was duly found guilty and put to death) is remarkable.

Laud's point that the reputation of the *Interpreter* was a matter of common knowledge, and that readers would therefore not be likely to accept its absolutist statements as the uncontroversial opinion of the learned, was a fair one. Readers were doubtless well aware in the 1630s that the dictionary had been found objectionable, and they continued to be. So, for instance, the printed report of a case of early 1648 in which the definition of the phrase *free chapel* became important notes that Cowell's thoughts on the matter are beside the point, 'for *Cowel* he is not fit to be cited, for his book was condemned by Parliament, and burnt as errone- ous, and scandalous'; this report was cited by an annotator of a copy of the *Interpreter*, who wrote at the entry for *parliament* that 'For y^s & such another passage tit. King ys book was condem'nd by Parliam^t & burnt.'[94] Another annotator, the dissident MP Sir Roger Twysden, had his copy interleaved, so that it is now bound in three volumes, enriched with material that he copied from printed editions of authorities for the early history of England and from manuscripts from his own library and from Cotton's.[95] Twysden's notes amount to a dictionary in their own right, with a different tenor and different concerns from those of the *Interpreter*. They often take off from the headwords of brief, uncontroversial entries,

---

[92] For Sheares' brush with authority before 1644, see Mendle, 'De facto freedom' 316–17.

[93] *History of the troubles and tryal of William Laud* 235–6.

[94] *Narrationes modernae* 82, citing Cowell, *Interpreter* (1607) sig. N4r (s.v. *chapel*); the marginalium (referring to 'Sty'. R. 82.' = Styles, *Reports* 82) is in the BL copy 507. d. 15 of the 1637 edition.

[95] Now British Library MSS Add. 24281–24283; fo. 1r cites manuscript collections of Edward Coke's, copied by 'my uncle Heneage' (Sir Heneage Finch, Speaker of the House of Commons) and editions including 'Matthew of Westminster', *Florilegus* (1570); Matthew Paris, *Historia maior* (1571); *Rerum Anglicarum scriptores post Bedam praecipui* (1596), and *Historiae normannorum scriptores antiqui* (1619). For Twysden's use of Cottonian manuscripts see Tite, *Early records of Sir Robert Cotton's library* 110, 156, 218.

such as that for *libertas*, where Twysden's remarks on liberty go far beyond Cowell's discussion of one technical sense of the word:

in what this *liberty, fraunchise*, and *Right* doth consist seemeth to me to be well worth yᵉ inquyry of some lerned man, I conceiue none will doubt the beelonging of them to bee eyther Pryueledges yᵗ perteyn to yᵉ body or goods of yᵉ subject, and both of them to bee so freede by yᵉ Lawes of it . . . yᵗ yᵉ King can not ad libitum suum leges mutare regni sui [change the laws of his kingdom at will]. see verb. *King* et *Parliament*.[96]

Here, Twysden's supplementation of Cowell is acute: he sees that the word *liberty* is a controversial one that calls, especially where the liberty of the subject is being set up against the authority of the governing power, for careful definition. This point appears to have passed Cowell by or to have seemed unimportant to him, just as it would to Samuel Johnson, whose dictionary of 1755 distinguishes liberty from the state of being enslaved or the state of being subject to necessity, but not from the state of being subject to arbitrary power.[97] Elsewhere, Twysden's annotations are equally interesting, for instance in the eleven columns of notes on the entry *parliament*, or in his reflections on the king's right to levy armies at the entry *armour*, or in his conclusion at the entry *prerogatiue* that 'yᵉ Kyng by Proclamation can create no offence wch was not one beefore, for then he might alter yᵉ Law . . . yᵉ Law of England is deuyded in to 3 parts *Common Law, statute law*, and *custome*, and yᵉ Proclamations of yᵉ Kyng are no part of them'.[98]

Owners of a number of extant copies of the successive editions of the *Interpreter* (of which there were six, from 1658 to 1727) likewise improved them by annotation. Books such as Thomas Tanner's copy of the 1701 edition, given to him by its editor, the antiquary and lexicographer White Kennett, and annotated by him with material from texts such as Rymer's *Foedera* and Thoresby's *Ducatus Leodiensis*, take the story of the *Interpreter* into the world of eighteenth-century antiquarianism, where this study cannot follow it.[99] Their existence makes it clear that Cowell's work has an importance beyond the controversies that arose from its first two editions: its maker's careful study of the language of medieval documents entitles him to be thought of as an antiquary like Tanner and Kennett, not simply as a political thinker. The Anglo-Saxonist Abraham Wheelock recognized him as such, giving him honourable mention in the company of such men as Lambarde, Leland and their successors.[100]

[96] BL Add MS 24282 fo. 128v.   [97] Smith, *Politics of language 1791–1819* 14ff.
[98] BL Add MS 24283 fo. 17r.
[99] Tanner's copy is Bodl. A 4. 5 Jur, citing Thoresby at sig. M4r and Rymer at sig. N1v; for Kennett and lexicography, see, e.g., Harris, *Chorus of grammars* 50.
[100] In Bede, *Historiae ecclesiasticae gentis anglorum libri* sig. B1v.

The scope of a rather different kind of dictionary of early English words, a glossary of post-classical Latin from English sources, published in 1626, is suggested by its long title, which can be translated:

Archaeologus: in the form of a glossary to post-classical antiquities, including Latino-barbarous words, loanwords, obsolete words, or Latin words used in non-classical senses, which occur in ecclesiastical and secular writers (including the ancient law-codes of various peoples, and charters and legal formulae) after the conquests of Europe by the Goths and Vandals, and illustrated with notes and commentaries in which many rites, magistracies, dignities, honours, offices, cultural phenomena, laws, and customs are expounded.[101]

Its author acknowledged a substantial debt to Cowell.[102] Unlike Cowell, however, he was not an academic but a private gentleman, Sir Henry Spelman.

Spelman has been called 'one of the main founders of English philological studies', not only on account of his lexicography and his contributions to Anglo-Saxon studies (not least the endowment of an Anglo-Saxon praelectorship at Cambridge) but also on account of his work as the editor of the records of the ecclesiastical councils and synods held in the British Isles, and as one of the principal rediscoverers of feudalism as an element in English legal and institutional history.[103] His background was rather like Guillaume Budé's, opsimathy and all. He was a member of a highly respectable gentry family with a strong legal tradition, who took up his most serious studies late in life, 'at the borders of old age', as he put it.[104] He went up to Cambridge in 1580, at the age of fifteen, when, as he later realized, he was still 'entirely unfitted for academic discipline'.[105] His father's death in the following year disrupted his studies. He inherited money from his father and, after taking his degree at Cambridge and spending three years at the Inns of Court, married an heiress, but his

---

[101] Spelman, *Archaeologus*, title-page, 'Archaeologus: in modum glossarii ad rem antiquam posteriorem, continentis latino-barbara, peregrina, obsoleta, et nouatae significationis vocabula, quae post labefactatas a Gothis Vandalisq[ue] res Europaeas, in ecclesiasticis profanisq[ue] scriptoribus, variarum item gentium legibus antiquis, chartis et formulis occurrunt, scholiis et commentariis illustrata, in quibus prisci ritus quam plurimi, magistratus, dignitates, munera, officia, mores, leges, et consuetudines en[a]rrantur.'

[102] Spelman, *Archaeologus* sig. π3r; cf. Pocock, *Ancient constitution* 91–2.

[103] For Spelman and English philology see Cronne, 'Study and use of charters by English scholars in the seventeenth century' 77 and for the Cambridge praelectorship see Lutz, 'Study of the Anglo-Saxon chronicle in the seventeenth century' 34–41; for his work on the councils and on feudalism, see respectively Powicke, 'Sir Henry Spelman and the "Concilia"' 351 and 355–67, and Pocock, *Ancient constitution* 91–123.

[104] Spelman, *Archaeologus* sig. π2r, 'ad senectutis confinia'.

[105] Ibid. 'Non dum xv. annorum puer e schola rapior Cantabrigiam: tenellus adhuc et Academicae disciplinae omnino inidoneus.'

wealth, although it enabled him to collect some interesting manuscripts (including an Old English glossed psalter, a copy of *Piers Plowman*, and, from his own day, an important collection of the poems of Donne), did not set him free for scholarly work.[106] Rather, he found himself oppressed by the business of a rich gentleman's life: property dealings, litigation, land management, a seat in Parliament, the high sheriffship of Norfolk, and more.

He was, however, able to spend some time studying, and to become with Camden one of the founding members of the Society of Antiquaries, a body whose members met to read each other papers on aspects of English cultural history, with an emphasis on philological methods and on the history of institutions: 'The Etymologie, Antiquity and Privilege of Castles' and the like.[107] Its other members included William Bowyer's son Robert, Richard Carew, William Lambarde and Sir Robert Cotton, who presented the paper on castles, and whose growing collection of manuscripts made him, as the years went by, able to comment with increasing authority on the history of English institutions – hence the closure of his library by royal order in 1629.[108] Spelman was one of a group who sought to revive its meetings in 1614 after they had lapsed for some years, a project which proved abortive because 'his Majesty took a little mislike of our Society, not being enform'd, that we had resolv'd to decline all matters of State'.[109]

Spelman's early but posthumously printed account of the history of heraldry may belong to the period of the regular meetings of the Society of Antiquaries.[110] His first printed publication, however, only appeared in the year before he hoped to revive the society. It was a treatise called

[106] For the psalter, now BL MS Stowe 2, see Ker, *Catalogue* 336–7 (item 271); for some of the other manuscripts, see *Bibliotheca selectissima: being the library of the late Sir Edmund King* 55–60, Macray, 'Manuscripts of the late John Henry Gurney', esp. 116 and 135, and Powicke, 'Sir Henry Spelman and the "Concilia"' 352–3 and 373–4; for the Donne manuscript, see Robinson, 'Seventeenth century miscellany'.

[107] For the society, see DeCoursey, 'Society of Antiquaries'; for the paper on castles, Hearne, *Collection of curious discourses* 166–73.

[108] See Sharpe, *Sir Robert Cotton*, esp. 48–83.

[109] Spelman, *Reliquiae Spelmannianae* 70; for the wording, cf. Van Norden, 'Sir Henry Spelman on the chronology of the Elizabethan College of Antiquaries' 155–6.

[110] Spelman, *Aspilogia* (1654): described A3v as 'non recentes sed aliquot ante annos sub odolescentiae [sc. adolescentiae] flore scriptas'. This statement is from Spelman's own dedicatory epistle, which must, since it belongs with the fomal co-dedication to Henry Howard as Earl of Northampton at sig. A3r, belong to the period 1604–14; the co-dedication to Philip Howard [attainted 1589] as Earl of Arundel is a scribal or compositorial blunder for Thomas Howard [restored to the earldom 1604]). The (holograph?) manuscript, Sleepy Hollow, NY: Rockefeller Archive Center, Rockefeller Family Archives, John D. Rockefeller, Jr., personal papers box 64, is undated, according to the online catalogue of the archive.

De non temerandis ecclesiis, addressed to his uncle Francis Sanders, which argued against the lay impropriation of church lands (Sanders was himself an impropriator, and Spelman had acquired the leases of two abbeys and been oppressed by a Chancery suit relating to them).[111] He referred in its preface to 'a greater Worke (much of the same Argument)' which he had written, and he continued to work on the topic for another twenty years, annotating a copy of *De non temerandis* and gathering further material, some of which was published posthumously.[112]

The history of the sacrilegious possession of church lands was only a part of the topic that engaged Spelman for much of his life, the history of landholding and law in general. For him, as for Lambarde and Cowell, the serious study of law entailed the study of old words. Coming across many *'strange* and *obsolete*' words in his reading of the texts that interested him, he decided to work on their interpretation: whenever he met such a word, he

set it down in it's proper order; with a distinct reference to the place: till by degrees he had collected a variety of instances, and by comparing ... was able to give a tolerable conjecture at the true signification ... [at last,] he began to digest his materials; and from the several quotations, to draw a judgement of the strict acceptation of each word, in the respective Ages wherein it was used.[113]

Although he did not claim to have begun reading seriously for his dictionary until around 1613, he had, by the end of 1616, advanced far enough in his work for one of its ideal potential readers, the German historian of law Friedrich Lindenbrog, to be excited by the prospect of its completion, and to suggest applying for an Imperial privilege to protect the work against unauthorized reprintings, perhaps thinking in particular of the unauthorized Wechel reprint of the *Rerum anglicarum scriptores* which had been edited by Sir Henry Savile.[114] His expectation that Spelman's big dictionary would be a natural target for unauthorized reprintings is a reminder of the attractiveness and importance of its subject to contemporaries in continental Europe as well as in England: nobody would pirate an unsaleable book.

[111] Spelman, *De non temerandis ecclesiis*; epistle to Sanders sigs. A3r–4r; For Spelman's abbeys, see Cronne, 'Study and use of charters by English scholars in the seventeenth century' 78.

[112] Spelman, *De non temerandis ecclesiis* sig. A2v; the annotated copy is British Library 875. b. 5 (1), filmed in the UMI series *English Printed Books, 1475–1640*, reel 2051 item 4; the posthumously published material appeared in 1698 as Spelman, *The history and fate of sacrilege ... wrote in the year 1632*; some of Spelman's manuscript collections for the work are in fact dated as late as 1634 (Macray, 'Manuscripts of the late John Henry Gurney' 135–6).

[113] Gibson, 'Life of Sir Henry Spelman' sigs. b2v–b3r.

[114] Bodl. MS Tanner 89, fo. 110r, letter from Lindenbrog to Spelman, 1 November 1616; a draft of such a privilege, in Lindenbrog's hand, is BL MS Add 34 599, fo. 73.

Lindenbrog's excitement at the dictionary project can be parallelled elsewhere in Spelman's correspondence. In 1619, he had been put in touch by Camden with Nicolas Fabri de Peiresc, who was apparently intrigued by the likeness of Spelman's coat of arms to that of his mother's family. Peiresc, like Spelman, was a gentleman, who had inherited substantial wealth, and was a member of a parliament (the *parlement* of Provence), and a trained lawyer. He was immensely learned, and a great correspondent with other learned persons; like his friend Robert Cotton and the members of the Society of Antiquaries, he was particularly interested in the collection and study of historical documents that bore on contemporary politics and society.[115] His correspondence with Spelman came at a point at which the dictionary project was moving slowly, and it is conceivable that Camden had suggested to Peiresc that a gentlemanly enquiry about the origins of coats of arms might encourage Spelman to start discussing his dictionary with one particularly well qualified to encourage it. Be that as it may, in the summer of 1619, Spelman's son Henry went on a tour of Europe and visited Peiresc, bringing with him not only genealogical material but also 'the first twenty quires' of the *Archaeologus*.[116] Peiresc showed the sample almost at once to four persons who he knew would be interested in it, and, in September, sent their observations to Spelman via Camden.[117] These showed, as Camden wrote in a covering letter when he sent them on to Spelman, 'wth what approbation yor *Glossary* was deseruedly applauded by *Peiresc, Bignon, Mausacus, Galminus* and *Rigaltius* the kinges Bibliothecarie, whoe desirously expect the edition thereof, as I my selfe and other your lo[uin]ge frendes here'.[118]

The letters in question did indeed show approbation. Everyone to whom Peiresc had shown his specimen had 'found such precious observations there, that they have not been able to put the book down and stop wondering at it'.[119] Philippe Jacques de Maussac, counsellor to the senate at Toulouse and editor of the *Lexicon* of Harpocration and of Michael Psellus' *De lapidum virtutibus*, had admired it and shown it to Gilbert

---

[115] See Miller, *Peiresc's Europe* 76–101.

[116] Peiresc, letter to Camden, 11 September 1628, quoted in Miller, *Peiresc's Europe* 200n86, 'l'autheur m'a envoyé les 20 premiers cahiers plus de dix ans y a'; the reference by Jérôme Bignon (see n121 below) to an 'exiguum ... specimen' and his criticisms only of the entries *abbas, abiectire, acceptor, adeling* and *adiective* suggest that Peiresc may have shown him a smaller sample.

[117] For the correspondence described here, see Van Norden, 'Peiresc and the English Scholars'.

[118] Camden, letter to Spelman, 19 September 1619, Bodl. MS Tanner 89, fo. 111r.

[119] Peiresc, letter to Camden, [September 1619], Bodl. MS Tanner 89, fo. 111v, 'ils ont troue de si rares obseruations qu'ils ne se pourront lasser de les veor et admirer'.

Gaulmyn. The latter, a lawyer, poet, orientalist and translator into Latin of such Byzantine texts as Psellus on demons and a biography of Moses, made suitably appreciative remarks about the work of 'that most noble knight, Henry Spelman, a hard-working man and, by Jove, a learned one'.[120] Jérôme Bignon, editor of the Merovingian formulary of Marculfus and author of a text on the divine right of kings, remarked in the course of a long and careful assessment that even such a short specimen demonstrated the excellence of the forthcoming book, and concluded that 'this glossary is a most beautiful and most useful piece ... you have made my mouth water with this specimen of the whole work, and I hunger avidly for the rest'.[121] The Latinist and Byzantinist Nicolas Rigault agreed that the completion of the work was much to be desired: 'the author must be urged to proceed with publication'.[122] Salmasius appears to have seen the sample a little later, and to have been greatly impressed by it.[123] Spelman was also encouraged in his work by closer neighbours. Robert Cotton lent him manuscripts, including Joscelyn's Old English grammar and dictionary.[124] John Selden annotated his presentation copy warmly 'A gift from the author, that most eminent and most learned man, a most dear friend'.[125]

The first part of the *Archaeologus* finally appeared in 1626, as a folio of 452 pages, covering about 1100 headwords in the range A–L. The complete dictionary was printed posthumously from Spelman's papers – the treatment of the latter part of the alphabet is therefore less polished than that of the former – as a folio of 576 pages and about 2400 headwords, prepared for the press under the title *Glossarium archaiologicum*.[126] The

---

[120] Gaulmyn, letter to Peiresc, [1619], BL MS Add. 34599, fo. 56r (copied BL MS Add. 34599, fo. 57r, and Bodl. MS Tanner 89, fo. 112r), 'Philippus Maussacus ... ostendit mihi Glossarium magna Industria & Immenso Labore scriptum Ab henrico Spelmanno nobilissimo Equite – Et Docto (Juppiter) ac Laborioso.'

[121] Bignon, letter to Peiresc, 31 August 1619, BL MS Add. 34599, fos. 51v–52r (copied Bodl. MS Tanner 89, fos. 114v and 115r), 'Exiguum quidem specimen operis sui vidi, sed ex quo (vt ex pedis Herculei planta, totius magnitudinem corporis metiri facile fuit) satis pateat libri genius ... Vt vno tandem verbo absoluam pulcherrimum est istud Glossarium atq[ue] utilissimum. Sane hoc specimine de toto opere mouisti saliuam, Doctissime Fabrici. Auide reliqua appeto.'

[122] Rigault, letter to Peiresc, [1619], Bodl. MS Tanner 89, fo. 116r, 'Il faut exciter l'auteur de continuer l'edition.'

[123] Van Norden, 'Peiresc and the English scholars' 382–3.

[124] Tite, *Early records of Sir Robert Cotton's library* 49, items 46.6–7.

[125] Bodl. O. 2. 18 Art. Seld., presented 12 May 1627, and inscribed with Selden's motto and the words 'Ex dono Viri clarissimi, doctissimi, amicissimi, autoris'.

[126] Some of the papers from which it was printed are Bodl. MS e Musaeo 48, fos. 5r–250v, materials for the range A–L (marked up from the 1626 edition: see Moore, *Primary materials* 32 and plates 48–9) and fos. 252r–592v, materials for the range M–Riota (manuscript: see Moore, *Primary materials* 24).

change in title from *Archaeologus* to *Glossarium archaiologicum* continued a debate that Spelman had conducted with himself before publication. Around 1619 he seems to have been circulating his specimen with the title *Glossary*. That is the word that Camden used of it in that year, and Peiresc and his circle generally referred to it as *glossarium*; Bignon called it *Glossarium archaeonomicum*, echoing the title of Lambarde's *Archaionomia* and implying that it was fundamentally concerned with legal words. It was in fact, as Maussac pointed out, much more than a glossary, and it was concerned with much more than the law.[127] Greek ἀρχαιολογία is used in Plato to mean the study of, *inter alia*, 'the genealogies of heroes and men, the traditions on the foundations of cities and the lists of eponymous magistrates of a city', and in later authors, such as Josephus and Dionysius of Halicarnassus, it appears as the title of historical works – hence the first occurrence of English *archaeology*, in a reference of 1607 to the Byzantine historian Sozomenos as writing 'all the Archaiology of the Iewes till SAVLS gouernment'.[128] So, the word *archaeologus* means 'the ancient historian' or 'the antiquary', and Spelman meant it to announce an interest not so much in language as in history: not the kind of history that is done by digging things up (this sense of words in *archaeol-* only developed in the eighteenth century), but the kind that is done by reading carefully.[129] An admirer of the book called its author 'Varro Anglicanus', identifying him as, like Budé, expert both in language and in antiquities.[130]

But the *Archaeologus* is no less a dictionary for its antiquarian content. Spelman's own statement that 'it was not so much my intention to provide a glossary to post-classical antiquity as to provide (to the best of my ability) wide-ranging commentaries' simply shows that his lexicographical practice was ahead of his theory: he had made a rich and discursive dictionary, but regarded the word *glossaria* as properly restricted to less discursive wordlists with greater entry-counts.[131] In fact,

---

[127] Maussac, letter to Peiresc, [after 5 September 1619], BL Add MS 34599, fo. 54r.

[128] For the Greek word, see Momigliano, 'Ancient history and the antiquarian' 287–8; the English attestation, the first cited in *OED*, is Hall, *Holy obseruations* sig. G3r.

[129] The change in the sense of the English word seems to have taken place in two stages: as early as 1707, Sir Robert Sibbald referred in his *Historical inquiries* sig. a2r to 'Archeologie, that is the Explication and Discovery of Ancient Monuments', but the restricted sense 'enquiry into the past carried out *by excavation*' was still emerging in, e.g., Thomas Warton, *Specimen of a history of Oxfordshire* (1783) vi, referring to the study of 'coins, pavements, barrows, fosses, roads, sepulchral utensils, and circumvallations' as 'our British, Roman, and Dano-Saxon archaeology' and Robert Bage's novel *Mount Henneth* (1788) 82, in which a 'Hall of Archaeology' contains the collection of coins, urns, mosaic pavements and other antiquities for which the owner 'has ransacked Wales'.

[130] Quoted Powicke, 'Sir Henry Spelman' 355.

[131] Spelman, *Archaeologus* sig. π3v, 'Cum nostri instituti esset, non tam Glossarium ad rem antiquam posteriorem, quam generales (prout potuimus) commentarios dare.'

when fullness of treatment rather than entry-count is considered, it can be argued that no dictionary of any of the language varieties of England had ever been undertaken on anything like this scale. Some of its entries were substantial essays in their own right: for instance, *heraldus* ran to nearly twenty-one columns, and *iustitia* to more than thirty-seven. *Feodum* was shorter than these at a little over fourteen columns, but had in it the nucleus of Spelman's extremely important discovery – perhaps a result of his correspondence with Peiresc – that the system of hereditary feudal tenures on which English land law was based was of Norman origin, not part of a supposedly immemorial common law.[132] A challenge to this analysis led to Spelman's writing a fuller version, the posthumously published 'Treatise of feuds and tenures by knight-service in England', and the fact that the dictionary entry could develop into a short monograph suggests its richness.[133] Indeed, Edmund Gibson, looking back on Spelman's dictionary at the end of the century, saw it as in large part a collection of 'discourses', like those of the Society of Antiquaries, observing that the second part was 'little more than a collection of Materials, out of which he intended to compose such Discourses, as he has all along given us in the First Part, under the words that are most remarkable.[134]

The fact that some of the entries were so extensive meant that, where they handled politically sensitive subjects, they could – again like the proceedings of the antiquaries – be dangerously explicit. 'I have heard it affirm'd', noted Gibson, 'that he stopped at the Letter *M*. because he had said some things under *Magna Charta*, and *Magnum Consilium*, that his Friends were afraid might give offence.'[135] Writing about the full *Glossarium* of 1664, Gibson felt it necessary to deny the claim that its editor had 'inserted many things of his own, that were not in Sir *Henry Spelman's* Copy; and particularly, some passages which tend to the enlargement of the *Prerogative* in opposition to the *Liberties* of the Subject'.[136] This claim had been made, for instance, by the Oxford don Obadiah Walker with reference to the entry *parliamentum*.[137] Walker was wrong in this respect – the text of the printed entry for *parliamentum* all corresponds with material in Spelman's own hand in the manuscript – but he was right to see the book as ideologically

[132] See Pocock, *Ancient constitution* 97–100, and cf. Pocock, 'Ancient constitution revisited' 280–1.
[133] Spelman, *Reliquiae Spelmannianae* 1–46, discussed Pocock, *Ancient constitution* 100–2.
[134] Gibson, 'Life of Sir Henry Spelman' sig. c1r.   [135] Ibid. sig. b3v.
[136] Ibid. sig. b4r; cf. Nicolson, *English historical library* 1:105–6.
[137] William Petyt, letter to a member of Queen's College, Oxford, 19 March 1676, in Macray, 'Manuscripts in the Inner Temple library' 244.

sensitive.[138] At about the time that Walker was arguing that material had been smuggled into it, and indeed projecting a new edition, a country gentleman called George Evelyn was telling a friend that 'the Licenser had dashed out a great part of the Epistle Dedicatory prefixed to his [i.e., Spelman's] Collection of Councils reflecting a little on Bishop Laud's designs of hierarchy, but ... he never complained of any injury done to him with respect to his Glossaries'.[139] So for Walker, Spelman's lexicographical work looked as if it had been made a vehicle for political propaganda, and Evelyn's friend appears to have asked whether it had been a target for censorship. For neither was it simply a neutral record of words.

Spelman's preface to the *Archaeologus* was, however, more a personal document than a political manifesto. He dedicated the book to 'God, the Church, and the Republic of Letters; as a suppliant in all humility, and with the protestation that additions, retractions, corrections and improvements shall be made to this work as far as shall be possible and shall on consideration appear appropriate'.[140] This modesty shaded into the heroic image of the dangerous voyage: lacking at one point knowledge and at another good judgement, 'here I am checked, uncertain, among the dangerous shoals; there I go out of my way and am dashed against the cliffs'.[141] Elsewhere in the preface, Spelman presented himself as a figure like Oedipus (in his capacity as solver of riddles), and as an Aeneas on the way to the underworld, recalling Henri Estienne's self-presentation as a conflation of Aeneas and Brutus: Bignon, Joannes Meursius and Lindenbrog had 'often proffered me the Golden Bough on my journeys into those Tartarean regions'.[142] He was, likewise, to see the lexicography of Old English as a matter of speaking with the dead, writing in a letter to the Dutch philologist Jan de Laet that he was glad that they would work

---

[138] Cf. Bodl. MS e Musaeo 48, fo. 471r, with Spelman, *Glossarium archaiologicum* (1664) s.v. *parliamentum*; some material in the manuscript is in Sir William Dugdale's hand, e.g., the definition of *mina* at fo. 358r, but this tends to be brief and uncontroversial, probably simply copied from loose slips of Spelman's which might otherwise have gone astray.

[139] For Walker's project, see Petyt in Macray, 'Manuscripts in the Inner Temple library' 244; for censorship, see Evelyn, letter to Roger James, 7 August 1676, ibid. 239. Spelman did indeed have trouble producing an acceptable text of the dedication to the *Concilia*: see BL MS Add. 34600 fos. 133ff., esp. 139–44 (first draft), 146–51 (second draft), 153–9 (third draft), and Powicke, 'Sir Henry Spelman and the "Concilia"' 362.

[140] Spelman, *Archaeologus* sig. πīv, 'Deo, Ecclesiae, Literarum Reipub[licae] sub Protestatione de addendo, retrahendo, corrigendo, poliendo, prout opus fuerit et consultius Videbitur ... Henricus Spelmannus omni supplex humilitate, D[ono] D[edit]'.

[141] Ibid. sig. π2r, 'hic inter syrtes dubius haero, illic deuius ad scopulos allidor'.

[142] Ibid. sig. π3r, 'saepe mihi ramum aureum ad tartareas istas regiones peragrandas, porrexerunt *Bignonius, Meursius, Lindenbrogius*.'

together 'to recall our obsolete Saxon language from its ashes, and to display it as best we can when we have brought it back to life'.[143] In the next sentence, he continued: 'I may say, with the poet, "why can we not join hand to hand, and hear words and exchange words" – "words", I say, meaning the ancient Saxon ones whose right interpretation I desire to hear from you.'[144]

The text he quotes is a melancholy one: the speaker is Aeneas on the shore near Carthage, calling to his mother Venus, who has appeared to him first in disguise and then momentarily in her full splendour, and is now leaving him distraught and exiled, cut off both from paternal and maternal heritage, unable to hear the words he desires to hear. Despite his awareness of its importance to his enquiries, Spelman 'never perfectly conquer'd' Old English.[145]

Although Spelman was cut off from the full enjoyment of Old English, he had access by other means to the Anglo-Saxon heritage – for instance, by the consideration of topography and toponymy. This naturally occurs in the *Archaeologus*, as in the entry for *heda* or *hitha* (more recently *hithe*, *hythe*), which Spelman glosses as *portus* 'wharf', noting that the Domesday Book says of the royal estate at Dartford in Kent that 'here are two *hede*, that is, wharves', and then adding that medieval place-names such as *Lamb-hith* and *Quene-hith* (modern Lambeth and Queenhythe) all have the same word as their final element.[146] Such entries show Spelman's place in the tradition of interplay between topography and lexicography that goes back to Lambarde, Nowell and Leland. It is no wonder that Camden had been such an enthusiastic supporter of the *Archaeologus* project, for its aims were evidently Camdenesque, and indeed its procedure was analogous to that of the *Britannia* – whereas Camden used the chorographical survey as a means by which to structure a large and varied body of factual knowledge about the past, Spelman was using the alphabetical wordlist to the same end. Spelman's connection with Camden continued posthumously: he was buried in Westminster Abbey 'at the foot of the Pillar over against Mr. *Camden's* Monument', and his life was written by Edmund Gibson, the editor of the revised *Britannia*

---

[143] Spelman, letter of 13 September 1638 to de Laet, BL MS Add. 34600 fo. 121r, 'te mecum obsoletam linguam nostram Saxonica[m] e cineribus revocare et qua possimus redivivam exhibere, multum gratulor'.

[144] Ibid., 'cum Poeta dicam – Cur dextram iungere dextra non datur: et vocas audire et reddere voces. Voces (inquam) priscas illas Saxonicas', quoting Virgil, *Aeneid* 1:408–9.

[145] Gibson, 'Life of Sir Henry Spelman' sig. b3r.

[146] Spelman, *Archaeologus* s.v. *heda*, '*Portus*. Domesd. in descriptione terrarum Regis Tarenfordiae in Comitatu Cantij. *Ibi sunt duo hede, id est, portus* ... Ex hoc, Lamb-hith, Quene-hith, ... etc.'

of 1695.[147] One of Spelman's areas of expertise was the study of charters, and these also brought land and language together, as William Lisle – who was Spelman's son-in-law – had remarked.[148] Spelman had other topographical interests as well. He wrote the description of Norfolk printed in John Speed's great atlas of the British Isles and a fuller post-humously published essay on the county, 'Icenia, sive Norfolciae descriptio topographica', and his name is associated with the gazetteer *Villare anglicum, or a view of the towns of England*.[149]

Gibson remarked in his life of Spelman that 'the Monuments of our Fore-fathers being neglected, we are depriv'd of a great deal of useful knowledge that might be drawn from them'.[150] These words sum up the motivation of Spelman's scholarly career. The monuments that he studied comprised two kinds of cultural heritage. As Lindenbrog, Peiresc, Bignon and others observed, he had important things to say about the legal history of northern Europe as a whole, and about the Latin in which many of the early legal texts had been written. He was, though, also strongly aware of the Englishness of his lexicographical study of Latin. The law he was investigating underpinned the law of his own day. Many early legal documents referred to particular hills and woods and streams which were still part of the physical shape of England, and still distinguished or bounded the estates of men of his own social class. Chaucer, whom he quoted, was for him 'our Chaucer'.[151]

OUR COUNTRYMEN (TO WHOME SO PROPERLY IT
BELONGETH): DUTCH AND ENGLISH LEXICOGRAPHERS
OF OLD ENGLISH 1605–1650

In the year in which Camden published the first edition of the *Remaines*, another landmark of English antiquarianism appeared: *A restitution of decayed intelligence in antiquities concerning the most noble and renowmed English nation*, by Richard Verstegan (formerly Rowlands). Both books had an Antwerp connection: Camden's was ultimately a result of the encouragement of Ortelius, and Verstegan's was written and published in Antwerp, to which the author, an English recusant of Dutch ancestry, had

---

[147] Gibson, 'Life of Sir Henry Spelman' sig. d1v.
[148] For Spelman and charters, see Cronne, 'Study and use of charters by English scholars in the seventeenth century' 80–7.
[149] Speed, *Theatre of the empire of Great Britaine* 35; Spelman, *Reliquiae Spelmannianae* 133–62; *Villare anglicum* title-page, 'collected by the appointment of Sir Henry Spelman'.
[150] Gibson, 'Life of Sir Henry Spelman' sig. b2v.
[151] Spelman, *Archaeologus* s.v. *leudis*, 'Et Chaucerus noster, *Blessed be the leud man*'.

moved in the 1580s after his publication of an account of the martyrdom of St Edmund Campion had made him liable to severe punishment if he remained in England.[152] An international intellectual background was as much of a strength for Verstegan as it was for Camden. Strongly as he insisted on his own Englishness in his text, he was also sensitive enough to the intellectual resources of the Continent to draw on the work of Cornelis Kiel, who addressed him in a liminary poem as 'restorer of the old English nation and language'; to discuss the work of Goropius Becanus with Ortelius; to read the epistle in which Lipsius published his Old Dutch wordlist; and to cite material from Flacius' Otfrid and Merula's Willeram.[153] Verstegan's contribution to antiquarian thought in England was to emphasize the importance of the Anglo-Saxon past (with a special interest in its paganism) rather than the largely mythical British past which many sixteenth-century scholars had found alluring.[154] His own Dutch ancestry doubtless encouraged him in this argument, which led him at one point into an interesting discussion of geomorphology as he set out the evidence that the British Isles had once been a peninsula of Europe.[155] Camden's example must have helped too: Verstegan was following the *Britannia* in seeing how etymology and verifiable historical data could work together. He was certain that the English language was that of the Anglian and Saxon conquerors of Roman Britannia, not least because he could see its affinities with Dutch and other continental Germanic languages, and he got some of his strongest arguments from this area of inquiry. 'The real hero of Verstegan's book', it has been said, 'is the English language.'[156] At the heart of the book is a wordlist of about 685 items, which Verstegan calls 'a number of our moste ancient English woords'.[157] This is the first printed wordlist of Old English – for although 'moste ancient' might be expected to denote a jumble of Old and Middle English, about 615 of the words in the list are indeed Old English.[158] Like Lipsius' Old Dutch wordlist, it selects words that differ from those of the current language; it is followed by the suggestion that poets might care to revive some of the words it registers rather than borrow from other

---

[152] Parry, *Trophies of time* 49–69.

[153] Verstegan, *Restitution* 149 (citation of Kiel) and sig. HH4r (Kiel's verses 'D. Ricardo Verstegano viro cl[arissimo] nationis et linguae veteris Anglicanae restauratori'), 190 (conversation with Ortelius), 194 (citation of Lipsius), 202 (extracts from Otfrid and Willeram).

[154] Kendrick, *British antiquity* 116–19; for his contributions to the study of paganism, see Bremmer, 'Anglo-Saxon pantheon'.

[155] Verstegan, *Restitution* 88–112; cf. Piggott, *Ancient Britons* 56–8.

[156] Parry, *Trophies of time* 64. [157] Verstegan, *Restitution* 206 (quotation), 207–39 (wordlist).

[158] Goepp, 'Verstegan's "most ancient Saxon words"'; word-count at 249.

languages, but it is by no means simply an archaizer's or purist's *vade mecum*.

Verstegan's wordlist is in fact a most impressive and interesting philological document. It handles morphological units other than the word, for instance in the entry for *ge-*: 'This preposition [i.e., prefix] was of our anceters much vsed & it is yet exceedingly vsed in the low-duitsh ... Wee haue since altered it from ge to y which yet wee sildome vse in prose, but somtymes in poetrie for the encreasing of sillables.'[159] It discusses the history of pronunciation, as s.v. *ic*: 'Our anceters pronounced the *Ich* not as now some of our westcountrie men do [i.e., like modern English *itch*], but as wee should do yf it were writte[n] Igh.'[160] The toponymic interests characteristic of earlier studies of Old English are also to be found here, for instance s.v. *caster* and in the discussions of *Dunkerk* s.v. *dune* and *Lichfield* s.v. *lic*.[161] Verstegan also handles dialect material, commenting, for example, s.v. *dugud* that 'it is also written *thugud* / whereof they vse in some partes of *England*, the woord thewghes or thewes, to wit, vertues good qualities or partes of the mynd. They say yet in the north when a thing hath lost his force or vertue, that it dowes not.'[162] This extends into a broad concern with popular antiquities and culture, from the discussion of early medieval crowns s.v. *cyne-helme* to that of werewolves s.v. *were-wulf*.[163]

Two words in Verstegan's defining text are particularly suggestive. The first is *framea*: the word *stafsweard*, which is only to be found in Ælfric's glossary, as a gloss on Latin *dolones*, is explained 'A *Stafswoord*, a short speare or iaueling the iron whereof was long and somwhat after the manner of a blade, *a framea*'.[164] The last word is very rare in early modern English; the only example in the *Oxford English Dictionary* is from Greenway's translation of Tacitus. Verstegan's decision to use it asserted a continuity of culture from the contemporaries of Ælfric to their continental ancestors. It also demonstrated his familiarity with an important continental wordlist, that of Lipsius, in which Old Dutch *staf-swert* is glossed 'Framea'.[165] The second is *Teutonic*, used in Verstegan's wordlist s.vv. *cemp*, in a reference to 'the name in Teutonic of kempfight', *dwolma*, 'A gulf, otherwise in Teutonic an *Inham*' and elsewhere.[166] This word appears to have been introduced to English by Verstegan. Sometimes, he uses it to mean an early ancestor of the living Germanic languages, 'such languages as depend on the Teutonic toung'.[167] Descent from this language unified

[159] Verstegan, *Restitution* 220.   [160] Ibid. 225.
[161] Ibid. 213, 217, 227.   [162] Ibid. 216.   [163] Ibid. 215, 236–7.   [164] Ibid. 232.
[165] Lipsius, letter to Schottius in *Epistolarum selectarum centuria tertia ad Belgas* 52.
[166] Verstegan, *Restitution* 213, 217.   [167] Ibid. 189.

English and Dutch. Verstegan states, following Lipsius, that 'About 900. yeare past our la[n]guage and the language of Saxonie and the Netherlands was all one', and pointed out that one could still find sentences that were almost the same in English and Dutch, comparing 'De string is losse / bind de string aen de wagen vast' with 'The string is loose / bynd the string on the wagon fast'.[168] Sometimes he even suggests that *Teutonic* can be a blanket term for the living Germanic languages, as in his wordlist s.v. *were*: 'the name of *man* / is now more known and more generally vsed in the whole Teutonic toung than the name of *Were*'.[169] The term was taken up by subsequent writers on the Anglo-Saxon heritage such as the 1640s political writer John Hare, whose remarks on Old English as 'most fruitfull and copious in significant and well-sounding rootes and Primitives' were quoted in the previous chapter. He wrote in *St. Edwards ghost, or anti-Normanisme* that 'There is no man that understands rightly what an English man is, but knowes withall that we are a member of the Teutonick Nation.'[170]

The *Restitution of decayed intelligence* has an attractive vignette of the dispersal of the nations from Babel on its title-page, and Verstegan explains in his text that 'the Teutonic toung' was the language 'which at the confusion of *Babel*, the Teutonic people (those I mean that were conducted by *Tuisco*) did speak'.[171] This myth of heritage derived from pseudo-Berosus; Verstegan was capable of seeing that this work might be a forgery, but did not realize that it was the ultimate authority for his grand historical narrative.[172] The myth was in fact an enabling one for him, allowing him to see the Germanic languages as a group that could be traced back to a single protolanguage of great antiquity. He decided not to follow Goropius in his claim that this protolanguage was that of Eden – indeed, he once asked Ortelius whether Goropius had been joking when he wrote the *Origines antwerpianae* – confining himself to the proposition 'that yf the Teutonic bee not taken for the first language of the world, it cannot bee denied to bee one of the most ancientest'.[173] He gave this proposition pictorial form in his engraving of a statue of the eponymous heroic leader of the Teutones, Tuisco, in the background of which Tuisco himself is to be seen leading a little group of people away from Babel.[174]

While Verstegan was printing his wordlist, the manuscript of John Joscelyn's *Dictionarium* had passed into the library of Sir Robert Cotton, where it could play a part in the politically charged intellectual world of

---

[168] Ibid. 147 (cf. Lipsius, letter to Schottius in *Epistolarum selectarum centuria tertia ad Belgas* 55), 199.
[169] Ibid. 236.　　[170] Hare, *St. Edwards ghost* 3 (shortly after a laudatory reference to Verstegan).
[171] Verstegan, *Restitution* 188.　　[172] Ibid. 112.　　[173] Ibid. 190–2 (quotation at 192).　　[174] Ibid. 71.

the seventeenth-century antiquaries. It was, most importantly, used in a dictionary project by the manuscript collector and member of the Long Parliament Sir Simonds D'Ewes, who came to the study of records at the end of the reign of James I, as he recalled in his *Autobiography*:

> on thursday the fowerth day of September [1623] in the afternoone I first begann my studijng Recordes at the Tower of London … I at first perused Recordes onlie to finde out the matter of law conteined in them; but afterwardes perceiuing other excellencies might bee obserued from them both Historicall and notionall, I alwaies continued the studie of the[m] after I had left the middle Temple & giuen ouer the studie of the Common Law it selfe, & especiallie searched the Recordes of the Exchecquer: intending if God shall permitt, & that I bee not swallowed vpp of euill times, to restore to Great Brittaine its true Historie, the exactest that euer was yet penned of anie nation in the Christian Worlde.[175]

He went on to study the records of his father's manor of Stowlangtoft, which he would inherit, with an interest perhaps all the keener for his knowledge that Stowlangtoft had not been in his family long: one might compare Rudyard Kipling's enjoyment in the poem 'The River-field' of the idea that his ownership of the land he had bought in Sussex, and his dealings with Hobson, the local expert in the management of that land, gave him a personal continuity of experience with its medieval owners. Whereas Kipling's talk with Hobson could provide a satisfying and immediate heritage experience, D'Ewes' study of the early records that made his recently purchased inheritance part of a centuries-old heritage called – just like Elizabeth I's study of Lambarde's summary of the archives in the Tower of London – for the help of a dictionary.

Since Joscelyn's death, a number of wordlists of or containing Old English had been undertaken. One of these was made by the antiquary Francis Tate, according to a letter by Sir Henry Spelman, which identifies it as a dictionary on the scale of Joscelyn's, but independent from it. It is now lost.[176] Another was at one time in the hands of John Bradshaw, one of the custodians of the exchequer archives in which D'Ewes studied; it is conceivable that this is to be identified with the dictionary made by Tate.[177] Two others, both known to D'Ewes and both lost, were a dictionary by

---

[175] D'Ewes, *The life of Sir Simonds D'Ewes written by himselfe*, BL MS Harley 646, fos. 69v–70r. The text edited by Halliwell in D'Ewes, *Autobiography and correspondence* (1845) is not to be trusted: in this passage, for example, it reads 'national' for 'notionall'.

[176] Spelman, letter of 13 September 1638 to de Laet, BL MS Add. 34600, fos. 121–2, at fo. 121v–122r; see also Camden, *Remaines* (1605) 20.

[177] D'Ewes, *Life*, BL MS Harley 646, fo. 130v.

William Lisle and a shorter 'Saxon vocabularie ... collected only out of the Four Evangelists, and one or two other small things, printed in that toungue', once owned by Sir William Boswell, the English resident at The Hague.[178] Three other glossaries, two written by Sir Robert Cotton's librarian, the antiquary (and lexicographer of Russian) Richard James, and one possibly owned by James, are preserved in the Bodleian Library, as is a slightly abbreviated transcript of the longest.[179] Abraham Wheelock, the first incumbent of the praelectorship endowed by Spelman, who produced a revised edition of Lambarde's *Archaionomia* and editions of the Old English version of Bede's *Ecclesiastical history* and the *Anglo-Saxon chronicle*, made two collections of Old English words, one of which, despite the heading 'Lexicon Sax.' at the top of the first page, is a working notebook rather than even a draft of a dictionary, and the other of which has few entries after the range A–B.[180] D'Ewes' references to these glossaries show his eagerness to find one that would help him with his antiquarian work. None of them was in fact the comprehensive work he wanted, so he started making his own.

In July of 1630, D'Ewes made the acquaintance of Sir Henry Spelman, and enjoyed 'much discourse touching our mutuall studies of Antiquities' with him.[181] It is probably not a coincidence that he first obtained a glossary of Old English within a few months of this meeting, borrowing it from John Bradshaw. Once he had it in his hands, he sat down to transcribe it, beginning on the first of January, 1631. 'I tooke care', he recorded in his autobiography, 'to penn it moore methodicalli then I found it, & intended to haue enlarged it'; he went on to describe the project as one 'of framing a Saxo[n] dictionarie with the Latine & moderne English added to it'.[182] The emphasis on the latter point suggests that D'Ewes was not simply interested in the interpretation of Old English texts, but in the relationship between their language and his own: in Old English as part of a continuous inheritance of language. He knew that his paternal great-grandfather had been a native speaker of Dutch, so that, although English

---

[178] Both are mentioned by Boswell in a letter to D'Ewes of 18 December 1636 in D'Ewes, *Autobiography and correspondence* (1845) II:228–9 at 229; the former is also mentioned in a letter of Lisle's to Sir Robert Cotton of 16 March 1630, quoted Pulsiano, 'William L'isle and the editing of Old English' 185–6n35, and de Laet enquired after it in a letter of 5 July 1638, cited Morris, *Correspondence* 177n49; see also D'Ewes, *Life*, BL MS Harley 646, fo. 130v.

[179] These are Bodl. MSS James 42, James 41, Selden supra 62, and Add. C. 250 respectively, discussed by Hetherington, *Beginnings* 69–76.

[180] These are BL MS Harley 761 and Cambridge, University Library MS Gg. 2.2 respectively, discussed by Hetherington, *Beginnings* 79–88.

[181] D'Ewes, *Life*, BL MS Harley 646, fo. 128v. [182] Ibid. fos. 130v–131r.

was his own native language, it was not something that he had from his distant ancestors. This gave him two reasons to study its history. First, as with the manor of Stowlangtoft, what his ancestors had not possessed could become retrospectively his intellectual possession as he studied it. Second, he may have had a sense that his very distant ancestors had spoken a language quite similar to Anglo-Saxon from which both Dutch and English were descended.

The same sense that the relationship of these two languages demonstrated that their speakers shared a heritage accounts for Spelman's writing to de Laet of 'our obsolete Saxon language' and for a poem published in an Oxford volume that celebrated the Anglo–Dutch peace treaty of 1654, one of the attempts at Old English referred to earlier in this chapter, 'On thære sibbe betweox Breotone & Holland' by Joseph Williamson.[183] Its first fourteen lines are written in Old English, the rest being in French. It is addressed 'To tham Hollandiscum', to the Dutch people, and begins by reflecting that the English and the Dutch are of the same ethnic origin, and that their initial division by the seas was followed by a long period of friendship until *sæs-cræft*, trade rivalries, became a source of dissension.[184] The poem's language is clearly meant to reflect this early affinity: by addressing the Dutch in the variety of English closest to the period when the ancestors of both nations lived amicably together in continental Europe, it seeks to re-invoke that amicable spirit. Examination of the odd word *sæs-cræft* 'seas-craft' strengthens this impression. The form of the first element is unusual, but even if it is emended to *sæ-cræft* 'sea-craft', it is neither an Old English word nor an early modern one. Williamson could conceivably have come across Middle English *seecraft* if he had read a certain fifteenth-century translation of Vegetius in manuscript, but it is much more likely that he was remembering the Dutch word *zeekracht* 'sea-power', which is attested from the 1650s. In that case, he believed so strongly in the affinity of Old English and Dutch that he was ready to turn to Dutch to supply a deficiency in the Old English lexical heritage.[185]

---

[183] *Musarum Oxoniensium* 'Ελαιοφορία, 91–2 (*recte* 71–72).

[184] Ibid. 91 (*recte* 71), 'Anne theod ætforan wæron we, | Anes modores sunu, oth thæt sæ | (Swa men secgeath) us todælod. | Æfter that anne heorte ond heafold | We begen hæfdon, oththæt æft | Totwæmth thruh graman us sæs-cræft.'

[185] Williamson's form in *sæs-* is no doubt by analogy with Old English *sæs-clif* 'cliff of the seas' or *sæs-grund* 'bed of the seas', both of which were known to Somner (*Dictionarium* s.vv.) but Old English compounds with the sense 'sea-' are regularly formed with *sæ-*. *OED* attests modern English *sea-craft* from 1727 onwards; *MED* attests Middle English *seecraft* (s.v. *sē* n.1 sense 3f) only from *Knyghthode and bataile*, a fifteenth-century paraphrase of Vegetius; *WNT* attests Dutch *zeekracht* from Vondel (1658).

In foregrounding the relationship of Old English and modern English in his dictionary, D'Ewes would demonstrate that modern English was doubly part of his heritage, as his own first language and as the cousin of the language of his Dutch-speaking ancestors. In 1640, Sir William Dugdale wrote to him that 'I am glad to heare of yor inclinac[i]on to print the Saxon Dictionarye, and especially the English therwth inasmuch as it hath soe much consonancye to the Saxon'.[186] By the time of this letter, D'Ewes' project had in fact been dropped and resumed. He would, according to the autobiography, have finished it within twelve months of its inception on New Year's Day of 1631 'but that I vnderstood of a Saxon Dictionarie intended to bee printed by one Mr Lisle'. This was William Lisle, whom D'Ewes described as 'most able to finish that worke', adding that 'if hee doe not, I may then againe perhaps by Gods assistance proceede with mine owne begunn resolution'.[187] These words were probably written in 1638, by which time D'Ewes must have been wondering if Lisle really was going to publish; on Lisle's death in that year, he supposed that the field was now clear for his own work. He had become aware of the existence of Joscelyn's *Dictionarium* in the Cottonian library, which was now in the possession of Sir Robert's son, and knew that he should use it if he was to proceed. Although he was unable to borrow the manuscript himself, he applied for help to Sir Henry Spelman, who asked the Earl of Bath to borrow it from Cotton, after which an amanuensis of Spelman's copied it for D'Ewes.[188]

By this time, however, D'Ewes had competition from another quarter; indeed, from another learned person with a Dutch family background and close connections with England. This was Jan de Laet, theologian, director of the Dutch West India Company, and maker of geographical and botanical compilations. Even within philology, de Laet's interests and expertise were broadly comparative. He was evidently interested in the lexicography of post-classical Latin, since his name appears, either as compiler or as owner or patron, at the end of the British Library manuscript Harley 3321, a glossary of medieval Latin that runs to about 2900 entries, many of them long and illustrated with numerous quotations. He owned a copy of Spelman's *Archaeologus*, together with many other dictionaries and philological books: the *Thesaurus graecae linguae*, Kiel's *Etymologicum* and van der Myl's *De lingua belgica*, Flacius' Otfrid and Merula's *Willeram*, Estienne Pasquier's *Recherches de France*, John

---

[186] Dugdale, letter to D'Ewes of 27 February 1640, in Dugdale, *Life, diary and correspondence* 194–5 at 194.
[187] D'Ewes, *Life*, BL MS Harley 646, fo. 130v.
[188] Spelman, letter of 17 April 1640 to D'Ewes, BL MS Add. 34601 fo. 6r; cf. Tite, *Early records of Sir Robert Cotton's library* 191–2.

Minsheu's polyglot *Ductor in linguas*, and so on.[189] In the course of a controversy with Hugo Grotius as to the origins of the native peoples of the Americas (Grotius believed that some of them were of Germanic origin, arguing for instance that the element *tlan* in New World place-names such as *Tenochtitlan* was in fact Germanic *-land*), he handled wordlists in languages from Huron and Nahuatl to Irish and Icelandic.[190]

De Laet's interest in the Germanic heritage led him into correspondence with the Danish antiquary Ole Worm, who presented him with a copy of his *Danicorum monumentorum libri*, and with a number of English Anglo-Saxonists, including Boswell, Spelman and D'Ewes himself; his first marriage, to a daughter of Pieter van Loor (Sir Peter Vanlore), a Dutch merchant resident in England, gave him several distinguished English brothers-in-law.[191] It was perhaps inevitable that he should have begun to think about the history of English. In 1616, he was reading the Gospels in Old English and was taking an interest in the early history of Dutch and Frisian, and in 1637–8 he began work on a dictionary of Old English.[192] He worked fast: by the middle of June 1638 he had 2600 head-words, and two months later he reported in a letter to Spelman that he had more than 3000.[193] Spelman replied with the polite and alarming message:

I do hope that you will gather your words from the most ancient of the old writers of Saxony, or from those of our country other than the ones which have been printed, and from which others labouring on the same work have already gathered the flowers, leaving meagre gleanings behind. For there are now two manuscript Saxon–Latin dictionaries [Nowell's and Joscelyn's?] available in England, full of material, and containing many thousands of words.[194]

This did not put de Laet off; in 1640, he was still working on his dictionary, now in consultation with Spelman.[195] Shortage of primary

---

[189] Hoftijzer, 'Library of Johannes de Laet' 208n35 (dictionaries), 211 (Otfrid and Willeram), and 202 (Pasquier).

[190] See Droixhe, 'Más ignorante que hereje'.

[191] For the presentation copy, see Hoftijzer, 'Library of Johannes de Laet' 216; for de Laet's English kinship network, see Bremmer, 'Laet'.

[192] For this, see Morris, *Correspondence* xviii–xxv and Hetherington, *Beginnings* 97–101.

[193] De Laet, letters to Boswell of 14 June 1638 and to Spelman of 15 August 1638, quoted Timmer, 'Introduction' 6.

[194] Spelman, letter of 13 September 1638 to de Laet, BL MS Add. 34600 fo. 121r–v, 'In Lexici autem quod moliris concinnatione, mallem vt ex antiquissimis veteris Saxoniae Scriptoribus, vel e nostratium alijs quam qui typis extant, et quos alij hanc navantes operam antea deflorauerunt (exile relinquentes spicilegiu[m]) tua collegas vocabula. Habentur enim iam nunc duo apud nos MSS. dictionaria Saxonica–Latina copiosa sane et multas continentia verborum chiliades.'

[195] Spelman, letter of 17 April 1640 to D'Ewes, BL MS Add. 34601 fo. 6r, identifies the dictionary as one which 'Mr Laët and my selfe haue bene longe about', but a draft letter of his to de Laet of 22 June 1640, BL MS Add. 34601 fos. 14–15, refers on 15r to 'Commune nostrum concilium de dictionario

materials was a problem, though de Laet owned some printed material in Old English and apparently had 'some Manuscripts' as well, but his friends in England helped him (James Ussher lent him the so-called Cædmon Manuscript of Old English poetry) and the list of sources that he is known to have used is quite impressive.[196] De Laet had nearly completed the dictionary by the time of his death in 1649, after which his heirs passed it on to the philologist Marcus Zuerius Boxhorn of Leiden, in the hope, in fact a vain one, that he would see it through the press.[197] The manuscript was destroyed by fire in the eighteenth century, but a wordlist apparently representing some of de Laet's early collections for it suggests that one of its significant features would have been the presentation of Dutch cognates, and if he was impressed by Spelman's suggestion that he should deal with words 'from the most ancient of the old writers of Saxony' as opposed to 'those of our country', some of these might have been taken from early medieval sources such as the Wachtendonck Codex.[198] Another feature would have been attention to some of the technical vocabulary of Old English: two other surviving wordlists, one of 473 items sent to D'Ewes and one of 84 items sent to Worm, are predominantly botanical, and in a letter to Spelman, de Laet says that he is working on the vocabulary of a collection of medical recipes.[199] A third feature would have been the presentation of poetic vocabulary, from the Cædmon Manuscript if no other.

While de Laet and Spelman were taking counsel together in 1640, D'Ewes had made good progress on his own dictionary, founded no longer on the glossary borrowed from Bradshaw but on his own transcript of the copy of Joscelyn's *Dictionarium* that Spelman had obtained for him.[200]

Saxonico–Latino edendo', cancelled and replaced by 'Commune studiu[m] nostrum de dictionario Saxonico–Latino concinnando', both of which forms suggest planning rather than drafting.

[196] For de Laet's Old English books, see Hoftijzer, 'Library of Johannes de Laet' 211–12; for his access to manuscripts in Leiden, see Timmer, 'Introduction' 6; for help from friends in England, see de Laet, letter of 16 December 1640 to Spelman, BL MS Add. 34601 fo. 38r; for his sources, see Morris, *Correspondence* xix–xxi, and for the Cædmon Manuscript in particular, Timmer, 'De Laet's Anglo-Saxon dictionary' 200f. (correcting Timmer 'Introduction' 8).

[197] See Morris, *Correspondence* xxv, Timmer, 'De Laet's Anglo-Saxon dictionary' 201–2, and Dekker, *Origins of Old Germanic studies* 216.

[198] The wordlist, of 28 Old English words with Latin glosses and explanatory material, citing 'Belgic' cognates eight times, is BL MS Harley 7579 fo. 129r.

[199] De Laet, list communicated to D'Ewes, BL MS Harley 7579 fos. 130–1; de Laet, letter of 4 April 1642 to Ole Worm, in Worm, *Epistolae* ii:808–9, and subsequent correspondence ibid. 810ff.; de Laet, letter of 16 December 1640 to Spelman, BL MS Add. 34601 fo. 38r, referring to work on the so-called *Liber medicus*, i.e., BL MS Royal 12. D. xvii.

[200] BL MSS Harley 8 and 9, described by Watson, *Library of Sir Simonds D'Ewes* 154, as 'largely in his [i.e., D'Ewes'] hand'. Spelman requested the return of the copy made by his amanuensis in a letter

The dictionary itself, *Dictionarium citeriorum saeculorum Anglo-Saxonico–Latinum*, survives in two manuscript volumes in folio, which are now in the British Library, still in the clasped armorial bindings for which D'Ewes paid eight shillings and eightpence in 1640.[201] The title-page of each volume is in D'Ewes' hand, and is rather striking, handsomely written in alternating red and black.[202] Not all of his manuscripts got this treatment: these were meant to be impressive books. The manuscripts of Joscelyn's *Dictionarium* were modest, but D'Ewes' dictionary is something much more like an *objet de luxe*, not only a treasury of culture but a treasure in its own right. It is identified as a product of the lexicographer's hard labour: the motto on a flyleaf of the first volume, written both in Old English and in Latin, means, with a hint of self-congratulation, 'nobody knows his own powers until he has had to use them.'[203] The first volume begins with a transcript, with collations, of Ælfric's *Grammar*, after which the dictionary proper runs to 531 leaves in folio, with about 31,500 entries and subentries, roughly half as many again as Joscelyn's *Dictionarium*.[204] The *mise-en-page* imitates Joscelyn's, though on a larger scale: the dictionary's short entries are evenly and generously spaced on double-column pages. To his transcript of the *Dictionarium*, D'Ewes added some modern English forms, although not many, and certainly not enough to fulfil the expectations raised by the title-page, which describes the dictionary as 'including the contemporary vernacular language of Great Britain'.[205] The reference here to Great Britain rather than England was a politically significant one in 1640; D'Ewes' point, that Old English was a heritage shared by England and Scotland, was made more explicitly in the next year when a poem in Old English by Abraham Wheelock on Charles I's return from a journey to gain support in Scotland was identified in the collection in which it was printed as having been composed *Anglo- & Scoto-Saxonice* 'in Anglo- and Scoto-Saxon'.[206]

By April 1640, Dugdale was able to write to Spelman that 'Sir S hath alreadie caused about two thousand new words to bee added to the

---

of 17 April 1640 and D'Ewes returned it later that year; by December, Spelman had communicated it to de Laet (see de Laet's letter of 16 December 1640 in BL MS Add. 34601, fo. 38r).

[201] For the date and cost of the binding of these books see Watson, *Library of Sir Simonds D'Ewes* 154 and 250, and for his bindings in general see ibid. 48–9 and frontispiece.

[202] Watson, *Library of Sir Simonds D'Ewes* 50–1 notes around thirty-five examples.

[203] BL MS Harley 8, fo. 2r, 'Nan man gecnawað his agene ellen ær þone neod wurðe þe he hit genotian sceal. Nemo novit proprias vires antequam cogatur iis uti.'

[204] Entry-count my own; Hetherington, *Beginnings* 116, gives a count of 737 entries to 22 pages (11 folios), which would give a total of 35,550 without allowing for blanks.

[205] BL MS Harley 8, fo. 3r, 'hodiernam etiam Magnae Britanniae vernaculam complectens'.

[206] *Irenodia Cantabrigiensis* sig. A4r.

Cottonian Dictionarie of which some are taken out of the Tower Recordes, & others out of originall Saxon monumentes he hath.'[207] Spelman immediately wrote D'Ewes a dignified letter, pointing out first that he and Jan de Laet had already been 'long about' their own dictionary project, and second that D'Ewes had only had access to Joscelyn's *Dictionarium* through Spelman's help, and had subsequently denied him access to the transcript that had been made when the dictionary was borrowed. He continued:

I know Mr Laët to be the ablest man for this purpose y^t we can lite on both for his knowledge & great travell in the Saxon tounge & also for the p[ro]ximitie wch his owne language and the *Frisian* haue to the auntient Saxon aboue our English. Yet was I alwaies & still continue of yor opinion & desire that neither he nor any fforaner may bereaue o^r Countrymen (to whome so p[ro]p[er]ly it belongeth) of the credit of y^t labour.[208]

Spelman had already identified Old English as a national heritage to be reserved for English scholars a couple of years earlier, writing that he was 'not willing that it [a dictionary of Old English] should be done by a stranger, and we here (to whome it more particularly belongeth) be pretermitted'.[209] This sentiment was, after his discussions with de Laet, balanced by the comparativist perspective of the continental tradition. To solve the problem that de Laet was the best man for the job but was unfortunately not an Englishman, he drew an example from the history, as he understood it, of continental philology: 'I wrotte vnto him . . . and desired . . . that he would contribute his endeavours hither and come in as an associate here amongst vs like *Budaeus* wth six other for edition of the Greeke *Lexicon*.' D'Ewes, he suggested unsuccessfully, should join the collaboration.[210]

Before he heard about de Laet's project, D'Ewes had had, in Dugdale's words, an 'inclinac[i]on to print the Saxon Dictionarye', and the news of a rival appears to have strengthened this inclination: by June, Spelman could write to de Laet that 'he makes haste even now to put a dictionary of the same sort as ours to press', adding caustically that D'Ewes would basically be printing Joscelyn's dictionary, 'inserting something of his own, I do not know what, and certainly failing to use other material'.[211]

[207] Dugdale, letter of 13 April 1640 to Spelman, in Watson, *Library of Sir Simonds D'Ewes* 10.
[208] Spelman, letter of 16 April 1640 to D'Ewes, BL MS Add. 34601 fo. 6r.
[209] Spelman, letter of 28 September 1638 to Wheelock, quoted Timmer, 'Introduction' 6.
[210] Spelman, letter of 16 April 1640 to D'Ewes, BL MS Add. 34601 fo. 6r–6v.
[211] Spelman, letter of 22 June 1640 to de Laet, BL MS Add. 34601 fo. 15r, 'eiusmodi dictionarium . . . e Cottoniana nactus bibliotheca, typis iam iam dare properat, sua nescio quae inserens, alia vero praetermittens'.

One kind of insertion that D'Ewes had in mind was of words from Germanic languages, but he did not understand that these were only relevant if they were cognate with the Old English word under discussion, a point which de Laet had to explain to him.[212] He then dropped this plan, and although he owned Kiel's dictionary, he never cited it in his own work in Old English.[213] He soon also changed his mind about printing his work: the expensive binding that he gave the manuscript in December 1640 was surely for a pair of volumes that would stay in his own library rather than being sent off as printer's copy. There was a reason for this. He had, a month earlier, been elected to Parliament, and had at once found that his knowledge of politically significant archival material gave him prestige: two weeks after taking his seat, 'I . . . vouched a Recorde which not onlie gaue great satisffaction to the house, but ended a waightie and perplexed dispute it was then controverting.'[214] Overtaking de Laet by publishing a learned dictionary may now have seemed less desirable than overtaking his fellow members of Parliament by decoding important records with a dictionary to which they would not have access. There are several reasons for a dictionary to remain unpublished: its maker may die, like Nowell, or lack publication funding, like Joscelyn, or lose interest in the project, as may have been the case with Wheelock. D'Ewes appears to exemplify another reason: its maker may be interested in the language described, not as a common heritage, but as a private resource.

While D'Ewes was nursing his dictionary and attending the Long Parliament in the 1640s, his correspondent William Dugdale was compiling his own in royalist Oxford. This is a reminder that the English Civil War was one in which men on both sides shared a cultural heritage and a commitment to its philological explication, as is Dugdale's work on county history, which belongs to a chorographical tradition capable (as in the case of Drayton's *Poly-Olbion*, a long chorographical poem with a partial commentary by Selden) of suggesting fundamentally anti-monarchical ideas.[215] Dugdale was, like Spelman and Lisle and D'Ewes, a landowner, and, like D'Ewes, he was the owner of recently purchased land. He was also a major antiquary, of whom it has been said that 'No man in England made more copious use of the manuscript heritage of

---

[212] D'Ewes, undated dictionary sample [summer, 1640?] in BL MS Add. 34601 fo. 7; de Laet, letter of 24 August 1640 to D'Ewes, BL MS Harley 374 fos. 164–5.

[213] For D'Ewes' ownership of Kiel's dictionary, see Watson, *Library of Sir Simonds D'Ewes* 181; for his failure to cite it, see Hetherington, *Beginnings* 135.

[214] D'Ewes, letter of 19 November 1640 to Anne D'Ewes in Watson, *Library of Sir Simonds D'Ewes* 6.

[215] For the politics of chorography in early modern England, see Helgerson, *Forms of nationhood* 107–47.

charters, deeds, and statutes, of parliamentary, judicial, and parish records'; his *Antiquities of Warwickshire* balances this interest in manu-script heritage, in the 'Records, Leiger-Books, Manuscripts [and] Charters' of its title-page, with an interest in genealogical heritage, the 'worthy Ancestors, to whose memory' the book is 'erected . . . as a *Monumentall Pillar*'.[216] His dictionary is a folio volume of 332 pages, now Bodleian MS Dugdale 29, which begins with a list of the manuscripts of Christopher Hatton's which, together with printed books from Lambarde to Wheelock, he had used as sources. It provides modern English glosses for its Old English headwords, and in that respect puts into practice the plan of D'Ewes' that Dugdale had praised before the outbreak of hostilities, and is also conscientious in the presentation of variant forms of Old English lexical items. However, it offers very little information about phraseology, and does not usually cite sources, let alone offer illustrative quotations, so that, although it registers some lexical items that had escaped other lexicographers, it does so rather more baldly than its most sophisticated contemporaries. The dictionary manuscript has in common with D'Ewes' that it appears to be designed to be used as a manuscript rather than sent off as printers' copy, each new letter of the alphabet being marked by a parchment tag for the convenience of future readers. Although its neatly written triple-column pages have white space left for the addition of entries, Dugdale would turn to his other projects rather than developing this one, and he therefore made it available to D'Ewes, whom he encouraged to keep working on lexicography.

By the late 1640s, D'Ewes had more time for this, having lost his influence in Parliament before being finally expelled in Pride's Purge at the end of 1648. It is to this period that most of the entries inserted in his dictionary in the spaces between those written in the period 1638–40 and in the wide margins left in the original page layout must belong. Despite his nationalistic protestations when de Laet's dictionary seemed to threaten his own, D'Ewes did now benefit from the learning of one continental scholar, Franciscus Junius, who stayed with him in 1648 and 1649, reading Old English manuscripts in his collection and supplying him with a collation of manuscripts of Ælfric's grammar and with words for the dictionary.[217] His dictionary also benefited from the work of other English scholars. Selden lent D'Ewes his manuscript of Nowell's

---

[216] Parry, *Trophies of time* 275, and see generally ibid. 217–48; Dugdale, *Antiquities of Warwickshire*, title-page and sig. a3r.

[217] Hetherington, *Beginnings* 107–9; cf. Junius, letter of 29 January 1649 to Isaac Vossius in F. Junius, *Correspondence* 758–67 at 764–75, and Watson, *Library of Sir Simonds D'Ewes* 43–4.

Vocabularium in 1648, and perhaps his manuscript of the dictionary of Richard James at the same time.[218] By March of 1650, D'Ewes was using Dugdale's dictionary, as we know from a letter to Dugdale from his collaborator Roger Dodsworth, referring to 'your Saxon Dictionary, wch the Beast undervalued to my Cosen (when [we] were wth him and saw it in his study window) in regard [to] what Hee had done to that purpose wch is finished by Mr Sumners hand'.[219]

'Mr Sumner', William Somner of Canterbury, began working with D'Ewes in or shortly before January of 1650; in that month, Dugdale wrote to D'Ewes that 'I hope now y^t you have ye advantage of that honest man, Mr Sumner, his helpe, you will speede ye impression of your Saxon Lexicon.'[220] Somner's hand appears in both Dugdale's and D'Ewes' dictionaries, and he seems on occasion to have used each to correct the other.[221] Dugdale's dictionary was in fact D'Ewes' major source after Joscelyn's: about 65 per cent of D'Ewes' wordlist appears to be from Joscelyn, and about a quarter from Dugdale, with more than half of the remaining 10 per cent from Richard James.[222] D'Ewes' achievement was, in other words, a compilation like the patchwork dictionaries despised by Henri Estienne, rather than a work of original learning. That is not to say that it was unpublishable. The dictionary as it stood at D'Ewes' death in 1650 covered the complete alphabetical range of the Old English vocabulary more comprehensively than any of the other manuscript dictionaries then circulating in England, and it would have made a respectable showing in print. Junius appears to have been preparing it for the press in 1651, but, whether because nobody was prepared to take on the financial risk of such a dictionary or because Junius was diverted by other projects, it never appeared.[223]

---

[218] Bennett, 'History of Old English and Old Norse studies in England' 359.

[219] Dodsworth, letter of March 1650 to Dugdale in Dugdale, *Life, diary and correspondence* 226–7 at 227.

[220] Dugdale, letter of 2 January 1650 to D'Ewes in ibid. 221–3 at 222.

[221] Giese, 'Anonymous seventeenth-century Bodleian manuscript dictionary'; Tornaghi, 'Certaine things to be considered'.

[222] Figures based on Hetherington, *Beginnings* 116.

[223] For Junius' preparation of an Old English dictionary, very probably this one, for the press, see Breuker, 'On the course of Franciscus Junius's Germanic studies' 144 and n58; the text to which Breuker refers here, a letter of 7 August from Christoph Arnold to Georg Richter, is most readily available in English in Masson, *Life of John Milton* IV:350–2.

CHAPTER 6

Vernacular heritages III: England and Scandinavia, circa 1650–1675

A MOST WISE INVESTIGATOR OF THE ANTIQUITIES OF HIS FATHERLAND: WILLIAM SOMNER AND OLD ENGLISH

William Somner now became the central figure in the study of Old English in England. He had been born and educated in Canterbury, and spent his life there, working for the diocese as a lay administrator. From an early age, he had a taste for antiquities: 'His visits within the City were to find out the Ancestors, rather than the present inhabitants; and to know the genealogie of houses, and walls, and dust.'[1] He developed a local reputation, so that for 'all the history of use and custom, he was consulted as a *Druid* or a *Bard*', a compliment recalling Celtis' to Trithemius in the previous century.[2] This expertise led to his first book, *The antiquities of Canterbury*, which appeared in 1640, founded on extensive archival work among 'old manuscripts, lieger-bookes, and other like records', some of which were printed in a documentary appendix, and on a lifetime's knowledge of a personal heritage of place: 'I have ... as bound in duty and thankfulnesse, applyed my selfe to the *Antiquities* of *Canterbury*, the place of my birth and abode.'[3] It also drew on earlier printed books, not least Lambarde's *Perambulation of Kent*.[4] One passage in it gives Somner the claim to be one of the first writers in English, perhaps the very first, to understand that styles of architecture had changed steadily in the Middle Ages, and that a given feature could therefore be dated on stylistic grounds.[5] He was, in other words, capable of seeing the medieval period

---

[1] Kennett, 'Life of Mr. Somner' 9.   [2] Ibid. 11.

[3] Somner, *Antiquities of Canterbury*, title-page and sig. **2v; for Somner's own collection of manuscripts of antiquarian and other interest, see Woodruff, *Catalogue* 42–51 (items 79–98) and cf. the list, less detailed but including printed books with substantial marginalia, in Kennett, 'Life of Mr. Somner' 119–20.

[4] See, e.g., Somner, *Antiquities of Canterbury* 151.

[5] Hunter, *John Aubrey and the world of learning* 166n1; cf., e.g., Somner, *Antiquities of Canterbury* 165, 'the work of the Steeple ... I hold elder then *Arundells* time, by comparing it with other pieces of that age' and other passages gathered Parry, *Trophies of time* 182–3.

as one in which development took place, rather than as a historical blur or singularity. The book was widely admired.[6]

   Canterbury was not a university town, but it was not an intellectual backwater either: it had been the site of a Benedictine priory with a great library until 1540, and books from that library must have fuelled the interest and augmented the libraries of local collectors.[7] There was an interesting circle of antiquaries in sixteenth-century Canterbury, and there were learned men among the cathedral clergy in the sixteenth and seventeenth centuries.[8] In his preface, Somner acknowledged the encouragement of one of these clergymen, Meric Casaubon.[9] Meric was the son of Isaac Casaubon, and hence the maternal grandson of Henri Estienne. One of his earliest publications was a defence of his father's memory against his calumniators, he identified himself on the title-pages of his Latin works as 'Mericus Casaubonus Is. F. ', i.e., 'son of Isaac', and he bequeathed a sense of the scholarly eminence of his ancestors to his own son John.[10] He translated Marcus Aurelius into English, presenting one of the first English archaeological reports in the commentary.[11] He also undertook a study of language, the *De quatuor linguis commentationes pars prior* of 1650. This had originally been planned as a 'tract on the origin of language', and was to have contained material on Hebrew, Greek, Latin and Old English.[12] After completing his material on Hebrew, however, Casaubon turned straight to Old English, and then decided that he would publish what he had rather than delaying further, so that his thoughts on Latin and Greek never appeared. They are suggested by a passage in the introduction: 'as for whether, as a number of learned men would have it, nearly all of the ancient Greek language stems from Hebrew – for nearly all of ancient English stems, as we show in this book, from Greek – that double theory would not be altogether unreasonable'.[13]

[6] See testimonies collected in Kennett, 'Life of Mr. Somner' 19–20.
[7] See de Hamel, 'Dispersal of the library of Christ Church, Canterbury' 271–2 and Watson, 'John Twyne of Canterbury'.
[8] For sixteenth-century Canterbury antiquaries, see Kendrick, *British antiquity* 105–8.
[9] Somner, *Antiquities of Canterbury* sig. **4r.
[10] M. Casaubon, *Pietas contra maledicos patrij nominis*; Hunter and Macalpine, 'Diary of John Casaubon' 52.
[11] Marcus Aurelius, *Meditations* (1634), with archaeological material 31–6 (last sequence of pagination), for which see Hunter, 'Royal Society and the origins of British archaeology' 119.
[12] M. Casaubon, *De quatuor linguis* sig. A2r, 'varia mecum … agitabam. Inter ea erat de ortu sermonis tractatus. ' For the material on the origins of language that did appear in the published book, see Borst, *Turmbau von Babel* 1316–17.
[13] Ibid. sig. A3v, 'Quanquam si quod plerique docti volunt, ex Hebraica tota fere vetus lingua Graeca fluxit; ex Graeca autem tota fere, quod hic docemus, Anglica vetus: non plane contra rationem fuerit haec conjunctio'; cf. Eros, '17th-century demonstration of language relationship'.

The section on 'the ancient English, or Saxon, language, and its relationship with Greek' was more than twice the length of that on Hebrew. Its opening pages are an account of the place of English in Casaubon's own heritage: he had grown up in a French-speaking household, though his father had urged him to learn German and had asked a friend to mark up a French dictionary to show which words in it were of Germanic origin.[14] After his father's short residence and death in England, he had remained in the country, and had become fluent in the language, about which he thought from an early age in etymological terms: he knew that it was related to German, but observed that it resembled Greek in certain respects.[15] On becoming a prebendary of Canterbury Cathedral, he had studied in its archives, in which there were documents in Latin and Old English, and had found the experience as intense as that of his grandfather's first acquaintance with Greek or Leland's first sight of the library at Glastonbury: 'I remember that when I touched those sacred pages, a kind of pious horror would thrill my soul, as if I gazed upon those who were speaking by means of their written monuments' – but 'I needed one thing to be perfectly happy: expertise in Old English.'[16] Like Budé eager to know Greek, 'I then began to burn with an extraordinary desire for a closer understanding of that language.'[17]

This desire was occasioned by the experience of archival work, but it was strengthened by a sense of the excellence of Old English. It was, he reflected, 'the true and genuine English language: as far as the present English language departs from Old English, so far has it degenerated from its native purity'.[18] But his understanding of it was not insular: he stated that English was substantially identical with the German and Dutch languages with which it so clearly shared an origin, and went on to describe the extent of the conquests of the barbarian peoples of late antiquity, all of whom he supposed to have been Germanic, in much the spirit of Beatus Rhenanus' identification with the triumphs of the Goths and Vandals.[19] He then touched on the possibilities that the Germanic languages might, as Goropius had suggested, be related to ancient Phrygian or, as had been proposed by philologists from de Smet and Joseph Scaliger onwards, to

[14] M. Casaubon, *De quatuor linguis* 127.   [15] Ibid. 128–9.
[16] Ibid. 130–1, 'Memini cum sacras illas membranas tangerem, religioso quodam horrore animum meum percelli solitum, quasi praesentes intuerer, qui monumentis illis loquebantur ... Unum deerat ad perfectam voluptatem, peritia linguae Saxonicae.'
[17] Ibid. 131, 'Miro tum coepi flagrare desiderio linguam istam proprius cognoscendi.'
[18] Ibid. 131–2, 'Saxonicam linguam, veram & genuinam esse linguam Anglicam, ut quantum a Saxonica vetere praesens Anglica recesserit, tantum a nativa puritate degeneravit.'
[19] Ibid. 132ff.

Persian; he asked whether the ancient Gauls had spoken a Germanic language; and he raised the question of the Germanic affinities of the languages of North America as debated by Grotius and de Laet.[20]

Old English, then, offered access to a local manuscript heritage but also to heritages of past conquests and migrations that had taken place across Europe, Eurasia or the world. But there was an anticlimax: Casaubon was a busy man and, much as he would have liked to, he had found himself making less progress than he wanted in the study of Old English, so that most of the argument about the *lingua saxonica* in the *De quatuor linguis*, including the 151-page wordlist in which Greek and English forms are compared and their supposed affinities discussed, is based on modern English evidence.[21] In order to have some help with Old English, he turned to Somner, noting his evident abilities and his extraordinary industry *in scrutandis patriis antiquitatibus*: 'in studying the antiquities of his native place'.[22] Somner did not at the time know Old English well, but with Casaubon's encouragement he made very rapid progress. He appears to have begun his studies in earnest shortly after the publication of the *Antiquities of Canterbury*, in which only a little Old English material is cited.[23] By 1644, he had produced a set of glossarial notes to forty-five Latin words in Sir Roger Twysden's edition of the 'Laws of Henry I', in which a knowledge of the language is already evident, as is a continuing interest in Kentish antiquities (Somner's contribution to the edition can be explained by Twysden's own connection with Kent).[24] By 1647, he was editing Old English charters in his historical and etymological study of the Kentish system of tenure and inheritance of land called gavelkind.[25] By 1650, as we have seen, his knowledge of Old English was so remarkable that he had been asked to collaborate with Simonds D'Ewes on his dictionary project. Nor was he limited to the study of Old English. In the 1640s, as Casaubon worked on his *De*

---

[20] Ibid. 135–9, alluding to Goropius Becanus, *Origines antwerpianae* 551f. and 959 and the Grotius–de Laet controversy, and quoting Salmasius, *De hellenistica commentarius* for Persian affinities; on this point, see Droixhe, *Linguistique et l'appel de l'histoire* 90f. for Salmasius and 56 for earlier discussions by de Smet and Lipsius.

[21] See Eros, '17th-century demonstration of language relationship' 2 and 7ff.

[22] M. Casaubon, *De quatuor linguis* 140.

[23] Two passages are printed (in Anglo-Saxon type) and translated in Somner, *Antiquities of Canterbury* 364–6.

[24] Somner, 'Glossarium' (1644): Kentish material at 222.

[25] Somner, *Treatise of gavelkind* (for the date of completion, see sig. A3r, 'this Preface and the following Treatise were both written more than twelve years agone' – the real date of publication, as noted on the BL (Thomason) copy E.1005(1), was 1659 – and see also the imprimatur dated 7 April 1647 at 216), presenting Old English texts 196–204, 206, and 211–16; see discussion in Lowe, 'William Somner, S 1622, and the editing of Old English charters'.

quatuor linguis, he came across a wordlist to another language, and asked Somner for his comments on it.

This was the collection of Old Dutch words from the Wachtendonck Codex which Lipsius had published in 1602. To Casaubon, a number of them 'seemed to have the taste of pure, genuine Saxonism', and he sent the list from his lodgings in London to Somner in Canterbury.[26] Somner's reply, a rich set of annotations on the wordlist, came back in a matter of days, and was printed as an appendix to the *De quatuor linguis*, running to seventy-two octavo pages and 462 entries, for about two thirds of which he supplied Old English cognates. This learned piece of work suggested the direction which the lexicography of early English was now ready to take. In it, Somner married insular material such as his own work on gavelkind with the work of major European scholars: Freher and Lindenbrog, Worm, Kiel (repeatedly, in contrast to D'Ewes). He used less obvious sources, such as an account of the so-called Roland statues to be found in Bremen and other German cities, which included discussions of many aspects of Saxon culture and language.[27] In a discussion of the obsolescent English word *wang-tooth* (which had also interested Verstegan), Somner referred to a fuller treatment in 'Glossar[io] nostro', a promise to the reader of more lexicographical publications to come.[28]

One of these was a contribution to a new project, Twysden's grand publication of ten unedited Latin sources for the history of England, including the chronicles of Symeon of Durham and William Thorne of Canterbury. This appeared in 1652 as *Historiae anglicanae scriptores decem*, with a glossary by Somner which runs to eighty-four columns in folio, in which 'obscure words ... are copiously explained, and many of them are traced back to their sources'.[29] As well as the ten texts and the glossary, the book features a substantial introductory essay by Selden, the *princeps* of the Old English poem called 'Durham' (in two texts, one transcribed by Twysden and the other edited by Somner), an appendix of variant readings, and a very detailed index: it is a splendid assertion of the dignity of English historical scholarship.[30]

---

[26] M. Casaubon, *De quatuor linguis* 143, 'inter legendum non pauca statim occurrerent, quae Saxonismum purum putum resipere viderentur'.

[27] Gryphiander, *De weichbildis saxonicis*, cited Somner, 'Ad verba vetera Germanica' 7, 18.

[28] Somner, 'Ad verba vetera Germanica' 44 (with this entry, cf. Verstegan, *Restitution* 223 s.v. *geweng*).

[29] Somner, 'Glossarium' (1652) sig. X3r: 'obscuriora quaeque vocabula ... copiose explicantur, & ad origines suas pleraque revocantur'.

[30] See Douglas, *English scholars 1660–1730* 167; for the texts of 'Durham', see O'Donnell, 'Junius's knowledge of the Old English poem *Durham*' 233, and for the place of the edition in the history of the publication of Old English verse, see Plumer, 'Construction of structure' 274–5.

Twysden's preface draws special attention to the glossary, as follows:

A word on the glossary, without which this work would be impoverished and limited in value. Understand that it was made for your sake by William Somner, a man of spotless probity and honesty, a most wise investigator of the antiquities of his fatherland, and most expert in this Anglo-Saxon language. If certain glossed words which are hardly to be found in these writers should nevertheless be met with by you in the glossary, know that ... those words, which nobody of whom I know has explained, will be met with by you in other historians of our nation, and you will be able to uncover their sense from this glossary.[31]

Twysden makes it clear that Somner was doing something significant here: rather than making a glossary to one particular book, he was already heading forwards towards the making of a dictionary of early English records as a whole. This was not yet a matter of making a dictionary of Old English; the glossary is, after all, of ten texts in Latin. But a number of the Latin words that needed to be glossed were unfamiliar because they were borrowings from English, so, in treating them, Somner was not far from his Old English studies, and was integrating the study of medieval Latin and a medieval vernacular into a single story of heritage, as was being done by other seventeenth-century lexicographers of post-classical Latin. Nor were his etymological observations confined to English: the European philologists on whose work he had drawn in the notes on Lipsius' wordlist reappear here, so that Anglo-Latin and Old English are drawn into the same story as the Netherlandic and Scandinavian language varieties presented by Kiel and Worm. In all, Somner cited 144 works in this glossary, of which 73 had been published in Europe and 71 in England.[32] What this suggests is that his own intellectual heritage was to a significant extent that of continental Europe.

The local heritage of Canterbury nevertheless remained close to his heart, as was shown in the next major book on which he worked. This was the *Monasticon anglicanum* of Roger Dodsworth and William Dugdale, a massive collection of records of all the houses of the religious orders in pre-Reformation England, to which Somner contributed translations of early English documents into Latin, the language in which the book was published. The preface to the *Monasticon* acknowledged his

[31] *Historiae anglicanae scriptores x*, sig. A6r, 'De Glossario verbum. Sine quo hoc jejunum & parum utile prorsus extitisset opus, illud a *Guilielmo Somnero*, pristinae probitatis & candoris viro, patriarumque antiquitatum indagatore sagacissimo, & ad hoc linguae Anglo-Saxonicae peritissimo, in tuam gratiam elaboratum intelligas. Quod si voculae quaedam glossatae, his scriptoribus minime repertae, in eo tamen tibi occurrunt, scias ... ut cum in aliis gentis nostrae historicis illae tibi fiant obviae, & a nemine quod scio explicatae, hinc earum sensum eruere possis.'
[32] Hetherington, *Beginnings* 136; the sources are listed ibid. 189–208.

work warmly (everyone seems to have spoken of Somner with marked respect) and noted that he was preparing the types for the publication of 'an extremely rich Old English–Latin dictionary'.[33] In a series of five liminary poems that appears after this preface in some copies, all by Canterbury men and therefore presumably gathered by Somner, he is actually treated as a co-editor, and the last of these, a remarkable piece written in what is really an imitation of Middle English rather than simply an archaic register, is addressed simply 'To the right ylered Clerks, Dan *William Sompner*, &c. on her makelesse werke, hight MONASTICON ANGLICANUM'.[34]

As a contributor to the *Monasticon*, Somner was part of a community engaged in the restoration of heritage. Not only did the title-page advertise the use of manuscripts from libraries formed by individuals – the 'Arundelliana, Cottoniana, Seldeniana, Hattoniana' and others – but its splendid plates were each sponsored by a different gentleman, bearing the coat of arms that he had inherited together with a short inscription, sometimes explaining that the donor of the plate was descended from the founder of the religious house that was illustrated.[35] This was a revival of the system of publication by subscription, the first use of which in England had supported a dictionary, the second edition of Minsheu's *Ductor in linguas*, published in 1625.[36] The community that supported the *Monasticon* was something of a beleaguered one in 1655, largely royalist and hence overshadowed by the experience of defeat in the Civil War, turning – like Twysden in his editing of the *Scriptores decem* – to scholarship at a time of enforced retirement from public affairs.[37]

Supporters of the parliamentarian side in the Civil War were responsible for the destruction of a great number of religious images in the 1640s

---

[33] Dodsworth and Dugdale, eds., *Monasticon anglicanum* I sig. d3r, 'vir nostrarum antiquitatum callentissimus, Gulielmus Somnerus Cantuariensis ... qui ad edendum copiosissimam Vocabularii Saxonico–latini nunc typos parat'. Cf. Somner's criticisms of an earlier version of this preface in a letter to Dugdale of 10 November 1654 in Dugdale, *Life, diary and correspondence* 282–3.

[34] Verses at Dodsworth and Dugdale, *Monasticon anglicanum* I, inserted after sig. d4 in copies including one in the Newberry Library, Case fD 7 .242 v. 1, filmed in the series *Early English Books 1641–1700* at reel 351 (I am grateful to Jill Gage and Will Hansen of the Newberry Library for verifying this), and one at Canterbury mentioned by Kennett, 'Life of Mr. Somner' 69; Joshua Childrey, 'To the right ylered Clerks' is on the verso.

[35] See Parry, *Trophies of time* 235–6; the royalist exile Sir Edward Walker offers, in a letter to Dugdale of 6 August 1655 (in Dugdale, *Life, diary and correspondence* 293–4 at 293) to sponsor a plate illustrating the abbey of Burton because it had been a former owner of the estate that had subsequently belonged to Walker's family.

[36] For Minsheu and subscription, see Williams, 'Scholarly publication in Shakespeare's day'; for subsequent publications by subscription, see Parry, 'Patronage and the printing of learned works for the author' 183ff.

[37] Cf. the list of antiquarian works of the 1650s in Parry, *Trophies of time* 19 and, for Twysden's circumstances, Jessup, *Sir Roger Twysden* 89–100.

and 1650s, including the great majority of English medieval stained glass (of all the parish churches in England, only one – Fairford in Gloucestershire – has retained its medieval glass intact to this day). The engraved frontispiece of the *Monasticon* associates the destruction of a built heritage with the need to conserve a textual heritage in the contrast between two of its panels. On one side of the composition, Pietas (whose name suggests both religious piety and the piety due to the memory of ancestors) points to a grand ecclesiastical building, with the motto *prisca fides* 'ancient faith' above her. In the corresponding position on the other side, Antiquitas sits before the ruins of the same building, her feet illuminated by the light shining from a book with Saxon lettering in it and her head in darkness, the motto *caput inter nubila*, 'head in the clouds' above her.[38] Elsewhere in the same picture, it is made clear that the villain of these contrasting scenes is Henry VIII, the dissolver of the monasteries; condemning parliamentarian iconoclasm explicitly in a frontispiece in 1655 would have been imprudent. However, quiet condemnation was another matter. One of the first foundations to be treated in the *Monasticon* is Canterbury Cathedral, whose windows and other images had been damaged by soldiers in 1642 and again by the preacher Richard Culmer and his associates, acting on parliamentary authority, in 1643–4.[39] A Latin poem is slipped into the account of Canterbury in rather an odd position, printed on the back of one of the engraved plates inserted into the book; such plates usually have their backs blank. The plate in question is a ground-plan of the cathedral, and the poem is by Charles Fotherby, grandson of a Dean of Canterbury of the same name. Its Latin title can be translated 'On the special devastation of the Metropolitan church called Christ Church, Canterbury: to that most faithful man, of ancient probity and most highly deserving of the clergy of England, William Somner'.[40] It catalogues the damage, identified as *Culmeriana*, done to the church: 'the sacred page of each of the windows is broken ... Now the peace of the tomb may be disturbed without punishment: one man hacks off a bishop's nose, and one a head.'[41] But one man, Fotherby continues,

---

[38] See Corbett, 'Title-page and illustrations to the *Monasticon anglicanum*'; the motto is Virgil, *Aeneid* 4:177, where the reference is to Fama, whose head is in the clouds because she has grown so tall, not because she is obscure.

[39] Spraggon, *Puritan iconoclasm during the English Civil War* 182–5.

[40] Dodsworth and Dugdale, *Monasticon anglicanum* i, reverse of plate inserted after p. 18, 'In direptionem Metropoliticae Ecclesiae *Christi Cantuariensis* particularem, ad fidissimum, & antiquae probitatis virum, deque Clero Anglicano optime meritum, *Guilielmum Somnerum*'.

[41] Ibid., 'Quaeque fenestrarum fracta est sacra pagina ... | Nunc impune licet pacem turbare sepulchri: | Amputat hic nasum Praesulis, ille caput.'

provides a defence against it. 'How much', he exclaims, 'the church owes to our Somner! This man gathers up the riches taken without law; this man restores the original glory of the temple which was about to fall, and its monuments are intact in his writings. Truly, he has erected a temple in paper.'[42] Fotherby had the *Antiquities of Canterbury* in mind, but what he said would also be true of Somner's next work.

This was the *Dictionarium saxonico–latino–anglicum* of 1659, a folio of 348 triple-column pages and about 15,400 entries. It was founded on the work of predecessors including Nowell (Selden lent the manuscript of the *Vocabularium* to Somner as he had to D'Ewes), D'Ewes, and Dugdale, but also on Somner's own reading and analysis of manuscript and printed sources.[43] It must already have been far advanced by the time of the publication of the first volume of the *Monasticon*: as early as 1656, Franciscus Junius referred to it as 'under the presse', and a year later he was writing impatiently that he would 'bee most glad to heare that Mr. Somner his Anglo-Saxonike Dictionarie is comming forth'.[44] The dictionary is handsomely laid out: Old English headwords in Saxon type are followed by Latin glosses in Roman type and modern English glosses in black-letter, sometimes with illustrative citations (though these are more richly provided in D'Ewes' dictionary) or added encyclopedic or etymological information. Like Somner's previous work, it responded to three kinds of heritage. The first was the local heritage of Canterbury, and more generally the insular cultural heritage of England, as accessible through topographical and antiquarian study. The second was the broader Germanic heritage of the English language, as accessible through the philological work of English and continental European scholars. The third was the personal heritage of scholarly tradition, generosity and friendship which had coloured Somner's work ever since he used the writings of William Lambarde and acknowledged the encouragement of Meric Casaubon in the *Antiquities of Canterbury*.

All three are evident in Somner's introduction to the dictionary, but it is the presence of the local that is particularly striking. Embedded in the

---

[42] Ibid., 'quantum nostro *Somnero* Ecclesia debet! | Hic raptas nulla lege recenset opes. | Hic priscum Templi ruituri instaurat honorem: | Integra sunt scriptis et monumenta suis. | Pro veris hic molitur chartacea templa.'

[43] See the acknowledgements and notes on sources at Somner, *Dictionarium* sigs. a4r–b1r. Cook, 'Developing techniques' gives overviews of the primary Old English sources 20–53 (and see Lutz, 'Zur Entstehungsgeschichte von William Somners *Dictionarium*' for Somner's use of his own transcripts from Old English manuscripts) and of other sources 54–84, 269–74 and 295; for Somner's use of the *Vocabularium*, see Marckwardt, 'Nowell's *Vocabularium saxonicum* and Somner's *Dictionarium*' and Kennett, 'Life of Mr. Somner' 76–7.

[44] Junius, letters of 25 February 1656 to Dugdale, in F. Junius, *Correspondence* 870–2 at 870, and of 2 March 1657 to the same, ibid. 878–81 at 880.

syntax of a passage that praises Meric Casaubon as 'indeed the worthiest canon of the venerable canons in our church of Canterbury' is the lament that, when Casaubon was installed there, Canterbury Cathedral 'was distinguished and flourishing, but it is now pitifully deformed by the appalling madness of innovation – that is, by the Culmerian (*Culmeriana*) violation of windows, tombs, and ornaments', with a sidenote identifying Culmer and reporting his nickname 'Blew Dick of Thanet'.[45] The first liminary poem in the book, by a poet and antiquary of strong royalist sympathies, Charles Fotherby's cousin John Boys of Hode Court, asks bitterly whether Somner expects 'That we (who have all famous Monuments | Raz'd, and defeated thus all good intents | Of former Piety) will honour give | To antique Characters?' and continues that Somner can no longer devote himself only to the antiquities of Canterbury: 'Loe; the whole Kingdome call's thee: in time save | It's falling Monuments.'[46]

The salvage that Somner was undertaking in the dictionary was the collection of old words but, for Boys, these could be considered together with ancient funerary monuments as part of an endangered heritage. Just the same had in fact been done by John Weever in his *Ancient funerall monuments* of 1631, a collection of epitaphs but also 'the most extensive anthology of medieval verse, as by Chaucer, Gower, Lydgate, and Hoccleve, that had so far appeared', early in whose splendid preface stands the lament that funeral monuments in England

are (to the shame of our time) broken downe, and vtterly almost all ruinated ... by which inhumane, deformidable act, the honourable memory of many vertuous and noble persons deceased, is extinguished, and the true vnderstanding of diuers Families in these Realmes (who haue descended of these worthy persons aforesaid) is so darkened, as the true course of their inheritance is thereby partly interrupted.[47]

This, Weever continued, was an injury 'offered as well to the liuing, as the dead'. His testimony to the heritage value of the monumental inscriptions that he gathered and the poems that he gathered alongside them also

---

[45] Somner, *Dictionarium* sig. a4r, 'in reverendi ... viri ... D. *Merici Casauboni, Is. F.* (vere venerabilium in nostra tunc temporis insigni & florente, nunc autem horrenda Novatorum rabie, *Culmeriana* [*sidenote*: Quidam enim *Richardus Culmerus, Blew Dick of Thanet*, vulgo dictus ...] scil. fenestrarum, sepulchrorum & ornamentorum violatione, misere deformata Ecclesia *Cantuariensi* Canonicorum Canonici dignissimi) ... amicitiam ... receptus sum'.

[46] Ibid. sig. b3r–v. For Boys' relationship to Fotherby, his royalist principles, and a reprinting of the liminary poem to Somner with the added subtitle 'A satyr', see Boys, *Aeneas his descent into hell* sig. A3r, 217ff., and 230–2, and for his antiquarian interests, cf. his unpublished poem 'Fasti cantuarienses, or the history of the renowned cathedral and metropolitical church of Christ Church in Canterbury', for which see Woodruff, *Catalogue* 8 (item 9).

[47] Weever, *Ancient funerall monuments* sig. π3r; for this book as collection of medieval verse, see Terry, *Poetry and the making of the English past* 89.

suggests the heritage value of the words that Somner collected in a project related to his devotion to the built monumental heritage of Canterbury.

A liminary verse in the *Dictionarium* calls Somner a fit peer for 'Our English *Varros*; whose *Herculean toile* | Hath crown'd *Themselves*, with *Glory*, and their native *Soilè*', and identifies those luminaries as Camden, Cotton and Dugdale.[48] The main text of the dictionary likewise makes the Englishness of its contents clear. Somner remarks from time to time on the presence of words derived from a given Old English form in the language of Chaucer or of his own century.[49] He also comments on their relationship to the English topographical heritage. For instance, *beorg* is

a hillock or little hill, a heap of earth, a tombe: such as those in several parts of *Wiltshire*, &c. mentioned of *Mr. Camden*, seconded by the learned *Wormius* in his *Monumenta Danica* . . . and hence our word of *burying*, whereof *Verstegan*, and *Sr. Hen. Spelman*, followed by *Wever*, in his ancient funerall monuments.[50]

Many other entries treat toponyms, often in some detail, as at *Holm* and *Searo-burg*, or questions of cultural history, as in the entries, each three columns long, for *gedrync* and *ordæl*.

In his treatment of the Germanic heritage, Somner gave a fresh demonstration of his familiarity with continental philology. About half of the printed books he cited were from continental Europe. So, for example, the first page of the main text of the dictionary cites four English imprints – Meric Casaubon's *De quatuor linguis*, Alexander Gill's *Logonomia anglica*, Wheelock's edition of Bede, and Spelman's *Archaeologus* – and five continental ones – Worm's *Runir*, Kiel's *Etymologicum*, Junius' edition of the Cædmon Manuscript, G. J. Vossius' *De vitiis sermonis et glossematis latino-barbaris*, and Gilles Ménage's *Origines de la langue françoise*. Germanic cognates are cited frequently, references to Kiel being particularly conspicuous as one reads through the dictionary, while Worm and the editions of Willeram and Otfrid are also, as Somner's preface promises, used regularly.[51]

Somner's dictionary bears comparison with those of continental contemporaries such as Worm, for whom its Latin defining text was meant: he hoped for 'good acceptation at home and abroad; at least, in the latter

---

[48] Somner, *Dictionarium* sig. b4r.
[49] Cook, *Developing techniques* counts 135 references to Chaucer (73; cf. ibid. 142, 'at least 135') and almost 200 to modern English (144).
[50] Citing Verstegan, *Restitution* 211–12; Spelman, *Archaeologus* 96 (s.v. *bergium*); Weever, *Ancient funerall monuments* 6.
[51] Somner, *Dictionarium* sig. B1r, 'quod adeo frequentem *Otfridi, Willerami,* . . . & aliorum quorundam venerandae antiquitatis scriptorum, fecerim mentionem'. Cook, *Developing techniques* identifies 'at least 679' references to Kiel (68) and another 615 labelled 'Belgis', which must for the most part be from Kiel as well (161); 73 to Worm (69); 49 to Otfrid (71); and 128 to Willeram (72).

case, among *Philoteutones*, in other words all those interested in Teutonic antiquities'.[52] A decade or so after it was published, however, Stephen Skinner was to reflect that it looked scanty compared to the Latin and Greek dictionaries of the previous century:

> Please consider, reader, how small a portion of our original language, like a few timbers from a great shipwreck, has come into our hands. For how great can the body of words be which is drawn out of three or four books (and not large ones)? Imagine, if from the Roman authors, nothing had been left to us but Cicero *De officiis* and the histories of Sallust and Tacitus, and from the Greeks, nothing but Herodotus, Thucydides and Xenophon, would Calepinus and Stephanus have grown to the same vast bulk? If you compare our Somner, in diligence inferior to neither of them, to that corpulent pair, would you not declare that here you saw a Hercules and there a Hylas, here a cyclops, and there a pigmy?[53]

This account not only reworked the narrative of devastation told by sixteenth-century classical scholars, suggesting that the pitiful ruins of Old English made the ruins of the classical heritage look fine and spacious, but reworked the tradition of self-presentation as Herculean and perhaps even Henri Estienne's brief, rueful self-identification with Polyphemus, pushing the ludicrous possibilities of the latter further: the word translated 'corpulent' is *ventriosus*, literally 'big-bellied', a comic word found in Plautus.

The making of the *Dictionarium* depended partly on support from an inheritance of money: when the incumbent of Spelman's praelectorship at Cambridge, Abraham Wheelock, died in 1653, Spelman's grandson Roger, 'heir to the philological gifts as to the fortune of that most noble hero', made part of its income available to Somner to support his work. The *Dictionarium* duly opens with an epistle to Roger Spelman: not a dedication, for the work is dedicated to 'each and every one of the students, at home and abroad, present and future, of the Saxon language, formerly the vernacular of the English', but an epistle that looks very like a dedication, and marks the book as one in which the addressee has a

---

[52] Somner, *Dictionarium* sig. A4v, 'non mediocri cum domi tum foris acceptatione; saltem (inter exteros) apud *Philoteutones*, (omnes scil. *Teutonicarum* Antiquitatum … studiosos …)'.

[53] Skinner, *Etymologicon* sig. C4r, 'quam exigua prisci nostri sermonis portio, tanquam e magno naufragio pauci asseres, ad manus nostras devenerit. Quantillum enim est verborum quod ex tribus vel quatuor non magnis libris depromi potest? Si enim ex *Romanis* Authoribus, nihil, puta, praeter *Tullium de officio* & *Sallusti, Tacitique* historias: ex *Graecis* nihil praeter *Herodotum, Thucididem* & *Xenophontem* superesset, nunquid *Calepinus* & *Stephanus* in immanem istam molem excrescerunt? Si *Somnerum* nostrum, diligentia neutri ipsorum secundum, duobus illis ventriosis conferas, quid aliud quam hinc *Herculem*, inde *Hylam*, hinc *Cyclopem*, inde *Pygmaeum* te videre jurabis?' Cf. the lightly adapted translation in Kennett, 'Life of Mr. Somner' 84–5.

personal as well as a hereditary interest.[54] The epistle to the reader that follows it identifies more obligations, for instance to James Ussher, who had (at Casaubon's and Dugdale's prompting) encouraged Roger Spelman to fund the dictionary, and, in pride of place, to Meric Casaubon.[55] Casaubon also takes up much of the first entry in the dictionary, for the prefix a- as in *abæran* 'to bear', in which Somner's statement that English borrows from Greek the aphaeresis of initial *a*- follows the phrasing of a passage in *De quatuor linguis* very closely, and is succeeded by the explanation that 'I was taught this, among many other things which are not widely known, by the one outstanding patron of my studies, Dr Meric Casaubon, the son of – and equal to – a great father, one to whom I am, like all students of this language, greatly indebted.'[56] Calling Meric Casaubon the equal of his father looks like laying it on with a trowel, but perhaps Somner really believed it. He identifies other contemporaries in other entries: the medical term *neþereoðan* is discussed with a reference to Dr William Jacob of Canterbury, who contributed a liminary poem to the dictionary, and the reader of the entry *hlæwe* 'hillock, tumulus' is referred, in English, to 'a large and learned discourse in that accurate and elaborate Description of *Warwickshire* by (the great retriever of our *English* Antiquities) my noble friend, Mr. *William Dugdale*: one (to do him right) without whose most active and effectual assistance in the publication of it, this work had never seen the light'.[57] Just as Somner honoured Meric Casaubon in the conspicuous first entry of the dictionary, so he ensured that this praise of Dugdale would be read, for there is a cross-reference to the entry for *hlæwe* on the last page of the book, in a list of the *philologi*, a number of them connected with Dugdale, who had sponsored its publication. There are eighty-three of them, together with fourteen Cambridge colleges (but no Oxford ones, although Bodley's Librarian is there, as is the late Provost of Queen's College, and the book

[54] Somner, *Dictionarium* sig. a4v describes the assignment of income as 'ab haerede tam philologicarum dorum quam fortunarum ejusdem nobiliss[imi] Herois, praeclaro scil[icet] ipsius *Henrici* nepote'; the epistle to Roger Spelman is ibid. sig. a3r–v, with another account of the assignment of income to Somner a3v (cf. also Kennett, 'Life of Mr. Somner' 73–4); the dedication proper is ibid. sig. a2r.

[55] Somner, *Dictionarium* sigs. b1r (Ussher), a4r (Casaubon); for Dugdale and Casaubon's persuasion of Ussher, see M. Casaubon, letter to Dugdale of November 5 1655, in Dugdale, *Life, diary and correspondence* 294–5 at 295.

[56] Somner, *Dictionarium* sig. A1r, 'quod, inter alia plura haud vulgaria, me docuit Studiorum meorum fautor ille unicus, D. *Mericus Casaubonus*, magni quidem patris non minor filius, ac de me, & omnibus istius linguae studiosis vir optime meritus'.

[57] Somner is citing Dugdale, *Antiquities of Warwickshire* 3–5 (in an account of the place-name *Knightlow*). Dugdale remembered this acknowledgement in his autobiography (in Dugdale, *Life, diary and correspondence* 5–37 at 37). For his interest in barrows see, e.g., Piggott, *Ancient Britons* 120.

was printed in Oxford): gentlemen antiquaries such as Sir Roger Twysden and Dugdale's friend Sir Simon Archer; Kentish gentry such as John Boys of Hode Court; learned men such as the lexicographer and orientalist Edmund Castell, the astrologer William Lilly, and the antiquary and polymath Elias Ashmole. Like Dodsworth and Dugdale's *Monasticon*, Somner's *Dictionarium* is a monument to a cultural heritage and to the community who valued it.

Between the dictionary and this list of supporters is an eighty-page appendix presented as the *editio princeps* of Ælfric's *Grammar* and *Glossary* (in fact, the glossary is a conflated transcript by Franciscus Junius of two other Old English glossaries).[58] Junius' source for the glossary was a manuscript that had for some years belonged to the Moretus family, but had been borrowed by the painter Rubens and was, when Junius had access to it, in the possession of Rubens' son.[59] Somner's account of the glossary betrays a sense of regret that such a work should have left England: whereas he had seen fine and ancient manuscripts of the *Grammar* in English collections, and had been able to use one from the royal library, 'The *Glossary* on the other hand has been sought from somewhat farther afield, inasmuch as it was copied in its entirety by Franciscus Junius FF ... [and, in the form of this transcript] brought back to its native land.'[60] It is to Junius that we now turn.

THE MAN WHO RESTORED ITS ANCIENT LANGUAGES
TO THE FATHERLAND: THE LEXICOGRAPHICAL
THOUGHT OF FRANCISCUS JUNIUS

Franciscus Junius (François du Jon) appeared earlier in this narrative as a visitor to the household of Sir Simonds D'Ewes in 1648 and 1649, who began, but did not complete, the preparation for print of D'Ewes' Old

---

[58] Its title-page (Somner, *Dictionarium* sig. Xx3r) presents it as 'Ælfrici, abbatis sui temporis dignissimi, grammatici vulgo dicti, grammatica latino–saxonica: una cum ejusdem, Ælfrici, glossario latino–saxonica, utrumque ante annos plus minus septingentos, scriptis mandatum, in gratiam linguae Anglo-Saxonicae studiosorum, nunc primum in lucem edidit Guliel[mus] Somnerus, Cantuarien[sis]'.

[59] Junius' transcript is now Bodl. MS Junius 71; its source has been divided, and is now partly Antwerp, Plantin-Moretus Museum MS 47, but partly BL Add. MS 32246 (a facsimile, Bodl. MS Facs. d. 76, reunites the two). For details, see Ladd, '"Rubens" manuscript'.

[60] Somner, *Dictionarium* sig. b2r, 'Pulchra quidem & perantiqua apud nostrates sunt ejusdem Grammaticae, quae vidimus & inspeximus, exemplaria: haec inter, Regium illud ad S. *Jacobi* [now BL MS Royal 15 B xxii], antiquum admodum & satis authenticum, omnino sequuti sumus. Glossarium autem illud paulo remotius petitum est, utpote quod ex pervetusto exemplari MS ... a *Francisco Junio, F. F.* ... integre descriptum, in patriam reductum ... fuerit,' quoted and translated Ladd, '"Rubens" manuscript' 354–5.

English dictionary. This modest philological activity, undertaken by a man already in his fifties, was very soon followed by the extraordinary achievements that led the Dutch antiquary and maker of wordlists Jan van Vliet to praise Junius as 'the man who restored its ancient languages to the fatherland, and restored beauty to the languages'.[61] Junius is remembered today as a founder of the comparative historical study of the Germanic languages, and as the owner and editor of one of the four principal manuscripts of Old English poetry, Bodleian MS Junius 11, the Cædmon or Junius Manuscript. He was also one of the most prolific lexicographers of his century, a scholar who, whenever he had a problem to think about, seemed to turn to the making of glossaries as a means of finding the way forward.

He was born at Heidelberg in 1591, the son of an eminent theologian of the same name. He is often identified as Franciscus Junius F. F., i.e., *Francisci filius*, distinguishing him both from his father and from his first cousin once removed, Franciscus Junius F. N., *Francisci nepos*, but at the same time identifying him as the son of a famous father, 'rival of his father's learning and reputation' as Somner put it.[62] The poet Joost van den Vondel was to see him as a member of a hereditary aristocracy of learning: 'When he looks back at his lineage, Junius does not pride himself on the nobility of his ancestors, acquired bravely by the gory rapier, but on their honour in letters, acquired by a pen.'[63] He grew up in Leiden, and therefore had native fluency in Dutch, although his father was French. As a young man, he lived for a while in the household of his brother-in-law G. J. Vossius. The latter's *De vitiis sermonis et glossematis latino-barbaris*, which as we have seen was used by Somner in his *Dictionarium*, is in effect a discursive dictionary of post-classical Latin, covering about 4200 words; in the tradition of Budé's *Commentarii*, it is not alphabetically ordered, but has a good alphabetical union index. It was the product of wide and critical reading, spanning the classical and vernacular languages. Vossius is to be found engaging with Robert Estienne on the etymology of *palefredus*, 'palfrey', and with Henri Estienne on the form *hebdomas*, 'week', but he also discusses questions raised by Goropius Becanus such as the etymology

---

[61] In Boethius, *Consolationis philosophiae libri v, anglo-saxonice redditi* (1698), frontispiece, 'Qui priscas patriae linguas linguisq[ue] decorem | Reddidit'; for van Vliet, see Dekker, *Origins of Old Germanic studies*, esp. 104 and n274 (verses on Junius) and 135–9 (wordlists).

[62] Somner, *Dictionarium* sig. a4r, '*Francisco Junio, F.F.* paternae laudis & eruditionis aemulo.'

[63] Van den Vondel, poem 'Aen den edelen heer Francois Junius, F. Z. ', in F. Junius, *Correspondence* 1074, 'Zoo Iunius te rugge ziet | Naer zijn geslacht; hy roemt zich niet | Op der vooroudren adel, fier | Verworven door 't bebloet rappier | Maer op hun lettereer, behaelt | Met eene pen', translation adapted slightly from ibid. 1075.

of *herberg* and by Kiel such as the sense of the word *tribunculus*.[64] As this suggests, his work often led him into Germanic material, and the following quotation is representative of many others:

Notnumfti is glossed *violence* in the *Glossarium latino–theotiscum*. There is also a heading *De notnumfti* in the laws of the Frisians, and indeed the law begins 'If anybody takes away anything by force'. Lindenbrog adds in his glossary that the same word is to be found in the *Speculum saxonicum* book 1 article 43 [etc.][65]

Vossius even touched on Gothic, discussing the one Gothic word that everybody knew, *atta* 'father', the first word of the Lord's Prayer.[66] The opportunity to see Germanic material handled like this may have been an influence on the young Franciscus Junius. In his mature work, Junius showed less interest than his brother-in-law in what he would call 'that corrupted barbarous Latin', but he admired the 'most compleat librarie of all manner of printed bookes and m[anuscripts], both in Greeke and Latin' formed by G. J. Vossius and augmented by his son Isaac, and was indebted to it for 'diverse Francike, Anglo-Saxonike, and Gothic Antiquities, no where else to be found'.[67]

Junius studied at the University of Leiden, where he must have attended the lectures of Bonaventure de Smet.[68] He was then the Calvinist minister of a parish near Rotterdam; after theological controversy made it impossible for him to continue in his ministry, he moved to England, where he lived for twenty years in the service of Thomas Howard, Earl of Arundel, the collector of art and antiquities whose library of manuscripts was one of the sources named on the title-page of the *Monasticon anglicanum*. As well as having access to Howard's books, Junius had a collection of his own, built up carefully and at some expense; by the time of his departure from the Low Countries in 1620, he had already acquired a copy of the *Thesaurus graecae linguae*.[69] His first major

---

[64] Vossius, *De vitiis sermonis* 151 (*hebdomada*), 256 (*palefredus*), 223 (*herberg*), 301 (*tribunculus*).

[65] Ibid. 253, '*Notnumfti* in Glossario Latino–Theotisco exponitur *violentia*. Ac in L. L. Frisiorum Titulus est *de Notnumfti*. Lex vero incipit: *Siquis rem quamlibet vi rapuerit*. Lindenbrogius addit in Glossario, legi eampse vocem in Speculo Saxonico lib. 1 Artic. XLIII. ' For Vossius and Germanic studies, see Dekker, *Origins of Old Germanic studies* 221f.

[66] Van de Velde, *Studie van het Gotisch in de Nederlanden* 131.

[67] For 'barbarous Latin', see Junius, letter of 29 May 1661 to Dugdale, in F. Junius, *Correspondence* 980–4 at 982; for the excellence of the Vossian library, see Junius, letter of 12 May 1656 to Dugdale, ibid. 874–6 at 874.

[68] He was certainly studying Greek diligently while de Smet was professor of Greek: see his letter of 1608 to G. J. Vossius in F. Junius, *Correspondence* 90–3 at 92–3.

[69] For his book-buying, see his letter of 14 February 1615 to G. J. Vossius, ibid. 116–23; for his ownership of the *Thesaurus graecae linguae*, see his letter of 10 June 1622 to Johanna Junius, ibid. 268–79 at 274–5.

work, an account of painting in the ancient world called *De pictura veterum* (1637), brought philological methods to the field of Arundel's interests. He returned to the Low Countries in 1641 as tutor to Aubrey de Vere, twentieth Earl of Oxford, who had been brought up with his Frisian mother's family after the early death of his father. This movement between England and the Low Countries had its consequences for Junius' philology. By the mid-1640s he had begun, like Verstegan, de Laet and D'Ewes before him, to reflect seriously on the connection between Dutch and English.[70] These two languages, both very well known to him, were so similar as to be evidently related to each other, and were moreover spoken in neighbouring countries with a long and close historical relationship. Around 1647, as his tutorship of Lord Oxford was coming to an end, he decided to further his understanding of both languages by learning a third that was closely related to them, Frisian, whose importance for historical Germanic philology had, as we have seen, already been glimpsed both by de Smet and by de Laet. He stayed in Friesland for some time, studying the language with the Frisian poet Gysbert Japix.[71]

Then or shortly thereafter, he began work on a Dutch etymological dictionary, now mostly lost, with the working title 'Etymologicum teutonicum', perhaps in response to the publication in 1642 of a new edition of Kiel's dictionary from which much of the etymological material had been excised.[72] The 'Etymologicum' cited Old English and Old Norse forms (Junius was studying material in both languages by the beginning of 1649), and was characterized by the argument that the vocabularies of these languages, together with Dutch, derived from Greek: by May 1650, it was well enough advanced for Junius to say that he was 'wholly applying myself to submitting to the press at the first possible opportunity ... an etymological dictionary, in which I have brought back several thousands of Dutch words (*vocum teutonicarum*) to their Greek origins'.[73] In the following year, the classicist Johannes Gronovius wrote

---

[70] Breuker, 'On the course of Franciscus Junius's Germanic studies' 139, quotes a document of October / November 1653 in which Junius claims that he 'had by eight or tenn yeeres studie made some Observations' on Germanic which he was now ready to print, in other words that, no later than 1645, he had begun studies that were serious enough to lead directly to publishable work on Germanic philology.

[71] For the date, see Breuker, 'Junius's Germanic studies' 139f.

[72] Ibid. 142–3; van Romburgh, 'Why Francis Junius ... became an Anglo-Saxonist' 8ff.

[73] For his first reference to Old Norse and Old English, see his letter to Isaac Vossius of 29 January 1649 in F. Junius, *Correspondence* 758–67 at 762–3; for the development of the dictionary, see his letter to Franciscus Junius F. N. of May 1650, ibid. 782–95 at 786–7, 'Totus nunc in eo sum ut prima quaque occasione ... praelo subiiciam etymologicum, in quo chiliades aliquot vocum Teutonicarum ad Graecas origines refero.'

to a friend that Junius 'has ready a lexicon of origins of the language of our country (*linguae patriae*), in which there is much excellent material from the ancient writings of the Anglo-Saxons: whether, however, all of our words can and must be derived from Greek, as he has decided, you shall judge'.[74] A sketch of a similar production survives among Junius' manuscripts: a short Scots vocabulary in which possible derivations from ancient Greek are presented, which may be a result of his visit to Scotland around 1648.[75] A couple of longer notes before the main sequence of this vocabulary give an idea of the degree of confidence of the argument. One, on *shypen*, begins by glossing the word with the Latin equivalent *bubile* and the English equivalents 'an oxe-stall, a cowe-house'; continues with two illustrations of the earlier form *scypen* from the Old English translation of Bede, together with the Latin originals of the cited passages; and then states that 'it is altogether probable that this word *scypen* is from σκέπω "I cover with a roof"'. Another observes that '*dal* once meant "father" among the Scots, as Bede attests in the first chapter of Book I of the *Ecclesiastical history*. Perhaps relevant here is the form δάλεμον, which Hesychius explains as equivalent to κηδεμών "guardian, tutor".'[76] These longer notes are then followed by roughly three hundred short entries. Some of these simply set two forms side by side, allowing their similarities to speak for themselves, so that for instance the word *stable* is glossed with its Latin equivalent *stabulum* and then followed without comment by Greek σταῦλος.[77] Others are slightly fuller: '*Snib* or *snip*: to exclaim against, to reprehend. From ἐνίσσειν, by a transposition of letters'.[78]

Junius' arguments for Greek as a mother-language were contemporaneous with those of his friend Meric Casaubon in *De quatuor linguis*, of which he owned and annotated a copy.[79] Both men were reacting against the well-established claim that the Germanic languages were independent

---

[74] Johannes Gronovius, letter of 17 October 1651 to Nicolaas Heinsius in Breuker, 'Junius's Germanic studies' 142, 'habet paratum Lexicon originum linguae patriae, in quo multo praeclara ex Anglosaxonum veteribus monumentis: an tamen ita omnia nostra possint, debeantque ad Graecos reduci, ut illi visum, tu judicabis'.

[75] Junius, letter to Isaac Vossius of 29 January 1649 in F. Junius, *Correspondence* 758–67 at 758–9, gives the date of the visit to Scotland. The glossary is Bodl. MS Junius 74 fos. 18–36.

[76] Bodl. MS Junius 74, fo. 17r, 'Shypen, Bubile. an oxe-stall, a cowe-house ... Omnino videtur *scýpen* istud esse a σκέπω, Tego ... Dal Scotis olim Patrem significabat, teste ven. Beda lib. 1 hist. eccles. cap. 1. Forte huc pertinet quod Hesychius δάλεμον exponit κηδεμόνα, curatorem, tutorem.'

[77] Ibid., fo. 34r, 'Stable, stabulu[m]. σταῦλος'.

[78] Ibid., fo. 33v, 'Snib vel snip, Increpare, reprehendere. ab ἐνίσσειν, literaru[m] transpositione'.

[79] Junius' copy of *De quatuor linguis* is now at Leiden: see Dekker, '*Vide Kilian*' 523–4 and F. Junius, *Correspondence* 959n65. Letters of his to Casaubon of 26 August 1630 and 28 February 1633 are ibid. 398–9 and 454–7.

from Greek and Latin. They might have had three objections to it. First, they had both grown up in households where Greek was studied at a high level of sophistication, and both therefore began their scholarly careers with a strong sense of its antiquity and of the dignity of scholarship directed towards it; both had, moreover, published on the Graeco-Roman world before turning towards Germanic studies. (Casaubon may have been aware of his grandfather's interest in the conformity of Greek and French, and Junius owned a copy of Henri Estienne's *De la precellence.*[80]) Second, they could see striking resemblances between Greek and the Germanic vernaculars, and reasoned that the similarity between two languages, one of which is attested by much earlier documents than the other, can be explained more elegantly by supposing one to be the parent of the other than by supposing that the two are siblings, one of which has no records of its early history. Third, they may have been unwilling to imagine their cultural heritage to go back either to the bloodthirsty and illiterate Germani described by Tacitus or to the post-Babelic followers of Tuisco described by the discredited pseudo-Berosus.

Both Junius and Casaubon handled material in more than one Germanic language, and both therefore had in front of them the evidence that those languages had much more in common with each other than with Greek. The implications of this evidence became stronger as more languages were considered: Casaubon could inspect Lipsius' Old Dutch wordlist and observe only that a number of the forms it registered 'seemed to have the taste of pure, genuine Saxonism', but Junius was fluent in English and Dutch, knew Old English well and had some knowledge of Frisian and Scots, so that he had the means to start building up a picture of relationships in which Greek was decreasingly relevant. Two manuscript rediscoveries in 1653–4, giving access to two more languages, finally forced Junius to discard the narrative of heritage that he had been telling in the 'Etymologicum teutonicum'.

In the first of these rediscoveries, Junius found himself revisiting his own past, and meeting Old High German:

In 1653, when I was at Heidelberg (where I took my very first breaths in this world), I chanced upon the harmony of the Gospels by Tatian in a Latin–Frankish version [i.e., both a Latin translation from the original Greek or Syriac and an Old High German translation from the Latin], which had been sent by Bonaventure de Smet to Marquard Freher, divided into 244 chapters, but suffering from the loss of about 76 chapters in the middle. But although such a grievous loss struck my heart

---

[80] Now Bodl. MS Junius 118: see Stanley, 'Sources of Junius's learning' 175.

with no trivial sorrow, yet by no means did it cast down my intention to survey what was still extant further and more deeply: rather, I decided to illuminate the whole work with what might be called a continuous commentary.[81]

This is the narrative of the partial, but only partial, recovery of a damaged textual heritage which is familiar from the careers of sixteenth-century classical philologists such as Henri Estienne and medieval philologists such as the early students of Old English. What called to Junius was precisely the damaged heritage precariously preserved in manuscript rather than the fuller and more readily accessible monument offered by Flacius' edition of Otfrid, of which he had in fact owned and given away a copy many years earlier.[82] Striking also is the emphasis on not being downcast by the damage: Junius wrote this note in Freher's Tatian manuscript as he was annotating it for publication, and preceded it with an epigraph from Cicero, 'I value antiquity highly; nor do I call more vigorously for what is lacking from antiquity than I praise what is extant, especially since, in my judgement, what is extant is superior to what is lost.'[83] The version of Tatian was not the only monument of Old High German that Junius encountered. In March 1654 he reported to Selden that, although he had not found many 'old *Francick monuments*' in Germany, he had encountered 'four *MS. glossaria*, besides *26 Hymnos veteris ecclesiae cum antiqua interlineatione Theotisca* [hymns of the early church, with an ancient Germanic interlinear gloss]': the hymns and three of the glossaries were part of the so-called Murbach Hymnal, which Junius' nephew Isaac Vossius had just bought from the heirs of Marcus Zuerius Boxhorn, and the fourth glossary was from another manuscript acquired from the same source. 'I begin', he continued, 'to think my self now so wel instructed with good subsidyes, as that I shal be bold to try how to ad something to what Goldastus and Freherus have commented in that kind.'[84]

---

[81] Freher's copy of Tatian, with interleaved additions by Junius, is Bodl. MS Junius 13 (for it see Ganz, 'MS. Junius 13 und die althochdeutsche Tatianübersetzung' 32–7); Junius' statement is ibid., fo. 5r, 'Incidi Heidelbergae (ubi primas hujus lucis auras ipse hausi) anno D[omini] M D C LIII in Tatiani Alexandrini harmoniam euangelicam Latino–Francica[m] a Bonaventura Vulcanio quondam ad Marquardum Freherum transmissam atque in capita CCXLIV distinctam, sed in medio sui LXXVI circiter capitum lacuna foedam. Ac licet jactura tam atrox non levi pectus moerore pulsaret, nequaquam tamen deposui animum altius aliquanto penitiusq[ue] percensendi quae supererant; sed universum opus perpetuo veluti commentario illustrare institui.'

[82] Rademaker, 'Young Franciscus Junius' 9–10.

[83] Bodl. MS Junius 13, fo. 1r, quoting Cicero, *Orator* 169, 'Antiquitas apud me valet plurimum: nec ego id, quod deest antiquitati, flagito potius, quam laudo, quod est; præsertim cum ea majora judicem, quae sunt, quam illa, quae desunt.' For the manuscript, see 'MSS. Junius' 966.

[84] F. Junius, letter to Selden of 8 May 1654 in his *Correspondence* 848–51 at 848. See Breuker, 'Junius's Germanic studies' 145–6 (but for the facts that the manuscripts were bought by Isaac Vossius and are not in the auction catalogue of the Boxhorn sale in 1654, see Palmer, 'Junius's blockbooks'

In the same year, newly excited by this Old High German material, he met another language in another manuscript. This was the Gothic of the Codex Argenteus, which had been acquired for the library of Rudolf II at Prague before 1600, and had then been taken as loot to Stockholm after Prague was overrun by Swedish troops in 1648. By this time, Isaac Vossius was in Stockholm as one of Queen Christina's court of scholars, and in the confusion after her abdication in 1654 he had chosen it as a payment for services rendered. He sent it to Amsterdam, where his uncle could read it.[85] Junius had owned Busbecq's Gothic wordlist for many years, and had known quite a lot about the Codex Argenteus since 1651, when James Ussher had described it to him in a letter about the resources for the study of Gothic.[86] Its arrival on his desk three years later was a remarkable stroke of good luck. Now he could see a Germanic language, evidently much more closely related to Dutch than Greek was, which was attested in texts over a thousand years old.

Further energized by this new access of information, Junius set to work. By mid-November, 'fired with an astonishing desire for haste', he had sent his *Observationes* on the Old High German Willeram to the press.[87] This book appeared in the following year, and sold well enough for Junius to be working on a second edition ten years later, although this was never published.[88] Its two series of wordlists show his lexicographical thought in transition. On the one hand, there are over a hundred pages of lists of Dutch, Old English, Gothic and Welsh monosyllables that appeared to him to derive from Greek words, and these echo, and incorporate material from, the 'Etymologicum teutonicum'.[89] On the other hand, the twenty-two-page glossed lexical index of Old High German and Old English at the end of the *Observationes* refers readers to passages in the commentary that contribute to a Germanic philology independent of narratives of

158n54 and 160n59); for the Murbach Hymnal, now Bodl. MS Junius 25, and the second manuscript, now MS Junius 83, see 'MSS. Junius' 969–71 and 981–2.

[85] For the *terminus ante quem* for Rudolf's acquisition of the Codex Argenteus, see Munkhammar, *Silver bibeln* 128; for its plunder in 1648, ibid. 130f.; for its travel to Amsterdam, see Breuker, 'Junius's Germanic studies' 145, 149.

[86] For Junius' copy of Busbecq, see his letter of 10 June 1622 to Johanna Junius in F. Junius, *Correspondence* 268–79 at 276–7; Ussher's letter to him on Gothic, of 3 July 1651, is ibid. 802–11.

[87] F. Junius, *Observationes* sig. X7v; for the date, see his letter of 12 November 1654 to Isaac Vossius, in his *Correspondence* 852–5 at 852–3.

[88] For the proposed second edition, see F. Junius, letter of 13 March 1665 to an unidentified correspondent, in his *Correspondence* 1000–7 at 1002–3, and for Junius' marked-up copies of the 1655 edition see Bremmer, 'Retrieving Junius's correspondence' 233, and Stanley, 'Sources of Junius's learning' 171.

[89] Junius, *Observationes* 176–233 ('monosyllaba Teutonica e Graecarum vocum initiis detruncata'); 233–58 ('monosyllaba Anglo-Saxonica e Graecarum vocum principio veluti abrupta'); 259–65 ('monosyllaba Gothica ex initialibus Graecorum vocabulorum literis abscissa'); 265–83 ('monosyllaba Cambro-Britannica e Graecarum vocum principio desumta').

supposed Greek heritage. Although these draw on Meric Casaubon's Greek etymologies, they also, and more importantly, use material from Otfrid, Tatian, Junius' glossarial manuscripts, the early Middle High German *Annolied* and so on; much of this material was unpublished, which tantalized van Vliet as he read the *Observationes*.[90] Anglo-Saxon types were cut for the Old English parts of this comparative Germanic material; these would be followed by 1663 by Gothic and runic, the whole set being known as the Junian types.[91] Only a few months after the *Observationes*, Junius' Anglo-Saxon types were used for his *princeps* of the Cædmon Manuscript, which had been given or lent to him by James Ussher in 1651–2. This edition was the first printed book of verse in Old English.[92] It lacked a commentary, although Junius made some manuscript notes towards one.[93] The publication was closely linked to Junius' programme of comparative work on the languages related to Dutch: the extant Old English texts were important to him because he supposed their language to be close to the common ancestor of Dutch, Frisian and English: the 'obsolete Saxon language' of Spelman's letter to de Laet.[94]

Junius regretted that the *Observationes* would not present its readers with more material from the Codex Argenteus, which he had had no time to integrate into his main commentary.[95] But he proclaimed the importance of Gothic in his dedicatory epistle:

The Frankish language [*lingua francica*, i.e., Old High German] is certainly old, Anglo-Saxon is older, but Gothic is in truth by far the oldest. Each of these three looks as if it was born to shed light miraculously on our vernacular, but comparing all three together with our language is specially suitable for embellishing and extending the glory of High German and Dutch.[96]

---

[90] For van Vliet's remarks, see his letter of 26 July 1659 to Isaac Vossius, quoted and translated Dekker, *Origins of Old Germanic studies* 91 and n215.

[91] For the types, see Lucas, 'Junius, his printers, and his types' and Dekker, *Origins of Old Germanic studies* 101.

[92] The *terminus ante quem* for his acquisition of the manuscript is given by Christoph Arnold's letter to him of November 1652 in F. Junius, *Correspondence* 836–41 (see esp. 836–7n5). For its place in the history of the printing of Old English verse, see Plumer, 'Construction of structure' 275.

[93] His marked-up copy of the 1655 edition, Bodl. MS Junius 73, is apparently only sparsely annotated (see Stanley, 'Sources of Junius's learning' 171), but he made ten leaves of fuller notes, now Bodl. MS Junius 73*, and compiled a volume comprising 'extemporaneae conjecturae et qualiscunque indiculus', now Bodl. MS Junius 113.

[94] See van Romburgh, 'Why Francis Junius … became an Anglo-Saxonist' 18f.

[95] F. Junius, letter of 12 November 1654 to Isaac Vossius, in his *Correspondence* 852–5; cf. his *Observationes* 259.

[96] F. Junius, *Observationes* sig. π2v, 'Antiqua certe est lingua Francica, antiquior Anglo-Saxonica, longe vero antiquissima est Gothica: quarum singulae ut ut mirifice vernaculam nostram illustrare natae sint, constat tamen mutuam trium istarum cum nostra collationem praecipue facere ad exornandum atque amplificandum superioris inferiorisque Germanicae decus.'

Before the end of the critical year 1654, Junius had transcribed the Codex Argenteus and had begun to plan an edition.[97] He may at first have imagined a plain-text edition like that of the Cædmon Manuscript, but he set to work before long on a glossary of Gothic words accompanied with the Greek words that they translated, and by the beginning of 1663 he was modestly announcing that he would like 'to shed some light on the Gothic text with a few notes', which would be lexical and phraseological, and would be accompanied by parallel texts in Greek, Old English and Latin.[98] What eventually appeared, printed with the Junian types and published in 1665, was a parallel text of the Gospels in Gothic and Old English (the latter edited by Thomas Marshall, chaplain to the English Merchant Adventurers at Dordrecht) with a long commentary, paginated continuously with the text.[99] The edition was accompanied by a discursive glossary of more than four hundred pages, the *Glossarium gothicum*, with its own half-title, dated 1664, and its own preliminaries, including a Latin poem by van Vliet, which is adorned with seventy-four footnotes.[100] Although the glossary is dated earlier than the edition, the title-page of the latter does specify that the glossary belongs with it, and the two appear always to have been issued together.[101]

By 1664, Junius had firmly rejected the theory of the Greek origin of Germanic words:

Although it is true that the origins of many appear to go back to Greek sources, yet I do not want to accept that our fathers drew, as it were, the dominant part of their language from the Greeks, when it seems nearer to the truth that ancient Greek and Scythian – and also Gothic itself, which came from ancient Scythian – developed from some common origin, and indeed a great many men of the most eminent learning think it likelier that Greek came from Scythian/Germanic than that Germanic came from Greek.[102]

---

[97] F. Junius, letter of 12 November 1654 to Isaac Vossius in his *Correspondence* 852–5 at 854–5; the transcript (or a fair copy thereof, as suggested by Dekker, *Origins of Old Germanic studies* 177) is now Bodleian MS Junius 55.

[98] For the shift from plain text to annotated edition, see F. Junius, letter to Isaac Vossius of 12 January 1663 in his *Correspondence* 996–1001 at 998, 'den Gotischen text met eenighe *notulis* wat lichts te geven'; for the early glossary, see Dekker, *Origins of Old Germanic studies* 114–15 and 177–8.

[99] It is discussed Van de Velde, *De studie van het Gotisch* 166–85.

[100] The poem, in Junius and Marshall, eds., *Quatuor . . . euangeliorum versiones perantiquae duae* sigs. *2r–**4v, is edited and translated with a commentary in Dekker, *Origins of Old Germanic studies* 388–429.

[101] Cf. Dekker, *Origins of Old Germanic studies* 99–100 for the order of completion: first texts, then glossary, then commentary, Marshall's contributions being the cause of delay.

[102] Junius, *Gothicum glossarium* xvii: 'Licet vero plurimas originationes videar ad fontes Graecos retulisse, non tamen hoc ita velim accipi, quasi potissimam linguae suae partem Patres nostri hauserint a Graecis; cum veritati magis videatur consentaneum veterem Graecam Scyticamq[ue]

Here we see him taking up ideas that had already been sketched by Goropius a century earlier, imagining a lineage for the Germanic languages in which Greek is their cousin, not their ancestor, wondering whether Germanic forms might not even be nearer to those of the common ancestor than Greek ones are, and identifying that ancestor tentatively as Scythian. This powerful model of linguistic heritage attracted Junius away from the study of the individual ancient texts that he had been publishing since 1655, towards the comparative study of the Germanic languages, for which he had Gessner and de Smet as models – and particularly towards lexicography.[103]

So, in the published edition of the Gothic Gospels, it was on lexicography rather than editing that his thoughts ran. It was the glossary that he provided with a foreword, not the edition proper, in which the only substantial prefatory item was the dedication to the Swedish nobleman who had, by 1665, bought the Codex Argenteus from Isaac Vossius. In the foreword to the glossary, he rehearses the difficulties of lexicography somewhat in the spirit of Henri Estienne, quoting the epigram in which Scaliger suggested it as the hardest form of penal servitude, and continuing that

for sure, the thoughts of humans are unable to imagine sufficiently and fully how much attention and diligence this business calls for; nobody can more truly tell the story of how many and how great are the embarrassments of most gloomy anxieties which surround the building up of a dictionary than he who has applied himself to this kind of writing.[104]

These are the words of someone who sees himself as committed to a daunting future of lexicographical work, not of an editor for whom the compilation of a glossary is a parergon to the establishment of a text. This commitment explains why Junius left his edition of the Old High German Tatian well advanced, but did not see it through the press.

The story being told in the *Glossarium* itself is not only about Gothic, as can be seen by examining a typical representative of the longer entries,

---

nec non ipsam quoque Gothicam ex vetere Scytica provenientem, a communi aliqua origine promanasse, multiq[ue] adeo viri longe doctissimi illam potius ex hac, quam hanc ex illa desumptam censeant.' Cf. Dekker, *Origins of Old Germanic studies* 260f.

[103] His copy of *Mithridates* is now Bodl. MS Junius 88 (he refers to it, e.g., in his letter of August 1660 to Johann Clauberg, in F. Junius, *Correspondence* 930–79 at 972–5) and his copy of *De literis et lingua getarum* is MS Junius 98; he cites de Smet's specimen of Gothic in *Quatuor . . . euangeliorum versiones* sig. *3r.

[104] F. Junius, *Gothicum glossarium* sig. ***3r, 'Humanae certe cogitationes nequeunt satis abundeque concipere, quantam curam diligentiamq[ue] postulet hoc negotium; ac nemo rectius narraverit quot quantaeq[ue] morossisimarum anxietatum difficultates circumstent Onomasticum aliquod molientem, quam qui animum suum ad hoc scribendi genus appulit.'

that for *thaurnjus*, 'thorns'. This begins with a note of two verses of the New Testament in which the word occurs, and then with quotations from three others, Gothic text being followed by Latin translation. Then come nine cognates: Old English *ðorn* and *ðyrn*; German *dorn* and *thorn*; Danish *torn* and *tiørne*; modern English *thorn*; Dutch *deurne* and *doorne*. After that, Junius proposes that 'it looks as if the origin of the word is to be sought in τορός "penetrating, piercing with a point". Others, however, derive it rather from τύρειν, which is the same as τείρειν "to torment".'[105] A passage follows on the possibility that the Greek word τύραννος 'tyrant, unconstitutional ruler' refers to such a ruler's tormenting the people. Then Junius returns to Germanic, explaining that the Dutch words *deurne* and *dorne* mean a pin or brooch to fasten a garment, as do Old Norse *thorn* and Icelandic *þørn*. Indeed, he reflects, Dutch also has a word *spelle* 'pin', associated with French *espingle* (modern French *épingle*) and Italian *spillo* and *spilletto*, all of which are clearly derived from *spinula* 'thorn'. There is an explanation for all this: 'in the more primitive age of our fathers, in place of pins, thorns were frequently used for fastening'.[106] This is backed up with a quotation from the *Germania* of Tacitus, in which the Germani are described as fastening garments with a brooch or, lacking that, a thorn. Junius' learning here is densely concentrated: he has cited twenty-two forms in a total of twelve languages – and indeed in seven language-specific typefaces, Gothic, Anglo-Saxon, runic, Greek, a large black-letter face for Dutch and English, a small one for German and modern Scandinavian, and roman for Latin and Romance. He has made a substantial digression into Greek, perhaps from the materials of the 'Etymologicum teutonicum', but has returned to Germanic, and to cultural history, showing how many of the major languages of Europe remember a time when a thorn rather than a brooch might fasten a garment.

Junius' comparative work on the Germanic languages, evident throughout the *Glossarium*, can also be seen taking shape in a number of his unpublished manuscripts. He compiled his own Icelandic–Latin vocabulary, based substantially on the lexical material in the only published grammar of Icelandic, Runólfur Jónsson's *Recentissima antiquissimae linguae septentrionalis incunabula, id est grammaticae islandicae rudimenta* (*The most newly published beginnings of the most ancient*

---

[105] Ibid. 346, 'Origo vocis videtur petenda ex τορός, Penetrans, acumine perfodiens. Alii tamen potius habent deducere à τύρειν, quod idem est τείρειν, Molestia afficere.'

[106] Ibid., 'rudior Patrum nostrorum aetas acicularum loco spinas frequenter adhibere solebat', citing Tacitus, *Germania* 17.

northern language, or the elements of Icelandic grammar) of 1651.[107] He also
acquired a manuscript of Guðmundur Andrésson's Icelandic dictionary,
completed before 1654 but not available in print in Junius' lifetime, and a
number of other sources for Scandinavian vocabulary.[108] He collected
glossaries in Old High German, four of which were mentioned above,
designating fourteen of them by letters so that he could refer precisely to
them in his own work; he also collected Old High German texts,
including a copy in his own hand of Flacius' edition of Otfrid.[109] To
these, he added an annotated transcript of Lipsius' Old Dutch glossary;
an incunabular Low German dictionary; a Frisian wordlist; and Old
English material which included a transcript of Nowell's 'Vocabularium',
two copies of Somner's dictionary and one of Spelman's *Archaeologus*.[110]

He then began to bring this mass of material together. One manuscript
in which he can be seen doing this is a union glossary closely written on
225 double-column leaves in quarto, and comprising about 30,000
entries.[111] This is described in the Bodleian *Summary Catalogue* as 'The
Latin–Anglo-Saxon dictionary of Francis Junius, compiled by him from
his glossaries', and this is so misleading as to call for comment.[112] There is

---

[107] Now Bodl. MS Junius 36; cf. Hickes, *Linguarum veterum septentrionalium thesaurus* 73–91 (3rd
    sequence of pagination, i.e., sigs. *T1r–*Z2r), which is identified by Bennett, 'Beginnings of
    Norse studies in England' 37 as 'really nothing more than the word-list Junius had made'.
[108] The manuscript of Andrésson is Bodl. MS Junius 120; Junius' other Scandinavian books included
    Worm's *Danicorum monumentorum libri sex* (now MS Junius 8) and his *Fasti danici* (now MS
    Junius 14), for both of which see F. Junius, *Correspondence* 763n9, and also a printed *Danske
    vrtebog* of 1647 (MS Junius 28), Simone Paulli's *Flora danica* of 1648 (MS Junius 30), and
    J. Loccenius' *Rerum suecicarum historia* of 1654 (MS Junius 87), from which he took information
    on runes (see Stanley, 'Sources of Junius's learning' 173).
[109] A–C (in Bodl. MSS Junius 116a, 116b) are the three glossaries from the Murbach Hymnal; D (MS
    Junius 116c) is from the other Boxhorn manuscript; of E–H (all in MS Junius 116d), E does not
    have a source indicated; F is from a manuscript owned by Vossius; G is from Goldast's *Rerum
    alamannicarum scriptores*; H is from a manuscript owned by Nicolaas Heinsius; there is no I or J;
    then K (in MS Junius 116e) is from the so-called Keronian glosses printed in Goldast; L is not Old
    High German; M is assigned both to a glossary of plant-names (in MS Junius 116f.) from a
    manuscript owned by Vossius and to a glossary of names for parts of the body (in MS Junius
    116d) in Goldast; of N–P (all in MS Junius 116f), N is a wordlist from Einhard's life of
    Charlemagne, O does not have a source indicated, and P is from a translation of Priscian. For
    these glossaries, see also the list in Junius, *Gothicum glossarium* sig. ***4r–v and the brief index in
    MS Junius 115b. The copy of Otfrid is MS Junius 17.
[110] The Lipsius wordlist, identified by Junius as item L in his series of glossaries, is Bodleian MS
    Junius 116f., fos. 3–116; the incunabular dictionary (Gherard van der Scheueren, *Theutonista*
    (1477)), annotated by Junius, is MS Junius 21 (for it, see Dekker, '*Vide Kilian*' 529); the Frisian
    wordlist is in MS Junius 115a (Junius also gave a Frisian wordlist to Jan van Vliet, presumably an
    earlier version of the one that he kept: see Dekker, *Origins of Old Germanic Studies* 121 and n53);
    Nowell's *Vocabularium* is transcribed as MS Junius 26; one copy of Somner is MS Junius 7; for
    the other, and the copy of *Archaeologus*, see Bremmer, 'Retrieving Junius's correspondence' 233.
[111] Now Bodleian MS Junius 112.   [112] 'Junius MSS' 985.

indeed Old English material in this glossary: Junius cites 'gr. Ælfr. ' and 'gl. Ælfr. ' and 'gl Cott' in some of the entries, keying them to Ælfric's grammar, his glossary (i.e., the Ælfrician glossary printed by Somner) and glossarial material that he had transcribed from Cottonian manuscripts. However, most of the lexical items registered are cited from a series of glossaries identified by letter, and these were the Old High German glossaries he had collected. So, this was not a 'Latin–Anglo-Saxon dictionary' but a union index, alphabetized by Latin headwords, of Junius' glossaries of Old English and Old High German alike. In his letter to Selden of 1654, he had announced an intention to collate the newly discovered Old High German glosses 'with the Anglo-Saxonick', making use of 'some of these Anglo-Saxonick monuments I transcribed by your favour out of divers Cottonian MSS, a process that would 'give much light to both'.[113] This was the result of the collation, and it was meant for publication: Junius was 'extremely busie to get my glossaries readie for the presse' in 1666, and referred two years later to 'my great worke of Teutonik Glossaries', which he had 'gott ... in a perfect order for the presse' but had since seen 'as it were lie dead by me', for want of willingness from publishers.[114]

He also made a fuller dictionary of early Germanic material. This has been called both an Old English dictionary and a 'Lexicon of the five old Northern Languages (whereof the *Saxon* [i.e., Old English] has the preference)', the latter being nearer the mark.[115] Confusion as to its identity has arisen because it is preserved in a composite manuscript, Bodleian MSS Junius 2 and 3, in which papers from four different stages of writing are assembled. In the first stage, Junius made an alphabetic dictionary, written in quarto booklets with their pages divided by folding into two columns, with a few entries for Old Norse and Gothic words (given in runes and the Gothic alphabet respectively) interspersed in a sequence dominated by entries for Old English, usually referenced to specific texts, and often illustrated by quotations. The defining language is Latin. In 1656, Junius wrote to Dugdale of this material that 'I keep my selfe ... busie with referring the most antient Gothike dialect, occurring

---

[113] F. Junius, letter to Selden of 8 May 1654, in his *Correspondence* 848–51 at 850. His transcripts of Cottonian glossaries are Bodl. MSS Junius 71, fos. 127 onwards (preceded by the Ælfrician vocabulary communicated by Junius to Somner), Junius 72, Junius 77, and Junius 84 fos. 45–51, for all of which see 'MSS Junius' 979–82 and Stanley, 'Sources of Junius's learning' 170–3; Nowell's *Vocabularium* is transcribed as MS Junius 26.

[114] F. Junius, letters of 23 July 1666 to Thomas Marshall, in his *Correspondence* 1018–23 at 1020, and of 3 February 1668 to Dugdale, ibid. 1030–3 at 1030.

[115] Dekker, "That most elaborate one" 301 and *passim*; Nicolson, *English historical library* 1:104.

in the Codex Argenteus, to that collection of an Anglo-Saxonike Dictionarie I have bene long gathering for mine owne private use.'[116] Since material from Somner's dictionary is quoted in entries that form part of this stage, its making must have continued until at least 1657. In the second stage, he interleaved his original quarto leaves, which were becoming rather full, with folio leaves a little over thirteen inches tall, also divided into double columns, on which he began writing more entries, with a somewhat higher proportion of Old Norse and Gothic entries. He now had fascicles for each of the letters of the alphabet as used to write the early Germanic languages, running to a total of 711 surviving leaves. It is this stage of the dictionary that Junius called 'my great Anglo-Saxonike Lexicon' in 1668, as part of a correspondence with Thomas Marshall about sources for the study of the early Germanic languages, adding that, by lending it to Marshall, he was sending 'what I could of them', the plural *them* indicating a collection of material bearing on more than one language.[117] To these fascicles, in a third stage, he added booklets of entries for Old High German words and other words from continental West Germanic in the alphabetical ranges T, TH, U and W / UU; others must have been lost.[118] In the fourth stage, after Junius' death, over 330 leaves of a transcript in several hands of his Old English materials from S onwards were added to MS Junius 3, making it bulky and unwieldy in a way that does not represent Junius' own work.[119]

As well as this 'Anglo-Saxonike' dictionary, Junius made wordlists of more recent varieties of English. After the disappointment with the 'Teutonik Glossaries' around 1666, he had started to study Chaucer, and since he found 'Chaucers old language' difficult, and 'knew not how to looke for a Commentator that should give anie light' to it, he read Gavin Douglas' *Eneados* to get acquainted with some of its features, just as William Lisle had done for Old English, and for the same reason: the Latin original could be used to explain the translation (for Chaucer's translations of Boethius and the *Roman de la rose*, Junius likewise read with the originals to hand).[120]

---

[116] F. Junius, letter to Dugdale of 28 January 1656, in his *Correspondence* 864–9 at 868.

[117] F. Junius, letter of 3 February 1668 to Dugdale, in his *Correspondence* 1030–3 at 1032.

[118] The booklets are now MS Junius 2, 552–5 (entries in T), and MS Junius 3, 349–58 (entries in TH), 360–72 (entries in U), and 450–63 (entries in W/UU).

[119] These additions are MS Junius 3, 24–66 (entries in Ð), 67–140 (entries in þ), 185–300 (entries in S), 301–48 (entries in T), 408–49 (entries in U), and 482–96 (entries in Y).

[120] For early modern difficulties with Chaucer's language, see Bremmer, 'Franciscus Junius reads Chaucer' 44 and 51–2; for the difficulty of finding a commentator, see F. Junius, letter of 3–4 June 1667 to Thomas Marshall, in his *Correspondence* 1024–7 at 1024; for Douglas as an introduction to Chaucer, see F. Junius, letter of 3 February 1668 to Dugdale, ibid. 1030–3 at 1030.

Native speakers of English in Junius' century also found Chaucerian
English more difficult than Latin: hence an English writer's praise of a
Latin version of the first two books of *Troilus and Criseyde* in 1635 tells the
translator that "Tis to your Happy cares wee owe, that wee | Read
Chaucer now without a Dictionary."[121] He ended up preparing wordlists
to both Chaucer and Douglas. The glossary to Douglas, MS Junius 114, is
probably the earlier of the two, and is the less elaborate: it comprises
about two hundred leaves, fasciculated into letter-ranges like MSS Junius
2 and 3, written in double columns with quite a lot of white space
between some entries and some strips or folded sheets of paper pasted
onto the leaves. There are about 2000 entries, keyed to a copy of a
sixteenth-century edition of Douglas' translation which Junius had
paginated (the original is foliated) to allow precise citation.[122] Some
simply direct attention to a lexical form: 'Paysit flesche. 391, m.'[123] Others
transcribe context for a lexical form and give Latin equivalents, though
not necessarily the Latin that Douglas translates: 'Pik, Ictus leviter per-
stringens ["a blow which touches lightly"]. the auld waikly but force or
dynte Ane dart did cast, quhilk wyth ane pik dit [*sc.* dyd] stint On his
harnes. 87, s.'[124] The master copy of Douglas is annotated, often with
notes on the treatment of the Latin original: so 'The fatale time, quham
na waling mai mend' is annotated '*Ineluctabile tempus.* So the translator
appears to have taken *ineluctabile* to be derived from *lugeo* ["I mourn"] or
luctus ["mourning"], not from *luctor* ["I wrestle", often used figuratively].'[125]

The glossary to Chaucer, a manuscript of eighty-four written leaves but
more than 3100 entries, is likewise based on a marked-up printed book, a
copy of Speght's edition of 1598, in which Junius numbered the columns
(the original is, like the printed *Eneados*, foliated) and added numerous
marginal cross-references based on this numbering.[126] So, for instance,
the description of the Knight in the General Prologue as 'meeke as is a
maid' has the note '64, i. 191, s.' in the margin, cross-referring to the
description of Nicholas in the Miller's Tale as 'like to a maiden meke to

[121] Cartwright, 'To the worthy author'; cf. Lisle, 'To the readers' sig. c3r.
[122] The printed text, Douglas, *Eneados* (1553), is Bodl. MS Junius 54.
[123] Bodl. MS Junius 114, fo. 160r, citing Douglas, *Eneados* fo. 202r.
[124] Ibid., fo. 161r, citing Douglas, *Eneados* fo. 43r; cf. Virgil, *Aeneid* 2:544–6, 'sic fatus senior
telumque imbelle sine ictu | coniecit, rauco quod protinus aere repulsum, | et summo clipei
nequiquam umbone pependit'.
[125] Bodl. MS Junius 54, fo. 37r, 'Ineluctabile tempus. Videtur itaque Interpres Ineluctabile accepisse
ut compositum a *Lugeo* vel *Luctus*, non a *Luctor*'; cf. Virgil, *Aeneid* 2:324.
[126] The glossary is now Bodl. MS Junius 6, keyed to Chaucer, *Workes* (1598), now MS Junius 9. The
entry-count is my own; cf. the count of 'about 4,000 entries' in Bremmer, 'Franciscus Junius
reads Chaucer' 58.

see' and to the Host's remark that the Clerk of Oxenford rides 'as still and coye, as doth a maide'.[127] Some, though not all, of these cross-references underlie entries in the glossary. The master copy is also marked up with emendations and references to classical and patristic authors, which suggest that, at one point, Junius may have projected a commentary, or at least a collection of animadversions, on Chaucer.[128] The glossary of 2034 entries printed in Speght's edition has been removed from the Junius copy, and was possibly cut up as the basis for the first stage of Junius' own Chaucer glossary, though the extant manuscript represents a subsequent stage written in double columns on folio leaves. Whereas Speght generally offers one-word glosses, Junius' glossarial entries can be rather more expansive: so, for instance, *A per se* is illustrated with a seven-line quotation from Henryson's *Testament of Cresseid* (printed as a sixth book to *Troilus and Criseyde* in Speght's edition), followed by an eight-line quotation from *Troilus and Criseyde* which gives the analogous image 'Right as our firste lettre is now an A, | In beautee first so stood she', then by the first eleven lines of the verse preface to Douglas' *Eneados*, in which 'A per se' occurs, and then by extracts from Martial (using *alpha* plus genitive to mean 'first among') and Revelation (the passage in which God is called the Alpha and the Omega).[129] The length of these quotations goes beyond what would be useful for private notes, and also suggests a projected publication, as perhaps does the 'syllabus operum Chauceri hoc libro con-tentorum', which assigns Latin titles to all the works.[130] A last clue as to the projected status of the Chaucer glossary is that there are references in it not only to lexicographers such as Spelman, but also to Junius' own *Etymolo-gicum anglicanum*: this suggests that the glossary was at one point intended to stand beside, rather than being subsumed into, the bigger work, as an independent publication or part of a commentary on Chaucer.[131]

The *Etymologicum anglicanum* itself had been in progress since the late 1650s, when Junius had shown Lord Hatton, on whose manuscripts Dugdale had drawn in making his dictionary, 'an alphabeticall collection of English words, whose proper signification and originall I had traced out and set downe as well as I could'; in 1661, he asked Dugdale if any Englishman would be interested in completing the work and publishing it

---

[127] Bodl. MS Junius 9, sig. A2r.   [128] Bremmer, 'Franciscus Junius reads Chaucer' 47–50, 54.

[129] Bodl. MS Junius 6 s.v. *A per se*, quoting *Testament of Cresseid* in Chaucer, *Workes* (1598) fo. 194v, *Troilus and Criseyde*, ibid. fo. 152v, Douglas, *Eneados* fo. 1r, Martial 2:57, Revelation 1:8.

[130] Bodl. MS Junius 9 fos. 398–403.

[131] For references to Spelman, see, e.g., Bodl. MS Junius 6 fo. 29v (s.v. *erke*) and Bremmer, 'Franciscus Junius reads Chaucer' 69n49; for references to the *Etymologicum anglicanum* see, e.g., MS Junius 6 fos. 72r (s.v. *ruse*) and 73v (s.v. *sable blake*) and Bremmer, ibid. 51 and 69n50.

'for the credit and honour of his owne countrie and language'.[132] It is not as extensive as the dictionary of Old English and early Germanic, comprising two volumes (Bodleian MSS Junius 4 and 5), amounting to just under five hundred folio leaves in total, written on one side only. Some of the entries are for words that had entered English only recently, as in the case of *artichoke*, a vegetable that was said to have been introduced in the reign of Henry VIII, for which Junius gives two forms, *artechoke* and *hartechoke*, then a Latin gloss, 'Carduus altilis, cinara, strobilus', then five cognates (French *artichaut*, Italian *articiocco, arciocco*, Spanish *artichosa*, Danish *artiskock* and Dutch *artischock*) before a reference to Salmasius' *Plinianae exercitationes*.[133] Other entries are naturally much closer to Junius' long-standing Germanic interests: *asunder* is glossed 'seorsum, sigillatim, separatim' and then compared to Gothic *sundro*, Old English *on sundran, on sundron*, Old High German *suntrigo* and Dutch *in't bÿsonder* before Old English *syndrian* 'to separate' is adduced as a parallel and the entry *seorsum* in Junius' Old High German glossary C is cited.[134] The Germanic material is sometimes presented in digressions from headwords of Romance origin, as s.v. *assist*, where a reference to the Dutch equivalent *bij-staen* leads Junius to reflect that Satan says in a poem in the Cædmon Manuscript 'bigstandað me strange geneatas. ða ne willað me at ðam striðe geswican' ('strong companions stand by me, who will not desert me in the battle') and to discuss this passage for five lines.[135]

The author to whom Junius refers most often in the *Etymologicum* is Chaucer. He also uses Douglas, as one might expect, and a range of Old English texts from manuscripts that he transcribed or owned, including the Old English translation of Orosius, the Rushworth Gospels, and glosses on the Psalms from the manuscript now called the Codex Vossianus.[136] There are likewise references to ancient primary sources such as the Old

---

[132] F. Junius, letter to Dugdale of 29 May 1661 in his *Correspondence* 980–5 at 980 and 982.

[133] Bodl. MS Junius 4, fo. 28v, citing the long discussion of thistles, cardoons and artichokes occasioned by Solinus' use of the plant-name *cynaris* in Salmasius, *Exercitationes Plinianae* (I have not seen the edition used by Junius; the passage is 159–60 (second sequence of pagination) in the 1689 edition); for the reputed date of the introduction of the artichoke, see Hakluyt, *Principal nauigations* (1599–1600) II:165 (first sequence of pagination), 'In time of memory things haue bene brought in that were not here before, as . . . the Artichowe in time of king *Henry* the eight.'

[134] Bodl. MS Junius 4, fo. 29r.

[135] Ibid., 'Assiste, Adjuvare, opitulari, assistere. Gall. assister. Belg. bij-staen. Huc faciunt verba Principis angelorum apostasiam a Creatore suo meditantis ac vires suas animo metientis. *bigstandað me strange geneatas. ða ne willað me at ðam striðe geswican. Mecum stant fortes coloni, qui me non deserent in pugna*; Cædmon 7, 12.'

[136] These three are now Bodl. MS Junius 15 (Orosius); MS Junius 76 (excerpts from Rushworth Gospels, for which see F. Junius, letter of May 1650 to Franciscus Junius F.N. in his *Correspondence* 783–95 at 788–9); MS Junius 27, now Bodl. MS Arch. F. d. 19 (Codex Vossianus).

High German glosses and the Codex Argenteus, and perhaps to personal observation. This last, however, is difficult to judge: he mentions the English idiom *a paire of bellowes* and the English word *blisterflie* without quoting authorities, but both had been registered in dictionaries.[137] Likewise, the note that 'in the vernacular, the aids for old men who have nearly lost their sight are called *brillen* by the Danes and the people of the Netherlands' may be glossarial in origin.[138] Among his numerous secondary sources are his own work on Willeram and on Gothic, and the standard English and continental authorities: Laurence Nowell, Spelman and Somner; G. J. Vossius, Kiel and Worm. The *Etymologicum anglicanum* is not Junius' most dramatic work, and it was vulnerable to criticism even before the advances of nineteenth-century Germanic studies, as in Samuel Johnson's comparison of it with the *Etymologicon linguae anglicanae* of Stephen Skinner (1671):

Junius appears to have excelled in extent of learning, and *Skinner* in rectitude of understanding. *Junius* was accurately skilled in all the northern languages, *Skinner* probably examined the ancient and remoter dialects only by occasional inspection into dictionaries; but the learning of *Junius* is often of no other use than to show him a track by which he may deviate from his purpose ... *Skinner* is often ignorant, but never ridiculous: *Junius* is always full of knowledge; but his variety distracts his judgment, and his learning is very frequently disgraced by his absurdities.[139]

Some of Junius' etymologies in which derivations from Greek occur follow in a footnote, and they are indeed most implausible; nor was it always Greek that led Junius astray, since, as the philologist George Hickes noticed a few years after his death, he had been willing to derive *girl* from Latin *garrula*, 'talkative'.[140] But as Johnson acknowledged, he had used Junius and Skinner extensively in his own work because no other attempt at a comprehensive etymological dictionary of English was available to him. As late as 1881, W. W. Skeat could observe that the etymological dictionaries of his day suffered from a tradition of uncritical borrowing from the same two sources.[141] Only after work such as Skeat's

---

[137] Bodl. MS Junius 4, fos. 43v 'vulgo Angli *a paire of bellowes* dicunt' and 50r 'Blisterflie vocatur etiam quibusdam Anglis insectu[m]'; cf. respectively Somner, *Dictionarium s.v. bilig* 'Follis ... a bladder, a pair of bellowes' and s.v. *blæst-belg* 'Follis, a pair of bellowes'; H. Junius, *Nomenclator* (1585) 72 'A whelke flie, or blister flie'.
[138] Bodl. MS Junius 4, fo. 44r, 'vulgo Danis ac Belgis haec senilium ac prope jam perditorum luminum subsidia vocabantur brillen'.
[139] Johnson, *Dictionary of the English language* sig. B1r, discussing Skinner, *Etymologicon*, for which see, e.g., Kerling, *Chaucer in early English dictionaries* 135–56.
[140] Hickes, letter to Arthur Charlett of 24 November 1694 in Harris, *Chorus of grammars* 151–3 at 152.
[141] Skeat, 'Preface to the first edition' xi.

had superseded Junius' *Etymologicum* could the latter be seen in historical perspective and appraised with detachment as 'the first systematic etymology of the English Language' with the additional reflection that 'from it stems the modern historical approach to lexicography'.[142]

Johnson was able to consult the *Etymologicum* because it had been published in 1743, edited by a learned country clergyman, Edward Lye. The Germanic dictionary was even slower to appear. John Fell, the great reinvigorator of learned printing at Oxford, had had MSS Junius 2 and 3 transcribed, with additions including Icelandic material from Junius' manuscript of Andréssen, shortly after Junius' death, but although the transcript survives in eleven volumes of tall folio, the edition was never published.[143] An unaugmented transcript of the same two Junius manuscripts was made for Lye in the next century.[144] This formed the basis for the dictionary published in 1772, after Lye's death, as *Dictionarium saxonico et gothico–latinum* (with Junius' name shamefully omitted from the title-page); Samuel Johnson was one of the subscribers. So, a hundred years after Junius' death, his lexicographical manuscripts were still worth printing. The distance between his knowledge of the Germanic languages and that of a very learned person of the next generation is suggested by an anecdote of 1697: the matrices and punches for the Junian types had been brought to the Bodleian in 1679 and had been put away, so that when Humfrey Wanley and Edward Thwaites sought them, they had to consult Bodley's Librarian, the orientalist Thomas Hyde:

> Dr Hyde knew nothing of them, but at last told them he thought he had some old Punchions about his study, but he did not know how they come there, and presently produces a small box full, and taking out one, he pores upon it and at last wisely tells them that these could not be what they look'd after, for they are Æthiopic: but Mr Thwaites desiring a sight of them found that which he look's upon to be Gothic, and in the box were almost all Junius's Saxon, Gothic and Runic Punchions.[145]

ARAMEO-GOTHIC: THE GERMANIC HERITAGE IN DENMARK AND SWEDEN

The Swedish delegate to the Council of Basel who claimed a seat in an honourable position on account of the Gothic and therefore exceptionally

---

[142] Barker, *Oxford University Press* 27.

[143] Now Bodl. MSS Fell 8–18; see Harris, *Chorus of grammars* 7–8 and Bennett, 'Beginnings of Norse studies' 37.

[144] Now BL Add MSS 4720–4722.

[145] Thomas Tanner, letter of 10 August 169, in Barker, *Oxford University Press* 26.

ancient descent of his sovereign was asserting a heritage that was of great significance to his countrymen.[146] To the early modern German assertion of descent from the Goths, a Swede or Dane might reply that, although all the Germanic peoples might participate to some extent in the Gothic heritage, it was first and foremost the property of his country. So, for instance, when Cluverius argued in the seventeenth century that the Gothic homeland was actually Prussia rather than Scandinavia, the Swedish response was outraged: the poet and antiquary Georg Stiernhielm wrote an *Anticluverius* of 128 pages denouncing this Prussian who had been 'carried away by a disordered love for his fatherland', asking sarcastically 'what has blinded you here, my dear Cluverius?' and concluding that the Scandinavian origins of the Goths were 'clearer than the sun at mid-day'.[147] According to Jordanes, after all, the Goths had their origin in a land called Scanzia in the far north of Europe, and this suggested strongly that they were Scandinavians.[148] The names of the Swedish provinces of Östergötland and Västergötland and of the Scandinavian island of Gotland supported the theory: they come from the name of a people called Götar, who, it was argued, were surely identical with the Goths.[149] The Götar were, with a people called the Svear, the officially recognized ancestors of the Swedes, and hence the early modern Latin equivalent of *Swensk* 'Swedish' was *Sueo-Gothicus*, a word that asserted a Gothic heritage whenever it was used.

The language of the Gothic past, or at least of a past remote enough to be called Gothic, was naturally studied in both Sweden and Denmark. This study took place in a context of vigorous lexicographical activity. The distinctive standardized forms of the Danish and Swedish languages that developed after political separation in the sixteenth century were codified in dictionaries, a substantial Swedish–Latin–Greek school dictionary of 1587 being followed by the first Danish–Latin dictionary, *Dictionarium Herlovianum*, in 1626, and by another Swedish–Latin dictionary, part of a big *Dictionarium latino–sueco–germanicum*, in 1640.[150] However, these practical works, compiled for use in grammar schools, were not the dictionaries in which the heritages of the Scandinavian peoples were most interestingly presented in the period. Much more

[146] Klindt-Jensen, *History of Scandinavian archaeology* 10f.
[147] Stiernhielm, *Anticluverius* 2, 'vir … praepostero in patriam amore raptus'; 4, 'Quid hic, mi Cluveri, te occaecat?'; 128, 'Sole meridiano clarius est.'
[148] Jordanes, *De getarum* (1597) 4.   [149] See, e.g., Stiernhielm, *Anticluverius* 1.
[150] For the beginnings of Danish lexicography, see Molbech, 'Historisk udsigt over de danske ordbogs-arbeider' 241–4; for the beginnings of Swedish lexicography, see Holm and Jonsson, 'Swedish lexicography' 1934f.

remarkable was the first dictionary of Norwegian, then the marginalized language variety of a country that was legally a province of Denmark, the *Norske dictionarium eller glosebog* of Christen Jenssøn, published in 1646.[151] But this assertion of a local linguistic heritage, like the Icelandic dictionary of Guðmundur Andrésson, the remarkable copy of the *Dictionarium* of Calepino to which some 37,000 Swedish lexical items were added in manuscript in the late seventeenth century, and the Danish dictionary projects of Peder Syv and Matthias Moth in the last quarter of the seventeenth century, belongs to a series of lexicographical developments many of which took place in the eighteenth and nineteenth centuries, and therefore cannot be treated here.[152] What will be discussed here is the way in which the development of strong Danish and Swedish national identities in the early modern period encouraged learned persons in both countries to examine early history and early linguistic material, sometimes in a competitive spirit.

This examination might, on the one hand, take the form of speculative writings on the Gothic past, such as those of the exiled Swedish bishop Johannes Magnus, whose national history began with the story, founded in Josephus and developed both in St Isidore's *Etymologiae* and *Historia gothorum* and in pseudo-Berosus, that the Goths were the progeny of Magog, grandson of Noah, as were the Scythians (this story was accepted generally enough for lists of the Swedish monarchy to begin with King Magog).[153] It might, on the other hand, take the form of archaeological work. Denmark and Sweden are rich in field-monuments such as barrows and dolmens, and especially in one kind of linguistically interesting medieval monument, the large stones that survive in their thousands with legible inscriptions carved on them in the runic alphabet. Since these rune-stones were ancient, and the ancient inhabitants of Scandinavia were thought to have been Goths, they were regarded as Gothic antiquities, and the runes as a Gothic alphabet. Deciphering the easier rune-stones was straightforward: the runic alphabet had been published with Roman

[151] Haugen, 'Introduction' 6.
[152] For Andrésson's dictionary, see Haugen, 'Introduction' 10; for the Swedish Calepino, see Holm, 'Schwedischer Calepinus'; for the projects of Syv and Moth, see Haugen, 'Introduction' 6 and 42.
[153] Johannes Magnus, *Historia de omnibus gothorum sueonumque regibus* 18–22, quoting pseudo-Berosus 19; cf. St Isidore, *Etymologiae* 9.2.26–7, 'Filii ... Iaphet septem nominantur: Gomer, ex quo Galatae, id est Galli. Magog, a quo arbitrantur Scythas et Gothos traxisse originem' (*PL* 82:330C) and St Isidore, *Historia de regibus gothorum, wandalorum, et suevorum* 1 (*PL* 83:1059A) and 66 (*PL* 83:1075A). For Johannes Magnus and pseudo-Berosus, see Schiebe, *Annius von Viterbo* 19–25 and Borst, *Turmbau von Babel* 1100–1, and for King Magog, see, e.g., Peer, *Een kort och nyttigh chrönica om alla Swerikis och Göthis konungar, ... ifrån then första konung Magogh.*

equivalents by Johannes Magnus in his history and by his brother Olaus in his chorographical *Historia de gentibus septentrionalibus*, and the language of the inscriptions was recognizably akin to the modern vernaculars.[154] Although later medieval Danish and Swedish manuscripts are quite numerous, and were read, the rune-stones had the same allure of antiquity as the remains of Old High German, Old English and Gothic. To this was added their place in the human landscape: texts in Old English might provide information about the continuity between Anglo-Saxon and contemporary England, but rune-stones could enact, rather than report, continuity. It was one thing to claim Gorm the Old as an ancestor of the Danish kings on the basis of chronicle evidence, and another to stand in the churchyard at Jelling in Jutland and see the great tenth-century stone that commemorated him, engraved with pictures and runes, *in situ* (as it still is). Rune-stones were heritage objects of a dramatic kind. Their study might go hand in hand with a lexicography that examined the national linguistic heritage.

It was already under way by the last decade of the sixteenth century. The Jelling field-monuments were published in 1591.[155] A couple of years later, a student of Hebrew called Joannes Bureus noticed a singular carved stone built into the Riddarholm Church in Stockholm: the design on it was a serpent, looping round in a figure 8, with characters inscribed on it.[156] Like Hans Dernschwam faced with his epigraphic puzzle in Constantinople a few decades earlier, he paid careful attention to the inscription; but, unlike Dernschwam, he was able to decode it, because it was runic.[157] Having done that, he went on to look for more rune-stones, further afield. In 1600, he engraved and published a very striking broadsheet, *Runakänslones lärespån / Elementa runica*, in which runic alphabets, calendrical material, a number of inscriptions (including one from the 1591 Jelling publication), images of ten rune-stones, inscriptions from nine others, and a couple of dozen Swedish coats of arms, with runic labels to identify them, are packed together in a dizzying mass of detail.[158] They surround a terse account of runes as the hereditary possession of the Gothic people – which remarks that runes had been suppressed for centuries during a period of degraded servitude to the Whore

[154] Johannes Magnus, *Historia de omnibus gothorum sueonumque regibus* 25; Olaus Magnus, *Historia de gentibus septentrionalibus* 57.
[155] Klindt-Jensen, *History of Scandinavian archaeology* 15 (plate 5).
[156] It is no longer *in situ*, and must have been lost when the old church tower was destroyed by fire; there is a reproduction in Bureus, *Monumenta sueo-gothica hactenus exsculpta* sig. O5r.
[157] Klindt-Jensen, *History of Scandinavian archaeology* 16; Svärdström, *Johannes Bureus' arbeten* 7.
[158] See Svärdström, *Johannes Bureus' arbeten* 11 (in Swedish) and 62–3 (in German).

of Rome – and a dedication to Karl, prince regent of Sweden, together with his nephew Johan and his son Gustavus Adolphus.[159] Karl, who was a protestant, and was indeed about to become king at the expense of his Catholic nephew Sigismund, was favourably impressed by the erudition and no doubt by the confessional orientation of this work, and in 1602 Bureus became Gustavus Adolphus' tutor. Thereafter, he conducted his researches under the benevolent eye of the monarch. In 1624, he and his research assistants published a collection of *Monumenta sueo-gothica hactenus exsculpta* (*Swedish monuments of which engravings have so far been made*), a collection of forty-eight woodcuts of rune-stones, including the one from the Riddarholm Church that had first interested Bureus. It was the result of extensive travel around Sweden surveying the monuments, and its title emphasized the riches that still remained unpublished.[160]

Archaeological and speculative approaches to antiquity could coexist comfortably in the work of a single antiquary. While Bureus was conducting excellent fieldwork in his survey of rune-stones, he was also devising an elaborate Rosicrucian and Kabbalistic philosophy which 'contained the view that an "Adulruna" exists in which the ancient Scandinavians had set their knowledge of the universe'; he 'claimed to have found the way to read this secret Rune by using genuine Kabbalist rules of replacement'.[161] Bureus' thought here belongs to some of the traditions that helped to shape the early modern work on universal languages: there is the same interest in cryptography, and the same sense that deciphering a powerful language might be used to unlock the whole human and material universe, opening ways to universal knowledge and peace. For him, then, the ancient linguistic monuments of Sweden were of both nationalistic and esoteric importance. His old pupil Gustavus Adolphus endorsed at least the former when he became king. He was interested both in lexicographical and in antiquarian inquiry: a memorandum of his written in 1629 records a plan for a dictionary of Swedish, and, in the following year, he established a royal antiquarian office, the *Riksantikvariat*, with Bureus at its head, and ordered a search for 'prehistoric artifacts, such as might shed light on the Fatherland[,] and in particular all old runic inscriptions, whether on stones or in manuscripts, complete or fragmentary'.[162] The survey of rune-stones

---

[159] Bureus, *Runakänslones lärespån*, top centre, 'aliquot seculis in Romanae meretrici prostitutam servitutem exauctoratas, proscriptas, neglectas'.
[160] Svärdström, *Johannes Bureus' arbeten* 12–14 (in Swedish), 63 (in German), and 72 figs. 2 and 3.
[161] Åkerman, *Queen Christina* 93.
[162] For the dictionary memorandum, see Holm and Jonsson, 'Swedish lexicography' 1934; for the *Riksantikvariat*, see Klindt-Jensen, *History of Scandinavian archaeology* 17.

continued until Bureus' declining health led to his withdrawal from the
project in 1648. It was never completed, and its results by the time it lapsed –
meticulous descriptions of 663 of the three thousand or so Swedish rune-
stones – were not fully published, although copperplates of about two
hundred of the stones were made, and there are a few collections of
impressions taken from them.[163]

Bureus' work on runes was interwoven with a more general interest in
language, which led him to collect materials for a dictionary. One volume
of these, now MS F a 13 in the Royal Library at Stockholm, was given the
title 'Göthiskt och Gammal-Svenskt Lexicon' ('Gothic and Old Swedish
lexicon') when it was bound in the eighteenth or nineteenth century, but
this is misleading, for it is far from being a dictionary as it stands: he
himself referred to it as 'Till Suänska Lexicon ... colligerat iuxta Alpha
Betha', i.e., '[Notes] towards a Swedish dictionary, collected in alphabetical order'.[164] It is in fact a collection of lexicographical notes including
medieval Latin (with a particular interest in the vocabulary of law-codes),
material from rune-stones, and some comparative observations such as
the suggestion that *afgud* 'idol' might have something to do with *pagoda*
'Asian temple'.[165] Other manuscripts of his show a similar set of interests:
MS F a 17 at Stockholm, for instance, is a collection of booklets in which
Bureus made a number of onomastical and lexicological lists, reminding
himself at one point to search for ancient Swedish names in the works of
Johannes and Olaus Magnus, and in the rune-stones.[166]

Before looking at Bureus' successors in Sweden, we should turn to his
most important contemporary in Denmark, Ole Worm. Worm's abilities, recalling Conrad Gessner's, ranged widely over natural philosophy,
medicine and philology. He held professorships both of Greek and of
medicine at Copenhagen, discovered a detail in the anatomy of the
human skull which is still named after him (the Wormian bones), and
formed a museum of natural history, ethnography and antiquities which
has remained famous because of the fascinating engraving of it that
appeared as frontispiece to its catalogue, published as *Museum Wormianum*

---

[163] Svärdström, *Johannes Bureus' arbeten* 15–25 (in Swedish), 63–4 (in German), and 73 figs. 4 and 5.
[164] Klemming, 'Anteckningar af Johannes Thomae Agrivillensis Bureus' 7 item 13.
[165] Stockholm, Kungliga Biblioteket MS F a 13 (which comprises a paginated sequence of leaves and a foliated sequence), p. 57 (medieval Latin); p. 158 (runic material, quoting the Jelling inscription; for more on the runic material in this volume, see Svärdström, *Johannes Bureus' arbeten* 35); fo. 14r (*afgud* and *pagoda*, citing J. J. Boissard, *Tractatus de divinatione* (1616?)).
[166] Stockholm, Kungliga Biblioteket MS F a 17, fo. 11v, 'Nomina propria Sveo gotica petenda sunt ex Johanne Magno Olao M. ... Et lapidibus sepulcralibus Runicis.'

in 1655. His correspondence with antiquaries in England and across the world of learning was very extensive.[167] It says much for the place of the ancient Germanic heritage in early modern Scandinavian high culture that this great virtuoso, so much a man of the seventeenth century, should have dedicated a book to the King of the Goths, as he did in 1643.

This book was a result of Worm's long-standing interest in Danish antiquities. By the mid-1620s, he was visiting and deciphering rune-stones, and in 1626, the year in which he published his first major monograph (the *Fasti danici*, on medieval runic calendars), he was able to arrange for the clergy of the whole kingdom, including Norway and Iceland, to be instructed, on royal authority, to report on rune-stones or other antiquities in their parishes.[168] This national survey continued for many years, urged on by Worm's energetic letters to fieldworkers and local authorities. Runes had intrigued scholars in Germany, England and the Low Countries for many years: Trithemius had printed runic material from a manuscript source in his work on writing systems; Lazius had also printed a runic alphabet; Robert Talbot had studied runic alphabets; Daniel Rogers had communicated runic alphabets and an inscription that he had seen in Denmark to de Smet, who reproduced them in *De literis et lingua getarum*; and Camden had reproduced a runic inscription from the north of England in the 1607 edition of *Britannia*.[169] But the scanty supply of field-monuments available outside Scandinavia, and the jejunity of the manuscript sources, had meant that none of these scholars had proceeded far in their study. Sir Henry Spelman had read a fragment of an English runic inscription in a copy shown him by Cotton, and corresponded with Worm on the subject of runes from 1628 onwards; his command of Old English and sense of cultural history were good enough for him to propose, rightly, to Worm that *rune* is cognate with Old English *ryne* 'secret thing'.[170] He hoped that the book that he knew Worm to be writing would add something to what Trithemius and de Smet had said 'about our obsolete Saxon letters

---

[167] For Worm and the English antiquaries, see, e.g., Parry, *Trophies of time* 284.
[168] Klindt-Jensen, *History of Scandinavian archaeology* 18ff.
[169] For Trithemius and Lazius as runologists, see Derolez, *Runica manuscripta* xxxiii–xxxvi and 295–8 and Ebel, 'Beginnings of runic studies in Germany' 177–8; for Talbot, see Graham, 'Robert Talbot's "old saxonice Bede"' 296 and 304–9; de Smet's runes are in his *De literis et lingua getarum* 43–7; for Rogers and Camden, see Bennett, 'Beginnings of runic studies in England' 268–9, and for Camden, see also Page, *Introduction to English runes* 3 and plate 16.
[170] Bennett, 'Beginnings of runic studies in England' 270–1; a draft of Spelman's letter to Worm of 7 May 1630 on the etymology of *rune* is BL Add. MS 34599, fos. 108–10.

and others': the existence of English runic inscriptions made runology part of the English heritage.[171]

In October 1636, Worm sent Spelman an abstract of the book, which was published in the same year with the title *Runir, seu danica literatura antiquissima, vulgo gothica dicta luci reddita* (*Runir, or the most ancient Danish literature, popularly called Gothic, brought to light*).[172] It comprised an introduction to the runic alphabet, with some discussion of early Scandinavian literature, comparative material extracted from Lipsius' Old Dutch wordlist, and a text of the Old Norse poem called 'Krákumál', the death-song of the Viking hero Ragnar Lodbrok. The first word of the book's title was set in runes, as was the text of the poem. This was because, although the extant Old Norse manuscripts, which are comparatively late, use the Roman alphabet, Worm thought that manuscripts contemporary with the rune-stones must have been written in runes. The text was provided with an interlinear Latin translation and a commentary. Worm was presenting a whole new field of inquiry to his readers, for he offered them not only an alphabet but a dramatic, although difficult, sample of an ancient literature, preceded by a wordlist of about 320 items, the first Old Norse vocabulary to be printed.

Worm's researches continued over the next few years, and were brought together in a collected edition of 1651, issued as *Antiquitates danicae*, which included four items: a new edition of the *Runir*; a reissue of a revised edition of the *Fasti danici* (1643); a reissue of *Danicorum monumentorum libri sex*, a collection of runic inscriptions (also 1643) with a new appendix; and a major glossary (1650). This was presented as *Specimen lexici runici*, with a long title which can be translated as:

A specimen of a runic lexicon, offering an explanation of some of the more obscure words which occur in the earliest Danish historians and poets, collected by the Revd. and most learned Magnús Ólafsson, pastor of Laufás in Iceland, and now reduced to order, enlarged, and expanded by Ole Worm, professor at the University of Copenhagen.[173]

---

[171] Spelman, draft of a letter to Worm in BL Add. MS 34599, fo. 146, 'si et quidpiam de Saxonicis nostris aliisq[ue] exoletis literis quas Tritemius Abbas in Polygraphiae suae libro V. et Bon. Vulcanius in suo de literis et lingua Getar[um] libello addideris'.

[172] Worm, letter to Spelman of 30 October 1636 in BL Add. MS 34600, fos. 74 (covering letter) and 75–84 (abstract); Worm, *Runir*, with Old Dutch wordlist 156–7 and wordlist to 'Krákumál' 160–7.

[173] Worm, *Antiquitates danicae*, half-title page of *Specimen* [beginning new pagination and register], 'Specimen lexici runici, obscuriorum qvarundam vocum, qvae in priscis occurrunt historiis & poetis Danicis, enodationem exhibens; collectum a Dn. Magno Olavio, pastore Lausasiensi in Islandia doctissimo, nunc in ordinem redactum auctum & locupletatum ab Olao Wormio, in Acad. Hafn. P. P.'

Ólafsson's glossary appears to have originated as a private project, and to have been pursued for some years before Worm asked him for a wordlist to help with the reading of Old Icelandic in 1635; after his death in 1636, the glossary was transcribed by Jón Magnússon, his successor at Laufás, and communicated to Worm.[174] By 1639, Worm had the transcript and had sent it to the historian Stephen Hansen Stephanius, who was at the time editing the Danish history of Saxo Grammaticus, and was impressed and delighted by it, asking for a transcript to be made 'by some Icelander', who would presumably be able to deal with Old Icelandic better than a Dane.[175] After some years of uncertainty, Worm decided to prepare an augmented version for publication.[176] One of the contributors at this late stage appears to have been Guðmundur Andrésson, whose own Icelandic dictionary would supersede the *Specimen lexici runici*.[177]

As published by Worm, the *Specimen* comprised a wordlist of about 1100 items, generously laid out in folio, with headwords set in runes, and illustrative quotations from the sagas (especially *Grettis Saga*) and a few other sources for more than two thirds of its entries.[178] The *Runir*, the *Specimen lexici runici*, the *Danica monumenta* with its appendix, and the *Fasti danici* were conceived as parts of an integrated publication, a collection showing off the lexical, literary and epigraphic riches of the early Danish (including Icelandic) heritage. Bureus was to claim that Worm had identified Swedish antiquities as Danish in his work.[179] The rights and wrongs of this dispute matter less than the fundamental agreement that underlay it: for both parties, lexicography and the study of the material heritage of landscape and monuments went together, and were associated with national identity.

To return to Sweden, Bureus' interests in the implications of ancient texts were carried forward into the reign of Queen Christina not only in his own continuing field surveys and study of the history of language, but also in the work of Cluverius' antagonist Georg Stiernhielm (Stjernhjelm). Stiernhielm, the son of a miner, came to be a powerful figure in Swedish

---

[174] Faulkes, 'Sources' 32ff.

[175] For circulation in manuscript, see Stephen Hansen Stephanius, letter of 16 May 1639, to Worm in Worm, *Epistolae* I:182–4 at 182 and 183, 'vehementer mihi placuit *Glossarium* istud priscae lingvae Danicae, a te ... communicatum ... rogo atqve obsecro, ut integrum illud *Glossarium*, a capite ad calcem, ab Islando quodam, vel meis sumptibus, describendum cures'.

[176] For the decision to print, see Worm, letters of 24 June 1646 and 16 June 1647 to Sven Jonsson in his *Epistolae* II:632–3 and 633–4 at 632–3, 'Labores *Dn. Magni Olavii*, penes me sunt, egregii sane, de qvibus publicandis non semel cogitavi' and 633, 'operam dabo, si faventes habuero Typographos, aliqvando in lucem ut prodeat'.

[177] Faulkes, 'Sources' 38–9.   [178] Ibid. 54–6.

[179] See Klindt-Jensen, *History of Scandinavian archaeology* 15f.

high culture. He is best known as a poet: his allegorical epic *Hercules* had a great influence on Swedish poetry, of which he has been described as the father. He also left philosophical writings, and studied Swedish antiquities: he was appointed Custos Archivis, responsible for the care of antiquities in the kingdom of Sweden, in 1649, just after writing an evidently Burean *Adulruna seu sybilla sueo-gothica virgula divinum.*[180]

He was also a lexicographer. In 1643, he published two interesting dictionary specimens. The first of these, *Gambla Swea- och Götha-måles fatebur* (*Storehouse of the old language of the Svear and Götar*), was heralded by an eight-page *Företahl*, a short philosophical preface to the dictionary, issued both by itself as a little pamphlet of four leaves in octavo, and accompanied by a specimen of the letter A.[181] No more appeared. The second specimen, *Magog arameo-gothicus*, will be discussed further at the very end of this book; for now, four brief points can be made about it. First, it cites one word each of Ulfila's Gothic (*atta* 'father' from de Smet) and Crimean Gothic (*jes* 'he').[182] Second, it gives a set of rules for etymological work, among which is a Goropian insistence on the primacy of monosyllables.[183] Third, it refers the reader to a forthcoming *Etymologicum* and *Lexicon antiquarium* of Stiernhielm's, the latter of which may be identical with the *Gambla Swea- och Götha-måles fatebur* – and to another forthcoming publication, which like the first two never appeared, a *Saga arameo-gothica.*[184] Fourth, it is dedicated on its title-page to Queen Christina as 'most serene queen of the Sueci and the Gothi': in the year that Worm was dedicating the fruits of his antiquarian and lexicographical work to the king of Denmark as King of the Goths, Stiernhielm was dedicating the first-fruits of his linguistic and lexicographical work to the queen of Sweden as Queen of the Goths.[185]

---

[180] Åkerman, *Queen Christina* 91–2.

[181] There is a copy of the 4-leaf pamphlet in the Kungliga Biblioteket, Copenhagen, shelfmark 191,247. For the fuller specimen, not seen by me, see Collijn, *Sveriges bibliografi 1600-talet* col. 885, identifying it as a quarto of 4 + 26 leaves, published in Stockholm by Peter von Selow, 1643.

[182] Stiernhielm, *Magog arameo-gothicus* sigs. A2v, 'ATTA ... Gothicu[m] esse testatur Bonavent. Vulcanius' and B3r, 'Dalekarl. *Issen* i. hic ille. & cognati nostri *Precopenses* in Taurica Chersoneso, Jes', drawing on Busbecq, *Legationis turcicae epistolae quatuor* fo. 136v, 'Ies Varthata. Ille fecit.'

[183] Stiernhielm, *Magog arameo-gothicus* sig. B1r, 'Radicem Primam [of a family of words] esse Monosyllabam'.

[184] Ibid. sigs. B1v, 'De nostris *Herre / Lavard / Drott* &c. inveniet curiosus Lector in meo Etymologico'; B2r, 'de quibus [sc. the words for nobility of lineage and character] plura in meo Lexico Antiquar.'; B4r, 'Tractatus meus, titulo SAGA ARAMEO-GOTHICA singula suo loco expediet singularius.'

[185] Ibid., title-page: 'Serenissimae Reginae Svecorum Gothorumq[ue] CHRISTINAE, GUSTAVI MAGNI F. dedicatus.' Cf., e.g., the reference to Christina as 'Gotthorum Regina' in Franciscus Junius F. N., letter of 1 April 1650 to Franciscus Junius F. F., in F. Junius, *Correspondence* 766–71 at 768.

Stiernhielm continued to work on language all his life, as we shall see – and as indeed books from his library such as his carefully annotated copy of Meric Casaubon's *De quatuor linguis* would show even if there were no other evidence.[186] His library was generally rich in historically oriented lexicography and lexicology, containing, for instance, material on the classical languages such as Scapula's *Lexicon* and a major Latin etymologicum, material on Germanic such as Goropius' *Origines antwerpianae* and posthumous *Opera* and Worm's *Danica monumenta*, and material of comparativistic interest such as Gessner's *Mithridates* in the edition augmented by Caspar Waserus, Hieronymus Megiser's and John Minsheu's polyglot dictionaries, and Rivola's *Dictionarium armeno–latinum*.[187]

Stiernhielm's interest in Sweden's Gothic heritage was shared by Queen Christina herself, who sent emissaries to France, Spain, Italy and Greece in search of Gothic inscriptions, and on one occasion apologized – perhaps not altogether seriously – to an Italian visitor for the behaviour of her ancestors at the sack of Rome in AD 410.[188] His broader interest in language and interpretation was likewise by no means unique in Christina's circle. For instance, her adviser Bengt Skytte was an associate of Comenius and the author of an unpublished scheme for a universal language.[189] This was, according to Leibniz, in whose correspondence Skytte's name recurs a number of times, a product of the study of numerous natural languages, of which it was some sort of generative underlying principle.[190] Skytte and Stiernhielm may in fact have worked on this together, since their marginal notes both appear in Stiernhielm's copy of a polyglot dictionary.[191] The interest of Leibniz in Skytte's work (and, indeed, in Stiernhielm's: he was anxious to obtain a copy of the *Magog arameo-gothicus*) is a reminder that seventeenth-century Sweden was not only a major political power but also, partly because of Christina's interest in learned men, an intellectual centre of European

---

[186] Walde, 'Om Georg Stiernhielms bibliotek' 110–11.
[187] Ibid. 120–5.   [188] Åkerman, *Queen Christina* 114–19.
[189] Ibid. 124ff.; see also M. M. Slaughter, *Universal languages and scientific taxonomy* 120 and 239n83.
[190] Leibniz, 'Miscellanea Leibnitiana pars altera, xxviii' in *Otium hanoueranum* 151–2, 'Dixit, ex omnibus fieri per abstractionem posse lingvam universalem matricem, radicalem, qvam nemo loqvatur, sed qvae sit omnium radix.' For Skytte in Leibniz' correspondence, see Leibniz, *Sämtliche Schriften und Briefe* 1.5:31 and 661; ibid. 1.6:442 and 564; ibid. 1.8:48 and 295; and Cram, 'John Ray and Francis Willughby' 230 for a letter from Leibniz to Kircher which says that Skytte is, 'maximis peregrinationis & sumtibus', collecting 'omnium prope orbis Linguarum radices' to bring them together 'in unam Harmoniam ac velut Linguam Universalem'. See also Schulenburg, *Leibniz als Sprachforscher* 31.
[191] For the dictionary, the *Thesaurus polyglottus* of Hieronymus Megiser, see pp. 292–3 below, and for this set of annotations to it, see Alston and Danielsson, 'Earliest dictionary of the known languages of the world' 10.

importance.[192] Grotius' arguments for a Germanic element in Mexican toponyms, for instance, were written while he was acting as Swedish ambassador to Paris, at a time when Sweden had commercial interests in the New World which might have been helped by a demonstration of ancient linguistic affinities. They, like some of the material in his history of the Goths, show one of the luminaries of the republic of letters in Swedish service, and directing his scholarly abilities to Swedish interests.[193] For a short while, it looked as if this intellectual vigour might be brought to bear on the study and cultivation of the Swedish language. An informal academy attended by Stiernhielm and others, including Isaac Vossius, began to meet at court at the beginning of 1650, and its meetings inspired Christina to commission René Descartes to write the statutes of a national academy later that year. Then, two years later, she proposed the establishment of an official academy for the specific purpose of the cultivation of the Swedish language, evidently with the Académie française as a model.[194] This plan appears to have lapsed after her abdication in 1654 – or perhaps to have been lost in her foundation of another academy, which was not concerned with the Swedish language, at Rome.

Stiernhielm followed his abortive *Gambla Swea- och Götha-måles fatebur* with a very important wordlist; this was a glossary to accompany his edition of the Codex Argenteus. As the principal monument of the Gothic language, the Codex Argenteus appealed strongly to Swedish Gothophilia. After Junius had made his transcript, the original had been purchased from Isaac Vossius by the Swedish Royal Chancellor, Count Magnus Gabriel De la Gardie. The purchase was made before Junius' edition was actually published in 1665, and De la Gardie therefore received the dedication. The whole manuscript was transcribed by the Uppsala professor Olaus Verelius, and this must have been after it had returned to Sweden but before Junius' edition.[195] In 1669, the Codex Argenteus found its present home when De la Gardie gave it to the University of Uppsala, bound in a silver cover on which, as well as an attractive scene of Time discovering Truth, and the donor's arms, is the inscription 'Ulfila revived, and restored to the fatherland by the offices of M. G. De la Gardie, Chancellor of the Kingdom of Sweden, 1669'.[196] The

[192] Leibniz, 'Miscellanea Leibnitiana pars prima, XLVIII: Memoire donné à un voyageur au nord' in *Otium hanoueranum* 97–8 at 97, 'Je souhaite d'obtenir une petite dissertation de *Stiernielmius*, qui n'est que de quelques pages, intitulée je crois, *Magog Aramaeus*.'

[193] For Grotius on the Goths, see Dekker, *Origins of Old Germanic studies* 225–7.

[194] Åkerman, *Queen Christina* 104.   [195] Kleberg, *Codex Argenteus* 17.

[196] Ibid. plate 2 (p. 11) 'Vlphila redivivus, et patriae restitutus cura MG De la Gardie R S Cancellarij Anno 1669'.

point that De la Gardie was restoring the codex to the fatherland is one of which he and others made much; the minutes of the Privy Council meeting at which he announced its acquisition note that the Lord High Chancellor 'heartily congratulated Sweden on the same', and at the ceremony of its presentation to the university De la Gardie expressed pride at having 'been able to restore it to the nation again, after it had been for so many hundreds of years in the hands of strangers'.[197] This was not his only contribution to the preservation of the heritage of the distant past: as Chancellor of the University of Uppsala he founded a College of Antiquities there in 1666, with Stiernhielm as director, Verelius as one of its senior members, and Olof Rudbeck the elder, discoverer of the lymphatic system and author of a famous treatise identifying Sweden with Atlantis, as another. He arranged in the same year for royal legislation to protect the monuments of the 'heroic achievements of the kings of Sweden and Gotland, their subjects, and other great men – the imposing castles, fortresses and dolmens, the stones bearing runic inscriptions, the tombs and ancestral barrows'.[198] Verelius was at this time editing sagas with an attentiveness to their vocabulary manifested in the discursive lexical index of forty-two pages in his edition of the saga of Bósa and Herrauðr in 1666.[199] The latter was followed by an unannotated list of about eight hundred personal names from the rune-stones, with a short preface in which Verelius remarks that 'I thought that so much *pietas* was owed to our ancestors' as to record their names; claims that a thorough survey of Swedish rune-stones and indexing of the names found in historical texts would enlarge the record tenfold; and reflects that even the sample he provides will, since all the names are formed from Old Swedish words, demonstrate 'how great the fecundity of our language once was'.[200] In the spirit of this work, the College of Antiquities was in 1667 assigned the task of publishing a dictionary of Old Swedish, though the only such dictionary that was actually produced in the seventeenth century, Verelius' own *Index linguae veteris scytho-scandicae sive gothicae* of 1691, was left unready for publication on its maker's death, and appeared posthumously in an edition which is not altogether satisfactory.[201]

---

[197] Ibid. 17–18.   [198] Klindt-Jensen, *History of Scandinavian archaeology* 27.

[199] *Herrauds och Bosa saga* (1666) 70–111 and 112–22.

[200] Ibid. 112, 'Deberi hoc pietatis majorum nostrorum putavi ... Si cui animus & otium foret lapides qui per totum regnum reperiuntur exscribere, nominibusque, quae in illis reperiuntur, ista addere, quae historiarum monumenta suppeditant, numerus decuplo major confici posset. Sed vel hic docuerit quanta lingua nostrae quondam fuerit ubertas.'

[201] See the editor's note at Verelius, *Index linguae veteris scytho-scandicae* sig. π2v, and Holm and Jonsson, 'Swedish lexicography' 1934.

Stiernhielm's revised version of Junius' edition and glossary was published in 1671, the cost of printing being defrayed by De la Gardie. It was
perhaps inevitable that the supposed repatriation of the codex should
have been marked in Sweden by such a publication, even though Junius'
was so recent and the work of so able a scholar. Stiernhielm was, however,
doing more than merely duplicating Junius' edition. Whereas Junius had
presented Gothic and Old English in parallel, Stiernhielm presented four
languages on each opening: first Gothic, in Roman letters; then Icelandic;
then Swedish; then Latin. This meant that the two editions facilitated
different kinds of comparative study: Junius' readers could compare the
two earliest translations of the Gospels into Germanic languages, and
Stiernhielm's could compare the Gothic text with Icelandic (understood
to be the most conservative Scandinavian language) and Swedish, to see
what Scandinavian and Gothic had in common, with the international
learned language, Latin, as a control. Some care was taken to ensure that
the book should be suitably grand in appearance: when the first gatherings had already been printed, Stiernhielm or a colleague appears to have
complained about the cheapness of the paper being used and the low
standard of compositorial accuracy, and a corrected text was then printed
on better paper, though copies with the uncorrected states of the gatherings in question are to be found.[202] The glossary had its own half-title,
reset in the second issue from the modest 'Glossary of Ulfila-Gothic with
related languages by Franciscus Junius, now enlarged with Swedish (*sueo-
gothica*) and improved by Georg Stiernhielm' to:

Glossary of Ulfila-Gothic with some related languages by Franciscus Junius, now
enlarged and improved with modern and ancient Swedish (*sueo-gothica moderna
& antiqua*) together with innumerable etymologies and forms from cognates in
the Eastern languages, Greek and the Slavonic languages, by Georg Stiernhielm
[a list of Stiernhielm's titles follows].[203]

The emphasis on historical depth given here by the specification of
modern and ancient Swedish, and the emphasis on comparative breadth
given by the specification of three classes of supposed cognate language,
are characteristic of Stiernhielm's thought. However, Stiernhielm did not

[202] Johansson, 'Variantexemplar.'
[203] Ibid. figs. 1 and 2 sets the two title-pages side by side. That of the first issue is dated 1670:
'Glossarium Ulphila-Gothicum, linguis affinibus, per Fr. Junium, nunc etiam Sueo-Gothica
auctum & illustratum per Georgium Stiernhielm.' That of the second is dated 1671: 'Glossarium
Ulphila-Gothicum, linguis aliquot affinibus, per F. Junium, nunc etiam Sueo-Gothica moderna
& antiqva, cui innumerae accesserunt etymologiae, & voces ex affinibus Orientalibus, Graeca, &
Slavonicis, locupletatum & illustratum per Georgium Stiernhielm [etc.]'

follow through on the ideas promised by the title-page in the making of this glossary: what he presented was basically an abridgement of Junius' glossary, with a few Swedish cognates added but much of the philological discussion removed. The promise to attempt the presentation of Eastern cognates was not entirely empty: for example, the forms *Gild* 'tribute' and *Gilstrameleins* 'tax census' are referred to Germanic forms such as German *Geld* 'money' by both Junius and Stiernhielm, after which Junius remarks that the word seems to have a great affinity with Greek κηλέω 'I beguile' while Stiernhielm prefers a word from Hebrew, 'the Japhetic sister of our Scythian language', which he cites as *gaal* and glosses as 'redeem'.[204] But for the most part, and particularly in the latter half of the alphabet, the glossary is an abridgement rather than a reworking.

One twentieth-century authority has described the whole edition as 'more a patriotic achievement than a philological one'.[205] It was – but Stiernhielm's patriotism, like that of Goropius Becanus, led him into philological speculations that were actually very suggestive. The reference to Hebrew as 'the Japhetic sister of our Scythian language', for instance, was suggestive in that it identified Hebrew as parallel to Swedish rather than as its ancestor, and the reference to 'our Scythian language, like the similar references made by Goropius Becanus, also had the potential to encourage interesting thought. This point will be explored further in the last section of this book, with reference to a last dictionary project of Stiernhielm's.

---

[204] F. Junius, *Gothicum glossarium* 131, 'Videtur vox magnam affinitatem habere cum κηλέω, 'Lenio, mulceo.' Stiernhielm, 'Glossarium Ulphila-Gothicum' 72 (separately paginated section in Stiernhielm, ed., *D. N. Jesu Christi SS. Evangelia*), 'Mihi proprior est Scythicae nostrae Iaphetica soror Hebr. . . . *gaal.*'

[205] Anders Grape, quoted in Kleberg, *Codex Argenteus* 17.

CHAPTER 7

Post-classical heritages: Du Cange and his world

THE MIDDLE TIME: THE SCHOLARLY DISCOVERY
OF POST-CLASSICAL LATIN AND GREEK

In parallel with the scholarly discovery of the vernacular languages of Europe in the sixteenth and seventeenth centuries was that of post-classical Latin and Greek. There were several advantages to working on these language varieties rather than on their classical predecessors. One was that the period between antiquity and the fourteenth or fifteenth century offered an abundance of texts. A glance at, for instance, the five hundred quarto pages of Philippe Labbé's *Nova bibliotheca mss. librorum* of 1653 shows how many post-classical *inedita* lay waiting for their editors, the manuscripts adequately catalogued and in major libraries, at a time when the supply of classical *inedita* had dwindled almost to vanishing-point. For a while, this abundance was strangely invisible to scholars looking for classical material – hence, for instance, Henri Estienne's decision to use the *Bibliotheca* of Photius as a quarry for classical texts rather than to edit it as a whole. But, gradually, the merits of post-classical literature, together with the wealth of *inedita*, encouraged editors and therefore lexicographers to overcome their prejudices.

This was all the more easily done because a classical training offered an immediate entrance to these texts. Their language was not purely classical – which is why they were of interest in their own right to lexicographers – but it was usually close enough to the classical for the divergences to be challenging rather than baffling. Moreover, the users of medieval Latin and Greek were for the most part Christians, whose writings were often more improving than those of the pagans whom Henri Estienne had regretted studying. Protestant scholars could find anticipations of their own beliefs, or proofs of the degeneracy of the Church of Rome, in post-classical writings in Latin, just as they could in vernacular writings such as those of Ælfric. And in Byzantine Greek, they could find Christian texts in an ancient but not Rome-centred tradition much more readily than in the Coptic or Armenian texts to which, as we have seen, the first lexica for scholars of Latin-reading Europe were being developed in the seventeenth century. As early as the 1550s, Hieronymus Wolf, a predecessor of Henisch's as city librarian of Augsburg, had turned from his early work on Isocrates – which would be reprinted by Henri Estienne in 1593 – to Byzantine studies, producing editions of the historians Ioannes Zonaras (for which one of the manuscripts had been obtained by Hans Dernschwam), Niketas Choniates, Nikephoros Gregoras and Laonikos Chalkokondyles.[1] This activity did not bring about an immediate flowering of Byzantine studies – the dictionary of loanwords in Byzantine Greek which Wolf identified in his Zonaras as desirable for such studies was not to be made in his lifetime or for some time afterwards – but it was a beginning.[2]

The turn to an interest in post-classical Latin and Greek often went hand in hand with a turn to an interest in the European vernaculars. So, for instance, Bonaventure de Smet, whose contributions to the comparative study of Germanic and other languages we have already seen, had begun his career with a revised edition and new translation of Arrian, published by Henri Estienne. He had gone on to edit other classical texts, but also addressed Byzantine theology in an edition of two Byzantine treatises, Nilus of Thessalonica on the primacy of the Pope and an anonymous author on the fire of purgatory, published in 1595. He then made a collection of glossaries, under the title *Thesaurus utriusque linguae*, which sounds conventionally classical in its implication that two languages – obviously Latin and Greek – are pre-eminently important. The wordlists in it, though, were all post-classical, including a revision of Henri Estienne's edition of pseudo-Cyrillus and pseudo-Philoxenus. In the introduction to his *Thesaurus*, de Smet made the same point about the enrichment of the surviving vocabulary of the ancient languages as Estienne had done: from the Latin and Greek texts he presents, 'it is possible to make a great addition to the Greek and Latin languages of words which are very rare and very worthy of being read'.[3] He also added

---

[1] Husner, 'Editio princeps des "Corpus historiae Byzantinae"'.

[2] For Wolf's sense that a dictionary was needed, see his preface to his edition of Zonaras, *Annales*, first published in 1557 and quoted in Baron, *Éloge de Charles Dufresne* 47, 'Rogo autem eos qui corruptae linguae periti sunt, ut propter scriptores, in quibus subinde barbara Vocabula occurunt barbaricum lexicon conficiant, vocibus barbaris praepositis & Graecis subjunctis, ne veteris duntaxat linguae periti ab eorum lectione deterreantur.'

[3] De Smet, *Thesaurus* sig. *2r, 'Glossaria ... e quibus maxima fieri potest ad Graecam & Latinam linguam lectissimorum & rarissimorum Vocabulorum accessio.'

that although his edition was not a *princeps*, it was the next best thing, since Estienne's was so full of errors as to be of very little use.[4] This was not entirely fair, and a modern judgement of his work is that 'he reproduced the edition of Estienne with certain errors corrected, but with more added'.[5] Copies of de Smet's edition were marked up just as copies of Estienne's had been, for instance by Isaac Vossius (transcribing Scaliger's annotations from his copy of Estienne's edition), and by the Dutch philologist Joannes Meursius.[6] Franciscus Junius had hunted eagerly for a copy, and was speechless with delight when G. J. Vossius found one for him.[7] These vocabularies were still generating excitement. But now the context of the excitement was changing.

This can be seen from a note in the prelims to de Smet's *Thesaurus*: 'There would have been, to close up this book, something of a glossary of barbarous Greek, a guide to the understanding of Zonaras and other historians of the later period, had not I not learned from a most learned and most amiable letter sent to me by the distinguished Nicolas Rigault that he was engaged in one.'[8] For de Smet, the place of an edition of Cyrillus and Philoxenus was not after a dictionary of ancient Greek, as it had been for Estienne, but before a dictionary of Byzantine Greek. Late antiquity was here being seen not as an end but as a beginning – though having said that, it should be added that later seventeenth-century editions of the lexicon of Scapula had, as will be shown below, a glossary of Byzantine words as an appendix. Rigault's dictionary appeared in the following year. Its author, whom we have already encountered as one of the savants to whom Peiresc showed specimens of Spelman's *Archaeologus*, was emerging at the time of his contribution to lexicography as a scholar of some note. His *editio princeps* of Onasander's first-century treatise on generalship had appeared in 1600 and that of a letter of Julian the Apostate (five quarto pages, in large type) would, like the dictionary, come out in 1601. Rigault subsequently widened his interests in the usual pattern from the meagre gleanings of classical *inedita* to post-classical

---

[4] Ibid., 'Glossaria ... opera mea si non primum e situ vetustatis eruta; certe, quod proximum est, ab innumeris foedissimisque errorum monstris quibus ita fuerunt obsita, ut exiguus ex ei fructus percipi posset expurgata.'

[5] Goetz and Gundermann, eds., *Corpus glossarium latinorum II* xix, 'Editio Stephani ... repetiit erroribus quibusdam correctis, sed pluribus adiectis.'

[6] Ibid. xx.

[7] F. Junius, letter of 25 November 1634 to G. J. Vossius, in his *Correspondence* 470–3 at 470–1.

[8] De Smet, *Thesaurus* sig. *4v, 'Accessissent Colophonis loco Glossae aliquot ἑλληνικοβάρβαροι, ad Zonarae aliorumque posterioris aevi Historicorum intelligentiam conducibiles; nisi Cl[arissimum] V[irum] Nicolaum Rigaltium hoc agere ex doctissimis amicissimisque ipsius ad me literis intellexissem.'

texts, such as a life of St Romanus, bishop of Rouen, of which he published the *princeps* in 1609, and a poem by the early Christian author Commodianus, of which his *princeps* would be published posthumously. He succeeded Isaac Casaubon as Royal Librarian in France in 1610. The pioneering wordlist that he produced was brief, only registering about 250 items. It was, in a French tradition of graciously typeset little classical books, printed in quarto, with centred lemmata, large type and ample use of white space; this stretched it to a little over two hundred pages. Although it only claimed to be a vocabulary of the imperial documents bearing on the art of war, especially the *Tactica of Leo VI* and the *Strategicon of Maurice*, it cited and excerpted fifteen manuscripts and seventy-three published works, so although it was short it was by no means slight. Of the unpublished texts, four are glossaries: one from the library of Claude Dupuy, two (including a manuscript of pseudo-Cyrillus) from that of Paul Petau, and one from that of François Pithou.[9] Distinguishing between published and unpublished sources was not a matter of course in 1601, and Rigault's decision to do so here suggests his sense of the wordlist as documenting the recovery in print of a textual heritage once concealed in manuscripts, as does his decision to make the same distinction in his catalogue of the Royal Library in 1622.[10]

Joannes Meursius, who was mentioned above as an annotator of de Smet's *Thesaurus*, was soon to take the record of post-classical Greek considerably further than Rigault had done. He had begun what would be a prolific philological career at an early age, publishing a volume of animadversions on the third-century Christian authors Arnobius and Minucius Felix when he was nineteen, with a second edition in the following year, identified as 'improved' on its title-page but not, as second editions usually were, 'augmented', since he had in fact cut a number of his rasher suggestions.[11] Late in his career, he published a little book on the lost works of Theophrastus, which begins, 'The works of Theophrastus, that most excellent philosopher, were many; but most have perished, and few have been saved.'[12] But, from its beginnings, he

[9] Nicolas Rigault, *Glossarium* 219: '[i] Glossarium in vetustiss[imis] membranis, graecolatinum: sed graeca latinis literis exarata. ex Bibliotheca Cl[audii] Puteani, V[iri] C[larissimi] [ii] Glossarium Cyrilli [and iii] Glossae Isidori [both] ex bibliotheca P[auli] Petauii, V[iri] C[larissimi] [iv] Glossarium Graecum vetustissimum. ex bibliotheca Fr[ancisci] Pithoei, I[uris] C[onsulti].'

[10] See McKitterick, *Print, manuscript and the search for order* 12.

[11] Meursius, *Criticus Arnobianus* (1598); Meursius, *Criticus Arnobianus . . . , editio altera, et melior* (1599). See Willems, *Les Elzevier* 16 (item 37) and 17 (item 40).

[12] Meursius, *Theophrastus: sive de illius libris, qui injuria temporis interciderunt* 5, 'Theophrasti, praestantissimi philosophi, Opera fuerunt plurima: sed quae, paucis conservatis, pleraque interciderunt.'

responded to the loss of the classical heritage which the loss of so many books by Theophrastus exemplifies, shaping his work to fit what could still be achieved. His corpus therefore included editions of minor classical authors such as Herodes Atticus, Phlegon of Tralles and some of the ancient authors on music; contributions to epigraphy; books about aspects of ancient culture such as funeral rites, luxury, festivals and dancing; editions and translations of Byzantine authors; and works on Dutch history, including the short but impressive history of his own university, Leiden. He worked at one time towards an edition of an important ancient lexicographer, Harpocration, which would have superseded that of Aldus, but this was still inchoate when Maussac published his own edition.[13] He also, like de Smet, followed in the footsteps of Henri Estienne in one of his publications: an edition of the minor works of Hesychius of Miletus, which succeeded Estienne's of the same author.[14] But, like de Smet's, his intellectual centre of gravity was more in the post-classical than the classical world.

His major contribution to lexicography was a glossary of Byzantine Greek, the *Glossarium graeco-barbarum*, which, although published only nine years after Rigault's, marked a considerable advance on it. It was, like the first two editions of pseudo-Cyrillus and pseudo-Philoxenus, received with great interest, and annotated by readers excited to have a tool for understanding Byzantine Greek and wanting to add improvements or register discoveries.[15] The first edition of the dictionary ran to a little more than eight hundred pages, still with the generous layout of Rigault's work: centred headwords, with text laid out across the page below them, and a tasteful profusion of white space. Meursius knew that, although he was presenting a great deal of new material, he still did not have enough to call for economy of layout. He must also have suspected that a dictionary of Byzantine Greek would be of most interest to a niche market for which there was no need to cut costs by saving paper; and he may have wanted to make it clear to anyone who saw the two side by side that his dictionary was much bigger than Rigault's. After the text was a double *index auctorum*, beginning with eighty-four works consulted in

---

[13] Harpocration, *Dictionarium in decem rhetores* (1614) sig. ẽ4r–v, 'Ecquis ita in literis tyro est vt ignoret viuere etiamnum hodie Ioannem Meursium indefessi laboris virum, qui in emendando et perpoliendo hoc auctore aliquid opera et laboris se impendisse publice professus est.'

[14] Estienne edited Hesychius with Diogenes Laertius, *De vitis* (1593); Meursius as Hesychius, *Opuscula* (1613).

[15] E.g., the Bodleian copy Mar. 42, quite heavily annotated, presumably by the donor, Thomas Marshall.

manuscript, and going on to eighteen pages of those consulted in print. On the very last page was a message:

PRINTER, WHOEVER YOU ARE: I want to ask you earnestly not to reprint this glossary of mine against my will or without consulting me. For I have not yet finished working on it, and it is sure to be republished at some time in a much more complete and better form. As you behave justly here, so may Mercury favour you.[16]

Perhaps Meursius' continuing work on the dictionary went faster than he expected, for the second edition appeared only four years later, now citing ninety-five works read in manuscript. Its text was in double columns, and although the headwords in each column were still surrounded by white space, and the entry-count had gone up from 3600 to 5400, the book could now be compressed to 670 pages, suggesting a sense that new buyers, less affluent than the small group targeted four years earlier, were in sight. The next appearance of Meursius' work was, indeed, aimed at a still larger market, the buyers of some of the later editions of Scapula's dictionary, to which a condensed version of the *Glossarium graeco-barbarum* was appended from 1652 onwards.[17] This was done, according to the publisher, 'so that young persons studying this language variety may also have a synopsis and taste of the modern Greek language' (*modern* meaning 'not ancient' rather than 'contemporary'), implying that undergraduates at the University of Leiden might by mid-century be engaged in Byzantine studies.[18]

To return to the first decades of the century, the tone of Meursius' prefaces to both editions is elegiac. Reflecting on the present state of what had been the Eastern and Western Roman empires, he observes that the Western Empire still clings to life in a mutilated form – in other words, as the Holy Roman Empire. But of the Eastern Empire, 'so completely has all its power collapsed, that we have nothing left but the memory of it which histories maintain. But histories represent to us nothing but the external appearance of the empire, and an account of things done at divers times; I sought, indeed, to inquire more deeply, and to look into its

---

[16] Meursius, *Glossarium* (1610) sig. ***6v, 'TYPOGRAPHE, QVISQVIS ES, Rogatum te serio volo, ne hoc Glossarium meum invito me, aut inconsulto, ad prelum reuoces. Nondum enim manum illi vltimam imposui, & certum est aliquando locupletius multo meliusque in publicum reducere. Ita tibi Mercurius faueat, vt tu Aequitati hic facies.'

[17] Scapula, *Lexicon graeco–latinum* (1652) (several issues, for which see Willems, *Les Elzevier* 173, item 706), cols. 312bis–366bis; subsequent editions of Scapula with this *glossarium contractum* appeared in 1663, 1687, 1816 and 1820.

[18] Louis Elzevier, prefatory epistle in Scapula, *Lexicon graeco-latinum* (1652) sig. *2r, 'ut et modernae *Graecorum* Linguae *Synopsin* quandam ac gustum haberet, Studiosa hujus sermonis *Juventus*'.

interior workings.'[19] And so he made a dictionary. Meursius' assertion that a dictionary actually preserves more of a vanishing culture than a historical narrative can do, and comes closer to its heart, is a bold one. In fact, he toned it down somewhat in the second edition, where he said that 'indeed, the Empire of the East has been so shattered that the memory of it scarcely remains. I have set myself the task of protecting that memory, as far as it is possible to do that using the monuments of the ancients. And in this book I have set out to re-present the state of the Empire.'[20] One way in which the second edition went about that re-presentation was to provide a fourteen-page subject-index, its first entries including 'acclamation at the coronation of an emperor'; 'guardian of the emperor's bedchamber' (i.e., *parakoimomenos*, the highest office conferred on eunuchs); and 'the *Book of Revelations of Adam*'.[21] It shows Meursius' awareness that his work really was an extensive guide to Byzantine culture rather than just a wordlist. In this feature of his dictionary as in others, he was in fact borrowing from Rigault, whose *Glossarium* of 1601 had also had such an index.

While the lexicography of Byzantine Greek was developing in France and the Low Countries, that of post-classical Latin was already well under way. Indeed, there is a sense in which it simply continued from the medieval period. Dictionaries such as the *Catholicon* had included many post-classical words, which sixteenth-century lexicographers whose focus was the classical canon had progressively excised from their dictionaries. However, there were areas, for instance law (especially canon law and the Roman law practised in much of continental Europe) and administration, in which the continuing existence of institutions whose practices had been codified in post-classical Latin made a knowledge of post-classical vocabulary necessary. Not only were the foundational texts of Roman law read in the sixth-century *Corpus iuris civilis*, but the language of their commentators needed to be taken into account: even after Budé, the Accursian tradition could not simply be ignored. So it was that medieval

---

[19] Meursius, *Glossarium* (1610) sig.)(2v–3r, 'adeo planissime imperium omne [Orientis] concidit, vt nihil praeter memoriam eius, quam Historiae vindicarunt, reliquum habeamus. Sed illae praeter externam quandam formam, & res varijs temporibus gestas, nihil nobis repraesentant, mihi vero penitius inquirere libuit, & in interiorem eius constitutionem.'

[20] Ibid. (1614) sig. *2v, 'Quippe in Orientem olim Occidentemque distributum; quod in Oriente fuit, nunc omnino nullum existit: quod in Occidente restat, valde etiam detruncatum, tantum sustinet se, ac tuetur. Et Orientis quidem Imperium ita intercidit, ut memoria vix supersit, Quam asserere, quantum e monumentis veterum fieri potuit, mihi proposui. Et hoc libro statum Imperii repraesentare conatus fui.'

[21] Ibid. (1614) 639, 'rerum in hoc glossario memorabilium index: acclamatio in coronationem imperatoris ... accubitores duo in aula ... Adami liber Revelationum.'

legal dictionaries such as the *Dictionarium iuris* of Albericus de Rosate continued to be reprinted decades after medieval general dictionaries such as the *Catholicon* had become obsolete.[22] So it was too that the huge sixteenth-century dictionaries of legal Latin that superseded them, such as Jacob Spiegel's *Iuris civilis lexicon* of 1538, Simon Schard's *Lexicon iuridicum* of 1582, and the *Lexicon iuridicum*, compiled in 1600 by Johannes Calvinus (Johann Kahl) and emulated by John Cowell, naturally included words from late antiquity and the Middle Ages: the 1549 edition of Spiegel, for instance, runs alphabetically, after entries for *a* and *ab*, from *abaces* (precious vases of a kind discussed in the *Digesta* of Justinian) to *zyzania* (tares, as mentioned in the Bible), neither of which is a classical word or indeed one registered in the *Latinae linguae thesaurus*.

The natural successors to dictionaries of juristic Latin rich in post-classical vocabulary were dictionaries of the juristic Latin found only in medieval texts. These were sometimes undertaken by scholars with strong interests in the vernaculars. So, for example, François Pithou collaborated with Spelman's correspondent Friedrich Lindenbrog on an edition of the *Lex Salica*, the law-code of the Salian Franks, with a substantial glossary, and also made a collection of about 1500 items from various post-classical Latin wordlists, published in 1622 as 'Excerpta Pythoeana'. He also took an interest in Old English, obtaining (on the journey to England on which he secured the manuscript containing excerpts from Macrobius which Henri Estienne failed to edit) a partial manuscript of the *Glossary* of Ælfric.[23] He communicated this material to the French diplomat and philologist Jacques Bongars, and to Friedrich Lindenbrog and Marquard Freher. Lindenbrog's transcript was itself transcribed by his brother Heinrich, and Heinrich's by Junius' friend Jan van Vliet.[24]

Friedrich Lindenbrog's glossarial interests led him to copy Old English glosses from other manuscripts, and to acquire a transcript of John Joscelyn's unpublished dictionary of Old English.[25] He also made a glossary of about two thousand post-classical Latin words, which forms the last 154 pages of the *Codex legum antiquarum*, a collection of early Germanic

---

[22] There were Venice editions of Albericus, *Dictionarium iuris tam civilis, quam canonici* in 1572, 1573 and 1581.

[23] Ker, *Catalogue* 470.

[24] See Dekker, *Origins of Old Germanic studies* 133 and nn. 112, 113.

[25] Ker, *Catalogue* 470–1, citing a manuscript copied by Lindenbrog, now Hamburg, Staats- und Universitäts-Bibliothek MS philol. 263, and ibid. 471n1, citing a manuscript owned by Lindenbrog, formerly Hamburg, Staats- und Universitäts-Bibliothek MS Germ. 32 fol., but stolen or destroyed during the Second World War, in which Joscelyn's dictionary was pp. 1–325, and was followed by Old English glosses and extracts from Latin–German glossaries.

law-codes which he published in 1613. As glossaries go, this is at first sight rather an odd one: the first substantial entry, for instance, *Abortiuus partus sine sacramento regenerationis traditur ad inferos* ('A miscarried foetus which is not baptized goes to hell') is not lexical at all, but gives the patristic authorities for this repellent but orthodox doctrine, which crops up in one of the legal codes.[26] Some entries are more obviously glossarial: the last, *Zurb*, documents the occurrence of this Old High German word embedded in the Latin of one of the law-codes, discusses its variants in different manuscripts, cites its treatment in a manuscript glossary, and ends with the explanatory note: 'In certain regions of Germany, lacking wood for the hearth, they use earth dug up from marshy places: they give this earth the name *Torff*, and the French call it *Tourbes*' (the reference is to peat, or *turf* as it is called in some varieties of English).[27] Overall, Lindenbrog's aim was not simply to explain hard words, and it was not to provide a subject-index (he did that separately) – it was to use an alphabetical wordlist to structure a wide range of cultural information which he perceived as ancillary to the *Codex legum antiquarum*.

Another glossary published in 1613 appears to have been the first to use the form *latino-barbarus* in its title: the 'glossarium latinobarbarum' of Johann Martin Lydius attached to his edition of the works of Nicholas de Clamanges, a late medieval advocate of church reform. This is a discursive alphabetical wordlist of about seven hundred lexical items, many of them from law-codes, in which, consistently with its maker's sense of medieval Latin as a mixed language, a number of analogous lexical items are adduced from contemporary Dutch and even English. Lydius, a minister of the Reformed Church and continuator of John Bale's historical survey of the papacy, was editing de Clamanges for the light he shed on the history of Romish error, but his work as a lexicographer was valuable in its own right to successors such as Spelman and Somner.[28] He was one of a number of early seventeenth-century antiquaries who took up the work of their predecessors of the Reformation period. Another, on whose early work Lydius drew, was Melchior Goldast, who edited the collection in which Dorat's poem on the household of Robert Estienne is preserved. His *Alamannicarum rerum scriptores* of 1616 made some of Joachim von Watt's unpublished writings available, and also included runic material and some important glossarial material, which was to be used by Junius: the Old

---

[26] *Codex legum antiquarum* II:1345.   [27] Ibid. II:1499.
[28] Lydius' continuation of Bale is *Scriptores duo Anglici, ... de vitis pontificum Romanorum* (1615); Spelman cites the 'Glossarium latinobarbarum' in *Archaeologus* sig. π3r; Somner's copy is Canterbury Cathedral Library, W/E-3-57.

High German glosses which have since his edition been called 'Keronian' after their supposed author; the 'Körperteilglossen' or glossary of words for parts of the body which is associated with the name of Walafrid Strabo; and glossaries of Goldast's own making.[29] Marquard Freher, who corresponded with Goldast about the 'Körperteilglossen', edited the important collection of primary sources *Germanicarum rerum scriptores aliquot insignes*, and had owned the manuscript of Tatian that passed to Junius, also edited the works of a sixteenth-century scholar, Trithemius.[30] Two related characteristics tend to distinguish these seventeenth-century scholars from their predecessors. The first is that Lindenbrog, Freher and Goldast had all been trained in the law, and had all come under the influence of the *mos gallicus* of legal history; Freher had indeed studied at Bourges. They were better placed than their predecessors to see the rigorous investigation of lexical items as a key to cultural history. The second is that they could see more clearly than their predecessors that the period extending roughly from the end of antiquity to the fifteenth century could be studied as a coherent and interesting entity. They could, in other words, choose to study the Middle Ages.

Goldast was in fact the first person to give this period the name *medium aevum* 'the middle age', in 1604.[31] A hundred years previously, no such term had been in general use. A sense that the period between the fall of the Western Roman Empire and the lifetime of Petrarch was unified by its darkness and ignorance is indeed present in Petrarch's own writings.[32] Flavio Biondo, writing in the mid-fifteenth century, saw the millenium beginning with the sack of Rome in 410 as an identifiable unit.[33] He did not, however, give it a name, and although forms such as *media tempestas* 'the middle time' are attested in the later fifteenth century, their reference is always to a vaguely conceived time between the present and the distant past rather than to a coherent and definable period.[34] Then, in the sixteenth century, forms such as *media aetas, media*

---

[29] For Goldast and the *Alamannicarum rerum scriptores*, see Hertenstein, *Joachim von Watt* 115–99, esp. 191f. for the Keronian glosses, 181–2 for the 'Körperteilglossen', and 140 for his own glossaries; for his runic studies, see Derolez, *Runica manuscripta* 303–5; for him and Lydius, see Spelman, *Archaeologus* sig. π3r.

[30] For Freher's correspondence with Goldast, see Hertenstein, *Joachim von Watt* 129.

[31] See Gordon, '*Medium aevum*' and Robinson, 'Medieval, the Middle Ages' 747–51.

[32] See Mommsen, 'Petrarch's conception of the "Dark Ages"'.

[33] Gordon, '*Medium aevum*' 5; Cochrane, *Historians and historiography* 36–7.

[34] Here, Gordon, '*Medium aevum*' 10 is superseded (especially in its treatment of Giovanni Andrea Bussi's use of *media tempestas* in the preface to the *princeps* of Apuleius) by Lehmann, 'Mittelalter und Küchenlatein' 203; Edelman, *Attitudes of seventeenth-century France toward the Middle Ages* 2 adds another example from Bussi.

antiquitas and *media tempora* were used by a few authors in senses that tended increasingly to define a period, often in discussions of the history of the Church from a Reformation perspective. G. S. Gordon's classic article on the subject records examples of these forms from the writings of von Watt, Beatus Rhenanus and Basel associates of theirs such as the printer Joannes Oporinus between 1522 and 1534, and of *media aetas* also from Hadrianus Junius' *Batavia* (completed by 1575 and published in 1588), but no others from the sixteenth century – though in fact a few can be found, notably an instance of *medium tempus* in Camden's *Britannia* of 1586. After 1600, however, Gordon could find a great wealth of examples: Marcus Welser used *media antiquitas* in a letter of 1600 to Scaliger; in 1601, the historian Henricus Canisius used *media aetas* twice; in 1604, Goldast used *media aetas*, *media antiquitas* and *medium aevum*; and so on.[35] The abrupt change in frequency of attestations suggests strongly that Goldast's contemporaries in Germany and England gave wide currency to a sense, inherited from a small group of their predecessors in the study of Germanic antiquities, that the centuries in question were a coherent period, and thereby made it possible to see what the seventeenth century had inherited from that period.

Apart from isolated occurrences of the German forms *mitler jaren* and *mitteljärigen* in von Watt and *mittel alters* in the Swiss historian Aegidius Tschudi, the first vernacular equivalents of these terms were in English and French.[36] John Foxe (who had lived in Basel as a guest of Oporinus) distinguished 'the primitiue tyme of the church, . . . the middle age, and . . . these our latter dayes of the church' as early as 1570.[37] Estienne Pasquier referred to 'l'Eglise sur son moyen aage' in a text published in 1596 but perhaps written earlier.[38] Using the phrase in a broader sense, Camden referred to the 'midle age, which was so ouercast with darke clouds, or rather thicke fogges of ignorance' in 1605, and Spelman to 'the middle ages' in 1616, translating this form into Latin as *media saecula* in 1625; a correspondent of Pierre Dupuy refers to 'quelques autheurs du moyen age' in 1626.[39]

---

[35] Gordon, '*Medium aevum*' 10–14 (the date 1518 in Gordon is corrected by Schaeffer, 'Emergence of the concept "medieval"' 21n2), to which can be added Camden, *Britannia* (1586) 76, 'medij temporis poeta' and examples from the late sixteenth century in Lehmann, 'Mittelalter und Küchenlatein' 205.

[36] For the chronological development of related forms in the European languages, see *OED* s.v. 'middle age'; for von Watt, see Gordon, '*Medium aevum*' 23 and for Tschudi, see Schaeffer, 'Emergence' 30.

[37] Foxe, *First volume of the ecclesiasticall history* 204 col. 1.

[38] Quoted Edelman, *Attitudes of seventeenth-century France toward the Middle Ages* 5.

[39] Camden, *Remaines* (1605) 2 (second sequence of pagination) and Spelman, *De non temerandis ecclesijs* (1616) 194, both cited in *OED3*; Spelman, *Archaeologus*, cited Gordon, '*Medium aevum*' 14; Jean Besly, letter of 1626 to Pierre Dupuy, quoted Edelman, *Attitudes of seventeenth-century France toward the Middle Ages* 5.

What this meant for lexicography was that, soon after the beginning of the seventeenth century, it became possible to see the usage of Latin authors from the post-Nicene fathers to the fifteenth century as forming an entity that corresponded to a historical period: whereas Lindenbrog and Lydius made glossaries for use with single books, Spelman could make something much more like a glossary to medieval Latinity in general. So could Charles du Cange, to whom we now turn.

THE CUSTOMS OF OUR FOREBEARS, NEARLY OBLITERATED AND BURIED IN OBLIVION: THE TEXTUAL HERITAGE OF CHARLES DU CANGE

A comprehensive survey of the seventeenth-century lexicographical study of medieval Latin and Byzantine Greek would proceed from the early wordlists of Lindenbrog and Lydius, Meursius and Rigault, to major mid-century works such as the *De vitiis* of G. J. Vossius. This narrative will move directly to the two monumental dictionaries of Charles Du Fresne, Sieur du Cange, the *Glossarium ad scriptores mediae et infimae latinitatis* (1678) and the *Glossarium ad scriptores mediae et infimae graecitatis* (1688). These dictionaries, neither of which has yet been altogether superseded, 'bear comparison', in Wilamowitz's opinion, 'with the *Thesaurus* of Stephanus'.[40] They resulted from the deep engagement of a phenomenally gifted scholar with the medieval heritage that had been defined by Goldast and his contemporaries.

Their maker was, like Budé and Spelman, a gentleman of independent means with a legal background. Born in 1610, he was the fifth son of Louis Du Fresne, sieur de Frédeval and du Cange, who had inherited a legal position in a town near Amiens.[41] He was educated at the Jesuit college in Amiens, where he showed academic promise, and then studied law at Orléans, being admitted to the bar before the Parlement of Paris in 1631. In 1638, Louis Du Fresne died, and Charles inherited a house in Amiens and other property from him, together with his title of sieur du Cange. In the same year, he married a well-born woman ten years younger than himself, Catherine Du Bos, who brought him a dowry of twelve thousand livres, and seven years later he purchased the lucrative post of *trésorier de France*, and thereby acquired the title of *conseiller du Roi*.[42]

---

[40] Wilamowitz-Moellendorff, *History of classical scholarship* 59; cf. Pfeiffer, *HCS* II, 133.
[41] For his family background, see Feugère, *Étude sur la vie et les ouvrages de du Cange* 3–5.
[42] Ibid. 6–9; Favre, 'Notice sur la vie et les ouvrages de Charles Dufresne du Cange' ii.

Du Cange at thirty-five, then, might have been mistaken for a typical member of his social class, comfortably wealthy, suitably married, well connected.

However, one anecdote that suggests his difference from his peers is transmitted in an eighteenth-century source: 'On dit que le jour de son mariage M. du Cange étudia six ou sept heures.'[43] The nineteenth-century French medievalist Léon Gautier is likewise said to have encouraged his students with the words 'Remember, gentlemen, that the great Du Cange worked for fourteen hours on his wedding day.'[44] Both versions of this unattractive story show du Cange being remembered as another Budé, but as surpassing his predecessor, who restricted himself to three hours' work on the day of his own wedding. The story may well be apocryphal, but the general point it makes is surely right: the well-born sieur du Cange was, long before his first printed publication, already a man whose life was shot through with the spirit of scholarship. He had, like Spelman, begun with heraldry. He researched and emblazoned a genealogy of his mother's family when he was twenty, and went on to write more on heraldry – notably a *Traité du droit et comportement des armes* in fifty-eight chapters, which has been praised highly in the twentieth century – and on Gaulish history.[45] A learned gentleman of his time might have been content to go on from those beginnings to devote a lifetime to antiquarian studies of his native province; du Cange did indeed leave extensive manuscript collections bearing on this subject.[46] But even in the 1630s he was reading voraciously in a very wide range of classical and post-classical Greek and Latin texts: his list of fifty-five Greek texts read between 1631 and 1636 begins with pseudo-Kodinos, a Byzantine treatise on church and court officials edited by Franciscus Junius' father, and goes on to Eunapios, a late pagan author of *Lives of the Sophists* (written apparently in a particularly unattractive style); Apollodorus on Greek mythology; the Byzantine romance *Hysmine and Hysminias* of Eustathios Makrembolites, edited by Spelman's admirer Gilbert Gaulmyn; and so

---

[43] Baron, *Éloge de Charles Dufresne* 45.

[44] Thompson, 'Age of Mabillon' 243; the figure of fourteen hours derives from Baron, *Éloge de Charles Dufresne* 7, 'Quatorze heures de travail au moins étoient son travail ordinaire.'

[45] Bloch, 'Charles Du Cange' 513 and 516–17; for the *Traité du droit et comportement des armes*, see Pastoureau, 'Du Cange héraldiste' 505f.

[46] See Hardouin, 'Liste des ouvrages de du Cange' xv ff. and Bloch, 'Charles Du Cange' 519–21; the history of Amiens from the fifth century to the thirteenth, with digressions on locally minted coinage and the history of the legal concept of the *régale*, was published in 1840 as *Histoire de l'état de la ville d'Amiens et de ses comtes.*

on, noting that he read some of them twice.[47] For many years, this reading was distilled in manuscript collections.

In 1657, however, he published a book of national importance, an edition of Geoffroy de Villehardouin's Old French history of the French crusaders' empire of Constantinople, with a facing text in modern French. This was published under royal sponsorship in a series of Byzantine historians, the *Corpus byzantinae historiae* or *Byzantine du Louvre*, which will be disussed below. Villehardouin had been published in 1584 and again in 1601, but du Cange's edition was textually better informed than either of its predecessors.[48] It was also greatly enriched with editorial material: the 208 folio pages of the edition itself were followed by another 145 pages of notes, a 17-page glossary of some of the Old French vocabulary that appears in the text, an index, 332 pages of supplementary historical and genealogical material and 86 pages of documents. An edition of the other major French historian of the crusades, Jean de Joinville, followed in 1668. This was, like the Villehardouin, a grand folio, published in the *Corpus byzantinae historiae*, and although it is not a *princeps*, and does not even draw on new manuscript evidence, it is also richly illustrated by editorial material. A seventeenth-century reader faced with du Cange's edition and uncertain as to whether to buy Joinville in 842 pages of folio might have turned instead to a second-hand copy of one of the duodecimo editions published seventy years earlier: the choice would have been that between historical narrative for its own sake, as pleasurable or instructive reading, and historical narrative as part of a larger antiquarian understanding of the past. At the end of the edition, hinting, like the glossary to Villehardouin, at future lexicographical interests, was a six-column index to 'termes de la basse latinité' which had been explained in du Cange's editorial matter.

In 1668, du Cange and his family fled Amiens to avoid an outbreak of bubonic plague. They went to Paris, and remained there.[49] Du Cange's personal library in Amiens had been good, but it could have offered

---

[47] BN ms fr 9495 fos. 2r and 3r; the list at 2r begins '1631. Codinus curop[alata] de offic[ialibus] g [raeco]l[atinus] f[olio] | 1634. Eunapius g[raeco]l[atinus] 8[vo] | 1634. Apollodorus g[raeco]l [atinus] 8[vo] 1634. | Eustath. κατ' ὑσμένην g[raeco]l[atinus] 8[vo]', i.e., pseudo-Kodinos, *De officialibus* (1588), Eunapios, *De vitis philosophorum et sophistarum* (1568 or a later edition), Apollodorus, *Bibliotheces* (1555 or a later edition), Makrembolites, *De Ismeniae et Ismenes amoribus* (1618). For the prose style of Eunapios, see *Oxford dictionary of Byzantium* ii:746.

[48] See Rickard, 'From Villehardouin to Du Cange' 114: du Cange's text was based on the 1584 edition, collated with that of 1601 (which is from a different manuscript), plus a fourteenth-century manuscript in the royal library (now BN fonds fr. 4972: see Bloch, 'Charles Du Cange' 518), plus a collation by Pierre Pithou of a lost printed edition and another manuscript.

[49] Samaran, 'Du Cange à Paris' gives a detailed account of the Paris household.

nothing like the daily opportunity of access to the superb manuscript collections in the institutional and private libraries of Paris.[50] To read a manuscript in the Louvre, he had previously had to travel for two days; now a leisurely half an hour's walk would bring him there.[51] He could now also participate fully in the vigorous learned life of the capital. He had apparently been a visitor to the meetings associated with the Dupuy brothers, with whom he was corresponding by 1651, and those over which the lexicographer Gilles Ménage presided, and some of these visits must have been made before the move to Paris, since the meetings of the Dupuy circle lapsed in 1661.[52] By 1666, Ménage was on good enough terms with du Cange to ask him to read early printed sheets of his *Origini della lingua italiana* before its publication.[53] But residence in Paris allowed him much more frequent contact with learned men, not least those who visited the house to which the Benedictines of the Congregation de Saint-Maur sent their most talented scholars, the abbey of Saint-Germain-des-Prés, just across the river from the Louvre. 'The learned reunion, the *conversazione*, was an essential feature of life at Saint-Germain,' as David Knowles, himself a monk and a historian, wrote. 'For almost a century, from the rise of Luc d'Achery [i.e., the late 1640s or early 1650s] to the death of Bernard de Montfaucon [1741], the abbey was the scene of regular weekly gatherings of all the scholarship and much of the connoisseurship of Paris and France.'[54] Du Cange became a leading participant in these meetings. The most illustrious of the Maurists, the palaeographer and historian Jean Mabillon, was coming into his powers just as du Cange arrived in Paris.[55] The two met regularly, and their intellectual relationship was close: hence the preface to Mabillon's *De re diplomatica* comes to a climax with thanks to du Cange, 'who forwarded this work with cautions and encouragements, just as if it had been your own, and who put your energies into spurring me on at times when I was reluctant'.[56] Hence also the anecdote of the visitor to the learned men of Paris, who was directed 'to the most learned of them all, to du Cange,

---

[50] For du Cange's library in 1658 see Paul Bonnefont, letter of 26 July 1658 to Jean Luc d'Achery, quoted Bloch, 'Charles Du Cange' 515.
[51] The journey time from Amiens to Paris before the improvements of the later eighteenth century is from Schama, *Citizens* 158.
[52] De Boer, 'Men's literary circles in Paris 1610–1660' 731, 768; for a letter from du Cange to the brothers Dupuy, dated Amiens, 16 May 1651, see Dorez, *Catalogue de la collection Dupuy* II:473.
[53] Emery Bigot, letter of 22 May 1666 to du Cange, in Doucette, *Emery Bigot* 106.
[54] Knowles, *Great historical enterprises* 41–2.
[55] Thompson, 'Age of Mabillon' 233 ff., 242; Barret-Kriegel, *Jean Mabillon* 52ff.
[56] Mabillon, *De re diplomatica* sig. ē2v, 'hancce lucubrationem nostram, non secus ac tuam, monitis & adhortationibus promovere, & mihi aliquando restitanti stimulos adhibere satagebas'.

who said to him 'It's Mabillon whom you should visit and consult'; but Mabillon sent him back right away, answering his inquiries by saying "Go back to du Cange: he has been, and is, my master, and he shall be yours." '[57]

Du Cange himself was now no longer the provincial scholar that he had been in Amiens but part of a brilliant metropolitan circle of learning. Because the Maurists were at the centre of that circle, he was in touch with a body whose aim was the recovery, by editorial, historical and antiquarian work, of medieval learned culture, with particular attention to monasticism, and therefore to texts in post-classical Latin.[58] His Latin dictionary would be revised by Maurist editors half a century after his death.

In parallel with the stimulus to read Latin which the Maurists provided, one of the long-running collective intellectual projects of seventeenth-century Paris, the editing of the Byzantine historians, attracted du Cange. Hieronymus Wolf's early project was revived in Paris in 1645 (though only given formal status as the *Corpus byzantinae historiae* in 1648), after which a series of important folio editions of historical authors issued from the Imprimerie Royale: Ioannes Kantakouzenos in three volumes (1645–6); Georgios Kedrenos in two, with extracts from the earlier work of Ioannes Skylitzes and a glossary (1647); Niketas Choniates, also with a glossary (1647); Theophylaktos Simokattes and Georgios Sphrantzes, also with a glossary (1647–8); and so on. The series emulated Wolf's in content, but another of its ancestors was the series of classical Greek *principes* produced by Robert Estienne as *imprimeur du roi* just a hundred years earlier. Du Cange's first contribution to this series was a double *editio princeps*, of the twelfth-century Byzantine historian Ioannes Kinnamos and of the sixth-century description of the cathedral of Hagia Sophia by Paulos Silentiarios. This, accompanied by du Cange's commentaries on Kinnamos and on his contemporaries Nikephoros Bryennios the younger and Anna Komnene, was published in 1670. By 1672, du Cange was at work on another twelfth-century Byzantine historian, Ioannes Zonaras, revising the text of Wolf's edition and illustrating it with a commentary so that the whole, published more than a decade later, comprises nearly 1200 pages in folio.[59] His edition of a seventh-century

---

[57] Baron, *Éloge de Charles Dufresne* 37–8, 'On l'addressa au plus sçavant de tous, à du Cange, qui lui dit: *C'est Mabillon que vous devez aller voir et consulter*; mais Mabillon le renvoya dans l'instant, en lui répondant: *Retournez à du Cange, il a été, il est mon Maître, et il sera le vôtre*'; a slightly different version, perhaps from an independent source, is in de Broglie, *Mabillon* 1:57.

[58] Knowles, *Great historical enterprises* 33–62, esp. 43ff.; for a checklist of Maurist editions of post-classical Latin, see Hurel, 'Benedictines of the Congregation of St.-Maur and the Church Fathers' 1031f.

[59] The edition was published 1686–7; a letter of 24 March 1672 from Louis Ferrand to Leibniz, in Leibniz, *Sämtliche Schriften und Briefe* 1.1:197, reports that 'M. du Cange ... travaille sur le Zonare.'

Byzantine chronicle, the so-called *Chronicon paschale*, was published posthumously in 1688.

The *Corpus byzantinae historiae* was a double project, whose focuses were, first, the recovery of a manuscript heritage by the production of *editiones principes* and the discovery of new manuscripts for collation (hence a number of title-pages specify the owners of the manuscripts on which the editions were based), and, second, the illumination of Byzantine civilization by the making of commentaries and glossaries. Du Cange's other contribution to it was a purely antiquarian work, the *Historia byzantina duplici commentario illustrata* of 1680. The two commentaries of its title are genealogical and topographical respectively; du Cange notes that two other subjects had previously called for commentary, namely a guide to civil and ecclesiastical dignities, achieved in the most recent edition of pseudo-Kodinos, and a guide to Byzantine Greek, supplied by the glossarial work of Rigault, Meursius, Charles Annibal Fabrot (particularly in his forty-three-page glossary to Kedrenos) and others.[60] The first commentary is a survey of the genealogies of a number of prominent families of the Byzantine world, including French, Albanian and Turkish families that played a part in Byzantine history, recalling du Cange's early genealogical researches and, more recently, the genealogical tables that formed part of the apparatus of his edition of Kinnamos. The second commentary is a detailed account of the buildings known to have stood in Constantinople, a subject on which du Cange had already touched in his edition of Paulos Silentiarios.

One other work of du Cange's should be mentioned in passing beside these contributions to Byzantine studies: his part in Charles Labbé's posthumous edition of the glossaries of pseudo-Cyrillus and pseudo-Philoxenus, which he saw through the press for publication. The edition itself has been criticized for its conflation of material from other glossaries with the two that it presented.[61] Its scholarly qualities aside, though, it is an explicit witness to du Cange's position as, in some ways, an heir to Robert and Henri Estienne, editor for a new generation of a glossary whose *princeps* had been edited by Henri by way of appendix to the *Thesaurus graecae linguae*. Noteworthy for the same reason is a Bodleian copy of the *Enchiridion* of Hephaestion, a handbook of metre from the second century AD that transmits some interesting verse fragments, which

---

[60] Du Cange, *Historia byzantina duplici commentario illustrata* 1–2, citing pseudo-Kodinos, *De officiis*; Rigault, *Glossarium*; Meursius, *Glossarium*; and Fabrot, 'Glossarium'.
[61] Goetz and Gundermann, eds., *Corpus glossarium latinorum II* xix.

bears the ownership signatures of Robert Estienne, written in the 1550s, and of du Cange, written in 1635.[62]

Du Cange's output would have been impressive without the great dictionaries of post-classical Latin and Greek, but it is for the dictionaries that he is remembered. He had begun work on a dictionary of post-classical Latin by 1666, though he must have been collecting material long before, and it was, to the excitement of a number of the learned, in press by the beginning of 1677, though it did not appear until the following year.[63] His collection of the materials that would constitute the dictionary of Greek must likewise have begun long before their publication, and must have been well advanced by the time he wrote in the *Historia byzantina duplici commentario illustrata* that there was no need for a new dictionary of Byzantine Greek – was his decision to publish his own work on the subject actually a consequence of making and reflecting on this assertion? He sent off the first batch of copy for the letter A in 1682, though the process of typesetting and correction took six whole years (one reason for this was that the *officina* of du Cange's printer, Jean Anisson, was at Lyons, a week's journey from du Cange in Paris), during which he compiled further material.[64] Both dictionaries are massive, complex responses to the post-classical textual heritage, and particularly to its extensiveness as experienced in the reading of printed books and manuscripts. They are, as Momigliano said, antiquarian works. Their title-pages suggest their range:

Glossary to the writers of middle and recent Latin: in which Latin words whose meaning has changed since the classical era, or which are uncommon [i.e., 'which were rare in classical authors but are more common in post-classical Latin'] or borrowed from the medieval vernaculars or elsewhere, have their meanings explained and their origins uncovered, and in which the following are reviewed, explained, and illustrated: many usages and customs of the Middle Ages; formulae and obsolete words belonging to laws, civic customs and post-classical jurisprudence; the dignities and offices both of the ecclesiastical and the secular orders; and many other things worthy of note – all taken from printed

---

[62] Now Bodl. Auct. S 2. 35.
[63] Emery Bigot, letters of 22 May 1666 to du Cange, in Doucette, *Emery Bigot* 106, and of 8 February 1677 to Antonio Magliabechi, ibid. 107n66; Leibniz, letter of 9 March 1677 to Ferdinand, bishop of Paderborn, in Leibniz, *Sämtliche Schriften und Briefe* 1.2:257–8 at 258; Louis Ferrand, letter of 23 March 1677 to Leibniz, ibid. II.2:260–1 at 260; Leibniz, letter of April (?) 1677 to Hermann Conring, ibid. II.1:324–5 at 325; Henri Justel, letter of 30 July 1677 to Leibniz, ibid. 1.2:284–8 at 287.
[64] Anisson acknowledged the receipt of slips for A in a letter of 14 August 1682 (Omont, *Lettres d'Anisson à du Cange* 9–11), and of a fair copy of A in five fascicles in a letter of 15 February 1683 (ibid. 17–18); cf. also Mabillon, letter of 1 September 1682 to Claude Nicaise in de Broglie, *Mabillon* 1:216–17 at 217, 'On va imprimer à Lyon le *Glossaire grec* de M. du Cange.'

and manuscript books and other documents, both in institutional and private collections.[65]

Glossary to the writers of medieval and later Greek, in which Greek words whose meaning has changed since the classical era, or which are uncommon or borrowed from the medieval vernaculars or elsewhere, whether ecclesiastical, liturgical, military, legal, medical, botanical or alchemical, have their meanings and origins uncovered, and in which the following are reviewed and explained: many usages and customs of the Middle Ages; the dignities of the church in general, the monastic orders, the palace and political life; and many other things worthy of note, and especially bearing on Byzantine history – all taken from printed and manuscript books and other documents.[66]

In both cases, it is made clear that encyclopedic material is to be expected, and thematic indexes make it possible to find, for instance, all the entries in the *Glossarium graecitatis* for titles of honour, a topic whose foregrounding here suggests that in some ways that dictionary is a sequel to the *Historia byzantina duplici commentario illustrata*. There are essay-length encyclopedic entries in the *Glossarium latinitatis*, for instance s.v. *annus*, which includes sixteen pages of elaborate calendrical tables (taken, with acknowledgement, from John Greaves' *Epochae celebriores* of 1650), and there are also a number of shorter disquisitive entries such as the five columns devoted to *eucharistia*, in which du Cange quotes a dissertation by his deceased brother Michel Du Fresne SJ. Entries in the *Glossarium graecitatis* tend to be terser, though the treatment of Κυριακή in the sense 'Sunday' runs to four columns. Du Cange was well aware that the length of such entries might lead to his being accused of self-indulgent digressiveness, and pointed out in the preface to the *Glossarium latinitatis* that 'it was our intention that this study of ours, such as it is, should not be a meagre publication in the manner of those lexica, old and new, which

---

[65] Du Cange, *Glossarium latinitatis* title-page, 'Glossarium ad scriptores mediae & infimae latinitatis: in quo latina vocabula novatae significationis, aut usus rarioris, barbara & exotica explicantur, eorum notiones & originationes reteguntur; complures aevi medii ritus & mores, legum, consuetudinum municipalium, & iurisprudentiae recentioris formulae, & obsoletae voces, utriusque ordinis, ecclesiastici & laici, dignitates & officia, & quamplurima alia observatione digna, recensentur, enucleantur, illustrantur; e libris editis, ineditis, aliisque monumentis cum publicis, tum privatis.'

[66] Du Cange, *Glossarium graecitatis* title-page, 'Glossarium ad scriptores mediae & infimae graecitatis: in quo graeca vocabula novatae significationis, aut usus rarioris, barbara, exotica, ecclesiastica, liturgica, tactica, nomica, jatrica, botanica, chymica explicantur, eorum notiones & originationes reteguntur: complures aevi medii ritus & mores; dignitates ecclesiasticae, monasticae, palatinae, politicae, & quamplurima alia observatione digna, & ad historiam byzantinam praesertim spectantia, recensentur ac enucleantur; e libris editis, ineditis veteribusque monumentis.'

simply comprise words and glosses'.[67] For some words, of course, a very brief treatment would be satisfactory, but the discussion of others should not be restricted by a rule of brevity, 'especially when we judged that the customs of our forebears, nearly obliterated and buried in oblivion, would uncover the meaning of texts and should be called back into the light'.[68] As well as the encyclopedic material within its lexical entries, the *Glossarium latinitatis* presents non-lexicographical material. The 4564 columns of dictionary entries at its heart, which provide over a hundred thousand illustrative quotations, are preceded by a preface *De causis corruptae latinitatis* of seventy-six pages and a 5000-item bibliography of medieval Latin writings, and followed by a long series of indexes – all this could be regarded as normal dictionary apparatus, though on a grand scale – but they are also followed by an appendix. This is a numismatic treatise, on which du Cange had been working for some years: 'A dissertation on the coins of the emperors of Constantinople, or of what is called the lower age, or the lower empire'. It comprises seventy-two pages of text, illustrated with eleven handsome engraved plates.[69] It is a classic antiquarian production, and it accompanies the text of the dictionary because that text was itself informed by antiquarianism. Du Cange had, as it turned out, no need to fear that the combination would be objectionable. A correspondent of Leibniz's who read part of the dictionary while it was still in press summed up the double achievement for which readers would value the *Glossarium*: on the one hand, 'a wonderful accumulation of erudition is to be seen there', and, on the other, this was 'quite apart from the explication of an infinite number of obscure words'. He concluded that 'it is a book which it will hardly be possible to surpass, and which will bring its author an immortal name'.[70]

The classical heritage made a readable corpus; a scholar could, in the spirit of Erasmus, set out to read everything that survived. The post-classical heritage could not be surveyed so systematically, partly because so much survived, and partly because so much was yet unpublished. The

---

[67] Du Cange, *Glossarium latinitatis* lix, 'eam nobis fuisse mentem, ut haec qualiscumque lucubratio nostra non ieiuna omnino prodiret in publicum, veterum, atque recentiorum Glossariorum more, quae verba cum sola explicatione complectuntur'.

[68] Ibid., 'praesertim cum veteres nostrorum mores, ac ferme obliteratos et oblivione sepultos ad Scriptorum intelligentiam detegendos, et rursum in lucem revocandos existimaremus'.

[69] Ibid., separately paginated and registered appendix, 'De imperatorum constantinopolitanorum seu de inferioris aevi, vel imperii, uti vocant, numismatibus, dissertatio'.

[70] Louis Ferrand, letter of 8 September 1678 to Leibniz, in Leibniz, *Sämtliche Schriften und Briefe* 1.2:360–1 at 361, 'l'on y voit un ramas prodigieux de Doctrine outre l'explication d'une infinité de mots que l'on ne scavoit pas. C'est un livre dont on ne sauroit guere se passer et qui va acquerir une reputation immortelle a son auteur.'

indices auctorum in both dictionaries locate them firmly in the process of the recovery of textual heritages. The sources of the *Glossarium latinitatis* are listed over 122 double-column folio pages; those of the *Glossarium graecitatis* only run to twenty-two pages, but these do include several hundred works read in manuscript, particularly in the royal library and that of the great minister and Maecenas Jean-Baptiste Colbert, but also in the collections of acquaintances from the circle of Saint-Germain-des-Prés such as the book-collector Antoine Faure and the orientalist Eusèbe Renaudot. Readers of the *Glossarium graecitatis* were themselves expected to need help as they handled manuscripts, and one of the appendices comprises twenty columns of manuscript abbreviations with their equivalents, some straightforward (μ with a stroke above it for μέγα 'great') and some puzzling (the chi-rho monogram for κρόκος 'purple crocus, saffron').[71] This table of abbreviations sums up the role of both dictionaries as series of reading notes and as handbooks for other readers.

Du Cange explains in the preface to the *Glossarium latinitatis* that, because so many of the texts he handled were newly edited or unedited, he found – like Spelman – that, they were full of difficult words that were not registered in the glossaries of post-classical Latin to which he had access. He made notes on them, which consisted in the end of a multitude of 'demies-feuilles volantes' or 'petits billets', in other words, citation slips, about six inches square.[72] Some of these are extant in the Bibliothèque Nationale: a typical one reads

> fatigiae
> molestiae, labores. Gall. fatigues.
>
> Chron Windesem lib. 1. c. 32. pro fatigis
> et expensis. lib. 2. c. 35. quantis laboribus
> et fatigijs. Occurit etiam In Lg ⌈legibus⌉ Hungaricis.[73]

It is clear how this was put together: du Cange found the word *fatigiae* with the sense 'inconveniences, labours' in Johann Busch's fifteenth-century

---

[71] Similar material circulated in manuscript and was discussed by du Cange and his correspondents: see Omont, *Lettres d'Anisson a du Cange* 20–1.

[72] 'Demies-feuilles volantes' is from Bonnefont, letter to d'Achery of 26 July 1658 in Bloch, 'Charles Du Cange' 515, and 'petits billets' is from Anisson, letters of 14 August 1682 and 23 August 1683, in Omont, *Lettres d'Anisson à du Cange* 9–11 and 23; see the sources gathered in Samaran, 'Du Cange à Paris' 168. The papers for the entry *bursa* are reproduced Bloch, 'Charles Du Cange' between 528 and 529 and discussed ibid. 530, and that for μονόζονοι is reproduced Omont, *Lettres d'Anisson a du Cange* 4.

[73] BN ms lat. 13036, slip 259; additions made as the slip was prepared for press are not transcribed here.

Chronicle of Windesheim, which was available to him in an edition of 1621, and wrote a slip for it, giving headword, definition, a French derivative with the same sense and two quotations. Both quotations appear to have been written at the same time, in which case marginalia or temporary notes probably underlie them. The reference to the occurrence in a Hungarian legal code, however, appears to have been added later; finding the word in that source, du Cange must have been able to put his hands on a previously written slip. These slips accumulated to the point at which, 'since I had a great many notes made from the huge number of writers whom I had, alike to relieve tedium or to avoid idleness, taken up, I decided to follow in the footsteps of so many learned men, and organize them, and put them, digested in some form, before the eyes of the public'.[74] The words 'in some form' suggest that an alphabetized lexical dictionary was not the only possibility du Cange considered: he might have turned his slips into a work like Budé's *Commentarii*, or into an alphabetically ordered encyclopedia.

The difference between du Cange and Budé, though, is that du Cange had amassed such an enormous body of lexical information in his reading that no other arrangement but alphabetical order would have made it accessible to readers. This is the difference that the knowledge explosion of the first full century of print had made to philology. As for the possibility of an alphabetically ordered encyclopedia, the survival of two sketches on this model compiled by du Cange from post-classical Latin and Greek sources shows the difference between what he could achieve in this format and what he did achieve in the *Glossarium latinitatis* and the *Glossarium graecitatis*. The first is a collection in two volumes, running to 820 folio pages, which has du Cange's Greek reading list of the 1630s prefaced to it. This includes entries on topics such as 'alliances of the King of France with the Turks' (an essay summarizing a defence of those alliances); 'archdeacon' (with material on the Eastern Church, some of it from Meursius' *Glossarium*); 'various styles and titles of honour of kings and magistrates' (with sub-headings in the margin such as *Majestas* and *serenitas*), and so on.[75] Much of the material here is, as these three headings suggest, concerned with the history of institutions, though there are also headings such as 'fear' and 'temperance' and 'theology'.[76]

---

[74] Du Cange, *Glossarium latinitatis* lvi: 'Cum igitur permulta ex ingenti Scriptorum, quos identidem levandi taedii vitandique otii causa in manus sumpseram, numero adessent animadversa, tot doctorum virorum insistendo vestigiis, ea recensere, et utcumque digesta in lucem emittere publicam decrevi.'

[75] BN ms fr 9494, fos. 8r–v, 'Alliances du Roy de france auec les Turcs' (drawing on du Ferrier, *Catholique d'estat*); 20r, 'Archidiaconus'; 23r–v 'Variae Regum aut Magistratuum Appella[ti]o[n]es ac tituli honorarij'.

[76] BN ms fr 9495, fos. 318r–v 'Timor'; 319r 'Temperantia'; 320r 'Theologia'.

A second collection, of which only two volumes out of three appear to survive (the whole would have run to about nine hundred pages), has headings such as 'investitures', 'oaths / formulae for swearing oaths' and 'characteristics of languages'.[77] The trouble with categories like these is that they could not accommodate a great deal of the information that du Cange had to hand, and he abandoned both collections long before their completion, leaving many headings with no material under them.

The first of the abandoned collections had a number of epigraphs on the importance of reading, such as the injunctions 'Read books; remember what you have read' from the so-called *Sayings of Cato*.[78] The *Glossarium latinitatis* collates the reading notes that would not fit into the subject-headed collections – what kind and range of reading, then, does it record? The bibliography prefaced to the dictionary might be used as evidence, but it does not say how often each item was used. A better picture can be taken by examining one column of dictionary entries, taken more or less at random, that from *bertonia* to *bestius*, and seeing what sources du Cange cites there. There are twenty-one citations in all. Four are glossarial. One of these is from the *Liber glossarum* attributed to St Isidore, which was available to du Cange in two printed collections of glossaries.[79] One is from the early thirteenth-century *Derivationes* of Hugutio of Pisa, which he used in a manuscript.[80] Two are from Balbi's *Catholicon*, which he appears to have used in manuscript rather than one of the early printed editions.[81] These citations were presumably added at a point when earlier reading notes were already being worked up into a dictionary. Elsewhere in the *Glossarium*, du Cange used the other big named-author dictionary of the Middle Ages, that of Papias, also in manuscript, and various other glossaries, of which his *index auctorum* specifies twelve as having been consulted in manuscript.[82]

The remaining nineteen citations tell us more about the textual heritage that du Cange encountered in his general reading. Two are patristic: one from Commodianus and the other from the sixth-century *Itinerarium*

---

[77] Paris, Bibliothèque de l'Arsenal MS 4815, fos. 56r–v 'Inuestitura'; 63–4 'jusjurandum' and 'Juresjurandi formulae'; 96r 'Lingua[rum] idiomata'.

[78] BN ms fr 9494, fo. 2r, 'Libros lege | quae legeris memento', quoting *Dicta Catonis*, sententiolae 26, 27.

[79] S.v. *bestiones*, citing 'Glossae Isidori', i.e., the *princeps* in de Smet, *Thesaurus utriusque linguae* cols. 667–98 at 671 or the reprinting in Godefroy, *Auctores latinae linguae* (1622) cols. 1bis–34bis (sigs. AAaa1r–BBbb1r) at 5bis.

[80] S.v. *bestiarium* (= *liber de bestiis compositus*), citing 'Ugutioni', identified in the *index auctorum* cxc as from a manuscript in the library of the Collège de Navarre in Paris.

[81] S.vv. *bestiarium* (= *liber de bestiis compositus*) and *bestius*; for the manuscript, see Bloch, 'Charles Du Cange' 530.

[82] Du Cange, *Glossarium latinitatis*, cols. clxxxix–cxc.

ascribed to Antoninus of Placentia, an account of a pilgrimage to the Holy Land.[83] Two are early medieval: one from Aldhelm's *De laude virginum* and the other from a Merovingian saint's life published in a five-volume collection of *inedita* from French libraries by du Cange's friend the Maurist Jean Luc d'Achery in 1661.[84] Among sources from the High Middle Ages, four citations are of a single manuscript in du Cange's possession, Guillaume Guiart's 20,000-line vernacular metrical chronicle *Branche des royaux lignages*, written at the beginning of the fourteenth century.[85] Three are of printed chronicles: one from France, that of Hugo de Flavigny; one from England, the annals of William Thorne of Canterbury from Twysden's *Historiae Anglicanae scriptores decem*; one from the borders of the Byzantine world, a fourteenth-century chronicle from what is now the city of Split.[86]

As important in du Cange's reading as chronicles were charters and other legal texts and documents. He cites four printed sources of this class. Three of these are of French origin, and all print the same passage from a twelfth-century charter.[87] The fourth is an English charter, printed in the *Monasticon anglicanum*.[88] To these can be added two thirteenth-century

---

[83] S.v. *bestius*, citing 'Commodianus instr. 34', i.e., Commodianus, *Instructiones* sect. 34, in the edition of 1650 or the reprint of its text in de la Bigne, *Maxima bibliotheca* 27:11–22; s.v. *Besca lingua*, citing 'Itinerarium Jerosolymitan. Antonini Monachi', i.e., *Itinerarium B. Antonini* (1640).

[84] S.v. *berua*, citing 'Althelmus de Laude virgin.', i.e., Aldhelm, *De laude virginum*, known to du Cange both from the *princeps* in Canisius, *Antiquae lectionis tomus* V (1604) part 2, 793–863 at 808 and from de la Bigne, *Maxima bibliotheca* 13:3–19 at 5 (in both, the reading in the text is *beluarum*, with *beruarum*, the form in which du Cange was interested, given as the MS reading in the margin); s.v. *besilium*, citing 'S. Audoenus lib. 2. de Vita S. Eligii c. 37', i.e., Audoenus, *Vita Sancti Eligii*, in Achery, *Veterum aliquot scriptorum . . . spicilegium* V:147–302.

[85] S.v. *besilium*, citing as a source for Old French *besil* and *besiller* 'Guill. Guiartum in Hist. Francor. MS.', i.e., Guiart, *Branche des royaux lignages*, presumably from what is now BN ms fr 5698 (see Bloch, 'Charles Du Cange' 525). Du Cange published extracts in his editions of Villehardouin, *Histoire de l'empire de Constantinople*, sig. ö2v, and Joinville, *Histoire de S. Louys IX*, 133–61.

[86] S.v. *bestia*, citing 'Hugo Flaviniac. in Chron. p. 245', i.e., Hugh, Abbot of Flavigny, 'Chronicon Virdunense' in Labbé, ed., *Nova bibliotheca manuscript[orum] librorum* (1657) 75–272 at 249; s.v. *bertonia*, citing 'Will. Thorn an. 1287. & 1313', i.e., William Thorne, 'Chronica' in *Historiae anglicanae scriptores* X cols. 1757–2296 at 1946 and 2019 (the latter is in fact an instance of the English form *berton*); and s.v. *bestiale, bestialia*, citing an occurrence of the form 'apud Michaëlem Madium de Barbezanis in Histor. cap. 20. 21', i.e., Mica Madius, 'De gestis Romanorum imperatorum et summorum pontificum', in Lučić, *De regno Dalmatiae et Croatiae* 371–81 at 378.

[87] S.v. *besenagium*, citing 'Charta Willelmi Comitis Cabilonensis an. 1180. in Bibliotheca Clun. p. 1441. & apud Gallandum de Franco alodio, & Chiffletium in Beatrice Cabil. p. 40', i.e., a charter of Guillaume, comte de Chalon, of 1180, printed in whole or in part in Marrier and Duchesne, *Bibliotheca cluniacensis* col. 1441; in Galland, *Du franc-aleu et origine des droicts seigneuriaux* 91; and in Chifflet, *Lettre touchant Beatrix comtesse de Chalon* 40.

[88] S.v. *bertonia*, citing 'Monasticon Anglic. to. 2. p. 887', i.e., an early thirteenth-century charter (supplied by John Aubrey from a cartulary no longer extant) in Dodsworth and Dugdale, *Monasticon anglicanum* II:887; for the date of the charter and the loss of the cartulary, see Pugh and Crittall, *History of Wiltshire* III:259f.

legal manuscripts: one, cited twice, is a collection of French royal documents from the beginning of the century, and the other is apparently one of the documents by which the king of Aragon guaranteed the liberties of Majorca after his reconquest of the island.[89]

This short section of the *Glossarium latinitatis* appears to be fairly representative of the whole except that it lacks material from law-codes and does not quote any Greek. The medieval Latin textual heritage as received by du Cange was, then, largely made up of ecclesiastical, annalistic and legal texts, and in this respect it resembles the Anglo-Saxon heritage as received by early students of Old English. Just as *Beowulf* is conspicuous by its absence from the early wordlists and dictionaries of Old English, so the medieval Latin from which we derive most pleasure today – secular lyric, hymnody, personal writings such as those associated with Abelard and Heloise, the *Gesta romanorum*, the bestiaries, the *Consolation of philosophy* – is largely absent from the *Glossarium latinitatis*. Here, du Cange's interests differ from those of William Camden, who evidently enjoyed the medieval Latin verse, including even extracts from the Archpoet, which he presented in the *Remaines*.[90] They are much closer to Spelman's or Twysden's: the history of the ownership of land and of the complex of rights and obligations that went with that ownership; the history of government, and particularly of the relationship between central and local government. The latter interest explains the manuscripts he was reading: the earliest collection of documents from the central administration of France, and a text recording the awareness of traditional local liberties in a kingdom subsequently merged into the strongly centralized kingdom of Spain.

A third interest, and a very important one, shows up when du Cange is compared with Erasmus. He cites Balbi's *Catholicon* as the source for two lexical items in the sample discussed above, and uses it quite frequently throughout the *Glossarium latinitatis*: perhaps two or three per cent of his

---

[89] S.v. *bestia* (in the phrase *venari ad magnam bestiam*), citing 'Vetus Inquisitio de foresta, in Regesto Philippi Aug. f. 114' and s.v. *bestia* (in the phrase *bestia mortua*), citing 'Charta Will. de Calviniaco 1212. in Regesto Philippi Aug. f. 74', identified in du Cange's *index auctorum* (col. cxciv) as 'Reg. Philippi Augusti Herouvallianum' and in his edition of Joinville, sig. Bbb 2v, as 'Reg. de Philippes Auguste de la Bibl. de M. de Herouual', i.e., BN, fonds fr. 9852.2, made available to du Cange by its then owner, Vyon d'Hérouval: see Delisle, *Catalogue des actes de Philippe-Auguste* xiii–xiv; s.v. *bestiarium* (= *pecus*), citing 'Libertates Regni Majoricar. an. 1248', almost certainly from a manuscript, though the nearest match in the *index auctorum* seems to be the one identified col. cxc as 'Libertates concessae Barcinonensibus a Petro Rege Arag. 1285'.

[90] Camden, *Remaines* (1605) 39f. (second sequence of pagination), quoting the verses beginning 'Mihi est propositum in taberna mori', with ascription to Walter de Mapes, i.e., Walter Map; cf. Piggott, 'William Camden and the *Britannia*' 37–8.

citations are to this text. This is a long way from its condemnation by Erasmus, whose self-definition required him to put as much distance as possible between his own work and that of the thirteenth century. By du Cange's time, the remoteness of the thirteenth century had been established: it was part of the *medium aevum*. He could therefore engage with Balbi with a new respect and a new interest, seeing the medieval dictionary as an object of inquiry rather than as a series of blunders.

Du Cange's understanding of *medium aevum* has been criticized on the grounds that he refers both to *scriptores medii aevi*, 'writers of the Middle Ages', and to *scriptores medii et infimi aevi*, 'writers of the Middle and later ages'; this, according to G. S. Gordon, 'seems, and is, a very clumsy and inconsistent manner'.[91] Du Cange knew perfectly well what period he was going to cover in his Latin dictionary: that from the latter years of the Western Empire to the fifteenth century. He generally referred to the period as *medium aevum*, but occasionally used *medium et infimum aevum* by analogy with the division of the post-classical Latin language into two stages, *media et infima latinitas*, the former ending around the ninth century.[92] This division was of purely theoretical importance for his lexicography, though: the *Glossarium latinitatis* treats medieval Latin as a single entity in the way that the development of the concept of *medium aevum* had made possible. The *Glossarium graecitatis*, by contrast, seems to have no clear *terminus ad quem*: du Cange asked Jacques Spon, who worked on the dictionary as corrector for Anisson in Lyons, to lend him a copy of an '*Histoire d'Athènes*, en grec vulgaire', and Spon and Anisson used a polyglot dictionary that included modern Greek to help them decipher du Cange's extremely difficult printer's copy.[93] The end of the Byzantine Empire is actually more clearly marked than the end of the Western Middle Ages: Constantinople fell in 1453, Trebizond in 1461, and after that there was no sovereign Byzantine state. But for du Cange and his contemporaries, the *medium aevum* was clearly defined because a distinct new culture had come after it, while Byzantine culture seemed rather to have gone into abeyance – the idea that it had been inherited by the Muslim rulers of the Ottoman Empire would have seemed most unattractive to them.

One might therefore say that medieval Latin and Byzantine Greek constituted two different kinds of heritage for du Cange and his

---

[91] Gordon, '*Medium aevum*' 16.

[92] See Edelman, *Attitudes of seventeenth-century France toward the Middle Ages* 8–9.

[93] Anisson, letters to du Cange of 1 March and 24 December 1683, in Omont, *Lettres d'Anisson à du Cange* 18–19 at 18 and 24–5 at 25.

contemporaries. The former belonged to a clearly defined past, by which it had been bequeathed to the present. The latter still continued, but without grandeur: its appropriation would be more a matter of revival than of rebirth. The ways in which it might be appropriated in seventeenth-century France will be examined in the next section.

HIS STUDIES WERE ALWAYS DIRECTED TOWARDS
THE HISTORY OF FRANCE: DU CANGE
AND THE FRENCH HERITAGE

Du Cange's great-nephew Jean-Charles Du Fresne D'Aubigni summarized the great man's scholarly achievement by saying that,

> in the vastness of his reading and of his literary undertakings, he nevertheless obeyed the unities of subject and indeed of place: in other words, from his earliest years his studies were always directed towards the history of France.[94]

Another eighteenth-century reader agreed:

> while he appeared only to occupy himself with the history of other nations, it was nevertheless the glory of his own, the majesty of the name of the French, and in short the general history of France, which had always been his principal object.[95]

The claim that his work was essentially a patriotic inquiry into French antiquities is on the face of it a remarkable one to have made about a Latinist and Byzantinist. For sure, du Cange was the editor of Villehardouin and Joinville. He was also a collector of French manuscripts such as the unique witness to a prose romance of Merlin.[96] In 1676, he sat on a commission instituted by Colbert to examine the possibility of publishing the medieval French historians after an earlier project of publishing the *Historiae francorum scriptores* had lapsed, and drew up a *Mémoire sur le projet d'un nouveau recueil des historiens de France*, which was not adopted (in the end, the Maurists took up the scheme in the

---

[94] *Mémoire sur les manuscrits de M. Du Cange* 7, 'Dans l'immensité de ses lectures et de ses travaux littéraires n'avoit cependant qu'une unité de sujet, et même une unité de lieu, c'està dire, que dès son plus bas âge il a toujours eu pour objet l'Histoire de France dans toutes ses parties et dans tous ses tems.'

[95] Baron, *Éloge de Charles Dufresne* 23, 'en paroissant ne s'occuper que de l'Histoire des autres Nations ... c'étoit la gloire de la sienne, la majesté du nom François, enfin l'Histoire générale de la France, qui avoit toujours été son objet principal'.

[96] Now BL Add. MS 38117; the British Museum *Catalogue of additions to the manuscripts in the years 1911–1915* notes *ad loc.* that it 'Apparently belonged to the philologist Charles Du Fresne, Sieur Du Cange ... a note on f. 1 being pronounced by a subsequent owner "de la main du fameux Mr Du Cange d'Amiens"'.

Rerum gallicarum et francicarum histories of 1737–86).[97] But this was by no means *all* of his work: Du Fresne D'Aubigni was claiming that du Cange's study of the history of Latin and his Byzantine studies were also contributions to French cultural and linguistic heritage.

A way to begin to examine the first part of that claim is to look at the fine engraved frontispiece of the *Glossarium latinitatis*, reproduced in part on the dustjacket of this volume. In the background of this composition, ancient Rome, adorned with obelisks and fine buildings, is burning. The Pantheon is surrounded by flames. In the middle distance is the figure of a man who has climbed a ladder to deface an inscription. Near the foot of the ladder, heavily cloaked figures, clutching large books, are in flight. One of them has been stopped by a soldier with a drawn sword, and turns towards him with an expression of anger and fear. More books lie on the ground near his feet. In front of him, two other figures are carrying books, but not to save them: the books are piled on the sort of stretcher used for carrying building materials, and the men are approaching a great fire attended by soldiers, who are throwing books into the flames, and poking them further into the fire with their spears. All this is backdrop; in the foreground, a female figure sits by the recent ruins of what was evidently a splendid building, her face partly covered, weeping. Her name is written at her feet: LATINITAS. Above her is a broken column, whose base is inscribed GLOSSARIUM *ad scriptores* MEDIAE & INFIMAE LATINITATIS.

The scene in this frontispiece must be the sack of Rome by the Goths. Nothing will ever be the same again after this: the literature of the ancient world will always be fragmentary, and the fabric of ancient Rome will always be broken. But the picture, despite the weeping of the personified Latinitas, is not one which the seventeenth-century reader need take as unrelievedly tragic. The Pantheon is surrounded by flames in the picture, but it is untouched by them; it survived the sack of Rome, and has survived since. The obelisks that adorned ancient Rome had, spectacularly, been re-erected a century before du Cange's work. The broken column stands on the same base as an apparently whole one. The fabric of Latinity has, this frontispiece states, been damaged, but not altogether destroyed. The *Glossarium latinitatis* is being presented as by no means a dictionary of a dead language.

This point is made again and again in the text. For one thing, the dictionary uses Latin, good classicizing Latin, as its defining language.

[97] The outline is edited in Hardouin, 'Liste des ouvrages de du Cange' xii–xiii (for the autograph, see Bloch, 'Charles Du Cange' 526) and discussed Feugère, *Étude sur la vie et les ouvrages de du Cange* 87–9; for the Maurist editions, see Knowles, *Great historical enterprises* 55.

It has a long preface written in Latin, an essay of great power; one eighteenth-century critic remarked of du Cange that 'the learned prefaces of his dictionaries are proof of a *génie philosophique*, and are in their genre the best one can read for their profundity and their style'.[98] This preface is not only an original composition in Latin, but also a catena of borrowings from other Latin authors, classical, patristic and modern: du Cange quotes Quintilian and St Augustine and St Jerome, Arnobius and Sir Thomas Smith, building their words into the structure of his own argument neatly and congruently, making it clear that he belongs to the same tradition as these authors, and writes their language, and so represents the continued survival of that language in France. The French neo-Latin poet Bernard de la Monnoie wrote that du Cange had unlocked post-classical Latin and Greek from their captivity, and exclaimed 'A wonder! Behold, a Gallic Camillus is here,' alluding to the role of Marcus Furius Camillus in Roman resistance to the Gauls in 390 BC.[99] Camillus was called the second founder of Rome, *parens patriae*, according to Livy.[100] Now a Frenchman was re-founding the heritage of Rome.

Furthermore, in its account of medieval Latin, the *Glossarium latinitatis* describes the language of many of the living institutions of Europe. Du Cange lived in a society whose laws and political arrangements had been shaped in Latin. He wrote in the preface that 'in our own country, France, it continued to be the case that both public and private records and most judgements of the highest courts were nearly always written down in the Latin language; this ended rather recently, in the reign of François I'.[101] The lived experience recorded by the vocabulary of medieval Latin landholding and administration underlay his own lived experience as landowner and administrator. 'The gentlemen of the *Chambre des Comptes*', noted an eighteenth-century account, 'always have M. du Cange's Latin glossary on their desk so that they can turn to it when ancient deeds present difficulties.'[102] In fact, du Cange attempted to register some of the Latin of early medieval France in what may have been his very first wordlist, a fascicle of twenty-one pages that gathers

---

[98] *Mémoire sur les manuscrits de M. Du Cange* I, 'Les doctes Préfaces de ses Glossaires sont encore preuve d'un génie philosophique, et sont en leur genre, ce qu'on peut lire de plus beau pour le fond et pour le style.' Cf. Baron, *Éloge de Charles Dufresne* 14–15.

[99] Quoted Baron, *Éloge de Charles Dufresne* 47, 'Res mira! e Gallis ecce Camillus adest.'

[100] Livy, *Ab urbe condita* 5.49.7, 'Romulus ac parens patriae conditorque alter urbis ... appellabatur.'

[101] Du Cange, *Glossarium latinitatis* xxxii, 'In Gallia nostra sic obtinuit, ut et acta publica ac privata plerique et suprema Curiarum iudicia, Latino fere idiomate semper describerentur, quod serius desitum Francisco I. regnante.'

[102] Baron, *Éloge de Charles Dufresne* 50.

about 630 lexical items under the title 'Glossarium francobarbarum'. Its principal sources are listed on its first page: Pierre Pithou on the Salic Law and the capitularies of Charlemagne; François Hotman on the vocabulary of feudal institutions; Jérôme Bignon's edition of the formulary of Marculfus; Jacques Sirmond on the capitularies of Charles the Bald.[103] If this sketch is the beginning of du Cange's collection of post-classical Latin vocabulary, it shows his lexicography growing from a French historiographical tradition, that of the philological study of French law and French institutions.

And, finally, the French language was derived from Latin. Du Cange was clear about this, writing firmly in the preface that 'I shall not dwell upon those who argue that the greater number of the vernacular languages owe their origins to Greek,' and adding that 'those who derive nearly all the vernaculars from Hebrew have no more right to a hearing'.[104] So, the study of post-classical Latin illuminated the history not only of French institutions, but of the origins of the French language itself: 'from those words which we call barbaric, there often comes material from which much of scholarly interest can be gathered, bearing both on the institutions and manners of our ancestors and also on the uncovering of the origins of common words'.[105] Du Cange's words sum up the understanding of the importance of post-classical Latin for the history of French that was being developed by others, for instance Gilles Ménage, who had written in his etymological dictionary of French (1650) that 'For a successful investigation of the origins of our language, one must have a perfect knowledge of Latin, and particularly of post-classical Latin, in which there are an infinite number of books, which make wearisome reading.'[106]

Writing Latin that conformed to classical standards, du Cange represented and enacted a learned tradition of continuity with the past, and, speaking French, he represented and enacted a popular, organic continuity

[103] BN ms fr 9486, fo. 1r, 'Glossarium | francobarbarum | Desumptum ex authorib. sequentibus | petro pithoeo ad Leg. salicam. – a | p. pithoeo ad capit. Caroli M. – b. | fr. hotomano In Comment. verb. feud. – c. | hier. bignonio ad formul. marculphi – d | jacob. sirmondo ad capit. Car. Calui.'

[104] Du Cange, *Glossarium latinitatis* xvi, 'Iis porro non immoror, qui plerasque ex vulgaribus Linguis Graecae ortus suos debere contendunt … Neque potiori iure audiendi illi qui omnes fere vulgares Linguas ab Hebraica accersunt.'

[105] Ibid. lv, 'Ex ipsis, quae barbara appellamus, vocabulis occurreret persaepe nescio quid unde plurimum perciperetur eruditionis, tum ad instituta moresque majorum nostrorum, tum ad vulgarias vocum origines retegendas.'

[106] Ménage, *Origines de la langue françoise* sig. ã4v, 'Pour reüssir en la recherche des Origines de nostre Langue, il faudroit auoir vne parfaite connoissance de la Langue Latine dont elle est venuë, & particulierement de la basse Latinité, dont les liures sont infinis et ennuieux à lire'; cf. Droixhe, 'Ménage et le latin vulgaire ou tardif' 143–64 and Dekker, *Origins of Old Germanic studies* 235–6.

with the same past. However, his work was not a simple celebration of continuity: there was a real tension in it between two possible narratives of the history of the Latin language. On the one hand, since the high literary Latin of the late Republic and the early Empire had so much prestige, it was possible to see a decline from its purity to the language of the early Middle Ages. On the other, it was possible to see the same change as a creative transformation of classical Latin through vulgar Latin to the romance vernaculars. This tension between narratives of decline and of progress keeps du Cange's long, brilliant preface moving to and fro for page after page. So, for instance, he exclaims, 'No wonder if in the Carolingian age, or a little before, the Latin language should have been so befouled successively in France, Italy, and Spain, since it had been so many times polluted by the flood of the barbarians.'[107] The texts written in early medieval Latin, he continues, would take an Oedipus to sort out their obscurities. But then the discussion moves from the language of Carolingian France to what du Cange calls the *lingua limosina*, in other words Old Occitan. Having touched on the question of its origins, he continues by remarking that 'that elegant language was considered so richly expressive, cultivated and refined that hardly any area survived into which it was not introduced, given above all that in the courts of princes the Provençal poets were held in high regard, and their poems, being endowed with singular genius, were read just about everywhere'.[108] By this point, du Cange's account of the language varieties that succeeded classical Latin has taken him to what we understand as the immediate origins of the Renaissance. Is his narrative, then, to be summed up as one of deterioration or rebirth? Du Cange really did not know for certain. In the case of Greek, the story was easy to tell, because its outcome only determined the evaluation of modern Greek, in which du Cange had no personal investment, rather than that of French. So, he was happy to say that the spoken language of the Eastern Empire simply 'became gradually but steadily worse' as a result of contact with other languages, and even the best writers, who tried to cultivate a pure style, found themselves bringing corrupt and foreign words into their written Greek.[109] But whereas the preface to the *Glossarium graecitatis* is

---

[107] Du Cange, *Glossarium latinitatis* xxvi, 'Non mirum igitur si Carolinis saeculis, vel paulo ante, in Gallia, Italia, et Hispania, sic deturpata deinceps fuerit Latina Lingua, quae barbarorum illuvie toties foedata fuit.'

[108] Ibid. xxix, 'Ea quippe Lingua nitida adeo, florida, culta ac polita habita est, ut nulla fere extiterit regio, in quam non immissa fuerit, cum maxime in Principium aulis magno in pretio haberentur Poetae Provinciales, eorumque poemata, ut genio quasi dotata singulari, ubique fere legerentur.'

[109] Du Cange, *Glossarium ... graecitatis* v, 'vulgaris ille sermo Graecus, quem κοινòν appellatum fuisse diximus, Latinorum, ac caeterarum deinde Gentium, quae in Orientis Provincias, Byzantiumque,

unequivocally a story of decadence, the preface to the *Glossarium latinitatis* is far more complex. It presents a vivid self-portrait of a lexicographer trying to understand, on the basis of the magnificently extensive reading distilled in his dictionary, whether or not he has a right to be proud of his cultural heritage.

In the end, du Cange's sense of growth triumphed over his sense of decline. Neologisms such as those that make some medieval authors so difficult, he reflected, were necessary in theology and philosophy; but also in medicine; and in sciences such as architecture, where the vocabulary available in Vitruvius was limited and sometimes obscure; and, for instance, in occupations such as falconry, for which there were no ancient texts. The linguistic changes of the early Middle Ages were fundamentally signs that the Latin language was, despite the impact of the barbarians, alive: they were signs of growth, of accommodation to lived experience. This narrative of growth, moreover, extended to the present day. To his account of the Latin origin of French, du Cange added an account of its medieval diffusion. Indeed, his dictionaries bring home the whole of the medieval French world to seventeenth-century France, including the empire of Constantinople, the kingdoms of Jerusalem and Cyprus, and the kingdom of England. This last Francophone outpost is given particular attention in the preface to the *Glossarium latinitatis*, ending with particular praise to the English antiquaries who have worked on the histories of institutions and of language:

Of those indeed who have undertaken to illustrate obsolete varieties of their own languages, worthy in the first place of particular praise are the English, who have expended so much sweat in the explication of the Saxon language, which was for a long time prevalent in nearly all of Great Britain, that without their sleepless nights we would hardly comprehend the laws of the Anglo-Saxon kings, even those which were subsequently translated by ancient writers into Latin, since they, and even the laws of the Norman kings, are everywhere sprinkled with Anglo-Saxon words and formulae. Those who have exercised themselves with the greatest success in this field are the most learned men Henry Spelman, Meric Casaubon, son of the great Isaac, and John [*sc.* William] Somner, and others, on whose commentaries we frankly acknowledge that we have extensively drawn, both in interpreting the English writers and even in revealing the origins of words of our own.[110]

ubi sedes erat imperij, commercij causa commeabant, deterior effectus, sensim semper in pejus abiit ... Byzantinae historiae Scriptores ... qui etsi sermonis munditiam coluerint, voces tamen corruptas vel barbaras, cum id aliter fieri posse non putarent, subinde inseruerunt.'

[110] Du Cange, *Glossarium latinitatis* xx, 'Ex iis vero qui Linguas suas obsoletas illustrare conati sunt, praecipuam imprimis laudem merentur Angli, qui in Saxonica, quae in tota fere majori Britannia diu obtinuit, enucleanda, ita insudarunt, ut absque eorum vigiliis, Anglo-Saxonum Regum Leges,

Du Cange was indeed, as English scholars noted in the decades after the publication of the *Glossarium latinitatis*, indebted to Spelman and Somner for a number of Anglo-Latin lexical items.[III]

The preface to the *Glossarium latinitatis* concludes, then, with a grand and generous picture of the recovery, certainly of a French cultural heritage, but also of a greater European heritage in which French and English have their part to play, in which the spider's web of philology, always extending new filaments and making new connections, has for part of its mesh all the languages within du Cange's grasp, the Latin and Greek of his great dictionaries, the varieties of English on which Somner worked, the Old French of Villehardouin's chronicle, the Old Occitan that became such a noble vehicle for so much poetry in the courts of high medieval Europe.

Likewise, the last appendix of the *Glossarium graecitatis*, following 250 columns of addenda to the Latin dictionary and to the treatise on Byzantine coins, is an sixty-five-column index to the places in both dictionaries at which the etymologies of French words have been discussed. The majority of these are naturally discussed in the *Glossarium latinitatis*, but words from *abricot* 'apricot' to *visier* 'vizier' are referred to discussions of Greek. Du Cange is not, however, always claiming that a French word whose origins are illuminated by an entry in the *Glossarium latinitatis* or the *Glossarium graecitatis* is ultimately from Greek or Latin. *Regarder*, for example, is referred to the word *warda*, which is transparently a Latin borrowing from a Germanic language. *Visier* is likewise referred to the word οὐιζήριος, clearly borrowed by Greek from a language of western Asia. Indeed, *visier* is also referred to another Greek word that means the same but is not formally related, πρωτοσυμβόυλος. The point is not simply to make a case for the ancestry of the French forms but to locate them in a polyglot network of cognates and semantic equivalents.

Du Cange's citation of vernacular texts such as Guiart in the *Glossarium latinitatis* is further evidence of his interest in the interlocking of

---

etiam quae Latio subinde donatae sunt a veteris Scriptoribus, haud perciperemus, cum eiusce Linguae vocabulis, ut formalibus, ubique aspersae sint, quemadmodum etiam Regum Normannicorum: in qua quidem palaestra maxima cum laude versati sunt viri eruditissimi Henricus Spelmannus, Emericus Casaubonus Magni Isaaci filius, Joannes Somnerus, aliique, ex quorum Commentariis hausisse nos multa ingenue agnoscimus, tum ad Anglos Scriptores illustrandos, tum etiam ad vocabulorum nostrorum origines retegendas.'

[III] See, e.g., Kennett, 'Life of Mr. Somner' 49, 'the diligent *Du-Fresne*, in explication of most of these terms, barely translates the *English* of this book [the *Treatise of Gavelkind*]' and the similar remarks in Nicholson, *English historical library* 1:106; cf. also Kennett, *Parochial antiquities* sig. b3v on du Cange's dependence on Spelman for 'all the old terms which were of more peculiar use in this Island'.

the learned and vernacular languages. He knew that adducing this sort of material as evidence for Latin usage would seem odd to some readers, and announced his intention to adduce it in a note in the preface.[112] Some may have been added after the collapse of the plan for a collection of the French historians in 1676; an eighteenth-century source records that du Cange, aware of his advancing age and of the improbability that the plans that had been discussed would come to anything, 'to save at least a moiety of the materials which he had amassed, decided to include them in his Latin glossary which he produced in 1678, and in a number of other works which he sent to the press in the remaining years of his life'.[113]

Du Cange was, then, conscious of linking Latin studies and the French heritage in a number of ways. The same was true of Byzantine studies, and not the least of the ways in which he connected them with the matter of France was by reflecting on his own role as historian. So, for instance, his justification of genealogy as a part of history in the *Historia byzantina duplici commentario illustrata* went far beyond a simple explanation of the historian's need to understand complex networks of familial relationships. He appealed to its place in tradition, seeing it as sanctioned by the example of the Biblical genealogies, but also by specifically French, or at least Gaulish, practice. So, he quoted Lucan on the bards of the ancient Gauls, who sang of the heroic deeds of ancestors in order to inspire their listeners before battle, and compared Taillefer's singing of the deeds of Roland before the Battle of Hastings. He then turned by way of analogy to Welsh bards, of whom he knew from Boxhorn's *Origines gallicae*, which quotes an account of bardic poetry by Giraldus Cambrensis in which, to complete the circle, Giraldus quotes Lucan.[114] For all the grandeur and urbanity of his book, a handsome folio, dedicated to Colbert, du Cange found it natural to compare his scholarly work with the heroic, even semi-magical, songs of an oral tradition. The passage from Lucan that he cited places bardic song in the explicit context of enmity to Rome, and follows the reference to the bards with a famous

---

[112] Du Cange, *Glossarium latinitatis* lix, 'non Latinos modo, sed etiam aevi supparis Scriptores vernaculos adhibuimus, erutos plerosque e manuscriptis codicibus'.

[113] *Mémoire sur les manuscrits de M. Du Cange* 9, 'pour sauver au moins une partie des matériaux qu'il avoit amassés, se détermina à les fondre dans son Glossaire Latin qu'il donna en 1678 et dans plusieurs autres Ouvrages qu'il fit imprimer depuis jusqu'à sa mort'.

[114] Du Cange, *Historia byzantina duplici commentario illustrata* 6, quoting Lucan 1:447–9 and citing William of Malmesbury, *De gestis regum anglorum* (no doubt from *Rerum anglicarum scriptores post Bedam praecipui* 57) and Albericus de Trium Fontium, *Chronicon* an. 1066 (p. 795 in the 1874 edition; read by du Cange in manuscript, presumably BN MS lat. 4896A; merely a quotation from William of Malmesbury) on Taillefer, and Giraldus Cambrensis, *Description of Wales* 1:12 from Boxhorn, *Originum gallicarum liber* 66 on Welsh bards.

account of Druidic practice, so that the allusion was balanced between participation in a classical tradition and keen, sympathetic attention to other, non-classical traditions that were apparently inimical to it.

The volumes of the *Corpus byzantinae historiae* were, moreover, clearly a credit to France, and the series received official sponsorship correspondingly. A good example of the necessarily delicate solicitation of that sponsorship took place in 1679, when du Cange wanted to offer Colbert the dedication of the *Historia byzantina duplici commentario illustrata*. The abbé Gallois, academician and professor of Greek at the Collège Royal, who was both a client of Colbert's and an associate of du Cange's from the circle of Saint-Germain-des-Prés, met with Colbert to make the offer, which was accepted. The dedicatory epistle urged that 'that truly regal edition of Byzantine authors, which foreigners everywhere admire as the monument *par excellence* of the magnificence of France, should be completed'.[115] Gallois read the epistle to Colbert and explained the merits of the project to him, adding that du Cange had laboured on it, and should be asked to continue doing so. This was well received, as Gallois explained in a letter to du Cange, which concluded by inviting him to put in a research proposal (the form of words is anachronistic, but that is what his suggestion amounted to), together with a list of the inedited Byzantine historical manuscripts in the royal library.[116] Du Cange's editions of Zonaras and the *Chronicon paschale* would duly be published from the Imprimerie Royale. The fact that the *Glossarium graecitatis* was, on the other hand, published by Jean Anisson of Lyons caused bad feeling in the Paris booktrade. Anisson was a learned man; he and his brother were known to du Cange from meetings at Saint-Germain, and have been described as 'continuing, at an even higher level, the tradition of the Estiennes'.[117] He was, however, accused of having snatched the printing of the *Glossarium* from his Parisian peers in order to prove his status as 'le plus grand libraire de l'univers', and there must have been great exasperation in Paris when he was awarded the title of *imprimeur royale* three

---

[115] Du Cange, *Historia byzantina duplici commentario illustrata* sig. ãₓv, 'ut Regia prorsus illa Byzantinorum Scriptorum editio, quam suspiciunt ubique gentium exteri ut eximium Gallicae magnificentiae monumentum, tandem absolvatur'.

[116] Jean Gallois, letter to du Cange of 11 October 1679, in Omont, 'Du Cange et la collection byzantine du Louvre' 34, 'comme j'ay vû que dans cette épistre vous tesmoignez avoir beaucoup d'envie que le Roy fasse continuer l'*Histoire byzantine*, j'ay entretenu Mgr Colbert de l'utilité de ce dessein ... Il a très bien reçeu tout ce que je lui en ay dit ... il seroit nécessaire que vous prissiez la peine de m'envoier un projet de ce que vous voulez faire et un catalogue succinct des principaux auteurs de cette histoire, dont les ouvrages n'ont pas encore été imprimés et qui sont à la Bibliothèque du Roy.'

[117] De Broglie, *Mabillon* 1:68, 'continuant, en la relevant encore, la tradition des Estienne'.

years after the dictionary appeared.[118] He and his enemies could see the prestige in dictionary publishing.

But quite apart from this sort of association, a significant part of the Byzantine past was, in a manner of speaking, French. 'In a manner of speaking', for the France of the crusader king Louis IX was not the same as that of Louis XIV, even though the latter was identified with his namesake by du Cange and others.[119] Nor was 'French' the right word for all the crusaders to whom it might loosely be applied: Villehardouin himself, to take one example, was a knight of the independent Comte de Champagne (and indeed had the office of Maréchal de Champagne), not of the King of France. He was a Frankish crusader, but not exactly a French one. Making the Frankish conquests in the eastern Mediterranean a point of national pride in seventeenth-century France was hence a matter of heritage-making rather than history. Language was an important feature of this story of heritage: Villehardouin may have served the Comte de Champagne, but the language variety in which he wrote was certainly French. Du Cange makes the point in the preface to the *Glossarium latinitatis* that French was spoken in the Byzantine Empire during the period of Frankish rule there, and he then adds that the Courtenay emperors who reigned in Constantinople from 1205 to 1261 were of French descent; s.v. *francia*, he remarks that the Greeks, Saracens and other peoples of the East called all Europeans *franci* (hence the modern English use of *Frankish* in the context of the crusades) because they were so impressed by the might of the French themselves.[120]

It is, then, in a general context of subsumption of the story of the Frankish crusaders' empire into the story of France that du Cange's Byzantine studies took place. His first two major editions were of Old French texts whose authors described contact with the Byzantine world, and his third was of a Byzantine text whose author, Kinnamos, described contact with Frankish crusaders (indeed Kinnamos is the authority for the emperor Manuel I Komnenos' introduction of Frankish practices like the use of the kite-shaped shield to Byzantine armies). Even before the edition

---

[118] For the accusation, see the open letter of 'Les imprimeurs et libraires de Paris à Messieurs les gens de lettres' drawn up around 1687–8 by members of the Paris booktrade in Omont, *Lettres d'Anisson à du Cange* 3n2 (for the heading, see Bloch, 'Charles Du Cange' 538).

[119] For the identification of Louis XIV with Louis IX, see Burke, *Fabrication of Louis XIV* 28, 113f., 192–3.

[120] Du Cange, *Glossarium latinitatis* s.v. *francia* (col. 520), 'Cum igitur tam late se se diffudisset Francorum nomen & virtus bellica, & in exteras ac remotas Europae regiones se se propagasset eorum Imperium, inde factum ut Graeci non modo, sed & Saraceni, Arabes, & Abyssini Europaeanos populos *Francoru[m]* nomine donarint.'

of Kinnamos, du Cange had edited Byzantine texts as appendices to his *Traité historique du chef de S. Iean Baptiste*. His argument there was that a certain relic preserved at the cathedral of Amiens was genuinely the head of St John the Baptist, removed from Constantinople during the period of Frankish rule by a crusader whose family lived near Amiens. Here, an interest in Byzantine antiquities came right home: the head displayed in du Cange's native town was an object inherited from the Frankish empire in Constantinople, and its former Byzantine owners were therefore a link between contemporary France and sacred history, between Amiens and the man who baptized Jesus.

France was not only a beneficiary of the Greek heritage but a possible reinvigorator of that heritage. The *Corpus byzantinae historiae* played its part in that work by the regeneration of texts. The public image of Louis XIV might echo those of Constantine the Great and of the Byzantine emperors.[121] And Constantinople might also, du Cange imagined, be restored to its status as a Christian seat of empire by war against the Turks who had been there since 1453 – so, like Henri Estienne, he vigorously promoted the cause of a crusade against the Turks. As early as the edition of Villehardouin, he was urging Louis XIV to reconquer Constantinople, hence the suggestive opening of his dedication to Louis, 'Sire, Ie ne presente pas à Vostre Maiesté des terres étrangeres, et de nouueaux mondes, quand ie luy offre l'Empire de Constantinople.'[122] Dedicating the *Historia byzantina duplici commentario illustrata* to Colbert, he reflected on the splendour of Christian Constantinople and its current desecration as seat of the Ottoman Empire, and expressed his confidence that Louis XIV was the man to drive the Turks out; at this point in the printed text of the dedication, something that Colbert disliked when he saw it in manuscript has been removed, suggesting that the old scholar's ardour led him further than the statesman thought appropriate.[123] In his account of the imperial Palaiologos family in this book, du Cange digresses to print a letter in which Konstantinos XI, the last Byzantine emperor of Constantinople, pleaded with the king of France to send him military support against the Turks.[124]

[121] Burke, *Fabrication of Louis XIV* 192–4.
[122] Du Cange, dedication in Villehardouin, *Histoire de l'empire de Constantinople* (1657) sig. ã3r; cf. Spieser, 'Du Cange and Byzantium' 200.
[123] Du Cange, *Historia byzantina duplici commentario illustrata* sigs. ã5v–6r; cf. Gallois, letter to du Cange of 11 October 1679, in Omont, 'Du Cange et la collection byzantine du Louvre' 34, 'j'ay achevé de luy lire vostre épistre, dont il a entendu la lecture avec plaisir et qu'il a agréée. Il vous prie seulement Monsieur, d'en vouloir retrancher à la fin ce que vous trouverez barré avec du crayon.'
[124] Du Cange, *Historia byzantina duplici commentario illustrata* 246.

The same point was made by the frontispiece to the *Glossarium graecitatis*, a companion piece to that of the *Glossarium latinitatis*.[125] There, in place of the weeping Latinitas, the goddess Athene sits in the foreground, helmeted, and holding a shield on which the title of the dictionary is inscribed. Three books lie closed at her feet, identified on their tail-edges as the works of Aristides, Isocrates and Demosthenes. The reason why these names are chosen is surely that they can be associated with the independence of Greece: an Aristides (not in fact the writer of that name) commanded against the Persians at Plataea, Isocrates' *Philippus* calls for war on the Persian Empire and Demosthenes' *Philippics* oppose the Macedonian hegemony. Behind Athene, a battle is going on; cannon are firing (so this is a modern battle), and some of the figures are wearing turbans. This is a dictionary that calls its reader to crusade against the Turk for the sake of the goddess of wisdom and Greek learning. The *Glossarium graecitatis* was, as du Cange's eighteenth-century admirers recognized, part of a whole web of historical scholarship and polemic designed to bring the Byzantine heritage, texts and lands alike, into French hands.

---

[125] For the intended relationship between the two, see Jean Anisson, letter to du Cange of 21 February 1688 in Omont, *Lettres d'Anisson à du Cange* 35.

CHAPTER 8

Shared heritages: Polyglot and universal dictionaries

PRAISE THE LORD ALL YE NATIONS: POLYGLOT DICTIONARIES

The dictionaries discussed in chapters 4, 5 and 6 dealt with languages that could be identified as part of the national heritage of one of the emerging nation-states of late medieval and early modern Europe. These, I have suggested, belong to a period when local heritages came to be invested with greater imaginative power than the shared heritage of classical antiquity. However, the late sixteenth and seventeenth centuries also saw three kinds of lexicographical work that engaged with multiple or universal heritages. These were the making of polyglot dictionaries; the making of dictionaries of artificial universal languages; and the use of dictionaries to illuminate the origins of all languages.

There were several major traditions of polyglot dictionaries in six-teenth- and seventeenth-century Europe.[1] One has been touched on above: that of dictionaries whose primary aim was to give an account of a single language but which were enriched with cognate forms from other languages. Such a dictionary would usually, as in the cases of Kiel's *Etymologicum teutonicae linguae* and Franciscus Junius' *Etymologicum anglicanum*, be offered explicitly as an etymologicon of the target lan-guage; the dictionary materials preserved in MSS Junius 2 and 3 are halfway between being a single-language etymologicon with generously provided cognates and being a union dictionary of multiple languages. Two other traditions, which account between them for about three hundred published dictionaries, are too important not to consider here, although they can only be treated cursorily. The first was that of small, thematically ordered dictionaries, characteristically in an oblong duo-decimo format, with different languages in parallel columns across an

[1] For an overview, see Haensch, 'Mehrsprachigen Wörterbücher', esp. 2909–16.

opening, many of which had the word *Vocabulista* in their titles. These ultimately derived from an Italian–German dictionary of 1477. One language after another was added to these *Vocabulista* dictionaries in the course of the sixteenth century, English entering the tradition in 1537, and ancient Greek in 1546. Eighty-nine editions had been printed, in a number of different countries, by 1636.[2] They must, for several reasons, have been of very limited practical use, and I have suggested elsewhere that their appeal must have been 'the pleasure of seeing the world divided up by language, and of being assured that the languages of Europe all divided it up alike'.[3] A similar series of dictionaries, more than ninety in all, derived from the French–Dutch dictionary of Noel de Berlaimont which was first published in 1536.[4] The second tradition that calls for specific mention is that of polyglot editions of Calepino, of which there were more than a hundred.[5] The polyglot Calepinos offered a bigger vocabulary than the *Vocabulista* dictionaries, keyed to an alphabetically ordered Latin wordlist. They must have been fairly useful reader's handbooks to the vocabularies of the major European languages, at least on those occasions when an equivalent in one or more vernaculars was wanted for a concept which the user could already express in Latin. They also conveyed the same message as did their smaller counterparts: that the languages of Europe could all express the same range of concepts, and hence that, whatever the linguistic differences of Europe might be, Europeans shared a heritage of concepts, and all, in that profound sense, spoke the same language. The one remarkable edition that added Japanese to its range widened this story.

The *Vocabulista* dictionaries and those descended from the work of Berlaimont were expansions of bilingual dictionaries, and the polyglot Calepinos were expansions of a monolingual work. A polyglot dictionary which was actually composed as such was that of Hadrianus Junius (Adriaan de Jonge), whose publishing career illustrates the way in which polyglot lexicography could, like the study of single vernaculars and post-classical Latin and Greek, be a development away from the classical philology of the sixteenth century. An early work of his, the *De anno* of 1553, was a study of some fundamentals of ancient culture loosely in the tradition of Budé, and it was followed in 1558 by a collection of *Adagia* modelled on that of Erasmus.[6] He continued to take an interest in Greek

---

[2] See Rossebastiano Bart, *Antichi vocabolari plurilingui*.
[3] Considine, 'Narrative and persuasion' 200.   [4] Haensch, 'Mehrsprachigen Wörterbücher' 291I.
[5] Labarre, *Bibliographie du Dictionarium d'Ambrogio Calepino*.
[6] For Erasmus as model, see H. Junius, *Adagiorum centuriae VIII cum dimidia* sig. a2v.

literature thereafter. His translation of Eunapios was read by du Cange, and another translation of his, that of the little collection of lives of philosophers by Hesychius of Miletus, was published to accompany the edition by Henri Estienne's correspondent Sambucus in 1572. He even worked on the lexicography of Greek: a *Dictionarium graecolatinum* of 1584 advertised its use of material of his on the title-page, and the notes he had made in the margin of his copy of the lexicon of Hesychius of Alexandria were published, together with material by Henri Estienne, in an edition of 1668.[7] But by the time he was translating Hesychius of Miletus, Junius had already turned from the ancient languages towards the vernaculars with the publication of his polyglot *Nomenclator: omnium rerum propria nomina variis linguis explicata indicans* in 1567.[8] This was a thematically ordered dictionary whose Latin headwords, of which there were about 8000, were followed by a short definition in Latin, and then equivalents in ancient Greek (where possible), German, Dutch, French, Spanish, Italian and occasionally English. Its thematic arrangement was well suited to use in education, for which it was patriotically intended, as the dedication to the son and heir of the great stadhouder Willem of Nassau, the thirteen-year-old Philips Willem, made clear (Junius' *Batavia*, as used by Kiel in his *Etymologicum*, was a product of the same patriotic spirit). Adaptations for use with other European languages such as English and Breton appeared in the sixteenth and seventeenth centuries.

Another major polyglot dictionary of the period was the *Ductor in linguas* of the English teacher of languages John Minsheu, a compilation of lexical and etymological information from a number of sources, including Cowell's *Interpreter*. This production, whose English headwords are followed with equivalents in Welsh, Dutch, German, French, Italian, Spanish, Portuguese, Latin, Greek and Hebrew, ran to five hundred folio pages. It has been criticized as derivative, but the compiler's claim that his work was laborious was surely true, and his claim that it was financially unprofitable is plausible: he announced on a list of purchasers of the first edition that '*by compiling and printing the same*, at his owne charge, *for the publicke good*, and the *aduancement of Learning and*

---

[7] Cellarius and Hönigerus, eds., Λεξικον Ἑλληνικορωμικον, title-page, 'post correctiones G. Budaei, I. Tusani, C. Gesneri, H. Iunii, R. Constantini, Io. Hartungi, Mar. Hopperi, Guil. Xylandri emendatum'; the use of material by Junius and Estienne in Hesychius of Alexandria, Λεξικον (1668) is briefly acknowledged there at sig. *4r–v, and discussed more fully in Hesychius of Alexandria, *Lexicon* (1746–66) I:xviii, xxiii.

[8] The numerous sixteenth-century editions and reworkings are summarized by Jones, *German lexicography* 444–5 (item 751), and sixteen seventeenth-century editions are listed ibid. 445–52 (items 752–67).

Knowledge hee hath not onely *exhausted and spent thereon all his stocke and substance*, but also runne himselfe into many and great debtes, *vnpossible for him euer to pay*'.[9] For Minsheu as for Henri Estienne, it seems that large-scale lexicography was a labour of love, something to be done out of delight in language rather than as a serious business proposition. He was not as learned as Estienne, and he was, like more famous polyhistors of his century, a consolidator of knowledge, not a theorist, but he brought together information not readily available elsewhere.

The dictionaries of the German scholar Hieronymus Megiser were in a different class. Megiser did substantial work in several fields: he wrote a history of the Imperial duchy of Carinthia, translated Marco Polo into Latin and made a number of contributions to lexicography. His first book was a *Dictionarium quatuor linguarum*, published in 1592, in which about 4700 German headwords were translated into Latin, Italian and Slovene, of which it was the first substantial dictionary.[10] Slovene was spoken in Carinthia, and Megiser's work therefore belongs to the same tradition of polyglot language study in the Holy Roman Empire as the fourteenth-century decree that the heirs of electors should be taught Latin, Italian and a Slavonic language to supplement their native German, or the trilingual Latin–German–Czech dictionary published in Vienna as early as 1513, or the polyglot dictionaries of Rudolfine Prague.[11] Megiser published two more dictionaries of considerable historical interest. The first was part of an introduction to Turkish, presenting information on spelling and grammar, a collection of 220 proverbs, and a Turkish–Latin and Latin–Turkish glossary of about 2200 entries, which was the first substantial printed dictionary of Turkish in western Europe.[12] The second was a Malagasy–German glossary of about 2000 entries, translated and put into alphabetical order from a Dutch original, accompanied by three dialogues in Malagasy from the same source.[13] The remarkable linguistic range evident here – Megiser

[9] For the dictionary and its sources, see Schäfer, 'John Minsheu: Scholar or charlatan?'; for the expense and difficulty of publication, see Williams, 'Scholarly publication in Shakespeare's day' and Minsheu, *Catalogue and true note of the names of such persons which haue receaued the etymologicall dictionarie of XI. languages* fo. 1r.

[10] See Stankiewicz, *Grammars and dictionaries of the Slavic languages* 84, 103.

[11] For the decree, see Bischoff, 'Study of foreign languages' 220–1; for the dictionary, *Dictionarius trium linguarum, latinae, teutonicae, boemicae, potiora vocabula continens*, see Claes, *Bibliographisches Verzeichnis* 61 (item 222) and Stankiewicz, *Grammars and dictionaries of the Slavic languages* 16.

[12] It was anticipated by the thematically ordered vocabulary of about 250 Turkish words in Crato, *Geheimnis der Türken* (1596) and, narrowly, by a manuscript Italian–Turkish dictionary of about 3300 entries, for which see Bombaci, 'Padre Pietro Ferraguto e la sua Grammatica turca (1611)' (word-count at 209).

[13] The source is Houtman, *Spraeck ende woord-boek inde Maleysche ende Madagaskarsche talen.*

must in fact have been just about the only person in the world who had a good acquaintance with Slovene, Turkish *and* Malagasy, even if he had the last of these at second hand – informed two further works.

The first was a successor to the texts of the Lord's Prayer that illustrated Gessner's *Mithridates*, a slim *Specimen quinquaginta linguarum* which brought forty-eight versions of the prayer together (one of its sources was de Smet's *De literis et lingua getarum*).[14] The second, the *Thesaurus polyglottus vel dictionarium multilingue*, also of 1603, is a much bulkier book, a dictionary of nearly 1600 octavo pages, which claims to document forms in about four hundred language varieties, following its Latin headwords with as many synonyms as possible.[15] The figure of four hundred is misleading, since a number of the varieties counted are certainly dialects: more than fifty of Greek alone. However, the scale of the work is still remarkable: for instance, equivalents for the word *pater* 'father' are given in sixty languages, and the total number of forms given must be about a hundred thousand. Different words are glossed with different thoroughness; *pater* is exceptionally well glossed, for instance, whereas there are fewer equivalents for other kinship terms, no doubt partly because Megiser had forty-eight equivalents for *pater* ready-made in his *Specimen quinquaginta linguarum*. What he could achieve depended very much on the materials he had to hand – as is, of course, true of all lexicography. For Malagasy, for instance, he had not yet encountered the source that he was later to translate, and could only use a list of twenty words in another Dutch travel narrative, which he may have read in manuscript.[16]

The languages catalogued in the *Thesaurus polyglottus* are classified in an introduction, which places them in nine main families: Hebrew (i.e., Semitic), Greek, Latin, Germanic, Slavonic, 'European' (a miscellaneous class including Finnic and Celtic languages, Hungarian and Basque), Asiatic, African and American. The sheer scope of Megiser's data enabled him to build up a remarkably full and complex picture of the languages of the world at a time when most comparative studies of language were confined to those of Europe and part of western Asia. When he encountered Malagasy, for instance, he was able to say with confidence that it was related to no known language, and although he was in fact mistaken (it is a member of the same family as Malay, though nobody identified it as such until the eighteenth century), that is less important than the fact that he was thinking

[14] For de Smet as a source, see Schulte, 'Gothica minora: Dritter Artikel' 326.
[15] See Jones, *German lexicography* 498–500 (items 832–3).
[16] See Grandidier and Grandidier, *Collection des ouvrages anciens concernant Madagascar* 322.

comparatively on the basis of a wide knowledge of non-European languages, and that he was one of the first Europeans to be able to do this.[17]

Megiser's *Specimen* and *Thesaurus polyglottus* were, at one level, restating the point implied by all the polyglot dictionaries: that the peoples of the world all had languages that expressed much the same set of concepts, and that all that was needed for all those peoples to talk to each other was patience and translation. Just as the *dictionarium quattuor linguarum* can be compared to the polyglot dictionaries of Rudolfine Prague, so the *Thesaurus polyglottus* has a place in that milieu, for it was dedicated to Rudolf II. Megiser's use of the Lord's Prayer as a text in the *Specimen* suggested as Gessner's had done that the speakers of different languages could pray together. The preface to the reader of the *Thesaurus polyglottus* says that the book began with a project to collect seventy-two languages.[18] The traditional account of the fall of Babel stated that seventy-two languages had been created at the confusion of tongues, and the inference must surely be that Megiser wondered if he could understand, and even reverse, that confusion. He may in part have been actuated by missionary zeal; the title-page of the *Specimen* proclaims 'Praise the LORD all ye nations; praise him every people' and the introduction to the Malagasy dictionary ends with the hope that the people of Madagascar will be converted to Christianity.[19] But he was not just making a handbook for Christian translators: he was offering a very powerful picture of linguistic relationship and diversity. His *Thesaurus polyglottus* was annotated by Georg Stiernhielm and Bengt Skytte as Skytte worked on his scheme for a perfect language, and data of his was also used by John Wilkins as he too considered how a perfect language could be made. Readers of Megiser could see more clearly than people had ever done before that human languages could be discussed together, and that a dictionary could be a vast unified record of the kinds of human linguistic behaviour.

BEYOND THAT OF ANY PARTICULAR COUNTREY OR NATION: UNIVERSAL DICTIONARIES

The multiplicity of languages with which the polyglot lexicographers engaged suggested the desirability of devising a single universal language,

---

[17] Megiser, 'Dictionarium der Madagarischen Sprach' 76; for the identification of Malagasy and Malay as cognate, see Droixhe, *Linguistique et l'appel de l'histoire* 43.

[18] Megiser, *Thesaurus polyglottus* sig.)(4r, and cf. ibid. sig.)(5r–v, quoting Goropius for Clement of Alexandria's rationale for this number.

[19] Megiser, *Specimen quinquaginta … linguarum* title-page, quoting Psalm 117, 'Laudate DOMINVM omnes gentes: laudate eum omnes populi'; Megiser, 'Dictionarium der Madagarischen Sprach' 78.

which would facilitate international communication. Whereas Latin had been a fairly satisfactory *de facto* universal language for centuries, the increasing importance of European contacts with peoples to whom it was quite alien raised the possibility that a truly universal language might take its place. Such a language might also be more purely rational in its structure than Latin or any other natural language, and might therefore become an important philosophical tool. There were a number of projects in the seventeenth century with the aim of making universal languages: these interested several of the lexicographers and philologists who have been mentioned above, for instance Comenius, Peiresc, Leibniz, Kircher and Sir William Boswell.[20] Many of them were decidedly sketchy, and therefore did not lead to the laborious making of dictionaries by which the relationship between their vocabularies and those of existing languages could be presented. So, for instance, Francis Lodwick's *A common writing* of 1646, a proposal for an ideographic writing system, ended with the promise of 'a *Lexicon* which is intended, God permitting', and which would have been indexed by an alphabetical 'collection ... of all the words extant in the English tongue', but although Lodwick was still writing about the lexicon as a possible publication six years later, nothing came of it.[21] The scheme would, as Robert Boyle remarked, have been viable only 'if the dictionary ... do not overswell and disease it of a tympany', and the dictionary would indeed have had to be enormous, including the whole vocabulary of English once in its equivalents for the ideographs and again in its index.[22] By 1652, Sir Thomas Urquhart, the translator of Rabelais, claimed to have made and lost 'the Grammar and Lexicon of an Universal Language', of which the lexicon had consisted of seven hundred pages in folio, but this claim was probably hyperbolic.[23]

   The first universal language to be published in completed form, with a grammar and dictionary, in England was the work of a clergyman called Cave Beck.[24] Beck was educated at Cambridge and Gray's Inn, and received an honorary MA at Oxford in 1643. Having been connected with all three of the major centres of English intellectual life, he moved away

---

[20] See Knowlson, *Universal language schemes*, surveying the seventeenth century 3–111 and discussing Comenius 10–11 and *passim*, Peiresc 68, Leibniz 107–11, Kircher 21 and Boswell 20.

[21] [Lodwick], *Common writing* sig. E3v, and cf. [Lodwick], *Ground-work or foundation laid* sig. C1r.

[22] Boyle, letter to Samuel Hartlib of 8 April 1647, quoted Slaughter, *Universal languages and scientific taxonomy* 119; see also Knowlson, *Universal language schemes* 57–61.

[23] Urquhart, Εκσκυβαλαυρον 5 (I am grateful to Sylvia Brown for the reference); Urquhart's claim there that the lexicon consisted of seven quires is clarified by the explanation ibid. 2 that the quires were each made up of 25 folio sheets, i.e., 100 folio pages.

[24] Salmon, 'Cave Beck' is now supplemented by Blatchly, 'Beck'.

from them to East Anglia, becoming master of Ipswich grammar school in 1650. In 1657, he published a short dictionary called the *Universal character*, which consisted of a list of 3996 English words to each of which a unique number was assigned, together with a preface explaining how these numbers could be used together with a simple system of alphabetically written inflections and prefixes to indicate their grammatical functions, and how a simplified pronunciation of numbers and letters could make the written 'character' into a spoken language.[25] Every other language in the world, Beck went on to suggest, could have a dictionary based on the same numeration of concepts made for it. The assignment of numbers to English words simply followed their alphabetical sequence, so that the same wordlist could be used to translate from English to numbers or vice versa; other languages would need a double list, first of their own words in alphabetical order with the numbers that corresponded to them, and then of the numbers in numerical order with the words that corresponded to them. The project lapsed after the publication of a French version of the book, and never really took on an international dimension; the imprint of the French version identified it as to be sold, like the original, by a bookseller in Ipswich. The frontispiece to the *Universal character* shows persons from all four continents, America, Africa, Asia and Europe, gathered round a table and apparently ready to communicate in the universal language.

A pair of rather different universal-language wordlists was published in England four years later, the 'Lexicon grammatico-philosophicum' and 'Lexicon latino-philosophicum' which formed part of George Dalgarno's *Ars signorum* of 1661.[26] Dalgarno was not impressed by Beck's work, which he regarded as 'nothing else, but an Enigmaticall way of writing the English Language'; his own was meant not to follow a natural language closely but to be 'more accommodated for an emphatick delivery of real Truths, and the grounds and precepts of Arts and Sciences, then any other Language'.[27] Its two wordlists are differently laid out. The 'Lexicon grammatico-philosophicum' is a single-sheet foldout of rather more than a thousand subject-grouped items. Those in each group share a root: so, the basic geometrical concepts have the root *m-m*, *mam* being 'a point', *mηm* (the Greek η and the Roman *e* indicated different vowels in Dalgarno's

[25] For context, see Knowlson, *Universal language schemes* 61f. and Slaughter, *Universal languages and scientific taxonomy* 120–1, 123–5.

[26] Dalgarno, *Ars signorum* 95–117.

[27] Dalgarno, letter to Samuel Hartlib of 20 April 1657 in *George Dalgarno on universal language*, ed. Cram and Maat, 417–18 at 418; Dalgarno, *News to the whole world* (1658?), ibid. 109–11 at 110.

language) 'a line', *mem* 'a surface' and *mim* 'a solid'.[28] The roots, Dalgarno explained in his main text, could be used to generate a full vocabulary by a combination of derivation and compounding: *fren* is 'vessel', from *fr-n* 'household item'; *ir* is 'spring', from *i-* 'body of water'; *em* is 'faeces' from *-m* 'thing or substance produced by the body'; so *frenirem* is 'chamberpot'.[29] The 'Lexicon latino-philosophicum' is a more conventional double-column wordlist which gives about 1500 Latin words with brief equivalents, some of them awkward and others obscured by misprinting, in the new language: *adorare* 'to reverence', for example, is *skaf tud stŋf,* literally 'cherish praise high-repute'.[30]

A much more ambitious universal-language dictionary was published later in the 1660s, compiled by the learned William Lloyd, who became one of the more colourful bishops of the later seventeenth century. Dalgarno and Lloyd knew each other, and Dalgarno's autobiography refers to his obligation to Lloyd for a number of favours, and 'more particularly for honouring me in taking the name of my Scholar'.[31] Lloyd's dictionary was part of a greater work, the *Essay towards a real character and a philosophical language* (1668) of John Wilkins, author of the cryptographical work *Mercury* and formerly warden of Wadham College, Oxford (and, briefly, master of Trinity College, Cambridge), who would also become a bishop. Dalgarno had collaborated with Wilkins on a language scheme in the 1650s, though the two had subsequently fallen out.[32]

Wilkins' *Essay* was one of the major early publications of the Royal Society: the society's arms appear on the title-page between text identifying him as a fellow of the society and text naming the printer to the society, and on the verso of the facing page is the society's own imprimatur. Although the society was to be 'a College for the Promoting of Physico-Mathematicall Experimentall Learning', its commitment to experimental science was not at first exclusive: its earliest fellows included polymaths like John Evelyn and Sir William Petty, who were joined later by men such as Francis Lodwick, Samuel Pepys and Isaac Vossius, and its intellectual life was correspondingly diverse.[33] So, for instance, it played an important part in the beginnings of archaeological thought in England.[34]

[28] Dalgarno, 'Lexicon grammatico-philosophicum' (foldout after sig. A8 of *Ars signorum*) col. 1, 'mam *punctum* | mŋm *linea* | mem *superficies* | mim *solidum*'.
[29] Dalgarno, *Ars signorum* 43.
[30] Examples are worked through in Shumaker, *Renaissance curiosa* 132–72.
[31] Dalgarno, autobiographical treatise in *George Dalgarno on universal language* 353–90 at 364.
[32] *George Dalgarno on universal language* 26ff.; for Dalgarno's own account, see ibid. 357f.
[33] De Beer, 'Earliest Fellows of the Royal Society'.
[34] Hunter, 'The Royal Society and the origins of British archaeology'.

Diverse as were the interests of its fellows, a shared ideal of the society was to communicate information. This might be done in the English language, and a committee was established in 1665 in order to investigate the possibility of language reform; one of its members was John Evelyn, who wrote to its chairman, Sir Peter Wyche, that year, proposing the making of 'a Lexicon or collection of all the pure English words' and 'a full catalogue of exotic words'.[35] A famous passage in Sprat's *History of the Royal-Society*, published two years later, likewise sets out the society's 'constant Resolution, to reject all the amplifications, digressions, and swellings of style: to return back to the primitive purity, and shortness, when men deliver'd so many *things*, almost in an equal number of *words*'.[36] The committee came to nothing, but its concerns were not forgotten. In 1685, Petty drew up a list of just over a hundred headwords for a 'Dictionary of sensible words', such as *God, liberty, fanatic, pleasure* and *wit*, to which he felt it should be possible to assign precise, illuminating definitions, following it the next year by a sketch of 'Twelve theological words'.[37] In 1689, Evelyn and Pepys were still talking 'of Academies and the Refining of our Language', leading Evelyn to transcribe his letter to Wyche of twenty-four years previously and send Pepys a copy.[38] The linguistic programme of the Royal Society is now, on the basis of this sort of activity, chiefly thought of as a matter of cultivating the plain style in English, but its members also considered whether the one-to-one correspondence of words and things might be obtained by other means. Wilkins' plans for a universal language, already adumbrated in *Mercury*, were therefore of interest to his colleagues and, as early as 1662, the minutes of the society record that 'Dr. Wilkins was put in mind to prosecute his design of an *universal language*.'[39]

The work that appeared six years later was a hefty folio of 636 pages.[40] It was divided into five parts. The first, 'Prolegomena', was a survey of natural languages and their shortcomings; 'The Second Part Containing

---

[35] John Evelyn, letter of 20 June 1665 to Sir Peter Wyche, most readily accessible in Spingarn, *Critical essays of the seventeenth century* II:310–13; this edition will be superseded by Douglas Chambers' forthcoming edition, *The letter copybooks of John Evelyn*.

[36] Sprat, *History of the Royal-Society* 113.

[37] For the 'Dictionary' and Petty's related writings, see his *Petty papers* I:147–66.

[38] Evelyn, letter to Pepys of 4 October 1689, in Pepys and Evelyn, *Particular friends* 206–10 (quotation at 207).

[39] Wilkins, *Mercury* ch. 13 (105–10), 'Concerning an universall Character, that may be legible to all nations and languages. The benefit, and possibility of this'; Bowen and Hartley, 'Right Reverend John Wilkins' 52.

[40] For it, see Knowlson, *Universal language schemes* 98ff. and Slaughter, *Universal languages and scientific taxonomy* 157–86.

Universal Philosophy' offered a detailed classification of things and qualities, summarized in a masterly fold-out table, larger and clearer than Dalgarno's; 'The Third Part Containing *Philosophical Grammar*' offered a theory of language; 'The Fourth Part Containing a *Real Character*, and a *Philosophical Language*' introduced Wilkins' proposed language and writing system. The last 162 pages, with their own half-title, comprised 'An alphabetical dictionary, wherein all English words according to their various significations, are either referred to their places in the philosophical tables, or explained by such words as are in those tables'.[41]

After an introduction, this dictionary presents about 11,500 words, often with careful distinction of senses.[42] It is not an index to the *Essay*: its wordlist originates not from the alphabetical ordering of the English equivalents of the philosophical language, but from those of English–Latin dictionaries of the seventeenth century.[43] It was compiled as a parallel work against which the philosophical language of the *Essay* might be tested and by means of which it might be improved. Wilkins wrote in his epistle to the reader that, among other contributions of Lloyd's, 'I must wholy ascribe to him that tedious and difficult task, of suting the Tables to the *Dictionary*, and the drawing up of the *Dictionary* it self.'[44] Gilbert Burnet was to make the further claim in the 1680s that 'Dr. Lloyd ... drew the Tables for Wilkins' Philosophicall language and Reall Character', and subsequently that 'in drawing the tables for that work, which was Lloyd's province, he had looked farther into a natural purity and simplicity of style, than any man I ever knew'.[45] The latter remark suggests the affinity between work on the development of the philosophical language and on the improvement of English, as does the fact that the manuscript of the dictionary marked certain current words 'which are yet very questionable as to their fitness and propriety' with an asterisk, although this distinction was overlooked in typesetting.[46]

The importance of Lloyd's dictionary, and its contribution to the English language, was acknowledged by a number of readers. Wilkins announced at the beginning of the *Essay* that 'the *Dictionary* ... I doubt not, will be found to be the most perfect, that was ever yet made for the

---

[41] Wilkins, *Essay* sig. aaa1r.
[42] Knappe, 'Theory meets empiricism' 85n67 gives a higher figure for main entries and subentries together, 'between 15,000 and over 20,000'.
[43] Ibid. 78f.   [44] Wilkins, *Essay* sig. c1r, discussed Knappe, 'Theory meets empiricism' 82–9.
[45] Burnet, 'Autobiography' 487 and Burnet, *History of my own time* 1:339.
[46] Wilkins, *Essay* sig. c1r; Lloyd complained that the dictionary would have been better 'had the printers kept to his directions' (quoted Lewis, 'Efforts of the Aubrey correspondence group' 356n44).

English Tongue'.[47] Its treatment of sense-divisions and phrasal verbs was of 'no small assistance' in the construction of the English–Latin part of Adam Littleton's *Linguae latinae liber dictionarius quadripartitus* of 1678.[48] The writer on grammar James Greenwood referred in 1711 to 'the Dictionary, wrote by the Right Reverend Father in God, Dr. *William Lloyd* ... (which is to be met with at the End of Bishop *Wilkin's* [*sic*] *Real Character*)' as 'the best *English* Dictionary that was ever published', and expressed an interest in republishing it 'in a more familiar Dress for the Sake of common Readers'.[49] The whole work, *Essay* and *Alphabetical dictionary* together, is of great lexicographical interest, as Wilkins himself recognized, comparing it to the dictionary of the Accademia della Crusca and the still incomplete dictionary project of the Académie française, and arguing that it would outshine them.[50]

Lodwick's 'common writing' and Beck's universal language had been predicated on the assumption that informed the polyglot dictionaries: that the concepts of a given language, in this case English, were universally valid, so that a word like *honour* names a social reality present without variation in all societies. Wilkins, like Dalgarno, abandoned that assumption to examine the whole system of human thought. He argued that all natural languages, including English, were so unstable as to be unsuitable for the expression of precise thought. Their instability was illustrated by an interesting discussion of language origins, diversity and change, including an early discussion of the phenomenon of language death, and a sketch of the history of English, illustrated with a chronological sequence of seven versions of the Lord's Prayer.[51] What Wilkins perceived as the fundamental disorder of natural languages, the fact that their words did not correspond as clearly and uniformly as they should to objects or concepts in a clearly analysed world, led in his opinion not only to various minor kinds of inadequacy and redundancy but to 'some of our Modern differences in *Religion*', and therefore even to wars of religion, by disguising 'many wild errors, that shelter themselves under the disguise of affected phrases; which being Philosophically unfolded, and rendered according to the genuine and natural importance of Words, will appear to be inconsistencies and contradictions'.[52] The project sketched in the *Essay* can therefore be seen, like Beck's, as a successor to the failed irenicism of which the dedication of the *Thesaurus graecae linguae* and the work of

---

[47] Ibid. sig. c1r.   [48] Littleton, *Linguae latinae liber dictionarius* sig. A3v.
[49] Greenwood, *Essay towards a practical English grammar* 26–7.   [50] Wilkins, *Essay* sig. a2r.
[51] Ibid. 1–10.   [52] Ibid. sig. b1r.

Comenius are monuments.[53] Hence Wilkins' contrast between the *Essay* and the national dictionary projects of the national academies, in which he claimed that his work was superior to theirs 'as the general good of mankind, is beyond that of any particular Countrey or Nation'.[54]

In place of the disorderly and unphilosophical languages of different nations, Wilkins offered a writing system and a spoken language that could be keyed to a great taxonomic articulation of all knowledge. So, the second part of the book divided all nameable things into forty major 'genera', to each of which an arbitrary syllable was assigned, for instance, *co* for economic relationship, *da* for world, *za* for fish.[55] Each of these genera could be subdivided into as many as nine 'differences', each indicated by one of the consonants b, d, g, p, t, c, z, s, n. Each 'difference' could be subdivided into up to nine 'species', each indicated by one of the vowels and diphthongs α, a, e, i, o, oυ, y, yi, yoυ. Opposition could be marked by semantically and morphologically determined rules: the simple opposite of a disyllable was marked with -*s*. These rules were cunningly constructed to make the language tolerably easy to pronounce. Wilkins demonstrated the point by presenting the Lord's Prayer in the philosophical language and forty-nine natural languages, drawing heavily on data from Gessner and Megiser, including two varieties of Sardic, Sami, Gothic, Basque, Malagasy and two North American languages.

There are, to give an example, six 'differences' of WORLD: (i) spiritual, (ii) celestial, (iii) land, (iv) water, (v) the class of animate objects and (vi) the class of imaginary geographical entities such as the equator. The first of these, the spiritual world, can be seen as consisting of (i) angels in general, (ii) special kinds of angel, (iii) souls in general, (iv) vegetative souls, (v) sensitive souls and (vi) rational souls. The class of special kinds of angel could be divided into the default, good angels, and their opposite, devils. So, a devil was an entity belonging to the genus WORLD (da-), difference 1 (-b-), species 2 (-a), opposed to the default (-s): the word for 'devil' was therefore *dabas*.[56] All of these divisions were set out on the folding table, and the alphabetical dictionary that followed made it possible to find an English word alphabetically and then see its place in the taxonomic scheme, from which its equivalent in the philosophical

---

[53] For universal languages and irenicism, see, e.g., Knowlson, *Universal language schemes* 10–11; for Wilkins and Comenius, see ibid. 96–7.

[54] Wilkins, *Essay* sig. a2r.

[55] Ibid. 22–3 for the genera themselves (which are then analysed 24–296); 415 for the syllables assigned to genera.

[56] Ibid. 51–5.

language could be worked out. So, for instance, *angel*, rather than being assigned a definition or an equivalent in the philosophical language, was classified 'W. I. 1', indicating that it belonged to the first species of the first difference of the genus WORLD, and *angel-fish* (meaning 'skate' rather than the tropical fish to which the name is now applied) was classified 'Fi. II. 5', indicating that it belonged to the fifth species of the second difference of the genus FISH. An adept would then know that the words in the philosophical language would be *daba* and *zado* respectively. The word *adore*, which came out so awkwardly in Dalgarno's language, was referred to the fourth difference of RELATION ECCLESIASTICAL: *syp*. Not every word was given its own analysis: *lash* was cross-referenced to *whip*, and *to lash out* was cross-referenced to *irregularity*, *excess* or *prodigality* (the sense 'strike out aggressively' was rare in the seventeenth century). Some of the cross-references called for highly periphrastic translations into the philosophical language: *root* in the mathematical sense was to be rendered by word for word equivalents of 'the Number which multiplied by it self produces that other number', and even *sink* was to be rendered as 'downition under water'.

Lloyd and Wilkins were sketching a dictionary that would survey and give an intellectual place to all knowable things: every kind of fish, every kind of economic relationship, every kind of happiness. At the same time, it would eliminate all ambiguity or redundancy from human thought. Such a project could not be executed by two men without help. An attempt to do something very similar was in fact being made by a single person at much the same time, in the form of Randle Holme's *Academy of armory*, which began as an illustrated handbook to all the possible patterns and objects that can be part of a coat of arms, but developed into something more like an illustrated dictionary of all objects, arranged in classes, whether or not they might conceivably appear in heraldry. But this, even though it confined itself to material objects, was an unfinishable labour. What was finished was, moreover, only marginally publishable. Holme published two and a half books, running to 1122 folio pages, apparently at his own expense, and advertised the rest of the third and a fourth as 'ready for the press ... if encouraged by liberal and free contributors'. These did not appear, and what Holme did publish was reissued twice, a sign that it was selling slowly. Parts of the *Academy* remained in manuscript until their final publication as a 543-page folio in 1905.

Wilkins and Lloyd were less ambitious than Holme, and they had more help. Some of the collaborative work that went into the *Essay*, much of it contributed by other fellows of the Royal Society, can be recovered.

This might be a matter of the fairly casual supply of wordlists: in June of 1666, Samuel Pepys lent Robert Hooke 'some of my tables of navall matters, the names of rigging and the timbers about a ship – in order to Dr. Wilkins's book coming out about the Universall Language', though he ended up dissatisfied by Wilkins' treatment of naval terminology.[57] It might be more substantial: John Ray and Francis Willughby gave Wilkins a great deal of help not only with the nomenclature of the natural world but also with the vocabularies of several European languages.[58] Ray was a particularly suitable person for Wilkins to appeal to since, like Gessner, he was not only a distinguished naturalist but also strongly interested in language. When he was helping Wilkins with zoological nomenclature, he was already at work on his *Collection of English proverbs*, which would be published in 1670, to be followed three years later by the *Collection of English words not generally used*, the first printed dictionary of English dialect words; nor did his lexicographical interests stop there, since he also produced a modest *Dictionariolum trilingue*, a subject-classed Latin and Greek dictionary for schoolboys, in 1675.[59] Ray's achievements were, like Wilkins' work, the result of communication with a wide circle of interested persons, 'my worthy friends, in several parts of this Kingdom', who read the first edition of the proverb collection, noted proverbs missing from it, and 'were pleased for the perfecting of the work frankly to communicate them to me ... amounting to some hundreds'.[60]

Wilkins was able to imagine his universal language scheme because he believed in the power of networks of sociability and correspondence such as that in which the Royal Society was an important node: if he did not know something, he hoped that he might know someone who knew it. He believed, in other words, that all human knowledge might be accessed, brought together and stored in a collaborative effort. This belief was a natural development of the polymathy of the late sixteenth and seventeenth centuries. The hugely compendious and richly indexed printed books that had been developed by the middle of the sixteenth century offered the imaginary possibility of storing all human knowledge in a suitably ordered text, a verbal equivalent of the collections of artefacts

---

[57] Pepys, *Diary* VII:148; cf. Pepys, *Naval minutes* 177, 'Consider the imperfections of that learned man Dr. Wilkins in his chapter of Naval Relation'; the entry is undated but shortly before one dated January 1683 (ibid. 180).

[58] See Cram, 'John Ray and Francis Willughby'.

[59] For the *Collection of English proverbs*, see Keynes, *John Ray* 24ff.; for the *Collection of English words* see ibid. 38ff.; for the school dictionary, published first as *Dictionariolum trilingue* and then as *Nomenclator classicus*, see ibid. 44f.

[60] Ray, *Collection of English proverbs* sig. A2r.

and natural wonders, such as those of Ole Worm or of the Royal Society itself, that proliferated in the period.[61]

How might this text be ordered? Major seventeenth-century encyclopedias were arranged thematically.[62] So were many of the small polyglot dictionaries of the period. This tended not to be true of larger dictionaries, though. The semi-etymological ordering of the dictionaries of Robert and Henri Estienne was a partial exception: it treated a number of the words in certain semantic fields together because of their etymological relationship. But natural languages do not always bring all the words in a given semantic field together in a single set of etymologically related derivatives. The *Latinae linguae thesaurus* could make an approach to being a *verbal concordance* to classical Latin, a book that brings together occurrences of the same word, but it could not be a *real concordance*, a book that brings together references to the same thing. In philosophical languages such as that proposed in Wilkins' *Essay*, on the other hand, derivational connection could always mirror semantic connection. David Cram has observed that 'from a *real* concordance it is but one step to a *real* character' and asked 'what else is a "real character" than a concordance to the book of nature?'[63] In Wilkins' philosophical language, the real and the verbal coincided. A dictionary of such a language could test a radical alternative to alphabetical ordering, and thus experiment with a different way of doing lexicography.

The experiment was not, in the end, successful. The theoretical advantage of universal languages such as that of the *Essay* was that their systems had very rational taxonomic structures built into them, but their practical disadvantages were obvious. An interesting digression in the *Essay* suggests one of these disadvantages; having started to put all living creatures in the compartments of a taxonomy, Wilkins' imagination turned to an occasion when all living creatures had to be put into real compartments, the stocking of Noah's Ark. He proved to his own satisfaction that, despite the objections of 'some hereticks of old, and some Atheistical scoffers in these latter times', this could actually have been done. There are, he explained, few enough species of animals – 'much fewer then is commonly imagined, not a hundred sorts' – for them all to fit into a feasible boat 450 feet long.[64] Pepys, who had a professional

---

[61] For the collections of the Royal Society, see Swann, *Curiosities and texts* 81–96.
[62] On alphabetization and early modern encyclopedias, see Considine, 'Our dictionaries err in redundancy' 198.
[63] Cram, 'Concordances of words and concordances of things' 90.
[64] Wilkins, *Essay* 162–8; text quoted from 162.

interest in the construction of ships, thoroughly enjoyed this part of the book, 'which doth please me mightily – and is much beyond whatever I heard of that subject'.[65] But it is not as neat as it looks: reptiles and amphibians are banished to 'the Drein or sink of the *Ark*', and 'As for those lesser Beasts, *Rat*[,] *Mouse, Mole,* as likewise for the several species of Insects, there can be no reason to question, but that these may find sufficient room in several parts of the *Ark*, without having any particular Stalls appointed for them.'[66] Wilkins was unwilling to admit it, but his imaginary ark did not have enough compartments; nor did the imaginary language of which it was an image. In the year after the *Essay* was published, John Ray wrote to the physician and naturalist Martin Lister that, although he had tried to present botanical information in accordance with its system, the attempt had been futile.[67] Some of the periphrases in Lloyd's dictionary suggested a related set of problems, the inadequacy of the philosophical language to handle technical language. Although work in continuation of the *Essay* continued after Wilkins' death, some of it done by Ray himself, nothing came of it in the end.[68]

What makes an inventory of kinds of fish and kinds of economic relationship and kinds of happiness possible is simply that they are namable; attempting to classify them turned out to be overwhelmingly, and in the end pointlessly, difficult.[69] Natural languages were actually better than universal ones at collecting and making sense of human understanding of the world. 'The search for a "key" to the harmony of the created universe', the 'pansophic striving' that drove the universal language projects, was thus diverted in the end to natural-language lexicography.[70] But the *Essay* and the universal-language tradition it represents were not a dead end in the history of lexicography: they left important legacies. Three can be treated briefly: Wilkins and Lloyd were 'the first lexicographers to use a highly systematic and methodological construction of entries'; 'their Alphabetical Dictionary was the first to have a self-defining lexicon (that is, words used for definitional purposes were also defined)'; and, since their work suggested the viability of classifying the words of a natural language in accordance with a rationally devised scheme, it led to the development of the thesaurus in the modern

[65] Pepys, *Diary* IX:215.　[66] Wilkins, *Essay* 165.　[67] Cram, 'John Ray and Francis Willughby' 231–2.
[68] See Salmon, 'John Wilkins' "Essay" (1668): Critics and continuators' and Lewis, 'Efforts of the Aubrey correspondence group'.
[69] Cf. Slaughter, *Universal languages and scientific taxonomy* 189ff. for the obsolescence towards the end of the seventeenth century of the taxonomic principles on which the universal languages were founded.
[70] Quotations from Evans, *Rudolf II* 177.

sense of the word, as a kind of lexicological work distinct from the dictionary.[71] Two others call for slightly fuller discussion. First, the universal-language tradition influenced the study of natural languages by emphasizing the fact that such languages are arbitrary, conventional systems. From that point, it follows that stories about languages are stories about the conventions agreed upon by given speech-communities, which can only be told by examining evidence for the usage of those speech-communities. And, from that, it follows that the study of language must be empirical, and must take the culture of a given language's speakers into account. This line of argument led towards the development of the highly empirical and culturally informative dictionaries of the nineteenth century. Second, the *Essay* and Lloyd's dictionary had, in common with other universal-language projects, the influential goals of the comprehensive coverage of words and the encyclopedic coverage of things. These goals are latent in vernacular dictionaries before the seventeenth century, but they are explicit in the universal-language tradition as early as the lexicon planned by Lodwick in 1646, and the *Essay* addresses them systematically. 'The Alphabetical Dictionary in John Wilkins' Essay', Fredric Dolezal observes, 'is the first monolingual English dictionary to include a broad range of the ordinary (i.e., non-technical and non-hard) English vocabulary in its lexicon.'[72] By the second quarter of the eighteenth century the goals of comprehensiveness and encyclopedism had become an important part of the tradition of making big English dictionaries.

The universal dictionary sketched in Wilkins and Lloyd's project therefore had a paradoxical relationship with heritage. On the one hand, it turned away from the linguistic heritages that we have seen discussed in so many ways by so many early modern lexicographers. On the other, it did so in order to embrace a new sort of heritage, not language but the knowledge of the natural world. The world itself was coming to be understood as a heritage in the seventeenth century: 'You never Enjoy the World aright, till you Perceiv yourself to be the Sole Heir of the whole World,' observed Thomas Traherne around 1670.[73] But knowledge of the world was seen as a heritage too, one that needed to be reconstructed just like the textual heritages of classical antiquity. Wilkins' interest in Noah's Ark is highly relevant here. 'The Ark', it has been argued, 'was an inspiration to collect animals and natural objects, and then to classify them as a step towards the

---

[71] Dolezal, *Forgotten but important lexicographers* 1.   [72] Ibid. 57.
[73] Traherne, *Centuries, poems, and thanksgivings* 1:15; cf. Lowenthal, *Heritage crusade* 227.

recreation of true knowledge … Inspired by the story of the Ark, many early modern authors and collectors saw themselves as rescuing human knowledge and understanding of the natural world from neglect and depravity.'[74] Wilkins imagined that revisions to the treatment of natural history in the *Essay* might provide a taxonomy for the collections of the Royal Society.[75] For him, collecting and ordering concepts made it possible to return to the pre-Babelic wisdom of Noah, and the philosophical language likewise made it possible to work against the confusion of tongues.[76] The dictionary of Wilkins and Lloyd reclaimed the Adamic heritage of wise knowledge of the natural world.

THE MOST ANCIENT LANGUAGE: COMPARATIVISM AND UNIVERSALISM

The universal-language projects which aimed to reverse the effects of the confusion of tongues at Babel were attempting to construct something like the Adamic language. To construct, or even to reconstruct: so, for instance, one shadowy projector whose work was known to Mersenne and Descartes 'prétendait avoir trouvé une langue matrice qui lui faisait entendre toutes les autres'.[77] The form of words here may suggest a claim to have discovered an ancestral language which would enable him to understand all the others, though it is likelier that *trouver* refers to invention rather than discovery, and *matrice* refers to the fruitfulness of the invention rather than claiming that an ur-language had been discovered, so that the sense is 'claimed to have constructed a matrix-language by means of which he was able to understand all other languages'. Obscure as that case is, the prospect of the rediscovery of a true *langue matrice* was certainly an exciting one in the early seventeenth century.

It was, for some investigators at least, a consequence of the Scythian hypothesis, as proposed in different forms by Goropius Becanus and Johannes Magnus, which had helped to open up the way to reflection on the likeness and possible affinity between the Germanic languages, other languages of Europe, and some of those spoken further to the east, in the general direction of Scythia, such as Persian. The 'Scythian' from which extant languages were supposed to descend was not so much the name of a known language variety as a shorthand for 'a lost language formerly

---

[74] Bennett and Mandelbrote, *The garden, the Ark, the tower, the temple* 8; cf. their comments on the Ark and wisdom 73–5 and their note on Wilkins' Ark 93–5.
[75] Wilkins, *Essay* sig. a1v.   [76] Cf. Knowlson, *Universal language schemes* 9–10.   [77] Ibid. 48–50.

spoken in south-western Asia and distinct from Hebrew'.[78] So, the Scythian hypothesis adumbrated the modern understanding that a number of European and Asian languages are indeed descended from a lost language which very probably was spoken in south-western Asia and was unrelated to Hebrew – the language now called Proto-Indo-European. Goropius' argument was vague, and he did not have the means to develop it; the work of the Indo-Europeanists who followed him was independent from his and methodologically quite different. But all the same, hindsight may lead us to take the comparativism of Goropius more seriously than did great scholars of a period closer to his, men such as Leibniz and Ihre: when Johannes Gronovius wrote that 'I would certainly rather see our [Germanic] words called Greek than Greek and Latin ones called Scythian,' he was further from what we now understand to be the true state of affairs than Goropius had been.[79]

The supposed Scythian origins of extant languages were discussed by a number of seventeenth-century scholars, for instance Boxhorn, Franciscus Junius and Salmasius.[80] One of the most striking of these discussions was that in Georg Stiernhielm's *Magog arameo-gothicus*, a pamphlet that took its title from the story of the Noachian descent of the Goths through Magog.[81] That story implied that Hebrew, the language of Noah, and Gothic, the language of the Goths, must be related, and the *Magog arameo-gothicus* explores the relationship in a short but remarkably ambitious series of etymological entries for Hebrew words, in which there are references to a projected – but never realized – etymological dictionary based on the same material. With Hebrew *ab* 'father' he compares forms from Aramaic, Syriac, Arabic and 'Saracenic', deriving them all from Hebrew *aba* or *avah* 'he wanted, he desired' (here and below, I cite Stiernhielm's forms and glosses without comment on their accuracy). Hence, he explains, *abbas* 'abbot' and also the words for 'father' in many languages: Hungarian *apa*, early Latin *papus* and more recent Latin *papa*, Sardic *babbu*, Turkish *baba* and indeed Czech *baba* and Polish *babka* 'grandmother'. Hence too other kinship terms such as Gothic and Icelandic *ave*, Latin *avus* and Malay *ibou*: they are all from the Hebrew

[78] Goropius Becanus, *Origines antwerpianae* 204, 213, 216; see Metcalf, 'Indo-European hypothesis', esp. 239f., and, for a less sympathetic account, Tavoni, 'Western Europe' 64–5.
[79] Gronovius, letter of 17 October 1651 to Nicolaas Heinsius in Breuker, 'On the course of Franciscus Junius's Germanic studies' 142, 'malo saltem nostra [vocabula] esse Graeca, quam Graeca & Latina esse Scythica'.
[80] For Boxhorn and Scythian, see Dekker, *Origins of Old Germanic Studies* 208–15; for Salmasius and Scythian (and even 'Indo-Scythian'), see ibid. 228–30.
[81] Context in Borst, *Turmbau von Babel* 1336.

word. But, Stiernhielm continues, those who derive words like Greek πητὲρ, Latin *pater*, English *father* and Persian *phedur* from the Hebrew are quite mistaken: these words are all from Swedish *fadher*.[82] The range of languages explained here is at first surprising, but it can be explained by Stiernhielm's access to the words for 'father' in Megiser's *Thesaurus polyglottus*. As for the statements about affinity, Stiernhielm understood the Scythian origins of the Noachides to imply that the two senior languages in the world must be Noah's Hebrew and Magog's (Scythian) Gothic, the latter being practically identical with Swedish. A consequence of that was that all other languages should come from one or other of those two.

A late stage of Stiernhielm's thoughts on the historical relationship between Swedish and other languages appears to be represented by a pamphlet of two leaves printed towards the end of his life, called *Babel destructa seu runa Suethica* (the second part of the title harks back to Bureus' *Adulruna*). The pamphlet offers an outline of a work that was never published, and was presumably circulated in an effort to arouse the interest of potential purchasers. It develops the argument of the *Magog* for the antiquity of Swedish, claiming that modern Swedish is the least altered representative of the ancient Scythian protolanguage. Its most important theses are as follows. (1) All the languages of the known world have arisen from one protolanguage and can be traced back to a set of roots which constitute the vocabulary of that protolanguage.[83] (2) This is the Adamic language, for there is nothing in the Bible to prove that new languages were created at Babel, or that any that were created there were anything but temporary; the variety of existing languages is the product of the kind of divergence from an original that can readily be observed, not of the creation of new languages after Babel.[84] (3) All the existing languages in the world, including those of Asia, northern Europe and western Europe, can be traced back to Scythian.[85] (4) The words spoken

---

[82] Stiernhielm, *Magog arameo-gothicus* sig. A2r, 'Heb. *ab, af* Chald. Syr. *Ab, abba.* Arab. *eb.* Saracen. *ebb.* Pater. ab . . . *aba, avah.* i.e., voluit, cupijt . . . Hinc Abbas, *Abbot* / & ap[ud] diversas gentes nomen Patris . . . Hungarice. Apa . . . Lat. antiq. *Papus.* Nov. Papa . . . Sardin. *babbu.* Turcic. *baba* . . . Sclav. & Bohem. Baba & Polon. Babka est Avia . . . Gothic. & Islandic. *Ave.* Lat. *Avus* . . . Malac. & Javens. in India *Ibou.* atq[ue] haec omnia ab Heb. *Ab.* & Syr. *abba.* Unde nonnulli etiam ducere laborant Graec. πητῆρ, Lat. *Pater* . . . Angl. *Father.* & Persic. *Phedur.* sed absurde: cum manifestam trahant haec originem a nostro *Fadher.*'

[83] Stiernhielm, *Babel destructa* fo. 1r, 'Videri omnes Linguas, quae in Orbe cognito extiterunt, & hodie extant, ortas ex una, & ad unam, *qua Radices,* posse reduci.'

[84] Ibid. 'Ex *Confusione Babylonica,* nullam ex SS. Scriptura demonstrari posse novam linguam exortam: & si qua exorta est, eam momentaneam, & ad breve tempus extitisse . . . Temporum & locorum intervallis, *Dialectos* abire in linguas, demonstratur experientia.'

[85] Ibid. fo. 1v, 'Ex *Scythica* ortas linguas primas, non minus Orientales, qvam Septentrionales, & Occidentales' (the origins of individual languages are spelt out fos. 1r–2r).

by Adam and his family, which are commonly said to have been Hebrew by the proponents of the seniority of that language, can just as well be called Scythian; and in fact they were more like Swedish than Hebrew.[86] (5) The contemporary Persian and Armenian languages (here Stiernhielm was putting his copy of the *Dictionarium armeno–latinum* to use) conform substantially with the Scythian language.[87] (6) In the Edenic language, the relationship between signifier and signified was not arbitrary.[88] The pamphlet ends with a reference to a projected 'Lexicon, or universal key to the first languages': this would present the roots of the Edenic vocabulary in so far as they could be reconstructed etymologically from extant languages, so that it would be at once the ultimate etymological dictionary of Swedish and the ultimate dictionary of a universal language.[89]

Perhaps no-one has ever seen dictionaries as a more powerful means for the reconstruction of heritage than Stiernhielm. The antiquity of Swedish was to be set out in the *Gambla Swea- och Götha-måles fatebur*; its affinity with Hebrew and other languages was sketched in the *Magog arameo-gothicus*, and would presumably have been expatiated on in the unrealized etymologicon to which that work refers; the wonderful dictionary imagined in the *Babel destructa* would have reached back to the origins of humankind, making the language of Adam himself a heritage for all people, especially speakers of Swedish. By the end of his life, he had gone far beyond Goropius in anticipating the conclusions and methods of nineteenth-century and subsequent comparative philology. He was not dazzled by the claims of Latin, Greek or Hebrew to primacy among languages, and saw no good evidence for the derivation of Swedish from any non-Germanic language. To make statements about the origins of Swedish, he turned to the runic texts and the Gothic of the Codex Argenteus, which he believed to be the most ancient attested language variety with any connection with Swedish. The ultimate ancestor of Swedish and Gothic must, he proposed, be reconstructed rather than being sought among extant languages. That ancestor, finally, was to be

[86] Ibid. fo. 2r, 'Voces *Adameas*, cujus generis sunt *Adam, Eva, Cain, Seth, Noah*, &c. quas pro antiquitate linguae Hebreae, vulgo, ejus Assertores adducu[n]t; non minus *Scythicas*, imo *Svehticas* esse magis qvam Hebraeas.'

[87] Ibid. 'Linguam *Persicam* hodiernam, ut & *Armenam* maximam partem constare ex lingua *Scythica*'.

[88] Ibid. 'patet Primigenias Vocum Radices non fortuito, sed ex Naturae & rationis fundo enatas'.

[89] Ibid. fo. 2v, 'Eruitur & aperitur certus numerus *Radicum* Universalium ... Ponuntur sigillatim singulae *Radices*, ex quibus, certo ordine, & methodo, in ipsa rerum genesi fundata, Rivi & Flumina vocum, in *Primas* & ex his *ortas* linguas educuntur. *Et hoc est, LEXICON, seu CLAVIS LINGVARUM PRIMARUM UNIVERSALIS*.'

sought in western Asia – for he observed that the languages of Europe had
affinities with each other and with some of the languages of western Asia,
including both Persian and Armenian.

Stiernhielm's lexicographical thought was not that of an isolated
visionary. To see how far ideas like his were diffused in Swedish intellectual life of the later seventeenth century, we may turn to Wittenberg in
February 1686, when a Swedish student, Andreas Jäger of Stockholm,
defended a magister's thesis under Georg Caspar Kirchmaier, *De lingua
vetustissima europae, scytho-celtica et gothica* (*On the most ancient language
of Europe, the Scytho-Celtic and Gothic*), which was subsequently published in the same pamphlet format as thousands of continental dissertations. Jäger never wrote a book: he returned to Sweden, became a
Lutheran pastor, and found himself in trouble with the church authorities
on at least one occasion.[90] But he gave such neat, unambiguous expression to his ideas in the printed form of his thesis that it has become a
minor classic, reviewed at length twice and reprinted once in the eighteenth century, and discussed in an important article in the twentieth.[91]

The thesis is adorned by liminary poems by Carstan Printz of
Gothenburg, who tells Jäger that he will receive the well-earned thanks of
the 'Gothic land', namely Sweden, for his work, and by Magnus Rönnow,
also a Swede (who subsequently held office in the Antikvitetsarkiv), who
observes that other nations have claimed that their own language is the
primordial one, but that it is Jäger who has proved the point for the
Scytho-Gothic language, and has thereby earned the honours of a grateful
fatherland.[92] Jäger's argument then begins briskly: we think with vener-
ation of the language of Adam and the holy patriarchs, and disagree with
the thoughts of Goropius and Cluverius on this subject; we do not,
however, think that the theory that all extant languages came forth from
that one as if from a womb (*veluti matrice*) at the confusion of tongues
has been proved.[93] Nor do we believe that Hebrew is to be identified with
the original language: over the course of time, it has surely changed, not

[90] Metcalf, 'Andreas Jäger' 489.
[91] For the eighteenth-century *fortuna* of the dissertation, see ibid. 491–3; it is now well known from its treatment in Metcalf, 'Indo-European hypothesis'.
[92] Both in Jäger, *De lingua vetustissima* sig. π4v, 'grates meritas Gothica terra dabit' and 'Extollant alii populi primordia linguae | Quisque suae ... | Salva tamen res est: SCHYTICAE [sic] GOTHICAEq[ue] vetustas | Praevalet ... | Hinc Tibi promeritos reduci decerneret honores | PATRIA grata.'
[93] Ibid. 1, 'Patriarcharum Lingvam SS. primam omnium & coaevam Protoplastis veneramur & agnoscimus adversus *Joh. Gorop. Becanu[m]* & *Phil. Cluverium*; ex illa vero, veluti matrice prodiisse in confusione tot lingvarum reliquas in universum, magis creditur, qvam demonstratur.'

least on account of contact with neighbouring languages.[94] Without rehashing Stiernhielm's arguments in his Gothic glossary, we do wish to make clear that the 'Celto-Scythic and Gothic' language is that of Japhet, that it takes priority over Latin, and that the Teutonic language derives from it, although we know that the latter has undergone a great deal of change since the days of Charlemagne.[95] After these preliminaries, he divides his dissertation into three chapters, dealing respectively with the origin of the Scythian language and people, the Celtic language and the Gothic language. Salmasius, Worm, Verelius and Rudbeck are cited as authorities for the identification of Scythians and Getae, and the migration of the Scythians from Ararat to Thrace and from Thrace to the far North is sketched.[96]

Then he comes to the Scythian language, which he has identified to his satisfaction with that of the children of Japhet, and opens his discussion boldly: 'let us begin by taking it for granted that the descendants of Japhet had no part in the insane Babylonian labour and building of the tower'.[97] Unaffected by the confusion of tongues, their language nevertheless diversified over the ages: 'The language of Japhet therefore continued among his descendants until the point where it diverged into different sections; in other words, the Scythian language split up into Phrygian [i.e., the progenitor of Greek], ancient Italic, Celtic, Gothic, Slavonic – for that is how many cardinal languages we recognize and discern in central and peripheral Europe.'[98] Two texts by Salmasius are then cited for the argument, based not only on lexical similarities but also on grammatical features such as similarities in the inflexional endings of verbs, that Persian and German are cognate (Leibniz was to cite the same texts for the same argument).[99] Salmasius, together with Stiernhielm, is

---

[94] Ibid. 2, 'Sed an tractu temporis *Ebraea* ista pura puta? nec *Phoenicia* vel *Cananaea, AEgyptia, Arabica, Aramaea, AEthiopica* commixta, manserit immunis? an in variam novamqve dialectum potius abierit?'

[95] Ibid., 'Penitus negavit & ingeniose admodum examinavit nuper in Glossario Ulphila-Gothico … Dn. Georgius Stiernhielmus … Nec recoqvimus hanc crambem. Istud unice curamus, ut appareat *vetustas* venerabilis (Latinae ac similibus anteponenda Lingvis) CELTO-SCYTHICAE & GOTHICAE; qvae & immediate prodiit a limine JAPHETI; veluti ex hac *Teutonica*, mirifice interpolata, mixta, aucta, perpolita, inde ab aetate Caroli M. maxime ad nostra usque tempora.'

[96] Ibid. 3ff.

[97] Ibid. 15, 'Praesupponimus initio, *Japheti* posteros insanae moli Babylonicae ac turri moliendae non interfuisse'; cf. Goropius Becanus, *Origines antwerpianae* 533–4.

[98] Jäger, *De lingua vetustissima* 16, '*Japheti* lingua igitur in posteris duravit usqve eo, dum in varias abiret alias: h. e. Lingua *Scythica* in *Phrygiam, Italicam* antiquam, *Celticam, Gothicam, Slavonicam*; tot cardinales etenim agnoscimus ac deprehendimus in media & extima *Europa*.'

[99] Ibid., citing Salmasius, *De hellenistica commentarius* 378 and Salmasius, 'Praefatio in Tabulam Cebetis arabicam' sig. *3r; cf. Leibniz, 'Miscellanea Leibnitiana pars altera, xxx' in *Otium hanoueranum* 152n.

also among Jäger's authorities for the argument that languages diverge into different dialects, which become independent languages in their own right. Latin is the mother who has brought forth Italian, Spanish, French, Rhaetic, Sardic and Romanian as daughters, and, similarly, the most ancient Scythian language disappeared as it turned into diverse others: Phrygian, Celtic (i.e., proto-Germanic), Old Italic, Gothic, Slavonic and Parthian (i.e., Old Iranian); then, for instance, the original Celtic language ramified in its turn.[100]

The further argument of Jäger's thesis continues to be interesting, not least for its suggestion that contemporary English preserved many elements of the language of 'Germania antiqva'.[101] This language was, in Jäger's terms, Celtic; the thesis ends with a densely packed mass of evidence for the close affinity of the *lingua Celtica* and the *lingua Gothica*, the latter being illustrated from Busbecq's report of Crimean Gothic, the Codex Argenteus, Willeram and other sources.[102] The disparity between the clarity of Jäger's vision of the relationship between languages and the confusedness of the empirical work that led him to classify Germanic data both as Celtic and as Gothic is significant. In the *De lingua vetustissima*, we can see not only what an impressive theory of the history of language shaped some of the most interesting seventeenth-century lexicographical thought but also how far that theory outstripped what was possible in lexicographical practice. The ideas in Jäger's dissertation, like those in the *Magog arameo-gothicus*, found expression in pamphlet form but never became the basis of a dictionary or monograph. Instead, they inspired another Wittenberg dissertation, also written by a Swedish student of Kirchmaier's, Johannes Michaelis Hepp, whose *Parallelismus & convenientia* XII *lingvarum ex matrice scytho-celtica* (*Parallel and concurrence of twelve languages of Scytho-Celtic origin*) was examined in 1697. Hepp acknowledged Jäger's work, and went beyond it particularly by providing a table of cognates of sixty-six German words in twelve parallel columns: one each for German, English, Czech, Croatian, Greek, French, Spanish, Italian, Latin, Polish, Swedish and Hungarian (sharing a column with the *lingua Taurica*, presumably Tatar).[103] However, neither he nor any contemporary could expand a little wordlist like this into a serious comparative historical dictionary.

---

[100] Jäger, *De lingua vetustissima* 17–18, 'Latina lingva mater filias & dialectos peperit *Italicam, Hispanicam, Gallicam, Rhaeticam, Sardicam, Walachicam* … dicimus, vetustissimam Europae linguam *Scythicam* in alias concessisse varias, *Phrygiam, Celticam, Italicam* antiquam (quae ex *Hetrusca, Osca,* & *Sabina* abiit in *Latialem* postea)[,] *Gothicam, Slavonicam,* & *Parthicam.* Deinde *Celtica* vicissim alios diffudit se in ramos.'

[101] Ibid. 36–8.   [102] Ibid. 42–8.

[103] Hepp, *Parallelismus et convenientia* XII *lingvarum* sigs. A3v (reference to Jäger), B4v–C2r (tables).

In order to make a dictionary that would show the history of any language group by illustrating the gradual divergence of one variety from another in the terms that Stiernhielm and Jäger were imagining, it would be necessary to use data from a large corpus of early texts that had been edited and dated. Such a corpus was not available for a single vernacular language in seventeenth-century Europe, let alone a group. There was, for instance, a larger body of Old English in print than of Old High German or Old Norse, enough for Somner and Junius to make their dictionaries, but very little scholarly work had been done on later medieval English, let alone Scots (hence Junius' glossaries to Chaucer and Douglas). The same was true for other medieval languages, Germanic and non-Germanic alike, and it would remain true until the nineteenth century.

The one language for which there was a large but coherent body of texts, covering centuries of linguistic change, with generally reliable dates assigned to them, was ancient Greek, and it was in a discussion of dialect differentiation in Greek that Salmasius had developed the principles that Jäger applied in his thesis. The monumental bulk and notorious commercial failure of the *Thesaurus graecae linguae* stood for two hundred years as a warning to lexicographers who might be interested in handling that set of data more historically than Henri Estienne had done. But it was as a contribution to the lexicography of ancient Greek that the ideas underlying Stiernhielm's dictionary projects and Jäger's thesis were revived, in the treatise *Über Zweck, Anlage und Ergänzung griechischer Wörterbucher* (*On the purpose, design and supplementation of Greek dictionaries*) of the German classicist Franz Passow, published in 1812. Passow would propose the chronological structuring of dictionary entries in such a way that each would tell the whole story of a word, from its earliest attestation to its latest, and his proposals would shape all serious diachronic lexicography thereafter.[104]

---

[104] See, e.g., Aarsleff, 'Early history of the *Oxford English Dictionary*' 419, 432.

Conclusion

People know two kinds of heritage: the personal and the cultural. The two merge into each other at some points. So, for instance, to register one's mother tongue in a dictionary is to register the language one learned literally from one's mother, the language that one was already acquiring with the discriminating ears and grammatical flair of early infancy – but it is also to register the language that links one to, and indeed binds one into, a speech-community far wider than the household of one's infancy. Henri Estienne learned French from his mother and his family, but his sense of being French and of being at home where French was spoken was more than a sense of his familial inheritance. Likewise, he acquired his Greek and Latin as a member of the extraordinary household in which he grew up, and developed his dedication to classical scholarship as a son of his inspiringly learned father, but, as a learned writer, he communicated with – in the senses of writing for and being part of – the whole commonwealth of the learned, and, as a reader of Latin and Greek, he communicated with the great tradition of the living and the dead who wrote in those languages. The learned languages were one of his personal heritages, and one of his cultural heritages. French was another of each of these. Reformed Christian belief and thought was a third.

Telling the stories of heritage is one way to tell the story of dictionaries. It is not the only one: we could, for instance, see the Estiennes' great dictionaries primarily as products of the maturing print culture that made so many sources readily available to them and provided the capital for the completion and dissemination of their own projects, and contextualize their work in the history of the book. We could see the Estiennes as following and modifying the work of earlier lexicographers, and contextualize their work in the technical history of lexicographical traditions. But I have tried to demonstrate in this book that an understanding of lexicography as shaped by ideas of heritage frees the history of dictionaries from too heavy a dependence on certain potentially arid kinds of narrative of the form '61 per cent of the entries in Y derive from entries in X', and engages it with broader and more humane questions about lexicology, the history of linguistics, the history of learned culture, indeed the history of culture in general.

That is not to say that the way in which early modern lexicographers understood and told their stories of heritage can be detached from the material circumstances of their work. It is possible, for instance, to see the sporadic expression of a sense of personal heritage in the work of medieval lexicographers: when Giovanni Balbi of Genoa used the entry *janua* in his *Catholicon* as a vehicle for autobiographical remarks founded on the supposed derivation of *Genoa* from *janua*, he was showing his awareness of his dictionary as a work that came out of his personal background. But it is only because of the material resources and information management strategies that could be exploited by early modern lexicographers that they were able to make dictionaries sufficiently rich and complex to tell stories both of personal and of cultural heritage. The former became particularly tellable in the space that became available for assertions of authorship in the prelims of the early modern printed book. The latter became tellable in fragments in great learned printed books of the late fifteenth and early sixteenth centuries like Perotti's *Cornu copiae* or Erasmus' *Adages* or Budé's *Commentarii*, which assembled part of what was known of the classical heritage in non-alphabetical order. Both could be inserted into the complex microstructure – the long entries enriched with discursive definitions and a carefully chosen array of quotations – which could be coordinated within the alphabetical macrostructure of dictionaries made in *officinae* like that of Robert Estienne, intellectual workplaces within which a great deal of paper could be written on, pushed about a table, moved from one pile to another, managed. It was Robert Estienne who first made a dictionary in which a vast cultural heritage was analysed into the stories told by individual words, made readily retrievable by being sorted into an alphabetical macrostructure, and both introduced and coloured throughout by the story of the lexicographer's personal heritage.

It was his son Henri who found ways to develop that narrative of heritage even further than Robert. For him, the story of ancient Greek culture was one that could best be told through the presentation of as many as possible of its texts, and for every text that he presented in an *editio princeps* or a newly castigated and emended edition, there was a personal story to be told in its prelims – in the prefaces and dedications that between them make up an autobiography written over forty years, surely one of the best of its century, from the anxious triumphs of the

1550s to the melancholy and aggressiveness of the 1590s. Pre-eminent above all the other prefaces of Henri Estienne's editions is that of the *Poetae graeci principes*, and pre-eminent above all the others of any kind is that of the *Thesaurus graecae linguae*. In both books, Henri Estienne was gathering the wonderful fragments of the heritage that had been transmitted from classical Greece to sixteenth-century France, and he prefaced both by explaining how that heritage had become part of him, flesh of his flesh, so that his great dictionary had from its prelims onwards something of the qualities both of an intellectual autobiography and of a love-letter to the distant past.

In the *Thesaurus latinae linguae* and the *Thesaurus graecae linguae*, the lexicography of the classical languages reached a height of achievement that would not be surpassed in the early modern period. But as the sixteenth century progressed, so did the means for the telling of stories of a different kind, those of the medieval linguistic heritages of the emerging nations of early modern Europe. The earliest forms or cognates of the European vernaculars – languages such as Old French, Old High German, Gothic and Old English – could not be registered with the same lexicographical techniques as the classical languages. Their texts were not as readily accessible, and they were not as well edited: indeed, the people who studied them encountered a circular problem, for the making of dictionaries depends on the availability of edited texts, and the editing of texts in obsolete language varieties depends on the availability of dictionaries. The early history of the lexicography of these language varieties therefore looks like an anticlimax after that of the great ordered registrations of the classical lexical heritages: a wordlist here, a glossary to a handful of freshly and imperfectly edited law-codes there, a few manuscript pages of onomastical notes, a series of dictionary projects that did not reach publication.

But these lexicographical essays show a marked forward impetus. One reason for this is that they coexisted, and to some extent interplayed, with the emerging lexicographical record of the standardizing languages of sixteenth-century Europe. So, while the first wordlists of early Germanic language varieties were being put together, a series of dictionaries of modern Dutch was being produced in the Plantin *officina* in Antwerp, notably by one of the most senior employees of the house, Cornelis Kiel, as skilful a manager of information as Robert Estienne, and a pioneer in the comparative etymological use of material from different varieties of Dutch and Low German. He and the Antwerp antiquary Goropius Becanus must have crossed paths as Goropius tried to understand the relationship between Dutch and the most ancient imaginable language. During their lifetimes, another Dutch-speaker, the diplomat Ogier van Busbecq, was interviewing one of the last speakers of Crimean Gothic in Constantinople and reflecting on the support which the Gothic language gave to one dialect of Dutch as opposed to another. More or less simultaneously, other Dutch-speakers were coming to grips with the thousand-year-old record of written Gothic in the Codex Argenteus. From Antwerp to Constantinople, the same story was being told in all these different lexicographical and lexicological projects: that of the language of the fatherland, the language inherited from the fathers.

Nor was this a story told only by Dutch-speakers. The manuscript hunting that led to the rediscovery of the Gothic of the Codex Argenteus was also being initiated in Germany by the generation of Aventinus and Celtis and in England by the generation of Leland. The ancient book was a monument of cultural heritage, but one whose stones could be reassembled into the edifice of a dictionary, and this process can be seen particularly clearly in the developing lexicographical record of Old English, from Leland to Nowell, from Nowell to Joscelyn, from Joscelyn via D'Ewes to Somner. The collection of manuscripts in private libraries made them not only cultural treasures but personal property, and from Erasmus onwards this privatization of heritage became a significant factor in lexicography. Spoken language itself was coming to be seen as an embodiment of cultural heritage as well: like Busbecq in Constantinople, lexicographers such as Nowell in England were listening to living language varieties and thinking hard about their relationship with the past. And the personal experience of listening was another way to make the recovery of the language of the fatherland an engagement with language as a personal inheritance as well as a cultural one. Nowell could draw on his knowledge of Lancashire; Anglo-Dutch lexicographers of Old English such as de Laet and Franciscus Junius could draw on their sense of the double personal heritage of the bilingual speaker as they thought about the shared origins of English and Dutch. Lexicography might be strongly allied with local studies, and dictionaries such as those of Dugdale and Somner were the work of distinguished local historians, firmly grounded in Warwickshire and Canterbury respectively, interested in the personal experience of place as well as in a wider cultural history. The presence of lexicographical raw material in the charters that recorded Anglo-Saxon landholding and in the inscriptions of the rune-stones which were such a striking feature of some Scandinavian landscapes strengthened this affinity, and indeed the use of runes to write early Scandinavian forms in lexicographical work such as that of Johannes Bureus, Ole Worm and Franciscus Junius privileged rune-stones above manuscripts in the Roman alphabet as transmitters of the linguistic heritage.

The classical heritage was a submerged stream in much of this work on the vernaculars: the wordlists of many vernacular dictionaries can be traced back to bilingual dictionaries of a given vernacular and Latin, often deriving ultimately from the first Latin–French and French–Latin dictionaries of Robert Estienne, and students of the vernacular languages might cut their teeth on classical philology, as did Conrad Gessner and Franciscus Junius. But the stories of post-classical Latin and Greek were also told in their own right. During the sixteenth century, manuscripts of local importance written in Latin, by authors from Hrotswitha of Gandesheim to Symeon of Durham, were brought to light and edited. Medieval law-codes, whether written in Latin or in the vernacular, were of fundamental importance to the historians of national institutions. The renewed interest in classical Latin literature that characterizes the Renaissance went hand in hand with a continuing use of post-classical Latin vocabulary in civil law and in the Church.

So it was that, by the early seventeenth century, increasingly elaborate work was being done on post-classical Latin, sometimes from the perspective of its importance as one of the living languages of legal institutions, as in Cowell's strongly controversial *Interpreter*, and sometimes from that of its importance as the language in which historical information was encoded, as in the glossaries of Friedrich Lindenbrog or in Spelman's widely admired *Archaeologus*. This work was underpinned by a developing sense that a period of roughly a thousand years had intervened between the end of classical antiquity and the age of humanistic Latin, and that this period was coherent, capable of being studied in its own right as a middle age, with its own cultural and linguistic characteristics, which had been inherited by the modern world but transformed in the inheritance. Manuscripts from the period could be sought out and studied, and its language could be registered in wordlists. Nor were Latin and the Western vernaculars the only languages from that period capable of being studied: from the mid-sixteenth century onwards, the Greek of the Byzantine Empire was an object of increasingly sophisticated inquiry. By the time Spelman was sending specimens of the *Archaeologus* to the learned correspondents of Peiresc in France, a number of them were editing Byzantine texts, and the first glossaries of Byzantine Greek were being published.

The recovery of the heritage of classical Latin and Greek led to the making of hundreds of dictionaries. The recovery of that post-classical

Latin and Greek led to the making of fewer dictionaries, for the schoolbook market was directed towards the classical language varieties, but the pre-eminent dictionaries of the post-classical language varieties, the *Glossarium latinitatis* and the *Glossarium graecitatis*, were achievements as astonishing as those of the Estiennes, and they were the work of one man, Charles du Cange. In his vast reading, the double textual heritage of the Western and Eastern Middle Ages came together in one man's lived experience. In his awareness of the Latin roots of French culture and of the ways in which the Christian eastern Mediterranean had belonged to French-speakers, the Western and Eastern Middle Ages came together again as a cultural inheritance for the France of Louis XIV in which he lived.

Three kinds of lexicography that were undertaken or imagined in the seventeenth century looked forward to the possibility of telling stories even more ambitious than those of the three heritages of the classical languages, the post-classical vernaculars, and post-classical Latin and Greek. The first of these was the making of polyglot dictionaries, which might for sure be the sort of intellectually unambitious project that made for little pocket dictionaries of multiple European languages, but might at its height, as practised in Hieronymus Megiser's *Thesaurus polyglottus*, attempt for the first time to survey all the languages in the world and to understand their relationships – to understand, indeed, speech as a common inheritance of all humans. The second was the making of dictionaries of artificial universal languages, a project most fully realized in William Lloyd's 'Alphabetical dictionary' which accompanied John Wilkins' *Essay towards a real character and a philosophical language*. This attempted to escape altogether from the confusion and irregularity of natural languages and to understand the knowable world as a common inheritance of all humans, nameable alike by all, the relationships of its material entities and abstract concepts equally perspicuous to all and capable of being documented in a book that would be at once a universal dictionary and a systematic universal encyclopedia. The third, and the furthest from any practical possibility even of partial achievement, was the project of making a dictionary of the most ancient language of humanity, a work that would combine the ambitions of Megiser and Lloyd, to make a universal etymological dictionary of all languages, documenting the words that might, however living languages transformed them, be a common inheritance for all peoples.

The most important documents for the study of this last dictionary project are scarcely more than pamphlets: a prospectus by the poet Georg Stiernhielm and a doctoral dissertation by the future pastor Andreas

Jäger. This brings the subject-matter of this book full circle, from the works by Erasmus and Budé that adumbrated the great achievements of the Estiennes without being strictly in dictionary form themselves to the short texts that voiced lexicographical thought far out of reach of lexicographical practice. The great advantage of reading dictionaries in a cultural context such as the context of the stories of heritage they tell is that one's reading is, as in both of these cases, inevitably led beyond the dictionaries themselves. So it must always be if we are to see why dictionaries matter.

Afterword

Since I completed this book, a number of additional sources have come to my attention, some of them newly published and some overlooked as I wrote, and I would like to draw the attention of readers to some of them.

On antiquarianism in general, with particular reference to the work of Momigliano: Peter N. Miller, ed., *Momigliano and antiquarianism: Foundations of the modern cultural sciences* (Toronto: University of Toronto Press, in association with the UCLA Center for Seventeenth- and Eighteenth-Century Studies and the William Andrews Clark Memorial Library, 2007).

On Henri Estienne: Judit Kecskeméti, Bénédicte Boudou and Hélène Cazes, under the direction of Jean Céard, *La France des humanistes: Henri II Estienne, éditeur et écrivain* (Turnhout: Brepols, 2003).

On dictionaries which registered Croatian lexical items, e.g., those of Gelenius, Georgievitz, Vrančić and Megiser: Branko Franolić, *A bibliography of Croatian dictionaries* (Paris: Nouvelles Editions Latines, 1985) 7–15.

On sixteenth-century Germanic philology: William Jervis Jones, *Images of language: German attitudes to European languages from 1500 to 1800*, Amsterdam Studies in the Theory and History of Linguistic Science ser. III, Studies in the History of the Language Sciences, vol. 89 (Amsterdam and Philadelphia: John Benjamins, 1999) 1–24.

On early modern dictionaries of Dutch: Nicoline van der Sijs, *Taal als mensenwerk: Het ontstaan van het ABN* (The Hague: SDU Uitgevers, 2004) 29–97 and 353–76.

On the English antiquaries of the seventeenth century, including Somner: Jan Broadway, *'No historie so meete': Gentry culture and the development of local history in Elizabethan and early Stuart England* (Manchester: Manchester University Press, 2006).

On Paris in the time of du Cange: Klaus Garber, 'Paris, capital of European late humanism: Jacques Auguste de Thou and the Cabinet Dupuy' (trans. Joe G. Delap), in Garber, *Imperiled heritage: Tradition, history, and utopia in early modern German literature*, ed. Max Reinhart (Burlington, VT: Ashgate, 2000) 54–72.

On Hieronymus Megiser: Eugenio Coseriu, *Von Genebrardus bis Hervás: Beiträge zur Geschichte der Kenntnis des Rumänischen in Westeuropa* (Tübingen: Gunter Narr Verlag, 1981), esp. 31–42.

I should also note that I have only had time to make very limited use of the recent work of Tom Deneire and Toon Van Hal on Lipsius and the Wachtendonck Psalms. Finally, my own article, 'Did Andreas Jäger or Georg Caspar Kirchmaier write the dissertation *De lingua vetustissima Europae* (1686)?', forthcoming in *Historiographia linguistica* 35.1 (2008), corrects my assumption in this book that the text in question was the sole work of its junior co-author.

Bibliography

MANUSCRIPT AND ARCHIVAL SOURCES, AND INDIVIDUAL
COPIES OF EARLY PRINTED BOOKS

Copenhagen, Koninglike Biblioteket.
175:2, 88. Otfrid, *Euangeliorum liber* (1571). Annotated by a Dutch-speaking
owner in the sixteenth or seventeenth century.

London, British Library.
507. d. 15. Cowell, *Interpreter* (1637). Annotated by an anonymous reader after 1648.
875. b. 5 (1). Spelman, *De non temerandis ecclesiis* (1613). Annotated by the author.
C. 95. c. 18. Leland, *Cygnea cantio* (1545). Annotated by Laurence Nowell and
William Lambarde.
E. 1005 (1). Somner, *Treatise of gavelkind* (1659). George Thomason's copy with
date of purchase marked by him.
Add. MSS 4720–4722. Eighteenth-century transcript of Oxford, Bodleian
Library MSS Junius 2 and 3.
Add. MSS 24281–24283. Cowell, *Interpreter* (1637). Interleaved and heavily
annotated by Sir Roger Twysden.
Add. MSS 34599–34601. Correspondence and working papers of Sir Henry
Spelman.
MSS Cotton Titus A. xv and xvi. John Joscelyn, *Dictionarium saxonico–latinum.*
MSS Harley 8 and 9. Simonds D'Ewes, *Dictionarium citeriorum saeculorum
anglo-saxonico–latinum.*
MS Harley 374. Includes letter from Jan de Laet to Simonds D'Ewes.
MS Harley 646. Simonds D'Ewes, *The life of Sir Simonds D'Ewes written by
himselfe.*
MS Harley 3321. Glossary of medieval Latin owned or compiled by Jan de Laet.
MS Harley 7579. Includes Old English wordlists by Jan de Laet.

Oxford, Bodleian Library.
30254 c. 2. Falconer Madan's collection of papers relating to the *Oxford English
Dictionary.*
A 4. 5 Jur. Cowell, *Interpreter* (1701). Annotated by Thomas Tanner.
Auct. S 2. 35. Hephaestion, Ἐγχειρίδιον (1553). With ownership signatures of
Robert Estienne and Charles du Cange.

B 2. 4 (2) Art. Seld. *Glossaria duo* (1573). Bound with vol. IV of a set of the *Thesaurus graecae linguae.*

Buchanan b. 8. *Glossaria duo* (1573). Bound as vol. VI of a set of the *Thesaurus graecae linguae.*

fol. Godw. 249. *Glossaria duo* (1573). Bound as vol. V of a set of the *Thesaurus graecae linguae.*

Mar. 42. Meursius, *Glossarium* (1610). Annotated by an early reader, presumably Thomas Marshall.

MS Dugdale 29. Dugdale's Old English dictionary.

MS e Musaeo 48. Printer's copy for Spelman, *Glossarium archaiologicum* (1664).

MSS Fell 8–18. Transcript by William Nicolson, with additions, of MSS Junius 2 and 3.

MSS Junius 2 and 3. Junius' large dictionary of early Germanic material, with post-Junian additions.

MSS Junius 4 and 5. Junius' *Etymologicum anglicanum.*

MS Junius 6. Junius' glossary to Chaucer.

MS Junius 9. Chaucer, *Workes* (1598), marked up by Junius and used as a source for MS Junius 6.

MS Junius 54. Douglas, *The .xiii. bukes of Eneados* (1553), paginated and annotated by Junius and used as a source for MS Junius 114.

MS Junius 74. Includes Junius' Scots vocabulary with notes on supposed derivations from ancient Greek.

MS Junius 112. Junius' index to his glossaries of Old English and Old High German.

MS Junius 114. Junius' glossary to Douglas' *The .xiii. bukes of Eneados.*

MS Tanner 89. Includes correspondence of Sir Henry Spelman.

MS Top. gen. c. 3. Collections by John Leland, partially edited by Hearne as Leland, *De rebus Britannicis collectanea.*

O. 2. 18 Art. Seld. Spelman, *Archaeologus* (1626). Author's presentation copy to John Selden.

Paris, Bibliothèque de l'Arsenal.

MSS 4815–4816. Alphabetically ordered encyclopedic collection of du Cange, entries beginning G–O and P–X.

Paris, Bibliothèque Nationale.

ms fr 9486. Du Cange, 'Glossarium francobarbarum'.

mss fr 9494–9495. Alphabetically ordered encyclopedic collection of du Cange, including a reading list of his from the early 1630s.

ms lat 13036. Guardbook containing 461 slips for the range *F–festuagium*, prepared as printer's copy for du Cange's *Glossarium latinitatis.*

Stockholm, Kungliga Biblioteket.

MS F a 13. Lexicographical notes by Johannes Bureus, alphabetically arranged.

MS F a 17. Lexicographical and onomastical notes by Johannes Bureus.

PRINTED SOURCES WRITTEN BEFORE 1800

Achery, Jean Luc de, ed. *Veterum aliquot scriptorum qui in Galliae bibliothecis, maxime Benedictinorum, latuerant, spicilegium.* 13 vols. Paris: apud Carolum Saureux *et al.*, 1657–77.

Ælfric. *A Saxon treatise concerning the Old and New Testament.* Ed. William Lisle. London: printed by Iohn Hauiland for Henrie Seile, 1623.

Albericus de Trium Fontium. *Chronicon.* Ed. P. Scheffer-Boichorst. *Monumenta Germaniae historica: scriptores* 23. 1874; rpt Stuttgart: Anton Hiersemann, 1963. 631–950.

Alciati, Andrea. *Emblematum libellus.* Venice: apud Aldi filios, 1546.

Ambrogio, Teseo. *Introductio in chaldaicam linguam, syriacam, atque armenicam, et decem alias linguas.* Pavia: excudebat Ioan. Maria Simoneta, sumptibus et typis authoris libri, 1539.

Anacreontis Teii odae. Ed. Henri Estienne. Paris: apud Henricum Stephanum [but printed by Guillaume Morel?], 1554.

Apollodorus. *Bibliotheces: siue de deorum origine, tam graece quam latine, luculentis pariter, ac doctis annotationibus illustrati, & nunc primum in lucem editi libri tres.* Ed. Benedetto Egio. Rome: in aedibus Antoni Bladi, pontif[ici] max[imi] excusoris, 1555.

Aurelius, Cornelius. *Batavia, siue de antiquo veroque eius insulae quam Rhenus in Hollandia facit situ descriptione & laudibus … libri duo … nunc primum in lucem edita.* Ed. Bonaventure de Smet. Leiden: ex officina Plantiniana, apud Franciscum Raphelengium, 1586.

Aventinus, Johannes. *Bayerische Chronik.* Ed. Matthias Lexer. In Aventinus, *Sämmtliche Werke* IV:1. Munich: Christian Kaiser, 1882.

[Baduel, Claude, ed.]. *Lexicon graeco–latinum, seu thesaurus linguae graecae.* [Geneva]: ex officina Ioannis Crispini, 1554.

Bage, Robert. *Mount Henneth: a novel, in a series of letters.* London: printed for W. Lowndes, 1788.

Barbaro, Ermolao. *Castigationes Plinianae.* Rome: impressit formis Eucharius Argenteus Germanus, 1492–3.

Baron, Jean-Léonore [writing as 'M. Lesage de Samine']. *Éloge de Charles Dufresne, Seigneur Du Cange, avec une notice de ses ouvrages: discours qui a remporté le prix de l'Académie d'Amiens en 1764.* Amiens: chez la veuve Godart, imprimeur du Roi et de l'Académie, 1764.

Bayle, Pierre. *Dictionaire historique et critique.* 2 vols. Rotterdam: chez Reinier Leers, 1697.

Beck, Cave. *Le charactere universel, par lequel toutes nations peuvent comprendre les conceptions l'une de l'autre.* London: chez A. Maxey, pour Guillaume Weekly, libraire en Ipswich, 1657.
  The universal character, by which all the nations in the world may understand one anothers conceptions. London: printed by Tho. Maxey for William Weekley … in Ipswich, 1657.

Bede. *Historiae ecclesiasticae gentis anglorum libri* v. Ed. Abraham Wheelock. Cambridge: excudebat Rogerus Daniel, 1643.

Bible. See R. Estienne, ed. (1550), *Gospels* (1571), F. Junius and T. Marshall, eds. (1665) and [Stiernhielm], ed. (1671).

Bibliotheca selectissima: being the library of the late Sir Edmund King, M. D. ... containing a collection of very valuable books in physick and other sciences ... also the library of that eminent and learned antiquary Sir H. S –, which will begin to be sold by auction at the Temple-change ... on Monday the 28th of November, 1709. London: sold for John Harding, 1709.

Binet, Claude. 'La vie de Pierre de Ronsard gentil-homme Vandomois'. In Ronsard, *Oeuvres* (1587). x:107–57.

Bochius, Joannes, ed. *Epigrammata funebria ad Christophori Plantini architypographi regii manes.* Antwerp: in officina Plantiniana, apud viduam et I. Moretum, 1590.

Bodin, Jean. *Methodus, ad facilem historiarum cognitionem.* Paris: apud Martinum Iuuenem, 1566.

Boethius. *Consolationis philosophiae libri* v, anglo-saxonice redditi. Ed. Christopher Rawlinson. Oxford: e theatro Sheldoniano, 1698.

Boxhorn, Marcus Zuerius. *Originum gallicarum liber.* Amsterdam: apud Joannem Janssonium, 1654.

Boys, John, trans. *Aeneas his descent into hell as it is inimitably described by the prince of poets in the sixth of his Aeneis ... to which are added some certain pieces relating to the publick, written by the author.* London: printed by R. Hodgkinsonne, 1660.

Bruni, Leonardo. *Epistolarum libri* viii. Ed. Laurentius Mehus. 2 vols. Florence: ex typographia Bernardi Paperinii, sumptibus Josephi Rigaccii, 1741.

Budé, Guillaume. *De transitu hellenismi ad christianismum.* Paris: ex officina Rob[erti] Stephani, 1535.

    Commentarii linguae graecae. Paris: ex officina Roberti Stephani typographi Regii, 1548.

    Opera omnia. Ed. Celio Secondo Curione. Basel: apud Nicolaum Episcopium Iuniorem, 1557.

Bureus, Joannes. *Runakänslones lärespån / Elementa runica.* Uppsala: [by the author], 1599. Facsimile reprint n.p., apparently for Sophus Bugge *et al.*, 1881

    Monumenta sueo-gothica hactenus exsculpta. 3rd edn. In Olaus Verelius, ed., *Itt stycke af Konung Olaf Tryggvasons saga.* Uppsala: af Henrich Curio, 1665.

Burnet, Gilbert. *History of my own time.* Ed. Osmund Airy. 2 vols. Oxford: Clarendon Press, 1897–1900.

    'Autobiography'. In H. C. Foxcroft, ed., *Supplement to Burnet's History of my own time.* Oxford: Clarendon Press, 1902. 451–514.

Busbecq, Ogier de. *Legationis turcicae epistolae quatuor.* Paris: apud Aegidium Beys, 1589.

Busch, Johann. *Chronicon canonicorum regularium ordinis S. Augustini capituli Windesemensis.* Antwerp: apud P. & I. Belleros, 1621.

Cædmon. *Paraphrasis poetica Genesios ac praecipuarum sacrae paginae historiarum, abhinc annos MLXX anglo-saxonice conscripta.* Ed. Franciscus Junius. Amsterdam: apud Christophorum Cunradi, typis & sumptibus editoris, 1655.

Calepino, Ambrogio. *Vocabularius: thesaurus copiosissimus.* Toscolano: apud Benacum in aedibus Alexandri Paganini, 1522.

Calvinus, Johannes. *Lexicon iuridicum ivris romani simvl, et canonici: fevdalis item, civilis, criminalis: theoretici, ac practici: et in schola, et in foro vsitatarum . . . simul & locorvm commvnivm, & dictionarii vicem sustinens.* Frankfurt: apud haeredes Andreae Wecheli, Claud[ium] Marnium & Ioan[nem] Aubrium, 1600.

Camden, William. *Britannia.* London: per Radulphum Newbery, 1586.

— *Britannia.* 3rd edn. London: [Printed at Eliot's Court Press] impensis Geor[gii] Bishop, 1590.

— 'Ad lectorem'. In *Britannia.* 5th edn. London: [Printed at Eliot's Court Press] impensis Georg. Bishop, 1600. 1–30 [last sequence of pagination].

— *Remaines of a greater worke, concerning Britaine.* London: printed by G[eorge] E[ld] for Simon Waterson, 1605.

— *Britain.* Trans. Philemon Holland. London: impensis Georgii Bishop & Iohannes Norton, 1610.

— *Remaines, concerning Britaine but especially England . . . reviewed, corrected, and encreased.* 2nd edn. London: [printed] by Iohn Legatt for Simon Waterson, 1614.

— *Britannia.* Ed. Edmund Gibson. London: printed by F. Collins for A. Swalle et al., 1695.

Canisius, Heinrich, ed. *Antiquae lectionis tomus v.* Ingolstadt: ex officina typographica Ederiana, apud Andream Angermarium, 1604.

Carew, Richard. 'The excellencie of the English tongue'. In Camden, *Remaines* (1614). 36–44.

Cartwright, William. 'To the worthy author'. In Geoffrey Chaucer, *Amorum Troili et Creseidae libri duo priores anglico–latini.* Trans. Sir Francis Kynaston. Oxford: excudebat Iohannes Lichfield, 1635. Sig. **1r.

Casaubon, Isaac. *Epistolae.* Ed. Theodorus Jansson ab Almeloveen. Rotterdam: typis Casparis Frisch et Michaelis Böhm, 1709.

Casaubon, Meric. *Pietas contra maledicos patrij nominis, & religionis hostes.* London: [W. Stansby] ex officina bibliopolarum, 1621.

— *De quatuor linguis commentationes pars prior, quae, de lingua hebraica et de lingua saxonica.* London: typis J. Flesher, sumptibus Ric. Mynne, 1650.

— *The case of Cornelius Bee and his partners.* Single-sheet broadside. [London, 1666].

Cellarius, Jacobus, and Nicolaus Hönigerus, eds. Λεξικον Ἑλληνικορωμικον: *hoc est, dictionarium graecolatinum, post correctiones G. Budaei, I. Tusani, C. Gesneri, H. Iunii, R. Constantini, Io. Hartungi, Mar. Hopperi, Guil. Xylandri emendatum.* Basel: per Sebastianum Henricpetri, 1584.

Celtis, Conrad. *Briefwechsel.* Ed. Hans Rupprich. Veröffentlichungen der Kommission zur Erforschung der Geschichte der Reformation und

Gegenreformation: Humanistenbriefe, Band 3. Munich: C.H. Beck'sche Verlagsbuchhandlung, 1934.

Chaucer, Geoffrey. *The workes . . . newly printed. In this impression you shall find these additions: . . . 4 Old and obscure words explaned. 5 Authors by him cited, declared. 6 Difficulties opened. 7 Two bookes of his, neuer before printed.* London: printed by Adam Islip, at the charges of Thomas Wight, 1598.

Chifflet, Pierre François. *Lettre touchant Beatrix comtesse de Chalon.* Dijon: chez Philibert Chavance, 1656.

Choniates, Niketas. *Historia, glossario graeco-barbaro auctior, et ope MSS. Reg. emendatior.* ed. C. A. Fabrot. Paris: e typographia regia, 1647.

Chronicon Paschale a mundo condito ad Heraclii imperatoris annum vicesimum . . . auctius et emendatius . . . cum nova latina versione & notis chronicis ac historicis. Ed. Charles du Cange. Paris: e typographia regia, 1688.

Codex legum antiquarum. Ed. Friedrich Lindenbrog. 2 vols. Frankfurt: apud Iohannem & Andream Marnios et consortes, 1613.

Coke, Roger. *A detection of the court and state of England.* London: [n.p.], 1694.

Commodianus. *Instructiones adversus gentium deos.* Ed. Nicolas Rigault. Toul: apud S. Belgrand & I. Laurentium, typographos regios, 1650.

Cowell, John. *The interpreter, or booke containing the signification of words: wherein is set foorth the true meaning of all, or the most part of such words and termes, as are mentioned in the lawe writers, or statutes of this victorious and renowned kingdome, requiring any exposition or interpretation.* Cambridge: printed by Iohn Legate, 1607.

    The interpreter: or booke containing the signification of words. London: printed [by Richard Hodgkinsonne] for William Sheares, 1637.

    The interpreter: or booke containing the signification of words. London: printed [by Augustine Mathewes] for William Sheares, 1637.

    The interpreter of words and terms, used either in the common or statute laws of this realm, and in tenures and jocular customs . . . further augmented and improv'd. Ed. White Kennett. London: printed for W. Battersby, J. Place, A. & J. Churchil, and R. Sare, 1701.

Crastone, Giovanni. *Lexicon graeco–latinum.* Milan: Buono Accorso, 1476?

    Dictionarium graecum copiosissimum secundum ordine alphabeti, cum interpretatione latina. Ed. Scipio Carteromachus and Marcus Musurus. Venice: in aedibus Aldi Manutii, 1497.

    Dictionum graecarum thesaurus copiosus . . . Dictionum latinarum thesaurus cum graeca interpretatione. Ed. Johannes Maria Tricaelius. Ferrara: per Joannem Maciochum Bondenum, 1510.

    Dictionarium graecum, vltra Ferrariensem aeditionem locupletatum locis infinitis. Ed. Valentinus Curio. Basel: apud Andream Cartandrum, 1519.

    Dictionarium graecum. Venice: Melchior Sessa & Petrus de Ravanis, 1525.

Crato, Adam. *Geheimnis der Türken von jrer Religion / Kriegsmanier / . . . sampt einem Dictionario dreyer Sprachen: Lateinisch / Persisch / welches die vnsern*

Türckisch nennen / vnd Deutsch. Magdeburg: gedruckt durch Paul Donat in Vorlegung Ambrosij Kirchners, 1596.

Crusius, Martin. *Turcograeciae libri octo*. Basel: per Leonardum Ostenium, Sebastiani Henricpetri impensa, 1584.

Dalgarno, George. *Ars signorum, vulgo character universalis et lingua philosophica*. London: excudebat J. Hayes, sumptibus authoris, 1661.

George Dalgarno on universal language: The art of signs (1661), The deaf and dumb man's tutor (1680) and the unpublished papers. Ed. David Cram and Jaap Maat. Oxford: Oxford University Press, 2001.

Dasypodius, Petrus. *Dictionarium latinogermanicum, voces propemodum uniuersas in autoribus latinae linguae probatis ... explicans ... nunc autem reuisum, castigatu[m] & auctum ... [cum] germanicae dictiones iuxta seriem literarum digestae*. Strasburg: per Wendelinum Rihelium, 1536.

Davanzati, Bernardo. *Opere*. Ed. Enrico Bindi. 2 vols. Florence: Felice le Monnier, 1852–3.

Davies, John. *Antiquae linguae britannicae ... et linguae latinae dictionarium duplex*. London: R. Young, impensis J. Davies, 1632.

Dekker, Thomas. *Lanthorne and candle-light: or the bell-mans second nights-walke in which hee brings to light a broode of more strange villanies than euer were till this yeare discouered*. London: printed for Iohn Busby, 1608.

de la Bigne, Margarinus, *et al.*, eds. *Maxima bibliotheca veterum patrum et antiquorum scriptorum ecclesiasticorum*. 27 vols. [Earlier editions of 1575–9 onwards were published as *Sacra Bibliotheca / Bibliotheca veterum patrum*.] Lyons: apud Anissonios, 1677.

Dernschwam, Hans. *Tagebuch einer Reise nach Konstantinopel und Kleinasien (1553/55)*. Ed. Franz Babinger. Studien zur Fugger-Geschichte 7. Munich and Leipzig: Verlag von Duncker & Humblot, 1923.

De Smet, Bonaventure, ed. *De literis et lingua getarum siue gothorum; item de notis lombardicis, quibus accesserunt specimina variarum linguarum*. Leiden: ex officina Plantiniana, apud Franciscum Raphelengium, 1597.

Thesaurus utriusque linguae. Leiden: excudebat Ioannis Patius, 1600.

See also Aurelius (1586), Jordanes (1597), Nilus of Thessalonica (1595).

D'Ewes, Sir Simonds. *The autobiography and correspondence of Sir Simonds D'Ewes during the reigns of James I and Charles I*. Ed. James Orchard Halliwell. 2 vols. London: R. Bentley, 1845.

Diogenes Laertius. *De vitis, dogm[atis] & apophth[egmatis] clarorum philosophorum, libri x*. Hesychius. *De iisdem philos[ophis] & de aliis scriptoribus liber*. Anon. *Pythagor[eorum] philosophorum fragmenta*. Ed. Henri Estienne, with translations by Hadrianus Junius and others. [Geneva?]: excud[ebat] Henr[icus] Steph[anus], 1593.

Dionysius of Halicarnassus. *Responsio ad Gn. Pompeii epistolam*. Ed. Henri Estienne. Paris: apud Carolum Stephanum, 1554.

Scripta quae exstant omnia. Ed. Friedrich Sylburg. Frankfurt: apud haeredes Andreae Wecheli, 1586.

Dodsworth, Roger, and William Dugdale, eds. *Monasticon anglicanum, sive pandectae coenobiorum benedictinorum, cluniacensium, cisterciensium, carthusianorum, a primordiis ad eorum usque dissolutionem.* 3 vols. London: typis Richardi Hodgkinsonne, 1655; typis Aliciae Warren, 1661; excudebat Tho. Newcomb, & prostant venales Ab. Roper, Joh. Martin, & Hen. Herringman, 1673.

Dorat, Jean. 'Ad Robertum Stephanum typographum nobilissimum'. In Melchior Goldast, ed., *Philologicarum epistolarum centuria una diuersorum a renatis literis doctissimorum virorum.* Frankfurt: impensis Egenolphi Emmelii, 1610. 235–43.

Douglas, Gavin, trans. *The .xiii.* [sic: Douglas' translation includes Maffeo Vegio's additional book] *bukes of Eneados of the famose Poete Virgill translatet out of Latyne verses into Scottish meter.* London: [William Copland], 1553.

Dubois, Jacques. *Introduction à la langue française.* Ed. Colette Demaizière. Textes de la Renaissance 22. Paris: Honoré Champion, 1998.

du Cange, Charles. *Traité historique du chef de S. Iean Baptiste.* Paris: chez Sebastien Cramoisy et Sebastien Mabre-Cramoisy, imprimeurs du roi, 1665.

Glossarium ad scriptores mediae et infimae latinitatis. Paris: typis Gabrielis Martini, prostat apud Ludovicum Billaine, 1678.

Historia byzantina duplici commentario illustrata. Paris: apud Ludovicum Billaine, 1680.

Glossarium ad scriptores mediae et infimae graecitatis. Lyons: apud Anissonios, Joan. Posuel., & Claud. Rigaud, 1688.

Glossarium ad scriptores mediae et infimae latinitatis: editio nova locupletior et auctior, opera et studio monachorum ordinis S. Benedicti e congregatione S. Mauri. 6 vols. Paris: sub oliva Caroli Osmont, 1733–6.

Histoire de l'état de la ville d'Amiens et de ses comtes. Amiens: Duval et Herment, 1840.

Glossarium latinitatis. Ed. L. Favre. 10 vols. Niort: L. Favre, 1887.

du Cange, Charles, ed. See also Villehardouin (1657); Joinville (1668); Kinnamos (1670); Zonaras (1686–7); *Chronicon Paschale* (1688).

du Ferrier, Jérémie. *Le catholique d'estat: discours politique des alliances du Roy très-Chrestien contre les calomnies des ennemis de son estat.* Paris: chez Ioseph Bouillerot, 1625.

Dugdale, Sir William. *The antiquities of Warwickshire illustrated from records, leiger-books, manuscripts, charters, evidences, tombes and armes, beautified with maps, prospects and portraictures.* London: printed by Thomas Warren, 1656.

Life, diary and correspondence. Ed. William Hamper. London: printed for Harding, Lepard, and Co., 1827.

See also Dodsworth and Dugdale, eds., *Monasticon anglicanum* (1655–73).

Eliot, John. *Communion of churches.* Cambridge [MA]: printed by Marmaduke Johnson, 1665.

Epistolae academicae Oxon[ienses] part 1 (1421–1457). Ed. Henry Anstey. Oxford Historical Society 35. Oxford: for the Oxford Historical Society, 1898.

Erasmus, Desiderius. *Adagiorum chiliades quattuor cum sesquicenturia*. Ed. Henri Estienne. [Geneva]: oliua Roberti Stephani, 1558.

[*LB*]: *Desiderii Erasmi Roterodami opera omnia*. Ed. Jean Le Clerc. 10 vols. Leiden: cura & impensis Petri Vander Aa, 1703–6.

Opus epistolarum Desiderii Erasmi. Ed. P.S. Allen. 12 vols. Oxford: in typographeo Clarendoniano, 1906–58.

[*ASD*]: *Opera omnia Desiderii Erasmi Roterodami*. Amsterdam and Oxford: North-Holland Publishing Company [subsequently Amsterdam: Elsevier], 1969– .

[*CWE*]: *Collected works of Erasmus*. Toronto: University of Toronto Press, 1974– .

Estienne, Charles. *De re hortensi libellus*. 2nd edn. Paris: ex officina Rob[erti] Stephani, 1539.

Estienne, Henri. *Ciceronianum lexicon graecolatinum: id est, lexicon ex variis graecorum scriptorum locis a Cicerone interpretatis collectum*. [Geneva]: ex officina Henrici Stephani, 1557.

Traicté de la conformité du language françois auec le grec. [Geneva]: Henri Estienne, [1565].

Introduction au traité de la conformité des merveilles anciennes avec les modernes ou traité préparatif à l'apologie pour Hérodote. Antwerp: par Heinrich Wandellin, 1567.

Henrici Stephani epistola, qua ad multas multorum amicorum respondet, de suae typographiae statu, nominatimque de suo thesauro linguae graecae. [Geneva]: excudebat Henricus Stephanus, 1569.

'Index librorum qui ex officina Henrici Stephani hactenus prodierunt'. In *Epistola ... de suae typographiae statu*. Sigs. a1–b8.

[*TGL*]: Θησαυρος της Ἑλληνικης γλωσσης: *Thesaurus graecae linguae, ab Henrico Stephano constructus, in quo praeter alia plurima quae primus praestitit, (paternae in thesauro latino diligentiae aemulus) vocabula in certas classes distribuit, multiplici deriuatorum serie ad primigenia, tanquam ad radices vnde pullulant, reuocata*. 4 vols. [Geneva]: excudebat Henr[icus] Stephanus, 1572.

Francofordiense emporium sive Francofordienses nundinae. [Geneva]: excudebat Henricus Stephanus, 1574.

De latinitate falso suspecta, expostulatio Henrici Stephani; eiusdem de Plauti latinitate dissertatio, & ad lectionem illius progymnasma. [Geneva]: excudebat Henricus Stephanus, 1576.

'De Plauti latinitate dissertatio'. In *De latinitate falso suspecta* (1576). 363–400.

Pseudo-Cicero, dialogus: in hoc non solum de multis ad Ciceronis sermonem pertinentibus, sed etiam quem delectum editionum eius habere, & quam cautionem in eo legedo debeat adhibere, lector monebitur. [Geneva]: apud ipsum [i.e., Henricum] Stephanum, 1577.

Nizoliodidascalus, siue, monitor Ciceronianorum Nizolianorum, dialogus. [Geneva]: apud Henricum Stephanum, 1578.

Deux dialogues du nouveau langage françois italianizé, et autrement desguizé, principalement entre les courtisans de ce temps. [Geneva: Henri Estienne, 1578].

Proiect du livre intitulé De la precellence du langage françois. Paris: par Mamert Patisson imprimeur du Roy, 1579.

Hypomneses de gall[ica] lingua. [Geneva: H. Estienne], 1582.

'Noctes aliquot Parisinae, Atticis A. Gelli seu vigillis invigilatae'. Separately paginated in Gellius, *Noctes atticae* (1585).

Les premices, ou le I. livre des proverbes epigramatizez ou des epigrammes proverbializez. [Geneva?: by or for Henri Estienne], 1594.

Oratio ad augustiss[imum] caes[arem] Rodolphum II ... adversus lucubrationem Vberti Folietae de magnitudine & perpetua in bellis felicitate imperij Turcici [and] *Exhortatio ad expeditionem in Turcas fortiter & constanter persequendam.* Frankfurt: typis Wechelianis, 1594.

De Lipsii latinitate (ut ipsimet antiquarii antiquarium Lipsii stylum indigitant) palaestra I. Frankfurt: [for H. Estienne?], 1595.

Thesaurus graecae linguae, ab Henrico Stephano constructus, post editionem anglicam novis additamentis auctum, ordineque alphabetico digestum. Ed. Charles Benoît Hase, Wilhelm Dindorf and Ludwig August Dindorf. 8 vols. in 9. Paris: excudebat Ambrosius Firmin Didot, 1831–65.

Estienne, Henri, ed. *Fragmenta poetarum veterum latinorum, quorum opera non extant.* [Geneva]: excudebat Henricus Stephanus, illustris viri Huldrici Fuggeri typographus, 1564.

   Poetae graeci principes heroici carminis, et alii nonnulli. [Geneva]: excudebat Henricus Stephanus, 1566.

Estienne, Henri, ed. or trans. See also *Anacreontis Teii odae* (1554); Moschus, Bion and Theocritus (1555); Erasmus (1558); Sextus Empiricus (1562); pseudo-Cyrillus and pseudo-Philoxenus (1573); Gellius (1585); Macrobius (1585); St. Justin Martyr (1592); Isocrates (1593); Diogenes Laertius (1593).

Estienne, Robert. [*LLT* (1531)]: *Dictionarium, seu latinae linguae thesaurus: non singulas modo dictiones continens, sed integras quoque latine & loquendi, & scribendi formulas ex optimis quibusque authoribus accuratissime collectas, cum gallica fere interpretatione.* Paris: ex officina Roberti Stephani, 1531.

   [*LLT* (1536)]: *Dictionarium, seu latinae linguae thesaurus: non singulas modo dictiones continens, sed integras quoque latine & loquendi, & scribendi formulas – ex Catone, Cicerone, Plinio auunculo, Terentio, Varrone, Livio, Plinio secundo, Virgilio, Caesare, Columella, Plauto, Martiale – cum latine grammaticorum, tum varii generis scriptorum interpretatione.* Paris: ex officina Roberti Stephani, 1536.

   Dictionarium latinogallicum, thesauro nostro ita ex adverso respondens, ut extra pauca quædam aut obsoleta: aut minus in usu necessaria vocabula, & quas consulto praetermisimus, authorum appellationes, in hoc eadem sint omnia, eodem ordine, sermone patrio explicata. Paris: excudebat Robertus Stephanus in sua officina, 1538.

Libri in officina Rob[erti] Stephani partim nati, partim restituti & excusi. [Paris: Robert Estienne, 1542].

[*LLT* (1543)] *Dictionarium, seu latinae linguae thesaurus: non singulas modo dictiones continens sed integras quoque latine & loquendi, & scribendi formulas ex optimis quibusque authoribus, ea quidem nunc accessione, ut nihil propemodum observatu dignum sit apud oratores, historicos, poetas, omnis denique generis scriptores, quod hic non promptum paratumque habeat, editio secunda.* Paris: ex officina Roberti Stephani typographi regii, 1543.

Traicte de la gram[m]aire francoise. [Geneva]: l'olivier de Rob[ert] Estienne, [1557].

Concordantiae Testamenti Novi graecolatinae. 1594; rpt Geneva, in officina Samuelis Crispini, 1599.

Thesaurus linguae latinae in iv tomos divisus: cui post novissimam Londinensem editionem, complurium eruditorum virorum collectis curis insigniter auctam, accesserunt nunc primum Henrici Stephani. Ed. Antonius Birrius. Basel: typis & impensis E. & J.R. Thurnisiorum, 1740–3.

Estienne, Robert, ed., *Sententiae et proverbia ex omnibus Plauti & Terentii comoediis.* Paris: ex officina Roberti Stephani, 1530.

Novum Iesu Christi D. N. Testamentum. Paris: ex officina Roberti Stephani, 1550. See also Virgil (1532).

Eunapios. *De vitis philosophorum et sophistarum, nunc primum graece & latine editus.* Trans. Hadrianus Junius. Antwerp: ex officina C[hristophori] Plantini, 1568.

Expositiones antiquae ac valde utiles ... ab Oecumenio & Aretha collectae. Verona: apud Stephanum & fratres Sabios, 1532.

Fabrot, Charles Annibal. 'Glossarium siue interpretatio obscurorum uerborum Cedreni'. In Kedrenos, *Compendium historiarum.* Sigs. ī3v–ōōīv.

Ferrarius, Philippus. *Lexicon geographicum.* London: ex officina Rogeri Danielis, 1658.

Foxe, John. *The first volume of the ecclesiasticall history contaynyng the actes and monumentes of thynges passed in euery kynges tyme in this realme.* London: printed by Iohn Daye, 1570.

Foxe, John, ed. See also *Gospels* (1571).

Freher, Marquard, ed. *Foederis Ludovici Germaniae, & Caroli Galliae regum ... apud Argentoratum, anno 842 percussi, formulae.* [Heidelberg?], 1611. See also *Germanicarum rerum scriptores* (1611–37), Trithemius (1601).

Galland, Auguste. *Du franc-aleu et origine des droicts seigneuriaux.* Paris: chez Estienne Richer, 1637.

Garrick, David. 'Talk of war with a Briton'. *Public Advertiser*, 22 April 1755, 2.

Gelenius, Sigismundus. *Lexicon symphonum, quo quatuor linguarum europae familiarum, graecae scilicet, latinae, germanicae ac sclauinicae concordia consonantiaq[ue] indicatur.* Basel: apud Hieronymum Frobenium et Nicolaum Episcopium, 1537.

Gellius, Aulus. *Noctes atticae.* Ed. Henri Estienne. Paris: [for the editor], 1585.

Georgievitz, Bartholomaeus. *De afflictione tam captivorum quam etiam sub Turcae tributo viventium christianorum ... similiter de ritu, de caeremoniis domi militiaeq[ue] ab ea gente usurpatis, additis nonnullis lectu dignis, linguarum slavonicae et turcicae, cum interpretatione latina, libellus.* Worms: excudebat G. Comiander, 1545.

Germanicarum rerum scriptores aliquot insignes, hactenus incogniti, qui gesta sub regibus & imperatoribus teutonicis, iam inde a Karolo M[agno] vsque ad Fridericum III. Imp[eratorem] perpetua fere serie, suis quique seculis, litteris mandatas posteritati reliquerunt, tomus vnus [etc.]. Ed. Marquard Freher. 3 vols. Frankfurt: typis Wechelianis, apud Danielem & Dauidem Aubrios, & Clementem Schleichium, 1611–37.

Gessner, Conrad. *Pandectarum siue partitionum uniuersalium libri XXI.* Zürich: excudebat Christophorus Froschouerus, 1548.

Gessner, Conrad. *Elenchus scriptorum omnium.* Ed. Conrad Lycosthenes. Basel: Joannes Oporinus, 1551.

Mithridates: de differentiis linguarum tum veterum tum quae hodie apud diversas nationes in toto orbe terrarum in usu sunt . . . observationes. Zürich: excudebat Froschoverus, 1555.

Gibbon, Edward. *The history of the decline and fall of the Roman empire.* London: printed for W. Strahan and T. Cadell, 1776.

Gibson, Edmund. 'Life of Mr. Camden'. In Camden, *Britannia* (1695). Sigs. b1r–d2r. 'The life of Sir Henry Spelman Kt'. In Spelman, *Reliquiae Spelmannianae.* Sigs. b1r–d1v.

Godefroy, Denis, ed. *Auctores latinae linguae in unum redacti corpus.* Editio postrema. Geneva: apud Iohannem Vignon, 1622.

Goropius Becanus, Joannes. *Origines antwerpianae, siue, cimmeriorum becceselana nouem libros complexa: atuatica, I. gigantomachia, II. Niloscopium, III. Cronia, IV. indoscythica, V. saxsonica, VI. gotodanica, VII. amazonica, VIII. venetica, & hyperborea, IX.* Antwerp: ex officina Christophori Plantini, 1569.

Opera . . . hactenus in lucem non edita: nempe, Hermathena, hieroglyphica, Vertumnus, gallica, francica, hispanica. Antwerp: excudebat Christophorus Plantinus architypographus regius, 1580.

The Gospels of the fower Euangelistes translated in the olde Saxons tyme out of Latin into the vulgare toung of the Saxons, newly collected out of auncient monumentes of the sayd Saxons, and now published for testimonie of the same. Ed. John Foxe. London: printed by Iohn Daye, 1571.

Greaves, John, ed. *Epochae celebriores, astronomis, historicis, chronologis, chataiorum, syro-graecorum, arabum, persarum, chorasmiorum, usitatae ex traditione Ulug Beigi, Indiae citra extraque Gangem principis.* London: typis Jacobi Flesher, & prostant apud Cornelium Bee, 1650.

Greenwood, James. *Essay towards a practical English grammar.* London: printed by R. Tookey, and are sold by Samuel Keeble [*et al.*], 1711.

Gryphiander, Joannes. *De weichbildis saxonicis, sive colossis Rulandinis urbium quarundam saxonicarum.* Frankfurt: typis Egenolphi Emmelij, impensis Petri Kopffij & Balthasaris Ostern, 1625.

Guarino di Favera, ed. *Thesaurus cornucopiae.* Venice: in domum Aldi Romani, 1496.

Hakluyt, Richard, ed. *The principall nauigations, voiages and discoueries of the English nation.* London: [printed] by George Bishop and Ralph Newberie, deputies to Christopher Barker, printer to the Queenes most excellent Maiestie, 1589.

The principal nauigations, voyages, traffiques and discoueries of the English nation. 2nd edn. 3 vols. London: imprinted by George Bishop, Ralph Newberie, and Robert Barker, 1599–1600.

Hall, Joseph. *Holy obseruations lib. 1, also some fewe of Dauids psalmes metaphrased, for a taste of the rest.* London: printed by H. L[ownes] for Samuel Macham, 1607.

The discovery of a new world. Trans. John Healey [from Hall's Latin *Mundus alter et idem*]. Ed. H. Brown. Cambridge, MA: Harvard University Press, 1937.

Hare, John. *St. Edwards ghost, or anti-Normanisme: being a patheticall complaint and motion in the behalfe of our English nation against her grand (yet neglected) grievance, Normanisme.* London: printed for Richard Wodenothe, 1647.

Harpocration. *Dictionarium in decem rhetores.* Ed. Philippe Jacques de Maussac. Paris: apud Claudium Morellum, 1614.

Hearne, Thomas, ed. *A collection of curious discourses written by eminent antiquaries upon several heads in our English antiquities.* Oxford: printed at the theater, 1720.

Henisch, Georg. *Teütsche Sprach vnd Weißheit / Thesaurus linguae et sapientiae germanicae: pars prima.* Augsburg: typis Davidis Franci, 1616.

Hephaestion. Εγχειρίδιον. Paris: apud Adrianum Turnebum typographum regium, 1553.

Hepp, Johannes Michael. *Parallelismus & convenientia* XII *lingvarum, ex matrice scytho-celtica.* [Wittenberg dissertation, *praeses* Georg Caspar Kirchmayer]. Wittenberg: prelo Schrödteriano, acad[emiae] typ[ographo], 1697.

Herrauds och Bosa saga. Ed. Olaus Verelius. Uppsala: excudit Henricus Curio, s[ueciae] r[egis] m[aiestatis] & acad[emiae] Vps[aliae] bibliop[ola], 1666.

Hesychius of Alexandria. Λεξικον *cum variis doctorum virorum notis.* Ed. Cornelius Schrevelius. Leiden and Rotterdam: ex officina Hackiana, 1668.

Lexicon, cum notis doctorum virorum integris, vel editis antehac, nunc auctis & emendatis, Hadr[iani] Junii, Henr[ici] Stephani, Jos[ephi] Scaligeri, Claud[ii] Salmasii, . . . etc. Ed. J. Alberti with David Ruhnken. 2 vols. Leiden: apud Samuelem Luchtmans et filium, academiae typographos, 1746–66.

Hesychius of Miletus. *De his qui eruditionis fama claruere.* Trans. Hadrianus Junius. Antwerp: ex officina Christophori Plantini prototypographi regii, 1572.

Περὶ τῶν ἐν παιδεια̣ διαλαμπσάντων σοφων. Ed. Janus Sambucus. Antwerp: ex officina Christophori Plantini prototypographi regii, 1572.

Opuscula, partim hactenus non edita, cum notis. Ed. Johannes Meursius. Leiden: ex officina Godefridi Basson, 1613.

See also Diogenes Laertius (1593).

Hickes, George, ed. *Linguarum veterum septentrionalium thesaurus grammatico-criticus et archaeologicus.* 2 vols. Oxford: e theatro Sheldoniano, 1703–5.

Historiae anglicanae scriptores x ... ex vetustis manuscriptis nunc primum in lucem editi. Adiectis variis lectionibus, glossario, indiceque copioso. Ed. Roger Twysden. London: typis Jacobi Flesher, sumptibus Cornelii Bee, apud quem prostant voenales, 1652.

Historiae normannorum scriptores antiqui. Ed. André Du Chesne. Paris: apud Robertum Foüet, Nicolaum Buon, Sebastianum Cramoisy, 1619.

The history of the troubles and tryal of William Laud. Ed. Henry Wharton. London: printed for R[ichard] Chiswell, 1695.

Holme, Randle. *The academy of armory, or, a storehouse of armory and blazon: containing the several variety of created beings, and how born in coats of arms, both foreign and domestick, with the instruments used in all trades and sciences, together with their terms of art, also the etymologies, definitions, and historical observations on the same, explicated and explained according to our modern language.* Chester: printed for the author, 1688.

    The academy of armory, or, a store-house of armory and blazon ... second volume. Ed. I. H. Jeayes [from BL Harleian MSS 2033–2035]. London: Roxburghe Club, 1905.

Holyoake, Thomas. *A large dictionary in three parts.* London: printed by W. Rawlins for G. Sawbridge [*et al.*], 1676.

Houtman, Frederick de. *Spraeck- ende woord-boek inde Maleysche Madagaskarsche talen.* Amsterdam: by Jan Ebertsz. Cloppenburch, 1603.

Ihre, Johann. *Glossarium Suiogothicum.* Uppsala: typis Edmannianis, 1769.

'Index codicum manuscriptorum bibliothecae Peutingerianae in collegium soc[ietatis] Iesu ad S. Saluatorem Augustae Vindelicorum'. *Journal zur Kunstgeschichte und zur allgemeinen Litteratur* 2 (1784): 311–18.

Irenodia Cantabrigiensis ob paciferum serenissimi Regis Caroli e Scotia reditum mense Novembri 1641. [Cambridge]: ex officina Rogeri Daniel, almae academiae typographi, 1641.

Isocrates. *Orationes et epistolae.* Ed. Henri Estienne and trans. Hieronymus Wolf. [Geneva]: excudebat Henricus Stephanus, 1593.

Itinerarium B. Antonini martyris de membranis veteribus descriptum, e musaeo Cl. Menardi, cum notationibus aliquot uocum obscurarum. Angers: apud Petrum Avril typographum, 1640.

Jäger, Andreas. *De lingua vetustissima europae, scytho-celtica et gothica.* [Wittenberg dissertation, *praeses* Georg Caspar Kirchmaier]. Wittenberg: typis Christiani Schrödteri, acad[emiae] typ[ographi], 1686.

James, Thomas. *Bellum Gregorianum.* Oxford: excudebat Josephus Barnesius, 1610.

Johnson, Samuel. 'Life of Dr. Boerhaave'. *Gentleman's Magazine* 9 (1739): 72–3, 114–16 and 172–6.

    The plan of a dictionary of the English language. London: for J. and P. Knapton *et al.*, 1747.

    The adventurer. London: printed for J. Payne, 1753.

A dictionary of the English language. London: W. Strahan for J. and P. Knapton [*et al.*], 1755.

Joinville, Jean de. *Histoire de S. Louys IX du nom roy de France, enrichie de nouuelles obseruations & dissertations historiques, avec les établissemens de S. Louys, le conseil de Pierre de Fontaines, & plusieurs autres pieces concernant ce regne, tirées des manuscrits.* Ed. Charles du Cange. Paris: chez Sebastien Mabre-Cramoisy, imprimeur du Roy, 1668.

Jordanes. *De getarum, siue gothorum origine & rebus gestis.* Isidore. *Chronicon gothorum, vandalorum, sueuorum, & wisogothorum.* Procopius. *Fragmentum, de priscis sedibus & migrationibus gothorum.* Ed. Bonaventure de Smet. Leiden: ex officina Plantiniana, apud Franciscum Raphelengium, 1597.

Julian the Apostate. 'Epistola ad Alexandrinos'. Ed. Nicolas Rigault. In Rigault, *Funus parasiticum.* Paris: apud Claudium Morellum, 1601. 1–14 [second sequence of pagination].

Junius, Franciscus. *Observationes in Willerami abbatis francicam paraphrasin Cantici Canticorum.* Amsterdam: apud Christophorum Cunradi, typis & sumtibus authoris, 1655.

Gothicum glossarium quo Argentei Codicis vocabula explicantur & illustrantur. Dordrecht: excudebant Henricis & Joannes Essaei, urbis typographi ordinarii, 1664. Issued with Franciscus Junius and Thomas Marshall, eds., *Quatuor D.N. Jesu Christi euangeliorum versiones perantiquae duae.*

Etymologicum anglicanum ex autographo [descriptum] & accessionibus permultis auctum [editum] ... praemittuntur vita auctoris et grammatica Anglo-Saxonica. Ed. Edward Lye. Oxford: e theatro Sheldoniano, 1743.

Dictionarium saxonico et gothico–latinum; accedunt fragmenta versionis Ulphilanae, necnon opuscula quaedam anglo-saxonica. Ed. Edward Lye and Owen Manning. London: Edm[und] Allen, 1772.

[Correspondence]: 'For my worthy freind Mr Franciscus Junius': an edition of the correspondence of Franciscus Junius F.F. (1591–1677). Ed. Sophie van Romburgh. Brill's Studies in Intellectual History 121. Leiden and Boston: E. J. Brill, 2004.

Junius, Franciscus, and Thomas Marshall, eds. *Quatuor D.N. Jesu Christi euangeliorum versiones perantiquae duae, gothica scil. et anglo-saxonica: quarum illam ex celeberrimo Codice Argenteo nunc primum depromsit Franciscus Junius F.F, hanc autem ex codicibus mss. collati emendatius recudi curavit Thomas Mareschallus, Anglus, cuius etiam observationes in utramque subnectuntur.* Dordrecht: typis & sumptibus Junianis, excudebat Henricus & Joannes Essaei, 1665.

Junius, Hadrianus. *De anno et mensibus commentarius, cui adiungitur fastorum liber.* Basel: per Henrichum Petri, 1553.

Adagiorum centuriae VIII cum dimidia. Basel: Froben, 1558.

Nomenclator: omnium rerum propria nomina variis linguis explicata indicans. Antwerp: ex officina Christophori Plantini, 1567.

The nomenclator, or remembrancer, written in Latine, Greeke, French and other forrein tongues: and now in English. Trans. John Higins. London: imprinted for Ralph Newberie and Henrie Denham, 1585.

Batavia: in qua praeter gentis & insulae antiquitatem, originem, decora, mores aliaque ad eam historiam pertinentia, declaratur quae fuerit vetus Batavia, quae Plinio, Tacito & Ptolemaeo cognita, quae item genuina inclytae francorum nationis fuerit sedes. Leiden: ex officina Plantiniana, apud Franciscum Raphelengium, 1588.

Nomenclator, communium rerum propria nomina gallico idiomate indicans, multo quam antea brevior & emendatior: en cette dernière édition a esté adioustée la langue Bretonne, correspondante à la Latine & Françoise. Ed. Guillaume Quiquier. Morlaix: chez G. Allienne, 1633.

Junius, Hadrianus, trans. See Eunapios (1568), Hesychius of Miletus (1572).

St Justin Martyr, *Epist[ola] ad Diognetu[m], & Oratio ad graecos.* Ed. Henri Estienne. [Geneva]: excudebat Henricus Stephanus, 1592.

Kantakouzenos, Ioannes. *Historiarum libri* IV, graece nunc primum prodeunt ex cod. MS. 500 bibliothecae Petri Seguierii. Trans. Jacobus Pontanus with a commentary by him and Jakob Gretser. Paris: e typographia regia, 1645–6.

Kedrenos, Georgios. *Compendium historiarum.* Ioannes Skylitzes *[Synopsis historiarum] nunc primum graece editus.* Trans. Guilielmus Xylander with a commentary by him and Jacobus Goar, and a glossary by Charles Annibal Fabrot. Paris: e typographia regia, 1647.

Kennett, White. 'The life of Mr. Somner'. In William Somner, *A treatise of the Roman ports and forts in Kent.* Ed. James Brome. Oxford: printed at the theater, 1693. 1–120.

Parochial antiquities attempted in the history of Ambrosden, Burcester and other adjacent parts in the counties of Oxon and Bucks. Oxford: printed at the theater, 1695.

Kiel, Cornelis. *Dictionarium tetraglotton, seu voces latinae omnes, et graecae eis respondentes, cum gallica & teutonica (quam passim flandricam vocant) earum interpretatione.* Antwerp: ex officina Christophori Plantini, sumptib[us] haeredum Arnoldi Bierckmanni, 1562.

Dictionarium teutonico–latinum, praecipuas linguae teutonicae dictiones latine interpretatas, seduloq[ue] cum germanicis & gallicis collatas, breuiter complectens. Antwerp: apud Christophorum Plantinum, 1574.

Etymologicum teutonicae linguae, sive dictionarium teutonico–latinum, praecipuas teutonicae linguae dictiones et phrases latine interpretatas, & cum aliis nonnullis linguis obiter collatas complectens ... opus germanis tam superioribus quam inferioribus, gallis, anglis siue anglosaxonibus, italis, hispanis & aliis lectu perutile. Antwerp: ex officina Plantiniana, apud Ioannem Moretum, 1599.

Kinnamos, Ioannes. *Historiarum libri sex, seu de rebus gestis a Joanne et Manuele Comnenis imp[eratoribus].* Paulus Silentiarios. *Descriptio Sanctae Sophiae, quae nunc primum prodit graece & latine, cum vberiori commentario.* Ed. Charles du Cange, with his 'notae historicae & philologicae' on Nikephoros Bryennios, Anna Comnene and Ioannes Kinnamos. Paris: e typographia regia, 1670.

Kircher, Athanasius, ed. and trans. 'Nomenclator aegyptiaco–arabicus, cum interpretatio latina'. In *Lingua aegyptiaca restituta*. Rome: sumptibus Hermanni Scheus, 1644. 41–493.

Knyghthode and bataile: A xvth century verse paraphrase of Flavius Vegetius Renatus' treatise 'De re militari'. Ed. Roman Dyboski and Zygfryd Marjan Arend. EETS 201. London: for the Early English Text Society, 1935.

Labbé, Philippe. *Nova bibliotheca mss. librorum*. Paris: apud Ioannem Henault, 1653.

Labbé, Philippe, ed. *Nova bibliotheca manuscript[orum] librorum*. [A different work, not a second edition of the *Nova bibliotheca* of 1653.] Paris: apud Sebastianum Cramoisy, regis et reginae architypographum, et Gabrielem Cramoisy, 1657.

Lambarde, William. *Dictionarium Angliae topographicum et historicum / An alphabetical description of the chief places in England and Wales*. London: for Fletcher Gyles, 1730.

Lambarde, William, ed. [with Laurence Nowell] and trans. Αρχαιονομια, *siue de priscis anglorum legibus libri sermone anglico, vetustate antiquissimo, aliquot abhinc seculis conscripti, atq[ue] nunc demum, magno iurisperitorum, & amantium antiquitatis omnium commodo, e tenebris in lucem vocati.* London: ex officina Ioannis Daij, 1568.

Αρχαιονομια ... *sexcentis in locis castigata ... cum multis aliis additionibus; accessere in hac nostra ultima editione leges Henrici primi nunc primum editae, ex manuscripto in fisco regis habito, una cum glossario earum antiquo ex manuscripto codice olim S. Augustini Doroborniensis.* Revised Abraham Wheelock [and Sir Roger Twysden]. Cambridge: ex officina Rogeri Daniel, celeberrimae Academiae typographi, 1644.

Leibniz, Gottfried Wilhelm von. *Otium hanoueranum, sive miscellanea ex ore & schedis illustris viri, piae memoriae, Godofr[idi] Guilielmi Leibnitii.* Leipzig: impensis Joann[is] Christiani Martini, 1718.

'Vita Leibnitii a se ipso breviter delineata'. In *Nouvelles lettres et opuscules.* Ed. A. Foucher de Careil. Paris: Auguste Durand, 1857. 379–86.

Sämtliche Schriften und Briefe. Darmstadt etc.: Akademie Verlag, 1923– .

Leland, John. *Naeniae in mortem Thomas Wyattis*. London: ad signem aenei serpentis [i.e., R. Wolfe], 1542.

Genethliacon illustrissimi Eäduerdi principis Cambriae, ducis Coriniae, et comitis palatini libellus ante aliquot annos inchoatus, nunc uero absolutus, & editus. London: apud Reynerum Wolfium, 1543.

Assertio inclytissimi Arturij regis Britanniae. London: apud Ioannem Herford, 1544.

Κυκνειον ασμα: *Cygnea cantio*. London: [R. Wolfe], 1545.

De rebus Britannicis collectanea. Ed. Thomas Hearne. 6 vols. Oxford: e theatro Sheldoniano, 1715.

Leland, John, and John Bale. *The laboryouse iourney & serche of Iohan Leylande for Englandes antiquitees, geuen of hym as a newe yeares gyfte to Kyng Henry the VIII in the XXXVII yeare of his reygne.* [London: by S. Mierdman for John Bale], 1549.

Lex frisionum sive antiquae frisiorum leges, a reliquis veterum germanorum legibus separatim aeditae & notis illustrata. Ed. Sibrandus Siccama. Franeker: apud Ioannem Lamrinck, ordinum Frisiae typogr[aphum], 1617.

Liber legis salicae; glossiarvm sive interpretatio rerum & verborum obscuriorum quae in ea lege habentur. Ed. François Pithou and Friedrich Lindenbrog. Paris: apud Iacobum Rezé, 1602.

Lindenbrog, Friedrich, ed. See *Codex legum antiquarum* (1613) and *Liber legis salicae* (1602).

Lipsius, Justus. *Epistolarum selectarum centuria tertia ad Belgas.* Antwerp: ex officina Plantiniana, apud Ioannem Moretum, 1602.

Lisle, William. 'To the readers'. In Ælfric, *Saxon treatise* (1623). Sigs. b1r–f4v.

Littleton, Adam. *Linguae latinae liber dictionarius quadripartitus.* London: printed for T. Basset *et al.*, 1678.

[Lodwick, Francis]. *A common writing, whereby two, although not understanding one the others language, yet by the helpe thereof, may communicate their minds one to another* [London]: for the Author, 1647 [really 1646].

    The ground-work or foundation laid (or so intended) for the framing of a new perfect language. [London: for the author?, 1652].

Lučić, Ivan, ed. *De regno Dalmatiae et Croatiae libri sex.* Amsterdam: apud Joannem Blaeu, 1666.

Lydius, Johann Martin. 'Glossarium latinobarbarum'. In Nicolas de Clamanges, *Opera omnia: accessit ejusdem glossarium latinobarbarum cum indice locupletissimo.* Ed. Johann Martin Lydius. Leiden: apud Iohannem Balduinum, impensis Lud[ovici] Elzeuirij & Henr[ici] Laurencij, 1613. 35–86 [3rd sequence of pagination].

Maaler, Josua. *Die Teütsch Spraach / Dictionarium germanicolatinum novum.* Zürich: excudebat Christophorus Froschouerus, 1561. Rpt Hildesheim: Georg Olms Verlag, 1971.

Mabillon, Jean. *De re diplomatica libri* vi. Paris: sumtibus Ludovici Billaine, in palatio regio, 1681.

MacCurtin, Hugh. *A brief discourse in vindication of the antiquity of Ireland, collected out of many authentick Irish histories and chronicles, and out of foreign learned authors.* Dublin: printed by S. Powell for the author, 1717.

    The elements of the Irish language, grammatically explained in English. Louvain: printed by Martin van Overbeke, 1728.

MacCurtin, Hugh, and Conor O'Begley. *The English Irish dictionary / An focloir bearla Gaoidheilge.* Paris: ar na chur acclodh le Seamus Guerin, 1732.

Macrobius. *In somnium Scipionis libri* ii [and] *Conuiuiorum saturnaliorum libri* vii. Ed. Henri Estienne. Paris: [for the editor], 1585.

    De verborum graeci et latini differentiis vel societatibus excerpta. Ed. Paolo de Paolis. Urbino: Quattro Venti, 1990.

[Madoets, André]. *Thesaurus theutonicae linguae / Schat der Nederduytscher spraken, inhoudende niet alleene de Nederduytsche woorden maer oock verscheyden redenen en manieren van spreken, vertaelt ende ouergeset int Fransois ende Latijn / Thresor du langage Bas-alman, dict vulgaireme[n]t*

Flameng, traduict en François & en Latin. Antwerp: ex officina Christophori Plantini prototypographi regij, 1573.

Magnus, Johannes. *Historia de omnibus gothorum sueonumque regibus.* Ed. Olaus Magnus. Rome: apud Ioannem Mariam de Viottis, 1554.

Magnus, Olaus. *Historia de gentibus septentrionalibus earumque diuersis statibus, conditionibus, moribus, ritibus, superstitionibus, disciplinis, exercitiis, regimine, victu, bellis, structuris, instrumentis, ac mineris metallicis, & rebus mirabilibus, necnon vniuersis pene animalibus in septentrione degentibus, eorumque natura.* Rome: apud Ioannem Mariam de Viottis, 1555.

Maittaire, Michael. *Stephanorum historia, vitas ipsorum ac libros complectens.* London: typis B. Motte, impensis C. Bateman, 1709.

Makrembolites, Eustathios. *De Ismeniae et Ismenes amoribus libri* XI. Ed. and trans. Gilbert Gaulmyn. Paris: sumptibus Hieronymi Drouart, 1618.

Malmenius, Andreas A. *Reliqui[ae] linguae Geticae* [Uppsala dissertation, *praeses* Johann Ihre]. Uppsala: excud[ebat] L. M. Höjer, reg[ii] acad[emiae] typogr[aphus], 1758.

Mancinelli, Antonio. *Epitoma seu regulae constructionis.* Venice: per Ioannem Rostium, 1492.

Manutius, Aldus. *Aldo Manuzio editore: Dediche, prefazioni, note ai testi.* Ed. Giovanni Orlandi. 2 vols. Milan: Edizioni il Polifilo, 1975.

Marcus Aurelius. *Meditations concerning himselfe treating of a naturall mans happinesse.* Trans. and comm. Meric Casaubon. London: printed by M. Flesher for Richard Mynne, 1634.

Marrier, Martin, and André Duchesne, eds. *Bibliotheca cluniacensis.* Paris: sumptibus Roberti Fouet, 1614.

'Matthew of Westminster'. *Florilegus.* London: ex officina Thomae Marshij, 1570.

Megiser, Hieronymus. *Dictionarium quatuor linguarum, videlicet germanicae, latinae, illyricae (quae vulgo sclavonica appellatur) & italicae, sive hetruscae.* Graz: a Iohanne Fabro, 1592.

    Specimen quinquaginta diversarum atque inter se differentium linguarum et dialectorum, videlicet Oratio Dominica et quaedam alia ex sacris literis, totidem linguis expressis. Frankfurt am Main: apud Ioachimum Bratheringium, 1603.

    Thesaurus polyglottus vel dictionarium multilingue, ex quadringentis circiter tam veteris quam novi (vel potius antiquis incogniti) orbis nationum linguis, dialectis, idiomatibus & idiotismis constans. Frankfurt am Main: [Joachim Brathering?], sumptibus authoris, 1603.

    'Dictionarium der Madagarischen Sprach'. In *Warhafftige, gründliche und ausführliche, so wol historische als chorographische Beschreibung der ... Insul Madagascar. ... Samt ... angehengtem Dictionario und Dialogis der Madagascarischen Sprach.* Altenburg: gedruckt in vorlegung Henning Grossen deß jüng[eres], 1609.

Institutionum linguae turcicae libri quatuor . . . quorum IV dictionarium est latino–turcicum et vicissim turcico–latinum. Leipzig: sumptibus authoris, 1612.

Mémoire sur les manuscrits de M. Du Cange. [N.p.]: 1752.

Ménage, Gilles. *Les origines de la langue françoise.* Paris: chez Augustin Courbe, 1650.

Meursius, Joannes. *Criticus Arnobianus tributus in libros septem; item hypocriticus Minutianus.* Leiden: ex officina Ludovici Elzevirii, 1598.

— *Criticus Arnobianus tributus in libros septem, editio altera, et melior.* Leiden: ex officina Ludovici Elzevirii, 1599.

— *Glossarium graeco-barbarum: in quo praeter vocabula amplius ter mille sexcenta, officia atque dignitates imperii Constantinop[olitani] tam in palatio, quam ecclesia aut militia, explicantur et illustrantur.* Leiden: ex officina Thomae Basson, 1610.

— *Glossarium graeco-barbarum: in quo praeter vocabula quinque millia quadringenta, officia atque dignitates imperii Constantinop[olitani] tam in palatio, quam ecclesia aut militia, explicantur et illustrantur. Editio altera, emendata, et circiter MDCCC vocabulis aucta.* Leiden: apud Ludovicum Elzevirium, 1614.

— *Theophrastus: sive de illius libris, qui injuria temporis interciderunt.* Leiden: ex officina Elseviriana, 1640.

Meursius, Joannes, ed. See Diogenes Laertius (1593).

Minsheu, John. *A catalogue and true note of the names of such persons which haue receaued the etymologicall dictionarie of XI. languages.* [London: by Edward Allde, available] at Mr [John] Brownes a booke-binder [12 variants issued between 1616 and 1621].

— Ηγεμων εις τας γλωσσας: *id est, ductor in linguas, the guide into tongues: cum illarum harmonia, & etymologijs, originationibus, rationibus, & deriuationibus in omnibus his vndecim linguis, viz: 1. anglica. 2. cambro-britanica. 3. belgica. 4. germanica. 5. gallica. 6. italica. 7. hispanica. 8. lusitanica seu portugallica. 9. latina. 10. graeca. 11. hebrea.* [London: printed by William Stansby and Eliot's Court Press] cum gratia & priuilegio regiae maiestatis, & vendibiles extant . . . apud Ioannem Browne bibliopolam, 1617.

More, Thomas. *The correspondence of Sir Thomas More.* Ed. Elizabeth Frances Rogers. Princeton, NJ: Princeton University Press, 1947.

Morris, John. *Correspondence of John Morris with Johannes de Laet (1634–1649).* Ed. Johannes A. F. Bekkers. Assen: Van Gorcum, 1970.

Moschus, Bion and Theocritus. *Idyllia.* Trans. Henri Estienne. Venice: Aldus, 1555.

Münster, Sebastian. *Cosmographei.* Intro. Ruthardt Oehme. Mirror of the World 1st ser. vol. 5. 1550; rpt Amsterdam: Theatrum Orbis Terrarum, 1968.

Musarum Oxoniensium Ελαιοφορία, *sive, ob faedera auspiciis serenissimi Oliveri.* Oxford: excudebat Leonardus Lichfield, academiae typographus, 1654.

Museum Wormianum, seu historia rerum rariorum, tam naturalium, quam artificialium, tam domesticarum, quam exoticarum, quae Hafniae Danorum in aedibus authoris servantur. Leiden: ex officina Elseviriorum, 1655.

Narrationes modernae, or, modern reports begun in the now upper bench court at Westminster in the beginning of Hillary term 21 Caroli, and continued to the end of Michaelmas term 1655. Ed. William Style. London: printed by F[rancis] L[each] for W. Lee, D. Pakeman, G. Bedel, and C. Adams, 1658.

Nicolson, William. *English historical library.* 3 vols. London: printed for Abel Swall, 1696–9.

Nilus of Thessalonica. *De primatu papae romani libri duo.* With [anonymous]. *De igne purgatorio.* Ed. Bonaventure de Smet. Leiden: ex officina Plantiniana, apud Franciscum Raphelengium, 1595.

Nizzoli, Mario, ed. *Dictionarium seu thesaurus latinae linguae . . . omnibus mendis diligenter expurgatus & locupletatus.* [Based on the work of Robert Estienne.] Venice: ex Sirenis officina, 1551.

Nowell, Laurence. *Vocabularium saxonicum.* Ed. Albert H. Marckwardt. Ann Arbor: University of Michigan Press, 1952.

Ortelius, Abraham. *Epistulae, cum aliquot aliis epistulis et tractatibus quibusdam ab utroque collectis (1524–1628).* Ed. John Henry Hessels. Cambridge: typis academiae, sumptibus ecclesiae Londino-Batavae, 1887.

Album amicorum. Facs. edn., trans. and comm. Jean Puraye. Amsterdam: A. L. Van Gendt & Co., 1969.

Otfrid of Weissenberg. *Euangeliorum liber: ueterum Germanorum grammaticae, poeseos, theologiae, praeclarum monimentum / Euangelien Buch, in altfrenckischen reimen . . . vor sibenhundertjaren beschriben, jetz aber mit gunst dess gestrenge ehrenuesten herrn Adolphen Herman Riedesel, Erbmarschalck zu Hessen, der alten Teutschen spraach vnd gottsforcht zuerlerne, in truck verfertiget.* Ed. Matthias Flacius Illyricus. Basel: [n.p.], 1571.

Paris, Matthew. *Historia maior, a Guilielmo Conquaestore, ad vltimum annum Henrici tertij.* London: excusum apud Reginaldum Wolfium, regiae maiest[atis] in Latinis typographum, 1571.

Peer, Petreius. *Een kort och nyttigh chrönica om alla Swerikis och Göthis konungar, som hafwa både in och vthrijkis regerat, ifrån then första konung Magogh, in til . . . nu regerande konungh Carl then IX.* Stockholm: Ch[ristoffer] Reusner, 1611.

Pepys, Samuel. *Naval minutes.* Ed. J. R. Tanner, Publications of the Navy Records Society 60. London: for the Navy Records Society, 1926.

Diary. Ed. R. C. Latham and W. Matthews. 11 vols. London: G. Bell and Sons, 1970–83.

Pepys, Samuel, and John Evelyn. *Particular friends: the correspondence of Samuel Pepys and John Evelyn.* Ed. Guy de la Bedoyère. Woodbridge, UK: Boydell Press, 1997.

Périon, Joachim. *Dialogorum de linguae gallicae origine, eiusque cum graeca cognatione, libri quatuor.* Paris: apud Sebastianum Niuellium, 1555.

Petrarch. *Epistolae de rebus senilibus xv.* In *Opera quae extant omnia.* Basel: excudebat Henricus Petri, 1554. 1046–65.

Petty, Sir William. *The Petty papers: Some unpublished writings of Sir William Petty edited from the Bowood papers.* Ed. Henry, Marquis of Lansdowne. 2 vols. London: Constable, 1927.

Philoponus, John. *On the accent of homonyms*. Ed. Lloyd W. Daly. Memoirs of the American Philosophical Society 151. Philadelphia: American Philosophical Society, 1983.

Pithou, François. 'Excerpta Pythoeana ex veteribus glossis'. In Godefroy, *Auctores latinae linguae* (1622). Appendix, cols. 33–80.

Pithou, François, ed. See *Liber legis salicae* (1602).

Pithou, Pierre, ed. *Annalium et historiae francorum ab anno Christi DCCVIII ad ann[um] DCCCCXC scriptores coaetanei XII*. Paris: apud Claudium Chappelet, 1588.

Plantin, Christophe. *Correspondance*. Maatschappij der Antwerpsche bibliophilen, uitgave nr 12, 15, 26, 29–34. Ed. Max Rooses (vols. I–III) and J. Denucé (vols. IV–IX). 9 vols. Antwerp: J.E. Buschmann (vols. I–II) and Antwerp: De Nederlandsche boekhandel; The Hague: M. Nijhoff (vols. III–IX), 1883–1918.

Pontanus, Jacobus. *Symbolarum libri* XVII Virgilii. Augsburg: ex officina typographica Ioann[nis] Praetorii, 1599.

'A proclamation touching D. *Cowels* booke called the Interpreter'. In *A booke of proclamations published since the beginning of his Maiesties most happy reigne ouer England, &c. vntill this present moneth of Febr. 3. anno Dom. 1609*. London: by Robert Barker, printer to the Kings most excellent maiestie, 1613. 225–7.

pseudo-Cyrillus and pseudo-Philoxenus. *Glossaria duo, e situ vetustatis eruta: ad utriusque linguae cognitionem et locupletationem perutilia*. Ed. Henri Estienne. With H. Estienne, 'De Atticae linguae seu dialecti idiomatis comment[arius]'. [Geneva]: excudebat Henr. Stephanus, 1573.

   Glossaria latino–graeca, & graeco–latina in duplicem alphabeticum ordinem redacta, cum variis emendationibus ex mss. codd. petitis, virorumque doctorum castigationibus ac conjectaneis: his accedunt glossae aliquot aliae latino–graecae ex iisdem codd. mss. quae nunc primum prodeunt. Ed. Charles Labbé; prepared for publication by Charles du Cange. Paris: cura & impensis Ludovici Billaine, 1679.

pseudo-Kodinos. *De officialibus palatii Constantinopolitani & officiis magnae ecclesiae*. Ed. Nadabus Agmonius, i.e., François du Jon the elder. [Heidelberg: apud I. Mareschallum], 1588.

   De officiis magnae ecclesiae et aulae constantinopolitanae. Ed. Jakob Gretser. *Notitiae graecorum episcopatuum*. Ed. Jacobus Goar. Paris: e typographia regia, 1648.

Rastell, John. *Exposicio[n]es t[er]mi[n]or[um] legu[m] anglor[um] ... collectis & breuit[er] compilatis p[ro] iuuinib[us] valde necessariis / The exposicions of [the] termys of [the] law of england ... gaderyd and breuely compyled for yong men very necessarye*. London: [J. Rastell, c. 1524].

Ray, John. *A collection of English proverbs: digested into a convenient method for the speedy finding any one upon occasion, with short annotations: whereunto are added local proverbs with their explications, old proverbial rhythmes, less known or exotick proverbial sentences, and Scottish proverbs ... enlarged by the addition of many hundred English, and appendix of Hebrew proverbs, with annotations and parallels*. 2nd edn. Cambridge: printed by John Hayes, printer to the university, for W. Worden, 1678.

Rerum anglicarum scriptores post Bedam praecipui, ex vetustissimis codicibus manuscriptis nunc primum in lucem editi. Ed. Sir Henry Savile. London: excudebant G[eorgius] Bishop, R[adulphus] Nuberie, & R[obertus] Barker typographi regij deputati, 1596.

Rerum anglicarum scriptores post Bedam praecipui, ex vetustissimis codicibus manuscriptis nunc primum in lucem editi. Ed. Sir Henry Savile. [A piracy of the above.] Frankfurt: typis Wechelianis apud Claudium Marnium & heredes Ioannis Aubrij, 1601.

Rhenanus, Beatus. *Briefwechsel.* Ed. Adalbert Horowitz and Karl Hartfelder. 1886; rpt Hildesheim: Georg Olms, 1966.

Rigault, Nicolas. *Glossarium* τακτικὸν μιξοβάρβαρον: *de verborum significatione, quae ad novellas imp[eratorum] qui in Oriente post Iustinianum regnauerunt, de re militari constitutiones pertinent.* Paris: apud Claudium Morellum, 1601.

Rigault, Nicolas, ed. See Commodianus (1650), Julian the Apostate (1601).

Rivola, Francesco. *Dictionarium armeno–latinum.* Milan: ex typogr[aphia] Collegii Ambrosiani, 1621.

Dictionarium armeno–latinum. Paris: [excudebat Antonius Vitray] impensis societis typographicae librorum officij ecclesiastici, iussu regis constitutae, 1633.

Ronsard, Pierre. *Les oeuvres de P. de Ronsard.* Ed. Jean Gallant and Claude Binet. 10 vols. Paris: chez Gabriel Buon, 1587.

Salmasius, Claudius. 'Praefatio in Tabulam Cebetis arabicam'. In Johannes Elichmann, ed., *Tabula Cebetis graece, arabice, latine.* Leiden: typis Iohannis Maire, 1640. Sigs. *2r–****iv.

De hellenistica commentarius, controversiam de lingua hellenistica decidens, & plenissime pertractans originem & dialectos graecae linguae. Leiden: ex officina Elseviriorum, 1643.

Plinianae exercitationes in Caji Julii Solini polyhistora. Utrecht: apud Johannem vande Water *et al.*, 1689.

Sambucus, Johannes. *Die Briefe des Johannes Sambucus (Zsamboky) 1554–1584.* Ed. Hans Gerstinger. Österreichische Akademie der Wissenschaften, philosophisch-historische Klasse, Sitzungsberichte, Band 255. Vienna: Hermann Böhlaus for the Österreichische Akademie der Wissenschaften, 1968.

Scaligeriana sive excerpta ex ore Iosephi Scaligeri. 2nd edn. The Hague: ex typographia Adriani Vlacq, sumptibus Iohanni Vlacq, 1669.

Scapula, Joannes. *Lexicon graeco–latinum ... accedunt lexicon etymologicum ... et Ioan. Meursii glossarium contractum, hactenus desideratum.* Ed. Cornelius Schrevelius. Amsterdam: apud Ioannem Blaeuw et Ludovicum Elzevirium, 1652.

Lexicon graecolatinum nouum in quo ex primitiuorum & simplicium fontibus deriuata atque composita ordine non minus naturali, quam alphabetico, breuiter & dilucide deducuntur. Basel: ex officina Heruagiana, per Eusebium Episcopium, 1580.

Schard, Simon. *Lexicon iuridicum iuris Rom[ani] simul & pontificij a doctorib[us] item & practicis in schola atque foro usitatarum vocum penus.* Basel: per Eusebium Episcopium & Nicolai fratris haeredes, 1582.

Scholia graeca in Homeri Iliadem. Ed. Hartmut Erbse. 7 vols. Berlin: de Gruyter, 1969–88.

Schroderus, Ericus. *Lexicon latino–scondicum.* Stockholm: sumptibus & typis Henrici Käysers regij typographi, 1637.

Scriptores duo Anglici, ... de vitis pontificum Romanorum. Ed. Johann Martin Lydius. Leiden: excudebat Georgius Abrahami a Marisse ... sumptibus Henrici Laurentij bibliopolae Amstelodamensis, 1615.

Selden, John. *Table Talk.* Ed. Frederick Pollock. London: Quaritch, 1927.

Sextus Empiricus. *Pyrrhoniarum hypotypωseωn libri III.* Trans. Henri Estienne. [Geneva]: excudebat ... Henricus Stephanus, illustris viri Huldrici Fuggeri typographus, 1562.

Shakespeare, William. *Works.* Ed. Stanley Wells, Gary Taylor *et al.* Oxford: Clarendon Press, 1986.

Sibbald, Sir Robert. *Historical inquiries, concerning the Roman monuments and antiquities in the north-part of Britain called Scotland.* Edinburgh: printed by James Watson, 1707.

Simokattes, Theophylaktos. *Historiarum libri viii, editio priore castigatior, et glossario graeco-barbaro auctior.* Georgios Sphrantzes. *Chronicorum de ultimis orientalis imperii temporibus, de Sultanorum Osmanidorum origine, successione, rebus gestis, usque ad Mahometem II. de rebus denique Peloponneciacis ante et post captam Constantinopolim libri III.* Georgius Trapezuntius. *Epistola, qua Joannem Paleologum Imp[eratorem] cohortatur ut ad synodum in Italia celebrandam proficiscatur: omnia ex bibliotheca ... Maximiliani utriusque Bavariae principis deprompta.* Trans. Jacobus Pontanus and ed. C. A. Fabrot. Paris: e typographia regia, 1647–8.

Skinner, Stephen. *Etymologicon linguae anglicanae seu explicatio vocum anglicarum etymologica.* London: typis T. Roycroft, & prostant venales apud H. Brome [etc.], 1671.

Smith, Thomas. 'Vita Camdeni'. In William Camden, *Epistolae cum appendice varii argumenti.* London: impensis Richardi Chiswelli, 1691. i–lxxvii.

Somner, William. *The antiquities of Canterbury, or a survey of that ancient citie, with the suburbs and cathedrall, containing principally matters of antiquity in them all; collected chiefly from old manuscripts, lieger-bookes and other like records, for the most part, never as yet printed; with an appendix here annexed, wherein (for better satisfaction to the learned) the manuscripts, and records of chiefest consequence, are faithfully exhibited.* London: printed by I[ohn] L[egat] for Richard Thrale, 1640.

'Glossarium'. In Lambarde, Αρχαιονομια (1644). 217–23.

'Ad verba vetera Germanica, a v[iro] cl[arissimo] Justo Lipsio collecta, notae'. In M. Casaubon, *De quatuor linguis* (1650). 1–72 [second series of pagination].

'Glossarium'. In *Historiae anglicanae scriptores x* (1652). Sigs. X3r–Dd8r.

Dictionarium saxonico–latino–anglicum. Oxford: excudebat Guliel[mus] Hall, pro authore, 1659.

A treatise of gavelkind, both name and thing, shewing the true etymologie and derivation of the one, the nature, antiquity and original of the other, with sundry emergent observations. London: printed by R. and W. Leybourn for the authour, 1660 [really 1659].

Speed, John, ed. *The theatre of the empire of Great Britaine.* London: imprinted [by William Hall] and are to be solde by Iohn Sudbury & Georg Humble, 1612.

Spelman, Sir Henry. *De non temerandis ecclesiis: a tracte of the rights and respect due vnto churches, written to a gentleman, who hauing an appropriat parsonage, emploied the church to prophane vses and left the parishioners vncertainly prouided of diuine seruice, in a parish neere there adioyning.* London: printed by John Beale, 1613.

De non temerandis ecclesijs: a tract of the rights and respect due vnto churches, written to a gentleman, who hauing an appropriate parsonage, imploied the church to prophane vses, and left the parishioners vncertainely prouided of diuine seruice, in a parish neere there adioyning. 2nd edn. London: printed by Iohn Beale, 1616.

Archaeologus: in modum glossarii ad rem antiquam posteriorem. London: apud Johannem Beale, 1626.

Aspilogia. London: typis Rogeri Norton [1654]. Issued, separately signed and paginated, in Nicholas Upton, *De studio militari libri quatuor.* Ed. Edward Bysshe. London: typis Rogeri Norton, impensis Johannis Martin & Jacobi Allestrye, 1654.

Glossarium archaiologicum continens latino-barbara, peregrina, obsoleta & novatae significationis vocabula. London: apud Aliciam Warren, 1664.

The history and fate of sacrilege, discover'd by examples of scripture, of heathens and of Christians ... wrote in the year 1632: a treatise omitted in the late edition of his posthumous works, and now published for the terror of evil doers. London: for John Hartley, 1698.

Reliquiae Spelmannianae: the posthumous works of Sir Henry Spelman, Kt., relating to the laws and antiquities of England, publish'd from the original manuscripts. Ed. Edmund Gibson. Oxford: printed at the theater for Awnsham and John Churchill, 1698.

Spiegel, Jacob. *Lexicon iuris civilis, postremo auctum & recognitum.* Rev. edn. [1st edn. 1538 as *Iuris civilis lexicon.*] Basel: apud Ioan[nem] Hervagium, 1549.

Sprat, Thomas. *The history of the Royal-Society of London for the improving of natural knowledge.* London: Printed by T[homas] R[oycroft] for J[ohn] Martyn and J[ames] Allestry, printers to the Royal Society, 1667.

Stiernhielm, Georg. *Företahl til dess gambla Swea och Götha-måles fatebur.* [Stockholm: Peter von Selow, 1643?]

Magog arameo-gothicus. Uppsala: imprimebat Eschillus Matthiae, 1643.

Babel destructa, seu runa Suethica. Stockholm: [n.p.], 1669.

Anticluverius, sive scriptum breve, Johanni [sic] Cluverio Dantisco-Borusso oppositum: gentis Gothicae originem et antiquissimam in Scandia vel Scandinavia sedem vindicans. Stockholm: sumptibus et typis Henrici Keysers, typogr[aphi] reg[ii], 1685.

Stiernhielm, Georg, ed. *D. N. Jesu Christi SS. Evangelia ab Ulfila gothorum in Moesia episcopo ... ex graeco gothice translata, nunc cum parallelis versionibus, sueo-gothica, norraena, seu islandica, & vulgata latina edita.* Stockholm: typis Nicolai Wankif regij typogr[aphi], 1671.

Strype, John. *The life and acts of Matthew Parker.* London: printed for John Wyat, 1711.

T[ooke], G[eorge]. *The Belides or eulogie and elegie of that truly honourable John Lord Harrington Baron of Exton.* London: [n.p.], 1647.

Toussain, Jacques, ed. *Lexicon graecolatinum, ingenti vocum accessione locupletatum.* Ed. Fédéric Morel. Paris: apud Carolam Guillard viduam Claudij Cheuallonij et Gulielmum Merlin, 1552.

Traherne, Thomas. *Centuries, poems and thanksgivings.* 2 vols. Ed. H. M. Margoliouth. Oxford: Clarendon Press, 1958.

Trippault, Léon. *Celt'hellenisme ou etymologic des mots francois tirez du graec: plus preuues en general de la descente de nostre langue.* Orléans: par Eloy Gibier, imprimeur et libraire iuré de l'vniuersité, 1581.

Trithemius, Johannes. *Opera historica.* Ed. Marquard Freher. 2 vols. Frankfurt: typis Wechelianis apud Claudium Marnium & heredes Ioannis Aubrij, 1601.

Urquhart, Sir Thomas. Εκσκυβαλαυρον: *or, the discovery of a most exquisite jewel, more precious then diamonds inchased in gold, the like whereof was never seen in any age.* London: printed by Ja[mes] Cotterel, and are to be sold by Rich[ard] Baddely, 1652.

van der Myl, Abraham. *Lingua belgica, siue de linguae illius communitate tum cum plerisque alijs, tum pr[a]esertim cum latina, graeca, persica ... ut & de ejus pr[a]estantia.* Leiden: excudebant Vlricus Cornelij & G. Abrahami pro bibliopolio Commeliniano, 1612.

Verelius, Olaus. *Index linguae veteris scytho-scandicae sive gothicae, ex vetusti aevi monumentis, maximam partem manuscriptis, collectus.* Ed. Ole Rudbeck. Uppsala: [n.p.], 1691.

Verstegan, Richard. *A restitution of decayed intelligence in antiquities concerning the most noble and renowmed English nation.* Antwerp: printed by Robert Bruney, and to be sold in London by Iohn Norton and Iohn Bill, 1605.

Vettori, Pietro. *Variarum lectionum libri xxv.* Florence: excudebat Laurentius Torrentinus, 1553.

Villare anglicum, or, a view of the townes of England collected by the appointment of Sir Henry Spelman. London: printed by R. Hodgkinsonne, 1656.

Villehardouin, Geoffroy de. *L'histoire de la conqueste de Constantinople par les barons français associez aux Venitiens, l'an 1204, d'un costé en son vieil langage & de l'autre en un plus moderne & intelligible.* Ed. Blaise de Vigenère. Paris: A. l'Angelier, 1584.

L'histoire, ou chronique, representee de mot à mot en ancienne langue françoise, d'vn vieil exemplaire escrit a la main, qui se trouue dans les anciens archiues de la serenissime Republique de Venise … de nouveau mise en françois. Lyons: par les heritiers de Guillaume Rouille, 1601.

Histoire de l'empire de Constantinople sous les empereurs françois. Ed. Charles du Cange. Paris: de l'imprimerie royale, 1657.

Virgil. *Opera* [with the commentary of Servius]. Paris: ex officina Roberti Stephani, 1532.

See also Douglas (1553).

Vives, Juan Luis. *Opera.* 2 vols. Basel: apud Nicolaum Episcopium iuniorem, 1555.

De tradendis disciplinis, in *Libri* XII *de disciplinis.* 1531; rpt [London: William Stansby], 1612.

Vossius, G. J. *De vitiis sermonis et glossematis latino-barbaris, libri quatuor.* Amsterdam: apud Ludovicum Elzevirium, 1645.

Vredius, Olivarius. *Historia comitum Flandriae.* Bruges: apud Lucam Kerchovium, 1650.

Warton, Thomas, *Specimen of a history of Oxfordshire.* 2nd edn. London: printed for J[ohn] Nichols, J[ames] Robson [*et al.*], 1783.

Waserus, Caspar. 'Ad Mithridatem commentarius'. In Conrad Gessner, *Mithridates: exprimens differentias linguarum, tum veterum, tum quae hodie per totum terrarum orbem in usu sunt.* Zürich: typis Wolphianis, 1610.

Webb, John. *An historical essay endeavoring a probability that the language of the empire of China is the primitive language.* London: printed for Nath[aniel] Brook, 1669.

Wedderburn, Robert [?]. *The complaynt of Scotland.* Ed. A. M. Stewart. Scottish Text Society, ser. IV, vol. II. Edinburgh: Scottish Text Society, 1979.

Weever, John. *Ancient funerall monuments within the vnited monarchie of Great Britaine, Ireland and the islands adiacent.* London: printed by Thomas Harper, and are to be sold by Laurence Sadler, 1631.

Wilkins, John. *Mercury, or the secret and swift messenger: shewing how a man may with privacy and speed communicate his thoughts to a friend at any distance.* London: printed by I. Norton for Iohn Maynard and Timothy Wilkins, 1641.

Ecclesiastes: or a discourse concerning the gift of preaching as it fals under the rules of art. London: printed by M.F. for Samuel Gellibrand, 1646.

An essay towards a real character and a philosophical language. London: printed for Sa[muel] Gellibrand, and for John Martyn, printer to the Royal Society, 1668.

Willeram. *In canticum canticorum paraphrasis gemina, prior rhythmis latinis, altera veteri lingua francica; addita explicatio lingua belgica et notae quibus veterum vocum francicarum ratio redditur.* Leiden: ex officina Plantiniana, apud C. Raphelengium, 1598.

Worm, Ole. *Fasti danici: universam tempora computanti rationem antiqvitus in Dania et vicinis regionibus observatam.* Copenhagen: apud Salomonem Sartorium regium et Academiae typographu[m], 1626.

Runir, seu danica literatura antiquissima, vulgo Gothica dicta luci reddita. Copenhagen: typis Melchioris Martzan, 1636.

Antiquitates danicae: literatura runica, lexicon runicum, monumenta runica, additamenta, fasti danici. Comprising: [1] Worm. *Runir, seu danica literatura antiquissima.* 2nd edn. Copenhagen: imprimebat Melch[ior] Martzan, suis & Georg[ii] Holst sumptibus, 1651. [2] Worm. *Fasti danici, universam tempora computandi rationem antiqvitus in Dania et vicinis regionibus observatam libris tribus exhibentes.* 2nd edn. Copenhagen: apud Ioachimum Moltkenium, 1643. [3] Worm. *Danicorum monumentorum libri sex, e spissis antiquitatum tenebris et in Dania ac Norvegia extantibus ruderibus eruti.* Copenhagen: apud Ioachimum Moltkenium, 1643. [4] Magnús Ólafsson. *Specimen lexici runici, obscuriorum qvarundam vocum, qvae in priscis occurrunt historiis & poetis Danicis, enodationem exhibens; collectum a Dn. Magno Olavio, pastore Lausasiensi in Islandia doctissimo, nunc in ordinem redactum auctum & locupletatum ab Olao Wormio, in Acad. Hafn. P. P.* [5] Worm. *Additamenta ad Monumenta danica.* Copenhagen: impressum a Melchiore Martzan acad[emiae] typog[raphus], 1650.

Epistolae. 2 vols. Copenhagen: [n.p.], 1751.

See also *Museum Wormianum* (1655).

Zonaras, Ioannes. *Annales.* Ed. and comm. Charles du Cange. Paris: e typographia regia, 1686–7.

PRINTED SOURCES WRITTEN AFTER 1800

Aarsleff, Hans. 'The early history of the *Oxford English Dictionary*'. *Bulletin of the New York Public Library* 66 (1962): 417–39.

Åkerman, Susanna. *Queen Christina of Sweden and her circle: The transformation of a seventeenth-century philosophical libertine.* Leiden: E. J. Brill, 1991.

Allen, Don Cameron. 'Donne among the giants'. *Modern Language Notes* 61.4 (1946): 257–60.

 The legend of Noah: Renaissance rationalism in art, science, and letters. Illinois Studies in Language and Literature 33.3–4. Urbana: University of Illinois Press, 1949.

Alston, R. C., and B. Danielsson. 'The earliest dictionary of the known languages of the world'. *English Studies* 45 (1964): Supplement, 9–13.

Armstrong, Elizabeth. *Robert Estienne, royal printer: An historical study of the elder Stephanus.* Cambridge: Cambridge University Press, 1954.

Asher, R. E. *National myths in Renaissance France: Francus, Samothes and the Druids.* Edinburgh: Edinburgh University Press, 1993.

Ashworth, William B., Jr. 'Natural history and the emblematic world view'. In David C. Lindberg and Robert S. Westman, eds., *Reappraisals of the scientific revolution.* Cambridge: Cambridge University Press, 1990. 303–32.

Babinger, Franz. 'Ein schriftgeschichtliches Rätsel'. *Keleti Szemle* 14 (1913–14): 4–19.

Barber, Peter. 'A Tudor mystery: Laurence Nowell's map of England and Ireland'. *The Map Collector* 22 (March 1983): 16–21.

Barker, Nicolas. *The Oxford University Press and the spread of learning: An illustrated history 1478–1978.* Oxford: Clarendon Press, 1978.

Barret-Kriegel, Blandine. *Jean Mabillon.* Paris: Presses universitaires de France, 1988.

Barroll, Leeds. 'A new history for Shakespeare and his time'. *Shakespeare Quarterly* 39.4 (1988): 441–64.

Beck, Hans-Georg. *Kirche und theologische Literatur im byzantinischen Reich.* Handbuch der Altertumswissenschaft sect. 12 part 2 vol. 1. Munich: C. H. Beck'sche Verlagsbuchhandlung, 1959.

Bennett, J. A. W. 'The beginnings of Norse studies in England'. *Saga-book of the Viking Society* 12 (1937): 35–42.

'The history of Old English and Old Norse studies in England from the time of Francis Junius to the end of the eighteenth century'. DPhil. thesis, University of Oxford, 1938.

'The beginnings of runic studies in England'. *Saga-book of the Viking Society* 13 (1950–1): 268–83.

Bennett, Jim, and Scott Mandelbrote. *The garden, the Ark, the tower, the temple: Biblical metaphors of knowledge in early modern Europe.* Oxford: Museum of the History of Science, 1998.

Benzing, Josef. *Bibliographie der Schriften Johannes Reuchlins im 15. und 16. Jahrhundert.* Bibliotheca Bibliographica 18. Bad Bocklet: Walter Krieg Verlag, 1955.

Berkhout, Carl T., and Milton McC. Gatch, eds. *Anglo-Saxon scholarship: The first three centuries.* Boston: G. K. Hall, 1982.

Berkowitz, Luci. 'Ancilla to the Thesaurus linguae graecae: The TLG canon'. In Jon Solomon, ed., *Accessing antiquity: The computerization of classical studies.* Tucson: University of Arizona Press, 1993. 34–61.

Bierbach, Mechtild. *Grundzüge humanistischer Lexicographie in Frankreich: Ideengeschichtliche und rhetorische Rezeption der Antike als Didaktik.* Kultur und Erkenntnis: Schriften der Philosophischen Fakultät der Heinrich-Heine-Universität Düsseldorf vol 18. Tübingen: A. Francke Verlag, 1997.

Bischoff, Bernhard. 'The study of foreign languages in the Middle Ages'. *Speculum* 36.2 (1961): 209–24.

Blair, Ann. 'Reading strategies for coping with information overload ca. 1550–1700'. *Journal of the History of Ideas* 64.1 (2003): 11–28.

Blatchly, J. M. 'Beck, Cave (*bap.* 1622, *d.* 1706)'. *Oxford dictionary of national biography.*

Bloch, Denise. 'Charles Du Cange (1610–1688): Exposition organisée a l'occasion du tricentenaire du Glossarium mediae et infimae latinitatis par la Bibliothèque Nationale'. In Yves Lefevre, ed., *La lexicographie du latin médiéval.* 509–47.

Boardman, John. *The archaeology of nostalgia: How the Greeks re-created their mythical past.* London: Thames & Hudson, 2002.

Bombaci, A. 'Padre Pietro Ferraguto e la sua Grammatica turca (1611)'. *Annali dell'Istituto Universitario Orientale di Napoli* n.s. 1 [1940]: 205–36.

Borchardt, Frank L. *German antiquity in Renaissance myth.* Baltimore: Johns Hopkins Press, 1971.

'Medievalism in Renaissance Germany'. In Leland R. Phelps with A. Tilo Alt, eds., *Creative encounter: Festschrift for Hermann Salinger.* Chapel Hill: University of North Carolina Press, 1978. 73–85.

Borst, Arno. *Der Turmbau von Babel: Geschichte der Meinungen über Ursprung und Vielhalt der Sprachen und Völker.* 4 vols. in 6, continuously paginated. Stuttgart: Anton Hiersemann, 1957–63.

Bowen, E. J., and Harold Hartley. 'The Right Reverend John Wilkins, F. R. S. (1614–1672)'. *Notes and Records of the Royal Society of London* 15 (1960): 47–56.

Brandon, Edgar Ewing. *Robert Estienne et le dictionnaire français au XVIe siècle.* Baltimore: J. H. Furst, 1904.

Brann, Noel L. *The abbot Trithemius (1462–1516): The renaissance of monastic humanism.* Studies in the History of Christian Thought 24. Leiden: E. J. Brill, 1981.

Breen, Quirinus. 'The *Observationes in M. T. Ciceronem* of Marius Nizolius'. *Studies in the Renaissance* 1 (1954): 49–58.

Bremmer, Rolf H., Jr. 'Laet, Johannes de (1581–1649)'. *Oxford dictionary of national biography.*

'Retrieving Junius's correspondence'. In Bremmer, ed., *Franciscus Junius F. F. and his circle.* 199–235.

'The Anglo-Saxon pantheon according to Richard Verstegan (1605)'. In Graham, ed., *Recovery of Old English.* 141–72.

'Franciscus Junius reads Chaucer: But why? how?' In Shippey with Arnold, eds., *Appropriating the Middle Ages.* 37–72.

Bremmer, Rolf H., Jr., ed. *Franciscus Junius F. F. and his circle.* Amsterdam: Rodopi, 1998.

Breuker, Ph. H. 'On the course of Franciscus Junius's Germanic studies, with special reference to Frisian'. In Bremmer, ed. *Franciscus Junius F. F. and his circle.* 129–57.

British Museum. *Catalogue of additions to the manuscripts in the British Museum in the years 1911–1915.* London: printed for the Trustees [of the British Museum], 1925.

Brough, Sonia. *The Goths and the concept of Gothic in Germany from 1500 to 1750.* Mikrokosmos: Beiträge zur Literaturwissenschaft und Bedeutungsforschung 17. Frankfurt etc.: Verlag Peter Lang, 1985.

Brown, Virginia. 'Caesar, Gaius Julius'. In F. Edward Cranz with Paul Oskar Kristeller, eds., *Catalogus translationum et commentariorum* III. Washington, DC: Catholic University of America Press, 1976. 87–139.

'Varro, Marcus Terentius'. In F. Edward Cranz with Paul Oskar Kristeller, eds., *Catalogus translationum et commentariorum* IV. Washington, DC: Catholic University of America Press, 1980. 451–500.

Brunschvicg, Léon. *Héritage des mots, héritage d'idées*. Paris: Presses universitaires de France, 1945.

Buckalew, Ronald E. 'Leland's transcript of Aelfric's *Glossary*'. *Anglo-Saxon England* 7 (1978): 149–164.

'Nowell, Lambarde and Leland: The significance of Laurence Nowell's transcript of Ælfric's *Grammar and Glossary*'. In Berkhout and Gatch, eds., *Anglo-Saxon scholarship: The first three centuries*. 19–50.

Budé, Eugène de. *Vie de Guillaume Budé, fondateur du Collège de France (1467–1540)*. Paris, Librairie academique Didier Emile Perrin, 1884.

Burgess, Anthony. 'The *OED* Man' [review of Murray, *Caught in the web of words*]. *Times Literary Supplement*, 30 September 1977. 1094–5.

Burgess, Glenn. *The politics of the ancient constitution: An introduction to English political thought, 1603–1642*. University Park, PA: Pennsylvania State University Press, 1993.

Burke, Peter. *The fabrication of Louis XIV*. New Haven: Yale University Press, 1992.

The art of conversation. Ithaca, NY: Cornell University Press, 1993.

'"Heu domine, adsunt Turcae": A sketch for a social history of post-medieval Latin'. In *The art of conversation*. 34–65.

'Language and identity in early modern Italy'. In *The art of conversation*. 66–88.

Languages and communities in early modern Europe. Cambridge: Cambridge University Press, 2004.

Burmeister, Karl Heinz. *Sebastian Münster: Eine Bibliographie mit 22 Abbildungen*. Wiesbaden: Guido Pressler, 1964.

Sebastian Münster: Versuch eines biographischen Gesamtbildes. Basler Beiträge zur Geschichtswissenschaft 91. Basel: Helbing & Lichtenhahn, 1969.

Achilles Pirmin Gasser 1505–1577: Arzt und Naturforscher, Historiker und Humanist. 3 vols. Wiesbaden: Guido Pressler Verlag, 1970–5.

Bursian, Conrad. *Geschichte der classischen Philologie in Deutschland von den Anfängen bis zur Gegenwart*. Geschichte der Wissenschaften in Deutschland Bd. 19. Munich and Leipzig: R. Oldenbourg, 1883.

Cameron, Alan. *The Greek anthology from Meleager to Planudes*. Oxford: Clarendon Press, 1992.

Carley, James P. 'Four poems in praise of Erasmus by John Leland'. *Erasmus in English* 11 (1981–2): 26–7.

'John Leland in Paris: The evidence of his poetry'. *Studies in Philology* 83 (1986): 1–50.

Carley, James P., and Pierre Petitmengin. 'Pre-Conquest manuscripts from Malmesbury Abbey and John Leland's letter to Beatus Rhenanus concerning a lost copy of Tertullian's works'. *Anglo-Saxon England* 33 (2004): 195–223.

Carley, James P., and Colin G. C. Tite, eds. *Books and collectors 1200–1700: Essays presented to Andrew Watson*. London: British Library, 1997.

Chandler, John. 'Introduction'. In John Leland, *Itinerary: Travels in Tudor England*. Ed. John Chandler. Far Thrupp, Glocs., and Dover, NH: Alan Sutton Publishing, 1993. xi–xxxvi.

Chrimes, S. B. 'The constitutional ideas of Dr. John Cowell'. *English Historical Review* 64 (1949): 461–87.

Chudoba, Bohdan. *Spain and the Empire 1519–1643*. Chicago: University of Chicago Press, 1952.

Claes, Franz. *De bronnen van drie woordenboeken uit de drukkerij van Plantin: Het Dictionarium tetraglotton (1562), de Thesaurus theutonicae linguae (1573) en Kiliaans eerste Dictionarium teutonico–latinum (1574)*. Bouwstoffen en studien voor de geschiedenis en de lexicografie van het Nederlands 12. [Brussels]: Belgisch Interuniversitair Centrum voor Neerlandistiek, 1970.

Lijst van Nederlandse woordenlijsten en woordenboeken gedrukt tot 1600. Nieuwkoop: B. de Graaf, 1974.

Bibliographisches Verzeichnis der deutschen Vokabulare und Wörterbücher gedruckt bis 1600. Hildesheim and New York: Olms, 1977.

Clément, Louis. *Henri Estienne et son œuvre française: étude d'histoire littéraire et de philologie*. Paris: A. Picard, 1899.

Cochrane, Eric. *Historians and historiography in the Italian Renaissance*. Chicago: University of Chicago Press, 1981.

Cohn, Leopold. 'Griechische Lexikographie'. In G. Autenrieth, *Griechische und lateinische Sprachwissenschaft*. 2nd edn. Munich: C. H. Beck'sche Verlagsbuchhandlung, 1890. 597–9.

Collijn, Isak. *Sveriges bibliografi, 1600-talet: Bidrag till en bibliografisk förteckning*. 5 fascicles. Skrifter utgivna av Svenska litteratursällskapet 10.19–23. Uppsala: Svenska litteratursällskapet, 1942–6.

Considine, John. 'Narrative and persuasion in early modern English dictionaries and phrasebooks'. *Review of English Studies* 52 (2001): 195–206.

'How much Greek did Philip Sidney know?' *Sidney Journal* 20.2 (2002): 57–78.

'Mennonite Low German dictionary' [review of Jack Thiessen, *Mennonite Low German dictionary / Mennonitisches-Plattdeutsches Wörterbuch* (2003)]. *Journal of Mennonite Studies* 22 (2004): 247–58.

'"Our dictionaries err in redundancy": The problem of encyclopedism, past, present and future'. In Gottlieb, Mogensen, and Zettersten, eds., *Symposium on Lexicography XI*. 195–205.

Considine, John, and Giovanni Iamartino, eds. *Words and dictionaries from the British Isles in historical perspective*. Newcastle: Cambridge Scholars Publishing, 2007.

Cook, Sister Mary Joan. 'Developing techniques in Anglo-Saxon scholarship in the seventeenth century as they appear in the Dictionarium saxonico–latino–anglicum of William Somner'. PhD thesis, University of Toronto, 1962.

Cooper, Richard. 'Numismatics in early Renaissance France'. In Crawford, Ligota and Trapp, eds. *Medals and coins from Budé to Mommsen*. 5–19.

Corbett, Margery. 'The title-page and illustrations to the *Monasticon anglicanum* 1655–1673'. *Antiquaries' Journal* 67.1 (1987): 102–10.

Cornell, T. J. 'Ancient history and the antiquarian revisited: Some thoughts on reading Momigliano's *Classical foundations*'. In Crawford and Ligota, eds., *Ancient history and the antiquarian*. 1–14.

Couvreur, Walter. 'Le déchiffrement du monument d'Ancyre'. In Rousseau, ed. *Sur les traces de Busbecq et du gotique.* 77–89.

Cram, David. 'John Ray and Francis Willughby: Universal language schemes and the foundations of linguistic field research'. In Werner Hüllen, ed., *Understanding the historiography of linguistics: Problems and projects.* Münster: Nodus Publikationen, 1990. 229–39.

'Concordances of words and concordances of things'. In Hüllen, ed. *World in a list of words.* 83–93.

C[raster], H. H. E. 'Index to Duke Humphrey's gifts to the old library of the University in 1439, 1441 and 1444'. *Bodleian Quarterly Record* 1 (1914–16): 130–5.

Crawford, M. H. 'Antoine Morillon, antiquarian and medallist'. *Journal of the Warburg and Courtauld Institutes* 61 (1998): 93–110.

Crawford, M. H., and C. R. Ligota, eds. *Ancient history and the antiquarian: Essays in memory of Arnaldo Momigliano.* Warburg Institute Colloquia 2. London: Warburg Institute, 1995.

Crawford, M. H., C. R. Ligota, and J. B. Trapp, eds. *Medals and coins from Budé to Mommsen.* Warburg Institute Surveys and Texts 21. London: Warburg Institute, 1990.

Cronne, H. A. 'The study and use of charters by English scholars in the seventeenth century: Sir Henry Spelman and Sir William Dugdale'. In Fox, ed. *English historical scholarship.* 73–91.

Curtius, Ernst Robert. *European literature and the Latin Middle Ages.* Trans. Willard R. Trask. Bollingen Series 36. New York: Pantheon Books, 1953.

Daly, Lloyd W., and B. A. Daly. 'Some techniques in mediaeval Latin lexicography'. *Speculum* 39 (1964): 229–39.

D'Amico, John F. *Theory and practice in Renaissance textual criticism: Beatus Rhenanus between conjecture and history.* Berkeley and Los Angeles: University of California Press, 1988.

de Beer, E. S. 'The earliest Fellows of the Royal Society'. *Notes and Records of the Royal Society of London* 7.2 (1950): 172–92.

de Boer, Josephine. 'Men's literary circles in Paris 1610–1660'. *Publications of the Modern Language Society of America* 53.3 (1938): 730–80.

de Broglie, Emmanuel. *Mabillon et la société de l'Abbaye de Saint-Germain des Prés a la fin du dix-septième siècle, 1664–1707.* 2 vols. Paris: Librairie Plon, 1888.

DeCoursey, Christina. 'Society of Antiquaries (*act.* 1586–1607)'. *Oxford dictionary of national biography.*

de Gruys, J. A. *The early printed editions (1518–1664) of Aeschylus: A chapter in the history of classical scholarship.* Bibliotheca humanistica et reformatorica 32. Nieuwkoop: B. de Graaf, 1981.

de Hamel, Christopher. 'The dispersal of the library of Christ Church, Canterbury, from the fourteenth to the sixteenth century'. In Carley and Tite, eds., *Books and collectors 1200–1700.* 263–79.

Dekker, Kees. '"*Vide Kilian* ...": The role of Kiliaan's *Etymologicum* in Old English studies between 1650 and 1665'. *Anglia* 114.4 (1996): 514–43.

The origins of Old Germanic studies in the low countries. Brill's Studies in Intellectual History 92. Leiden: E. J. Brill, 1999.

'Franciscus Junius (1591–1677): Copyist or editor?' *Anglo-Saxon England* 29 (2000): 279–96.

'"That most elaborate one of Fr. Junius": An investigation of Francis Junius's manuscript Old English dictionary'. In Graham, ed. *Recovery of Old English.* 301–43.

Delaruelle, L. *Guillaume Budé (1468–1540): Les origines, les débuts, les idées maîtresses.* Bibliothèque de l'École des Hautes Etudes: Sciences historiques et Philologiques 162. Paris: Librairie Honoré Champion, 1907.

'Le dictionnaire greco–latin de Crastone: Contribution à l'histoire de la lexicographie grecque'. *Studi italiani di filologia classica* n.s. 8.3 (1930): 221–46.

Delisle, Léopold. *Catalogue des actes de Philippe-Auguste.* Paris: Auguste Durand, 1856.

Demaizière, Colette. 'Deux aspects de l'idéal linguistique d'Henri Estienne: Hellénisme et Parisianisme'. In *Henri Estienne.* 63–75.

'Les réflexions étymologiques d'Henri Estienne de la *Conformité* (1565) aux *Hypomneses* (1582)'. In Jean-Pierre Chambon and Georges Lüdi, eds., *Discours étymologique: Actes du colloque international.* Tübingen: Max Niemeyer Verlag, 1991. 201–10.

See also Dubois (1998) in the second section above.

Demerson, Geneviève. *Dorat et son temps: Culture classique et présence au monde.* Clermont-Ferrand: Adosa, 1983.

Deneire, Tom, and Toon Van Hal, eds. *Lipsius tegen Becanus, over het Nederlands als oertaal: Editie, vertaling, en interpretatie van zijn brief aan Hendrik Schotti (19 december 1598).* Amersfoort: Florivallis, 2006.

Derolez, R. *Runica manuscripta.* Rijksuniversiteit te Gent: Werken uitgegeven door de faculteit van de wijsbegeerte en letteren 118. Bruges: De Tempel, 1954.

de Smet, Gilbert. 'Invloed van Junius' Batavia op Kiliaans Woordenboek'. *Tijdschrift voor Nederlandse Taal- en Letterkunde* 74 (1956): 44–59.

'Einführung'. In Petrus Dasypodius, *Dictionarium latinogermanicum.* 1536; rpt Hildesheim: G. Olms, 1974. [v]–[xiv].

Devereux, E. J. *Bibliography of John Rastell.* Montreal and Kingston: McGill-Queen's University Press, 1999.

Dionysius of Halicarnassus. *Opuscula.* Ed. Hermann Usener and Ludwig Radermacher. 2 vols. Leipzig: Teubner, 1899.

Diringer, David, with Reinhold Regensburger. *The alphabet: A key to the history of mankind.* 2 vols. 3rd edn. London: Hutchinson, 1968.

Dolezal, Fredric. *Forgotten but important lexicographers: John Wilkins and William Lloyd: A modern approach to lexicography before Johnson.* Lexicographica series maior 4. Tübingen: Max Niemeyer, 1985.

Donaldson, B. C. *Dutch: A linguistic history of Holland and Belgium.* Leiden: Martinus Nijhoff, 1983.

Dorez, Léon, ed. *Catalogue de la collection Dupuy.* 2 vols. Paris: E. Leroux, 1899.

Doucette, Leonard E. *Emery Bigot: Seventeenth-century French humanist*. Toronto: University of Toronto Press, 1970.

Douglas, David. *English scholars 1660–1730*. 2nd edn. London: Eyre and Spottiswoode, 1951.

Droixhe, Daniel. *La linguistique et l'appel de l'histoire (1600–1800): Rationalisme et révolutions positivistes*. Geneva: Librairie Droz, 1978.

'La crise de l'hébreu langue-mère au XVIIe siècle'. In Chantal Grell and François Laplanche, eds., *La république des lettres et l'histoire du judaïsme antique, XVIe–XVIIIe siècles*. Mythe, critique et histoire 6. Paris: Presses de l'Universitaire de Paris-Sorbonne, 1992. 65–99.

'Ménage et le latin vulgaire ou tardif'. In R. Baum *et al.*, eds. *Lingua et traditio: Geschichte der Sprachwissenschaft und der neueren Philologien: Festschrift für Hans Helmut Christmann zum 65. Geburtstag*. Tübingen: Narr, 1994. 143–64.

'"Más ignorante que hereje"': De Laet, Acosta et l'origine linguistique des Américains'. In Gerda Hassler and Jürgen Storost, eds., *Kontinuität und Innovation: Studien zur Geschichte der romanischen Sprachforschung vom 17. bis zum 19. Jahrhundert. Festschrift für W. Bahner zum 70. Geburtstag*. Münster: Nodus Publikationen, 1997. 73–88.

Dunn, R. D. 'General introduction'. In William Camden, *Remains concerning Britain*. Ed. R. D. Dunn. Toronto: University of Toronto Press, 1984.

Ebel, Else. 'The beginnings of runic studies in Germany: A survey'. *Michigan Germanic Studies* 7 (1981): 176–84.

Eco, Umberto. *The search for the perfect language*. Trans. James Fentress. Oxford, UK and Cambridge, MA: Blackwell, 1995.

Edelman, Nathan. *Attitudes of seventeenth-century France toward the Middle Ages*. New York: King's Crown Press [a division of Columbia University Press], 1946.

Eros, John F. 'A 17th-century demonstration of language relationship: Meric Casaubon on English and Greek'. *Historiographia linguistica* 3.1 (1976): 1–13.

Evans, R. J. W. *Rudolf II and his world*. Oxford: Clarendon Press, 1973.

'Rantzau and Welser: Aspects of later German humanism'. *History of European Ideas* 5 (1984): 257–72.

Fairbanks, Sydney, and F. P. Magoun, Jr. 'On writing and printing Gothic'. *Speculum* 15.3 (1940): 313–30.

Faulkes, Anthony. 'The sources of *Specimen lexici runici*'. *Íslenzk tunga* 5 (1964): 30–138.

Favre, Léopold. 'Notice sur la vie et les ouvrages de Charles Dufresne du Cange'. In du Cange, *Glossarium latinitatis* (1887). ix:i–xi.

Feugère, Léon. 'Essai sur Henri Estienne'. In Henri Estienne, *Conformité du langage français avec le grec*. Ed. Léon Feugère. New edn. Paris: J. Delalain, 1853. v–ccxxxvi.

Étude sur la vie et les ouvrages de du Cange. 1852; rpt Geneva: Slatkine Reprints, 1971.

Fisher, John H. *The emergence of standard English*. Lexington, KY: University Press of Kentucky, 1996.

Floridi, Luciano. 'The grafted branches of the Sceptical tree: *Noli altum sapere* and Henri Estienne's Latin edition of *Sexti Empirici Pyrrhoniarum Hypotyposeon libri III'*. *Nouvelles de la République des Lettres* 11 (1992): 127–66.

Flower, Robin. 'Laurence Nowell and the discovery of England in Tudor times'. In E. G. Stanley, ed., *British Academy papers on Anglo-Saxon England*. Oxford: Oxford University Press for the British Academy, 1990. 1–27.

Foley, Stephen Merriam. *Sir Thomas Wyatt*. Twayne's English Authors Series 475. Boston, MA: Twayne, 1990.

Forster, C. T., and F. H. B. Daniell. *The life and letters of Ogier Ghiselin de Busbecq*. 2 vols. London: C. Kegan Paul & Co., 1881.

Fox, Adam. *Oral and literate culture in England, 1500–1700*. Oxford: Clarendon Press; New York: Oxford University Press, 2000.

Fox, Levi, ed. *English historical scholarship in the sixteenth and seventeenth centuries*. London: Oxford University Press for the Dugdale Society, 1956.

Friedman, Jerome. *The most ancient testimony: Sixteenth-century Christian-Hebraica in the age of Renaissance nostalgia*. Athens, OH: Ohio University Press, 1983.

Gandolfo, Maria Delfina. 'Roman Slavdom'. In Lepschy, ed., *History of linguistics III*. 108–23.

Ganz, Peter. 'MS. Junius 13 und die althochdeutsche Tatianübersetzung'. *Beiträge zur Geschichte der deutschen Sprache und Literatur* 91 (1969): 28–76.

[Gasnault, Pierre, and Jeanne Veyrin-Forrer]. *Guillaume Budé* [catalogue of an exhibition to commemorate the quincentenary of Budé's birth]. Paris: Bibliothèque Nationale, 1968.

Geanakoplos, Deno J. *Greek scholars in Venice: Studies in the dissemination of Greek learning from Byzantium to western Europe*. Cambridge, MA: Harvard University Press, 1962.

Geary, Patrick J. *The myth of nations: The medieval origins of Europe*. Princeton, NJ: Princeton University Press, 2002.

Geiger, Ludwig. *Johann Reuchlin, sein Leben und seine Werke*. Leipzig: Duncker & Humblot, 1871.

Gerstinger, Hans, ed. *Codex Vindobonensis med. gr. 1 der Österreichischen Nationalbibliothek*. Graz: Akademische Druck- und Verlagsanstalt, 1965–70.

Giese, L. L. 'An anonymous seventeenth-century Bodleian manuscript dictionary: Its authorship and significance to Old English studies'. *Bodleian Library Record* 14.2 (1992): 145–57.

Gilliver, Peter. '*OED* personalia'. In Lynda Mugglestone, ed., *Lexicography and the OED: Pioneers in the untrodden forest*. Oxford: Oxford University Press, 2000. 232–52.

Ginzburg, Carlo. 'The high and the low: The theme of forbidden knowledge in the sixteenth and seventeenth centuries'. *Past and Present* 73 (1976): 28–42.

  Clues, myths, and the historical method. Baltimore: Johns Hopkins University Press, 1989.

Goepp, Philip H., II. 'Verstegan's "most ancient Saxon words"'. In Thomas A. Kirby and Henry Bosley Woolf, eds., *Philologica: The Malone anniversary studies*. Baltimore: Johns Hopkins Press, 1949. 249–55.

Goetz, Georg, and Gotthold Gundermann, eds. *Corpus glossariorum latinorum II: Glossae latinograecae et graecolatinae*. Leipzig: B. G. Teubner, 1888.

Gordon, G. S. '*Medium aevum* and the middle age'. In *S.P.E. Tract 19*. Oxford: Clarendon Press, 1925. 3–28.

Gordon, Phyllis Walter Goodhart, ed. and trans. *Two Renaissance book hunters*. New York: Columbia University Press, 1974.

Gottlieb, Henrik, Jens-Erik Mogensen, and Arne Zettersten, eds. *Symposium on lexicography XI: Proceedings of the eleventh international symposium on lexicography May 2–4, 2002, at the University of Copenhagen*. Lexicographica series maior 115. Tübingen: Max Niemeyer, 2005.

Grafton, Anthony. *Defenders of the text: The traditions of scholarship in an age of science, 1450–1800*. Cambridge, MA: Harvard University Press, 1994.

'Tradition and technique in historical chronology'. In Crawford and Ligota, eds., *Ancient history and the antiquarian*. 15–31.

Commerce with the classics. Ann Arbor: University of Michigan Press, 1997.

Grafton, Anthony, ed. *Rome reborn: The Vatican Library and Renaissance culture*. Washington: Library of Congress; New Haven and London: Yale University Press, 1993.

Graham, Timothy. 'The earliest Old-English word-list from Tudor England'. *Medieval English Studies Newsletter* 35 (December 1996): 4–7.

'Robert Talbot's "old saxonice Bede": Cambridge University Library, MS Kk. 3. 18 and the "alphabetum norwagicum" of British Library, Cotton MSS, Domitian A. IX'. In Carley and Tite, *Books and collectors 1200–1700*. 295–316.

'John Joscelyn, pioneer of Old English lexicography'. In Graham, ed. *Recovery of Old English*. 83–140.

Graham, Timothy, ed. *The recovery of Old English: Anglo-Saxon studies in the sixteenth and seventeenth centuries*. Kalamazoo, MI: Medieval Institute Publications [of] Western Michigan University, 2000.

Grandidier, Alfred, and Guillaume Grandidier, eds. *Collection des ouvrages anciens concernant Madagascar, tome 1: Ouvrages ou extraits d'ouvrages ... 1500 à 1613*. Paris: Comité de Madagascar, 1903.

Gransden, Antonia. *Historical writing in England II: c.1307 to the early sixteenth century*. London: Routledge & Kegan Paul, 1982.

Grimm, Jacob. 'Vorwort'. In Jacob Grimm and Wilhelm Grimm, eds., *Deutsches Wörterbuch* 1. Leipzig: S. Hirzel, 1854. i–lxviii.

Gumbert, J. P. 'The Williram goes to print'. *Quaerendo* 5.3 (1975): 205–17.

Haensch, Günther. 'Die mehrsprachigen Wörterbücher und ihre Probleme'. In Hausmann *et al.*, *Wörterbücher*. III:2909–37.

Hamilton, Alistair. 'Eastern churches and Western scholarship'. In Grafton, *Rome reborn*. 225–49.

Hardouin, M. H. 'Liste des ouvrages de du Cange'. In du Cange, *Glossarium latinitatis* (1887). IX:xi–xviii.

Harris, Richard L., ed. *A chorus of grammars: The correspondence of George Hickes and his collaborators on the Thesaurus linguarum septentrionalium.* Publications of the Dictionary of Old English 4. Toronto: Pontifical Institute of Medieval Studies, 1992.

Hastings, Adrian. *The construction of nationhood: Ethnicity, religion and nationalism.* Cambridge: Cambridge University Press, 1997.

Haudricourt, A. G. 'Ogier de Busbecq, botaniste'. In Rousseau, *Sur les traces de Busbecq et du gotique.* 55–60.

Haugen, Einar. 'The Scandinavian languages as cultural artefacts'. In Joshua A. Fishman, Charles A. Ferguson, Jyotirindra Das Gupta, eds., *Language problems of developing nations.* New York: Wiley, 1968. 267–84.

The Scandinavian languages: An introduction to their history. London: Faber and Faber, 1976.

'Introduction'. In Eva L. Haugen, *A bibliography of Scandinavian dictionaries.* White Plains, NY: Kraus International, 1984. 1–61.

Hausmann, Franz Josef, Oskar Reichmann, Herbert Ernst Wiegand, and Ladislav Zgusta, eds. *Wörterbücher: Ein internationales Handbuch zur Lexikographie / Dictionaries: An international encyclopedia of lexicography / Dictionnaires: Encyclopédie internationale de lexicographie.* 3 vols. Berlin and New York: Walter de Gruyter, 1989.

Heesakkers, Chris. 'Lipsius, Dousa and Jan van Hout: Latin and the vernacular in Leiden in the 1570s and 1580s'. In Karl Enenkel and Chris Heesakkers, eds., *Lipsius in Leiden: Studies in the life and works of a great humanist on the occasion of his 450th anniversary.* Voorthuizen: Florivallis, 1997. 93–120.

Helgerson, Richard. *Forms of nationhood: The Elizabethan writing of England.* Chicago: University of Chicago Press, 1992.

Henri Estienne. Cahiers V.-L. Saulnier 5. Paris: Presses de l'École normale supérieure de jeunes filles, 1988.

Hepple, Leslie W. 'William Camden and early collections of Roman antiquities in Britain'. *Journal of the History of Collections* 15.2 (2003): 159–74.

Hertenstein, Bernhard. *Joachim von Watt (Vadianus), Bartholomäus Schobinger, Melchior Goldast: Die Beschäftigung mit dem Althochdeutschen von St. Gallen in Humanismus und Frühbarock.* Berlin and New York: Walter de Gruyter, 1975.

Hetherington, M. Sue. *The beginnings of Old English lexicography.* Spicewood, TX: published by the author, 1980.

Hieronymus, Frank. *Griechischer Geist aus Basler Pressen.* Publikationen der Universitätsbibliothek Basel 15. Basel: Universitätsbibliothek Basel, 1992.

Hirstein, James S. *Tacitus' Germania and Beatus Rhenanus (1485–1547): A study of the editorial and exegetical contribution of a sixteenth century scholar.* Studien zur klassischen Philologie 91. Frankfurt: Peter Lang, 1995.

Hobsbawm, Eric, and Terence Ranger, eds. *The invention of tradition.* Cambridge: Cambridge University Press, 1983.

Hobson, Anthony. *Great libraries.* London: Weidenfeld and Nicolson, 1970.

Hoftijzer, Paul G. 'The library of Johannes de Laet (1581–1649)'. *Lias* 25.2 (1998): 201–16.

Holm, Lars. 'Ein schwedischer Calepinus aus dem 17. Jahrhundert'. In Gottlieb, Mogensen and Zettersten, *Symposium on lexicography XI.* 303–23.

Holm, Lars, and Hans Jonsson. 'Swedish lexicography'. In Hausmann *et al.*, *Wörterbücher.* 11:1933–43.

Horodisch, A. 'Die Geburt eines Kinderbuches im 16. Jahrhundert'. *Gutenberg-Jahrbuch* (1960): 211–22.

Hüllen, Werner, ed. *The world in a list of words.* Lexicographica series maior 58. Tübingen: Niemeyer, 1994.

  English dictionaries 800–1700: The topical tradition. [Corrected paperback reprint; 1st edn. 1999.] Oxford: Clarendon Press, 2006.

Hunter, Michael. 'The Royal Society and the origins of British archaeology'. *Antiquity* 65 (1971): 113–121 and 187–192.

  John Aubrey and the world of learning. London: Duckworth, 1975.

Hunter, Richard, and Ida Macalpine. 'The diary of John Casaubon'. *Proceedings of the Huguenot Society of London* 21 (1965–70): 31–57.

Hurel, Daniel-Odon. 'The Benedictines of the Congregation of St.-Maur and the Church Fathers'. In Irena Backus, ed., *The reception of the Church Fathers in the West from the Carolingians to the Maurists.* 2 vols. Leiden: E. J. Brill, 1997. 11:1009–38.

Husner, Fritz. 'Der editio princeps des "Corpus historiae Byzantinae": Johannes Oporin, Hieronymus Wolf und die Fugger'. In *Festschrift Karl Schwarber: Beiträge zur Schweizerischen Bibliotheks-, Buch- und Gelehrtengeschichte.* Basel: Benno Schwabe & Co. Verlag, 1949. 143–62.

IJsewijn, Jozef. *Companion to Neo-Latin studies.* 2nd edn. 2 parts (part 2 with Dirk Sacré). Supplementa Humanistica Lovaniensia v; xiv. Louvain: Leuven University Press, 1990; 1998.

Iversen, Erik. *The myth of Egypt and its hieroglyphs in European tradition.* Copenhagen: GEC Gad Publishers, 1961.

Jardine, Lisa. *Erasmus, man of letters.* Princeton: Princeton University Press, 1993.

Jenkyns, Richard. *The Victorians and ancient Greece.* Oxford: Basil Blackwell, 1980.

Jessup, Frank W. *Sir Roger Twysden 1597–1672.* London: Cresset Press, 1965.

Johansson, J. Viktor. 'Variantexemplar av Stiernhielms Ulfilas-edition: en bokhistorisk undersökning'. *Göteborgs Högskolas Årsskrift* 45.4 (1939) [separately paginated fascicle].

Jones, Richard Foster. *The triumph of the English language: A survey of opinions concerning the vernacular from the introduction of printing to the Restoration.* Stanford: Stanford University Press, 1953.

Jones, William Jervis. *German lexicography in the European context: A descriptive bibliography of printed dictionaries and word lists containing German language (1600–1700).* Studia linguistica Germanica 58. Berlin: W. de Gruyter, 2000.

Kämper, Heidrun. 'Einführung und Bibliographie zu Georg Henisch, Teütsche Sprach und Weißheit. Thesavrvs [sic] lingvae et sapientiae Germanicae (1616)'. In Helmut Henne, ed. *Deutsche Wörterbücher des 17. und 18. Jahrhunderts: Einführung und Bibliographie.* 2nd edn. Hildesheim and New York: Georg Olms, 2001. 39–73.

Karrow, Robert W., Jr. *Mapmakers of the sixteenth century and their maps: Biobibliographies of the cartographers of Abraham Ortelius, 1570.* Chicago: Speculum Orbis Press for the Newberry Library, 1993.

Kau-Too, Sau. *Thesaurus of Karen knowledge.* Ed. Jonathan Wade. Tavoy: Karen Mission Press, 1847–50.

Kelley, Donald R. *Foundations of modern historical scholarship: Language, law and history in the French Renaissance.* New York: Columbia University Press, 1970.
'History, English law and the Renaissance'. *Past and Present* 65 (1974): 24–51.
'Civil science in the Renaissance: Jurisprudence Italian style'. *Historical Journal* 22.4 (1979): 777–94.
'*Tacitus noster*: The *Germania* in the Renaissance and Reformation'. In T. J. Luce and A. J. Woodman, eds., *Tacitus and the Tacitean tradition.* Princeton: Princeton University Press, 1993. 152–67.

Kendrick, Thomas Downing. *British antiquity.* 1950. Rpt with additions. London: Methuen, 1970.

Kenney, E. J. *The classical text: Aspects of editing in the age of the printed book.* Sather Classical Lectures 44. Berkeley: University of California Press, 1974.

Ker, N. R. 'Medieval manuscripts from Norwich Cathedral Priory'. *Transactions of the Cambridge Bibliographical Society* 1 (1949–53): 1–28.
Catalogue of manuscripts containing Anglo-Saxon. Oxford: Clarendon Press, 1957.

Kerling, Johan. *Chaucer in early English dictionaries: The old-word tradition in English lexicography down to 1721 and Speght's Chaucer glossaries.* Leiden: Leiden University Press, 1979.

Keynes, Geoffrey. *John Ray: A bibliography.* London: Faber and Faber, 1951.

Kidd, Colin. *British identities before nationalism: Ethnicity and nationhood in the Atlantic world, 1600–1800.* Cambridge and New York: Cambridge University Press, 1999.

King, V. 'Clever Talk' [review of A. Richards, *An Iban–English dictionary* (1981)]. *Times Literary Supplement*, 3 September 1982: 952.

Kleberg, Tönnes. *Codex Argenteus: The Silver Bible at Uppsala.* Trans. Neil Tomkinson. 6th edn. Uppsala: Uppsala University Library, 1984.

Klemming, G. E. 'Anteckningar af Johannes Thomae Agrivillensis Bureus'. *Samlaren* 5 (1884): 5–26.

Klindt-Jensen, Ole. *A history of Scandinavian archaeology.* Trans. G. Russell Poole. London: Thames and Hudson, 1975.

Knapp, M. E. *A checklist of verse by David Garrick.* Charlottesville: University of Virginia Press for the Bibliographical Society of the University of Virginia, 1955.

Knappe, Gabriele. 'Theory meets empiricism: English lexis in John Wilkins' philosophical language and the role of William Lloyd'. *Archiv für das Studium der neueren Sprachen und Literaturen* 241.1 (2004): 69–89.

Knowles, M. D. *Great historical enterprises: Problems of monastic history.* London: Thomas Nelson and sons, 1963.

Knowlson, James. *Universal language schemes in England and France 1600–1800.* Toronto: University of Toronto Press, 1975.

Krömer, Dietfried. 'Lateinische Lexikographie'. In Hausmann *et al.*, *Wörterbücher* 11:1713–22.

Kyes, Robert L., ed. *The Old Low Franconian psalms and glosses.* Ann Arbor: University of Michigan Press, 1969.

Labarre, Albert. *Bibliographie du Dictionarium d'Ambrogio Calepino (1502–1779).* Bibliotheca Bibliographica Aureliana 26. Baden-Baden: Éditions Valentin Koerner, 1975.

Ladd, C. A. 'The "Rubens" manuscript and *Archbishop Ælfric's Vocabulary*'. *Review of English Studies* n.s. 11 (1960): 353–64.

Law, Vivien. *The history of linguistics in Europe from Plato to 1600.* Cambridge: Cambridge University Press, 2003.

le Bourdelles, Hubert. 'En marge de la communication de A. Haudricourt: Réflexions sur Busbecq et la botanique'. In Rousseau, ed., *Sur les traces de Busbecq et du gotique.* 61–3.

Leedham-Green, Elizabeth, and David McKitterick. 'A catalogue of Cambridge University Library, 1583'. In Carley and Tite, *Books and collectors 1200–1700.* 153–235.

Lefevre, Yves, ed. *La lexicographie du latin médiéval et ses rapports avec les recherches actuelles sur la civilisation du moyen-âge.* Colloques Internationales du CNRS 589. Paris: CNRS, 1981.

Lehmann, Paul. 'Mittelalter und Küchenlatein'. *Historische Zeitschrift* 137.2 (1928): 197–213.

Leinbaugh, Theodore H. 'Ælfric's *Sermo de sacrificio in die Pascae*: Anglican polemic in the sixteenth and seventeenth centuries'. In Berkhout and Gatch, *Anglo-Saxon scholarship: The first three centuries.* 51–68.

Lepschy, Giulio, ed. *History of linguistics III: Renaissance and early modern linguistics.* London and New York: Longman, 1998.

Le Roy Ladurie, Emmanuel. *Montaillou: The promised land of error.* Trans. Barbara Bray. New York: George Braziller, 1978.

Lewis, Rhodri. 'The efforts of the Aubrey correspondence group to revise John Wilkins' *Essay* (1668) and their context'. *Historiographia linguistica* 28.3 (2001): 331–64.

Lloyd-Jones, Hugh. 'Rudolf Pfeiffer'. In *Blood for the ghosts: classical influences in the nineteenth and twentieth centuries.* London: Duckworth, 1982. 261–70.

Lodge, R. Anthony. *French: From dialect to standard.* London and New York: Routledge, 1993.

Louthan, Howard. *The quest for compromise: Peacemakers in Counter-Reformation Vienna.* Cambridge: Cambridge University Press, 1997.

Lowe, Kathryn A. 'William Somner, S 1622, and the editing of Old English charters'. *Neophilologus* 83 (1999): 291–7.

Lowenthal, David. *The heritage crusade and the spoils of history.* Paperback edn [1st edn 1996]. Cambridge: Cambridge University Press, 1998.

Lowry, Martin. *The world of Aldus Manutius: Business and scholarship in Renaissance Venice.* Ithaca, NY: Cornell University Press, 1979.

Lucas, Peter J. 'Junius, his printers, and his types: An interim report'. In Bremmer, *Franciscus Junius F.F. and his circle.* 177–97.

Lutz, Angelika. 'Zur Entstehungsgeschichte von William Somners *Dictionarium saxonico–latino–anglicum*'. *Anglia* 106 (1988): 1–25.

'The study of the Anglo-Saxon chronicle in the seventeenth century and the establishment of Old English studies in the universities'. In Graham, *Recovery of Old English.* 1–82.

[MacCunn, John, and Florence MacCunn]. *Recollections of W. P. Ker by two friends.* Glasgow: printed for private circulation by Maclehose, Jackson & Co., 1924.

Maclagan, Michael. 'Genealogy and heraldry in the sixteenth and seventeenth centuries'. In Fox, *English historical scholarship.* 31–48.

Macray, W. D. 'The manuscripts in the Inner Temple library'. In *Historical Manuscripts Commission eleventh report, appendix, part VII: The manuscripts of the Duke of Leeds, the Bridgewater Trust, Reading Corporation, the Inner Temple, &c.* London: Her Majesty's Stationery Office, 1888. 227–308.

'The manuscripts of the late John Henry Gurney, Esq., of Keswick Hall, Norfolk'. In *Historical Manuscripts Commission twelfth report, appendix, part IX: The manuscripts of the Duke of Beaufort and others.* London: Her Majesty's Stationery Office, 1891. 116–64.

Malkiel, Yakov. *Etymology.* Cambridge: Cambridge University Press, 1993.

Marckwardt, Albert H. 'Nowell's *Vocabularium saxonicum* and Somner's *Dictionarium*'. *Philological Quarterly* 26.4 (1947): 345–51.

'An unnoted source of English dialect vocabulary'. *Journal of English and Germanic Philology* 46 (1947): 177–82.

'The sources of Laurence Nowell's *Vocabularium saxonicum*'. *Studies in Philology* 45 (1948): 21–36.

See also Nowell, *Vocabularium* (1952) in the second section above.

Marsden, R. G. 'A Virginian minister's library, 1635'. *American Historical Review* 11 (1906): 328–32.

Masson, David. *The life of John Milton.* 7 vols. London: Macmillan, 1873–94.

Matras, Yaron. *Romani: A linguistic introduction.* Cambridge: Cambridge University Press, 2002.

McCabe, Richard. 'Translated states: Spenser and linguistic colonialism'. In Jennifer Klein Morrison and Matthew Greenfield, eds., *Edmund Spenser: Essays on culture and allegory.* Aldershot, UK, and Burlington, VT: Ashgate, 2000. 67–88.

McKitterick, David. *Print, manuscript and the search for order, 1450–1830.* Cambridge: Cambridge University Press, 2003.

McNeil, David O. *Guillaume Budé and humanism in the reign of Francis I.* Geneva: Librairie Droz, 1975.

Meier, E. A., *et al. Andreas Cratander: Ein Basler Drucker und Verleger der Reformationszeit.* Basel: Druckerei Cratander AG, 1966.

Mendle, Michael. 'De facto freedom, de facto authority: Press and Parliament, 1640–1643'. *Historical Journal* 38.2 (1995): 307–32.

Menhardt, Hermann. 'Die Nibelungenhandschrift c, der Laurin und die Historia Gothorum des Lazius'. *Zeitschrift für deutsches Altertum und deutsche Literatur* 84 (1952/3): 152–8.

Metcalf, George J. 'Abraham Mylius on historical linguistics'. *Publications of the Modern Language Association of America* 68 (1953): 535–54.

'Konrad Gesner's views on the Germanic languages'. *Monatshefte für deutschen Unterricht, deutsche Sprache und Literatur* 55.4 (1963): 149–56.

'Andreas Jäger and his *De lingua vetustissima Europae* (1686)'. *Modern Language Notes* 81.4 (1966): 489–93.

'The Indo-European hypothesis in the 16th and 17th centuries'. In Dell Hymes, ed., *Studies in the history of linguistics: Traditions and paradigms.* Bloomington: Indiana University Press, 1974. 233–57.

Miller, Peter N. *Peiresc's Europe: Learning and virtue in the seventeenth century.* New Haven: Yale University Press, 2000.

Molbech, Christian. 'Historisk udsigt over de danske ordbogs-arbeider, i det 17de og 18de aarhundrede, af Geheimeraad Matthias Moth, F. Rostgaard og J. Langebek'. *Nye Danske Magazin* 5.4 (1827): 241–88.

Momigliano, Arnaldo. 'Ancient history and the antiquarian'. *Journal of the Warburg and Courtauld Institutes* 13 (1950): 285–315.

The classical foundations of modern historiography. Sather Lectures 54. Berkeley: University of California Press, 1990.

Mommsen, Theodore E. 'Petrarch's conception of the "Dark Ages"'. *Speculum* 17.2 (1942): 226–42.

Moody, T. W., and W. E. Vaughan, eds. *A new history of Ireland IV: Eighteenth-century Ireland 1691–1800.* Oxford: Clarendon Press, 1986.

Moore, J. K. *Primary materials relating to copy and print in English books of the sixteenth and seventeenth centuries.* Oxford: Oxford Bibliographical Society, 1992.

Moss, Ann. *Renaissance truth and the Latin language turn.* Oxford and New York: Oxford University Press, 2003.

'MSS. Junius'. In Falconer Madan, H. H. E. Craster, and N. Denholm-Young, eds., *A summary catalogue of western manuscripts in the Bodleian Library at Oxford.* Vol. 2.2. Oxford: Clarendon Press, 1937. 962–90.

Mund-Dopchie, Monique. 'Le premier travail français sur Eschyle: Le *Prométhée enchaîné* de Jean Dorat'. *Les lettres romanes* 30 (1976): 261–74.

Munkhammar, Lars. *Silver bibeln: Theoderiks bok.* Stockholm: Carlssons, 1998.

Murray, James A. H. 'Ninth annual address of the president to the Philological Society'. *Transactions of the Philological Society* (1880): 117–55.

Murray, K. M. Elisabeth. *Caught in the web of words: James Murray and the Oxford English Dictionary.* New Haven: Yale University Press, 1977.

Mylett, A., ed. *Arnold Bennett: The Evening Standard years.* London: Chatto and Windus, 1974.

Nicole, Jules. *Les scolies genevoises de l'Iliade.* 2 vols. Paris: Librairie Hachette, 1891.

Nolhac, Pierre de. *Ronsard et l'humanisme.* Bibliothèque de l'École des Hautes Études 227. 1921; rpt Paris: Librairie Honoré Champion, 1966.

O'Brien, John. *Anacreon redivivus: A study of Anacreontic translation in mid-sixteenth-century France.* Ann Arbor: University of Michigan Press, 1995.

Ó Cuív, Brian. 'Irish language and literature, 1691–1845'. In Moody and Vaughan, eds., *A new history of Ireland IV.* 374–423.

O'Donnell, Daniel Paul. 'Junius's knowledge of the Old English poem *Durham*'. *Anglo-Saxon England* 30 (2002): 231–45.

Omont, H. *Lettres d'Anisson à du Cange relatives à l'impression du Glossaire grec (1682–1688).* Paris: Ernest Leroux, 1892.

'Du Cange et la collection byzantine du Louvre'. *Revue des études grecques* 17 (1904): 33–4.

Osselton, N. E. *Branded words in English dictionaries before Johnson.* Groningen: J. B. Wolters, 1958.

Owen, A. L. *The famous druids: A survey of three centuries of English literature on the druids.* Oxford: Clarendon Press, 1962.

Oxford dictionary of Byzantium. Ed. Alexander P. Kazhdan. 3 vols. New York and Oxford: Oxford University Press, 1991.

Pade, Marianne. 'Niccolò Perotti's *Cornu copiae*: Commentary on Martial and encyclopedia'. In Marianne Pade, ed. *On Renaissance commentaries.* Noctes neolatinae: Neo-Latin Texts and Studies 4. Hildesheim, etc.: Georg Olms Verlag, 2005. 49–63.

Padley, G. A. *Grammatical theory in western Europe: Trends in vernacular grammar I–II.* Cambridge: Cambridge University Press, 1985–8.

Page, R. I. *An introduction to English runes.* London: Methuen, 1973.

Palmer, Nigel F. 'Junius's blockbooks: Copies of the *Biblia pauperum* and *Canticum canticorum* in the Bodleian Library and their place in the history of printing'. *Renaissance Studies* 9.2 (1995): 137–65.

Parry, Graham. *The trophies of time: English antiquarians of the seventeenth century.* Oxford: Oxford University Press, 1995.

'Patronage and the printing of learned works for the author'. In John Barnard and D. F. McKenzie with Maureen Bell, eds., *The Cambridge history of the book in Britain IV: 1557–1695.* Cambridge: Cambridge University Press, 2002. 174–88.

Partridge, Eric. *The gentle art of lexicography, as pursued and experienced by an addict.* London: André Deutsch, 1963.

Passow, Franz. *Über Zweck, Anlage und Ergänzung griechischer Wörterbucher.* Berlin: bey Friedrich Maurer, 1812.

Pastoureau, Michel. 'Du Cange héraldiste'. In Lefevre, *Lexicographie du latin médiéval.* 501–8.

Pattison, Mark. 'Classical learning in France: The great printers Stephens'. *Quarterly Review* (1865): 323–64.

Isaac Casaubon. 2nd edn. Oxford: Clarendon Press, 1892.

Pedersen, Holger. *The discovery of language: Linguistic science in the nineteenth century.* Trans. John Webster Spargo. [Danish original, *Sprogvidenskaben i det nittende aarhundrede: Metoder og resultater,* 1924.] 1931; rpt Bloomington: Indiana University Press, 1962.

Penny, Ralph. *A history of the Spanish language.* 2nd edn. Cambridge: Cambridge University Press, 2002.

Peters, Manfred. 'Einleitung'. In Conrad Gessner, *Mithridates* [facs. rpt]. Aalen: Scientia Verlag, 1974. 7–84.

Pfeiffer, Rudolf. [*HCS* I]: *History of classical scholarship from the beginnings to the end of the Hellenistic age.* Oxford: Clarendon Press, 1968.

[*HCS* II]: *History of classical scholarship from 1300 to 1850.* Oxford: Clarendon Press, 1976.

Piggott, Stuart. 'Antiquarian thought in the sixteenth and seventeenth centuries'. In Fox, *English historical scholarship.* 93–114.

'William Camden and the *Britannia*'. In *Ruins in a landscape: Essays in antiquarianism.* Edinburgh: Edinburgh University Press, 1976. 33–53.

Ancient Britons and the antiquarian imagination: Ideas from the Renaissance to the Regency. London: Thames and Hudson, 1989.

Plumer, Danielle Cunniff. 'The construction of structure in the earliest editions of Old English poetry'. In Graham, *Recovery of Old English.* 243–79.

Pocock, J. G. A. *The ancient constitution and the feudal law: A study of English historical thought in the seventeenth century.* Cambridge: Cambridge University Press, 1957.

'The ancient constitution revisited: A retrospect from 1986'. In *The ancient constitution and the feudal law . . . a reissue with a retrospect.* Cambridge: Cambridge University Press, 1987. 253–387.

Powicke, F. M. 'Sir Henry Spelman and the "Concilia"'. *Proceedings of the British Academy* 16 (1930): 345–79.

Price, Glanville, ed. *Encyclopedia of the languages of Europe.* Oxford: Blackwell, 1998.

Přívratská, Jana. 'Dictionary as a textbook – textbook as a dictionary: Comenius' contribution to Czech lexicography'. In Hüllen, *World in a list of words.* 151–8.

Prospectus novae editionis Thesauri graecae linguae ab Henrico Stephano constructi. Paris: excudebat Ambrosius Firminus Didot, 1830.

Pugh, R. B., and Elizabeth Crittall. *A history of the county of Wiltshire.* Victoria County History. In progress. London: Oxford University Press for the Institute of Historical Research, 1953– .

Pulsiano, Phillip. 'William L'isle and the editing of Old English'. In Graham, *Recovery of Old English.* 173–206.

Rademaker, C. S. M. 'Young Franciscus Junius: 1591–1621'. In Bremmer, *Franciscus Junius F.F. and his circle.* 1–17.

Raumer, Rudolf von. *Geschichte der Germanischen Philologie, vorzugsweise in Deutschland.* Geschichte der Wissenschaften in Deutschland Bd. 9. 1870; rpt New York: Johnson Reprint Corporation, 1965.

Renouard, A. A. *Annales de l'imprimerie des Estienne, ou histoire de la famille des Estienne et de ses éditions.* 2 vols, continuously paginated. 2nd edn. Paris: J. Renouard et cie, 1843.

Reynolds, L. D., and N. G. Wilson. *Scribes and scholars: A guide to the transmission of Greek and Latin literature.* 3rd edn. Oxford: Clarendon Press, 1991.

Rickard, Peter. 'From Villehardouin to Du Cange via Vigenère'. *Zeitschrift für französische Sprache und Literatur* 103.2 (1993): 113–43.

Riddle, John Marion. 'Dioscorides'. In F. E. Cranz with Paul Oskar Kristeller, eds., *Catalogus translationum et commentariorum IV.* Washington, DC: Catholic University of America Press, 1980. 1–143.

Ridé, Jacques. *L'image du Germain dans la pensée et la litterature allemandes de la redécouverte de Tacite à la fin du XVIème siècle: contribution à l'étude de la genèse d'un mythe.* Thesis, Université de Paris IV, 1976. 3 vols. Lille: Atelier de reproduction des thèses, université de Lille III; Paris: Librairie Honoré Champion, 1977.

Riemann, Erhard, ed. *Preussisches Wörterbuch* vol. I fasc. I, 'Einführung'. Neumünster: Karl Wachholtz Verlag, 1974.

Roberts, R. Julian. 'Madan, Falconer (1851–1935), librarian and bibliographer'. *Oxford dictionary of national biography.*

Robinson, A. M. Lewin. 'A seventeenth century miscellany (Grey Collection 7A 29)'. *Quarterly Bulletin of the South African Library* 35.3 (1981): 74–91.

Robinson, Fred C. 'Medieval, the Middle Ages'. *Speculum* 59.4 (1984): 745–56.

Robinson, Orrin W. *Old English and its closest relatives.* Stanford: Stanford University Press, 1992.

Rockefeller Archive Center. 'Rockefeller family archives: John D. Rockefeller, Jr. personal papers, 1874–1961'. Online catalogue. www.archive.rockefeller. edu/collections/family/jdrjr/. Viewed 9 February 2006.

Rosier, James L. 'A new Old English glossary: Nowell upon Huloet'. *Studia Neophilologica* 49 (1977): 189–94.

 'The sources of John Joscelyn's Old English–Latin dictionary'. *Anglia* 78 (1960): 28–39.

Rossebastiano Bart, Alda. *Antichi vocabolari plurilingui d'uso popolare: La tradizione del 'Solenissimo vochabuolista'.* Alessandria: Edizioni dell'Orso, 1984.

Rouse, Robert Allen. *The idea of Anglo-Saxon England in Middle English romance.* Woodbridge, UK, and Rochester, NY: Boydell and Brewer, 2005.

Rousseau, André, ed. *Sur les traces de Busbecq et du gotique.* Lille: Presses universitaires de Lille, [1991].

Rūķe-Draviņa, Velta. *The standardization process in Latvian: 16th century to the present.* Acta universitatis Stockholmiensis: Stockholm Slavic Studies II. Stockholm: Almqvist & Wiksell International, 1977.

Rydberg-Cox, Jeffrey A. 'Automatic disambiguation of Latin abbreviations in early modern texts for humanities digital libraries'. In Catherine C. Marshall, Geneva Henry and Lois Delcambre, eds., *Proceedings [of the] joint conference on digital libraries, 27–31 May 2003.* Los Alamitos, CA: IEEE Computer Society, 2003. 372–3.

Salmon, Vivian. 'John Wilkins' "Essay" (1668): Critics and continuators'. *Historiographia linguistica* I.2 (1974): 147–63.

'Cave Beck: a seventeenth century Ipswich schoolmaster'. In *The study of language in 17th-century England*. Amsterdam studies in the theory and history of linguistic science, ser. 3, vol. 17. Amsterdam: John Benjamins, 1979. 176–90.

'Missionary linguistics in seventeenth century Ireland and a North American analogy'. *Historiographia linguistica* 12.3 (1985): 321–349.

'Arabists and linguists in seventeenth-century England'. In G. A. Russell, ed., *The 'Arabick' interest of the natural philosophers in seventeenth-century England*. Leiden: E. J. Brill, 1994. 54–69.

Samaran, Charles. 'Du Cange à Paris, Rue des Écouffes: D'après son testament et son inventaire après décès'. 1920. Reprinted in *Recueil d'études*. Geneva: Librairie Droz, 1978. 163–81.

Sanders, Willy. *Der Leidener Willeram: Untersuchungen zu Handschrift, Text und Sprachform*. Medium Aevum: Philologische Studien 27. Munich: Wilhelm Fink Verlag, 1974.

Schaeffer, Peter. 'The emergence of the concept "medieval" in central European humanism'. *Sixteenth Century Journal* 7.2 (1976): 21–30.

Schäfer, Jürgen. 'John Minsheu: Scholar or charlatan?' *Renaissance Quarterly* 26.1 (1973): 23–35.

Schama, Simon. *The embarrassment of riches: An interpretation of Dutch culture in the Golden Age*. London: Fontana Press, 1987.

Citizens: A chronicle of the French Revolution. London: Penguin, 1989.

Landscape and memory. New York: Alfred A. Knopf, 1995.

Schiebe, Marianne Wifstrand. *Annius von Viterbo und die schwedische Historiographie des 16. und 17. Jahrhunderts*. Skrifter utgivna av Kungl. Humanistiska Vetenskaps-Samfundet i Uppsala 48. Uppsala: K. Humanistiska vetenkaps-samfundet, 1992.

Schmitz, Thomas A. Review of O'Brien, *Anacreon redivivus*. *Bryn Mawr classical review* [1996] 96.8.14. Online at <http://ccat.sas.upenn.edu/bmcr/1996/96.08.14.html>.

Schneider, Rolf. *Der Einfluß von Justus Georg Schottelius auf die deutschsprachige Lexikographie des 17 / 18. Jahrhunderts*. Theorie und Vermittlung der Sprache 21. Frankfurt: Peter Lang, 1995.

Schoeck, Richard J. 'Early Anglo-Saxon studies and legal scholarship in the Renaissance'. *Studies in the Renaissance* 5 (1958): 102–10.

Schöffer, I. 'The Batavian myth during the sixteenth and seventeenth centuries'. In J. S. Bromley and E. H. Kossmann, eds., *Britain and the Netherlands V: Some political mythologies: Papers delivered to the fifth Anglo-Dutch Historical Conference*. The Hague: Martinus Nijhoff, 1975. 78–101.

Schreiber, Fred. *The Estiennes: 300 highlights*. New York: E. K. Schreiber, 1982.

The Hanes collection of Estienne publications: From book collecting to scholarly resource. Chapel Hill: Library of the University of North Carolina at Chapel Hill, 1984.

E. K. Schreiber: Catalogue twenty-nine. New York: E. K. Schreiber, [1993].

E. K. Schreiber: Autumn 2005 list. New York: E. K. Schreiber, 2005.

Schulenburg, Sigrid von der. *Leibniz als Sprachforscher*. Veröffentlichungen des Leibniz-Archivs herausgegeben von der niedersächsischen Landesbibliothek 4. Frankfurt am Main: Vittorio Klostermann, 1973.

Schulte, J. W. 'Gothica minora: Erster Artikel'. *Zeitschrift für deutsches Alterthum* 23 (1879): 51–64.

'Gothica minora: Zweiter Artikel'. *Zeitschrift für deutsches Alterthum*, 23 (1879): 318–36.

'Gothica minora: Dritter Artikel'. *Zeitschrift für deutsches Alterthum* 24 (1880): 324–55.

Sharp, Thomas, ed. *Illustrative papers on the history and antiquities of the city of Coventry*. Revised William George Fretton. [N.p.]: for the subscribers, 1871.

Sharpe, Kevin. *Sir Robert Cotton 1586–1631: History and politics in early modern England*. Oxford: Oxford University Press, 1979.

Shippey, Tom, with Martin Arnold, eds. *Appropriating the Middle Ages: Scholarship, politics, fraud*. Studies in medievalism XI. Cambridge: D. S. Brewer, 2001.

Shumaker, Wayne. *Renaissance curiosa: John Dee's conversations with angels, Girolamo Cardano's horoscope of Christ, Johannes Trithemius and cryptography, George Dalgarno's universal language*. Medieval & Renaissance Texts & Studies 8. Binghamton, NY: Center for Medieval and Early Renaissance Studies, 1982.

Silver, Isidore. *Ronsard and the Hellenic Renaissance in France I: Ronsard and the Greek epic*. St Louis, MO: Washington University Press, 1961.

The intellectual evolution of Ronsard I: The formative influences. St Louis, MO: Washington University Press, 1969.

Ronsard and the Hellenic Renaissance in France II: Ronsard and the Grecian lyre. Travaux d'humanisme et Renaissance 182, 208, 218. 3 vols. Geneva: Librairie Droz, 1981–7.

Simms, J. G. 'The Irish on the Continent, 1691–1800'. In Moody and Vaughan, *A new history of Ireland IV*. 629–56.

Simpson, James. *1350–1547: Reform and cultural revolution*. Oxford English Literary History 2. Oxford: Clarendon Press, 2002.

Simpson, Percy. *Proof-reading in the sixteenth seventeenth and eighteenth centuries*. London: Oxford University Press, 1935.

Siraisi, Nancy G. 'Life sciences and medicine in the Renaissance world'. In Grafton, *Rome reborn*. 168–97.

Sisam, Kenneth. *Studies in the history of Old English literature*. Oxford: Clarendon Press, 1953.

Skeat, W. W. 'Preface to the first edition'. In *An etymological dictionary of the English language*. 4th edn. Oxford: Clarendon Press, 1909. viii–xv.

Slaughter, M. M. *Universal languages and scientific taxonomy in the seventeenth century*. Cambridge: Cambridge University Press, 1982.

Smith, Olivia. *The politics of language 1791–1819*. Oxford: Clarendon Press, 1984.

Sonderegger, Stefan. 'Ansätze zu einer deutschen Sprachgeschichtsschreibung bis zum Ende des 18. Jahrhunderts'. In Werner Besch, Anne Betten, Oskar

Reichmann, and Stefan Sonderegger, eds., *Sprachgeschichte: Ein Handbuch zur Geschichte der deutschen Sprache und ihrer Erforschung.* Handbücher zur Sprach- und Kommunikationswissenschaft 2. 2nd edn. Berlin and New York: Walter de Gruyter, 1998. 1:417–42.

Spieser, Jean-Michel. 'Du Cange and Byzantium'. In Robin Cormack and Elizabeth Jeffreys, eds., *Through the looking glass: Byzantium through British eyes.* Aldershot: Ashgate Publishing, 2000. 199–210.

Spingarn, J. E., ed. *Critical essays of the seventeenth century.* 3 vols. Oxford: Clarendon Press, 1908–9.

Spitz, Lewis W. *Conrad Celtis: The German arch-humanist.* Cambridge, MA: Harvard University Press, 1957.

The religious renaissance of the German humanists. Cambridge, MA: Harvard University Press, 1963.

Spraggon, Julie. *Puritan iconoclasm during the English Civil War.* Woodbridge, UK: Boydell Press, 2003.

St John's College, Cambridge. 'Catalogue of post-medieval manuscripts'. www.joh.cam.ac.uk/library/. Accessed 19 September 2005.

Stankiewicz, Edward. *Grammars and dictionaries of the Slavic languages from the Middle Ages up to 1850: An annotated bibliography.* Berlin: Mouton Publishers, 1984.

Stanley, Eric. *In the foreground: Beowulf.* Cambridge: D. S. Brewer, 1994.

'The sources of Junius's learning as revealed in the Junius manuscripts in the Bodleian library'. In Bremmer, *Franciscus Junius F.F. and his circle.* 159–76.

Starnes, DeWitt T. *Renaissance dictionaries, English–Latin and Latin–English.* Austin: University of Texas Press; Edinburgh: Thomas Nelson and Sons, 1954.

Robert Estienne's influence on lexicography. Austin: University of Texas Press, 1963.

[STC]. *A short-title catalogue of books printed in England, Scotland & Ireland and of English books printed abroad, 1475–1640.* First compiled by A. W. Pollard and G. R. Redgrave; 2nd revised and enlarged edn begun by W. A. Jackson and F. S. Ferguson, completed by Katharine F. Pantzer. 3 vols. London: Bibliographical Society, 1976–91.

Stearns, MacDonald, Jr. *Crimean Gothic: Analysis and etymology of the corpus.* Studia linguistica et philologica 6. Saratoga, CA: Anma Libri, 1978.

Stein, Gabriele. *The English dictionary before Cawdrey.* Lexicographica series major 9. Tübingen: Max Niemeyer, 1985.

'The emergence of lexicology in Renaissance English dictionaries'. In Considine and Iamartino, *Words and dictionaries.* 25–38.

Steinmeyer, Elias von. *Die kleineren althochdeutschen Sprachdenkmäler.* 1916; rpt Dublin and Zürich: Weidmann, 1971.

Stoker, David. 'Doctor Collinges and the revival of Norwich City Library 1657–1664'. *Library History* 5.3 (1980): 73–84.

Strauss, Gerald. 'Topographical-historical method in sixteenth-century German scholarship'. *Studies in the Renaissance* 5 (1958): 87–101.

Historian in an age of crisis: The life and work of Johannes Aventinus 1477–1534. Cambridge, MA: Harvard University Press, 1963.

Svärdström, Elisabeth. *Johannes Bureus' arbeten om Svenska runinskrifter.* Kungl. Vitterhets Historie och Antikvitets Akademiens Handlingar 42.3. Stockholm: Wahlstrom & Widstrand, 1936.

Swann, Marjorie. *Curiosities and texts: The culture of collecting in early modern England.* Philadelphia: University of Pennsylvania Press, 2001.

Swerdlow, N. M. 'The recovery of the exact sciences of antiquity: Mathematics, astronomy, geography'. In Grafton, *Rome reborn.* 125–67.

Tate, Robert B. 'Mythology in Spanish historiography of the Middle Ages and the Renaissance'. *Hispanic review* 22.1 (1954): 1–18.

Tavoni, Mirko. 'Western Europe'. In Lepschy, *History of Linguistics III.* 2–108.

Terry, Richard. *Poetry and the making of the English past, 1660–1781.* Oxford: Oxford University Press, 2001.

Thiessen, Jack. *Mennonite Low-German dictionary / Mennonitisches Wörterbuch.* Marburg: N. G. Elwert Verlag, 1977.

Thompson, James Westfall. 'The age of Mabillon and Montfaucon'. *American Historical Review* 47 (1942): 225–44.

Tilley, Morris Palmer. *A dictionary of the proverbs in England in the sixteenth and seventeenth centuries.* Ann Arbor: University of Michigan Press, 1950.

Tilmans, Karin. *Historiography and humanism in Holland in the age of Erasmus: Aurelius and the Divisiekroniek of 1517.* Bibliotheca humanistica & reformatorica 51. Nieuwkoop: De Graaf, 1992.

Timmer, B. J. 'Introduction'. In B. J. Timmer ed., *The Later Genesis, edited from MS. Junius 11.* Oxford: Scrivener Press, 1948. 1–75.

  'De Laet's Anglo-Saxon dictionary'. *Neophilologus* 41 (1957): 199–202.

Tite, Colin G. C. *The early records of Sir Robert Cotton's library: Formation, cataloguing, use.* London: British Library, 2003.

Tornaghi, Paola. 'Certaine things to be considered & corrected in Will. Dugdales Saxon-lexicon'. In Considine and Iamartino, *Words and dictionaries.* 50–80.

Toscano, Silvia. 'Orthodox Slavdom'. In Lepschy, *History of linguistics III.* 123–48.

Trapp, J. B. 'The conformity of Greek and the vernacular: The history of a Renaissance theory of languages'. In R. R. Bolgar, ed., *Classical influences on European culture A. D. 500–1500: Proceedings of an international conference held at King's College, Cambridge, April 1969.* Cambridge: Cambridge University Press, 1971. 239–44.

Trinquet, Roger. *La jeunesse de Montaigne: Ses origines familiales, son enfance et ses études.* Paris: A. G. Nizet, 1972.

Tunberg, Terence. 'The Latinity of Erasmus and medieval Latin: Continuities and discontinuities'. *Journal of Medieval Latin* 14 (2004): 147–70.

Turner, Alberta. 'Another seventeenth-century Anglo-Saxon poem'. *Modern Language Quarterly* 9 (1948): 389–93.

Ulery, Robert W., Jr. 'Tacitus, Cornelius'. In F. Edward Cranz with Virginia Brown and Paul Oskar Kristeller, eds., *Catalogus translationum et commentariorum* VI Washington, DC: Catholic University of America Press, 1986. 87–174.

Ullmann, B. L. 'Manuscripts of Duke Humphrey of Gloucester'. *English Historical Review* 52. 208 (1937): 670–2.

University of Oxford Early Printed Books Project. 'Background' (subheading 'Database'). www.lib.ox.ac.uk/icc/. Viewed 23 October 2005.

Utley, Francis Lee. 'Two seventeenth-century Anglo-Saxon poems'. *Modern Languages Quarterly* 3 (1942): 243–61.

van den Branden, Lode, Elly Cockx-Indestege and Frans Sillis. *Bio-bibliografie van Cornelis Kiliaan.* Nieuwkoop: B. de Graaf, 1978.

Van De Velde, R. G. *De studie van het Gotisch in de Nederlanden: Bijdrage tot een status quaestionis over de studie van het Gotisch en het Krimgotisch.* Gent: Secretariaat van de Koninklijke Vlaamse Academie voor Taal- en Letterkunde, 1966.

Van Hal, Toon. 'Een "geurtje" rond de Wachtendonkse Psalmen?: Een omstreden bijdrage van Justus Lipsius tot de Germaanse filologie'. *De Gulden Passer* 84 (2006): 27–44.

Van Norden, Linda. 'Peiresc and the English scholars'. *Huntington Library Quarterly* 12.4 (1949): 369–89.

'Sir Henry Spelman on the chronology of the Elizabethan College of Antiquaries'. *Huntington Library Quarterly* 13.2 (1950): 131–60.

van Romburgh, Sophie. 'Why Francis Junius (1591–1677) became an Anglo-Saxonist, or, the study of Old English for the elevation of Dutch'. In Shippey with Arnold, *Appropriating the Middle Ages.* 5–36.

Voet, Leon. *The golden compasses: A history and evaluation of the printing and publishing activities of the Officina Plantiniana at Antwerp.* 2 vols. Amsterdam: Vangendt; London: Routledge & Kegan Paul, 1969.

von Martels, Zweder R. W. M. 'On His Majesty's service: Augerius Busbequius, courtier and diplomat of Maximilian II'. In Friedrich Edelmayer and Alfred Kohler, eds., *Kaiser Maximilian II: Kultur und Politik im 16. Jahrhundert.* Wiener Beiträge zur Geschichte der Neuzeit 19. Vienna: Verlag für Geschichte und Politik; Munich: R. Oldenbourg Verlag, 1992. 169–81.

Wagner, A. R. *English ancestry.* London: Oxford University Press, 1961.

Walde, O. 'Om Georg Stiernhielms bibliotek: Några anteckningar'. *Donum Grapeanum: Festskrift tillägnad överbibliotekarien Anders Grape på sextiofemårsdagen den 7 mars 1945.* Uppsala: Almqvist & Wiksell, 1945. 107–41.

Walker, Keith. 'Johnson's Dictionary' [letter to the editor]. *Times Literary Supplement,* 7 October 1977, 1149.

Warnicke, Retha M. *William Lambarde: Elizabethan antiquary 1536–1601.* Chichester: Phillimore, 1973.

Waterman, John T., trans. and comm. *Leibniz and Ludolf on things linguistic: Excerpts from their correspondence (1688–1703).* University of California Publications in Linguistics 88. Berkeley and Los Angeles: University of California Press, 1978.

Watson, Andrew G. *The library of Sir Simonds D'Ewes.* London: British Library, 1966.

'John Twyne of Canterbury (d. 1581) as a collector of medieval manuscripts: A preliminary investigation' *The Library,* ser. 4, 8.2 (1986): 133–51.

Weiss, Roberto. *Humanism in England during the fifteenth century*. 3rd edn. Oxford: Blackwell, 1967.

Wellisch, Hans. *Conrad Gessner: A bio-bibliography*. Zug: IDC, 1984.

Wells, C. J. *German: A linguistic history to 1945*. Oxford: Clarendon Press, 1985.

Wernham, R. B. 'The public records in the sixteenth and seventeenth centuries'. In Fox, *English historical scholarship*. 11–30.

Wilamowitz-Moellendorff, Ulrich von. *Geschichte der Philologie*. 3rd edn. 1927; repr. Leipzig: B. G. Teubner Verlagsgesellschaft, 1959.

History of classical scholarship. Trans. Alan Harris. London: Duckworth, 1982.

Will, Samuel F. 'Camille de Morel: A prodigy of the Renaissance'. *Publications of the Modern Languages Society of America* 51.1 (1936): 83–119.

Willems, Alphonse. *Les Elzevier: Histoire et annales typographiques*. Brussels: G.-A. Van Trigt, 1880.

Williams, Franklin B., Jr. 'Scholarly publication in Shakespeare's day: A leading case'. In James G. McManaway, Giles E. Dawson, and Edwin E. Willoughby, eds., *Joseph Quincy Adams memorial studies*. Washington, DC: Folger Shakespeare Library, 1948. 755–73.

Index of dedications and commendatory verses in English books before 1641. London: Bibliographical Society, 1962.

Williams, Haydn. 'George Borrow: The word-master as hero'. In T. L. Burton and Jill Burton, eds., *Lexicographical and linguistic studies: Essays in honour of G. W. Turner*. Cambridge: D. S. Brewer, 1988.

Williams, Raymond. *Keywords: A vocabulary of culture and society*. London: Fontana, 1976.

Witt, Ronald G. *'In the footsteps of the ancients': The origins of humanism from Lovato to Bruni*. Leiden etc.: Brill, 2000.

Woodruff, C. Eveleigh. *A catalogue of the manuscript books which are preserved in study X.Y.Z and in the Howley-Harrison collection in the library of Christ Church, Canterbury*. Canterbury: Cross & Jackman, 1911.

Wooldridge, Terence Russon. *Les débuts de la lexicographie française: Estienne, Nicot et le Thresor de la langue françoyse (1606)*. Toronto: University of Toronto Press, 1977.

Woolf, D. R. *Reading history in early modern England*. Cambridge: Cambridge University Press, 2000.

Wright, C. E. 'The dispersal of monastic libraries and the beginnings of Anglo-Saxon studies'. *Transactions of the Cambridge Bibliographical Society* 1 (1949–53): 208–37.

Fontes Harleiani: A study of the sources of the Harleian collection of manuscripts preserved in the Department of Manuscripts in the British Museum. London: British Museum, 1972.

W[right], E. M. *The life of Joseph Wright*. 2 vols. London: Oxford University Press, 1932.

Index